Ala

adventure guide

Ala
adventure

ska
guide

Melissa DeVaughn

MENASHA RIDGE PRESS
Your Guide to the Outdoors Since 1982

Alaska Adventure Guide

Copyright © 2011 by Melissa DeVaughn
All rights reserved
Printed in the United States of America
Published by Menasha Ridge Press
Distributed by Publishers Group West
First edition, first printing

Library of Congress Cataloging-in-Publication Data

    DeVaughn, Melissa.
        Alaska adventure guide / by Melissa DeVaughn. —1st ed.
           p. cm.
        Includes index.
        ISBN-13: 978-0-89732-906-4
        ISBN-10: 0-89732-906-6
        1. Alaska—Guidebooks. I. Title.
        F902.3.D48 2011
        917.98'05204—dc22

                      2010041094

Cover design by Scott McGrew
Interior design by Annie Long
Cover photo © Alaska Stock LLC/Alamy
Author photo by Andy Hall
Maps by Steve Jones
Indexing by Galen Schroeder

Menasha Ridge Press
P.O. Box 43673
Birmingham, AL 35243
menasharidge.com

Please note that prices fluctuate over time and that travel information changes because of the many factors that influence the travel industry. Every effort has been made to ensure the accuracy of information throughout this book, and the contents of this publication are believed to be correct at the time of printing. Nevertheless, the publishers cannot accept responsibility for errors or omissions, changes in details provided in this guide, or the consequences of any reliance on the information provided by the same.

To help ensure an uneventful trip, please read carefully the relevant planning and safety sections of this book, and perhaps get further information and guidance from other sources. Acquaint yourself thoroughly with the areas you intend to visit before venturing out. Ask questions and prepare for the unforeseen. Also familiarize yourself with current weather reports, maps of the area you intend to visit, and any relevant area regulations.

▲ CONTENTS

▲ CONTENTS (continued)

▲ LIST OF MAPS

▲ ACKNOWLEDGMENTS

GETTING THIS BOOK from its original concept to reality proved to be an awesome—sometimes overwhelming—task. Doing it on my own would have been impossible. Thankfully, many people helped me along the way; without them, this project could not have been completed. Your friendship, expertise, guidance, and recommendations helped shape the book, and I want to thank each of you: Charlie Sassara, one of Alaska's most accomplished mountaineers and an all-around nice guy; Tim Woody, a cycling fanatic whose attention to detail was much appreciated; and Craig Medred, my colorful coworker and former Outdoors editor at the *Anchorage Daily News,* with whom I worked for so many years. I'm also grateful to my friends—the "gang," as we call ourselves— Colleen Mueller, Liz Shen, and Dee Ginter, who always were willing to watch my children when I got superbusy. You're truly my "Alaska family." Special thank-yous go to my editor, Molly Merkle, who encouraged me to keep this book alive after so many years, and Ritchey Halphen, Amber Henderson, and Julie Hall Bosché, who patiently waded through my copy and helped turn it into the book you are now holding. And most of all, I want to thank my husband, Andy Hall, and my children, Reilly and Roan, for supporting me along the way.

▲ ABOUT THE AUTHOR

MELISSA DeVAUGHN was on staff at the
Anchorage Daily News, Alaska's largest daily newspaper, for more than 10
years, covering outdoors and sports in
Alaska. She now splits her time between
freelance writing and as editor at the
Alaska Star, a longtime weekly newspaper in her community—a place surrounded by the wilderness of Chugach

State Park. She has been covering outdoors-related topics for newspapers
and magazines since 1990 and has also worked at the *Roanoke Times*
in Virginia; the *Peninsula Clarion,* on Alaska's Kenai Peninsula; and The
Associated Press's Anchorage bureau. Her work has also appeared in *Alaska,*
Backpacker, Canoe & Kayak, and *Women's Sports & Fitness* magazines, among
other publications. She hiked the Appalachian Trail in 1993 before moving to
Alaska, and she continues to enjoy backpacking throughout the state. In addition, she enjoys mountain and road biking in the summer, and in the winter
she spends her time mushing with her team of Alaskan huskies. She lives in
Chugiak, Alaska, with her husband, Andy Hall; 9-year-old daughter, Reilly;
12-year-old son, Roan; nine dogs; one cat; five fish; and a tortoise. She can be
reached at her Web site, **melissadevaughn.com.**

PART ONE

UNDERSTANDING ALASKA

▲ The Last Frontier

EVERYTHING IS BIG in Alaska.

The fish are huge. The mountains are tall. The rivers are wide. Go fishing or hiking, and these symbols of grandness can be rationally comprehended. They can be measured and photographed and bragged about when you get back home. It's an adventure traveler's paradise.

But to fully comprehend just what *big* means in Alaska, consider this: while you can drive your car across some states in the continental U.S.

in a few hours, here it would take you that much time to get from end to end by jet.

Alaska is a land that offers unlimited opportunities for the traveler who is willing to get off the beaten track and explore the nooks and crannies that make the state remarkable. Whether it's a deep fjord or a meandering river, a massive ice field or a steep mountain, Alaska is where the most adventurous of travelers are drawn.

Alaska Adventure Guide offers you some insight into this vast land with a section-by-section outline of the state's best outdoor adventures—from rafting a Class V river and paddling a hidden cove to hiking a scenic trail and cycling across the state. We realize that Alaska's vastness alone makes it alluring to the thousands of adventure travelers who come here each year, but we also know from experience that it can be an overwhelming place to take in all at once.

Alaska is the largest state in the union: one-fifth the size of the contiguous United States and larger than California, Montana, and Texas combined. The land covers some 586,000 square miles and is home to North America's tallest mountain—Mount McKinley, also known as Denali—and many other peaks that are among the highest in the United States. Statistics are even more mind-boggling: Alaska boasts some 3,000 rivers, 10,000 glaciers, and, incredibly, more than 3 million lakes. And wildlife roams through it all: bears, moose, and, in the waters, whales and fish.

Yet Alaska is one of the least populated states in the country, with fewer than 700,000 residents, most of whom live in the state's three largest cities and outlying areas.

These qualities combined give the outdoor traveler even more incentive to come here. This is a place where, despite progress and all that comes with it—high-rises, smart phones, buses, cars—you can still reach the wilderness relatively easily. It is entirely conceivable, in fact, to land at one of Alaska's international airports, grab a taxi, and drive as few as 5 miles to the nearest state wilderness park. Pay the driver, slip on your backpack, and your adventure begins. It really doesn't get any better than this.

Of course, there are many more-elaborate trips that can be taken in Alaska, and those are the ones that make truly memorable moments. But it's fun to dream of a place in the United States where the wilderness remains so predominant.

More than a century ago, Alaska's population wasn't nearly as large as it is today, but the gold rush brought people by the thousands, setting the foundation for today's population. When hardy miners, searching the land and water for glistening rock, hit the jackpot in the late 1800s, this harsh land suddenly had something irresistible to offer. Prospectors flocked here in search of riches beyond their wildest dreams. Some found them, others died trying.

Today, adventure travelers the world over come to Alaska with the same zeal those prospectors had—only what these visitors seek is priceless. It is Alaska's unyielding beauty that draws those who come to climb its highest peaks, travel its longest rivers, and visit its most isolated villages. They drive limited roads, photograph plentiful wildlife, and cruise glacier-studded waterways. After experiencing the Last Frontier, those visitors often become residents. And it's easy to understand why.

The landscape of Alaska was wild and awe-inspiring for millennia before the discovery of gold, and it has remained so since. Indigenous peoples were the first to recognize the grandeur of this place. They worshiped the land for the riches it gave: not gold, but food and shelter. Despite the challenges of this extreme country, these people survived and thrived. Today, their songs and stories tell of a time when they spoke directly to the land and the land spoke back.

Early outsiders such as authors Jack London and Robert Service also appreciated the country for its rugged splendor. Their stories and poems romanticize the place, and can we argue with them? If we imagine London, cozy in his Yukon cabin, watching the aurora borealis on a frigid winter evening, it's no surprise that he was inspired to pen *The Call of the Wild*.

After all these years, the world has realized that the true wealth of Alaska remains. In contrast to our cramped and hurried lives, in which high-rises

continued on page 14

MILEAGE CHART (approximate driving distances in miles between cities)	Anchorage	Circle	Dawson City	Eagle	Fairbanks	Haines	Homer	Prudhoe Bay	Seattle	Seward	Skagway	Tok	Valdez
Anchorage	–	520	494	501	358	775	226	847	2,234	126	832	328	304
Circle	520	–	530	541	162	815	746	1,972	2,271	646	872	368	526
Dawson City	494	530	–	131	379	548	713	868	1,843	619	430	189	428
Eagle	501	541	131	–	379	620	727	868	1,974	627	579	173	427
Fairbanks	358	162	379	379	–	653	584	489	2,121	484	710	206	364
Haines	775	815	548	620	653	–	1,001	1,142	1,774	901	359	447	701
Homer	226	746	713	727	584	1,001	–	1,073	2,455	173	1,058	554	530
Prudhoe Bay	847	1,972	868	868	489	1,142	1,073	–	2,610	973	1,199	695	853
Seattle	2,243	2,271	1,843	1,974	2,121	1,774	2,455	2,610	–	2,493	1,577	1,931	2,169
Seward	126	646	619	627	484	901	173	973	2493	–	958	454	430
Skagway	832	872	430	579	710	359	1,058	1,199	1,577	958	–	504	758
Tok	328	368	189	173	206	447	554	695	1,931	454	504	–	254
Valdez	304	526	428	427	364	701	530	853	2,169	430	758	254	–

Chukchi Sea

Little Diomede Island

Nome

Norton Sound

Yukon Delta National Wildlife Refuge

Bethel
Yukon Delta National Wildlife Refuge

Bering Sea

Nunivak Island

Attu Island

Pribilof Islands

Bristol Bay

Cape St. Stephen   Rat Islands

Alaska Peninsula

Unimak Island   Cold Bay

Adak
Adak Island   Atka Island
Atka

Unalaska–Dutch Harbor

Aleutian Islands

PACIFIC

Alaska

0   100 mi
0   100 km

Arctic Ocean

Beaufort Sea

Barrow

Prudhoe
Bay

Deadhorse

Cape Krusenstern
National Monument

Noatak National
Preserve

Brooks Range

Anaktuvuk
Pass

Arctic National
Wildlife Refuge

United States
Canada

Kobuk Valley
National Park

Gates of the Arctic
National Park and Preserve

Dalton Hwy.

Brooks Range

Kotzebue

Coldfoot

8

Dempster Hwy.

Arctic Circle

Bering Land Bridge
National Preserve

Bettles

Fort Yukon

Yukon Flats
National Wildlife
Refuge

5

Galena

Chena
Hot Springs   6

Circle

Yukon-Charley Rivers
National Preserve

CANADA

Unalakleet

Manley
Hot Springs   2

Fairbanks
North Pole

Eagle

YUKON

Nenana

Denali
National Park

Delta
Junction

5

Dawson City

McGrath

Mt. McKinley

Alaska   Range

3

8

Tok

9

4   1

United States
Canada

6

Kuskokwim River

Yukon River

Talkeetna

Willow

Glennallen
Wrangell Mts.

1

4

Wasilla

Palmer

1

McCarthy

2

4

ANCHORAGE

Valdez

Wrangell–St. Elias
National Park and Preserve

1

Whitehorse

1

Lake Clark National
Park and Preserve

Kenai
Soldotna

10

Whittier

7

Dillingham

Homer

Seward

Cordova

Prince
William
Sound

Skagway

BRITISH
COLUMBIA

King
Salmon

Halibut Cove

Seldovia   Kenai Fjords
National Park

Yakutat

Haines

Juneau

Katmai National
Park and Preserve

Alaska
Marine
Highway

Gulf of Alaska

Glacier Bay National
Park and Preserve

Gustavus

Admiralty Island
National Monument

Kodiak

Chichagof Island

Admiralty Island

Baranof Island

Sitka

Petersburg

Kodiak Island

Alaska Marine Highway

Wrangell

Aniakchak National
Monument and Preserve

Prince of Wales Island

Craig
Ketchikan

Misty Fjords
National Monument

Prince Rupert
B.C.

To Seattle

O C E A N

Unpaved road	———
Ferry	– – –
Paved road	———
State or provincial route	—①—

Southcentral Inland Alaska

■ BACKPACKING	■ CYCLING	16. Gold Mint Trail
1. Crow Pass	8. Anchorage–Valdez	17. Pioneer Ridge–
2. Kesugi Ridge	9. Bird–Gird Trail	Austin Helmers
	10. Eklutna Lake	18. Reed Lakes
■ CANOEING	11. Hatcher Pass	19. Winner Creek
3. Lynx Lake Loop	12. Kenai Peninsula Tour	Gorge
	13. Tony Knowles	
■ CLIMBING	Coastal Trail	■ DOG MUSHING
4. Mount Blackburn		20. Chugach Express
5. Mount Bona	■ DAY HIKING	Dog Sled Tours
6. Mount Sanford	14. Bird Ridge	
7. Mount St. Elias	15. Flattop	

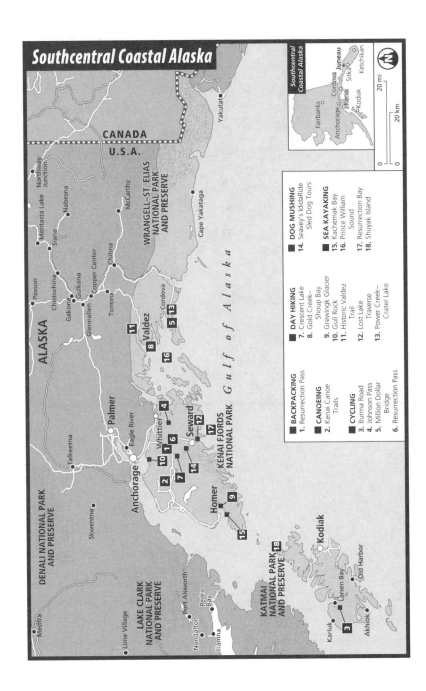

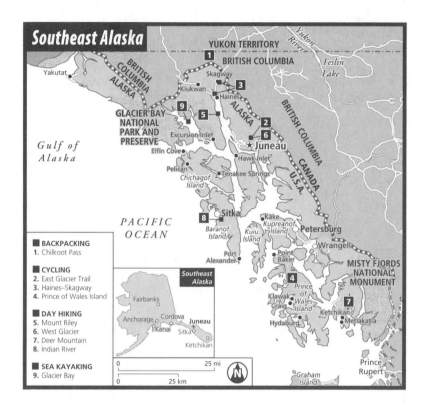

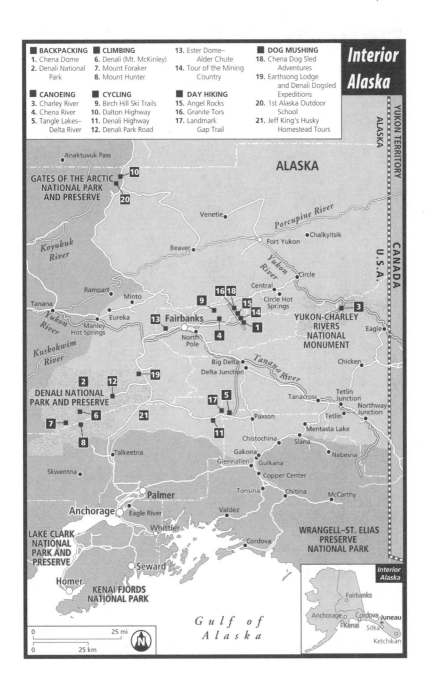

■ **BACKPACKING**
1. Chena Dome
2. Denali National Park

■ **CANOEING**
3. Charley River
4. Chena River
5. Tangle Lakes– Delta River

■ **CLIMBING**
6. Denali (Mt. McKinley)
7. Mount Foraker
8. Mount Hunter

■ **CYCLING**
9. Birch Hill Ski Trails
10. Dalton Highway
11. Denali Highway
12. Denali Park Road

13. Ester Dome– Alder Chute
14. Tour of the Mining Country

■ **DAY HIKING**
15. Angel Rocks
16. Granite Tors
17. Landmark Gap Trail

■ **DOG MUSHING**
18. Chena Dog Sled Adventures
19. Earthsong Lodge and Denali Dogsled Expeditions
20. 1st Alaska Outdoor School
21. Jeff King's Husky Homestead Tours

Interior Alaska

Bush Southwest Alaska

Nome
Golovin
Shaktoolik
Unalakleet
Stebbins
St. Michael
Kotlik
Anvik
Pilot Station
Yukon River
Bethel
Tanunak
Napakiak
Kuskokwim River
Toksook
Kipnuk
Kwigillingok

Bering Sea

St. Paul

St. George

■ **BACKPACKING**
1. Lake Clark National Park

■ **CANOEING**
2. Wood River

■ **SEA KAYAKING**
3. Katmai Coast

Cold Bay
Sand Point
King Cove
False Pass

Unalaska
Akutan
Biorka
Kashega

Nikolski

Pacific

See Inset
← Atka

Bush Southwest Alaska

Fairbanks
Anchorage
Cordova
Juneau
Kenai
Sitka
Kodiak
Ketchikan

0 — 20 mi
0 — 20 km

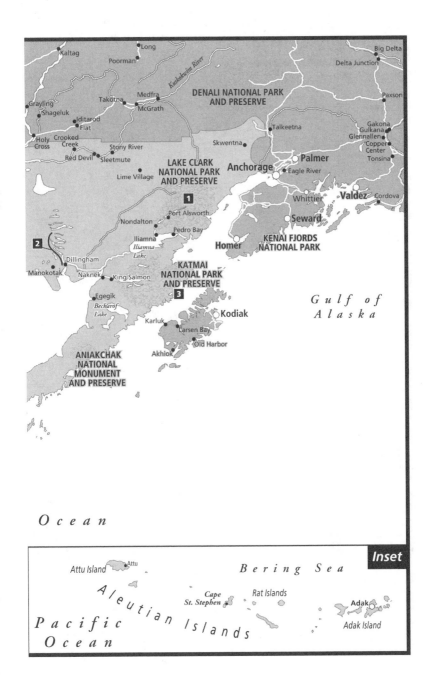

Kaltag
Long
Big Delta
Poorman
Delta Junction
Kuskokwim River
Grayling
Takotna
Medfra
DENALI NATIONAL PARK
AND PRESERVE
Paxson
Shageluk
McGrath
Iditarod
Flat
Talkeetna
Gakona
Gulkana
Holy Crooked
Cross Creek
Stony River
Skwentna
Glennallen
Copper
Center
Red Devil Sleetmute
LAKE CLARK
NATIONAL PARK
AND PRESERVE
Anchorage
Palmer
Tonsina
Lime Village
Eagle River
1
Port Alsworth
Whittier
Valdez
Cordova
Nondalton
Seward
Pedro Bay
2
Iliamna
*Iliamna
Lake*
Homer
KENAI FJORDS
NATIONAL PARK
Dillingham
Manokotak Naknek King Salmon
KATMAI
NATIONAL PARK
AND PRESERVE
*G u l f   o f
A l a s k a*
Egegik
*Becharof
Lake*
3
Karluk
Kodiak
Larsen Bay
Old Harbor
ANIAKCHAK
NATIONAL
MONUMENT
AND PRESERVE
Akhiok

O c e a n

Inset
Attu Island
Attu
B e r i n g   S e a
A l e u t i a n
*Cape
St. Stephen*
Rat Islands
Adak
*P a c i f i c
O c e a n*
I s l a n d s
Adak Island

Bush Far North Alaska

■ **BACKPACKING**
1. Brooks Range

■ **CYCLING**
2. Anvil Mountain

■ **DOG MUSHING**
3. Jerry Austin's Alaska Adventures

Arctic

Wainwright

Chukchi Sea

Brooks Range

Point Hope

NOATAK NATIONAL PRESERVE

Kivalina

CAPE KRUSENSTERN NATIONAL MONUMENT

Kiana

Kotzebue

Noorvik

RUSSIA

BERING LAND BRIDGE NATIONAL PRESERVE

Buckland

Taylor

Wales

2

Koyuk

Elim

Shaktoolik

Golovin

Nome

Unalakleet

St. Lawrence Island

3

Stebbins   St. Michael

Kotlik

Grayling

Anvik

Bering Sea

Yukon River

Pilot Station

Bush Far North Alaska

Fairbanks

Anchorage   Cordova   **Juneau**

Kenai   Sitka

Kodiak   Ketchikan

Tanunak

Bethel

Kuskokwim River

Napakiak

0   20 mi

0   20 km

Nunivak Island

Toksook

Kipnuk

Kwigillingok

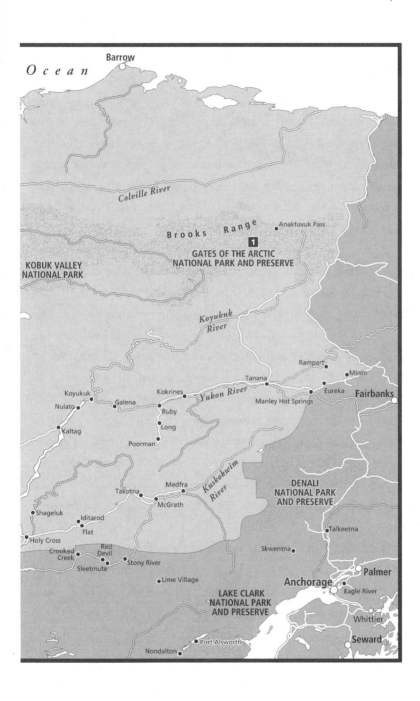

Ocean

Barrow

Colville River

Brooks Range

Anaktuvuk Pass

1

**GATES OF THE ARCTIC
NATIONAL PARK AND PRESERVE**

**KOBUK VALLEY
NATIONAL PARK**

Koyukuk
River

Rampart

Minto

Tanana

Kokrines

Yukon River

Eureka

Fairbanks

Koyukuk

Manley Hot Springs

Nulato

Galena

Ruby

Kaltag

Long

Poorman

Kuskokwim
River

Medfra

Takotna

McGrath

**DENALI
NATIONAL PARK
AND PRESERVE**

Shageluk

Iditarod

Flat

Talkeetna

Holy Cross

Crooked
Creek

Red
Devil

Skwentna

Sleetmute

Stony River

Lime Village

Anchorage

Palmer

Eagle River

**LAKE CLARK
NATIONAL PARK
AND PRESERVE**

Whittier

Port Alsworth

Seward

Nondalton

continued from page 3

block the skies, highways bisect the ground, and crowds fill every space, Alaska lets us breathe, slow down, and appreciate the earth. It's a good way to live.

Unfortunately, the very things that make this state so alluring—its endless possibilities and unlimited destinations—can also intimidate visitors who don't know where to begin. That's where *Alaska Adventure Guide* comes to the rescue. The most-often-heard lament among travelers to this state is that they didn't get to see everything they wanted. Believe us, they're not alone. There are lifelong Alaskans who *still* haven't seen the entire state, so what's the hurry for those of you seeing it for the first time?

This guide strives to narrow your focus, readjust your internal rules of measurement, and help you see that the bigness of Alaska does not have to be overwhelming. Slow down. Enjoy the special moments. Watch the sun set behind a snowcapped mountain, or peer through binoculars at a pair of bear cubs frolicking on a hillside. Sip some locally brewed beer and listen to street musicians perform. Set up camp and roast some marshmallows by the fire. Paddle to a remote cove and stop to watch sea otters play.

TRAVELER'S TIP

▶ Adjust your perspective and think s-l-o-w.

In other words, think of Alaska as more than just a one-time vacation. This state is larger than most European countries, and there is no way you'll be able to see it all in a week, two weeks, or even three.

Take time to absorb the breadth and depth of a place that still retains a bit of Last Frontier wildness despite the ever-quickening encroachment of progress.

No matter which part of Alaska you visit, you will experience a sense of epic scale. The distinct regions each have their own climate, culture, and geography, with unique opportunities for adventure—from rafting to backpacking to dog mushing to kayaking. The one aspect they all share, however, is room to roam.

▲ A Quick Glimpse at Our Regions

WHEN PLANNING a visit to Alaska based on outdoor adventure, the most important question to ask is, "What do I want to do?" How you get there, which region of the state you'll need to go to, and how to organize the logistics will fall into place quite easily after that first question is resolved. *Alaska Adventure Guide* is set up with this premise in mind, offering a breakdown of activities and outfitters in our special-interest chapters.

However, if your trip happens to be limited to a specific region—for example, if your great-uncle on your father's side has sent you a ticket to Fairbanks, or if you have just enough frequent-flier miles to get you to Anchorage—start by simply perusing our region-by-region chapters. More details on each area are available in their respective chapters, but here's a quick overview.

SOUTHCENTRAL INLAND ALASKA

Southcentral Inland Alaska begins with the state's largest population center, the municipality of **Anchorage,** and moves inland toward **Talkeetna** to the north and the **Copper River–Glennallen** corridor to the west. At just fewer than 300,000 people—more than 40% of the state's residents—Anchorage is the hub of Alaska's economy. With its port, train station, and international airport, it serves as a gateway for travelers from around the globe. Yet the sprawling metropolis is surrounded by wilderness: the waters of **Cook Inlet** and the dense spruce, birch, and aspen forest of **Chugach State Park.** It is entirely conceivable, then, to have an outstanding outdoor adventure without ever leaving the city limits.

Naturally, Anchorage has a cosmopolitan side. Even the most discriminating travelers will find shopping, theater, art galleries, museums, and fine dining to suit their tastes. A short drive south brings you to the world-class ski resort at **Mount Alyeska.** To the north lie such gems as the **Matanuska-Susitna Valley,** which affords incredible rafting, hiking, and biking options, as well as a chance for mountaineering even in the summer.

SOUTHCENTRAL COASTAL ALASKA

The coastal waters and communities that make up **Prince William Sound,** the **Kenai Peninsula,** and **Kodiak Island** are included in the region we call Southcentral Coastal Alaska. These areas are overwhelmingly the best places for water recreation such as adventure cruising and sea kayaking, but don't overlook the superior hiking, biking, and wildlife viewing. The Kenai Peninsula satisfies just about any outdoor dream, which is why it is known as Alaska's playground to residents who flock there when they have their own vacation time to spend.

SOUTHEAST ALASKA

Often referred to as "The Panhandle," which reflects its status as the long, thin branch of the state holding everything together, Southeast Alaska is an especially diverse region, offering lush forests, rich native culture, and limitless coastline. It is the ideal place for adventure cruising as well as kayaking, wildlife viewing, birding, fishing, and biking. Of its communities, only **Skagway** and **Haines** connect to the road system, but it is an easy area to visit by air and water. The region's largest city in area, **Juneau,** is also the state capital. From here, day trips to outlying waterfront villages can easily be arranged. The state ferry system forms an integral part of life for those who call Southeast Alaska home.

THE INTERIOR

Point smack-dab in the middle of the state, and you've got the Alaska of most visitors' imaginations: the Interior. Towering mountain ranges extend forever along the Parks Highway toward **Fairbanks,** the Interior's largest city. In the north of the state looms the wild **Brooks Range** and, in the south, the **Alaska Range.** In between is land so wide open that when you pass a cabin or small business along the road, you wonder how on earth the people survive.

But survive they do. The Interior is home to hardy Alaskans who brave cold and isolation for the reward of a simple, uncluttered way of life. In summer, constant sunlight and temperatures in the 80s bring a blessed reprieve, a time to play. This is a region rich in dog-mushing expertise, and in wilderness-hiking and backpacking opportunities galore. And if you want to see wildlife, this is the place to go.

THE BUSH

Fanning out from the Interior is land so remote that it is simply called the Bush. The majority of Alaska's native people choose to reside here, often living off the land by fishing, hunting, and gathering as their ancestors did before them. The largest communities are **Barrow, Nome, Kotzebue,** and **Bethel,** augmented by dozens of villages scattered across the region. We have included **Southwest Alaska** as part of our Bush chapter because of its remoteness and sparse population.

The Bush's Inupiat, Yup'ik, and Aleut natives depend on boats, snowmobiles, and dog teams to get around the mostly roadless communities. In winter the rivers freeze, creating ribbon highways for snowmobile and dog-team travel; in summer, boats provide transportation. Today, most communities also have airplane service, connecting the world to these once-inaccessible places. The Bush is where some of the most adventurous of adventurers roam, rafting rivers that see perhaps fewer than a dozen people in any given year, or fishing lakes that don't know the feel of human footsteps.

▲ A Brief History of a Big State

TWO CENTS AN ACRE.

That's what William H. Seward, the man responsible for purchasing Alaska from Russia in 1867, negotiated for the United States.

At the time, that rate, which totaled $7.2 million, was called outrageous. Critics said Seward was a foolish man. They called the purchase Seward's Folly and the land Seward's Icebox.

But oh, what a bargain it was. Today, not only is Alaska one of the most beautiful states in the country, but it also boasts a wealth of natural resources

and a growing economy that is dependent on tourism. It's still lightly populated compared with other states, and it maintains a frontier attitude in many
smaller communities.

The Russians were among the first to explore the area, and vestiges of
their presence remain today. From their first ventures to Alaskan lands back
in the 1700s, the Russians have shown that they may have sold the territory,
but many of them never stopped calling it home.

Vitus Bering was the original Russian explorer. The year was 1741, and he
and his crew reached what is now called Kayak Island. However, Bering and
many of his fellow voyagers perished in a shipwreck on the return trip. Those
who survived the disastrous event brought home luxurious sea-otter skins that
spurred other Russian explorers to rush to Alaska. Grigori Shelekhov was one
of those entrepreneurs; in 1784 he founded the first permanent settlement in
Alaska on Kodiak Island and sent Aleksandr Baranov to manage his company.

Kodiak is, in fact, the first place the Russians settled, first in secluded Three
Saints Bay and later in present-day Kodiak. Their influence is evident during
a modern-day walking tour of the city, including the museum, Holy Resurrection Russian Orthodox Church, and the Saint Innocent Veniaminov Research
Institute Museum. A yearly event celebrates the canonization of a Russian
priest, Saint Herman, in an area outside of town called Monk's Lagoon.

As the Russians became involved with the sea-otter-skin industry, they
inevitably clashed with Alaskan natives, who saw the foreign influx as an
intrusion on their lives and livelihoods. By 1786 Russian fur traders had
made their way to the Kenai Peninsula and by 1791 had settled in the area.
Russian Orthodox priests arrived and began introducing the natives to Chris-
tianity, and their churches grew.

But tensions mounted, and in 1797 a battle for the Kenai erupted between
the Dena'ina Athabascans and the Lebedev Company, the fur-trading company based on the Kenai. More than 100 Russians, Dena'ina, and other
natives were killed.

Meanwhile, the majority of Russians had moved east toward Sitka and
other Southeast communities, where they continued to trade furs. By 1796

they had arrived in Yakutat, later settling in Sitka, which became their capital. The Tlingit people living in the area knew that submitting to the Russians meant allegiance to their czar and slave labor for their fur-trade company. A battle between the Tlingits and the Russians ensued in 1802, and nearly all the Russians and their Aleut slaves were killed.

In 1804, undaunted by the battle, Aleksandr Baranov arrived ready to fight. For six days he fought the Tlingits, this time overpowering them. The Russians named their newly acquired land New Archangel, and the site known as Castle Hill evolved.

Sitka is one of the best places to learn about Russia's influence on Alaska. Just take a walk around the city. Enjoy lofty views of the surrounding islands and ocean from Castle Hill (where, incidentally, "Russia America" officially became Alaska, USA, in 1867); see a re-created Russian blockhouse; visit the old Russian cemetery and the Lutheran cemetery, where Princess Aglaida Maksutov, wife of Alaska's last Russian governor, lies buried; pass many historical houses; check out Saint Michael's Russian Orthodox Cathedral; and visit the Russian Bishop's House, which is part of Sitka National Historical Park.

By the time the United States took ownership of Alaska, much of the Russian conflict had subsided. The next wave of activity to reach the state had nothing to do with war and a lot to do with wealth. Gold was discovered near Sitka in 1872, prompting the beginning of a gold rush that would peak at the turn of the 20th century. In 1897 the largest discovery was made in the Klondike, stretching from Canada's Yukon Territory into Alaska and attracting thousands of gold seekers. In 1898 prospectors found gold on the beaches in Nome, sparking another rush to the western part of the territory. The gold rush turned one-street towns into bustling cities of thousands, seemingly overnight.

By 1906 gold production was at its peak, and Alaska got its own nonvoting delegate to Congress. Gold mining was on the decline, but with the influx of so many new residents, other exciting prospects emerged. Copper mining at the Kennicott mine began, and oil production was already under way at select spots throughout the land. In 1912, Alaska was named an official U.S. territory.

Although still just a territory, Alaska played a significant role in the nation's economy, bringing in money from natural-resource development. Construction of the Alaska Railroad began in 1914, and logging in Southeast Alaska was becoming a large industry around the same time. In 1935 Depression-era farming families came to Alaska as part of the Matanuska Valley Project. The government-backed effort to create a self-sustaining farming community in Alaska gave poverty-stricken families free land in exchange for their sweat and toil in making it arable. While many abandoned the project, intimidated by the harsh winters and crude living conditions the first few years, others thrived. Today, countless generations of those first families still call the Matanuska-Susitna Valley in Southcentral Alaska their home. Visitors to the area frequently come to gawk at the giant cabbages, massive carrots, and other vegetables and fruits that grow so huge during the summer.

As those valley farmers settled into their new homes, another region of the Alaska territory came to the forefront of the public eye. Today, it's a little-known fact that the Japanese invaded the territory of Alaska during World War II, but in 1942 it was headline news. On a June day on the remote archipelago that makes up the Aleutian Chain in Southwest Alaska, just six months after the attack on Pearl Harbor in Hawaii, the Japanese struck. Planes from a Japanese aircraft carrier bombed the Naval Station and Fort Mears in Dutch Harbor, then occupied nearby Attu and Kiska islands. It was the first time since the War of 1812 that foreign forces had occupied American territory.

Forty-two people from the islands were taken to Japan as hostages. Seventeen of them died in captivity. Meanwhile, the U.S. government evacuated the remaining Aleuts from their homes in the Aleutian and Pribilof islands. American troops destroyed many homes on the islands to prevent the Japanese from settling in too easily. Many of the natives who once called this remote region home were not able to return for years. Much of their settlement had been burned to the ground, leaving them with nothing.

Fortunately, U.S. forces did not tolerate the occupation for too long. By May 1943, the Japanese had been mostly defeated, but at a high cost to American soldiers. In the end, more than 20 U.S. pilots and 2,500 troops perished.

With the war came better access to Alaska. Recognizing the need to reach this remote territory, the government approved funds in 1942 to build the Alaska Highway. U.S. Army engineer troops designed and built the primitive 1,400-plus-mile road in a mind-boggling nine months and six days, from Dawson Creek, British Columbia, to what is now Delta Junction in Alaska. It was the first and only overland connection to the Lower 48 states and still one of the primary ways of reaching Alaska today.

Alaska gained statehood in 1959, becoming the 49th state to join the nation. Over the years, defining moments put Alaska in the spotlight: On March 27, 1964, a Good Friday afternoon, a 9.2-magnitude earthquake rattled the state, wiping out the village of Chenega in Prince William Sound and the community of Portage on Turnagain Arm. Other communities suffered millions of dollars in damage. In the end, the 4-minute-long earthquake killed 131 people in Alaska, along with 14 others in Oregon and California who were swept away by tidal waves.

In 1971 Congress approved the Alaska Native Claims Settlement Act, which gave 40 million acres and $900 million to Alaskan natives, officially recognizing their aboriginal ownership of the land. For years the government had been vague about its acknowledgement of natives' land ownership, but the discovery of oil brought incentive for settling the longstanding claim. The signing of the Alaska Native Claims Settlement Act then cleared the way for construction of the Trans-Alaska Pipeline System, an 800-mile raised tube that carries oil from the North Slope oil fields to Valdez. The construction of the pipeline brought thousands of workers to the state, creating a wave of activity. A boom of construction followed, and for a time Alaskans were living large.

In 1980 the Alaska legislature, led by then-Governor Jay Hammond, recognized the value of the oil resource and created what it called the Permanent Fund, which held a quarter of all oil royalties for future generations and was paid out as a dividend to each qualified Alaskan once a year. The first checks, mailed in 1982, paid each qualified Alaskan, including babies and children, $1,000. Today the legislature is attempting to raid the Permanent Fund to pay for government. If you visit Alaska and read the newspapers or watch the news, you'll likely see countless reports about the ongoing debate. So far, voters have kept attempts to tap into the fund at bay. In 2000 the dividend to each Alaskan reached a record high of $1,963.86. In 2004 it dropped to $919.84, the first time since 1995 that it was below $1,000. By 2007 it was back up to $1,654, but in 2010 it fell to $1,281.

Through it all, Alaskans—both those native to the land and those who moved north for a bit of adventure but decided it was a pretty good place to call home—have persevered. They have proved that the critics who called Alaska Seward's Folly or Seward's Icebox all those years ago were simply wrong. Seward just may have been the most brilliant man of his time, recognizing in Alaska a potential that continues to shine today. Oil production, commercial fishing, and tourism are industries that offer Alaskans a way to earn a living in a ridiculously beautiful setting. But above all, Alaska's biggest asset is its natural environment. It is something to be celebrated, enjoyed, and, most of all, protected for generations to come.

▲ Alaska's Native Peoples and Cultures

UNLESS YOUR OUTDOOR adventure includes travel in some of the remotest sections of the state, you likely won't cross paths with many of Alaska's native people. It's a surprisingly true and unfortunate phenomenon: natives make up only 16% of the population of today's Alaska, although there are 11 distinct cultures and 20 languages among the group as a whole.

Many natives still live in the most remote and wild areas of the state, putting them off the radar for the traveler who blows by only the larger cities. Even though a fair number of natives live in the cities too, they share these places with tens of thousands of people of all nationalities. In fact, Anchorage is technically the largest native village in the state, considering that nearly 29,000 American Indians and Alaska natives call it home. That's a larger population than any of the more remote, mostly native communities.

It would be a shame to come all the way to Alaska, though, and not learn more about the indigenous peoples who first called this land home. Their

When in Alaska: Native Etiquette

When you visit an area whose residents are predominantly natives, above all, be respectful. Just as you would while traveling in any other country, whether you're encountering shepherds in Ireland leading their sheep home or aborigines in Australia working on their ranches, avoid the temptation to gawk. In general, treat them as you would want to be treated.

If you are close enough and able to, ask before taking photographs.

Native cultural events are steeped in tradition. Many of them represent the living or the dead and are religious in nature. The same goes for native burial sites.

You may notice that native Alaskans speak slowly and often take their time in responding to a question or comment. Do not become unnerved by this or assume they do not hear you.

Likewise, try not to interrupt when conversing with native Alaskans. It is purely a Western tendency to try finishing another person's thoughts or to jump in with your own opinions. By Alaska native standards, it is considered rude—although it would also be rude to point it out.

When traveling, especially in remote areas, be sure to secure the proper permits for visiting native-owned land. With the advent of the Alaska Native Claims Settlement Act, more than 40 million acres of Alaska land is native-owned. That means it is private. Some native corporations require a fee for use of their land; others require only that visitors get permission, and a few prohibit public access. (For details, see Part Three, "Native Lands: What You Should Know," on page 62.)

cultures are fascinating and impressive yet humbling and challenging. A good number of today's natives, especially those in the villages, still live entirely by the same means as their ancestors. They catch fish, harvest berries, and hunt for most of their food. They go whaling and hold potlatches. Their connection to the land is as close now as it was hundreds of years ago, despite the arrival of electricity, running water, and the convenience of four-wheel-drive vehicles in lieu of dogsleds.

In general, there are three groups of Alaska natives: Indian, Eskimo, and Aleut. The terms *Inuit* and *Native American* are sometimes used in place of *Eskimo* and *Indian* in an effort to be considerate, but that doesn't always work in Alaska. It is true that in many other places, *Eskimo* is considered a derogatory word because it is said to mean "eater of raw meat"; however, using the term *Inuit* is not accurate in an Alaskan context because the Inuit language is restricted to the peoples of Arctic Canada and portions of Greenland. In Alaska and Arctic Siberia, where Inuit is not spoken, the comparable terms are *Inupiat, Yup'ik,* or one of the other cultural names within that region.

For the most part in Alaska, *Indian* and *Eskimo* are not offensive words. In fact, Eskimos pride themselves on their heritage. Still, if you feel uncomfortable using such terms, simply ask a native which culture he or she comes from. The natives of the northern reaches of Alaska will not use the word *Eskimo* when answering. Instead they likely will name a more specific culture, such as Inupiat, Yup'ik, or Cup'ik.

These three designations are further divided into five cultures, based on similarities in tradition, language, and proximity. At the **Alaska Native Heritage Center,** considered the defining authority on the subject, there are houses representing each of the five cultures, and visitors to the Anchorage-based center can learn how the varying native groups lived. These groups include Athabascan; Yup'ik and Cup'ik; Inupiat and St. Lawrence Island Yupik; Aleut and Alutiiq; and Eyak, Tlingit, Tsimshian, and Haida. As the state continues to grow and new residents from all over the United States and other nations arrive, Alaska's first peoples are finding it more important than ever to celebrate their heritage and educate those who want to know more about them.

ATHABASCAN

You'll see the word *Athabascan* spelled two ways, with a *c* and with a *k*, but don't be confused—they are one and the same. The geographic region for the

Athabascan people traditionally begins in the Interior, just south of the Brooks Range, and follows all the way to the Kenai Peninsula, which is described in more detail in the Southcentral Coastal chapter (page 331). Before the advent of modern transportation, the Athabascans lived along five major rivers: the Copper, Yukon, Tanana, Susitna, and Kuskokwim. They were a nomadic people, often traveling hundreds of miles to follow their best sources of food, depending on the time of year and severity of the seasons.

Today, Athabascan people live throughout the entire state, as well as in the Lower 48 states. According to the Alaska Native Heritage Center, "the Athabascan people call themselves 'Dena,' or 'the people.' " They are taught a respect for all living things; hunting is for subsistence only. They also are taught to share, perhaps a throwback to a time when combining resources was the only way groups could survive. Sharing is a community-wide belief, and those who have, give.

When you see the name *Denali*—and, believe us, if you set foot in this state, you will—give a nod to the Athabascan people. Denali, the native name for Mount McKinley, North America's largest peak, is an Athabascan term meaning "high one."

TLINGIT, HAIDA, EYAK, AND TSIMSHIAN

The Haida, an Indian group of about 800 who emigrated from Canada, now live in Southeast Alaska, Prince of Wales Island, and surrounding areas. The Tlingit, about 11,000 strong, live mostly in the Southeast. The Tsimshian are a small group from Metlakatla living in the area on their own reservation. The Eyak are related to the Athabascans but influenced greatly by the Tlingits. The Eyak language died in 2008 with the death of its last known speaker.

INUPIAT AND ST. LAWRENCE ISLAND YUPIK ESKIMOS

The Inupiat and the St. Lawrence Island Yupik people call themselves the "Real People," according the Alaska Native Heritage Center, and their homelands are in northern and northwestern Alaska. They depend largely on subsistence, still hunting whales, seals, walruses, and other large animals and gathering berries seasonally. They also hunt birds and fish when the conditions are right. These groups of natives are in the same category because of their similar subsistence patterns, the way they construct their homes, and the tools they use to survive.

St. Lawrence Island Yupiks speak Siberian Yupik, which is different from the languages spoken by other Yup'ik Eskimos (thus the difference in the spellings *Yupik* and *Yup'ik*).

YUP'IK AND CUP'IK

These groups of Eskimos live in Southwest Alaska in such communities as Nome, Unalakleet, and Perryville. Their names come from the dialects of the languages they speak. Like the Yupiks of St. Lawrence Island and the Inupiat of north and northwestern Alaska, they depend on a subsistence lifestyle for their livelihood, and elders tell stories of traditional ways of life to teach younger generations about their heritage.

ALEUT AND ALUTIIQ

South and Southwest Alaska are the original regions of the Aleut and Alutiiq peoples, although today they live all over the state and beyond. Traditionally, Aleuts and Alutiiqs depended on the ocean for their livelihoods, living off what they could catch from the sea, creeks, rivers, or even lakes. Their territory ranged from the North Pacific and Bering Sea, from Prince William Sound to the end of the Aleutian Chain. In places such as Kodiak Island, the influence of Russians, which began in the 18th century, can still be seen today. The Orthodox Church became the focal point of every village, and the native people in these communities adopted many of the Russian traditions and the language.

WANT TO KNOW MORE? The **Alaska Native Heritage Center,** which provided the bulk of information for this section, can be contacted at 8800 Heritage Center Dr., Anchorage 99506; 800-315-6608 or 907-330-8000; **alaskanative.net.**

PART TWO
PLANNING YOUR TRIP

▲ Is It Cold All the Time?
The Truth about Alaska's Seasons

YOU'VE SEEN THE pictures. You've heard the stories. Now that you have a copy of *Alaska Adventure Guide*, you have the facts.

One key fact is that living in Alaska isn't that much different from living in any other four-season state. The winters, while very, very cold on occasion, really aren't that punishing once you get used to them. The summers, while admittedly shorter than and not quite as humid as summers in the Lower 48, truly are warm enough for shorts and sandals. And the shoulder seasons of fall and spring are

Alaska's Climate

Take a look at the chart to the right, based on information from the Alaska Climate Research Center and data from the National Oceanic and Atmospheric Administration, and you may conclude that Alaska is a perennially cold place—the warmest average temperature in July does not exceed 63°. The truth is, these numbers can be deceiving, though they can give you an idea of which areas generally have milder climates than others.

Remember that these are averages, taken over a 24-hour period, and they reflect the day's high and low temperatures. On a sunny July day in Anchorage, for example, the temperature could easily reach the low 70s. However, it could be only 50°F in the morning or the middle of the night.

So don't be daunted by the numbers. In general, Alaska is comfortable in the summer. As for winters, however, we'll let you be the judge.

shorter, squeezed into just a few weeks rather than a few months. Blink and you could miss the changing colors of the leaves in the fall. In spring it sometimes seems that there's snow on the ground one week and fully greened-up trees the next.

The real difference between Alaska's climate and that of other places is its variety. The coastal weather that envelops so much of the state collides with the mountainous terrain, making Alaska's weather a bit tumultuous. It may be sunny and dry at the beginning of the day but rainy by afternoon. Snowstorms in July are not unheard of. At the base of a hiking trail, the temperature might be in the high 60s, but once you get above the tree line and hit the summit, it can drop by 20 degrees or more. In more ways than one, especially when it comes to weather, Alaska is a land of extremes.

▲ AVERAGE DAILY TEMPERATURES

City	JAN	APR	JUL	OCT	Overall
Anchorage	14.9°F	35.8°F	58.4°F	36.6°F	35.9°F
Barrow	−13.4°F	−2.2°F	39.3°F	13.5°F	9.4°F
Fairbanks	−10.1°F	30.7°F	62.5°F	25.1°F	26.9°F
Homer	22.7°F	35.4°F	53.4°F	37.5°F	37.4°F
Juneau	24.2°F	39.7°F	56.0°F	42.2°F	40.6°F
Kodiak	29.9°F	37.5°F	54.4°F	40.7°F	40.8°F
Nome	7.0°F	17.6°F	51.5°F	28.0°F	26.2°F
Valdez	20.5°F	37.1°F	54.9°F	38.1°F	37.7°F

Then there is the geographic distance. The weather in Barrow, at the northern edge of Alaska, and Ketchikan, on the Southeast Panhandle, can be bizarrely different. On an average July day in Southeast Alaska, highs can reach 61°F; in Barrow, you're lucky if it rises above 45°F. That's why deciding on your destination within the state is so important.

▲ How to Stay Safe in the Wilderness

THE MOST IMPORTANT thing to remember about visiting Alaska's backcountry is that it is wild. A trail that starts at the edge of the metropolitan city of Anchorage, for example, can be just as dangerous as a wilderness setting in the middle of the Bush. In fact, animal–human encounters are more likely to happen close to towns, the direct result of humans' ever-encroaching presence into the woods that bears, moose, and other wild animals call home.

However, we encourage you not to be fearful of Alaska's outdoors. Bears do not lurk around every bush; mosquitoes do not carry West Nile virus (not yet, anyway). It will not snow in the middle of a 70° sunny day in July, despite the temperamental weather the state often experiences.

To borrow a phrase from the Boy Scouts, be prepared. With a few simple precautions, you should have no problem in the woods and tundra and rivers and oceans of Alaska.

BEARS

We could write an entire book on the issues surrounding bears—how to avoid them, how to watch them, and how to protect yourself against them should it come to that. But let's just give you this first bit of advice: encountering a bear of any kind is very unlikely. If you go into the Alaska wilderness preoccupied with a fear of bears, your apprehension will take much of the enjoyment out of your trip. This isn't to say that bears aren't a threat at all, but if you follow these guidelines, your chance of an encounter is quite slim.

Experts agree that bear repellents are your best protective option, especially for those unaccustomed to using firearms. Repellent sprays cost anywhere from $20 to $70 and can reach varying distances. Do not carry a firearm unless you are skilled at using it and have ascertained that it is allowed in the particular area you are traveling.

Never approach bears. This seems almost absurd to mention, but it has happened before. Most Alaskans can tell you the story of the Australian tourist who thought Binky the polar bear at the Alaska Zoo was so cute that she decided to climb into the cage with him. Binky, needless to say, chewed on the woman for a while before she was eventually rescued. Even if bear watching is your goal, view the beasts *from a distance*.

Keep a very clean camp, and store food, toothpaste, and anything else that has even a slight scent in a bear-proof container at least 30–50 yards from your sleeping camp. Do not bury your trash, because it will attract bears and thus accustom them to humans (not to mention you'll be littering). Avoid camping

TRAVELER'S TIP

▶ We acknowledge that bear bells, which can be strapped onto packs to create noise, are popular, but we find that they distract from the wilderness experience and are not at all necessary. The incessant jingling also diminishes your chance of seeing other wildlife that you might be seeking, such as birds, moose, or small mammals.

near streams and other spawning areas when salmon are running—bears will be there.

Make noise, sing, or clap your hands when traveling through areas that are densely populated with trees and brush that makes visibility a challenge. Bears generally attack only when frightened, when protecting their food, or when you approach a sow with cubs. Making noise can give the bear a chance to run off, thus avoiding an encounter.

The chances of encountering a polar bear are close to zero unless you are wandering the Chukchi Sea or some other Far North destination. Instead, brown or black bears are the ones to watch out for. Brown bears can range in color from honey to cinnamon and have platter-wide faces with short snouts; black bears, by contrast, have long, skinny faces and snouts, and range in color from jet black to a bluish gray.

If a brown bear charges, stand your ground until the animal is approximately 3 feet away. If an attack is imminent, drop and play dead, locking your hands behind your neck and balling up to protect your vital organs. If you are wearing a pack or riding a bicycle, try to position yourself so that the gear is between you and the animal. Do not run. You will not get away.

If a black bear charges, fight back. These animals attack to kill and are not deterred by passive behavior. We can't promise that you'll win the fight, but it is worth a try. The upside: black bears rarely attack.

MOOSE

Although moose can seem as benign as cows chewing their cud in a pasture, these lanky ungulates can be quite dangerous, attacking seemingly without reason and charging or stomping pets and people. Like bears, they mainly attack when they're provoked,

TRAVELER'S TIP

▶ If you encounter a moose, give it wide berth. If the animal sets its ears back or flattens them against its head, it may be getting angry. If the hair on its back bristles, it could be about to charge. Move slowly. If you happen upon a young moose, look around for the mother. You do not want to get between her and her young. Most moose prefer to be left alone. If they are grazing on trees or shrubs and do not respond to your presence, you should be able to pass without incident.

frightened, or defending their young, but sometimes they just seem to not want people around.

You're much more likely to see a moose than a bear—moose wander the streets of Anchorage, browse in lawns (just check YouTube), and use trails as their own personal pathways. The popular Tony Knowles Coastal Trail, which skirts the city's edge, is a veritable moose hangout.

If a moose does charge, your best bet is to try placing an obstacle such as a tree or a bush between yourself and the animal, so that the moose's flailing hooves cannot make contact. As with bears, do not run.

OTHER WILDLIFE

Alaska also teems with creatures such as squirrels, mice, martens, hoary marmots, beavers, and muskrats. Larger mammals such as mountain goats, caribou, wolves, and Dall sheep are usually shy but sometimes unpredictable. Among the most irksome are porcupines, which are not aggressive creatures but will chew on your gear. If you leave your sweat-soaked, salty-tasting backpack outside, chances are that a porcupine will snack on it; the same goes for leather boots or rubber bike tires. And for obvious reasons, don't startle a porcupine—you could end up with a face full of quills. As a plus, though, we have no snakes!

BUGS

Alaskans often joke that the state bird is not the ptarmigan but the mosquito. From the feel of their bites, these irritating insects can certainly seem as large as birds. Alaska has 25 types of mosquitoes, none of which carry disease but any of which can easily spoil your outdoor experience. They arrive each spring in the state by the millions—a cruel joke to those of us who yearn to be outdoors in short sleeves and shorts.

Mosquitoes can become overwhelming as you get farther away from civilization, and they can turn a serene camping experience into a cramped, stuck-in-your-tent nightmare. June and July are the worst months for mosquitoes, but these suckers can appear as early as late April and hang around through

August in some places. They can be brutal on lakes and streams as well as in wet, swampy areas and brushy ones, which you may come upon while backpacking. Pack bug spray—the most powerful kind you can stand—along with a head net and long-sleeve shirts and pants. If you don't like the chemicals in bug sprays, consider a citrus- or eucalyptus-based formula rather than forgoing repellent altogether.

Other bugs to look out for include biting flies and various bee species. Happily, we have no dangerous spiders or scorpions to worry about.

WEATHER

Perhaps the greatest threat to an outdoor vacation is the weather. If you aren't dressed properly or if you become too wet and cold, you risk developing hypothermia, a life-threatening drop in your core body temperature, even in the summer. This is a very real danger in Alaska, especially in the mountains, where temperatures drop as you move higher. Hypothermia can sneak up on you, making you feel as if you're just slightly cold, before rapidly developing into a disorientation that can lead to more-dangerous problems.

Avoiding hypothermia is simple: don't get wet. Even a shirt damp with perspiration can be dangerous if it's all you're wearing while you stand atop a windy summit. As comfortable as cotton is, resist the temptation to wear it—the saying "cotton kills" is well known in Alaska, and most people opt for synthetics or woolen sweaters and fleece instead.

Wear polypropylene or other moisture-wicking underwear against your skin and quick-drying layers over that; add layers as the conditions warrant. Always carry a spare pair of undergarments in case you get submerged in water or otherwise wet. Bring

TRAVELER'S TIP

▶ If you must pack cotton clothes, save them for town, not the wilderness.

along a hat and at least a pair of glove liners for unexpected cold weather, again even in the summer. And make sure to pack a waterproof raincoat and pants as an outer shell. (See "How to Pack Smart," page 35, for additional tips.)

WATER

Alaska's cold water can turn a simple slip in a stream into a potentially deadly situation. Hypothermia can set in quickly. When crossing streams and rivers, always pick the route that seems the most shallow and least swift. Cloudy water, made gray by glacial silt, can hide possible dangers such as rocks and deep spots, so if you're not sure, don't try to cross. If possible, cross streams and rivers while linking arms with a partner or partners to reduce the chance of getting swept away. If you're in a group of more than two hikers, form a triangle and pivot your way across the river, thus creating enough disturbance in the river's flow to ease walking. Walk parallel to the current, and unhook your backpack from your waist in case you slip and get pulled under—this way you can get out of it without as much of a struggle. Morning is the best time to cross a stream or river, when the water tends to be at its lowest. If possible, shoot for an early-morning crossing.

NAVIGATION

A map and compass are obvious necessities for anyone traveling into the backcountry, even on trails. In Alaska, many trails are quite primitive and can overlap game trails and other unmarked paths, possibly creating confusion when you're trying to travel a main trail. Farther out, in the roadless areas, there often are no trails at all. Acquaint yourself with how to use a topographical map and how to read a compass. The U.S. Geological Survey produces the most-often-used maps, but commercial maps of various regions of Alaska also can be purchased. Many outdoor travelers can read a global-positioning system (GPS) and rely on them for backcountry travel. They can be particularly useful tools for travel in trailless areas.

ADVANCE PLANNING

Don't leave home without telling someone where you're going and when you expect to be home. Write down your plans, and leave them with someone you trust. If they change at the last minute, as can often happen if planes get delayed or the weather turns, call someone—anyone—and let him or her know your alternative travel plan. It's a simple thing to do and will make it easier for rescuers to zero in on your location if you get into trouble. Many trails and recreation areas have a sign-in sheet at the trailhead. Use it.

Alaska doesn't have the all-encompassing cell-phone coverage common to the Lower 48, so don't assume that you'll be able to call for help in an emergency. Emergency Location Transmitters and satellite phones can be rented and are worth the peace of mind if you plan to travel through remote areas where you don't expect to see others.

▲ How to Pack Smart

THE BEST WAY to prepare for a visit to Alaska is to pack in layers, a tenet that most outdoor travelers already know well. Not only does this method make sense, but it also allows you to stay warm and dry while mixing and matching outfits to your heart's content.

The following is a suggested clothing packing list for the general outdoor traveler. Adjust your list according to the activities you plan to tackle.

UNDERWEAR   Synthetic or woolen long underwear wicks moisture away from the skin and serves as a good barrier against mosquitoes and sun in the summer. Because Alaska is prone to frequent rainstorms, long underwear is a must. Depending on the length of your trip, bring one to three pairs.

SOCKS   Synthetic or woolen socks work best. Bring one to three pairs.

SHIRTS   Two long-sleeve shirts, preferably made of a quick-drying material available at sport shops all over, are the best choice. They double as town shirts and don't wrinkle as easily as cotton. Pack two quick-dry T-shirts too, for warmer days.

PANTS   Fleece pants work well at night for camping; quick-drying hiking pants can be worn for many outdoor adventures, from biking to backpacking.

SHORTS   Despite widespread beliefs to the contrary, many days are warm enough for hiking in shorts, which are good for fording shallow streams or rivers. Pack one to two pairs. We prefer shorts with lots of pockets for keeping maps, a compass, bug spray, and other necessities close at hand. Some people prefer shorts that have belt loops, so they can strap on a knife, bear spray, or other safety items.

FOOTWEAR   Your choice of shoes will be based largely on what types of trips you plan to take, but in general boots are best. Today's boot makers have developed boots that are light yet tough enough to handle trailless hiking and trekking. However, heavier leather boots will provide more support for longer treks when carrying more weight. Plan, too, on boots that will keep your feet warm. Bring a pair of boots and a pair of comfortable camp shoes, preferably ones that can double as town shoes. We prefer **Teva** river sandals because they can be used to ford streams and rivers but also dry out quickly enough to be worn in town. **Crocs**—those ugly but lightweight foam-style shoes—are popular alternatives.

FOR THE EXTREMITIES   Even if you're traveling to the warmest place in Alaska at the height of summer, a knit hat and a pair of glove liners are must-haves. For travel during the shoulder seasons, bring heavier mittens and a balaclava to cover your face.

RAINGEAR   Rain pants and an outer shell for the upper body are probably the most important pieces of gear for anyone planning to spend time outdoors. Your parka can be lightweight or beefy, depending on the trip and duration, but above all it should keep you dry.

▲ When to Go

SUMMER TRAVEL

Summer is by far the most popular time to visit Alaska, so be prepared to pay for the privilege. Plane-ticket prices go up in the summer, as do rates for lodging at hotels and bed-and-breakfasts and prices at restaurants. In fact, many hotels and restaurants and most outdoor outfitters close during the winter or switch gears to a secondary business.

Summertime trips require careful planning because you are sharing this time with tens of thousands of other travelers. The lines at the airports, especially Ted Stevens Anchorage International Airport, can be overwhelming. You'll have to wait for seats in the most popular restaurants, and you'll likely need advance reservations to find a place to stay. So bring patience, and lots of it.

But don't let this dissuade you from coming to Alaska in the summer. Long called the Land of the Midnight Sun for its long days and very brief sunsets, Alaska is a magical place this time of year. You can sense the energy among the residents, who, after spending a winter wrapped in a cocoon of darkness, are squeezing every possible ounce of activity out of the summer. Don't be surprised to see folks riding bikes at 11 p.m., grilling dinner at midnight, or mowing their lawns at 5 a.m. Their internal clocks are so attuned to daylight that it is nearly impossible to let a good sunshiny day go to waste.

Maximum daylight during the summer ranges from 17 hours, 28 minutes in the Southeast community of Ketchikan to 19 hours, 21 minutes in Anchorage to around the clock in far-north Barrow, which has continuous daylight from May 10 to August 2 every year. Even when the sun finally does set, it's as if someone has simply dimmed the lights, not completely snuffed them out.

It can be difficult to sleep in this setting if you're used to pitch darkness at night. If so, bring a sleeping mask for camping, or ask for rooms with blackout curtains when you book your lodging.

WINTER TRAVEL

Surprisingly, winter travel is on the rise in Alaska, and those adventurous enough to take advantage of an Alaska vacation this time of year are in for a real treat. As stated earlier, most of the state is not unbearably cold in the winter. Sure, temperatures in such places as Barrow and the North Slope can stay below 0°F for weeks as a time, but in the main cities and outlying communities, they're more manageable. The average high in Anchorage in January, for example, is 21°F; in Fairbanks, it's 2°F.

Perhaps, too, Alaska is gaining more attention for its assortment of wintertime activities. With the growing popularity of the 1,000-mile Iditarod Trail Sled Dog Race, for example, dog mushing is becoming more and more mainstream. Visitors from around the world pay thousands of dollars to follow world-class racers from checkpoint to checkpoint by plane. Others opt to take their own dog-sledding trips, and plenty of reputable guides can teach them how.

In the Interior of Alaska, a celestial pastime is now gaining momentum. Visitors flock here in the winter to watch the mystical aurora borealis, or northern lights, dance across the sky. Entire travel packages center on such viewings, complete with hot-springs lodging, photography lessons, and the like. Admittedly, it's a one-of-a-kind undertaking.

Of course, Alaska is prime ski country, but it still lacks the overpopulation that many ski resorts elsewhere are encountering these days. The state boasts only one world-class ski resort, although fine skiing can be found at any number of regional spots. More important, it offers true adventure skiing, with heli-skiing options available throughout the state and cross-country skiing just about anywhere you go. Alaska is still a place where the activity is affordable; skiing is simply a way of life for Alaskans. Slip on some skis and head to the local bike trails, which are groomed for skiing in the winter, and you have the ideal winter getaway.

When you're traveling in the winter, there are a few basic things to remember. First of all, much of the state shuts down for the season, so don't expect to see and do all of the touristy things you may have read about. Second, dress for the weather. Bring heavy winter boots, a parka, and gloves, and always wear long underwear, even when walking around town. It may not be the most stylish of attire, but at least you'll be able to enjoy yourself.

Also, if traveling in a vehicle, especially on remote roads, make sure to have your cold-weather clothing items with you. Better yet, bring a sleeping bag or an extra blanket just in case your vehicle breaks down. In most cities and towns, this might be considered overkill, but on side roads during the winter in Alaska, it could be hours before a car happens by.

The bright side of winter travel in Alaska is that it is much more affordable: plane tickets plummet to half their summer rates, and hotels often offer discounted rooms and meals. You may find service a bit better too, as overworked summer employees have a little more breathing room and time to spend with their hotel and restaurant guests. You'll also be sharing the state with the locals, so you get a true sense of what it's like to live here.

SHOULDER SEASONS

Slip in an Alaska adventure during this time of year, usually right after Labor Day and just before Memorial Day, and you just may have the best of both worlds: lower prices and summerlike weather. As we've said, Alaska weather is unpredictable.

Springtime in Alaska, unlike in many states, tends to be drier, while fall is when the rain comes. It's not uncommon for late April to early May to be dry and unseasonably warm, making such activities as road cycling, birding, and hiking a real treat. Even better, the mosquitoes generally haven't hatched yet, giving you one less thing to worry about.

Fall, though it can be rainy, is a gorgeous time of year to visit. It is a short season, with only about three weeks of good fall foliage to enjoy. Still, if you hit fall during its peak, when the birch trees turn bright yellow and the alpine bushes go fiery red, there is nothing quite like it.

Hotels, restaurants, and outfitters have been working overtime during the busy summer season, and fall is a reprieve. Many are eager for the smaller crowds, the breaks between bookings, and the chance to slow down and relax. It's the ideal time to shop for bargains; get in on more intimate, custom-planned tours; and enjoy end-of-season outings such as backpacking and canoeing, wildlife viewing, and biking.

▲ Should I Travel Independently or with a Group?

WITH OUTDOOR RECREATION the focus of the typical adventurous traveler's vacation, we recommend that you plan your trip accordingly: choose your desired activity or activities, and then narrow your visit to the best region or regions of the state for those activities. After you've made these decisions, you'll need to make another, equally important one: will you travel independently or go with a group?

This seemingly minor detail can have a lasting effect on the quality of your adventure. Whether you're backpacking to an unnamed peak in the Brooks Range, rafting across a remote river, or cycling across Southeast Alaska, the wrong guide or the wrong group dynamic can turn any adventure to disaster. But what if you rely on your own limited knowledge of Alaska and things go wrong anyway?

We've experienced both travel options. While it can be risky, traveling with a group can add a pleasurable dimension to your adventure that you never thought possible. Having a guide along can offer peace of mind; he or she knows the land well and has presumably troubleshot potential problems many times before. While you will pay slightly more for a guided trip, consider the value of having someone else organize food, gear, and logistics while you just enjoy the flight (or drive or boat trip) north.

On the other hand, traveling alone is exciting, an accomplishment of which to be proud, especially in Alaska, where everything is so big and far away and unnamed. The frugal traveler can experience thrills at a lower cost, but he or she must be savvy and quite organized.

Take a few moments to consider the scenarios in the box on the following page. If you answer them truthfully, they should help you determine which traveling style is right for you.

OK, so this isn't a complete psychological evaluation, but in general, if you answered mostly A's, chances are you should go it alone. You will prefer the

What Kind of Traveler Are You?

▶ How do you feel when returning from a party, nightclub, or social event in which you must mingle with many people?
   a. Exhausted
   b. Exhilarated

▶ Just how organized are you?
   a. My checkbook is always balanced.
   b. Where *is* my checkbook?

▶ In my daily life . . .
   a. I have a routine that I follow every morning before going to work.
   b. I hit the snooze button three times and shower when I have time.

▶ When spending money . . .
   a. Every penny counts, and I cut coupons daily.
   b. I spend a few extra dollars and worry about it later.

▶ When taking risks . . .
   a. I think through a situation, eliminate the risk, and then move forward.
   b. I feel hesitant and second-guess my decisions.

control you have over your day-to-day activities by planning your own trip, and you will be careful enough to do it wisely.

Someone who answered mostly B's may be more flexible, more extroverted, and more open to the idea of traveling with people they don't know.

▲ Special-interest Trips

IT WAS WHEN the bear came within 3 feet, sniffing at us and our packs before nonchalantly wandering away, that I realized just how life-changing that nine-day backpacking trip in Denali National Park and Preserve would be. No matter how many mountains we climbed or how many rivers we forded, the "bear story" was the defining moment of that trip, more than a decade ago. That pale pink tongue sticking out to catch our scent; the small, yellowish eyes that seemed to be straining to see us; the wide, clawed feet that clicked over the gravelly riverbank—they are details held still in our memories, never to be erased by time.

This is what happens when you tighten the lens that encompasses all of Alaska and bring it into focus on one objective: "I *will* raft that river"; "I *will* climb that mountain"; "I *will* see those glaciers." Of course, it would be nice if you could avoid a bear encounter; even though ours turned out to be disaster-free, that isn't always the case. But the point is, every single nook and cranny in Alaska is filled with such memorable moments if only you take the time to embrace them.

Starting on page 64, we share a collection of our favorite outdoor activities in Alaska and where to find them. Our destinations will allow you to sample your choice of exciting options in Alaska and take the time to sample them well. Look them over. Think about what appeals to you. Compare the time commitment required for, say, a remote wilderness-backpacking trip versus an easily accessible river-rafting jaunt. Each has its own level of appeal, depending on your particular needs and preferences.

▲ Gathering Information

IF YOU'RE STILL trying to figure out where you want to go in Alaska, these resources may help. Some cater to the whole state, others to just a particular region. All of the accompanying Web sites are useful. Most of the cities and towns represented will send a complimentary visitors' guide if you fill in a request online. Allow a few weeks for them to actually deliver, though. Additional postage may be required for overseas requests.

STATEWIDE

ALASKA MAGAZINE   907-272-6070; **alaskamagazine.com.** A good place to read about the most interesting places and people in Alaska and get a feel for regional communities.

ALASKA GEOGRAPHIC   866-257-2757 or 907-274-8440; **alaskageographic.org.** A good source for regional publications, guidebooks, and maps of Alaska's public lands.

ALASKA TRAVEL INDUSTRY ASSOCIATION   travelalaska.com. This site has some great interactive maps to explore, and it often advertises travel deals.

ALASKA WILDERNESS RECREATION AND TOURISM ASSOCIATION   2207 Spenard Rd., Suite 202, Anchorage 99503; 907-258-3171; **awrta.org.**

ANCHORAGE DAILY NEWS   800-478-4200 or 907-257-4200; **adn.com.** The state's largest daily newspaper, with more statewide coverage than any other. One of the paper's Web sites, alaska.com, serves as a visitor resource, but the main news site is worth reading too.

FAIRBANKS DAILY NEWS–MINER   907-459-7566 (to order) or 907-459-7572 (newsroom); **news-miner.com.** The Interior's daily newspaper of choice, with an emphasis on this region and points north.

JUNEAU EMPIRE   907-586-3740; **juneauempire.com.** This longtime newspaper in the state capital, with an emphasis on Southeast Alaska issues, publishes some entertaining local-government stories.

THE MILEPOST   907-272-6070 ($29.95; to order, 907-726-4707 or **themile post.com**). This phone-book-size periodical is updated every year and, true to its name, gives a good milepost-by-milepost breakdown of all roads in Alaska, including the lesser-traveled ones. It also features mini-profiles of some Bush and off-the-road-system communities.

SOUTHCENTRAL INLAND ALASKA

Anchorage

ANCHORAGE CONVENTION AND VISITORS BUREAU   524 W. 4th Ave., Anchorage 99501-2212; 800-478-1255 or 907-276-4118; **anchorage.net.** Look for the sod-roofed Log Cabin and Downtown Visitor Information Center at the corner of F Street and Fourth Avenue.

Copper Valley–Glennallen

GREATER COPPER VALLEY CHAMBER OF COMMERCE   907-822-5558; traveltoalaska.com.

Matanuska-Susitna Valley

MAT-SU CONVENTION AND VISITORS BUREAU   7744 E. Visitors View Ct., Palmer 99645; 907-746-5000; **alaskavisit.com**. The visitor center is at Mile 35.5 Parks Hwy. (take the Trunk Road exit).

Talkeetna

TALKEETNA CHAMBER OF COMMERCE   907-733-2330; **talkeetnachamber.org**.

SOUTHCENTRAL COASTAL ALASKA

Anchor Point

ANCHOR POINT CHAMBER OF COMMERCE   907-235-2600; anchorpointchamber.org.

Cordova

CORDOVA CHAMBER OF COMMERCE AND VISITORS CENTER 907-424-7260; **cordovachamber.com**.

Homer

HOMER CHAMBER OF COMMERCE   907-235-7740; **homeralaska.org**.

Kenai

KENAI VISITORS AND CULTURAL CENTER   11471 Kenai Spur Hwy., Kenai 99611; 907-283-1991; **visitkenai.com**.

Kenai Peninsula

KENAI PENINSULA TOURISM MARKETING COUNCIL   35477 Kenai Spur Hwy., Suite 205, Soldotna 99669; 907-262-5229; **kenaipeninsula.org**.

Kodiak Island

KODIAK ISLAND CONVENTION AND VISITORS BUREAU   100 Marine Way, Suite 200, Kodiak 99615; 800-789-4782 or 907-486-4782; **kodiak.org**.

Seldovia

SELDOVIA CHAMBER OF COMMERCE   907-234-7612; **xyz.net/~seldovia**.

Seward

SEWARD CHAMBER OF COMMERCE   907-224-8051; **seward.com.**

Soldotna

GREATER SOLDOTNA CHAMBER OF COMMERCE   907-262-9814; **soldotnachamber.com.**

Valdez

VALDEZ CONVENTION AND VISITORS BUREAU   200 Chenega St., Valdez 99686; 907-835-2984; **valdezalaska.org.**

Whittier

GREATER WHITTIER CHAMBER OF COMMERCE   whittieralaskachamber.org.

SOUTHEAST ALASKA

Haines

HAINES CONVENTION AND VISITORS BUREAU   907-766-2234 or 800-458-3579; **haines.ak.us.**

Juneau

JUNEAU CONVENTION AND VISITORS BUREAU   1 Sealaska Plaza, Suite 305, Juneau 99801; 800-587-2201 or 907-586-1737; **traveljuneau.com.**

Ketchikan

KETCHIKAN CONVENTION AND VISITORS BUREAU   131 Front St., Ketchikan 99901; 800-770-3300 or 907-225-6166; **visit-ketchikan.com.**

Prince of Wales Island

PRINCE OF WALES CHAMBER OF COMMERCE   907-755-2626; **princeofwalescoc.org.**

Sitka

SITKA CONVENTION AND VISITORS BUREAU   907-747-5940; **sitka.org.**

Skagway

SKAGWAY CONVENTION AND VISITORS BUREAU   907-983-2854; **skagway.com.**

THE INTERIOR

Delta Junction and Points North

DELTA JUNCTION INFORMATION CENTER   Where the two highways meet; 907-895-5068.

Denali Area

DENALI CHAMBER OF COMMERCE   907-683-4636; **denalichamber.com.**

Denali National Park

DENALI NATIONAL PARK   907-683-2294; **nps.gov/dena.**

Fairbanks

FAIRBANKS CONVENTION AND VISITORS BUREAU   101 Dunkel St., Suite 111, Fairbanks 99701; 800-327-5774; **explorefairbanks.com.**

Nenana

NENANA VISITOR CENTER   A Street at the Parks Highway; 907-832-5435.

Tok

TOK "MAINSTREET ALASKA" VISITORS CENTER   At the junction of the Alaska Highway and Tok Cutoff; 907-883-5775; **tokalaskainfo.com.**

THE BUSH

Barrow

Visitor information is not readily available, but these agencies could be of help:

CITY OF BARROW   907-852-5211; **cityofbarrow.org.**
NORTH SLOPE BARROW PUBLIC INFORMATION DIVISION   907-852-0215.

Bethel

BETHEL CHAMBER OF COMMERCE   907-543-2911; **bethelakchamber.org.**

Dillingham

DILLINGHAM CHAMBER OF COMMERCE AND VISITOR CENTER   907-842-5115; **dillinghamak.com.**

King Salmon

KING SALMON VISITORS CENTER   907-246-4250.

Kotzebue

KOTZEBUE VISITOR INFORMATION CENTER   154 2nd St.,
Kotzebue 99752; 907-442-3890.

Nome

NOME CONVENTION AND VISITORS BUREAU   907-443-6624;
nomealaska.org.

Unalaska–Dutch Harbor

UNALASKA/PORT OF DUTCH HARBOR CONVENTION AND
VISITORS BUREAU   877-581-2612 or 907-581-2612; unalaska.info.

PART THREE
GETTING AROUND

▲ Coming into the State

THE BOTTOM LINE on travel to Alaska is that it will take some time. A typical flight from the East Coast to Alaska takes at least 10 hours; from Europe it will be even longer. Those coming from another country must now fly through one of the cities in the Lower 48 states, because the polar route from Asia is no longer a routine flight.

The other methods of travel, by land or sea, take even longer, but they constitute a trip in themselves, which can be filled with adventure along the way. The **Alaska Marine Highway,** which connects 30 coastal communities in Alaska, accommodates travelers with or without their own vehicles. Or take a cruise to reach the great land. Either way will be memorable.

The third option is to drive. The **Alaska Highway** is the main artery into the state, traveling some 1,400 miles from Yukon Territory, Canada, to Alaska. Popular modes of road travel to Alaska include recreational vehicle, automobile, and bus.

BY AIR

Carriers

Regardless of your ultimate destination, you'll likely pass through **Ted Stevens Anchorage International Airport,** the state's largest hub of airline activity. With connections from all over the world and more than 280 flights arriving daily, the Anchorage airport—named after the late longtime U.S. senator Ted Stevens—serves as the gateway to Alaska. The Anchorage airport is served by several major carriers to the rest of the United States and sometimes flights from Japan or Korea. It's also possible to fly into Fairbanks or Southeast Alaska. Most passengers come into Anchorage through Seattle, but for a bit more money you can fly nonstop to Anchorage from various major cities. There are many more flights in the summer than in the winter.

Alaska Airlines (800-426-0333; **alaskaair.com**) has more flights than all other airlines combined, with as many as 20 a day to Seattle in summer and summer nonstops to various other destinations, including Washington, D.C.; Chicago; Dallas–Fort Worth; Los Angeles; Minneapolis–St. Paul; Portland, Oregon; Vancouver, British Columbia; and La Paz, Mexico. Alaska Airlines is the only jet carrier with more than token coverage anywhere in Alaska other than Anchorage, and it has arrangements with commuter airlines that fan out from its network to the smaller communities. Other major airlines that serve Anchorage at the time of this writing include **American** (800-433-7300; **aa.com**), **Continental** (800-525-0280; **continental.com**), **Delta** (800-221-1212; **delta.com**), **US Airways** (800-428-4322; **usairways.com**) and **United** (800-241-6522;

TRAVELER'S TIP

▶ If you're willing to drop everything and go, sign up for **My Alaska Air,** an online newsletter that announces fare specials weekly, with tickets sometimes less than $100 from Seattle to Anchorage (go to **alaskaair.com** for details).

ual.com). Overseas airlines include **Asiana Airlines** (800-227-4262; **us.flyasiana.com**), **China Airlines** (907-248-3603; **china-airlines.com**), **Japan Airlines** (800-525-3663; **jal.com**), and **Korean Airlines** (800-438-5000; **koreanair.com**), as well as **Air Canada** (888-247-2262; **aircanada.com**) in the summer only. *Note:* Flight line-ups and airlines change too fast to keep track of here, so know that all of this is subject to change.

Fares

Flying in Alaska is simply a way of life: we do it so much that it comes naturally, and we've become savvy bargain-finders as a result. Fares vary wildly, so watching for sales can pay off. It's almost always cheapest to change planes in Seattle due to the competition on the Seattle–Anchorage route, and it seems the more complicated you're willing to make your route, the less you'll pay. So finding a good ticket price is a balancing act between efficiency and maintaining your sanity. If you can find a round-trip ticket for $400 or so, consider yourself lucky. Occasionally, you can nab a $300 ticket, but those are fairly restricted flights and destinations. International travelers should expect to pay a higher premium for their tickets—overseas travel runs more in the $500–$700 range when booked far in advance, although, again, the occasional bargain can be found. The airlines seem to watch each other closely, and when one offers a summer sale, often in April or early May, the others usually follow suit. If you get one of these tickets, count yourself lucky, because this seems to be happening less and less.

Getting to the Bush

To fly to Alaska's most remote roadless places, collectively known as the Bush, you'll have to jump on another plane, usually a small prop-driven aircraft that can hold just a few passengers. These planes have weight limits, so the pilots and crew will ask you how much you weigh. (This is not your driver's

🦌 Air-travel Tips

▶ **Small planes can be loud.** If you're sensitive to noise, be sure to have earplugs handy. Most small-plane operators are aware of this and will provide earplugs or headphones, but be prepared with your own 50¢ pair.

▶ **Check ahead with airline operators** both big and small for the rules regarding transport of potentially hazardous materials, such as fuel for cookstoves, lighters, bear spray, or any other combustibles.

▶ **When traveling with a backpack** as your primary gear, ask for or bring a large plastic bag in which to wrap it. It's not uncommon for packs to get wet, especially in floatplanes, as they land. Also, many commercial airlines require a bag to prevent backpack straps from getting caught in baggage carousels. If landing in the Bush, you can remove your plastic bag and give it to the pilot to carry back so you don't have to lug it around the wilderness.

license—resist the urge to fudge the numbers, because an overloaded plane is neither a good nor a safe thing.) Small air taxis like this are situated all over the state; Alaska has 10,932 registered aircraft, according to 2010 Federal Aviation Administration statistics. The state has 387 public-land-based airports, 33 heliports, and about 640 recorded landing areas. **Lake Hood** in Anchorage is the world's largest and busiest seaplane base. It accommodates an average of 110 takeoffs and landings daily, and more than 600 on a peak summer day. In fact, Alaska has 121 seaplane bases, more than any other state in the country.

Depending on your destination, the plane in which you fly will be equipped with floats for landing on water, skis for landing on snow or ice, or wheels for landing on remote runways. Bush planes and their pilots can take you to isolated fishing spots, wilderness lodges, cabins, or anywhere else you might want to go. In addition to the registered and known landing sites, skilled

Bush pilots are able to land on unnamed gravel bars and rivers or lakes all over the state, offering a truly unique experience. Some adventurers like to be dropped off at one remote location and hike, raft, or bike to another location for pickup; others prefer to be dropped off for an entire season, along with a summer's or winter's worth of gear. Whatever it is you have in mind, there likely is an Alaskan Bush pilot willing and able to help.

Be aware that the price for these Bush adventures can rival what you paid to reach Alaska on a jet (flying from Kodiak to Homer on most small planes, for example, will cost upward of $350 round-trip). A sometimes-less-expensive way to travel is by tagging along on the numerous mail planes that fly into some of the more remote villages on a twice- or three-times-a-week basis. While it will save money, these are trips of necessity, and you will be at the whim of the mail-carrier-cum-pilot's schedule. Check with local carriers in towns such as Kodiak, Homer, Fairbanks, Nome, and Barrow to see what the options are.

BY SEA

While it may take a bit longer to reach Alaska via the many cruise ships that sail north, it's definitely a pleasant way to reach the Last Frontier. There are several choices and just as many destinations.

Carriers

Start searching and you'll find an abundance of cruising options, especially in Southeast and Southcentral Coastal Alaska. But to arrive in Alaska from Canada or the Lower 48 states, your choices are more limited. The most affordable option is the **Alaska Marine Highway System** (800-642-0066; **ferry alaska.com**), a government-funded transportation system that not only offers an enjoyable way to reach Alaska but also serves as a vital link among coastal communities throughout Alaska. The Alaska Marine Highway is the only water-based transportation system recognized as a national scenic byway, taking passengers through the Inside Passage of Southeast Alaska, across the Gulf of Alaska, into Prince William Sound in Southcentral Coastal Alaska, and out to the Aleutians in Bush Alaska. It also brings passengers from the ports of Prince Rupert, British Columbia, and Bellingham, Washington. Passengers can come as they are or reserve a spot for their vehicles or RVs. Other choices providing transport from out-of-state include **Carnival Cruise Lines** (888-227-6482; **carnival.com**), which debarks from Vancouver, British Columbia; **Holland America Line** (877-724-5425; **hollandamerica.com**), which also leaves from Vancouver; and **Princess Cruises** (800-774-6237; **princess cruises.com**), which offers one-way destinations that begin in Vancouver, British Columbia, or Alaska and sail south.

Fares

While the Alaska Marine Highway is not vastly less expensive than private cruise companies, the real value lies in the fact that travelers can bring their own vehicles, thus saving money during their stay in Alaska. It's our favorite way to see Alaska because it allows us to travel at our own pace with no schedules to follow, and gives us the freedom to roam once we've reached our destination. Plus, it's a great way to meet real Alaskans, who depend on the Marine Highway much as Lower 48 folks depend on interstates. The one-way fare for one person traveling with a vehicle from Bellingham, Washington, to Skagway, Alaska, for example, is $1,200 without a private cabin (add at least another $350 for that privilege, as cabins are hard to come by). Add another $400 or so for recreational vehicles, and another $250–$350 per person, and your round-trip rate could go as high as $1,900 for a two-person getaway complete with recreational vehicle. Compare that price with the average price per person of a private cruise—$2,500—and you have quite a bargain, albeit much less lavish. You can also check the cruise-line and ferry-system Web sites for occasional specials from varying ports. Some of the deals can be up to 50% off, depending on your willingness to drop everything and go.

Getting to the Bush

Logistically, it's close to impossible to reach some of Alaska's roadless areas via cruise ship. However, small cruise-boat operators offer personalized treks into unexplored areas of Alaska aboard 5- to 15-passenger yachts and boats

Ferry-travel Tips

▶ If traveling on the Alaska Marine Highway with a car, keep in mind that the ferry has directional loads—the heavier the load, the slower the ferry travels. In general, loads are heavier going north until about mid-July; by August, loads are heavier going south. Plan your travel accordingly.

▶ Walk-on reservations are almost never needed. But if you want a private cabin or want to ensure a spot for your vehicle, you should definitely call ahead of time. Cabins are comfortable but small; beds are in a bunk arrangement. If you need two beds for sleeping but neither person in your party can climb to a top bunk, get a four-berth cabin with two bunks.

▶ Kayaks, bicycles, and other outdoors gear are allowed, but there is a fee. Call ahead for details. Pets may travel with you but must have current health certificates (within 30 days) in order to travel through Canada or into Alaska from another state. The cost for pets is $10–$25, depending on your port of departure. Pets must stay in carriers or in your vehicle.

and even small ships. These operators work at a premium: a cruise into the remotest parts of Alaska requires extremely careful planning and specialized equipment for navigating shallow waterways. **Cruise West** (888-851-8133; **cruisewest.com**), a small-ship cruise company, travels to popular Southeast destinations, and **Discovery Voyages** (800-324-7602; **discoveryvoyages.com**) offers personalized trips in Prince William Sound. Again, the Alaska Marine Highway System is best equipped to get you to such far-flung places as Dutch Harbor and Kodiak Island. Fares for wilderness cruises vary widely depending on your planned activities and destination. Ten days of birding in Prince William Sound will run about $3,500 per person; the two-week trip to the Bering Sea ranges $11,000–$19,000 per person.

(For more information on cruising as an adventure in itself rather than as a means to another destination, see Part Four.)

BY RAIL

Although there are two railways in Alaska, the aptly named **Alaska Railroad** and the **White Pass–Yukon Route,** they can't get you to the Lower 48 states. The Alaska Railroad, with hubs in Anchorage, Fairbanks, and Seward, carries passengers from the Interior through the Southcentral Inland and Coastal areas. The White Pass–Yukon Route, for visitors to Skagway who want to briefly relive the life of the gold-rush era, travels only as far as Whitehorse, Yukon Territory, Canada.

Carriers

The closest you'll get to Alaska by mainstream railway is by taking **Amtrak** (800-872-7245; **amtrak.com**) from the West Coast to Bellingham, Washington, and connecting with the Alaska Marine Highway System, which is quite close to the railroad depot. From the east, reserve a seat with **Via Rail** (888-842-7245; **viarail.ca**) out of Canada. The transcontinental route starts in Toronto and has a connection in Jasper that will take you to Prince Rupert, British Columbia, another launching point for the Alaska Marine Highway System.

Fares

The four-day journey from Toronto to Prince Rupert on Via Rail costs approximately $600 Canadian for a round-trip ticket, plus one stopover at which you must pay your own lodging. On Amtrak, it's even more complicated. For example, a round-trip ticket from Albuquerque, New Mexico, to Bellingham takes three days and requires two train changes, one in Los Angeles and the other in Seattle. That trip, with a small room, is $1,500, slightly less if you travel coach. Both railway Web sites above have special online deals, so be sure to check for those. There also are discounts for booking at least five days in advance.

BY LAND

On the average map, the distance between Alaska and the rest of the United States really doesn't look that far. Washington state, for example, appears to

TRAVELER'S TIP

▶ We suggest that you forget all preconceived notions of interstates and high-speed travel.

be quite close. But don't be fooled: Alaska is so big that it's difficult to draw it to scale on most maps. The truth is, driving to Alaska, whether in a lumbering recreational vehicle or in the speediest of sports cars, will take time. Lots of time. The distance between Seattle and Anchorage is 2,435 miles; from Chicago, it's 3,818 miles. Compare that with the distance between Miami and Los Angeles—2,720 miles—and, well, you get the picture.

Driving Your Own Car

If you're planning a road trip to Alaska, it will be a grand journey. Many an outdoor adventurer prefers traveling this way; the flexibility of driving on your own allows you to stay at that great campground longer, explore that wilderness area you just discovered, pull off and enjoy a sunset, or watch moose browse in a kettle lake as long as you please.

While many of Alaska's main highways are paved, they also are two- and sometimes four-lane throughways that cannot accommodate high speeds. On average, you'll be traveling 45–55 miles per hour, sometimes faster, sometimes slower. Be on the lookout for moose, which can destroy a vehicle when struck even at slow speeds. Also be aware that because of Alaska's arctic climate, the roads develop persistent frost heaves, which feel like giant speed bumps if you hit them too fast. Road crews spend entire summers repairing these dips and divots, so don't be surprised if you encounter frequent construction.

The main artery into Alaska is the 1,400-mile **Alaska Highway,** which is gorgeous in some spots, boring in others. Services such as fuel are adequately spaced, but it's a good idea to carry an extra 5-gallon container of gas just in case. Auto service is harder to come by, so be sure to bring along a working spare tire and basic travel necessities such as jumper cables, flares, and flashlights. Food is also available at small cafes and convenience stores along the way, but don't count on anything very good. In fact, we prefer to pack a large cooler and carry our own hard-to-get items—fresh greens, fruits, and other snacks—and splurge on overpriced bottles of water at these stores along the way. Oddly, there is the occasional Subway sandwich shop in the remotest of towns, offering a reprieve from the fried food found at most local diners.

A good resource while driving any of the roads into Alaska and the Yukon is *The Milepost* (Morris Communications, $29.95; **themilepost.com**), which has good maps and mile-by-mile logs of each road. It's strictly an informational book, with basic descriptions of what you'll see along the way. It's updated yearly too, so it often includes anticipated construction projects to give you an idea of the day's driving ahead of you.

Renting a Vehicle

Of course, you can accomplish the same goal of reaching Alaska by renting a vehicle instead of putting wear and tear on your own. Be sure to check with the company from which you plan to rent to make sure crossing state lines and entering Canada is permitted.

If you reach Alaska by plane or ship and want to get around while here, you can also rent cars locally in just about any community (see the "Getting Around" sections of our regional chapters). All the major national car-rental companies are represented in Anchorage and Fairbanks, and there are a few local dealers as well. Sometimes the latter are a bit more expensive, but they also allow driving on gravel roads, which you will soon see are quite common in Alaska. This is an important item to notice on your rental contract: many of Alaska's most scenic roads, such as the Denali Highway, are mostly gravel. If you plan to drive roads such as these, check the rental company's fine print before signing. Rates vary depending on the vehicle you want and the company you use, but on average, prices start at $45 a day. Renting a vehicle by the week also cuts the price. Or check **Travelocity (travelocity.com)** to get a comparison of prices. This site has begun to outperform other competitors such as **Priceline (priceline.com)**, particularly when it comes to Alaska flights and rentals. Another source of good car-rental comparisons is **Orbitz (orbitz.com)**, which will call up all available car rentals in a given location in an easy-to-read layout. Once you research the rate online, though, call the company to see if it will honor the rate, thus saving you a surcharge to Orbitz.

Word of warning: We once, out of necessity, rented a vehicle in Homer and drove it one-way to Anchorage. The distance: 226 miles. The rental period: 24 hours. The price: $170. Renting vehicles for one-way travel tends to be too expensive to make much sense. Instead, plan your road trip from Anchorage or Fairbanks or wherever you happen to fly or sail in from, and return the car to its home location.

CAR-RENTAL COMPANIES   There are more than a dozen rental options for the Anchorage area, but we've found **Budget** (800-527-0700; **budget.com**), **Denali Car** (907-276-1230; **denalicarrentalak.com**), **Enterprise** (800-261-7331; **enterprise .com**), and **Hertz** (800-654-3131; **hertz.com**) among the best. In Fairbanks, try **Affordable New Car Rental** (907-452-7341), **Arctic Rent-A-Car** (907-479-8044; **arcticrentacar.com**), **Budget, Dollar Rent A Car** (800-800-4000 or 907-451-4360), or **Heindl's Car & Truck Leasing** (907-451-0004), which offers truck and van rentals and camper packages. In Juneau, **Hertz** (907-789-9494; **hertz.com**), **National Car Rental** (800-CAR-RENT or 907-789-9814; **nationalcar.com**), and **Rent A Wreck** (800-535-1391 or 907-789-4111; **rentawreck.com**) can provide a good price comparison. If Skagway is your first stop, there's **Sourdough Car Rentals** (907-983-2523; **sourdoughrentals.com**). If you're stopping in Haines first, try **Eagle's Nest Car Rentals** (907-766-2891; **alaskaeagletours.com**); if you're arriving by cruise ship in Ketchikan, there's **Southeast Auto Rental** (907-225-8778), which has gotten mixed reviews for service but the price is right.

By RV

Whether you're in your own RV or a rental, you'll soon figure out why so many people travel this way: it just makes sense.

You can be as close to nature as possible yet still have the comfort of a dry bed if the weather should turn. You can change your itinerary at a moment's notice. For the outdoor traveler, an RV can be a good base of operations, a portable home that can store your climbing gear, mountain bike, kayak, and everything else you need for off-the-beaten-path destinations.

The key, though, is figuring out if it makes financial sense. RVs rent for about $250 per day—about the same price as a room at one of the better

RV-rental tips

▶ **Consider your goals before costs.** Rent an RV for the additional experience it will give you, serving as a house on wheels and allowing for access to some far-off places. RV-rental rates and the current price of gasoline combined can rival the cost of staying in hotels and eating out every night.

▶ **If you're willing to travel last-minute** during the shoulder seasons of spring and fall, RV companies sometimes look for drivers to deliver their vehicles to their home locations.

▶ **Most RV rentals come with additional items** such as bed linens, cooking utensils, and pots and pans, as well as unlimited mileage. Make sure these things are included before reserving your RV. Some rental companies still have cleaning charges, but as the companies compete for business, they've begun waiving that fee.

▶ **If you're a nonsmoker,** make sure you get a nonsmoking vehicle. Some companies claim their RVs are smoke-free but won't guarantee it. Ask ahead of time to avoid having to return your vehicle.

hotels during the height of summer. Considering a budget of $5,000, a family of four could rent a spacious RV for two weeks (the rates drop with longer-term rentals), buy all their groceries and gas, and still have money left over for a few guided activities such as day cruises, rafting, biking, or kayaking. A mega-cruise-ship excursion for a family of four, however, would be in the $10,000 range. Staying at that fine hotel in the city, dining out every night, and renting a car for day trips would be about $7,000.

While active, outdoors-oriented families will most definitely benefit from the $250-per-day RV rental, we think it's overkill for solo travelers and couples. But there is another option. Finally, the travel industry has discovered that not all RV travelers want to sit in a generator-equipped campground every night grilling hot dogs. Some of us want to get *way* out there. A few companies, such as **ABC Motor Home Rentals** in Anchorage 800-421-7456 or 907-279-2000; **abcmotorhome.com**), rent pickup trucks with camper shells to help adventurers reach even farther into the backcountry. The rates range from $170 per day for high-season travel to $90 per day for winter use.

Yet another option is to sample just a bit of Alaska by RV. **Alaska Travel Adventures** (800-323-5757; **alaskarv.com**), one of the state's longest-running outdoor-tour companies, offers a package it calls the Alaska Highway Cruise. In these trips you take a one-way cruise to Alaska, then hop into a reserved RV for a drive along some of the state's more scenic routes. The trips range $2,599–$3,599 per person, 11–22 days. It's a great way to experience the luxury of a cruise ship yet still have some private "real Alaska" time on the road. We jokingly refer to it as the "marriage-saver tour," as it is a great, and surprisingly affordable, compromise in all Alaska has to offer.

As with car rentals, one-way RV rentals are more expensive yet still available. **Cruise America** (800-671-8042 or 907-349-0499; **cruiseamerica.com**) offers one-way rentals between Anchorage and rental centers around the country.

RV ROAD ETIQUETTE   Being behind the wheel of a 21-foot recreational vehicle, especially if you're used to sports cars or pickups, can be daunting at first. It is only natural, and safe, to slow down a bit. However, drive according to the speed limit.

TRAVELER'S TIP

▶ The law in Alaska is that if five or more vehicles are trailing behind your RV, you must pull over.

Because Alaska is such a popular travel destination, the roads during the summer can become clogged with RVs and visitors who slow to a snail's pace to take in the mountains, oceans, and wildlife that seem to be around every bend. Not only can this be dangerous but it can also lead to short tempers. Locals use the roads to get to and from work and other destinations. Most of the scenic roads have overlooks spaced along the road for slower vehicles to pull into. It takes only a moment and allows you all the time you need to shoot that great photo or take a break from driving.

RV-RENTAL COMPANIES   In Anchorage, **ABC Motor Home and Car Rentals** (800-421-7456 or 907-279-2000; **abcmotorhome.com**) has a range of RVs as well as a luxury van for large groups and camper rentals for smaller parties. No smoking or pets allowed.

Alaska Affordable Motor Home Rental (907-349-4878 or 907-306-2923; **alaska-rv-rental.com**) is much less expensive than its competitors, with rates at $175 per day with free, unlimited miles in Alaska. Vehicles are not as fancy but are quite functional. No smoking or pets allowed. **Alaska Best RV Rentals** (907-223-9123; **alaskabestrvrentals.com**) offers rates of $150–$175, which is lower than the large-company averages. Again, no smoking or pets allowed.

▲ Where to Stay

IN EACH OF our regional chapters, we go into more detail on the best camping and lodging options for a particular area. In roadless areas such as the Bush, lodging opportunities can be scarce, but you'll still be able to find a place to sleep in most any town or village you come to. Charts within each chapter provide an alphabetical listing of the campgrounds, lodges, bed-and-breakfasts, and hotel accommodations, with rankings for quality, value, and price.

▲ Visiting the Parks and Refuges

ONE OF THE things you'll notice about Alaska is that the land seems to go on forever. It would seem easy to just step out into it and go for an adventure. The truth is, though, nearly three-quarters of Alaska is protected as public land through the passage of the Alaska National Interest Lands Conservation Act. Tribal corporations own another large chunk, the result of the passage of the Alaska Native Claims Settlement Act. Because these lands are protected, there are limitations on their use, and restrictions are set by the various owners. One of the most important planning aspects of your trip should be investigating land-use regulations. Some agencies allow online reservations or phone reservations up to six months in advance. Others work on a first-come, first-served basis. Still others require you to show up in person to register or pay for access.

STATE LANDS: GETTING MORE INFORMATION

ALASKA STATE PARKS   For information on all of Alaska's state parks, including the popular Chugach State Park, call 907-269-8400 or 907-451-2705. The Web site is **alaskastateparks.org.**

FEDERAL LANDS: GETTING MORE INFORMATION

NATIONAL PARK SERVICE   Four **Alaska Public Lands Information Centers** in the state have details on all 19 of Alaska's nationally managed areas (as well as state-park, refuge, and national-forest information). Access them online at **alaskacenters.gov,** or visit any of the following locations: **Anchorage** (605 W. 4th Ave., Suite 105, Anchorage 99501; 888-869-6887 or 907-644-3661); **Fairbanks** (101 Dunkel St., Suite 110, Fairbanks 99701; 907-459-3730); **Ketchikan** (Southeast Alaska Discovery Center, 50 Main St., Ketchikan 99901; 907-228-6234); or **Tok** (907-883-5667).

NATIONAL REFUGES   These vast public lands are managed by the U.S. Fish and Wildlife Service, which can be reached at 907-786-3309 or **r7.fws.gov.**

U.S. BUREAU OF LAND MANAGEMENT   For Fairbanks-area information, which is regulated by the BLM, call 907-474-2200 or visit **blm.gov/ak/st/en.html.** The Alaska state offices are at 222 W. 7th Ave., Suite 13, Anchorage 99513; 907-271-5960.

U.S. FOREST SERVICE   There are two national forests in Alaska: **Tongass** and **Chugach.** Information on the Tongass can be accessed at the Tongass National Forest office, 648 Mission St., Ketchikan, 99901; 907-225-3101; **fs.fed.us/r10/tongass.** Chugach National Forest information is available at 3301 C St., Anchorage 99503; 907-743-9500; **fs.fed.us/r10/chugach.**

NATIVE LANDS: WHAT YOU SHOULD KNOW

There are 13 regional native corporations, all of which own certain lands throughout Alaska. Many of these corporations allow public use of their lands, but it is always prudent to check ahead of time if you know your trip will pass private property. Contact the **Alaska Native Heritage Center** in Anchorage (907-330-8000; **alaskanative.net**) to learn more about the area in which you plan to travel, or contact the corporations directly. Most of the following Web sites have maps that illustrate the land and region owned by a particular corporation.

▶ **AHTNA, Inc.**: Based in Glennallen (Southcentral Inland). 907-822-3476; ahtna-inc.com.

▶ **Aleut Corporation**: Based in Western Alaska and the Aleutians (Bush). 907-561-4300; **aleutcorp.com**.

▶ **Arctic Slope Regional Corporation**: Based in Barrow (Bush). 907-339-6000; asrc.com.

▶ **Bering Straits Native Corporation**: Based in Nome (Bush). 907-443-2985; beringstraits.com.

▶ **Bristol Bay Native Corporation**: Based in Bristol Bay (Bush). 907-278-3602; **bbnc.net**.

▶ **Calista Corporation**: Based in Southwest Alaska (Bush). 907-279-5516; calistacorp.com.

▶ **Chugach Alaska Corporation**: Based in Copper River Delta (Southcentral Coastal, Southcentral Inland). 907-563-8866; **chugach-ak.com**.

▶ **Cook Inlet Region, Inc.**: Based in Southcentral Inland and Coastal Alaska. 907-274-8638; **ciri.com**.

▶ **Doyon, Ltd.**: Based in Yukon Interior region. 888-478-4755 or 907-459-2000; **doyon.com**.

▶ **Koniag, Inc.**: Based in Kodiak (Southcentral Coastal). 888-658-3818 or 907-486-2530; **koniag.com**.

▶ **NANA Regional Corporation**: Based in Kotzebue (Bush). 907-442-3301; nana.com.

▶ **Sealaska Corporation**: Based in Southeast Alaska (Southeast). 907-586-1512; sealaska.com.

▶ **Thirteenth Regional Corporation**: Based in Seattle, this corporation represents out-of-state Alaskans. You'll likely not need to contact them, but here's the information just in case: 206-575-6229; **the13thregion.com**.

PART FOUR
ADVENTURE CRUISING

THINK OF CRUISING, and you might imagine one of those behemoths lumbering across the ocean carrying thousands of people in crate-size staterooms. You might also think of all-night gambling, Vegas-style entertainment, and dinner buffets that are nothing short of an over-the-top smorgasbord.

If you're an independent outdoor traveler, this might not sound like much fun.

The truth is, cruising on giant luxury ships such as those run by Holland America, Princess Cruises, and Carnival Cruise Lines is not what it used to be. Sure, you can have the glitz and glamour of those fancy packages, but you can also enjoy your own mini-adventures, leaving the ships at their ports of call and embarking on land adventures that range from four-wheeling across an old logging road to dog mushing on a glacier. The larger cruise-ship companies are realizing that today's travelers are more active, more adventurous, and more willing to create their own entertainment.

This chapter strives to introduce you to a different type of cruising, though. Sure, those large cruise ships can sometimes seem a bargain, and there is plenty onboard to keep you busy. But we think the true adventure traveler is looking for something a bit more "out there."

The trips listed in this chapter run the gamut. The vessels are small and their destinations sometimes quite remote. You don't need to pack a tux or an evening gown, but don't forget your hiking boots. This is a different mode of cruising, a true outdoor traveler's vacation. We call it adventure cruising.

The two most popular places to find an adventure cruise are the coastal waters of **Prince William Sound** in Southcentral Coastal Alaska and the island-studded waters of the **Southeast Panhandle.** Southeast Alaska is one of the best places to watch whales breech and glaciers calve; however, its popularity draws the larger ships too. Prince William Sound also gets big-cruise-ship traffic, but not as much. The city of **Seward,** at the tip of the Kenai Peninsula in Southcentral Coastal Alaska, is also a hot spot for cruisers.

▲ Adventure-cruising Tips and Resources

Add-on Trips

While some of the land-based tour companies in Alaska team up with the larger cruise ships to offer special add-on trips not available to other travelers, be aware that you'll pay a premium for these trips. Most are offered at a discounted group rate to the cruise companies, but the savings aren't always passed on to the traveler.

WHAT TO BRING

One of the joys of cruising is that while you are undoubtedly venturing into Alaska's wilderness, you can still go inside your heated cabin if its gets too cold. On adventure cruises, though, you should be prepared for whatever activities are included in the trip. Some companies will provide cold-weather gear or other equipment necessary for the trip, but most do not. Check with the cruise company, asking what they provide and what you'll need to bring for each activity. For example, on some cruises, you may need to bring a sleeping bag for overnight onshore camping trips.

Also remember that you may be out at sea for a few days or even a couple of weeks. These are wilderness adventures, and there are no stores, so be prepared with everything you'll need for the break from civilization.

Most of these ships are smaller than the luxury liners too, so you'll probably need to pack lighter than you normally would.

The following items are essentials:

✔ All necessary prescription medications

✔ Binoculars

✔ Brimmed hat

✔ Camera with extra digital storage cards or batteries and film

✔ Good walking shoes or lightweight hiking boots

✔ Insect repellent

✔ A journal and a pen to document your experiences. While bringing a laptop might seem tempting, resist the urge unless you have a place to stash it.

✔ Layered clothing

✔ Polarized sunglasses (polarized lenses are better for seeing into water)

✔ Sunscreen

✔   Waterproof, windproof raingear

✔   Lightweight winter hat and gloves (yes, even in the summer)

RESOURCES

For the best in-depth information about travel and activities, visit or call the local visitor bureaus and chambers of commerce of the communities at which you will be stopping. Here's a sampling.

STATEWIDE   Anchorage Convention and Visitors Bureau, 524 W. 4th Ave., Anchorage 99501-2212; 907-276-4118; **anchorage.net.**

SOUTHCENTRAL COASTAL ALASKA   Greater Whittier Chamber of Commerce; whittieralaskachamber.org; Kodiak Island Convention and Visitors Bureau, 100 Marine Way, Suite 200, Kodiak 99615; 800-789-4782 or 907-486-4782; **kodiak.org; Seward Chamber of Commerce;** 907-224-8051; **seward.com.**

SOUTHEAST ALASKA   Juneau Convention and Visitors Bureau, 1 Sealaska Plaza, Suite 305, Juneau 99801; 800-587-2201 or 907-586-1737; **travel juneau.com; Ketchikan Convention and Visitors Bureau,** 131 Front St., Ketchikan 99901; 800-770-3300 or 907-225-6166; **visit-ketchikan.com; Sitka Convention and Visitors Bureau;** 907-747-5940; **sitka.org; Skagway Convention and Visitors Bureau;** 907-983-2854; **skagway.com.**

Web Sites

Several useful sites can offer insight on cruising in Alaska, whether you decide to travel with a large cruise ship or you select a smaller, adventure-based excursion.

▶   **adn.com**   This Web site is the *Anchorage Daily News*'s daily online edition. Three-month subscriptions are an option for those who want to bone up on local happenings before visiting their area of choice.

▶   **alaska.com**   Hosted by the state's largest newspaper, the *Anchorage Daily News*, this site offers travel tips, special booking savings, and other links of interest for potential visitors to the state.

▶   **alaskamagazine.com**   Like its print counterpart, the Web site of *Alaska* magazine covers life on the Last Frontier through travel features, personality

▲ TEN TIPS FOR A GREAT CRUISE

To get the most for your money, consider the following advice:

1. *Go off the beaten path.* Don't make this an ordinary trip; instead, do something new and adventurous. It is, after all, an adventure, so make it a memorable one.

2. *Check out the crew,* the boat, and the company's credentials and testimonials. Make sure you know what you're getting and that you'll get what you pay for.

3. *Look for Web specials throughout the year.* Also ask about specials and current discounts when you call to make reservations. There may be unlisted deals, and it never hurts to ask.

4. *Consider traveling during shoulder seasons,* when tickets can be bought at reduced rates. You may also get unique opportunities to see and do things not offered during peak seasons.

5. *Look for specialized tours* or companies that will build a tour to fit your travel needs and desires.

6. *Shop judiciously.* Cruise-ship shops have you as their captive audience. Resist buying from them. If you must shop, wait until the last day to buy, when items usually go on sale.

7. *Make it a family trip.* You may get a group discount, and your adventure will be more memorable if you share it with your friends and family.

8. *Find out exactly what is and what isn't included* in the cost of the cruise. Add-ons can multiply rapidly.

9. *Book early in the season.* Smaller ships have very limited space and are often booked a year or more in advance. You might also get early-booking discounts.

10. *Find out ahead of time* if your ship's room has outlets for plugging in electrical items such as hair dryers, irons, computers, and so on. Many staterooms have only one outlet, so if having access to several electrical items at once will be an issue, bring your own power strip.

profiles, community issues, and other bits and pieces of interest to both local and outside readers.

▶ **alaskatia.org**   The Alaska Travel Industry Association's Web site lists member groups that offer cruising options throughout the state. The organization's visitor-targeted site, **travelalaska.com,** offers maps, resources, and stories about traveling in Alaska, either on a cruise or on your own.

▶ **cruisecritic.com**   This cool site allows you to get the down and dirty on cruise ships. Which ones really are the best? Let those who've been cruising themselves tell you. The site can also help you find cruises that cater to specific demographics, such as seniors, families, or gays and lesbians. The Independent Traveler sponsors the site.

▶ **cruise411.com**   Here you'll find unbiased reviews on ships and cruises across the world, including Alaska. The site also offers Web specials and last-minute travel specials for those ready to toss a few items in a bag and go.

▶ **juneauempire.com**   For those traveling to Southeast Alaska, the *Juneau Empire* is the newspaper of choice. Online subscriptions are available.

▶ **themilepost.com**   This periodical is one of the most accurate Alaska travel resources because it is updated annually, unlike many guidebooks that are updated only every two to three years. *The Milepost* covers the road systems of Alaska in mile-by-mile increments and contains special features on such off-the-road communities as Cordova, Nome, and Unalaska.

▶ **weather.com**   This Web site will give you an idea of what sort of weather to expect in the communities through which you will be traveling. However, we can give you a general idea: rain. It rains often in the coastal areas, so come prepared for that. When you get the occasional sunny day—and you will—it makes your trip even more glorious.

Booking Companies

▶ **Alaska Cruises**   800-201-6937; **alaskacruises.com.** The site alone is worth checking out—it's a visitors' brochure packed with information on all the things to do and see in Alaska. Another good thing about this site is that the selection of cruises is larger than that of other booking companies.

▶ **Alaska Visitors Center–Alaska Statewide Marketing**   888-655-4020 (reservations) or 907-929-2822 (other questions); **alaskavisitorscenter.com.** This independent company books trips, lodging, and rentals for more than 150 businesses and outfitters throughout the state. A good resource for finding out more about local attractions in any given town or city you plan to visit.

▶ **All Alaska Tours**   877-317-3325 or 907-277-3000; **alaskatours.com.**In Anchorage, this company offers a handful of cruises, with early-booking discounts.

Book

▸ *The Milepost* $29.95 at **themilepost.com.** A mile-by-mile guide to Alaska and western Canada; publishes up-to-date information on cruise-ship travel to (and in) Alaska.

▲ Adventure-cruise Outfitters

▸ **ALASKA PASSAGES ADVENTURE CRUISES** ›› *Petersburg* 888-434-3766; **alaska passages.com.** Alaska Passages provides the ideal trip for small groups of six or fewer cruisers. The intimate and family-oriented atmosphere aboard the **M/V Heron** makes for a unique experience, and the adventures and activities are customized for you and your companions. This private charter yacht offers sea kayaking, glacier cruises, wildlife viewing, fishing, hiking, whale watching, and more. Hosts Scott and Julie Hursey are Alaska naturalists, ex–commercial fishers, and longtime residents of Petersburg. Tours range from 5 to 10 days, and rates are $3,700–$5,600 per person.

▸ **AMERICAN SAFARI CRUISES** ›› *Lynnwood, Washington–Inside Passage* 888-862-8881 or 206-284-0300; **amsafari.com.** Luxury and hospitality are the themes of these yacht-based adventures, as guests are greeted at the dock with Champagne, hors d'oeuvres, and warm smiles. Alaska tours range from four to eight days and start at around $5,500 per person; activities include kayaking, heli-hiking, air tours, and exploration. The truly rich and famous can even rent the entire yacht for a mere $250,000 and entertain up to 38 other guests. Uniquely northern-inspired gourmet meals and comfortable staterooms round out the experience. American Safari also focuses on education and green cruising, as the company's expedition leaders offer lectures and tour narratives for each location.

▸ **ANADYR ADVENTURES** ›› *Valdez* 800-TO-KAYAK or 907-835-2814; **anadyradven tures.com.** Anadyr offers two- to five-day trips around Prince William Sound out of Valdez from its yacht-based vessel. Kayak or hike by day, and sleep in comfort each night. Trips cost $1,080 per person for the three-day adventure or $1,900 for five days and include gourmet meals and a casual atmosphere amid the spectacular scenery and wildlife of the sound. Adventures center on sea kayaking; however, hiking, berry picking, wildlife viewing, beachcombing, fishing, and glacier exploration also fill your days on these excursions.

▸ **THE BOAT COMPANY** ›› *Poulsbo, Washington–Inside Passage* 360-697-4242; **theboatcompany.com.** This outfitter takes visitors on eight-day journeys up the Inside Passage, doing it in style aboard the 157-foot **M/V Mist Cove** and the 145-foot **M/V Liseron.** The ships offer spacious and luxurious accommodations;

Alaska naturalists and a crew of 10–12 take care of your every need. Fishing, hiking, birding, nature walks, naturalist tours, kayaking, wildlife viewing, beach-combing, and a variety of other leisure activities are led by experienced Alaska guides. Unique to this company are its early-morning kayaking, hiking, and fishing trips, which allow guests to greet the beauty and tranquility of an Alaska sunrise. Prices range $4,895–$7,000, double occupancy.

▶ **DISCOVERY VOYAGES »** *Whittier* 800-324-7602; **discoveryvoyages.com.** Offers a great selection of tours that range 7–13 days. Itineraries vary, and activities change with the seasons, encompassing seasonal wildlife viewing, photography, kayaking, hiking, birding, and even a sea-life-centered natural-history tour. The spring birding tour, guided by a local naturalist, is one of the company's finest. You won't go hungry on these adventures, either, with their emphasis on fresh Alaska seafood and delicious desserts. Custom tours are also available, with prices starting at $2,100 per person.

▶ **PANGAEA ADVENTURES »** *Valdez* 800-660-9637 or 907-835-8442; **alaska summer.com.** Pangaea offers unique adventures aboard a four-person sail-boat or a powerboat. These relaxing trips are like no others in the area, as guests explore Prince William Sound at their own pace, stopping to hike, comb the beaches, kayak, and enjoy the wildlife, glaciers, and world-famous scenery of the area. With your crew of three, you will also be very well taken care of and very well fed. The vessels range from the near-luxurious **M/V Raven** to the more functional **Tempest,** a working boat that is ideal for hardened adventurers who just want a dry, comfortable place to sleep after a day's outing. Pangaea Adventures are entirely customized—dates, activities, and all—to your party's desires. Trips range from four to eight days and start at $2,100 per person per day.

▶ **SEA WOLF ADVENTURES »** *Elfin Cove* 907-957-1438; **seawolfadventures.net.** This company provides accessible adventures for people of all ages, interests, and abilities aboard the **M/V Sea Wolf.** With several guides on board to cater to your every whim, and with a chef who also leads the kayak excursions, your six-day adventure is sure to be memorable. At around $3,200 per person for all activities, rooms, and meals, it's also a pretty good bargain. This is a good choice for those adventurers who use wheelchairs—one of the vessel's staff is a paraplegic adventurer and has tested its comforts himself.

▶ **SIKUMI CUSTOM ALASKA CRUISES »** *Girdwood–Prince William Sound, Inside Passage* 425-806-2083; **sikumi.com.** This is truly an intimate luxury cruise aboard the 67-foot **M/V Sikumi,** which sleeps 12 and includes private state-rooms (each with its own bathroom), spacious decks, and a richly appointed salon and dining room. If you can pull yourself away from the relaxing atmo-sphere of the boat, the company's guides offer a multitude of only-in-Alaska

adventure-cruise outfitters @ a glance

Alaska Passages Adventure Cruises

888-434-3766 | alaskapassages.com

REGION » Southeast
COST » $$
SUITABLE FOR KIDS? » Yes
ACTIVITY LEVEL » Moderate
TRIP LENGTH » 5–10 days

American Safari Cruises

888-862-8881 or 206-284-0300
amsafari.com

REGION » Southeast
COST » $$$
SUITABLE FOR KIDS? » Yes
ACTIVITY LEVEL » Light
TRIP LENGTH » 4–8 days

Anadyr Adventures

800-TO-KAYAK or 907-835-2814
anadyradventures.com

REGION » Southcentral Coastal
COST » $$$
SUITABLE FOR KIDS? » Older kids
ACTIVITY LEVEL » Moderate
TRIP LENGTH » 2–5+ days

The Boat Company

360-697-4242 | theboatcompany.com

REGION » Southeast
COST » $$$$
SUITABLE FOR KIDS? » No
ACTIVITY LEVEL » Light
TRIP LENGTH » 8 days

Discovery Voyages

800-324-7602 | discoveryvoyages.com

REGION » Southcentral Coastal
COST » $$$
SUITABLE FOR KIDS? » Yes
ACTIVITY LEVEL » Light
TRIP LENGTH » Varies

Pangaea Adventures

800-660-9637 or 907-835-8442
alaskasummer.com

REGION » Southcentral Coastal
COST » $$
SUITABLE FOR KIDS? » Older kids
ACTIVITY LEVEL » High
TRIP LENGTH » 4–8 days

Sea Wolf Adventures

907-957-1438 | seawolf-adventures.com

REGION » Southeast
COST » $$$
SUITABLE FOR KIDS? » Older kids
ACTIVITY LEVEL » Moderate
TRIP LENGTH » 6 days

Sikumi Custom Alaska Cruises

425-806-2083 | sikumi.com

REGION » Southeast
COST » $$$$
SUITABLE FOR KIDS? » No
ACTIVITY LEVEL » Light
TRIP LENGTH » 4–8 days

The World Outdoors

800-488-8483 or 303-413-0938
theworldoutdoors.com

REGION » Southeast
COST » $$$
SUITABLE FOR KIDS? » Yes
ACTIVITY LEVEL » Moderate
TRIP LENGTH » Varies

adventures throughout the Inside Passage and Prince William Sound. Kayaking, hiking, beachcombing, birding, and fishing are just a few of the activities offered. One trip even features a soak in a natural hot spring. Sikumi's cruises range from four to eight days and cost about $4,5000 per person, double occupancy. Book early, as cruise dates sell out quickly. Deals often are available for May and June cruises.

▶ **THE WORLD OUTDOORS** ➤ *Boulder, Colorado—Inside Passage* 800-488-8483 or 303-413-0938; **theworldoutdoors.com.** Hiking, sea kayaking, and zodiac excursions are the highlights of these adventure cruises through the Last Frontier. This company explores the vast wilderness of the Inside Passage, which includes forays off-board to hike; pick berries; or go beachcombing, kayaking, or tidepooling. Rates start at $5,650. The ship, which holds up to 62 guests, is larger than some of the previous options and includes a library and lecture/slide-show room for the naturalist in all of us.

PART FIVE

BACKPACKING

IT'S NO EXAGGERATION to say that backpacking in Alaska will be unlike any other backpacking experience you've ever had. In most backpacking excursions, hikers follow a marked trail to an ultimate destination—a mountaintop, remote lake, or ocean view. Think of the East Coast's Appalachian Trail, which stretches from Georgia to Maine, or the West Coast's Pacific Crest Trail, from Mexico to Canada. These are clearly marked, well traveled, and designed to meet the needs of hikers.

This type of backpacking experience does exist in Alaska, and this section will highlight some of the finest marked-trail options in the state. But Alaska is not called the Last Frontier without reason: it's a place where there is land so remote that nary a clue of human interference exists. The majority of Alaska's backcountry is trailless and accessible only by plane or boat—no roads, no trailheads, no signs to mark the trail. Backpackers in Alaska must rely on their own outdoors skills and their ability to read maps, compasses, and GPS units to make their way across the wilderness.

In this chapter we've focused on the mostly marked trails throughout the state, ranging from overnight destinations to trips that will take several days to complete. They will serve as a guide for planning your adventure. We have rated them from easy—meaning the trails are well marked and maintained with bridges, bog barriers, and other means of navigational assistance—to difficult, meaning you'll have to do some bushwhacking and follow ridgelines to travel from end to end.

But don't limit your exploration of the Last Frontier to these suggestions. Backpacking in country that is truly wide open and without trails is exhilarating and exciting, challenging and rewarding. We could never lay out one of these trips for you because each one is unique. Just before the individual trail descriptions, however, we've included a general section on trailless backpacking and how to go about planning your own excursion.

▲ Checklist for Success

✔ **BE WEIGHT-CONSCIOUS.** We're not talking about cutting the handle off your toothbrush or tearing chapters out of your reading book (although these techniques really do shave off ounces!), but traveling in backcountry Alaska is hard work. You're often bushwhacking and navigating among thick brambles and brush, crossing rivers and scaling bumpy alpine slopes. Bringing along too much gear can turn one of these adventures into a slow, painful slog. A pack that snags on branches and other brush can also be cumbersome.

✔ **DRESS APPROPRIATELY.** We acknowledge the need for weight-conscious backpacking but also respect the necessity of having enough clothing for the duration. Do not travel into the backcountry ill-prepared. Wear polypropylene

alaska backpacking @ a glance

Brooks Range

REGION ❯❯ The Bush
DISTANCE ❯❯ Varies
TRAIL/TRAILLESS? ❯❯ Trailless
DIFFICULTY ❯❯ ★ ★ ★ ★ ★
TIME TO HIKE ❯❯ Varies
CONFIGURATION ❯❯ Varies
SUITABLE FOR KIDS? ❯❯ No
GUIDE SUGGESTED?
❯❯ Highly recommended

Chena Dome Trail

REGION ❯❯ The Interior
DISTANCE ❯❯ 30 miles
TRAIL/TRAILLESS? ❯❯ Trail
DIFFICULTY ❯❯ ★ ★ ★ ★
TIME TO HIKE ❯❯ 2–4 days
CONFIGURATION ❯❯ Loop
SUITABLE FOR KIDS? ❯❯ Teens
GUIDE SUGGESTED? ❯❯ No

Chilkoot Pass Trail

REGION ❯❯ Southeast
DISTANCE ❯❯ 33 miles
TRAIL/TRAILLESS? ❯❯ Trail
DIFFICULTY ❯❯ ★ ★ ★ ★
TIME TO HIKE ❯❯ 3–5 days
CONFIGURATION
❯❯ End-to-end
SUITABLE FOR KIDS? ❯❯ Age 10 and older
GUIDE SUGGESTED? ❯❯ No

Crow Pass–Historic Iditarod Trail

REGION ❯❯ Southcentral Inland
DISTANCE ❯❯ 26 miles
TRAIL/TRAILLESS? ❯❯ Trail
DIFFICULTY ❯❯ ★ ★ ★
TIME TO HIKE ❯❯ 2–3 days
CONFIGURATION ❯❯ End-to-end
SUITABLE FOR KIDS? ❯❯ Teens
GUIDE SUGGESTED? ❯❯ No

Denali National Park and Preserve

REGION ❯❯ The Interior
DISTANCE ❯❯ Varies
TRAIL/TRAILLESS? ❯❯ Trailless
DIFFICULTY ❯❯ ★ ★ ★ ★
TIME TO HIKE ❯❯ Varies
CONFIGURATION ❯❯ Varies
SUITABLE FOR KIDS? ❯❯ No
GUIDE SUGGESTED? ❯❯ No

Kesugi Ridge Trail

REGION ❯❯ Southcentral Inland
DISTANCE ❯❯ 27.4 miles
TRAIL/TRAILLESS? ❯❯ Trail
DIFFICULTY ❯❯ ★ ★ ★ ★
TIME TO HIKE ❯❯ 2–4 days
CONFIGURATION
❯❯ Out and-back/end-to-end
SUITABLE FOR KIDS? ❯❯ Age 10 and older
GUIDE SUGGESTED? ❯❯ No

Lake Clark National Park

REGION ❯❯ The Bush
DISTANCE ❯❯ Varies
TRAIL/TRAILLESS? ❯❯ Trailless
DIFFICULTY ❯❯ ★ ★ ★ ★ ★
TIME TO HIKE ❯❯ Varies
CONFIGURATION ❯❯ Varies
SUITABLE FOR KIDS? ❯❯ No
GUIDE SUGGESTED? ❯❯ Recommended

Resurrection Pass Trail

REGION ❯❯ Southcentral Coastal
DISTANCE ❯❯ 39 miles
TRAIL/TRAILLESS? ❯❯ Trail
DIFFICULTY ❯❯ ★ ★ ★
TIME TO HIKE ❯❯ 2–5 days
CONFIGURATION
❯❯ Out and-back/end-to-end
SUITABLE FOR KIDS? ❯❯ Age 10 and older
GUIDE SUGGESTED? ❯❯ No

backpacking outfitters @ a glance

ABEC's Alaska Adventures

877-424-8907 or 907-457-8907
abecalaska.com

REGION ›› The Interior/The Bush
COST ›› $$$
SUITABLE FOR KIDS? ›› No
ACTIVITY LEVEL ›› High
TRIP LENGTH ›› 8–19 days

Alaska Alpine Adventures

877-525-2577 or 907-781-2253
alaskaalpineadventures.com

REGION ›› Statewide
COST ›› $$
SUITABLE FOR KIDS? ›› Varies
ACTIVITY LEVEL ›› Moderate
TRIP LENGTH ›› 7–10 days

Alaska Mountain Guides and Climbing School

800-766-3396
alaskamountainguides.com

REGION ›› Southeast
COST ›› $
SUITABLE FOR KIDS? ›› Older kids
ACTIVITY LEVEL ›› Moderate–high
TRIP LENGTH ›› 4–5 days

Arctic Wild

888-577-8203 or 907-479-8203
arcticwild.com

REGION ›› Statewide
COST ›› $$$
SUITABLE FOR KIDS? ›› No
ACTIVITY LEVEL ›› Moderate–high
TRIP LENGTH ›› 10+ days

1st Alaska Outdoor School

907-590-5900
1stalaskaoutdoorschool.com

REGION ›› The Interior
COST ›› $
SUITABLE FOR KIDS? ›› Varies
ACTIVITY LEVEL ›› Moderate
TRIP LENGTH ›› 2+ days/custom

Sea to Sky Expeditions

800-990-8735 or 604-583-3318
seatoskyexpeditions.com

REGION ›› Southeast
COST ›› $$
SUITABLE FOR KIDS? ›› Yes
ACTIVITY LEVEL ›› Moderate
TRIP LENGTH ›› 7 days

Wilderness Birding Adventures

907-694-7442
wildernessbirding.com

REGION ›› The Bush
COST ›› $$
SUITABLE FOR KIDS? ›› Varies
ACTIVITY LEVEL ›› Moderate
TRIP LENGTH ›› 3+ days

or other moisture-wicking underwear against your skin and quick-dry layers over the top. Add layers as conditions warrant. Always carry a spare pair of undergarments in case you get wet. Bring a hat and at least a pair of glove liners for unexpected cold weather, even in the summer. And make sure to have a waterproof raincoat and pants. But resist the urge to overpack—if you have the proper waterproof shell, you can get by with the same basic outer layer for an entire week or more. Another tip: long-sleeve shirts and long pants are great for keeping mosquitoes at bay.

✔ **KNOW HOW TO NAVIGATE.** A map and compass are obvious necessities for anyone traveling into the backcountry, even on trails. In Alaska, many trails are quite primitive and can overlap game trails and other unmarked paths that are potentially confusing when trying to travel a main trail. Farther out, in the roadless areas, there often are no trails at all. Acquaint yourself with a topographical map and compass. The **U.S. Geological Survey** has the most-often-used maps, but commercial maps of various regions of Alaska also can be purchased. Many outdoor travelers can read global-positioning systems and rely on them for backcountry travel. These can be particularly useful tools for travel in trailless areas.

✔ **BE BEAR-AWARE.** See "How to Stay Safe in the Wilderness" (page 30) for our tips on avoiding the beasts and maximizing your safety in case of an encounter.

✔ **USE CARE WHEN CROSSING STREAMS AND RIVERS.** Alaska's cold water can turn a simple slip in a stream into a life-threatening situation. Hypothermia (see next page) can set in quickly. When crossing water, always pick the route that seems the most shallow and least swift. Cloudy water, made gray by glacial silt, can hide possible dangers such as rocks and deep spots, so if you're not sure, don't chance it. If possible, link arms with a partner or partners while crossing to reduce

TRAVELER'S TIP

▶ Morning is the best time to cross a stream or river because the water tends to be at its lowest. If possible, shoot for an early-morning crossing.

the risk of getting swept away. If there are more than two hikers, form a triangle and pivot your way across the river, thus creating enough disturbance in the river's flow to ease movement. Walk parallel to the current. We always unhook our backpacks from our waists in case we slip and get pulled under; if packs are unhooked and loosened, we can get out of them without as much of a struggle.

✔ **AVOID GIARDIASIS.** The intestinal parasite *Giardia lamblia* occurs in Alaska lakes and streams despite our remoteness. You can get it from drinking untreated water in areas of beaver and other water-mammal activity. It's not fun: symptoms are diarrhea and severe cramping, and they may appear up to two weeks after exposure. Treat water by boiling or using chemical tablets or a portable water filter.

> **TRAVELER'S TIP**
>
> ▶ June and July are the worst times of year for mosquitoes and biting flies, but the pests can appear as early as late April and stick around through August in some places.

✔ **GUARD AGAINST MOSQUITOES.** You won't necessarily get sick from too many mosquito bites, but they sure can ruin an otherwise unforgettable outdoor adventure.

The general rule of thumb is that the farther out you travel into the backcountry, the more mosquitoes you're likely to encounter. On lakes and streams, they can be brutal, as well as in wet, swampy areas and brushy spots. Pack bug spray—the most powerful kind you can withstand—along with a head net, long-sleeve shirts, and pants.

✔ **BEWARE OF HYPOTHERMIA.** When the body gets so cold that its core temperature drops, this is called hypothermia, and it can kill. It is a very real danger in Alaska, especially in the mountains, where temperatures drop the higher you go, even in the summer. Hypothermia can also sneak up on you, rapidly developing into a disorientation that can lead to even-worse problems. Avoiding hypothermia is simple: don't get wet. Even a shirt damp from perspiration can be dangerous if it's all you're wearing while standing atop a windy summit.

✔ **CARRY THE ESSENTIALS.** We've mentioned clothing. We've stressed the importance of having the proper guidance equipment. Here are a few more items to pack:

1. A **first-aid kit** that can patch up minor cuts and bruises, as well as any specific medications that may be needed for anyone in your traveling party. The longer the trip, the better stocked this kit should be.

2. A **campstove** that is light and can heat water quickly. This is a better choice than building fires, which can be hard to do in treeless areas and is more damaging to the landscape. In some places, fires are prohibited.

3. **Matches** or a **lighter** that will work even in extreme cold and/or wind. When camping in winter, you're better off with matches, as lighters can become temperamental.

4. **Headlamps** (unless you're traveling in the far, far north at the height of summer) are useful tools to have and can also double as SOS devices. Other signaling devices you may consider carrying include flares, whistles, and guns.

5. A **tent**. Sleeping under the stars may sound romantic, but as soon as the mosquitoes start biting, you'll be dreaming of shelter. Tents also keep you warm and dry, thus protecting against hypothermia. Bring a tent that is easy to pitch, because staking one down in the tundra can be tricky. Make sure the fly is completely waterproof. If you truly want to sleep outside, we prefer the milder nights of winter, when gazing up at the northern lights sans mosquitoes is a wondrous experience.

▲ Trailless Hiking

MORE THAN 75% of Alaska's land belongs to the public—in the form of national parks or preserves, wildlife refuges, state parks, and even city-owned parkland. This opens up backcountry travel like no other place on earth, but it also can be a bit overwhelming. Do you need permits? How do you gain access? When do you travel? All these questions have different answers too, depending on which public agency's land you plan to travel.

To start, get in touch with one of the four **Alaska Public Lands Information Centers** throughout the state (for contact information, see "Federal Lands:

Getting More Information" in Part Three, page 62).

The centers are a great source for maps and other details of the areas in which you will be traveling, or for getting information on which maps you will need. *Note:* Although topographical maps can sometimes be purchased at such places as sporting-goods stores and map shops, the best sources for detailed maps of trailless areas in Alaska are the **Geophysical Institute at the University of Alaska Fairbanks;** 907-474-7558; **gi.alaska.edu;** and the **ESIC Map Office,** U.S. Geological Survey, on the Alaska Pacific University Campus; 907-786-7011.

As mentioned in Part Three, five main agencies control public land in Alaska:

> **TRAVELER'S TIP**
>
> ▶ The **Alaska Public Lands Information Centers** circulate information about all of the publicly owned land in the state and direct you more specifically to the particular agencies that handle permits, reservations, and other trip-planning details within their land ownership.

ALASKA STATE PARKS   The Alaska Department of Natural Resources' Division of Parks and Outdoor Recreation protects and interprets areas of natural and cultural significance and supports the state's tourism industry in park units as small as a half acre and as large as 1.6 million acres. One of the most popular facilities is **Chugach State Park** (Potter Section House, Mile 115 Seward Hwy., Anchorage; 907-345-5014), covering 495,000 acres just outside of Anchorage and offering some excellent marked-trail backpacking. Other state parks, such as **Wood-Tikchik** outside of Dillingham, are a bit harder to reach. One of our favorites is **Kachemak Bay State Park** (Mile 168.5 Sterling Hwy., Homer 99603; 907-235-7024), located on the Kenai Peninsula in Southcentral Coastal Alaska. Here you can combine the best of land and sea, with snowcapped mountains the setting for one day's adventures while gentle ocean waves provide the next day's. To get general contacts for all of Alaska's state parks, see "State Lands: Getting More Information" in Part Three (page 62).

NATIONAL PARK SERVICE   National parks compose more than 45 million acres of public land in Alaska—an astonishing number if you stop to think about it. **Denali National Park** alone, for instance, is 6 million acres, about the size of Massachusetts. Alaska has 17 national-park sites, most of which contain very few maintained trails. Access is quite remote, and travelers here must be very well equipped to handle backcountry travel on their own: in emergencies it can be days before help arrives. All Alaska national parks allow firearms except in buildings such as visitor centers. Some require backcountry travel permits; others don't. Be sure to check with each park individually when planning your trip. For more information on Alaska national parks, visit **nps.gov** and link to the "Alaska" section.

U.S. BUREAU OF LAND MANAGEMENT   This federal agency oversees approximately 85 million acres. These lands offer many opportunities for remote recreation and solitude. Millions of acres are found away from the primary highway system, but some—such as the **Steese National Conservation Area,** the **White Mountains National Recreation Area,** the **Brooks Range,** historic **Fort Egbert** in Eagle, and the **Fortymile Wild and Scenic River**—can be accessed by road. For information on the Bureau of Land Management in Alaska, contact the **Alaska State Office** (907-271-5960), the **Anchorage Field Office** (907-267-1246), the **Glennallen Field Office** (907-822-3217), or the **Fairbanks District Office** (907-474-2200). Or visit **blm.gov.**

U.S. FISH AND WILDLIFE SERVICE–NATIONAL WILDLIFE REFUGES   There are 16 national wildlife refuges in Alaska totaling nearly 77 million acres, the most well known of which is the **Arctic National Wildlife Refuge,** which sits at the center of an oil-drilling debate that has been going on in Washington, D.C., for decades. In general, these lands are less developed (and in most cases not developed at all) than their national-park counterparts. Our favorites are the **Alaska Maritime National Wildlife Refuge** (907-235-6546; **alaska .fws.gov/nwr/akmar/index.htm)** for its kayak-paddling opportunities; the **Kenai National Wildlife Refuge** (907-262-7021; **alaska.fws.gov/nwr/kenai)** for its wildlife viewing, canoeing, and backpacking; and the **Arctic National Wildlife Refuge** (800-362-4546 or (907-456-0250; **alaska.fws.gov/nwr/arctic)** for its rafting and backpacking. To see an overview of all the national refuges in Alaska, visit **alaska.fws.gov/nwr/nwr.htm.**

U.S. FOREST SERVICE Alaska is home to only two national forests, but combined they are vast—the largest in the nation. **Chugach National Forest** surrounds Prince William Sound and is close to Anchorage, while **Tongass National Forest** includes the islands of Southeast Alaska and surrounds the cities of Ketchikan, Sitka, and Juneau. To get contact information for both parks, see "Federal Lands: Getting More Information" in Part Three (page 62).

▲ The Best Trailless Hiking in Alaska

SURE, YOU CAN step off into the woods for a great trailless-backpacking experience, but we have a few favorites that we'd like to share. These are places of unparalleled beauty that offer a little bit of the best of Alaska. Our listings include contact information so you can tailor your trip to your needs—how far you want to travel, which route you want to take, and so on. First, here's a little advice to help get you started.

Travel with a Guide?

If ever there's a time to consider paying a guide to lead a backpacking trip, it's when traveling in remote backcountry. Even the most seasoned backpacker can benefit from traveling with a guide, and for several reasons.

First, guides know the area like most folks know their backyards. When venturing into the wilderness for the first time, backpackers must carry maps, compasses, and GPS units. While guides will do the same, they often don't need to, instead relying on their own years of experience and knowledge of the area to lead them. Having a guide can take a lot of pressure off you and let you enjoy the trek rather than, say, fretting over whether you crossed the correct mountain pass.

Second, there's safety in numbers. While you probably want to maintain a sense of peace and solitude on a backcountry excursion, it also is wise to have at least a few companions in case of emergency. In the Alaska backcountry, you could go months without encountering another human.

TRAVELER'S TIP

▶ Having more than two people in your group—but no more than seven for the sake of the fragile ecosystems—can be a lifesaver if something goes wrong.

And the more people in your group, the smaller your chances of having dangerous encounters with wildlife such as bears.

Third, it can be cost-effective. You do the math. We'll use a trip to the Brooks Range as an example. An eight-day backpacking trip in the Arctic National Wildlife Refuge starts at around $3,000 depending on the guide you choose. Those trips include ground transportation and use of gear and guiding skills, as well as Bush plane airfare and food. Flying in the Bush on your own can cost hundreds of dollars, and food can be equally expensive: rates vary by the type of plane used and the number of passengers, as well as the distance between points. As for food, expect to pay at least 25% more for perishables such as produce and milk than you would in, say, Anchorage or Fairbanks.

BROOKS RANGE

Nine mountain systems make up the whole of the Brooks Range, which passes through the **Arctic National Wildlife Refuge** and **Gates of the Arctic National Park,** two masses of federally protected land the size of South Carolina and West Virginia, respectively. There are so many incredible places to see here that it may be difficult to decide in which direction to go. The **Romanzof Mountains,** where Dall sheep graze peacefully, is one choice. Or go to the rugged mountains of the **Arrigetch Peaks.** Gates of the Arctic is a mind-blowing option as well. The Brooks Range extends east to west from one end of Interior Alaska to the next and separates the far-north Arctic land from Interior Alaska, which is more centrally located and not quite as extreme in its climate.

Traveling in either the Arctic National Wildlife Refuge or Gates of the Arctic requires great skill and knowledge of backcountry travel and navigation. Access is via plane or off the Dalton Highway. Refuge managers encourage small groups—no more than seven backpackers at a time—to minimize impact on the fragile Arctic terrain. When hiking in groups, travel in a fan pattern to avoid creating long-lasting trails. Fires are discouraged because there is little to no wood in the Arctic, but if you do choose to build a fire, remove all evidence of it upon leaving.

Permits are not required for travel in the Brooks Range, with the exception of Gates of the Arctic National Park and Preserve, in which travelers are required to attend a backcountry orientation at the Anaktuvuk, Bettles, or Coldfoot ranger stations (see Resources following). But even if you're traveling in another part of the range, always file a trip plan with someone who knows when you are due to return.

Resources

▶ For more details on travel in the Brooks Range within Gates of the Arctic National Park, contact one of the park offices. They are open year-round, but hours vary, so call ahead of time to make sure someone is around. The **Anaktuvuk Pass Ranger Station** (907-661-3520; **nps.gov/gaar/index.htm**) has a year-round outside visitor display, but the ranger station hours vary, so call ahead. The **Bettles Ranger Station/Visitor Center** (907-692-5494) is open daily from mid-June to Labor Day but sometimes closes for lunch; it's open 8 a.m.–5 p.m. the rest of the year except holidays. The **Coldfoot Visitor Center** (907-678-5209) is open Memorial Day–Labor Day, 10 a.m.–10 p.m. The **Fairbanks Headquarters** (907-457-5752) is open weekdays 8 a.m.–4:30 p.m. and closed holidays.

▶ For further information on travel in the Brooks Range within the **Arctic National Wildlife Refuge,** call 800-362-4546 or 907-456-0250, or visit **alaska .fws.gov/nwr/arctic.**

▶ **U.S. Geological Survey (USGS)** maps can be used for travel in the Brooks Range (check with one of the **Alaska Public Lands Information Centers** listed in Part Three, page 62, or go to **usgs.gov** and click on "Maps, Imagery, and Publications"). Shaded relief maps are available at the **Arctic National Wildlife Refuge** Web site (**alaska.fws.gov/nwr/arctic/index.htm**). A single all-inclusive map of the refuge is not available because the area is too vast; instead, figure out which section you plan to travel in and order those indexed maps accordingly.

Brooks Range Backpacking Outfitters

▶ **ABEC'S ALASKA ADVENTURES ▸▸** 877-424-8907 or 907-457-8907; **abecalaska .com.** This Fairbanks-based guide company has been in business since 1980, offering some ultra-remote backpacking trips in the area. The outfitter also offers paddling trips. Best suited for active travelers. Trips range from 8 to 19 days, $2,950–$5,750.

▶ **ARCTIC WILD ➤➤** 888-577-8203 or 907-479-8203; **arcticwild.com.** The company has been around for more than 10 years, and its guides have 30-plus years of experience in the far north of Alaska. This environmentally conscious guide outfit is highly recommended for the most adventurous of travelers, with trip offerings as long as 20 days and most in the category of challenging (think real adventure). Options include base camp, backpack, rafting, or canoeing. Prices, per person, range $2,750–$4,300.

▶ **WILDERNESS BIRDING ADVENTURES ➤➤** 907-694-7442; **wildernessbirding .com.** One of the best outfitters in the state, as evidenced by its abundance of "wait list" trips. Although its trips are focused on birding, you will enjoy the guides and their expertise in the area. The company offers a gray-headed-chickadee trip in the Arctic National Wildlife Refuge as well as a base-camp birding trip, also in the refuge. Trips start at $1,700 for three days; the ANWR chickadee trip is eight days at $3,400.

DENALI NATIONAL PARK AND PRESERVE

This park's 6 million acres beckon travelers. You need a permit to travel within the park, which is divided into 87 numbered units. A limited number of campers are allowed in nearly half of those units at a time in an effort to maintain a wilderness environment for the wildlife that frequents this world-class park.

TRAVELER'S TIP

▶ You must apply in person for permits no sooner than one day before you plan to leave; no phone reservations are accepted.

Self-reliance is absolutely necessary. You must be prepared to travel cross-country through remote terrain in harsh weather, and to rescue yourself if there are emergencies. You must also travel responsibly, leaving no fire rings, trash, human waste, or other traces of your presence. This protects the habitat for wildlife as well as other backpackers out to enjoy a wilderness experience.

Obtaining a permit requires first planning your trip. A backcountry unit map is necessary to do this, so you can travel from one unit to the next without interruption. At the height of the backpacking season, many units fill up, so plan several itineraries before obtaining your permit.

Resources

▶ **Alaska Geographic** sells two books that are useful to backcountry hikers: *The Backcountry Companion* by Jon Nierenberg and *Backcountry Bear Basics* by Dave Smith. Both are available through this nonprofit (**alaskageographic.org**).

▶ For general information, call **Denali Backcountry Operations** at 907-683-2294 or 907-683-9510, or visit **nps.gov/dena** and go to the page on backpacking. There is a free, downloadable Backcountry Camping Guide too.

▶ **USGS** maps can be used for travel within the park.

Denali National Park Backpacking Outfitter

▶ **ALASKA ALPINE ADVENTURES »** 877-525-2577 or 907-781-2253; **alaskaalpine adventures.com.** The company offers two trips through Denali—a shorter, moderate weeklong trip and a more-challenging 10-day version. The cost is $2,995 for the former and $3,350 for the latter. A four-day family adventure can be had for $1,899 per adult, with discounts for kids. The company also offers a great tour of Denali State Park to the south. That seven-day trip starts at $1,850—a better option in our view because there are fewer people and the scenery is just as spectacular.

LAKE CLARK NATIONAL PARK AND PRESERVE

Lake Clark offers an impressive cross-section of Alaska. Here, you can walk along the shores of Cook Inlet, hike close to volcanoes, and see impressive lakes and rivers all in one trip. Backcountry permits are not required here; however, there are generally accepted rules of travel for the area. Leave no trace when camping—this includes removing all signs of fires and carrying out trash to avoid attracting wildlife.

The park's western end offers the easiest hiking because the drier tundra enables hikers to travel without getting as wet or tangled in bushes. Farther south, where there is more timber and brush, count on more bushwhacking but also more-remote hiking, where you'll be less likely to encounter other people.

Twin Lakes is one of the more popular places to hike and fish. The park service has a backcountry patrol cabin on the lower lake that is usually staffed all summer. **Turquoise Lake** is higher in elevation, with tundra vegetation and generally less wildlife, but it has great scenery and hiking in all directions.

For hardcore hikers, there is the multiday option of accessing **Telaquana Lake.** This will require serious knowledge of backcountry travel but can be an epic adventure for the truly rugged traveler.

Access to Lake Clark National Park can be expensive because of air-taxi costs, which range $300–$600, depending on where you land. Unlike road-accessible Denali National Park, Lake Clark is truly remote but, as a reward, far less frequented by travelers.

Resources

▶ For more details on Lake Clark, call headquarters at 907-644-3626 or 907-781-2218, or visit **nps.gov/lacl** and go to the page on backpacking.

▶ **USGS** maps can be used for travel in Lake Clark.

Lake Clark Backpacking Outfitter

▶ **ALASKA ALPINE ADVENTURES** ➤ 877-525-2577 or 907-781-2253; **alaskaalpine adventures.com.** The company's experienced guides—who are not only excellent recreational backpacking leaders but also trained mountaineers— offer three trips in the Lake Clark region, ranging from 7 to 10 days. Prices start at $3,150. There are four family-trip offerings too, from 6 to 7 days, starting at $2,695.

▲ The Best Hiking Trails in Alaska

IF HIKING OFF-TRAIL into the backcountry makes you just a little too uncomfortable, don't worry. There are some world-class trails in Alaska that are well marked (at least by Alaskan standards!) and well established, making for an excellent Alaska vacation for those who love to travel on foot. There are dozens of such trails throughout the state, but many of them are best suited as day hikes because they are not long enough to constitute a multiday trip (for more on day hiking, see Part Eight, page 167). We're sharing our five favorite trips, which are long enough to include at least one night's camping and usually more. For experienced hikers, a 35-mile trail will seem like a simple overnighter, but if we can convince you of anything, it is to slow down and really enjoy these trails. If you must make miles, set up camp early and explore the region around you. All of the trips we suggest afford you this opportunity.

Travel with a Guide?

Guided trips are excellent when traveling into the trailless backcountry, where intimate knowledge of the area and excellent orienteering skills are absolutely necessary. But, honestly, anyone with previous backpacking experience will be able to handle the marked trails in Alaska that we suggest. If you follow leave-no-trace practices and are careful to protect yourself against wildlife, traveling Alaska's marked trails can be a grand adventure.

Still, if you feel the need to travel with a guide, we've included, where applicable, a few suggestions at the end of each trail description. Not many wilderness guides cater to marked-trail hiking, so the choices are few. The ones we suggest are the best you'll find.

CHENA DOME TRAIL

Region The Interior.	**Best time of year to hike** Mid-June–early Sept.
Distance 30 miles.	
Trail configuration Loop.	**Traffic level** Light–moderate.
Difficulty ★★★★.	**Facilities** Marked trailheads within a mile and a half of each other; one trail shelter located within Chena River State Recreation Area.
Suitable for kids? Teens.	
Time to hike 2–4 days.	

TRAIL SUMMARY   This loop hike offers great alpine hiking and views, with great berry-picking late in the summer. The longest hike in the **Chena River State Recreation Area,** it's best suited to conditioned hikers. It has a total 8,500-foot elevation gain, one of the highest of any trail in Alaska. It's well marked in most places until it reaches the open treeless areas, and then is designated by mileposts and cairns. It can get dry late in the season, so carry plenty of additional water if traveling in late summer. Fires are prohibited; wildlife is plentiful.

DIRECTIONS TO TRAILHEAD   The trailheads are only 1.5 miles away from each other, one at Mile 49 and the other at Mile 50.5 of Chena Hot Springs

Road, 55 miles east of Fairbanks. Take the Steese Highway north 5 miles to Chena Hot Springs Road, and turn east. The trailheads are on the west side of the road, just beyond the trailhead for **Angel Rocks,** another day-hike option at about 2 miles one-way on a steep out-and-back trail.

TRAIL DESCRIPTION   The Chena Dome Trail is one of those treks that will be imprinted in your mind. The views are so expansive that it feels as if you are perched on top of the highest ridgeline in Alaska. The trail circumnavigates the **Angel Creek watershed** but can be dry at times because of its elevation. Resupply your water at every opportunity. Most people start from the north-end trailhead at Mile 50.5 because the climbing is spread out. But traveling this way also means that you'll end up doing most of your climbing later in the trip. You decide. If you want to get the worst over, start on the south end. However, if you like to climb hills with a lighter pack, save it for the end.

The trail is well marked in some places, not so much in others, so be prepared with backup navigational tools. A compass and map are musts. In poor weather, be prepared to travel by compass or GPS, or set up camp and wait for conditions to clear. After the first mile of climbing, a view of the **Angel Creek Valley** opens up; by Mile 3, you're about at tree line. The ridgeline is at 3,700 feet and follows dips and climbs until you reach **Chena Dome,** the high point, at 4,421 feet. The only trail shelter is at Mile 17, and there are no reservations required—it's first-come, first-served, although if you have already set up camp here, by all means welcome newcomers or those in distress. After the shelter, the trail dips and climbs like a yo-yo, offering some steep and challenging hiking, but still with open views. Sometimes this section of trail can be hard to follow, but on clear days it should be pretty self-explanatory. The descent to the south-end trailhead begins about 3 miles out and is pretty quick traveling.

Resources

▶ **The Chena Dome Trail** is located in the **Chena River State Recreation Area,** which is part of Alaska State Parks. For details on specific regulations within the area, visit **dnr.alaska.gov/parks/units/chena.** The **Alaska Public Lands Information Center** can help (907-459-3730; **alaskacenters.gov/fairbanks.cfm**)

▶ **USGS** topographic maps—in particular Circle A-5 and A-6, and Big Delta D-5 —will come in handy on this route, especially in poor weather. Check with one of the **Alaska Public Lands Information Centers** listed in Part Three (see page 62), or go to **usgs.gov** and click on "Maps, Imagery, and Publications." Alaska State Parks also publishes a hiking pamphlet, "Chena Dome Trail," available at **Alaska Public Lands Information Centers.**

Chena Dome Outfitter

▶ **1ST ALASKA OUTDOOR SCHOOL ➺** 907-590-5900; **1stalaskaoutdoorschool .com.** This adult-education-oriented guide service can get you started on your own adventure or guide you along the way. Owner Ralf Dobrovolny was born in Germany and has experienced extreme northern adventures throughout Canada and Alaska. He offers custom trips, including Chena Dome, which vary in price but tend to be in the very affordable $150-per-day range.

CHILKOOT PASS TRAIL

Region Southeast Alaska.	**Facilities** Marked trailheads and designated campsites with toilets, cooking shelters, and caches to keep food safe from bears. Fees and permits are required to hike on the Canada side but not on the U.S. side. A permit is required for all overnight backpackers regardless of where you're hiking.
Distance 33 miles.	
Trail configuration End-to-end.	
Difficulty ★★★★.	
Suitable for kids? Age 10 and older.	
Time to hike 3–5 days.	
Best time of year to hike June–Sept.	
Traffic level Moderate–heavy.	

TRAIL SUMMARY   The trail is historical as well as scenic, following the route of gold seekers during the gold rush of 1898–1900. It begins at the Taiya River bridge, near the community of **Dyea,** and travels over the Chilkoot Pass to the much prettier side, at **Lake Bennett in Canada.** The route passes through forests and past streams and lakes, and opens into high alpine country.

DIRECTIONS TO TRAILHEAD   From downtown Skagway, drive 2 miles north on the Klondike Highway to the Dyea Road. Turn left and drive 7 miles to the trailhead, which is marked and has a ranger station nearby. Reaching Lake Bennett is more complicated, as there is no road access. Drive north on the Klondike Highway 27 miles to a parking area on the left side of the road for Log Cabin.

You can follow the railroad tracks to a spur trail to Chilkoot Pass, or walk along the tracks all the way to Lake Bennett to start the hike from the north. When the White Pass and Yukon Route train is running, it is a better and safer option.

TRAIL DESCRIPTION   Because the Chilkoot Pass Trail is such an important historical asset to Southeast Alaska and Canada, a permit is needed to hike it, and everyone is asked not to remove artifacts they may come across: old rusting cook pans, wagon wheels, mining equipment, and the like. These are all evidence of one of the grandest rushes for gold in North America, when in 1898 gold was discovered and tens of thousands of prospectors flocked to the area, intent on claiming their share of the riches. The trail was the shortest and best-known route to the Klondike gold fields, and these hardscrabble prospectors traveled the route year-round in wind, rain, and snow.

TRAVELER'S TIP

> ▶ The Chilkoot Pass Trail is one of the best examples of Alaska's varied climates.

While hiking the Chilkoot Pass Trail from end to end, you'll experience everything from lush rainforests to rocky, craggy cliff sides and alpine valleys. There are lakes and streams, and snow is in the pass year-round. For these reasons, it can become a popular place at the height of the hiking season, and it will be quite unlike Alaska's more-remote hikes. Still, it is a mind-blowing experience, imagining what it must have been like for the thousands of souls who lugged their belongings over it in search of riches.

If you want to trace the steps of the 30,000 gold miners of 1898, you'll want to travel from Dyea to Lake Bennett, although either direction is OK. We prefer traveling from the Dyea side because it is actually easier climbing up the steepest section of the trail, known as **The Scales,** than it is to climb down. The first 5 miles of the Chilkoot Trail travel along a creek, with some climbing to reach **Finnegan's Point,** which is the first place to camp. The next uphill section travels through an area known as **Canyon City,** which was the base for hauling supplies over the pass during the gold rush. The old town site is practically gone now, and if you continue another 2 miles or so, you will reach **Pleasant Camp,** at Mile 10.5, which tends to be less crowded than other camps.

Sheep Camp is at Mile 13, and most people overnight here before climbing **The Scales,** which tops out at about Mile 18. Between these miles, expect steep climbing and boulder hopping. Take breaks often to look over your shoulder and enjoy the view. On clear days, it is breathtaking. On foul-weather days, though, the hike can be almost scary. Watch your footing, and dress in plenty of layers. Despite the high traffic level here, the route can still be quite dangerous if you take a fall. The distance from Sheep Camp to the Pass is only 3.5 miles, but it sometimes feels practically vertical.

The Scales is so named because it's where miners would stop and reweigh their gear for the climb upward (miners called the slope the Golden Stairs for its sharp 45-degree grade). These days, no one will weigh your pack, but try to keep it as light as possible while still carrying the appropriate gear. Your lungs will thank you. When you reach the pass, at 3,535 feet, you've also reached the border between the United States and Canada, and frankly, the prettiest, best-kept side of the park. During the gold rush, the Royal Canadian Mounted Police stationed themselves at this point, checking to make sure each person who passed the area had enough supplies to last them for the year. If they did, they were allowed through. If not, they had to turn around and go back down.

The next best camping location from the pass is 4 miles north of the summit at **Happy Camp,** but an emergency shelter is at **Stone Crib,** just a few hundred feet below the pass, for those caught in bad weather atop the pass. The area used to be an anchor for the aerial tramway.

Reaching Happy Camp is a nice but rocky walk, marked by cairns and temporary poles that the National Park Service and Parks Canada remove each winter. There is snow in the region year-round, often even in July, so be aware of the weather. You'll be in open country and pass a few streams, including Morrow Lake and a small waterfall at Mile 20. Staying at Happy Camp can be a fun experience, with campers celebrating their accomplishments and relating stories of survival.

> **TRAVELER'S TIP**
>
> ▶ We like Happy Camp because it tends to be less crowded than Deep Lake, 3 miles farther down the trail, where the majority of hikers stay.

The last 10 miles are your reward for all your hard work to reach this area. The trail follows a gradual descent along **Deep Lake** and the canyon that drops into **Lindeman City.** Today, the area is a campground and Canadian ranger station, but during the Klondike gold rush more than 10,000 people at a time set up tents and lived here while building the boats they would use to take them to the gold fields. On the way to Lake Bennett are a couple of campgrounds, and you hike through a forested area that drops in elevation until you reach the end of the trail.

Resources

▸ The U.S. portion of the trail is part of **Klondike Gold Rush National Historical Park.** For general information, contact the National Park Service at 907-983-2921 or **nps.gov/klgo/chilkoot.htm.** The **Southeast Alaska Discovery Center** in Ketchikan can also help (50 Main St., Ketchikan 99901; 907-228-6220; **alaska centers.gov/ketchikan.**cfm). The Canadian leg is part of the **Chilkoot Trail National Historic Site.** For general information, contact **Parks Canada** (888-773-8888; **pc.gc.ca/lhn-nhs/yt/chilkoot/index_e.asp**). (*Note:* When crossing the border into Canada, adults must present a passport and another form of picture ID; children must show a passport or birth certificate, plus a letter of authorization if one or both parents are absent.)

▸ Every person camping on the Chilkoot Pass Trail must have a permit, and it's best to get one months in advance because this hike is so popular. Only eight permits a day are held for hikers without reservations. Day users in Canada must also have a permit (day hikers in the United States do not need one). All fees are payable at the time of reservation, or at the time permits are obtained if no reservation is made. Permit fees are refundable up to a month before your planned departure; reservation fees are nonrefundable. Rates are $50.80 for adults, $25.35 for children ages 6–16. The reservation fee is an additional $11.70 per hiker. Those hiking in the United States pay only $16.50 per adult and $8.25 per youth (in Canada, the rate is $34.30 for adults and $17.10 for youth). Canadian day-use permits are $9.80. Pick up a permit at the **International Trail Center** in Skagway (at Second and Broadway; 907-983-9234). You are required to present the permit upon request by rangers and wardens. The center also offers a useful 12-minute video on hiking the Chilkoot Pass Trail.

▸ **USGS** topographic maps for the area are Skagway C-1 (SW, NW) and Canadian topo maps White Pass (104 M/11), Homan Lake (104 M/14), and Tushi Lake (104 M/15). **"A Hiker's Guide to the Chilkoot Trail,"** an illustrated guide that includes everything backpackers need to know before heading onto the trail, is more convenient than the full topo maps. A **USGS** topo map with side scale shows the trail's elevation gain to help hikers plan their days. It also includes detailed historical descriptions of major points along the way and basics such as customs, permits, and weather info, along with an equipment checklist. The guide is available for $3.95 at **alaskageographic.org** or at the National Park Service Visitor Center information desk in Skagway (291 2nd Ave.; 907-983-9200 or 907-983-2921; **nps.gov/klgo**).

▶ The **White Pass and Yukon Route** (800-343-7373 or 907-983-2214; **whitepass railroad.com**) offers rail transportation from the end of the trail at Lake Bennett to Skagway, Alaska, or Fraser, British Columbia.

Chilkoot Pass Trail Outfitters

▶ **ALASKA MOUNTAIN GUIDES AND CLIMBING SCHOOL** ➤ 800-766-3396; **alaskamountainguides.com.** This Haines-based outfit can do it all, and hiking the Chilkoot Trail is offered as a four-day ($790) or five-day ($890) trek with as many as 10 participants at a time. The price is reasonable, covering everything from gear rentals to permit fees to transportation and lodging in Whitehorse, Yukon Territory, on the way back.

▶ **SEA TO SKY EXPEDITIONS** ➤ 800-990-8735 or 604-583-3518; **seatosky expeditions.com.** Another excellent choice, organized by a company that offers a slightly longer itinerary for those who want to see Skagway in more depth. A seven-day trip ($1,495) includes stays in Whitehorse and Skagway.

CROW PASS–HISTORIC IDITAROD TRAIL

Region Southcentral Inland Alaska.	**Best time of year to hike** June–late Sept.
Distance 26 miles.	**Traffic level** Light.
Trail configuration End-to-end.	**Facilities** Marked trailheads and one cabin on the south end.
Difficulty ★★★.	
Suitable for kids? Teens.	*Currently no guides are available for this hike.*
Time to hike 2–3 days.	

TRAIL SUMMARY   This hike connects the **Eagle River Valley** to **Girdwood**, on the other end of the municipality of Anchorage, and passes through some of the most scenic land in **Chugach State Park** and **Chugach National Forest**. The route loosely follows the old Iditarod mail route, a dogsled path and footpath traveled by those going from Seward northward at the turn of the 20th century. While many Alaskans step up to the challenge of covering the Crow Pass Trail in one day, it is best enjoyed as an overnight trip, or even as a two-night trip if you really want to take in the scenery.

DIRECTIONS TO TRAILHEAD   From Anchorage, reach the south-end trailhead by driving south on the Seward Highway and turning left on the Alyeska Highway, at Mile 90 of the Seward Highway. Drive 2 miles and turn left onto Crow Creek Road. Drive 5 miles and turn right at the fork in the road. The trailhead and parking area are about a mile up the road. To reach the north-end trailhead, drive north on the Glenn Highway out of Anchorage until you reach the Hiland Road–Eagle River Loop exit just before Eagle River. Take that exit, staying to the right, and follow Eagle River Loop to the intersection of Eagle River Road (there is an oddly placed Walmart at this intersection). Follow Eagle River Road all the way to the end, about 10 more miles, and park at the Eagle River Nature Center. The trail is behind the center. Parking at the center is $5.

TRAIL DESCRIPTION   Most people choose to travel the Crow Pass Trail from south to north, so our descriptions will also follow this route. The climb out of Crow Creek Road is steep, reaching 2,500 feet to the pass and offering great views of **Raven Glacier.** About 2 miles in, you'll see the remains of an old gold mine that operated from the early 1900s to 1948. Feel free to explore the area, but be careful because the buildings are in rough shape. At 3,550 feet is the sole U.S. Forest Service cabin, which is available on a fee basis, so don't assume it's OK to stay there. The cabin sleeps up to six; a loft upstairs can squeeze in additional people.

After the cabin, you'll be following rock cairns that mark the trail to the pass. One of the most popular places to camp is right at the pass, at Raven Glacier, although it can get windy and foul weather can blow in quickly. But the views rival any in the state, and the mountains and glacier provide great contrast to the greens of the summer foliage.

From the pass, the trail continues along the edge of Raven Glacier, eventually reaching **Clear Creek** at Mile 6. You'll have to ford this creek, but in less than a mile you'll pass over Raven Creek via bridge. The next creek crossing is at

Mile 9.5. The trail then begins a climb, opening to a view of **Eagle Glacier,** before descending again toward the biggest water crossing of the trip, **Eagle River.**

Fording Eagle River can be very easy if the water is low or challenging if it is roaring fast and deep. The ford, at Mile 13 and halfway through the trip, requires sure footing and more than one person. Most times, it is about knee-deep and not very difficult, so if you reach it after heavy rains or the spring thaw, consider camping overnight and crossing in the morning, when it tends to be lower. **Thunder Gorge,** at Mile 14, is a good place for camping and has a metal ring for contained fires.

Mile 16.5 brings you to **Twin Falls,** another camping option. Beyond this you'll travel on fairly benign terrain, with a slight decline and a few small stream crossings. At Mile 23 is the **Echo Bend** campsite, a popular spot in winter for ice climbers. From here the hike continues through a pretty birch-and-aspen forest dotted with old cottonwoods. You'll arrive at the **Eagle River Nature Center (ernc.org)**, a nonprofit organization that offers interpretive and educational programs for budding naturalists, and helps maintain the trails in the area.

Resources

▶ The **Crow Pass Trail** passes through **Chugach State Park** and **Chugach National Forest** lands. For details on specific regulations within the state-park area, visit **dnr.alaska.gov/parks/units/chugach.** For details on the Chugach National Forest end to the south, visit **fs.fed.us/r10/chugach** and click on the "Glacier Ranger District" link. National-forest employees cannot make reservations for the cabin (see below) but can answer questions better than reservation agents; call 907-783-3242.

▶ **Chugach National Forest** manages the **Crow Pass Cabin,** which rents for $35 per night by permit only. Reservations may be made up to 180 days in advance (877-444-6777; **recreation.gov**). The **Alaska Public Lands Information Center** in Anchorage can also help (866-869-6887 or 907-644-3661; **alaska centers.gov/anchorage.cfm**).

▶ **Eagle River Shuttle** (907-332-1742 or 907-694-8888; **eaglerivershuttle.com**) will take you pretty much anywhere you want to go; the newest van accommodates up to nine people at a time. Rate for passage to the south trailhead of Crow Creek Trail is $175 for up to four people; for larger groups, the rate per person goes down.

▶ **USGS** topographic maps for the area are Anchorage A-6 and A-7 (NE). The **Glacier Ranger District** (907-783-3242) also has information.

KESUGI RIDGE TRAIL

Region Southcentral Inland.	**Time to hike** 2–4 days.
Distance 27.4 miles.	**Best time of year to hike** Mid-June– late Sept.
Trail configuration Out-and-back or end-to-end.	**Traffic level** Light–moderate.
Difficulty ★★★★.	**Facilities** Marked trailheads on either end and a campground at the south-end trailhead.
Suitable for kids? Age 10 and older.	

TRAIL SUMMARY   The majority of this hike lies amid alpine meadows offering open vistas and stunning views of Mount McKinley and the **Alaska Range.** Accessing the high ridges is a strenuous climb but well worth the effort, and once you're above tree line, the ridges climb and drop frequently. Although the trail is marked, foul weather can sock the entire alpine trail in a shroud of fog and mist.

TRAVELER'S TIP

▶ The gentler approach to the tree line is from the north end at Little Coal Creek, but we prefer the Byers Lake route because of its base- camp options.

DIRECTIONS TO TRAILHEAD   The south-end trail-head is at **Byers Lake Campground,** off the Parks High-way at Mile 147. Turn east into the campground and park near the boat launch. Be sure to check for closures, as the trail is sometimes closed due to bear activity. The north-end trailhead is at **Little Coal Creek,** at Mile 164 of the Parks Highway. A sign on the east side of the road directs you to the trailhead.

TRAIL DESCRIPTION   Kesugi Ridge is located in **Denali State Park,** between the Talkeetna Mountains and **Alaska Range,** an hour and a half south of its national-park big sister. The state park was established in 1970 and expanded to its present size (comparable to Rhode Island) in 1976; its western boundary meets the boundary of Denali National Park and Preserve. Denali State Park is less traveled but offers great ridgeline hiking, fishing, and other activities. Wildlife is plentiful here, including black and grizzly bears, moose, lynx, coyotes, foxes, and even wolves. *Kesugi* is a Tanaina Indian word meaning "the ancient one," and getting to this place may make you feel ancient—the climb to the tree line is steep and hard, but well worth it.

The high point is also at the north end, about 4 miles in and at 3,500 feet. The trails are well used as they approach tree line and, once you're in the alpine areas, are marked only by a well-worn path or an occasional cairn. In poor weather, be prepared to travel by compass or GPS or set up camp and wait for things to clear up.

Resources

▶ **Alaska Backpacker Shuttle** (907-344-8775) provides a van shuttle between Seward and Anchorage and Anchorage and Denali.

▶ For fishing regulations in the waters along the trail—Skinny Lake, Byers Lake, Byers Creek, and Little Coal Creek—contact the **Alaska Department of Fish and Game** or the **Alaska Public Lands Information Center** in Anchorage (866-869-6887 or 907-644-3661; **alaskacenters.gov/anchorage.cfm**).

▶ In case of an emergency, contact the **Alaska State Troopers** at the Talkeetna Post, Mile 12.5 Talkeetna Rd. (911 or 907-733-2256), or in Cantwell, Mile 209.6 Parks Hwy. (907-768-2202).

▶ **Denali State Park** is part of the Alaska State Parks system, managed by the Department of Natural Resources. More information about the area is available at **dnr.alaska.gov/parks/units/denali1.htm.** The Denali Ranger, through the **Mat-Su/CB Area Headquarters,** can answer specific questions (907-745-3975).

▶ **USGS** topographic maps include Talkeetna C-1, C-2, and D-1, and Talkeetna Mountains C-6 and D-6. For Kesugi Ridge only, you will need Talkeetna C-1 and Talkeetna Mountains C-6 and D-6. Maps are also available at the Visitor Contact Station at the Alaska Veterans Memorial, Mile 147.1 Parks Hwy. (907-745-3975).

Kesugi Ridge Outfitter

▶ **ALASKA ALPINE ADVENTURES** ≫ 877-525-2577 or 907-781-2253; **alaskaalpine adventures.com.** These guides are among the few to offer trips to Kesugi Ridge. A seven-day trip starts at $1,850.

RESURRECTION PASS TRAIL

Region Southcentral Coastal.

Distance 39 miles.

Trail configuration Out-and-back or end-to-end.

Difficulty ★★★.

Suitable for kids? Age 10 and older.

Time to hike 2–5 days.

Best time of year to hike Mid-June–Sept.

Traffic level Moderate–heavy.

Facilities Established tent sites, U.S. Forest Service cabins, and marked trailheads with parking and out-houses.

(*Currently no guides are available for this hike.*)

TRAIL SUMMARY   Resurrection Pass, a national recreation trail, is one of the most popular road-accessible hikes on the Kenai Peninsula. Its scenery ranges from forested riverside habitat to high alpine meadows. The highest elevation is at the pass itself, at about 2,600 feet. It offers good lake fishing for rainbow and lake trout, Dolly Varden, and some burbot.

DIRECTIONS TO TRAILHEAD   From Anchorage, take the Seward Highway south to reach either end of the trail. The north-end trailhead is in the community of **Hope,** 70 miles from Anchorage. Look for the Hope turnoff; turn right onto the Hope Highway, and travel about 16 miles to a left-hand turn onto Palmer Creek Road. Follow this gravel road until it branches to the right onto Resurrection Creek Road. The trailhead is on the right, with plenty of parking. The south end of the trail is in **Cooper Landing,** off the Sterling Highway. From Anchorage, follow the Seward Highway south to Mile 90, at its junction to the Sterling Highway. Follow the Sterling Highway about 15 miles to Mile 52, and turn right (north) into the marked trailhead parking area.

TRAIL DESCRIPTION   From the north end of the trail, near the community of Hope, the path climbs continuously along **Resurrection Creek,** where gold seekers once panned for gold. A cabin is at Mile 7, but we like **Fox Creek Cabin,** about 12 miles in, which offers a reprieve from an even-steeper climb out of the woods to Resurrection Pass. The **Devil's Pass Trail** connects to the Resurrection Pass Trail at the pass. The **Devil's Pass Cabin** here is an excellent base for a few days of exploring. The southern end of the hike is a more gradual downhill route through lakes and the **Juneau Creek** basin. Look for wildlife including bears, moose, and porcupines in this section. The prettiest part of the hike, in our opinion, occurs from **Swan Lake,** at about Mile 26 from the Hope direction, to the trailhead in Cooper Landing. Through this area, you will pass Juneau Lake and its two lakeside U.S. Forest Service cabins, and **Juneau Falls,** 4 miles from the southern terminus of the trail. The falls are a great place for tent camping but can get busy on weekends.

Resources

▶   For fishing regulations in the waters along the trail—Trout, Juneau, and Swan lakes, as well as Resurrection and Juneau creeks—contact the **Alaska Department of Fish and Game** (907-262-9368; **sf.adfg.state.ak.us**).

▶   Cabins in **Chugach National Forest** cost $25–$45 per night and must be reserved in advance either online or over the phone. Reservations can be made up to 180 days (six months) in advance of the first night's stay; 877-444-6777; **recreation.gov.** For details about the cabins, in the Seward Ranger District, call 907-271-2500 or visit **fs.fed.us/r10/chugach/cabin_web_page/ cabin_files.** Check this site before making reservations online or by phone, because the agents at **recreation.gov** are located somewhere in the Lower 48 states and don't know much about the cabins. The **Alaska Public Lands Information Center** in Anchorage can also help (866-869-6887 or 907-644-3661; **alaskacenters.gov/anchorage.cfm**).

▶   **USGS** maps for the area are Seward B-8, C-8, and D-8. Kenai National Wildlife Refuge maps can be downloaded online at **kenai.fws.gov/maps.htm** or purchased through **Alaska Geographic** ($9.95; **alaskageographic.org**).

PART SIX
CANOEING

MOST VISITORS TO Alaska will not venture beyond the fringes of development. Planes can carry you to isolated lodges, parks, and communities, but even
when you set out from a remote airstrip, there often are established routes and
trails that you must follow. Stay on these and you'll most likely share your wilderness experience with others. It's easy to leave the tour-package travelers behind,
but you'll have to work a little harder to shake the backcountry hikers and campers. Rather than paring your supplies to the bare minimum and trying to get
farther off the beaten path, why not leave the path behind altogether?

Alaska has far more river than road or trail and, with more than a million, lakes outnumber people at least two to one. Put a canoe in the water,

and a few paddle strokes will pull you into the solitude many seek and few find without tremendous effort.

Take, for example, a family weekend trip we spent exploring the **Kenai Canoe Trails** near Sterling on the tourist-heavy Kenai Peninsula. While the main roads, campgrounds, and popular fishing holes were packed with people, the entrance to the canoe system held just a few vehicles. We passed several canoeists on the first two lakes but soon found ourselves alone. We camped that night on an island and enjoyed a spectacular sunset accompanied only by the crackle of the campfire and the haunting call of a loon. While other Kenai Peninsula visitors likely were stacked camper to camper in the surrounding campgrounds, we had the place to ourselves. Over the course of the entire weekend, we spotted only a half-dozen other people.

This chapter explores some of the canoeing options in Alaska, focusing on a few of our favorite trips. In some cases, you'll be able to go with a guide; in many cases, you'll have to organize the expedition yourself. But we're confident you can do it. Canoeing in Alaska is a great way to explore regions of the land not easily seen from the road, and, luckily, many of our best canoeing destinations are road-accessible.

The Alaska boating season generally extends from June through August, as many lakes do not become ice-free until that time. Water levels are unpredictable, so paddlers are encouraged to get information on levels from local residents, the district office of the land-managing agency for that river, air-taxi operators, or the **Alaska River Forecast Center** in Anchorage (907-266-5160).

▲ Checklist for Success

WHEN IT COMES to Alaska weather, you can count on one thing: it *will* change. We've seen wind-driven rain arrive even before clouds had a chance to obscure the sun, and we've awakened to snow early on a June morning. Combine the unpredictable weather with the inherent risks that come with canoeing in colder waters, and the need for solid preparation becomes clear.

alaska canoeing @ a glance

Charley River

REGION ▸▸ The Interior
DISTANCE ▸▸ 88–151 miles
TRAFFIC LEVEL ▸▸ Light
DIFFICULTY ▸▸ Class II–V
CONFIGURATION ▸▸ One-way
SUITABLE FOR KIDS? ▸▸ No
GUIDE SUGGESTED? ▸▸ Recommended

Chena River

REGION ▸▸ The Interior
DISTANCE ▸▸ 100 miles
TRAFFIC LEVEL ▸▸ Moderate–heavy
DIFFICULTY ▸▸ Class I
CONFIGURATION ▸▸ One-way
SUITABLE FOR KIDS? ▸▸ Teens
GUIDE SUGGESTED? ▸▸ No

Kenai Canoe Trails

REGION ▸▸ Southcentral Coastal
DISTANCE ▸▸ 64 miles
TRAFFIC LEVEL ▸▸ Light
DIFFICULTY ▸▸ Class I
CONFIGURATION ▸▸ Out-and-back
SUITABLE FOR KIDS? ▸▸ Yes
GUIDE SUGGESTED? ▸▸ No

Lynx Lake Loop

REGION ▸▸ Southcentral Inland
DISTANCE ▸▸ 8 miles
TRAFFIC LEVEL ▸▸ Moderate–heavy
DIFFICULTY ▸▸ Class I
CONFIGURATION ▸▸ Lake
SUITABLE FOR KIDS? ▸▸ Yes
GUIDE SUGGESTED? ▸▸ No

Tangle Lakes–Delta River

REGION ▸▸ The Interior
DISTANCE ▸▸ 29–114 miles
TRAFFIC LEVEL ▸▸ Light
DIFFICULTY ▸▸ Class I–III
CONFIGURATION ▸▸ Lakes/river
SUITABLE FOR KIDS? ▸▸ Yes
GUIDE SUGGESTED? ▸▸ No

Wood River

REGION ▸▸ The Bush
DISTANCE ▸▸ 115 miles
TRAFFIC LEVEL ▸▸ Light
DIFFICULTY ▸▸ Class I–II
CONFIGURATION ▸▸ Lake/river
SUITABLE FOR KIDS? ▸▸ Yes
GUIDE SUGGESTED? ▸▸ No

Here is a checklist of must-haves for canoeing Alaska waters—whether you're setting off down the Yukon or exploring a small lake you've discovered along the highway.

What to Bring

✔ **PERSONAL FLOTATION DEVICE (PFD).** There are more ways to tip a canoe than can be listed here. Canoe long enough and it will happen, usually with no warning, so wear your PFD whenever you're in the boat. Take the time to get a jacket that fits, and you'll be more likely to wear it.

✔ **PADDLE.** It might seem obvious, but you'll move more efficiently with a paddle that is fitted to you. Height and arm length are just part of the equation. Whether you sit or kneel, the height of the canoe seat and the style of paddle all

canoeing outfitters @ a glance

Alaska Outdoor Rentals and Guides

907-457-2453
2paddle1.com

REGION ▸▸ The Interior
COST ▸▸ $
SUITABLE FOR KIDS? ▸▸ Yes
ACTIVITY LEVEL ▸▸ Moderate
TRIP LENGTH ▸▸ Custom

Fresh Water Adventures

907-842-5060
freshwateradventure.com

REGION ▸▸ The Bush
COST ▸▸ $$
SUITABLE FOR KIDS? ▸▸ Yes
ACTIVITY LEVEL ▸▸ Moderate
TRIP LENGTH ▸▸ Custom

Arctic Wild

888-577-8203 or 907-479-8203
arcticwild.com

REGION ▸▸ The Interior
COST ▸▸ $$
SUITABLE FOR KIDS? ▸▸ No
ACTIVITY LEVEL ▸▸ Moderate–difficult
TRIP LENGTH ▸▸ Varies

Great Alaska Safaris

800-544-2261 or 907-262-4515
greatalaska.com

REGION ▸▸ Southcentral Coastal
COST ▸▸ $$$
SUITABLE FOR KIDS? ▸▸ Yes
ACTIVITY LEVEL ▸▸ Easy–moderate
TRIP LENGTH ▸▸ 3–9 days

Canoe Alaska

907-883-2628
canoealaska.net

REGION ▸▸ The Interior
COST ▸▸ $$
SUITABLE FOR KIDS? ▸▸ Yes
ACTIVITY LEVEL ▸▸ Light–moderate
TRIP LENGTH ▸▸ Custom

Weigner's Backcountry Guiding

907-262-7840
alaska.net/~weigner

REGION ▸▸ Southcentral Coastal
COST ▸▸ $$
SUITABLE FOR KIDS? ▸▸ Yes
ACTIVITY LEVEL ▸▸ Moderate
TRIP LENGTH ▸▸ Varies

come into play. So take your time when buying or renting, and make sure the fit is right for you and the canoe you will be using.

✔ **CANOE.** Few visitors to Alaska will bring their own canoe, so you'll have to make the best of it once you're here. You'll be faced with aluminum versus fiberglass or Kevlar, wider lake vessels versus narrower riverboats. Choose based on the type of trip you'll be taking and your skill level. If you're going to make a lot of portages, be sure the canoe has a comfortable yoke. If you have one you like, bring it along. Packing a yoke is a lot easier than bringing the whole canoe, and you can always pack it away or mail it home if it doesn't fit.

Many of the guides, outfitters, and charter companies licensed to do business on public lands also rent boats. Listings of these companies are available from the **Alaska Public Lands Information Center** (605 W. 4th Ave., Suite 105, Anchorage 99501; 866-869-6887 or 907-644-3661; **alaskacenters.gov/canoeing.cfm**).

✔ **RAINGEAR.** Rain is inevitable, so be prepared for it. Because you'll be sitting with your legs exposed to the rain and the runoff from your rain jacket, don't skimp on rain pants. Breathable fabrics help battle sweat buildup while deflecting rain, so look for fabrics like Gore-Tex and Sympatex when shopping for gear. A raincoat also will double as a Windbreaker, so make sure it's comfortable enough to spend a lot of time in.

✔ **FOOTWEAR.** Touting one type of footwear over another is a good way to start a fight between canoeists. Hip boots that can be rolled down are versatile but can be tough to walk in while portaging, and they're dangerous if you fall into deep water while wearing them. Knee boots probably do the job most efficiently. Many Alaskans swear by XtraTuf brand neoprene boots. They're expensive (about $75 per pair), but they're comfortable and durable.

✔ **BUG REPELLENT.** Unless you're canoeing in early May or September, you'll probably be greeted at every portage and campsite by hundreds of bloodthirsty insects, notably mosquitoes, white socks, and no-see-ums. Bring a head net and plenty of bug spray. Repellents containing DEET are the most effective, but some people are wary of the health risks that can come with its use. Consider a citrus- or eucalyptus-based product before forgoing repellent altogether. Halfway down a wilderness river is no place to discover that the bugs are unbearable.

✔ **SLEEPING BAG.** Summer temperatures can dip below freezing, so use that as your guide when choosing a bag. Synthetic material might be more bulky than down, but it has the advantage of maintaining its insulating ability when wet. It's too easy to get wet traveling over water in rainy country, so leave the down bag at home and make more room for the synthetic. You won't regret it.

✔ **STOVE.** Bring a light, portable stove. Campfires are one of the pleasures of wilderness travel where they're allowed, but weather and the availability of wood can make a fire more work than it's worth. And when the weather is at its worst, a warm drink and a hot meal are most enjoyable. If you're going to be flown out to a remote launching point, be sure to discuss any rules regarding transport of flammable liquids well before you leave.

✔ **FIRE STARTER.** Waterproof, strike-anywhere matches ought to be in every backcountry traveling kit. They're light and easy to pack, and they don't run out of fuel. Bring a butane lighter too, but the matches are a sure thing, so don't forget them.

✔ **LAYERED CLOTHING.** Temperatures can fluctuate dramatically in a matter of hours, so dressing in layers is the best way to cope with the changing weather. Polypropylene, fleece, and other synthetics don't absorb water, and they provide good insulation, but they don't block the wind. Wool is bulkier but has many of the same qualities and provides some water repellency. However, if wool gets wet, it takes forever to dry. A knitted wool sweater or thick fleece sweater combined with a wind-blocking jacket or vest will get you through all but the most extreme conditions. Long pants will help keep the bugs off and keep you warm.

✔ **TENT.** Make sure it's large enough to accommodate your party and that its rain fly has been waterproofed recently.

What to Do

▶ **SHARE YOUR DESTINATION.** Don't leave home without telling someone where you're going and when you expect to be home. Write it down and leave it with someone you trust. It's an easy thing to do, and it will help rescuers to zero in on your location if you get into trouble. Many canoe areas have a sign-in sheet at the trailhead. Use it.

Alaska doesn't have the plentiful cell-phone coverage common to the Lower 48, although it is getting better each year. Don't expect to call for help in an emergency. Emergency Location Transmitters and satellite phones can be rented and are worth the peace of mind if you are going to be traveling through remote areas.

▶ **SET REALISTIC TRAVEL GOALS.** Give yourself enough time to make the trip. A good rule of thumb is 10–15 miles per day. That'll give you enough time to cover the distance while indulging in sportfishing, photography, and the many other enjoyable activities one might encounter along the way. And with the long days of the Alaska summer, you'll have plenty of daylight, even if you get a late start.

▶ **FILTER YOUR WATER.** Giardia is ubiquitous in Alaska, so don't take any chances. Water filters are light and compact, and using one is easier than boiling water and produces better-tasting results than iodine pills. Treating water might seem like an inconvenience, but one bout of gut-wrenching giardia will convince you otherwise.

▶ **PACK EFFICIENTLY.** Canoe travel allows you the option of bringing a few more conveniences along than you would on a backpacking trip. Just remember that you'll probably have to portage your gear at some point, so don't overdo it—for example, coolers may sound great, but on a three-day canoe trip with multiple portages, they will get old quickly. Most canoeing experts agree that packing all of your gear in one canoe backpack (a watertight stuff-sack that comes with shoulder straps) makes for the easiest portaging.

▶ **CARRY WATERPROOF MAPS.** You'd be surprised how easy it is to miss a portage, even on a well-marked canoe system. A map will keep you oriented on even the most convoluted river or lake system. Modern GPS units have maps built in, but a paper map won't run out of batteries or quit working if it's dropped in the water. Carry your map in a Ziploc bag with the day's route showing, or treat it with waterproofing chemicals available at most sporting-goods stores.

Find maps for the route you'll be visiting at **alaskacenters.gov/canoeing .cfm.** There you'll be able to click the route you're planning to travel. Trip-planning pages for specific public lands usually identify the maps needed for specific rivers.

▶ **GET A FISHING LICENSE.** If you're traveling over water anywhere in Alaska, the fishing is probably exceptional, but sportfishers tend to focus on a handful of rivers. Fishing licenses are required. You can pick one up at local fishing and game offices and most sporting-goods stores, grocery stores, or even gas stations throughout Alaska. While you're there, pick up a regulation book, as many lakes and rivers are designated for catch-and-release only.

▶ **SECURE ALL PERMITS, AND PAY ALL FEES.** Alaska has some of the most pro-gressive water-rights laws in the country, ensuring public access to virtually all navigable waters in the state. But camping regulations change as rivers pass through various public and private lands. Research your route and check with the government agencies that control the lands through which you will pass. Native corporations own large swaths of land in remote Alaska and often require permits for camping, so be sure you've got permission before setting up camp.

Travel with a Guide?

The following trips can be made by those with moderate canoeing skills. Guide services are available, but whether or not you need them is largely up to you. For some, venturing into the wilds of Alaska without a guide is unthinkable. However, if you're going to hire a guide, do your homework. When investigat-ing a guide service, here are a few tips.

▶ **ASK FOR REFERENCES.** You'll get an unvarnished evaluation from past clients. Don't go by testimonials on an outfitter's Web site, because those are only the best of the best.

▶ **MAKE SURE YOUR GUIDE HAS EXPERIENCE** on the river or lake system you'll be traveling. There's nothing worse than discovering that you're paying a guide who has less experience than you.

▶ **LISTEN TO WORD-OF-MOUTH REFERRALS.** Call sporting-goods shops in the areas in which you want to travel. They know the lakes, rivers, and people who travel them as well as past customers.

▶ **LOOK FOR FEDERAL CERTIFICATION.** Guides licensed to operate in national parks and refuges must prove they are capable. If you choose a guide from these listings, you can be reasonably sure they know what they are doing.

▲ Alaska's Best Canoeing

CHARLEY RIVER

Region The Interior.	**Difficulty** Class II–IV.
Distance 88 miles to confluence with the Yukon River, additional 63 miles to the town of Circle.	**Suitable for kids?** No.
	Best time of year to go June–Sept.
	Traffic level Light.
Trail configuration One-way.	**Facilities** None.

DESTINATION SUMMARY   For the advanced paddler, the Charley River offers many challenges over the 88-mile run from put-in until it joins the Yukon River. The river descends through rock gardens at an average of 31 feet per mile at a speed of 4–6 miles per hour.

DIRECTIONS TO TRAILHEAD   There is no direct road access into the Charley River basin. The region surrounding the basin is accessible by the Taylor and Steese highways, which terminate at Eagle and Circle, respectively. Access to the river is by fixed-wing aircraft with short takeoff and landing. The most popular airstrip is **Gelvin's** (907-443-3879), an unmaintained gravel landing area located in the upper portion of the Charley, just above Copper Creek. Take out at the Yukon or paddle to Circle, 63 miles downriver. The **Eagle field office** (907-547-2233) can provide details on river conditions as well.

DESCRIPTION   The Charley is a National Wild and Scenic River flowing through the **Yukon-Charley Rivers Preserve.** Snowmelt usually keeps the river high during May and June, making the upper river a challenging passage. In late summer and fall, low water exposes boulders and gravel bars, so paddlers must be vigilant and willing to scout before running some stretches of whitewater.

The river originates in the Yukon-Tanana uplands and flows northward about 108 miles to the **Yukon River.** The river passes through three distinct environments—open alpine valleys, entrenched river, and open floodplain—offering spectacular scenery as well as unspoiled wilderness. The upland valleys drain a rugged mountain area where peaks taller than 6,000 feet are common.

Average float time to the Yukon River is six days. An additional two to three days are needed to float the Yukon River to Circle. No rapids are on this section of the Yukon.

The river passes through rolling alpine tundra, mountainous terrain, and high, river-carved bluffs. Rustic cabins and historical sites from the 1898 gold rush are preserved along its path. Paleontological and archaeological sites are also plentiful. Peregrine falcons nest in the high bluffs that overlook the river, while the rolling hills that make up the preserve are home to a vast array of wildlife. The Charley descends from 4,000 feet above sea level to 700 at the Yukon River. It is considered by many to be the most spectacular river in Alaska.

Resources

▶ **Alaska Outdoor Rentals & Guides** (907-457-2453; **2paddle1.com.** This outfit gets our highest recommendation for shuttle support and canoe rentals. It can also provide some guide service.

▶ The **Alaska Public Lands Information Center** (101 Dunkel St., Suite 110, Fairbanks 99701; 907-459-3730; **alaskacenters.gov/fairbanks.cfm**) can advise you on good local trails and places to find rental equipment.

▶ **Go North Alaska Travel Center** in Fairbanks (866-236-7272 or 907-479-7272; **paratours.net**) rents RVs and camper trucks if you want a SAG (support and gear) vehicle for road support. Their rates are affordable too, ranging $137–$319 per day depending on the vehicle you choose.

▶ **U.S. Geological Survey** (**USGS**) maps include Charley River A-4, A-5, B-4, B-5, B-6, Circle D-1, Eagle C-6, D-5, and D-6. Check with one of the **Alaska Public Lands Information Center**s listed in Part Three (page 62), or go to **usgs.gov** and click on "Maps, Imagery, and Publications."

Charley River Outfitter

▶ **ARCTIC WILD** ➤ 888-577-8203 or 907-479-8203; **arcticwild.com.** This Fairbanks-based outfitter leads multiday trips on the Charley River starting at the headwaters of the river, and through Class II and III rapids for 108 miles of extraordinary scenery. The cost is $2,900 per person.

CHENA RIVER

Region The Interior.	**Suitable for kids?** Teens.
Distance 100 miles.	**Best time of year to go** June–Sept.
Trail configuration One-way, down-river.	**Traffic level** Moderate–heavy.
Difficulty Class I.	**Facilities** None; camp on your own.

DESTINATION SUMMARY   This clear-water river runs west from Chena Hot Springs and flows into the Tanana River near Fairbanks. It's a Class I stream, but sweepers and logjams can upset the unwary canoeist.

DIRECTIONS TO TRAILHEAD   From Fairbanks, drive 10 miles out Chena Hot Springs Road. Turn right on Nordale and leave one car at the Chena River Bridge. Continue down Chena Hot Springs Road for 48 miles and put in at the Angel Rocks trailhead. If you prefer a shorter trip, start at one of several spots between Mile 30 and Angel Rocks.

DESCRIPTION   The Chena's braided headwaters join to form a narrow, moderately difficult river that cuts through forested mountains and hills and muskeg lowlands, meandering close to the road for much of its length. This westerly flowing river drains 2,000 square miles and draws moderate-to-high amounts of recreational use due to its proximity to Fairbanks. There's no whitewater, but be alert for logjams and sweepers that can span the narrow channel. Even though you see and hear automobile traffic on parts of the river, don't forget that this is wild country. Use of bear-proof containers is recommended for food. Campsites are plentiful along the banks and on gravel bars. Expect high, fast-moving water during May and early June due to snowmelt. August rains can also raise water levels, so watch the weather and choose your campsite carefully. A floodwater-abatement dam spans the upper river. Contact the **Army Corps of Engineers** (907-488-6359; **poa.usace.army.mil/co/chena/index.html**) to see if the floodgates are open.

Resources

▸ The **Alaska Public Lands Information Center** (101 Dunkel St., Suite 110, Fairbanks 99701; 907-459-3730; **alaskacenters.gov/fairbanks.cfm**) can advise you on good local trails and places to find rental equipment.

▸ Canoe rentals are available at **Alaska Outdoor Rentals and Guides** (907-457-2453; **2paddle1.com**). They offer foldable and lightweight vessels as well as river-worthy boats.

▸ The **Fairbanks Convention and Visitors Bureau** (101 Dunkel St., Suite 111, Fairbanks 99701; 800-327-5774; **explorefairbanks.com**) can help book lodging and rentals.

▸ **USGS** maps for the area are Circle A-5, Big Delta D-5, D-6, and Fairbanks D-1 and D-2.

Chena River Outfitter

▸ **ALASKA OUTDOOR RENTALS AND GUIDES** ≫ 907-457-2453; **2paddle1.com**. Offers guided floats on the Chena as well as other locations.

KENAI CANOE TRAILS

Region Southcentral Coastal Alaska.	**Best time of year to go** Mid-May–Sept.
Distance 64 miles.	**Traffic level** Light.
Trail configuration Out-and-back and end-to-end.	**Facilities** Unimproved campsites; fires are allowed within fire rings, marked portages with some board-walks.
Difficulty Class I.	
Suitable for kids? Yes.	

DESTINATION SUMMARY   Located on the Kenai Peninsula between Sterling and the Cook Inlet shoreline, the Kenai Canoe Trails consist of two canoe routes: **Swan Lake Trail,** which winds 60 miles through spruce and birch forest, connecting 30 lakes and three forks of the Moose River; and the **Swanson River Trail,** an 80-mile-long route that connects more than 40 lakes with 46 miles of the Swanson River. Both trail systems offer multiple route options, so canoeists can make excursions of various lengths, from overnights to week-long meanders through the lakes and lowland forest. Portages vary in length from a couple of hundred yards to three-quarters of a mile.

DIRECTIONS TO TRAILHEAD   From Anchorage, take the Seward Highway South to Mile 90, where it joins the Sterling Highway. Follow the Sterling Highway to Mile 80.3 and turn right on Swanson River Road. Follow Swanson River Road to Swan Lake Road at Mile 17. The Swan Lake system has two entrances, the first at Mile 3 and the second at Mile 9.5. Farther on, at Mile 17.5, you'll find the entrance to the Swanson River system at Paddle Lake.

DESCRIPTION   Start at the west (Mile 3) entrance on Canoe 1 Lake. The portage between Canoe 1 and Canoe 2 is a wet one. We wouldn't call it a water portage because you can't exactly paddle it, and walking is difficult because water levels vary from ankle- to hip-deep. Hip boots are valuable here, allowing one person to drag the canoe while the other paddles. The passage between **Spruce** and **Marten lakes** is a true water portage, a beautiful channel through a marshy landscape, wide enough for a canoe and not much more. Low, birch-covered hills and lowlands thick with black spruce surround the lakes. Glacial erratics stand out of the water in several lakes throughout the system.

Portages are clearly marked, wide, and well maintained, with boardwalks spanning the wettest portions of the trail. Watch for roots that can trip up the unwary canoe carrier.

The biggest danger for canoeists on this system is wind. Some of the larger lakes, such as **Gavia** and **Swan,** can get pretty choppy when the wind blows, so head for the shoreline if the wind starts to build. It's better to paddle the long way around than to swim.

In addition to fine canoeing, the area is rich in wildlife; moose are common, as are black and grizzly bears, wolves, ptarmigan, grouse, beaver, mink, and numerous waterfowl.

Resources

▸ The Kenai Trails lie within the **Kenai National Wildlife Refuge.** For more information, visit **kenai.fws.gov/VisitorsEducators/visiting/canoe/canoeing.htm.**

▸ For fishing regulations, contact the **Alaska Department of Fish and Game;** 907-262-9368; **sf.adfg.state.ak.us** (click on "Licenses and Permits").The page offers maps of area lakes, fishing regulations, and dates of open fisheries. Or call 907-267-2218. The **Alaska Public Lands Information Center** in Anchorage can also help (605 W. 4th Ave., Suite 105, Anchorage 99501; 866-869-6887 or 907-644-3661; **alaskacenters.gov/anchorage.cfm**).

▶ **Alaska Canoe and Campground** (907-262-2331; **alaskacanoetrips.com**) rents canoes for $32.50 per night for three nights or more, and **Weigner's Backcountry Guiding** (907-262-7840; **alaska.net/~weigner**) also rents gear.

▶ The most comprehensive guide to the trails is *The Kenai Canoe Trails,* by Daniel Quick, published by Northlite Publishing Company. The 168-page book sports a water-resistant cover and provides a tremendous amount of practical information gathered by Quick over 30 years of paddling the trail system. Inside you'll find detailed maps and descriptions of every lake and trail, campsite locations, and fishing information, as well as advice on what to wear, how to choose a canoe, and more. To order ($15.95 plus $3.85 shipping and handling), call 907-262-5997 or visit **northlite.biz/canoe.**

▶ **USGS** maps for the area are Kenai C-2 and C-3. Kenai National Wildlife Refuge maps can be downloaded online at **kenai.fws.gov/maps.htm** or purchased through the Alaska Natural History Association ($9.95; 907-274-8440; **alaskageographic.org**).

Kenai Canoe Trails Outfitters

▶ **GREAT ALASKA SAFARIS ≫** 800-544-2261 or 907-262-4515; **greatalaska.com.** Sterling-based operator with a solid reputation.

▶ **WEIGNER'S BACKCOUNTRY GUIDING ≫** 907-262-7840; **alaska.net/~weigner.** This longtime guide knows the area extensively and is recommended by locals. Weigner also rents Old Town canoes and provides a shuttle service for those on independent trips. Cost is $180 per day for day trips and $230 per day for multiday trips.

LYNX LAKE LOOP

Region Southcentral Inland Alaska.	**Best time of year to go** June–Sept.
Distance 8 miles.	**Traffic level** Moderate–heavy.
Trail configuration Lake.	**Facilities** Designated campsites and
Difficulty Class I.	public-use cabins.
Suitable for kids? Yes.	

DESTINATION SUMMARY   The Lynx Lake Loop is an easy paddle through a chain of small, undeveloped lakes. It's a good place for novice paddlers to test their skills. More-experienced boaters will also enjoy the scenery and peaceful-ness of the lake-speckled region. It's an ideal weekend trip, although it can be paddled in a full day.

DIRECTIONS TO TRAILHEAD   The turnoff for Nancy Lake State Recreation Area is located at Mile 66.5 of the Parks Highway. From Anchorage, take the Glenn Highway north toward Wasilla, and turn on the Parks Highway interchange.

DESCRIPTION   The **Nancy Lake State Recreation Area** contains an 8-mile chain of lakes called the Lynx Lake Loop, in the Matanuska-Susitna Valley region of Southcentral Inland Alaska. The canoe trail consists of easy lake pad-dling through small, wild lakes; well-marked portages; and designated camp-sites. Public-use cabins are also available for rent. A longer trip can be made by continuing south from **Lynx Lake** to **Butterfly and Skeenta lakes** before returning on the same route to rejoin the loop. Cabins are located on **Red Shirt, Lynx, Nancy, James, and Bald lakes.**

Ten thousand years ago, this area, like much of Alaska, was covered with ice. Though the ice has retreated, it still bears the marks of the recent glacia-tion. As the glaciers melted, they left an impermeable layer of glacial silt and clay that underlies the region. Water trapped above that layer saturates the landscape, creating the many lakes that cover the region.

For those who prefer river canoeing, there is a put-in via the **Little Susitna River,** at Mile 57 Parks Hwy., in Houston. The river is mostly easy traveling, but some canoeing experience is advisable, as sweepers and powerboat traffic are common. Travel time on the river is 4–5 hours.

Resources

▶   **Alaska Public Information Center:** 550 W. 7th Ave., Suite 1260, Anchorage 99501; 907-269-8400; **alaskastateparks.org.** The **Alaska Public Lands Information Center** (605 W. 4th Ave., Suite 105, Anchorage, 99501; 866-869-6887 or 907-644-3661; **alaskacenters.gov/lynx-lake-loop.cfm**) also has information on the trip.

▶   Canoe rentals are available through **Tippecanoe Rentals** (907-495-6688; **paddlealaska.com**).

▶   **USGS** maps for the area are Tyonek C-1 and Anchorage C-8.

▶   No guides are available for this area, but the paddling is reasonably easy and
    good for beginners.

TANGLE LAKES—DELTA RIVER

Region The Interior.	**Suitable for kids?** Yes.
Trail configuration Lake crossings and river passage.	**Best time of year to go** May–Sept.
	Traffic level Light.
Distance 29–114 miles.	**Facilities** None.
Difficulty Class I–III.	

DESTINATION SUMMARY   Designated as a National Wild and Scenic River,
the Delta begins at Lower Tangle Lake and flows north through the Amphitheater Mountains to the foothills of the **Alaska Range.** The trip length can vary
29–114 miles depending on the takeout. It offers some of the best grayling
fishing in the state.

DIRECTIONS TO TRAILHEAD   From the Richardson Highway, turn west
onto the Denali Highway. Follow the Denali 21 miles to the put-in at the Tangle Lakes Campground, on the right. Take out along the Richardson Highway
at either Mile 212.5 or Mile 229 across from Ann Creek (see Resources, next
page, for shuttle information). Take out at Big Delta if you choose to make
the longer float.

DESCRIPTION   The float begins with a 16-mile-long chain of lakes that
requires no portages, but water can be low in spots, so be careful of the line
you choose. Watch for wind on the lake crossings. The first mile of river is
shallow and rocky. At Mile 2, the river enters a half-mile-long canyon with an
impassable waterfall. Watch for the portage on the right. The half-mile trail is
rocky, narrow, and slippery when it's rainy out, and is interrupted by a small
pond, so gear must be reloaded in the boat, ferried across, and then carried
to the put-in point below the canyon. Below the falls, the only tricky section
includes Class III rapids stretch on for almost 2 miles before smoothing out
into Class I and some easy Class II rapids for the remaining 12 miles. Camp

spots are easy to find along the bank and on gravel bars. Six miles before the takeout at Mile 212.5, the river becomes braided. Look for the takeout on the right bank below the confluence of **Phelan Creek.** The Class IV, 20-mile stretch of river between Ann and One Mile creeks is known as **Black Rapids,** and portaging around it by car is recommended (plus, kids shouldn't travel this section). Put in again around Mile 230, and float Class III water through braided channels for about 30 miles before the waters calm to Class I. Take out at Big Delta.

Resources

▶ From Fairbanks, vehicle rentals are available through **Alaska Outdoor Rentals & Guides** (907-457-2453; **2paddle1.com**) and **Go North Alaska Travel Center** (866-236-7272 or 907-479-7272; **paratours.net**). Rates start at $108 per day, depending on the vehicle.

▶ The **Alaska Public Lands Information Center** in Anchorage can help with details on the best places to camp or stay along the road (605 W. 4th Ave., Anchorage 99501; 907-644-3661; **alaskacenters.gov/delta-and-gulkana.cfm**), as can the Fairbanks location (101 Dunkel St., Suite 110, Fairbanks 99701; 907-459-3730; **alaskacenters.gov/fairbanks.cfm**).

▶ The **Fairbanks Convention and Visitors Bureau** (101 Dunkel St., Suite 111, Fairbanks 99701; 800-327-5774; **explorefairbanks.com**) can help you plan lodging and transportation. The **Anchorage Convention and Visitors Bureau** (907-276-4118 or 907-274-3531; **anchorage.net**) is a good option if your trip is starting from the south.

▶ Canoe rental and shuttle service available at **Tangle River Inn** (907-822-3970, **tangleriverinn.com**). The $125 (depending on current gas prices) shuttle is a great time-saver and well worth it, but the lodge owners can be hard to reach, so start planning well in advance.

▶ **USGS** maps for the area include Mount Hayes A-4, A-5, B-4, C-4, D-4, and Big Delta A-4.

Tangle Lake Canoe Outfitter

▶ **CANOE ALASKA »** 907-883-2628; **canoealaska.net.** Based in Tok, this outfitter offers customized guided trips in the Interior. The family-owned business has been operating since 1980.

WOOD RIVER

Region The Bush.	**Suitable for kids?** Yes.
Distance 115 miles.	**Best time of year to go** June–Sept.
Trail configuration Lake/river.	**Traffic level** Light–moderate.
Difficulty Class I–II.	**Facilities** None.

DESTINATION SUMMARY   A classic lake-and-river journey through pristine, fjordlike lakes teeming with world-class fishing.

DIRECTIONS TO TRAILHEAD   Commercial air to Dillingham Airport; air charter from Dillingham Airport to trailhead. The area is operated by Alaska State Parks.

DESCRIPTION   Part of **Wood-Tikchik State Park,** the route descends the Wood River Lake system, five lakes varying 20–45 miles long and interconnected by short, rocky, and swift rivers. The state park allows powerboats and contains several fishing lodges, but the wild nature of the region is largely preserved.

The surrounding terrain includes spired peaks, rolling mixed upland forest, and large, open tundra fields. Bounded on one side by the spruce-, birch-, and alder-covered **Wood River Mountains** and on the other by the muskeg-covered **Nushagak Lowlands,** the variety and beauty of the terrain is remarkable.

From **Lake Kulik,** follow the **Wind River** to **Mikchalk Lake.** From Mikchalk, follow the **Peace River** to **Lake Beverly.** From Beverly, follow the **Agulukpak River** to **Nerka Lake,** which flows into the **Agulowak River** and finally to **Aleknagik Lake.** Short stretches of Class II whitewater can be found on several of the interconnecting rivers. The trail terminates at the community of **Aleknagik.**

Open fires are permitted only on gravel beaches and bars. Use dead and down wood only. Extinguish fully and bury completely before leaving the site. The use of portable campstoves is permitted throughout the park and is encouraged. Live-tree cutting is not permitted.

All five species of Pacific salmon—king, red, pink, silver, and chum— spawn in the Wood River and Tikchik systems. Rainbow trout, grayling, lake trout, arctic char, Dolly Varden, and northern pike also are present and bring many sportfishermen to the region.

Moose, caribou, and brown bears can be seen throughout the park. Birds nesting in the area include a wide variety of waterfowl, gulls, bald eagles, golden eagles, arctic terns, various loons, spotted and least sandpipers, semi-palmated plovers, willow ptarmigan, and spruce grouses.

Resources

▶ **Alaska State Parks**, Wood-Tikchik District, can supply information on conditions and places to camp. The main office is open year-round (550 W. 7th Ave., Suite 1380, Anchorage 99501; 907-842-2641; **dnr.alaska.gov/parks/units/woodtik.htm**); the ranger station is open seasonally, late May through late September (907-842-2641).

▶ Visitor information is available at **Dillingham Chamber of Commerce and Visitor Center** (907-842-5115; **dillinghamak.com**).

▶ **USGS** maps for this area are Dillingham C-8, C-7, and D-8; 1-inch-to-the-mile scale (1:63,360) recommended.

Wood-Tikchik Outfitters

▶ **FRESH WATER ADVENTURES** ➤ 907-842-5060; **freshwateradventure.com**. A longtime operator in the area that can fly you in and guide you.

▶ The **WOOD-TIKCHIK RANGER STATION** (see Resources, above) has information on other guides licensed to lead trips into the area.

PART SEVEN
CYCLING

YOU MIGHT NOT be able to climb Mount McKinley on a bike in Alaska, but there is no shortage of other scenic places to check out by means of pedal power. Ride from the coastal communities of the Kenai Peninsula clear to the Interior. Pedal mountain passes and wide-open valleys. Or get really adventurous and wait until wintertime, when a few studs in your tires will give you plenty of traction for riding on ice and snow.

Cycling in Alaska requires preparation as well as good conditioning. This is not Kansas, and by that we mean that just about any road, trail, or path that you choose to follow will eventually climb a hill. Some mountains, so small as to not even be named, can challenge even the fittest of cyclists. Still, the reward is justified when you've climbed a long stretch of road or trail and are greeted by a view that will knock your cycling socks off.

This chapter will share with you some of our favorite cycling destinations and give you some tips on how best to prepare for the trip. We have focused one section on road riding, which includes touring with panniers or trailers. The next section covers routes that are best traveled on mountain bikes, including overnight camping on singletrack trails while hauling gear to roadways that are mostly gravel and best suited for beefy bikes. We've also included a section on our favorite day rides for those of you who prefer to keep your bike as light as possible and sleep in comfort at night.

Our rides vary in difficulty, but the truth is that just about all of them will be challenging. For example, we list a day jaunt on a paved bike path skirting Anchorage as easy, but that's just because it's paved and well traveled, and it requires very little planning to experience. Still, there are some hilly climbs and windy sections that will take at least average biking skills to navigate. At the other end of the spectrum, we rate a mountain-biking camp trip on the Resurrection Pass as moderate to difficult because you'll be carrying all of your gear and experiencing roots, rocks, mud, and overgrown singletrack quite often. Still, it is a very manageable ride for a mountain biker with off-road cycling skills.

All that said, don't let yourself become too intimidated by the ratings, and consider instead the type of cycling experience you want. Look at the mileage of the trip, its level of technical challenges (for the mountain-bike section), and its accessibility and affordability. Some trips, such as a tour of the Nome Road System, offer quite pleasant riding but require an out-and-back ride, which some cyclists don't like. It gets expensive to reach Nome too, so keep your budget in mind.

▲ Checklist for Success

✔ **PLAN AHEAD.** Even if your cycling adventure will keep you on the road system, where there is easy access to telecommunications, it's still a good idea to

▲ alaska cycling @ a glance

The Anchorage–Valdez Loop

**REGIONS ›› ** Southcentral Inland, Coastal
**DISTANCE ›› ** 360 miles
**MOUNTAIN/ROAD? ›› ** Road
**DIFFICULTY ›› ** ★★★★
**CONFIGURATION ›› ** Loop
**TIME TO RIDE ›› ** 6–9 days
**SUITABLE FOR KIDS? ›› ** No
**GUIDE SUGGESTED? ›› ** No

Anvil Mountain

**REGION ›› ** The Bush
**DISTANCE ›› ** 9 miles
**MOUNTAIN/ROAD? ›› ** Mountain
**DIFFICULTY ›› ** ★★★
**CONFIGURATION ›› ** Out-and-back
**TIME TO RIDE ›› ** Day trip
**SUITABLE FOR KIDS? ›› ** Yes
**GUIDE SUGGESTED? ›› ** No

Birch Hill Ski Trails

**REGION ›› ** The Interior
**DISTANCE ›› ** Varies
**MOUNTAIN/ROAD? ›› ** Mountain
**DIFFICULTY ›› ** ★★★
**CONFIGURATION ›› ** Loops/out-and-back
**TIME TO RIDE ›› ** Day trip
**SUITABLE FOR KIDS? ›› ** Varies
**GUIDE SUGGESTED? ›› ** No

Bird-Gird Trail

**REGION ›› ** Southcentral Inland
**DISTANCE ›› ** 24 miles
**MOUNTAIN/ROAD? ›› ** Mountain/road
**DIFFICULTY ›› ** ★★
**CONFIGURATION ›› ** Out-and-back
**TIME TO RIDE ›› ** Day trip
**SUITABLE FOR KIDS? ›› ** Yes
**GUIDE SUGGESTED? ›› ** No

Burma Road

**REGION ›› ** Southcentral Coastal
**DISTANCE ›› ** 12 miles one-way
**MOUNTAIN/ROAD? ›› ** Mountain
**DIFFICULTY ›› ** ★★★★★
**CONFIGURATION ›› ** Loop
**TIME TO RIDE ›› ** Day trip
**SUITABLE FOR KIDS? ›› ** No
**GUIDE SUGGESTED? ›› ** Recommended

The Dalton Highway

**REGION ›› ** The Interior
**DISTANCE ›› ** 414 miles
**MOUNTAIN/ROAD? ›› ** Mountain
**DIFFICULTY ›› ** ★★★★★
**CONFIGURATION ›› ** End-to-end
**TIME TO RIDE ›› ** 8–12 days
**SUITABLE FOR KIDS? ›› ** No
**GUIDE SUGGESTED? ›› ** No

The Denali Highway

**REGION ›› ** The Interior
**DISTANCE ›› ** 134 miles
**MOUNTAIN/ROAD? ›› ** Mountain
**DIFFICULTY ›› ** ★★★
**CONFIGURATION ›› ** End-to-end
**TIME TO RIDE ›› ** 2–4 days
**SUITABLE FOR KIDS? ›› ** Teens
**GUIDE SUGGESTED? ›› ** No

Denali Nat'l. Park & Preserve Road

**REGION ›› ** The Interior
**DISTANCE ›› ** 170 miles
**MOUNTAIN/ROAD? ›› ** Mountain
**DIFFICULTY ›› ** ★★★★
**CONFIGURATION ›› ** Out-and-back
**TIME TO RIDE ›› ** 2–4 days
**SUITABLE FOR KIDS? ›› ** Teens
**GUIDE SUGGESTED? ›› ** No

more alaska cycling @ a glance

East Glacier Trail

REGION ›› Southeast
DISTANCE ›› 4.5 miles
MOUNTAIN/ROAD? ›› Mountain
DIFFICULTY ›› ★ ★ ★
CONFIGURATION ›› Loop
TIME TO RIDE ›› Day trip
SUITABLE FOR KIDS? ›› No
GUIDE SUGGESTED? ›› No

Eklutna Lake

REGION ›› Southcentral Inland
DISTANCE ›› 32 miles
MOUNTAIN/ROAD? ›› Mountain
DIFFICULTY ›› ★ ★ ★
CONFIGURATION ›› Out-and-back
TIME TO RIDE ›› Day trip
SUITABLE FOR KIDS? ›› Yes
GUIDE SUGGESTED? ›› No

Ester Dome and Alder Chute

REGION ›› The Interior
DISTANCE ›› 9.5 miles round-trip
MOUNTAIN/ROAD? ›› Mountain
DIFFICULTY ›› ★ ★ ★
CONFIGURATION ›› Loop
TIME TO RIDE ›› Day trip
SUITABLE FOR KIDS? ›› No
GUIDE SUGGESTED? ›› No

Haines–Skagway (Golden Circle)

REGION ›› Southeast
DISTANCE ›› 355 miles
MOUNTAIN/ROAD? ›› Road
DIFFICULTY ›› ★ ★ ★
CONFIGURATION ›› Loop option
TIME TO RIDE ›› 5–9 days
SUITABLE FOR KIDS? ›› Teens
GUIDE SUGGESTED? ›› Recommended

Hatcher Pass–Gold Mint Trail

REGION ›› Southcentral Inland
DISTANCE ›› 18 miles
MOUNTAIN/ROAD? ›› Mountain
DIFFICULTY ›› ★ ★ ★ ★ ★
CONFIGURATION ›› Out-and-back
TIME TO RIDE ›› Day trip
SUITABLE FOR KIDS? ›› No
GUIDE SUGGESTED? ›› No

Johnson Pass Trail

REGION ›› Southcentral Coastal
DISTANCE ›› 20 miles
MOUNTAIN/ROAD? ›› Mountain
DIFFICULTY ›› ★ ★ ★ ★
CONFIGURATION ›› Out-and-back
TIME TO RIDE ›› Day trip
SUITABLE FOR KIDS? ›› Teens
GUIDE SUGGESTED? ›› Recommended

Kenai Peninsula Tour

REGIONS ›› Southcentral Inland, Coastal
DISTANCE ›› 302 miles
MOUNTAIN/ROAD? ›› Road
DIFFICULTY ›› ★ ★ ★
CONFIGURATION ›› Y-shaped
TIME TO RIDE ›› 4–8 days
SUITABLE FOR KIDS? ›› No
GUIDE SUGGESTED? ›› No

Million Dollar Bridge

REGION ›› Southcentral Coastal
DISTANCE ›› 48 miles
MOUNTAIN/ROAD? ›› Mountain
DIFFICULTY ›› ★ ★
CONFIGURATION ›› Out-and-back
TIME TO RIDE ›› Day trip
SUITABLE FOR KIDS? ›› Yes
GUIDE SUGGESTED? ›› No

more alaska cycling @ a glance

Prince of Wales Island

REGION ›› Southeast
DISTANCE ›› 60–300 miles
MOUNTAIN/ROAD? ›› Mountain
DIFFICULTY ›› ★★★
CONFIGURATION ›› Varies
TIME TO RIDE ›› 3–6 days
SUITABLE FOR KIDS? ›› No
GUIDE SUGGESTED? ›› No

Tony Knowles Coastal Trail

REGION ›› Southcentral Inland
DISTANCE ›› 20 miles
MOUNTAIN/ROAD? ›› Mountain/road
DIFFICULTY ›› ★★
CONFIGURATION ›› Out-and-back
TIME TO RIDE ›› Day trip
SUITABLE FOR KIDS? ›› Yes
GUIDE SUGGESTED? ›› No

Resurrection Pass Trail

REGION ›› Southcentral Coastal
DISTANCE ›› 39 miles
MOUNTAIN/ROAD? ›› Mountain
DIFFICULTY ›› ★★★
CONFIGURATION ›› Varies
TIME TO RIDE ›› 1–3 days
SUITABLE FOR KIDS? ›› Teens
GUIDE SUGGESTED? ›› No

Tour of the Mining Country

REGION ›› The Interior
DISTANCE ›› 46 miles
MOUNTAIN/ROAD? ›› Mountain
DIFFICULTY ›› ★★★★
CONFIGURATION ›› Out-and-back
TIME TO RIDE ›› Day trip
SUITABLE FOR KIDS? ›› No
GUIDE SUGGESTED? ›› Yes

let someone you trust know where you are going, when you are coming back, and how often you plan to make contact. On some of the more-deserted sections of road in Alaska, you could crash off the side of the road and not be discovered for days. When traveling the backcountry by mountain bike, it's even more important to file a trip plan with someone you know, as well as with the managing agency on whose land you will be traveling: national forest, state park, and so on.

✔ **KNOW YOUR EQUIPMENT,** and how to make repairs if necessary. Know how to change or patch tires, fix broken chains, and adjust brakes and other movable parts.

✔ **ALWAYS WEAR A HELMET** and appropriate safety gear. That means reflective gear for road trips and knee or elbow pads if traveling in extreme downhill-mountain-bike areas.

✔ **KEEP A LIGHT LOAD.** There's nothing like an extra 5 or 10 pounds of unnecessary gear to really bog down what could otherwise be an enjoyable ride. Resist the urge to load your panniers or bike trailer down with every imaginable amenity. Also, load up with the gear you will be bringing before you even leave for your trip, and ride around with it to get a feel for how it will affect your maneuverability.

cycling outfitters @ a glance

Alaska Backcountry Bike Tours

866-354-2453 or 907-746-5018
mountainbikealaska.com

REGIONS ▸▸ Southcentral Coastal,
Southcentral Inland, Interior
COST ▸▸ $$
SUITABLE FOR KIDS? ▸▸ Teens
ACTIVITY LEVEL ▸▸ Moderate–high
TRIP LENGTH ▸▸ 1–8 days

Alaska Outdoor Rentals and Guides

907-457-2453 | akbike.com

REGION ▸▸ The Interior
COST ▸▸ $$
SUITABLE FOR KIDS? ▸▸ Teens
ACTIVITY LEVEL ▸▸ Moderate
TRIP LENGTH ▸▸ Custom

Alaskan Bicycle Adventures

907-245-2175 | alaskabike.com

REGION ▸▸ Southcentral Coastal/Inland
COST ▸▸ $$$
SUITABLE FOR KIDS? ▸▸ Teens
ACTIVITY LEVEL ▸▸ All levels
TRIP LENGTH ▸▸ 7–8 days

Alaska Ultra Sport

907-745-6680
alaskaultrasport.com

REGIONS ▸▸ Southcentral Coastal, Inland
COST ▸▸ $$$
SUITABLE FOR KIDS? ▸▸ Teens
ACTIVITY LEVEL ▸▸ Light–high
TRIP LENGTH ▸▸ Custom

Denali Outdoor Center

888-303-1925 or 907-683-1925
denalioutdoorcenter.com

REGION ▸▸ The Interior
COST ▸▸ $
SUITABLE FOR KIDS? ▸▸ Teens
ACTIVITY LEVEL ▸▸ Moderate
TRIP LENGTH ▸▸ Day trips

Sockeye Cycle Co.

877-292-4154 | cyclealaska.com

REGION ▸▸ Southeast
COST ▸▸ $$
SUITABLE FOR KIDS? ▸▸ Teens
ACTIVITY LEVEL ▸▸ Moderate
TRIP LENGTH ▸▸ 2–9 days

✔ **DRESS APPROPRIATELY.** The most important pieces of gear you'll need for any cycling trip are a wind- and waterproof rain jacket and pants. We prefer pants that zip open at the ankles so you can get them on and off without having to remove your shoes. We also like arm and leg warmers, which are good options in the flaky Alaska weather we encounter.

✔ **KNOW HOW TO NAVIGATE.** When traveling in the backcountry, carry a map of the trails you are riding. If you're in trailless areas, bring along a compass as well, or a GPS unit. On road rides, a road map, available at any convenience store, should suffice. We are in the middle of nowhere, but it's pretty hard to get lost because there aren't that many roads in Alaska.

TRAVELER'S TIP

▶ It is important, especially with panniers, to distribute weight evenly. This lessens the chance of losing control or braking too much on either the rear or front brakes.

✔ **GUARD AGAINST MOSQUITOES.** Even cyclists riding at 20 miles per hour will want to be prepared for mosquitoes, because the minute you stop, they will be on you. This is even more apparent when mountain biking. The same precautions in Part Five (see page 79) apply here.

✔ **BRING ALONG FIRST AID.** Carry basic emergency-care items, including bandages, antibiotic ointment, self-stick bandages, and a space blanket for warmth. We've been known to dissolve ibuprofen in our water bottles, which really helps for those next-day aches and pains, too.

✔ **CARRY BASIC BIKE-REPAIR EQUIPMENT.** This includes:

1. A park tool with Phillips and flathead screwdrivers attached.
2. A patch kit.
3. At least one spare tube. (We recommend one spare for each week of planned riding. If you're traveling for six weeks at a time, consider mailing tubes to yourself at post offices in towns along the way.)
4. A chain tool and/or missing-link adapter that can be used in place of a broken chain.
5. Extra lubricant for long rides to keep the chain working smoothly and quietly.
6. A tire wrench or wrenches to help remove tires from rims in case of a flat.
7. An old sock or bandanna to use as a cleaning rag during repairs.
8. A small pump that can fit in an under-the-seat bag or day pack.
9. A Swiss Army knife.

Travel with a Guide?

Whether or not you travel with a guide will depend on two things: how much experience you have and how much planning you're willing to do.

FOR ROAD BIKING Experienced road cyclists needn't use a guide unless they desire the camaraderie of numbers and the ease of not carrying their own gear.

Now, on to the next question: how much work are you willing to invest to plan your trip? There aren't that many cycling guides in Alaska, and those who do exist do a superb job of working out all the details so all you have to do is show up and hop on your bike or one they provide for you. Many cyclists like this option because it eliminates the unknown: how much food you should pack, what type of camping gear works best, and such. Also, traveling with a guide provides safety in numbers. For some, this is reassuring; for others it feels invasive. This is a question only you can answer because your cycling experience will be vastly different traveling with a group than if you are traveling alone.

Traveling with a guide also eliminates the need to carry your own gear. Road cyclists might be particularly happy with this option because it allows them to see more of the state traveling more miles per day than if they were hauling their gear in panniers or a trailer.

FOR MOUNTAIN BIKING   If you've ridden backcountry singletrack trails many times and can handle the technical difficulties that come with them, then by no means should you be intimidated by Alaska's trails. They are a challenge, to be sure, but anyone who has ridden in Utah, Colorado, or any of the other popular off-road riding spots in the country will be able to handle Alaska trails just fine.

So far, so good? Now ask yourself these questions:

1. Can I confidently navigate in places where the trails may disappear—where I may be traveling across trailless high-country tundra or the banks of dried-out riverbeds?

2. Am I comfortable with the fact that I could very well run into a bear or moose that is not too happy to see me? Do I know how to defend myself properly and reduce the chances of such an encounter?

3. Do I recognize other trail hazards specific to Alaska, such as devil's club, a prickly plant that is hell to land on, or cow parsnip, which if rubbed against the skin can cause a red, itchy burn that can last for months?

Still feeling good? Then go it alone. We say you'll be fine on Alaska's mountain-biking trails.

▲ Road Biking

TRUE, IT'S THE largest state in the country, but Alaska is noticeably lacking in roads. There are only a few main paved ones, and some of our so-called highways are still gravel in some places. For Alaskans, this is a good thing—it keeps the state rugged and natural, and lessens the tendency for traffic to fill up every lane. We pride ourselves on our remoteness.

For cyclists, this can create a road-touring challenge. The ability to travel on skinny tires is limited to just a few places in the state. But they are beautiful places. The travel options we suggest here will allow you to stay on your road bike, although you may want to upgrade to 25-millimeter tires to navigate the sometimes-gravelly sections of road that constantly seem to be under construction in Alaska. You will notice two of the three routes we suggest begin in Anchorage, the state's most-populated city and thus the one with the most developed road system. Other "highway" riding options are listed in the more extensive mountain-biking section because they will require mountain bikes to navigate.

THE ANCHORAGE–VALDEZ LOOP

Region Southcentral Inland and Southcentral Coastal Alaska.

Distance 360 miles, connecting three roads (Seward, Richardson, and Glenn highways).

Route configuration This loop ride is made possible by a pleasant ferry passage between the communities of Whittier and Valdez, putting the cyclist back in Anchorage at the end.

Difficulty ★★★★.

Suitable for kids? No.

Time to ride 6–9 days.

Best time of year to ride Early June–late-August.

Traffic level Moderate–heavy in summer; lightest in early June.

Facilities Most amenities available along the way, although they are spread out in some places.

ROUTE SUMMARY   The Anchorage–Valdez Loop offers it all—a train ride, a ferry trip, and some of the most awesome road-climbing challenges in the state. The loop also offers relatively well-shouldered roads and all-pavement riding.

DIRECTIONS TO ANCHORAGE   The Anchorage–Valdez Loop starts in Anchorage. For particulars on how to get here, see our profile for the Kenai Peninsula Tour (page 136).

DESCRIPTION   There are two ways to do the Anchorage –Valdez Loop. We prefer the first option, though it requires a bit of hitchhiking, and that is a personal choice.

This option involves riding the Seward Highway from Anchorage to the turnoff for the Whittier–Portage Glacier Access Road, at Mile 48. Turn here and ride another 12 miles to the entrance to the **Anton Anderson Memorial Tunnel,** which will take you to Whittier. Due to safety concerns, cyclists are not allowed to ride through the tunnel. The trick is to find someone with a pickup or fifth wheel that will allow you to ride through the tunnel with him or her. Offer to share or even pay the $12 toll. There is no shortage of pickups, and plenty of people line up for the every-half-hour departures.

The second option, and the only other way through the tunnel with a bike, is to take the regularly scheduled train trips through the tunnel. You can board the train at the **Alaska Railroad** depot in downtown Anchorage (but you will miss some of the most scenic riding of the entire trip) or take the Seward Highway from Anchorage to Mile 46 and the Alaska Railroad parking area. The rate for passage from here is $22 one-way, plus a $20 fee for carrying bikes. (For more information on the Seward Highway section of the road, see the relevant part of the Kenai Peninsula Tour route, on page 136.)

In Valdez there are many places to camp, lodge, or resupply (see the South-central Coastal chapter for our suggestions, starting on page 360). The bike ride out of Valdez begins relatively flat on the Richardson Highway but soon climbs the spectacular 2,678-foot **Thompson Pass,** at about Mile 26, which is one of the highest mountain climbs on the road system in Alaska, as well as one of the snowiest road-accessible areas in the state. After the pass you'll enjoy a steep 7.5-mile descent, but beware of trucks and other fast-driving vehicles. This section of road has incredible views, including glimpses of **Worthington Glacier,** which is accessible by road.

TRAVELER'S TIP

▶ Once you've arrived in Whittier, it will be time to board the **Alaska State Ferry** for passage across Prince William Sound to Valdez. Enjoy a relaxing 7-hour ride across the sound (or 3½ hours if you're lucky enough to be on the fast ferry M/V *Chenega*), complete with naturalist narration along the way. Watch for sea lions, otters, whales, and other marine mammals.

Squirrel Creek State Recreation-site, at Mile 80, is a good place to stop for the night if you're camping, with campsites right by the creek. Just across the road is a place to buy some snacks.

The ride from Squirrel Creek to Glennallen is wide open, with rolling hills and some large climbs, but nothing as challenging as Thompson Pass. **Glennallen,** at Mile 119, is a good resupply point, but if you continue past the town, there are some beautiful camping options farther south. One such choice is the **Tolsona Wilderness Campground,** about 20 miles from Glennallen and right by the creek. Lake Louise Road is another 10 miles away and an excellent option if you're up to riding your bike another 20 miles to **Lake Louise State Recreation Area.** The camping is wonderfully peaceful, with loons and other birds keeping you constant company.

From Lake Louise Road, you'll still have 150 miles left to reach Anchorage, and the last 75 miles are some of the most harrowing as traffic picks up and the road narrows in places. **Eureka Summit,** 20 miles from Lake Louise Road and the highest point on the Glenn Highway at 3,322 feet, will be a challenge, especially if you experience the infamous head- and side winds that seem to prevail in the area. Just after the summit, you'll descend to **Sheep Mountain.** Be sure to stop at **Sheep Mountain Lodge** (877-645-5121; **sheepmountain. com**) for some of their baked goods to keep you going. Owner Zack Steer is familiar with the cycling scene, hosting the annual Fireweed 400 bike race from the lodge each year. The lodge has great little cabins (and a welcome hot tub for those sore legs) if you want to take another day off and enjoy the view.

From Sheep Mountain Lodge, the road narrows. Even after you've reached Palmer, you will still be 45 miles from Anchorage. Some cyclists like to end their trip here and schedule a ride into Anchorage. For those who prefer to pedal all the way back to the state's largest city, just keep heading south on the Glenn until you reach Peter's Creek, at which point you can hook up with a bike path that parallels the highway (with one confusing jog through Eagle River—just ask the locals for directions) for the next 20 miles into downtown Anchorage.

Resources

▸ *The Alaska Bicycle Touring Guide,* by Pete Praetorius and Alys Culhane, is available through various outlets if you do a Google search. But it is about 20 years old, so many of the businesses in the more populated areas will no longer be around. We like it for its elevation-profile information, though.

▸ The **Alaska Marine Highway** (800-642-0066; **ferryalaska.com**) offers ferry service from Whittier to Valdez, and vice versa. Fare is $89 one-way for adults; $12 extra for bicycles.

▸ To book yourself and your bike on the **Alaska Railroad,** call 800-544-0552 or visit **alaskarailroad.com.** Rates are $22 from Portage to Whittier; bikes cost an extra $20.

▸ The **Anchorage Convention and Visitors Bureau** (907-276-4118 or 907-274-3531; **anchorage.net**) has plenty of brochures for places to stay and things to do while in the state's largest city. The nearby **Alaska Public Lands Information Center** (605 W. 4th Ave., Suite 105, Anchorage 99501; 866-869-6887 or 907-644-3661; **alaskacenters.gov/anchorage.cfm**) can help with details on the best places to camp or stay along the road.

▸ Anchorage's **Arctic Bicycle Club** supports the annual **Fireweed 400,** a road race that begins at Sheep Mountain Lodge on the Glenn Highway and travels to Valdez (visit **fireweed400.com** for details). Teams and individuals can sign up for distances of 50, 100, 200, or 400 miles, testing their grit against Alaska's toughest section of road riding. The race attracts participants from around the world and is a qualifying event for the grueling Race Across America ultra-endurance-cycling challenge.

▸ For detailed mile-by-mile information on the roads and amenities along the way, a great resource for all the trips in this chapter (but not one you want to take with you on your bike because it's as big as a phone book) is *The Milepost,* published by Morris Communications ($29.95; **themilepost.com**). We suggest photocopying the pages that cover a particular trip and bringing them with you. If you're camping along the way, they can be burned as you go.

▸ Anchorage has many bike shops from which to choose if you need last-minute supplies or repairs. We like **Chain Reaction Cycles** (12201 Industry Way, Unit 2 Anchorage, 99515; 907-336-0383; **chainreactioncycles.us**); **The Bicycle Shop** (1035 W. Northern Lights Blvd., Anchorage 99503; 907-272-5219); and

Paramount Cycles (1320 Huffman Park Dr., Anchorage 99515; 907-336-2453). Chain Reaction accepts your bike shipment and will put your bike back together for you if you're flying in from out of state. You can pick it up once you arrive. This is a safer option than shipping your bike via the airlines. Just call the shop ahead of time to arrange. **Downtown Bicycle Rental** in Anchorage (333 W. 4th Ave., Suite 206, Anchorage 99501; 907-279-5293; **alaska-bike-rentals.com**) is the only place that rents road bikes (dated but functional), along with shoes and pedals without clips. Rates are $43 for 24 hours, but ask about discounts for rentals by the week.

HAINES–SKAGWAY (GOLDEN CIRCLE) ROUTE

Region Southeast Alaska.	**Time to ride** 5–9 days.
Distance 355 miles, connecting three roads (Haines, Alaska, and South Klondike highways).	**Best time of year to ride** Early June–October.
Route configuration Can be made into a loop by taking a fast ferry between communities of Skagway and Haines.	**Traffic level** Moderate in summer; light in June, September, and October.
Difficulty ★ ★ ★.	**Facilities** Most amenities available along the way, including lodging, food, and camping.
Suitable for kids? Teens.	

ROUTE SUMMARY   This cycling trip takes in some of the most scenic areas of Southeast Alaska and affords the vacationing cyclist a chance to take the ferry and see parts of the Inside Passage.

DIRECTIONS TO HAINES   You can reach Haines from the Lower 48 states via the **Haines Highway,** which connects to the **Alaska Highway.** The **Alaska Marine Highway** ferry also travels to Haines regularly, offering access from the Lower 48 and other Alaska communities. Three regional airlines serve Haines, each with several scheduled flights daily throughout the year, which can connect you to Juneau. From there, you're linked through **Alaska Airlines** to Canada and the rest of the United States.

DESCRIPTION   From Haines, the cyclist riding the Golden Circle Route will travel three highways: 146 miles on the Haines Highway to Haines Junction, 100 miles on the Alaska Highway to Whitehorse, and 109 miles to Skagway on the South Klondike Highway. The first 20 miles out of Haines will ease you into the cycling rhythm. The road is flat and well paved, and follows the river for an added bit of scenery. For the next 10–15 miles, the road rises slightly, but passes through the **Chilkat Valley Bald Eagle Preserve,** which is home to thousands of bald eagles, and even more during the fall salmon-spawning season. A roadhouse at about Mile 33 is a good stopping spot.

From the aptly but not-so-creatively named **33 Mile Roadhouse** (907-767-5510, **33mileroadhouse.com**), the road gets a bit more challenging, and there is some climbing all the way to the Canada border, at Mile 40.5.

From the customs station, the route climbs gently for about 10 more miles, to tree line (be aware that measurements will be in kilometers while in Canada, but we'll stick to miles for sanity's sake). At about Mile 50, you'll begin climbing steeply to **Three Guardsmen Lake,** a beautiful spot with dramatic views, followed by a short descent and a final climb to **Chilkat Pass.**

The pass is 59 miles into the trip and, at 3,510 feet, an impressive place to stop and take in the view. One of the few access points from the Pacific for explorers, gold miners, and adventurers, Chilkat today is appreciated for its beauty and ruggedness. It is windy here almost constantly, and snow remains in the pass longer than in other areas, as late as early June.

The ride from the summit begins to descend, with wondrous views of the St. Elias Mountains beginning to dominate the background over the next 15–20 miles. You'll also be at the **Tatshenshini-Alsek Wilderness Provincial Park** (**env.gov.bc.ca/bcparks**), which is one of the most popular places for rafting and kayaking.

At Mile 85, you'll pass from British Columbia into the Yukon Territory. **Million Dollar Falls,** at Mile 93.5, boasts more than 30 campsites, water spots, a kitchen shelter, and fishing opportunities in the nearby rivers.

From Million Dollar Falls, it's a 55-mile ride to **Haines Junction** and the Alaska Highway. Haines Junction also is the first town of mention since leaving Haines, and a good place to resupply (unless you can hold off one more day and get your supplies in Whitehorse, which has even more services). The **Kluane Range** dominates the background for this section of ride.

TRAVELER'S TIP

▶ Canada customs will likely stop you at the border and quiz you carefully—at least that's what's happened to everyone we know who's cycled it. This is mostly to find out how well prepared you are. It is not uncommon to see bears, overestimate your cycling abilities in the conditions, or underestimate the availability of supplies along the way. Be patient, answer their questions, and you will soon be on your way.

The ride from Haines Junction to Whitehorse is 100 miles—a good place to attempt a century ride if that's part of your goal. The route is flat and mostly smooth, with only an occasional steep but short hill. The shoulder is narrow for the first half of the ride, so be careful when being approached by RVs and vehicles hauling trailers. The route follows through forest and is a good place for spotting bears, which with any luck will run away if they see you.

Whitehorse offers every amenity imaginable, plus some interesting visitor attractions. The **S/S Klondike,** a giant boat that plied the Yukon River until 1955, is a nice stop, with tours daily. The visitor center has many suggestions for things to do and places to see. If you've planned a recovery day in your trip, this is the place to stop.

From Whitehorse you will begin traveling the last 109 miles of your route, first getting back onto the Alaska Highway to connect with the **South Klondike Highway,** south of Whitehorse. The last established campground is at Carcross, but that is only 33 miles into the trip (a better option exists at scenic **Tutshi Lake,** at about Mile 60). At Mile 48, you'll cross back into British Columbia, headed for Alaska.

The last 50 miles into Skagway begin to climb up and over **White Pass,** but you'll be rewarded by some nice downhills too. Six miles outside of Skagway is the U.S. border station, where you will have to stop and present identification.

Skagway, you'll immediately notice, is tourist-oriented, with lots of shops selling trinkets and catering to the 7,000-plus cruise-ship passengers who disembark almost daily. But on your bike you'll be able to uncover some of its charm too. Drive the back streets and get outside the visitor-center area, and you can get a glimpse of the town it once was.

Resources

▶ The **Alaska Marine Highway** (800-642-0066; **ferryalaska.com**) offers ferry service from the Lower 48 states to Haines and/or Skagway. From Belling-ham, Washington, to Haines, a two-day trip, expect to pay $353 one-way (Haines Ferry Terminal: 907-766-2113) plus an extra $60 for your bike. For fast-ferry service between Haines and Skagway, choose one of the following, both of which can accommodate bicycles: the **Haines–Skagway Fast Ferry** offers up to 26 crossings per day for $35 one-way or $68 for a round-trip (888-766-2103 or 907-766-2100; **hainesskagwayfastferry.com**), while the **Silver Eagle Transport** can also transport a few vehicles at a time (907-766-2418; **alaskaferry@hotmail.com**).

▶ The **Haines Convention and Visitors Bureau** (800-458-3579 or 907-766-2234; **haines.ak.us**) offers options aplenty for lodging and eating, and can mail its annual travel planner.

▶ The **Kluane Chilkat International Bike Relay** is an option for those who want to turn their cycling trip into a 150-mile competition or fun run (**kcibr.org**). It's also the largest cycling event in the state, attracting more than 1,200 riders of all ages and abilities. The race is usually held in mid-June.

▶ The **Southeast Alaska Discovery Center** in Ketchikan (50 Main St., Ketchikan 99901; 907-228-6220; **alaskacenters.gov/ketchikan.cfm**) can help with details on the best places to camp or stay along the road.

▶ **Wings of Alaska** (at the Haines Airport Terminal; 907-766-2030; **wingsof alaska.com**) has $218 round-trip flights from Juneau to Haines. Check with the airline to see if there is added cost for carrying your bike.

Haines-Skagway Cycle Outfitter

▶ **SOCKEYE CYCLE CO. ➻** 877-292-4154; **cyclealaska.com.** This longtime South-east company has a reputation for hosting some of the most fun trips in Alaska. They offer guided tours in locations throughout Southeast, including an overnight mountain-bike trek to Chilkat Pass that we love. But its Golden Circle Tour is the best: at nine days and $2,225 from Haines to Skagway, you'll travel 360 miles through this very route. The company also is the only one around that offers bike service if you're traveling independently and have mechanical problems.

THE KENAI PENINSULA TOUR

Region Southcentral Inland–Southcentral Coastal Alaska.	**Suitable for kids?** No.
	Time to ride 4–8 days.
Distance 302 miles, connecting two road systems, the Seward and Sterling highways; 127 miles to Seward, 37 back to cutoff, 138 to Homer on Sterling.	**Best time of year to ride** Late May–late Sept.
	Traffic level Heavy in summer, moderate in May and Sept.
Route configuration Y-shaped.	**Facilities** Most amenities available along the way, including lodging, food, and camping.
Difficulty ★★★.	

ROUTE SUMMARY   The Kenai Peninsula Tour skirts one of the most breath-taking scenic routes in Alaska, following the waters of **Turnagain Arm** and climbing into the **Chugach National Forest** to **Seward.** The **Seward Highway** is designated a National Scenic Byway. The Sterling Highway section, connecting to **Homer,** also has expansive views of **Cook Inlet** and the volcanoes that make up the **Alaska Peninsula.**

DIRECTIONS TO ANCHORAGE   The Kenai Peninsula Tour starts in **Anchorage,** the state's largest city, in Southcentral Inland Alaska (for more on Anchorage amenities, see the Southcentral Inland Alaska chapter, starting on page 292). It's accessible via daily jet service to Anchorage's **Ted Stevens International Airport** from any number of carriers, including **Alaska Airlines** (800-252-7522; **alaskaair.com**), **Continental** (800-523-3273; **continental.com**), United (800-864-8331; **ual.com**), and **Delta** (800-221-1212; **delta.com**). Overseas airlines include **Korean Airlines** (800-438-5000; **koreanair.com**), **China Airlines** (907-248-8605; **china-airlines.com**), and **Asiana Airlines** (800-227-4262; **us.flyasiana.com**), as well as **Air Canada** (888-247-2262; **aircanada.com**), among others. The flight line-ups change constantly, so be sure to check ahead of time to make sure a specific carrier is still serving the state.

Access to Anchorage from the Lower 48 states also is via road. Travel into the state on the **Alaska Highway,** which connects to the **Richardson Highway,** and then the **Glenn Highway,** which travels directly into Anchorage.

DESCRIPTION   Traveling the Kenai Peninsula affords an all-encompassing sample of what Alaska is about. This section of the state ranges from coastal tidewater habitat to snow-covered glaciers and mountains. You'll travel through forests and along open valleys above the tree line.

Our route will take you first to Seward, minus the 37-mile backtrack to the turnoff for the Sterling Highway and Homer. Some cyclists like to get a ride back to this cutoff, while others prefer to depend on their own pedaling power the whole way. We suggest getting a ride for this section, however, because there is a 5- to 10-mile section of road that is probably the most hazardous along the entire Kenai Peninsula route. The road is winding and the shoulders nonexistent. Travelers in the summer tend to drive too fast, making for some scary riding during that particular section. The Department of Transportation is constantly upgrading this section of road, and in some places the shoulder is wide and inviting. But until the entire 37 miles from the Sterling Highway cutoff to Seward is upgraded, we suggest hitching a ride back to the turnoff. In the Resources section (page 143), we've suggested a few outfits that will get you back to the cutoff safely.

The Seward Highway   Now, on to the road: You will start by riding south out of Anchorage on the Seward Highway, named an All-American Road in 2000 and a National Scenic Byway in 1998. The first third of the road travels along the base of the **Chugach Mountains.** The shoulders are wide and the cycling can be enjoyable, despite the numerous recreational vehicles, fifth wheels, and trucks that whiz by. Look for Dall sheep to the left and beluga whales in the water to the right. This section also can get vicious headwinds, so prepare to be blasted. (*Hint:* Start your travel in the morning, when the winds tend to be gentler.)

About 24 miles into the ride, you'll cross a bridge over **Indian Creek** and notice a parking and rest area adjacent to the Indian Creek ball fields. We suggest you get off the road here and begin following the bike path that is right next to the highway. This newly constructed trail travels 12 miles to the intersection of the Alyeska and Seward highways. Most of the trail is alongside the highway, but some of it dips into the woods and climbs the surrounding mountains, giving cyclists an incredibly scenic diversion from their road ride while still on pavement.

At the Alyeska Highway cutoff, there is a gas station and cafe with coffee, fresh baked goods, and other goodies. It's a great place for a power snack. Get back onto the Seward Highway, heading south. Beware this area: it is often crowded with traffic and pedestrians and can get a bit hectic with drivers jockeying for position on the road.

The Seward Highway continues on a relatively flat (and often windblown) stretch but climbs await past the 50-mile mark. Leaving Turnagain Arm behind, the road winds up and over **Turnagain Pass,** reaching an elevation that takes you from sea level to 988 feet in a matter of 6 miles. It doesn't sound like much, but it's a long, slow climb. Beware, too, of fast drivers on this straightaway.

The junction with the Hope Highway is the next major intersection at about 70 miles, and you'll enjoy a high-rise ride over a new bridge that spans **Canyon Creek,** a natural wonder carved deep into the mountains and rushing swiftly from the surrounding glacier-fed creeks and rivers. This is another good place to take a break, enjoy the views, and use the restroom facilities.

After an extended climb to **Summit Lake,** you will begin a well-earned descent—and then another short but steep climb—that will bring you to **Summit Lake Lodge** (907-244-2031; **summitlakelodge.com**), at Mile 80.5 in bike miles. This is a good place to camp and eat—the **Chugach National Forest Tenderfoot Creek Campground** ($18) is adjacent to the lodge, and the lodge offers reasonable cabin rentals for $90 per night.

In less than 10 miles, you will reach a Y-intersection that branches off toward Homer and the Sterling Highway or stays straight and continues south on the Seward Highway to Seward. Stay straight and begin riding defensively, because two-thirds of the way into this section of road is narrow and winding, and cars drive too fast.

You'll soon come to the roadside town of **Moose Pass,** which will make its existence known with obvious signs warning drivers to slow down, at about

Mile 97. Moose Pass residents like peace and quiet, and the hustle and bustle of summertime activity can be overwhelming at times. The town is surprisingly well stocked with a general store, lodging, food, and a hotel. There's even a campground and a few nicely appointed artists' studios.

Beyond Moose Pass, the road alternately widens and narrows, and it won't be until you reach Mile 110 that the shoulders will become broad enough to comfortably accommodate your bike and let other drivers pass without feeling the force of their speed as they go by. Road improvements have made the last 20 miles into town an enjoyable ride, with awesome views.

At Mile 110 is the quaint **Primrose Campground,** off Primrose Road. We like it for its smallness—only 10 sites with pit toilets at either end—and its scenery, from its perch right on the side of the lake. It's a quiet place to camp (for only $11) and maintains the Alaska-wilderness feel that you won't get in the town-centered campgrounds in Seward.

TRAVELER'S TIP

▶ If you're traveling to Seward in mid-August, you may be competing with Silver Salmon Derby fishermen for the best lodging spots.

Still, most people will opt to continue on to Seward, which is a few hill-climbs away but nothing too challenging. Be on the lookout for moose or bears along the roadsides and by the **Snow River,** which you'll ride alongside for a while. The road takes you straight into town, and the **Seward Chamber of Commerce** visitor center is on the right-hand side of the road, not to be missed. If you have any questions on camping, they can surely help. There is almost always an open site, and plenty of bed-and-breakfasts and hotels from which to choose.

The Sterling Highway   This road travels nearly 143 miles to what we consider the prettiest town in all of Alaska: **Homer,** a seaside community that is as eclectic in its personality as it is in its inhabitants. Here, farmers, artists, fishermen, and people from all political, personal, and religious backgrounds live harmoniously (at least most of the time). This is a place where the mountains meet the ocean, where the best of Alaska comes together to be explored in one compact location. We could easily spend an entire summer in Homer and never run out of things to do.

Cycling to Homer will be an adventure. The route passes first through the scenic lakeside community of **Cooper Landing,** tucked into the mountains and quickly becoming a tourist destination itself. Just 10 years ago, this sleepy little town hosted a few river-rafting companies and a bed-and-breakfast or two. Today it bustles with visitors, there for the famed Kenai River king salmon. Anglers, rafters, and nature lovers come here during the summer, so when you cycle through the first 15 miles of the Sterling Highway, don't be surprised by the crowds. The aquamarine water of **Kenai Lake,** around which Cooper Landing is based, is breathtaking. It almost doesn't look real, but it certainly is. There are plenty of places to stop for a bite to eat or fill up water bottles, and the 350 or so year-round residents are superfriendly. A visitor-information center operates during the summer right off the Kenai River bridge. The **Cooper Creek Campground,** 14 miles into the Sterling, is a good place to camp ($11).

Beyond Cooper Landing, things get a little quieter, and the route follows gentle hills that gain and lose elevation, but not at the alarming rates of Turnagain Pass. The **Russian River Campground** is 2 miles out of town, but it often is full during the summer due to the rush of king-salmon fishermen. Bears are seen often, so be on the lookout. The trailhead to the **Resurrection Pass Trail,** a mile beyond the campground, is a good option for mountain bikers (see page 157 of the "Mountain Biking" section for details).

The road is relatively flat for the next 5 miles, leading into the **Kenai National Wildlife Refuge,** the most visited of the 16 national wildlife refuges in Alaska. The shoulder is not bad in this section, but because it is straight, drivers are eager to make up time and often speed. Ride defensively.

Sterling, the community for which the highway was named, is surprisingly small, given the signs you'll notice of its impending arrival. The road widens at about Mile 43, and lampposts line the street, giving one the impression that the town is somehow metropolitan. That is far from the reality of Sterling, a community of about 4,900 people, most of them living on side streets and off in the woods, not along the well-lit and lightly traveled road.

Sterling is another good place to stop for a snack. The cinnamon buns at

Cook's Corner (907-262-6021), near Mile 82, are locally famous and will jump-start your engine if you're beginning to tire from the miles.

Another 15 miles of riding will bring you to the city of **Soldotna,** a tourist destination centered on fishing the Kenai River, but also offering some wonderful jaunts into the Kenai National Wildlife Refuge. Here, you can get anything you need—groceries, camping supplies, and even a charter flight the rest of the way to Homer if you're ready to stop cycling. There is no real charm to the place, but it is functional, with the grocery stores and fast-food restaurants that so many travelers seem to want. Soldotna has a visitor center with a database of places to stay and things to do. If you're going to stop and sample some of life on the Kenai, this is a good place to call it a day. The ride from Soldotna to Homer has some decent hills and outstanding views to enjoy, and it's best to start off early in the morning, when the traffic is not so heavy.

Leaving Soldotna, you will continue along the Sterling Highway, although another option is to take **Kalifornsky Beach Road** on the south end of town toward Homer. It reconnects with the Sterling Highway at the town of Kasilof and is slightly less traveled and less hilly, with wider shoulders. They are both beautiful (we prefer Kalifornsky Beach, or K-Beach as it is called locally) because of the views of **Cook Inlet.**

Kasilof (Kuh-**SEE**-lof), located at about Mile 72 and reached from either road, is another funky little community, although you can't appreciate its character from the main road. It's home to nearly 600 year-round residents, most of whom depend on fishing for their living.

The road continues with slight ups and downs and passes several points of interest, including campgrounds and recreation-sites that draw visitors all summer. **Clam Gulch State Recreation-site,** at Mile 81, is very popular. Time your ride with the tides, and you can stop, camp on the beach, and dig for wrist-thick clams to cook over a fire and eat fresh. (You need a fishing license for this, though, so make sure to get one when in Soldotna.)

Farther down the road, at about Mile 99, is **Ninilchik Village,** at the mouth of the Ninilchik River. The **Holy Transfiguration of Our Lord Russian Orthodox**

Church sits atop a hill overlooking Cook Inlet and the river, dominating the landscape. Images of this ornate green-and-white church show up in books and magazines all over the world.

From Ninilchik, there are more than 40 miles of up-and-down cycling ahead of you, and they seem to go on forever. To the left are the **Caribou Hills,** mountains that become snow-covered early in the season and remain that way until late in the spring. It is a winter-sports lover's destination—dog mushers, snowmobile riders, and skiers flock there in winter.

To the right of the road, you'll enjoy views of several volcanoes that all have been active at one time or another. There's **Mount Augustine,** far to the south and sometimes hidden from view, which has been spewing ash off and on since 2006; **Iliamna; Redoubt;** and **Spurr.** Mount Redoubt is the most impressive of the four and was the latest to erupt, in April 2009. On a sunny day, it appears to loom almost directly in front of you. While the riding itself might begin to feel monotonous, the views never get old.

Ten miles outside of Homer, you'll pass through **Anchor Point;** it has a few amenities, but we don't quite consider it a destination. If you do decide to stop here, it's worth the extra 2 miles of riding to reach the **Halibut Campground,** at the end of Anchor River Road. The state recreation area is right at the water and has 20 camp spots, toilets, water, and other facilities. Camping is $10.

Prepare for your arrival in Homer as you climb the last hill that offers a pull-out to the west overlooking **Kachemak Bay.** You'll still have another 9 miles or so before you reach the very end of the road, at the **Homer Spit,** which literally peters out into the sea. But at the overlook, you have officially greeted Homer.

TRAVELER'S TIP

▶ We suggest bringing your own bike with you for long trips, as it's better to ride a bike with which you are familiar.

Riding down the hill into Homer will be a well-earned achievement. Reward yourself by staying here as many days as possible. The recreation opportunities are vast—hiking, birding, beachcombing, fishing, kayaking, and more. There are museums, restaurants, and gift shops too. You won't find a bicycle shop in town, but basic repair supplies can be purchased at the local hardware stores.

Resources

▶ The **Homer Chamber of Commerce** (907-235-7740; **homeralaska.org**) can help you find food and lodging. Ask for its annual visitor guide if you sign up online.

▶ **Seward Bike Shop** (411 Port Ave.; 907-224-2448) services bikes and sells Kona, KHS, and Specialized products. They rent mountain bikes, comfort bikes, and cruisers as well, with half-day and daily rates.

▶ The **Seward Chamber of Commerce** (907-224-8051; **seward.com**) can give you plenty of options for lodging and eating.

▶ The **Tenderfoot Creek Campground** at Summit Lake at Mile 46; **Bertha Creek Campground** at Mile 61.5; **Granite Creek Campground** at Mile 64; and **Primrose Campground** at Mile 110 are all managed by **Chugach National Forest** (907-743-9500; **fs.fed.us/r10/chugach**). Camping is $11 per night. **Chugach State Park** (907-345-5014; **dnr.alaska.gov**) is in charge of the **Bird Creek Campground,** just outside of Anchorage. Some cyclists like to stay here before heading into Anchorage on the last day of their ride; sites are $15. Chugach State Park also manages the **Halibut Campground,** in Anchor Point. The **Alaska Public Lands Information Center** in Anchorage (605 W. 4th Ave., Suite 105, Anchorage 99501; 866-869-6887 or 907-644-3661; **alaskacenters.gov/anchorage.cfm**) can help with details on the best places to camp or stay along the road.

Kenai Peninsula Route Outfitters

▶ While a few companies out there offer day trips and overnighters on the Kenai Peninsula, they are strictly mountain-biking adventures. Those who opt for this trip must go it alone.

▲ Mountain Biking

Riding off-trail or on the gravel roads of Alaska can be one of the best ways to see the state. On these treks, you get a good dose of the outdoors with the efficiency of following a path that covers more ground than walking. While road-bike trips are few and limited to city centers, where pavement is more commonplace, mountain bikes open up a whole new world of cycling. Great roads and trails for cycling stretch from as far south as Prince of Wales Island to as far north as Nome, in western Alaska.

This section outlines a few of our favorite cycling destinations, ranging from camping trips on remote trails to vehicle-supported road rides along scenic gravel "highways." We think of Alaska as a mountain biker's paradise. There is no shortage of places in which to ride and explore, from day trips just outside the city centers to weeklong treks into the wilderness.

There is, however, a shortage of experienced mountain-bike outfitters to guide you on your journey. We have listed the few that we know to be reputable and have excellent outdoors skills. You will find them at the end of the mountain-biking trip suggestions (see "Mountain-bike Outfitters," page 165).

THE DALTON HIGHWAY

Region The Interior.

Distance 414 miles one-way.

Route configuration Bike out and arrange a ride back, or go out-and-back.

Difficulty ★★★★★.

Suitable for kids? No.

Time to ride 8–12 days.

Best time of year to ride June–Aug.

Traffic level Steady tourist traffic as well as heavy trucks.

Facilities Very few; food and lodging are available at the **Yukon River Camp** (Mile 56; 907-474-3557; **yukonrivercamp.com**), in **Coldfoot** (Mile 175; 866-474-3400 or 907-474-3500; **coldfootcamp.com**), and in **Deadhorse,** at the northern end of the road.

   Two lodging and food options are in **Wiseman,** just a few miles north of Coldfoot Camp: **Arctic Getaway Cabin and Breakfast** (907-678-4456; **arcticgetaway.com**), which is rustic but authentic; and **Boreal Lodging** (907-678-4566; **boreallodge.com**), which is scenic and well kept.

Otherwise, services are not available.

The **Bureau of Land Management** (907-474-2200; **blm.gov/ak/dalton**), which manages much of the land along the road, has four campgrounds, three of which are primitive camping areas. Download its 35-page Dalton Highway guide online.

A private campground is in **Coldfoot.** In **Deadhorse,** your options are the **Arctic Caribou Inn** (866-659-2368; **arcticcaribouinn.com**) or **Deadhorse Camp** (877-474-3565; **deadhorsecamp.com**).

Camping options include **Finger Mountain** (Mile 98), Arctic Circle (Mile 115), **Gobblers Knob** (Mile 131), **Grayling Lake** (Mile 150), **South Koyukuk River** (Mile 156), **Marion Creek** (Mile 179), **Middle Fork Koyukuk River** (Mile 204), **Last Spruce Tree** (Mile 235), **Galbraith Camp** (Mile 274), and **Last Chance** (Mile 355). Some have pit toilets and other amenities.

ROUTE SUMMARY   The Dalton Highway, built in 154 days in 1974 to provide access to the oilfields of the North Slope, is a rugged 414-mile road that begins 84 miles north of Fairbanks and crosses the **Brooks Range** to **Prudhoe Bay.** The first 100 miles of the road are paved, but from there it is rough gravel. Views are outstanding. The Dalton Highway is known locally as the "Haul Road" because it is used to convey supplies to and from the North Slope oilfields.

DIRECTIONS TO FAIRBANKS   Reach Fairbanks by driving north on the Richardson or Parks highways, or by flying in to the Fairbanks International Airport via daily jet service from Seattle or Anchorage, as well as other cities. **Alaska Airlines** is the primary service provider (800-252-7522; **alaskaair.com**). Reach the Dalton Highway by taking the Elliott Highway 84 miles north out of downtown Fairbanks.

DESCRIPTION   The Dalton Highway, or State Route 11, was for decades—and still is today—used as a supply route for oilfield work. However, in 1995, the state opened the once-closed road to tourist traffic as well, and travelers will notice the constant truck and tourist traffic. Note that the term *constant* in Alaska is relative. This means that perhaps one truck and a half-dozen cars will pass by every half hour or so. And that's on busy days.

Cycling the Haul Road, as it is known locally, is an epic ride involving steep climbs (as much as 10–12% in some places), rough gravel, and, in the summer, some of the state's fiercest mosquitoes. But don't let that description deter you from riding this road, because it also offers an awesome glimpse of Alaska, as you travel through the Brooks Range and past the Arctic Circle to reach the farthest-north point in Alaska. It's a superlative-filled journey. The scenery includes views of the mighty **Yukon River,** the **Arctic Circle** (just past Mile 115), **Atigun Pass** (at the crest of the Continental Divide), the caribou of the **North Slope plains,** 375-million-year-old limestone-filled **Sukakpak Mountain** (elevation 4,459 feet at Mile 203.5), and any number of sweeping mountain vistas opening into the **Brooks Range, Gates of the Arctic National Park,** or **Arctic National Wildlife Refuge.**

From the Elliott Highway, the road travels north near the community of Livengood. The **Trans-Alaska Pipeline System** parallels the road along the way, rising and falling with the contours of the hills and valleys. The road crosses the Yukon River at Mile 56, and passes through **Gates of the Arctic National Park** and the **Arctic National Wildlife Refuge,** the same refuge at the heart of controversy among conservationists who want to protect it and big-oil interests who want to develop it. Look for caribou, moose, and bears throughout this area. The road passes the Arctic Circle at Mile 115. (Incidentally, the Dalton is the only highway in the United States and one of only two in North America that crosses the Arctic Circle.) The next place to

TRAVELER'S TIP

▶ No matter the road or trail you travel, it's a good idea to have tires beefy enough to withstand gravel, dirt, roots, and rocks. On roads such as the Dalton Highway, 700-by-35 tires are a good choice.

resupply is **Coldfoot,** 175 miles into the drive. There is an RV campground with hookup, food, and lodging. Just up the road is **Wiseman,** which also has a couple of lodging options. Travel services are limited—north of Coldfoot is the longest service-free stretch of highway in North America: 244 miles.

A good camping option is **Galbraith Lake,** at Mile 274. The terrain gets a little rough here, as the road changes course and begins crossing drainages. There will be occasional slow climbs and a few good descents before you reach pavement again at Mile 334. The pavement continues until you're about 50 miles outside of Deadhorse, where it again turns to gravel. This section also gets muddy from the heavy traffic coming in and out, so be prepared for a bumpy last 50 miles.

Deadhorse is on the shores of the Arctic Ocean. It's not much to write home about as far as visitor amenities go: there are only a couple of hotels, a store, and gas station, and the majority of people you'll see live there only a few weeks at a time for their jobs in the oilfields. But the community is as far north as you can go on Alaska's primary road system. And it is worth exploring, especially if your goal is to dip a toe into the Arctic Ocean.

Resources

▶ **Alaska Outdoor Rentals and Guides** (907-457-2453; **akbike.com**) gets our highest recommendation for shuttle support and rentals. The outfitter rents bicycles and gear for all your Interior adventures. They also can provide SAG (support and gear) and/or deliver you wherever you want to go with your bike or one of theirs.

▶ The **Alaska Public Lands Information Center** (101 Dunkel St., Suite 110, Fairbanks 99701; 907-459-3730; **alaskacenters.gov/fairbanks.cfm**) can advise you on good local rides and places to find rental equipment.

▶ **Arctic Outfitters Auto Rentals** (907-474-3530; **arctic-outfitters.com**) is one of the few companies that rent vehicles that can be used on the Haul Road, including all the necessary gear to help you along if you break down. The vehicles even come equipped with CB radios in case of problems. The rates are $229 per day for Ford Escapes and $199 per day for two or three days.If you rent for four or more days, it goes to $179. The company also can arrange shuttles and lodging.

▶ We like **Dalton Highway Express** (907-474-3555; **daltonhighwayexpress.com**) because it caters to independent travelers with their own equipment. This small company will take you anywhere along the Dalton Highway from Fairbanks and drop you off wherever you want to be left. They will pick you up at a later, prearranged time, as well. It's $221 to get to Deadhorse, $106 to Coldfoot; bicycles cost extra.

▶ The **Fairbanks Convention and Visitors Bureau** (101 Dunkel St., Suite 111, Fairbanks 99701; 800-327-5774; **explorefairbanks.com**) can help you plan lodging and transportation.

▶ **Go North Alaska Travel Center** in Fairbanks (866-236-7272 or 907-479-7272; **paratours.net**) rents RVs and camper trucks if you want a SAG vehicle for road support. Their rates are affordable too, starting at $137 (with unlimited miles), depending on the vehicle you rent. There is a gravel dent fee for RVs, though, so be prepared to be "dinged," so to speak, an extra $200 for that.

▶ Access to the Arctic Ocean is limited due to ongoing oilfield work, but many cyclists like the idea of dipping their tires into the northernmost ocean. Contact the **Northern Alaska Tour Co.** (907-474-1986; **northernalaska.com**) to make it happen. Its guides also can show you around if you want to see more of the oilfield at Deadhorse.

THE DENALI HIGHWAY

Region The Interior.

Distance 134 miles one-way.

Route configuration End-to-end, or loop if connected with the Richardson and Parks highways. Identified as Alaska State Route 8; 85% gravel, 15% paved.

Difficulty ★★★.

Suitable for kids? Preteens and up.

Time to ride 2–4 days.

Best time of year to ride Late June–August.

Traffic level Light.

Facilities Food and lodging are available intermittently throughout the road.

Much of the land surrounding the Denali Highway is managed by the **Bureau of Land Management** (907-822-3217; **blm.gov/ak/st/en/fo/ado.html**), which allows camping all along the road.

There are a few campgrounds and three lodging options, but pulling off to find your own spot makes for a more remote-feeling experience.

Some nice campgrounds in the area include the **BLM Tangle Lakes Campground** at Mile 21.5, which offers 25 tent and RV sites with toilet facilities, water, picnic tables, and fire rings; and the **BLM Brushkana Creek Campground** at Mile 105, which has 12 sites, toilet facilities, water, picnic tables, garbage barrels, and fire rings.

Located on either end of the highway, the camps make good places to stop on each end of the ride.

For those not interested in camping, we like the lodging options at **Tangle River Inn** (907-822-3970 or 907-892-4022; **tangleriverinn.com**) on the Paxson end of the highway; **Maclaren River Lodge** (at Mile 42; 907-822-5444; **maclarenlodge.com**), and **Gracious House Lodge** (at Mile 82; 907-333-3148 or 907-259-1111; **alaskaone.com/gracious**).

ROUTE SUMMARY   The Denali Highway, State Route 8, is on mostly gravel roads but takes in some of the most scenic country in the state. There are cavernous potholes. The washboards are relentless. And the services—a couple of lodges here and a campground or two there—are few. But those who do venture onto this frontier highway are blessed with a rolling self-guided tour of Alaska bisecting some of the state's most spectacular mountain ranges. The area, with its open tundra and countless kettle lakes, attracts thousands of birds, including the rare arctic warbler and Smith's longspur.

TRAVELER'S TIP

▶ The Denali Highway can get dry and dusty, so carry good riding glasses with changeable lenses for the conditions.

Anglers are drawn to the tranquil fishing, where grayling and trout are abundant at the height of summer.

DIRECTIONS TO DENALI HIGHWAY   From Fairbanks, drive south on the Richardson Highway until you reach Paxson. The Denali Highway connects to the right and is well marked. From Anchorage, drive north on the Glenn Highway to the Parks Highway. Travel north on the Parks Highway until you reach Cantwell. The turnoff for the Denali Highway is on the right and well marked.

DESCRIPTION   When it first opened in 1957, the Denali Highway was the only road link to Denali National Park, replacing the Alaska Railroad as primary access. Then the Parks Highway opened in 1971, and the Denali Highway became obsolete. Today the road is still used as a summertime link for those who choose to drive it. It closes in mid-fall, when the snow gets too deep, and doesn't reopen until spring, usually in mid-May. It's a piece of history that hasn't changed much since the day it was first carved across Alaska.

The highway is a mostly gravel road—only the first 20 miles on the eastern end and 3 miles on the western end are paved. **Maclaren Summit** is the highest point of the highway—4,086 feet at about Mile 40 from the eastern end. From there the road gets narrower and windier, and potholes and washboards can be numerous. Mountain bikers can make good time on the road, although we recommend the three-night, four-day option. Cycling at this pace allows you to stop at some of the better camping and lodging locations and gives you driving time on either end to travel to Fairbanks or Anchorage, depending on your ultimate destination.

From Paxson, the road starts out on pavement, but within 20 miles gives way to gravel. The **BLM Tangle Lakes Campground,** at Mile 21.5, is a good place to camp if you've gotten a late start. There is no fee for the 25 established campsites with picnic tables.

Once the gravel begins, you will slow down a bit, but the scenery is stunning. The Denali Highway is popular with off-road vehicles, so you may see four-wheeler trails going off into the woods. Those routes are open to mountain bikes too, and many cyclists like to explore off-road. If you do go, take a

GPS, compass, and map, because it can get confusing once you get back in the mountains.

Maclaren Summit is the highest climb of the trip, at Mile 40. The 4,086-foot pass is the second highest on the road system (**Atigun Pass,** on the Dalton Highway, is the highest). Look for a pullout here with views of the **Susitna River Valley, Mount Hayes,** and the rest of the **Alaska Range.** It can be windy and cold, though—not conducive to camping.

At Mile 43.5, a side road called the **Maclaren River Road** leads to **Maclaren Glacier.** Mountain bikers like this road too. The glacier is 12 miles in, and you have to cross the **Maclaren River.** This is for very experienced cyclists only.

The next 20 miles follow winding roads with numerous kettle lakes and creek crossings. You'll find plenty of pullouts for taking breaks or camping. The **Susitna River Bridge,** at Mile 79, is impressive to look at with its multiple trusses and 1,036-foot length. The bridge can get extra-slippery when wet, so slow down and ride carefully here. There's just one lane, so be on the lookout for oncoming traffic.

Camping or lodging is available at Mile 82 at the **Gracious House Lodge.** From there, expect relatively gradual climbs until Mile 94, which begins a steep, well-deserved descent.

After crossing the Brushkana Creek Bridge, near Mile 105, you'll see the entrance to the **BLM Brushkana Campground.** Camping is $6, and there are a few trails around the campground to explore. Store your food well. Bears and curious squirrels can be eager to raid your stash.

Leaving Brushkana Creek will lead to a nice climb that begins a steep descent at Mile 110. From there the riding is relatively easy, although washboards can get rough in this section due to frequent flooding. The pavement picks up again at Mile 131 and is smooth riding all the way into **Cantwell,** a small community at the intersection of the Denali and Parks highways. Lodging, food, gas, and other amenities are available here.

Resources

▸   From Fairbanks, bike rentals are available through **Alaska Outdoor Rentals and Guides** (907-457-2453; **akbike.com**). If you want SAG support, vehicles can be rented through **Go North Alaska Travel Center** (866-236-7272 or 907-479-7272; **paratours.net**). Rates start at $137 per day, depending on the vehicle.

▶ The **Alaska Public Lands Information Center** in Anchorage can help with details on the best places to camp or stay along the road (605 W. 4th Ave., Anchorage 99501; 866-869-6887 or 907-644-3661; **alaskacenters.gov/anchorage.cfm**), as can the Fairbanks location (101 Dunkel St., Suite 110, Fairbanks 99701; 907-459-3730; **alaskacenters.gov/fairbanks.cfm**).

▶ From Anchorage, bike rentals and bicycle trailers are available through **Downtown Bike Rentals** (907-279-5293; **alaska-bike-rentals.com**). Rates start at $32 per day.

▶ The **Fairbanks Convention and Visitors Bureau** (101 Dunkel St., Suite 111, Fairbanks 99701; 800-327-5774; **explorefairbanks.com**) can help you plan in-town lodging and transportation. The **Anchorage Convention and Visitors Bureau** (907-276-4118 or 907-274-3531; **anchorage.net**) is a good option if your trip is starting from the south.

▶ *Mountain Bike Alaska* by Richard Larson features a one-page chapter on riding the Denali Highway. Although nearly 15 years old, the guide will provide some additional details on the road. It's available at **Amazon.com** or local Alaska bookstores for around $15. Another good resource is the BLM's Denali Highway brochure, available online at **blm.gov/ak/st/en/fo/gdo/denali_highway_points.html** and including a map with points of interest.

DENALI NATIONAL PARK AND PRESERVE ROAD

Region The Interior.	**Best time of year to ride** June–August.
Distance 85 miles one-way to Wonder Lake, 91 miles to Kantishna.	**Traffic level** Moderate–heavy; mostly tour buses.
Route configuration Out-and-back.	**Facilities** Six primitive campgrounds, most of which require advance registration.
Difficulty ★★★.	
Suitable for kids? Teens.	
Time to ride 2–4 days.	

ROUTE SUMMARY   The Denali National Park and Preserve Road is a narrow, sometimes-one-lane dirt-and-gravel road that meanders through the **Alaska Range** in some of the most pristine land in the world. Vehicle traffic is limited to permitted tour buses and those traveling to and from the mining community of

Kantishna, at the far end of the road. The scenery is simply stunning, providing the cyclist a glimpse of wild Alaska from the chirping of ground squirrels to the purposeful lumbering of grizzly bears.

DIRECTIONS TO DENALI NATIONAL PARK AND PRESERVE   From Fairbanks, drive 124 miles south on the Parks Highway until you reach the entrance to the park, at Mile 237. From Anchorage, take the Glenn Highway north to the intersection of the Parks Highway, and drive north on the Parks until you reach the park entrance. Charter flights are available from Anchorage, Talkeetna, or Fairbanks. Visit the **National Park Service** Web site (**nps.gov/dena**) for details on qualified air-taxi services. The **Alaska Railroad** also offers daily summer service into the park, either from Fairbanks or Anchorage (800-544-0552; **alaskarail road.com**). For more rail details, go to the Resources section (page 154). The park Web site also features a cycling section to help you plan, at **nps.gov/dena/ planyourvisit/cycling.htm.**

DESCRIPTION   Riding the Denali Park Road is an adventure suited for cyclists who are more concerned about enjoying the scenery than getting in a lot of miles. The road is only 91 miles long, but it is challenging. It is narrow, winding, and steep in many places, and the gravel is better in some spots than in others. In the summer, it can also get dry, and passing tour buses create a lot of dust that you have to drive through.

There are a few rules of the road. First, if you plan to camp along the way, you must have a campground reservation or a backcountry permit. You cannot simply pull over and camp where you wish. The backcountry buses that take passengers into the park for sightseeing can also transport cyclists and their bikes on a first-come, first-served basis.

Bikes are allowed only on the roads. They cannot be taken onto trails, riverbeds, and so on. If you have a backcountry permit to camp, you must park your bike at established rack, at any campground, the Toklat Rest Stop, or the Wonder Lake Ranger Station. Park officials recommend cyclists reserve campsites well ahead to ensure they can be at least close to their bicycles. Because of the dust, you should carry good riding glasses with changeable lenses for the conditions.

Now, for the road. Travel begins at the intersection of the Parks Highway and the entrance to the park. The first 15 miles are paved to the **Savage River Campground.** All vehicles are allowed on this section, so traffic may be heavy until you reach the gravel part of the road. From here, traffic is limited to the park-service backcountry shuttle buses, which take passengers into the park. A fair number of private tour buses also travel the road.

Across the **Savage River,** the road follows the base of **Primrose Ridge,** staying mostly above tree line until it reaches the **Sanctuary River** at Mile 23. The road climbs briefly and then turns along the **Teklanika River.** This is a good spot for viewing grizzly bears, which often forage along the braided riverbed. The **Teklanika Campground** is a popular stopping point for cyclists because

TRAVELER'S TIP

▶ Cyclists on the Denali Park Road are asked to stop whenever a bus passes, which can be every 5–10 minutes at the height of the summer travel season. So don't be intent on making miles. Instead, soak in the scenery of the most-visited national park in Alaska, and see if you can spot any wildlife along the way.

it is a third of the way into the trip. **Igloo Creek Campground,** 4 miles farther along the road, is another option, but check to see if it is open. Both have been temporarily closed in recent seasons because of wildlife activity (visit **nps.gov/dena/planyourvisit/campgrounds.htm** for the latest information).

The next 10 miles are some of the most scenic along the entire road. First is **Sable Pass,** at Mile 40, 3,900 feet in elevation. It doesn't sound high, but when you're riding it, you'll appreciate the views. At Mile 43, you'll go over the **Toklat River.** This portion of road is known for its prime bear-viewing. The Toklat River bears of the park are somehow more impressive than any you'll see along the route. From the bridge you will begin a steep climb up **Polychrome Pass,** at Mile 46 and 3,700 feet high. A rest stop here provides a good place to hook up your bike and take a hike in the open tundra. In the early fall, the pass lives up to its name, coming alive in vibrant hues of orange, red, and yellow. Even in the summer and winter, the terrain has a multicolored appearance. Dall sheep are common along this section of road. We once spotted seven just off the road and spent a half hour watching them graze on the rugged slopes.

Highway Pass, at Mile 58 and 3,980 feet in elevation, is the highest point along the road. From there it is a gentle ride to Mile 66 and the **Eielson Visitor Center,** which has reopened after a complete rebuild in 2008. From the visitor center, the summit of **Mount McKinley,** also known as **Denali**—North America's tallest peak, at 20,320 feet—is just 33 miles away, according to the *Denali Road Guide.* On a clear day, it will feel even closer. The mountain dominates the landscape, and from this close, it feels as if it is literally towering over you.

Beyond Eielson, the terrain changes dramatically, opening up to a tundra plain that seems to go on forever. **Wonder Lake Campground,** at Mile 85, is a picturesque place to pitch a tent. For those who want to add a few more days of adventure to their trip and cycle back out, **North Face Lodge–Camp Denali** and **Denali Backcountry Lodge** are good places to rest and explore the interior of the park through hiking or other activities.

Resources

▶ The **Alaska Public Lands Information Center** (101 Dunkel St., Suite 110, Fairbanks 99701; 907-459-3730; **alaskacenters.gov/fairbanks.cfm**) can advise you on good local rides and places to find rental equipment. The **Fairbanks Convention and Visitors Bureau** (101 Dunkel St., Suite 111, Fairbanks 99701; 800-327-5774; **explorefairbanks.com**) can help you plan your trip.

▶ The **Alaska Railroad** offers daily summer service into the park, from either Fairbanks or Anchorage (800-544-0552; **alaskarailroad.com**). From Anchorage, the train ride is about 7 hours. From Fairbanks, it will take 3 hours. Rates are $146 from Anchorage and $64 from Fairbanks; bikes are $20 extra.

▶ The **Denali Chamber of Commerce** (907-683-4636; **denalichamber.com**) can provide you with information on local sights and happenings.

▶ The **Denali National Park and Preserve** Web site offers some more details on biking. Go to **nps.gov/dena/planyourvisit/cycling.htm.**

▶ The *Denali Road Guide,* by Kris Capps and published by **Alaska Geographic**, is a great companion to take along on your ride. Light and informative, it offers insight into the flora and fauna that you see along the way. It also helps let you know what is coming ahead with each mile. It's available in the park visitor headquarters or through **Alaska Geographic** ($6.95; **alaskageographic .org**). You can also order a *Trails Illustrated* map of the park through **Alaska Geographic** ($11.95)—good to have on hand if you plan to go off-road at all.

PRINCE OF WALES ISLAND

Region Southeast Alaska.	**Time to ride** 3–6 days.
Distance Varies 60–300 miles round-trip or more.	**Best time of year to ride** Early June–late Sept.
Route configuration Out-and-back, with numerous side-trip options.	**Traffic level** Light.
Difficulty ★★★.	**Facilities** Campgrounds, bed-and-breakfasts, and resupply points are all available. Remote routes have fewer amenities.
Suitable for kids? No.	

ROUTE SUMMARY   Prince of Wales Island is part of the 16.9-million-acre **Tongass National Forest** and for years has been central to the logging industry in Southeast Alaska. As a result, there are thousands of miles of logging roads, both paved and gravel, on which to cycle. Views, while often scarred by clear cuts, also are breathtaking.

There is no specific route to follow, although the most common would be to travel from **Hollis** to **Coffman Cove** and back for a 150-mile round-trip. However, the adventure is yours to create. You can even travel as far north as **Labouchere Bay** and **Port Protection** at the northwest tip of Prince of Wales Island, essentially adding another 100 miles to your overall mileage.

DIRECTIONS TO PRINCE OF WALES ISLAND   The easiest way to get to the island with bikes is to fly to Ketchikan and then take the **Inter-Island Ferry** (866-308-4848 or 907-826-4848; **interislandferry.com**) to Hollis. Be clear about your plans to include a bicycle. The folks in this small town don't get many cyclists, so be sure they don't charge you the same rate that they would a car. Access to Ketchikan is through **Alaska Airlines** (866-252-7522; **alaskaair.com**).

DESCRIPTION   Prince of Wales Island is the third-largest island in the United States after the Big Island of Hawaii and Kodiak Island in Southcentral Coastal Alaska. It has a wet maritime climate and affords travels through some of the largest forests you will see in Alaska, despite the years of logging it has undergone. It boasts more roads than anywhere else in Southeast Alaska, with 105 miles of paved road, 155 miles of improved gravel, and more than 2,000 miles of rough-cut logging roads, most of which experienced mountain-bikers can easily handle.

Starting from the ferry terminal at Hollis, you'll first ride the paved and aptly named **Craig-Klawock-Hollis Highway,** 23 miles west to Klawock, then turn south for the remaining 8 miles into **Craig.** The town has most amenities, including a bank, a post office, restaurants, a laundry, and a supermarket.

To head north on the island to the North Prince of Wales Road (the main connector of all the main roads), backtrack on the Craig-Klawock-Hollis Highway to the intersection of Boundary Road, which becomes Big Salt Lake Road. That road travels 16 miles to a T-intersection that will take you north up the island, or east on the paved Thorne Bay Road. We recommend checking out **Thorne Bay.** It's an easy 17 miles of low grades and gentle curves. Plus, it's right on the water and has several nice lodging and camping options, a few restaurants, and a post office.

You'll backtrack again to reach **North Prince of Wales Road,** also known as the "island highway" by locals. The 78-mile-long road is well maintained but narrow in places with no shoulders. There are some challenging climbs that are rewarded with winding downhills, and several spots where you can branch off and explore the local communities, including **Coffman Cove, Tuxekan,** and **Naukati.**

If you opt to ride all the way to **Labouchere Bay,** be prepared for a less-than-exciting end to your trip. There's not much there other than a sign and a rocky, sandy beach. No one lives there.

Resources

▶ The easiest way to get to the island with bikes is to fly to Ketchikan and then take the **Inter-Island Ferry** (866-308-4848 or 907-826-4848; **interislandferry .com**) to Hollis. Bikes are free. Adult passage is $37.

▶ The **JT Brown General Store** in Craig (907-826-3290) is the local Trek dealer and might have a couple of spare parts such as tires or brake pads. They likely won't have disc-brake parts or anything else fancy, though, so be prepared to do your own repairs.

▶ The **Prince of Wales Chamber of Commerce** (907-755-2626; **princeofwalescoc .org**) in Klawock can help you set up lodging—if they're open, that is. We suggest trying to reserve your spots ahead of time, because in the summer you can never count on people being around. The Web site also has a helpful printable map that is good to take with you.

▶ For details on **Thorne Bay,** visit the great Web site **thornebayalaska.net.** You can see photos and check out local businesses for reservations.

▶ Cabins in **Tongass National Forest** cost $25–$45 per night and must be reserved in advance either over the phone or online (877-444-6777; **recreation .gov**). Reservations can be made up to 180 days (six months) in advance of the first night's stay. For details about the 19 cabins in the Craig and Thorne Bay ranger districts, call 907-826-3271 (Craig) or 907-828-3304 (Thorne Bay), or visit **fs.fed.us/r10/tongass/cabins/cabins.shtml.** Check this site before making reservations online or over the phone, because the agents at **recreation .gov** are located somewhere in the Lower 48 states and don't know much about the cabins. The **Alaska Public Lands Information Center** in Anchorage can also help (605 W. 4th Ave., Suite 105, Anchorage 99501; 866-869-6887 or 907-644-3661; **alaskacenters.gov/anchorage.cfm**), as can the **Southeast Alaska Discovery Center** in Ketchikan (50 Main St., Ketchikan, 99901; 907-228-6220; **alaskacenters.gov/ketchikan.cfm**).

▶ Camping also is available through **Tongass National Forest,** and private campgrounds are scattered across the island. Of the five U.S. Forest Service campgrounds on Prince of Wales, only two have running water. Rates are $8 per night at **Harris River Campground** in Craig and $5 per night at **Eagle's Nest Campground** in Thorne Bay. The other three, all in Thorne Bay, are free. Call 907-826-3271 in Craig or 907-828-3304 in Thorne Bay, or visit **fs.fed.us/r10/ tongass/recreation/rec_facilities/campground_info.html.**

RESURRECTION PASS TRAIL

Region Southcentral Coastal Alaska.	**Best time of year to ride** Mid-June– Sept.
Distance 39 miles.	
Route configuration Out-and-back or end-to-end.	**Traffic level** Moderate–heavy.
Difficulty ★★★.	**Facilities** Established tent sites, U.S. Forest Service cabins, and marked trailheads with parking and outhouses.
Suitable for kids? Preteens and up.	
Time to ride 1–3 days.	

ROUTE SUMMARY   The Resurrection Pass Trail is a National Recreation Trail that is one of the most popular routes on the Kenai Peninsula, attracting hikers, mountain bikers, equestrians, and hunters. Its scenery ranges from forested riverside habitat to high alpine meadows. The highest elevation is at the pass itself, at about 2,600 feet and in an open alpine valley. The area has good lake fishing for rainbow and lake trout, Dolly Varden, and some burbot.

DIRECTIONS TO RESURRECTION PASS   From Anchorage, take the **Seward Highway** south to reach either end of the trail. The north-end trailhead is in the community of **Hope,** 70 miles from Anchorage. Look for the Hope turnoff. Turn right onto the Hope Highway and travel about 16 miles to a left-hand turn onto Palmer Creek Road. Follow this gravel road until it branches to the right onto Resurrection Creek Road. The trailhead is on the right, with plenty of parking. The south end of the trail is in **Cooper Landing,** off the Sterling Highway. From Anchorage, follow the Seward Highway south to Mile 90, at its junction to the Sterling Highway. Follow the Sterling Highway about 15 miles to Mile 53, and turn right (north) into the marked trailhead parking area.

DESCRIPTION   From the north end of the route, near the community of Hope, the dirt singletrack trail climbs continuously along **Resurrection Creek,** where gold seekers once panned for gold (people still try it today). About 12 miles in is **Fox Creek Cabin,** which offers a reprieve to an even-steeper climb out of the woods to Resurrection Pass (this section is one of the best for blueberry picking in late summer). The **Devil's Pass Trail** connects to this trail at Resurrection Pass. The nearby **Devil's Pass Cabin** is an excellent place to spend a few days exploring through day hikes. The southern end of the ride is a more gradual downhill through lakes and the Juneau Creek basin. Look for wildlife including bears, moose, and porcupines in this section. The prettiest section of the ride, in our opinion, occurs from **Swan Lake,** at about Mile 26 from the Hope direction, to the trailhead in Cooper Landing. Through this area you will pass **Juneau Lake** and its two lakeside U.S. Forest Service cabins, along with **Juneau Falls,** 4 miles from the southern terminus of the trail. The falls are a great place for tent camping but can get busy on the weekends with large groups.

Resources

▸   Before gearing up, head to one of the many bike shops in Anchorage (see our picks in the Kenai Peninsula Tour, page 136), and drop by the **Anchorage**

Convention and Visitors Bureau (907-276-4118 or 907-274-3531; **anchorage.net**) to find out what's going on in the city.

▶ Cabins in **Chugach National Forest** cost $25–$45 per night and must be reserved in advance either over the phone or online (877-444-6777; **recreation .gov**). Reservations can be made up to 180 days (six months) in advance of the first night's stay. For details about the cabins in the Seward Ranger District, call 907-271-2500 or visit **fs.fed.us/r10/chugach/cabin_web_page/cabin_files**. Check this site before making reservations online or over the phone, because the agents at **recreation.gov** are located somewhere in the Lower 48 states and don't know much about the cabins. The **Alaska Public Lands Information Center** in Anchorage can also help (605 W. 4th Ave., Suite 105, Anchorage 99501; 866-869-6887 or 907-644-3661; **alaskacenters.gov/anchorage.cfm**).

▶ *Mountain Bike Alaska* by Richard Larson features a one-page chapter on riding the Resurrection Pass Trail. Although nearly 15 years old, it will provide some additional details on the trail. It's available at **Amazon.com** or local Alaska bookstores for around $15.

▶ One option to lengthen your journey is to connect with the **Resurrection River–Russian Lakes Trail System,** which travels another 32 miles and comes out on Exit Glacier Road off the Seward Highway, outside of Seward. This trip is for experienced mountain bikers only: bears, rough terrain, and frequent blowdowns are common, but the trip is unforgettable. The best source on details for the ride are available in the book **55 *Ways to the Wilderness in Southcentral Alaska*** by Helen Nienhueser and John Wolfe Jr., available at **Amazon.com** or through local bookstores for around $17.

▶ **U.S. Geological Survey (USGS)** maps for the area are Seward B-8, C-8, and D-8 (visit **usgs.gov**). **Kenai National Wildlife Refuge** maps can be downloaded online at **kenai.fws.gov/maps.htm** or purchased through **Alaska Geographic** (**alaskageographic.org**).

▲ Our Favorite Day Trips

If you don't have enough time for a multiday adventure, you still have several other great options for biking in Alaska. Here is just a sampling. Our best advice is to stop in the local bike shops and ask for current recommendations, because trail conditions vary with the weather.

SOUTHCENTRAL COASTAL ALASKA

BURMA ROAD WITH OPTIONAL OLD WOMEN'S MOUNTAIN RETURN

Closest town Kodiak.	**Difficulty** Moderate on Burma Road; difficult for Old Women's Mountain return. ★★★★★
Configuration Loop; old road and some gnarly singletrack.	
	Suitable for kids? No.
Distance 12 miles one-way.	**Riding time** 2–3 hours.

DIRECTIONS   Take Rezanof Drive West out of town to Anton Larsen Bay Road, on the right. Ride until you cross Buskin Bridge Number 6. Burma Road is on the far side. *Note:* Part of this route is on U.S. Coast Guard property, so you'll need to get advance permission to ride (907-487-5372). The *Kodiak Island Mountain Bike Guide,* available at **58 Degrees North Bike Shop** in Kodiak (907-486-6249), has a complete log of the ride.

JOHNSON PASS TRAIL

Closest town Seward.	**Difficulty** ★★★★
Configuration Out-and-back; narrow singletrack.	**Suitable for kids?** Teens and older.
	Riding time 3–5 hours.
Distance Up to 20 miles.	

DIRECTIONS   From Anchorage, take the Seward Highway south to Mile 63.8, the Granite Creek trailhead, or drive to the Upper Trail Lake trailhead, at Mile 32.7. Both trailheads are on the left side of the road. **Chugach National Forest** (907-271-2500) has more information.

MILLION DOLLAR BRIDGE TO CHILD'S GLACIER

Closest town Cordova.	**Difficulty** ★★
Configuration Out-and-back; gravel road.	**Suitable for kids?** Yes.
	Riding time 4 hours.
Distance 48 miles.	

TRAVELER'S TIP

▶ A great logbook for Anchorage trails is *Mountain Bike Anchorage* by Rosemary Austin ($17.95; available at local bookstores and bike shops or online at **nearpointpress.com**), which gives detailed descriptions of these and other popular Anchorage-area rides. We highly recommend it.

DIRECTIONS   The only access to Cordova is via air or ferry; once you're in town, take Whitshed Road, which turns into the Copper River Highway. The **Cordova Chamber of Commerce** (907-424-7260; **cordovachamber.com**) has more information.

SOUTHCENTRAL INLAND ALASKA

BIRD-GIRD TRAIL

Closest town Anchorage.	**Difficulty** ★★
Configuration Out-and-back; paved pathway.	**Suitable for kids?** Yes.
	Riding time 2 hours.
Distance 12 miles one-way.	

DIRECTIONS   Mile 103 of the Seward Highway. This trail is a misnomer because the newly improved and repaved bike path actually spans 12 miles from the community of Indian to Girdwood, rather than Bird Creek to Girdwood, where it used to begin. Cross a bridge over Indian Creek, and park in the parking and rest area adjacent to the Indian Creek ball fields immediately on your right. (Parking is $5.) Most of the trail is alongside the highway, but some of it dips into the woods and climbs the surrounding mountains, giving cyclists an incredibly scenic road ride. **Chugach State Park** (907-345-5014) has more information.

EKLUTNA LAKE

Closest town Eagle River.	**Difficulty** ★★★
Configuration Out-and-back; dirt-and-gravel nontechnical trail.	**Suitable for kids?** Yes.
	Riding time 3–4 hours.
Distance 13 miles one-way.	

DIRECTIONS Take the Glenn Highway north through Eagle River to about Mile 25, the Thunderbird Falls exit. Take this exit and follow the road about a half mile to the Eklutna Lake Road. Follow Eklutna Lake Road to its end. Parking at **Chugach State Park** (907-345-5014) is $5.

HATCHER PASS–GOLD MINT TRAIL

Closest town Palmer.	**Difficulty** ★★★★★
Configuration Out-and-back; technical singletrack.	**Suitable for kids?** No.
	Riding time 2 hours.
Distance 9 miles one-way, but gets pretty brushy after 5 miles.	

DIRECTIONS Take the Glenn Highway north through Palmer to about Mile 49, and then turn left on Hatcher Pass Road (Fishhook-Willow). The Gold Mint trailhead is 13 miles up the road, just past the Motherlode Lodge. **Mat-Su State Parks** (907-745-3975) has more information.

TONY KNOWLES COASTAL TRAIL

Closest town Anchorage.	**Difficulty** ★★
Configuration Out-and-back; paved pathway.	**Suitable for kids?** Yes.
	Riding time 1 hour.
Distance 10 miles one-way.	

DIRECTIONS From downtown Anchorage, head north at the intersection of Fifth Avenue and H Street. At Third Avenue, H Street becomes Christensen Drive. Follow it down the hill, and turn left onto Second Avenue. The trailhead is not large, but there is a sign and parking is alongside the road. The **Anchorage Convention and Visitors Bureau** (907-276-4118 or 907-274-3531) has more information.

SOUTHEAST ALASKA

EAST GLACIER TRAIL

Closest town Juneau.	**Difficulty** ★★★
Configuration Loop.	**Suitable for kids?** No.
Distance 4.5 miles.	**Riding time** 1 hour.

DIRECTIONS   The trail leaves from behind the visitor center at Mendenhall Glacier. *Warning:* Many hikers are on it during the peak tourist season, so be considerate of those users. **Mountain Gears Bike Shop** (907-586-4327) has more information.

THE INTERIOR

BIRCH HILL SKI TRAILS

Closest town Fairbanks.	**Difficulty** ★★★ (an average; some choices are more difficult than others).
Configuration Loops and out-and-back; a variety of singletrack and dualtrack riding choices.	
	Suitable for kids? Depends on the trail.
Distance Varies depending on the loops and routes you take.	**Riding time** 1–4 hours will pretty much cover the whole area.

DIRECTIONS   Drive north on the Steese Highway to Fairhill Road. From Fairhill, turn left on Birch Hill Road to the sign for the cross-country skiing trails. **Alaska Outdoor Rentals and Guides** (907-457-2453, **akbike.com**) has more information.

ESTER DOME AND ALDER CHUTE

Closest town Fairbanks.	**Difficulty** ★ ★ ★
Configuration Loop; singletrack and old fire roads.	**Suitable for kids?** No.
	Riding time 1 hour.
Distance 9.5 miles.	

DIRECTIONS   From Fairbanks, drive south to the little community of Ester and turn right. Park at the Ester Community Park, near the firehouse. Bike back up the highway about 100 yards to the entrance to the mining area. An old dirt road heads up the hill. This road winds up Ester Dome about 4 miles. The Alder Chute follows a power line for 2.5 miles downhill and is very steep. **Alaska Outdoor Rentals and Guides** (907-457-2453, **akbike.com**) has more information.

TOUR OF THE MINING COUNTRY

Closest town Fairbanks.	**Difficulty** ★ ★ ★ ★
Configuration Out-and-back; singletrack and fire roads.	**Suitable for kids?** No.
	Riding time 3–6 hours.
Distance 46 miles.	

DIRECTIONS   Take Chena Hot Springs Road; when it meets up with Steele Creek Road, park and start the ride from the bike path there. The route is complicated, so ask at local bike shops for details. **Alaska Outdoor Rentals and Guides** (907-457-2453; **akbike.com**) has more information.

THE BUSH

ANVIL MOUNTAIN

Closest town Nome.	**Distance** 9 miles round-trip.
Configuration Out-and-back; gravel road that goes from sea level to 1,062 feet.	**Difficulty** ★ ★ ★
	Suitable for kids? Yes.
	Riding time 1 hour.

DIRECTIONS   From downtown Nome, drive north onto the Teller Road. After the road curves west, about 3.5 miles from town, watch for a turn to the right for Glacier Creek Road. Follow Glacier Creek Road directly up Anvil Mountain. On a clear day you will have an expansive view of the city of Nome, the Bering Sea, Sledge Island, and the surrounding tundra. The **Nome Convention and Visitors Bureau** (907-443-6555; **visitnomealaska.com**) has more information.

▲ Mountain-bike Outfitters

▶ **Alaska Backcountry Bike Tours** (serving Kenai Peninsula, Denali National Park Road, and other statewide locations): 866-354-2453 or 907-746-5018; **mountain bikealaska.com.** This Palmer-based company is one of our favorites for any biking adventure from Denali National Park south to the Kenai Peninsula. They offer a seven-day Denali Park Road Riding tour that includes transfers, park fees and admissions, bike rental, road trips through other national parks, and all meals except one dinner. The cost is $2,695 per person. They also offer singletrack trips that range from two to eight days and cost $445–$2,695. Day trips to such locations as Eklutna Lake and the Tony Knowles Coastal Trail (see pages 161 and 162) begin at $69.

▶ **Alaska Outdoor Rentals and Guides** (serving Dalton Highway, Denali Highway, and Denali National Park Road): 907-457-2453; **akbike.com.** They can guide you on whichever route you choose to ride, including singletrack trips in the Interior. The outfitter also can provide SAG support and/or deliver you wherever you want to go, with your bike or one of theirs on the Dalton or Denali highways (there is no vehicle support on the Denali Park Road, however).

▶ **Alaskan Bicycle Adventures** (serving Kenai Peninsula, Denali Highway, and other state locations): 907-245-2175; **alaskabike.com.** The outfitter offers a Bicycle Alaska trip for serious cyclists. The eight-day tour costs $2,995; cyclists average 65 miles a day, with an opportunity to skip portions if they like. The less-strenuous Alaskan Adventure is seven days, costs $2,995, and averages 30 miles of riding per day, plus some kayaking to mix things up.

▶ **Alaska Ultra Sport** (serving Denali Highway, Nome, Kenai Peninsula, Prince of Wales Island, and other locations): 907-745-6680; **alaskaultrasport.com.** Longtime adventurers Bill and Kathi Merchant guide mountain bikers in the summer and winter to locations throughout Alaska. Recognized as among the most accomplished cyclists in the state, the Merchants also organize the annual Iditarod Trail Invitational, a winter mountain-bike race that travels 1,100 miles from Southcentral Alaska to Nome, in the Bush, using mountain bikes designed for riding on the snow and ice. Custom trips are available; most range from one to nine days and average about $250 per day. They offer an eight-day Denali Highway tour for $3,200. Our top pick for guided tours.

▶ **BicyclingWorld.com:** 610-683-5000; **bicyclingworld.com.** This Web site won't guide a trip for you, but you can often book discounted trips through its online specials.

▶ **Denali Outdoor Center** (serving Denali National Park Road): 888-303-1925 or 907-683-1925; **denalioutdoorcenter.com.** The center rents bikes on a multiday basis and offers guided day trips into the park for $50.

PART EIGHT
DAY HIKING

WHETHER YOU'RE WARMING up for a wilderness hike or just looking to stretch your legs after a long drive, a day hike is great way to leave the crowds behind and get a feel for the region you're visiting.

Many good trails can be found close to Alaska's population centers, so don't assume that one won't be interesting or challenging because of its proximity to town. **Indian River,** for instance, starts within walking distance of downtown Sitka and quickly delivers the willing hiker into the heart of the rainforest, where black bears, deer, and eagles are commonly spotted. In Anchorage, trail-laced **Chugach State Park** offers many trails that will take you into truly wild country and lead you back to town in time for dinner at one of the city's fine restaurants. continued on page 170

▲ alaska day hiking @ a glance

Angel Rocks–Chena Hot Springs

REGION ›› The Interior
DISTANCE ›› 3.5–8 miles
TIME TO HIKE ›› 6–9 hours
DIFFICULTY ›› ★★★★
CONFIGURATION ›› End-to-end
SUITABLE FOR KIDS? ›› No
GUIDE SUGGESTED? ›› No

Bird Ridge

REGION ›› Southcentral Inland
DISTANCE ›› 4–12 miles
TIME TO HIKE ›› 2–5 hours
DIFFICULTY ›› ★★★★
CONFIGURATION ›› Out-and-back
SUITABLE FOR KIDS? ›› Older kids
GUIDE SUGGESTED? ›› No

Crescent Lake

REGION ›› Southcentral Coastal
DISTANCE ›› 12.5 miles
TIME TO HIKE ›› 3–6 hours
DIFFICULTY ›› ★★★
CONFIGURATION ›› Out-and-back
SUITABLE FOR KIDS? ›› Yes
GUIDE SUGGESTED? ›› No

Deer Mountain

REGION ›› Southeast
DISTANCE ›› 6 miles
TIME TO HIKE ›› 3 hours
DIFFICULTY ›› ★★★
CONFIGURATION ›› Out-and-back
SUITABLE FOR KIDS? ›› Yes
GUIDE SUGGESTED? ›› No

Flattop

REGION ›› Southcentral Inland
DISTANCE ›› 3 miles
TIME TO HIKE ›› 1–3 hours
DIFFICULTY ›› ★★★★
CONFIGURATION ›› Out-and-back
SUITABLE FOR KIDS? ›› Yes
GUIDE SUGGESTED? ›› No

Gold Creek–Shoup Bay

REGION ›› Southcentral Coastal
DISTANCE ›› 7–22 miles
TIME TO HIKE ›› 3–14 hours
DIFFICULTY ›› ★★★
CONFIGURATION ›› Out-and-back
SUITABLE FOR KIDS? ›› First half OK
GUIDE SUGGESTED? ›› No

Gold Mint Trail

REGION ›› Southcentral Inland
DISTANCE ›› 18 miles
TIME TO HIKE ›› 4–6 hours
DIFFICULTY ›› ★★★
CONFIGURATION ›› Out-and-back
SUITABLE FOR KIDS? ›› Yes
GUIDE SUGGESTED? ›› No

Granite Tors

REGION ›› The Interior
DISTANCE ›› 15 miles
TIME TO HIKE ›› 6–8 hours
DIFFICULTY ›› ★★★★
CONFIGURATION ›› Loop
SUITABLE FOR KIDS? ›› No
GUIDE SUGGESTED? ›› No

Grewingk Glacier Lake

REGION ›› Southcentral Coastal
DISTANCE ›› 6.5 miles
TIME TO HIKE ›› 4 hours
DIFFICULTY ›› ★★★
CONFIGURATION ›› Out-and-back
SUITABLE FOR KIDS? ›› Yes
GUIDE SUGGESTED? ›› No

Gull Rock

REGION ›› Southcentral Coastal
DISTANCE ›› 11 miles
TIME TO HIKE ›› 3–5 hours
DIFFICULTY ›› ★★
CONFIGURATION ›› Out-and-back
SUITABLE FOR KIDS? ›› Yes
GUIDE SUGGESTED? ›› No

more alaska day hiking @ a glance

Historic Valdez Trail

REGION » Southcentral Coastal
DISTANCE » 8 miles
TIME TO HIKE » 4–5 hours
DIFFICULTY » ★★
CONFIGURATION » End-to-end
SUITABLE FOR KIDS? » Yes
GUIDE SUGGESTED? » No

Indian River Trail

REGION » Southeast
DISTANCE » 8 miles
TIME TO HIKE » 2–5 hours
DIFFICULTY » ★★
CONFIGURATION » Out-and-back
SUITABLE FOR KIDS? » Yes
GUIDE SUGGESTED? » No

Landmark Gap Trail

REGION » The Interior
DISTANCE » 5 miles
TIME TO HIKE » 3 hours
DIFFICULTY » ★★★
CONFIGURATION » Out-and-back
SUITABLE FOR KIDS? » Yes
GUIDE SUGGESTED? » No

Lost Lake Traverse

REGION » Southcentral Coastal
DISTANCE » 15 miles
TIME TO HIKE » 6–9 hours
DIFFICULTY » ★★★
CONFIGURATION » End-to-end
SUITABLE FOR KIDS? » Yes
GUIDE SUGGESTED? » No

Mount Riley

REGION » Southeast
DISTANCE » 8 miles round-trip
TIME TO HIKE » 2–5 hours
DIFFICULTY » ★★★
CONFIGURATION » Out-and-back
SUITABLE FOR KIDS? » Yes
GUIDE SUGGESTED? » No

Pioneer Ridge–Austin Helmers

REGION » Southcentral Inland
DISTANCE » 9 miles
TIME TO HIKE » 6–7 hours
DIFFICULTY » ★★★★
CONFIGURATION » Out-and-back
SUITABLE FOR KIDS? » Teens
GUIDE SUGGESTED? » No

Power Creek–Crater Lake

REGION » Southcentral Coastal
DISTANCE » 12.5 miles
TIME TO HIKE » 4–6 hours
DIFFICULTY » ★★★★
CONFIGURATION » End-to-end
SUITABLE FOR KIDS? » Teens
GUIDE SUGGESTED? » No

Reed Lakes

REGION » Southcentral Inland
DISTANCE » 9 miles
TIME TO HIKE » 4–7 hours
DIFFICULTY » ★★★
CONFIGURATION » Out-and-back
SUITABLE FOR KIDS? » Yes
GUIDE SUGGESTED? » No

West Glacier

REGION » Southeast
DISTANCE » 6.5 miles
TIME TO HIKE » 4 hours
DIFFICULTY » ★★
CONFIGURATION » Out-and-back
SUITABLE FOR KIDS? » Yes
GUIDE SUGGESTED? » No

Winner Creek Gorge

REGION » Southcentral Inland
DISTANCE » 6 miles
TIME TO HIKE » 2–3 hours
DIFFICULTY » ★★
CONFIGURATION » Out-and-back/loop
SUITABLE FOR KIDS? » Yes
GUIDE SUGGESTED? » No

▲ day-hiking outfitters @ a glance

Alaska Nature Tours

907-766-2876
alaskanaturetours.net

REGION ›› Southeast
COST ›› $$
SUITABLE FOR KIDS? ›› Yes
ACTIVITY LEVEL ›› All levels
TRIP LENGTH ›› Day trip

Gastineau Guiding

907-586-8231
stepintoalaska.com

REGION ›› Southeast
COST ›› $$
SUITABLE FOR KIDS? ›› Yes
ACTIVITY LEVEL ›› Light–moderate
TRIP LENGTH ›› Day trip

The Ascending Path

907-783-0505
theascendingpath.com

REGION ›› Southcentral Inland
COST ›› $
SUITABLE FOR KIDS? ›› Yes
ACTIVITY LEVEL ›› Light–moderate
TRIP LENGTH ›› Day trip

Kodiak Treks

907-487-2122
kodiaktreks.com

REGION ›› Southcentral Coastal
COST ›› $$$
SUITABLE FOR KIDS? ›› Yes
ACTIVITY LEVEL ›› Light–moderate
TRIP LENGTH ›› Day/overnight

1st Alaska Outdoor School

907-590-5900
1stalaskaoutdoorschool.com

REGION ›› The Interior
COST ›› $$
SUITABLE FOR KIDS? ›› Yes
ACTIVITY LEVEL ›› Light–moderate
TRIP LENGTH ›› Day trip

Pangaea Adventures

800-660-9637 or 907-835-8442
alaskasummer.com

REGION ›› Southcentral Coastal
COST ›› $$
SUITABLE FOR KIDS? ›› Yes
ACTIVITY LEVEL ›› Light–moderate
TRIP LENGTH ›› Day trip

continued from page 167

Other great trails begin with little fanfare along remote highways with nothing more than a trail marker to indicate what wonders lie down the path.

Turn to Part Five, Backpacking, which begins on page 74, if you're intent on a remote wilderness expedition or a multinight hike. In this chapter, we stick to short hikes that can be done in a day or less. We'll tell you how to find a few of our favorites and give you the resources to find others in the regions you'll be visiting. Remember, these are just a sampling. Entire guidebooks can be—and have been—written about the hiking in various regions of the state. These represent our favorites, some very popular, a few not quite as well known.

Late spring or early summer is the best time for hiking in most parts of Alaska. The weather tends to be drier, and the vegetation isn't high enough to obscure the scenic views and the less-than-pleasant surprises that might be lurking along the path. Most animals will avoid humans at all costs, but it's easy to surprise an animal in heavy brush, and inadvertently stepping between a mama and baby, whether it's a bear or a moose, can be life-threatening.

Spring hiking also means that you're more likely to encounter snow in higher elevations, so plan your hike based on the time of year in which you are visiting. Early May may be perfect for a lower-elevation hike, while trails up high might keep snow until June or even July.

That said, don't be intimidated if you're hiking later in the season, either. In Part Two, Planning Your Trip (page 27), we provide a few specifics to help you avoid an unpleasant wildlife encounter, so be sure to read it before you head down the trail.

▲ Checklist for Success

✔ **LET OTHERS KNOW YOUR WHEREABOUTS.** Tell someone where you're going and when you plan to return. If the trailhead doesn't have a sign-in sheet, leave a note in your car.

✔ **BE BEAR-AWARE.** See "How to Stay Safe in the Wilderness" (Part Two, page 29) for our tips on avoiding the beasts and maximizing your safety in case of an encounter.

✔ **DON'T COUNT ON YOUR CELL PHONE** for emergency communication. While cell-phone coverage is getting better in Alaska all the time, it is still spotty in many parts of the state, particularly the backcountry.

✔ **CARRY EMERGENCY FOOD AND WATER.** You never know when you might need it.

✔ **BRING ALONG A GOOD RAIN JACKET.** It will keep you dry and provide wind (and bug) protection.

✔ **ALLOW ABOUT 1 HOUR FOR EVERY 2.5 MILES OF HIKING.** Some people hike faster than that, others slower, but on average this will give you an idea of how long a hike on established trails should take you.

If you are an experienced backpacker who has hiked extensively in the Lower 48, you pretty much know what to expect from a hike. But if you're relatively new to the pursuit or you're just not sure, there's no shame in hiring a guide to help you get the lay of the land. Besides, most guides have local knowledge about the flora, fauna, geography, and geology of the area. We offer a few suggestions for guides in our recommended areas. Not all of them cover our suggested hikes, but there are plenty of trails from which to choose. Most Alaska guides will arrange custom hikes too, so if you have a particular hike in mind, don't hesitate to ask. Most likely, they can accommodate you.

▲ Southcentral Inland Day Hikes

BIRD RIDGE

Location South of Anchorage.

Distance 4–12 miles round-trip.

Trail configuration Out-and-back.

Difficulty ★★★★.

Suitable for kids? Yes, but not young ones.

Time to hike 2–5 hours.

Best time of year to hike Mid-May–Sept.

Traffic level Moderate at lower levels, light up top.

Facilities Large parking lot; Alaska State Parks $5 parking fee required.

Maps U.S. Geological Survey (USGS) Quads Seward D-7 (NW) and Anchorage A-7.

TRAIL SUMMARY   The hike climbs gently and then emerges from the trees after a mile. It has a steep uphill and offers fine alpine hiking and views of **Turnagain Arm** and **Bird Creek Valley** as it ascends to **Bird Peak** (elevation 3,505 feet). At this point, you've traveled about 2 miles and can turn around, or you can keep going another 4 miles or so along the ridgeline.

TRAVELER'S TIP

▶ The Bird Ridge Trail is snow-free earlier than others in the area, especially in the lower elevations.

DIRECTIONS TO TRAILHEAD   From Anchorage, take the Seward Highway South 25 miles to Mile 102. Look for the large parking lot and trailhead on the inland side of the highway.

FLATTOP

Location Anchorage.	**Traffic level** Heavy.
Distance 3 miles round-trip.	**Facilities** Well-maintained trail, man-
Trail configuration Out-and-back.	made stairsteps on the lower
Difficulty ★★★★.	mountain, parking area; Alaska
Suitable for kids? Yes.	State Parks $5 parking fee.
Time to hike 1–3 hours.	**Maps** USGS Quad Anchorage A-8.
Best time of year to hike Mid-June–Sept.	

TRAIL SUMMARY   Flattop is the most-climbed mountain in Alaska due to its proximity to Anchorage and spectacular views of **Cook Inlet, downtown Anchorage,** the **Chugach Mountains** to the east, and, on a clear day, **Denali (Mount McKinley)** to the north. The trail climbs gradually at first, then ascends steeply via man-made steps. A few hundred feet below the summit, the path gives way to a boulder scramble marked sparsely with orange paint. If you can't find the paint, don't worry; there are usually plenty of people up there whom you can follow. It's an overused trail, but one you'll be glad you hiked.

DIRECTIONS TO TRAILHEAD   From downtown Anchorage head south 6 miles on the Seward Highway. Take the O'Malley Road exit. Turn left, following O'Malley for 4 miles to Hillside Drive. Turn right on Hillside, drive 1 mile, and turn left on Upper Huffman. Then turn right on Toilsome Hill Road to the Glen Alps parking lot at Mile 2. A shuttle is available from downtown (for details, see Southcentral Inland Resources, page 176).

GOLD MINT TRAIL

Location Matanuska-Susitna Valley.	**Best time of year to hike** Mid-June–Sept.
Distance 18 miles round-trip.	
Trail configuration Out-and-back.	**Traffic level** Moderate.
Difficulty ★★★.	**Facilities** Parking lot.
Suitable for kids? Yes.	**Maps** USGS Quad Anchorage D-7.
Time to hike 4–6 hours.	

TRAIL SUMMARY   Level but rocky trail can be wet early in the year and after heavy rains, although trail work has been done in some of the wetter sections. The trail climbs alongside the **Little Susitna River** through a beautiful mountain valley to the river's source at **Mint Glacier.** Mountain bikers as well as hikers use it.

DIRECTIONS TO TRAILHEAD   From Anchorage, take the Glenn Highway north through Palmer. Turn left on Fishhook Road and drive 13.8 miles toward Hatcher Pass. The Gold Mint Trailhead parking lot is directly across from the now-closed Motherlode Lodge.

PIONEER RIDGE–AUSTIN HELMERS TRAIL

Location Matanuska-Susitna Valley. **Distance** 9 miles round-trip. **Trail configuration** Out-and-back. **Difficulty** ★★★★. **Suitable for kids?** Teens. **Time to hike** 6–7 hours.	**Best time of year to hike** Mid-June–Sept. **Traffic level** Moderate–light. **Facilities** Well-maintained trail with benches. **Maps** USGS Quads Anchorage B-5, B-6.

TRAIL SUMMARY   Named after a Mat-Su Valley visionary trail builder, this challenging route accesses the main ridge that connects with **Pioneer Peak.** Starting about 300 feet above sea level, the trail ascends to 5,330 feet over its 4.5-mile length. Spectacular views make it worth the effort.

DIRECTIONS TO TRAILHEAD   Head north from Anchorage on the Glenn Highway. At Mile 30, take the Old Glenn Highway exit and drive 8.5 miles to the intersection of Knik River Road. Stay straight on Knik River Road; the trailhead is at Mile 3.9 on the right. An Austin Helmers trailhead sign, added in 2004, adorns the parking lot.

REED LAKES

Location Matanuska-Susitna Valley.	**Time to hike** 4–7 hours.
Distance 9 miles round-trip.	**Best time of year to hike** Mid-June– Sept.
Trail configuration Out-and-back.	**Traffic level** Moderate.
Difficulty ★★★.	**Facilities** Marked trailhead.
Suitable for kids? Yes.	**Maps** USGS Quad Anchorage D-7.

TRAIL SUMMARY   The trail begins with a 1.5-mile hike on an old mining road. At the old **Snowbird Mine** village you'll pass a decrepit cabin. Cross **Glacier Creek** and then **Reed Creek** before ascending via well-made switchbacks; then rock-hop through a boulder field. Follow Reed Creek through meadows to **Lower Reed Lake.** Visit the waterfall on the way to **Upper Reed Lake.** Both lakes are small but situated in a perfectly notched valley with amazing views.

DIRECTIONS TO TRAILHEAD   From Anchorage, take the Glenn Highway north through Palmer. Turn left on Fishhook Road and drive 14.5 miles toward Hatcher Pass. About a half mile past the switchback at the now-closed Motherlode Lodge, you'll see Archangel Road on the right. Follow it for 2.3 miles. Look for the pullout and trailhead marker on the right. In the early season, Archangel Road may be gated, in which case just park across the road and hike in the 2.3 miles.

WINNER CREEK GORGE

Location Girdwood.	**Time to hike** 2–3 hours.
Distance 6 miles round-trip.	**Best time of year to hike** June–Oct.
Trail configuration Out-and-back (see loop option in summary).	**Traffic level** Moderate.
	Facilities Trailhead; hand-pull tram over Winner Creek Gorge.
Difficulty ★★.	
Suitable for kids? Yes.	**Maps** USGS Quad Seward D-6 (NW).

TRAVELER'S **TIP**

▶ The trees you'll see along the Winner Creek Gorge Trail are huge compared with others in the South-central Inland region, which is why we like this hike so much.

TRAIL SUMMARY   This easy hike winds through the northernmost rainforest in Alaska, composed of big spruce and hemlocks and carpeted in giant ferns.

At Mile 1.5, the trail splits at a bluff above **Winner Creek.** Go left to see the crashing water of the gorge. A right turn takes you upstream past the remains of an old miner's cabin to a pretty alpine basin. You can create an 8-mile loop connecting to the historic **Iditarod Trail** by using the hand tram at the gorge and crossing to the trail. It comes out at **Crow Creek Mine Road** and follows a bike path and road back into Girdwood. Local guide service is available for this hike (for details, see Southcentral Inland Resources, below).

DIRECTIONS TO TRAILHEAD   From Anchorage, take the Seward Highway south 35 miles to Mile 90. Turn inland onto the Alyeska Highway. At Mile 3 the highway ends at an intersection with Arlberg Road. Go left on Arlberg, past Alyeska Resort, and park in the area across from the shuttle-bus stop. Cross the road; there is a bike path with a sign for the trail. Or park at the hotel and walk around either side of the building beneath the tram. Follow the access road to the edge of the forest where the trail begins.

Southcentral Inland Resources

▶   The **Alaska Public Lands Information Center** (605 W. 4th Ave., Anchorage 99501; 866-869-6887 or 907-644-3661; **alaskacenters.gov/anchorage.cfm**) can offer advice on dozens of area hikes ranging from 1-mile beginner walks to 15-mile all-day treks.

▶   **Downtown Bicycle Rentals** (333 W. 4th Ave., Suite 206; 907-279-5293; **alaska -bike-rentals.com**) offers a hike-bike combo for $35 that combines a hike to Flattop with a ride down to Anchorage on the return. Take a shuttle to Flattop with your rented bike, hike to the top, and then ride back down afterward.

▶   The **Chugach National Forest** (3301 C St., Suite 300, Anchorage 99503; 907-743-9500) includes many great trails for hiking, most of which are located in Southcentral Coastal Alaska. The Winner Creek Gorge Trail, however, is partly on Chugach land.

▶   Without **Chugach State Park** (Potter Section House, Mile 115, Seward Highway; 907-345-5014; **dnr.alaska.gov**) there would not be the incredible trail system surrounding the municipality that we have today. The Bird Ridge, Flattop, and Pioneer Ridge–Austin Helmers trails are part of this great swath of land.

▶ The **Division of Natural Resources Public Information Center** (550 W. 7th Ave., Suite 1260, Anchorage 99501; 907-269-8400; **dnr.alaska.gov**) can answer questions about Alaska State Parks lands, which include all of Chugach State Park and state recreation areas such as Hatcher Pass.

▶ The **Finger Lake State Recreation-site** (907-745-3975 or 907-269-8400; **alaskastateparks.org**), in our opinion, contains some of the most underused and underappreciated lands in the state—for example, the Hatcher Pass area, where the Reed Lakes and Gold Mint trails, among many others, are located. The hiking and views are outstanding, and access is easy.

Southcentral Inland Outfitter

▶ **THE ASCENDING PATH** » *At the yurt at Alyeska Resort* 907-783-0505; **theascendingpath.com.** This experienced guide company specializes in ice climbing and glacier trekking, but they also take time out to lead day hikes on the popular Winner Creek Trail. It's a good family destination. The hike takes 4 hours and is $79 for adults, $69 for kids 17 and younger. The outfit can arrange guided hikes to other Southcentral Inland areas as well. Just ask.

▲ Southcentral Coastal Day Hikes

CRESCENT LAKE

Location Cooper Landing.	**Best time of year to hike** June–Sept.
Distance 12.5 miles round-trip (see end-to-end option in summary).	**Traffic level** Moderate–heavy.
	Facilities U.S.
Trail configuration Out-and-back.	Forest Service cabins and marked trailhead with parking.
Difficulty ★★★	
Suitable for kids? Yes.	**Maps** USGS Seward Quads B-7, C-7,
Time to hike 3–6 hours.	and C-8.

TRAIL SUMMARY   The trail makes a long, gradual climb through spruce and hemlock forest to **Crescent Lake,** which sits right at tree line. From the lake, the country is wide open for exploring above tree line, and some like to continue on around Crescent Lake to the **Crescent Saddle Cabin,** past the lake, and on to **Carter Lake,** which spits you out on the Seward Highway, Mile 33. That makes

TRAVELER'S TIP

▶ Crescent Lake is a great place to stop and fish. Grayling is the resident species.

for a 19-mile end-to-end trek. The trail gets heavy use in the summer, so it's not uncommon to cross paths with mountain bikers and horseback riders. A local guide leads horsepacking trips out here often.

DIRECTIONS TO TRAILHEAD   From Anchorage, take the Seward Highway south to the cutoff for the Sterling Highway. Follow the Sterling Highway to Mile 44.9. Turn left onto Quartz Creek Road (just past the **Sunrise Inn;** (907-595-1222; **alaskasunriseinn.com**) and drive a little more than 3 miles to the trailhead. It is well marked.

GOLD CREEK–SHOUP BAY

Location Valdez.	**Best time of year to hike** May–Sept.
Distance 7–22 miles round-trip.	**Traffic level** Light.
Trail configuration Out-and-back.	**Facilities** Marked trailheads with outhouses and sign-in kiosk; two public-use cabins and campgrounds.
Difficulty ★ ★ ★	
Suitable for kids? First half OK.	
Time to hike 3–14 hours.	**Maps** USGS Valdez A-7.

TRAIL SUMMARY   The trail can be muddy, but spectacular views of **Valdez, Shoup Glacier,** and **Shoup Bay** make any mess worthwhile. A campsite, latrine, and food-storage locker can be found at **Gold Creek,** which is a wonderful place to camp among the giant spruce and hemlock trees. The trail becomes more rugged beyond Gold Creek; for day hikers this is a good place to turn around, a 7-mile round-trip. For endurance hikers, the trip is just beginning and starts to climb and turn, eventually offering spectacular views of Shoup Glacier. Two public-use cabins and a camping area are at the end of the trail. Flood damage to the trail in 2006 created some particularly challenging areas, so this hike is not for the faint of heart.

DIRECTIONS TO TRAILHEAD   Follow Egan Drive west through Valdez. The road dead-ends just past Mineral Creek. Look for a small parking lot with outhouses and a trail marker.

GREWINGK GLACIER LAKE

Location Homer.	**Time to hike** 4 hours.
Distance 6.5 miles round-trip.	**Best time of year to hike** June–Sept.
Trail configuration Out-and-back.	**Traffic level** Light.
Difficulty ★★★	**Facilities** Marked trailhead and an
Suitable for kids? Yes.	outhouse on Glacier Spit.

DIRECTIONS TO TRAILHEAD **Homer** lies at the end of the Kenai Peninsula, 226 miles south of Anchorage. The Grewingk Glacier Lake Trail is across Kachemak Bay from Homer. Note that this trip takes extra planning to arrange water transportation. Water taxis are available from the Homer Spit for as little as $50 (see our Resources listing on page 182).

GULL ROCK

Location Hope.	**Best time of year to hike** June–Sept.
Distance 11 miles round-trip.	**Traffic level** Light.
Trail configuration Out-and-back.	**Facilities** Starts at the Porcupine
Difficulty ★★	Campground area, and is signed.
Suitable for kids? Yes.	**Maps** USGS Quad Seward D-8.
Time to hike 3–5 hours.	

TRAIL SUMMARY The route is an old wagon trail along **Turnagain Arm** providing occasional ocean views. The remains of an old cabin, stable, and bridge can still be seen at **Johnson Creek.** The trail stays well above the tide line, climbing to 620 feet before dropping down **Gull Rock.** It's rooty and rocky in places, so wear good boots.

DIRECTIONS TO TRAILHEAD From Anchorage, take the Seward Highway South 70 miles to Mile 56.7. Follow the 18-mile-long Hope Highway to Porcupine Campground, where you'll find the trailhead.

TRAVELER'S TIP

▶ The Gull Rock Trail is a great place to spot sea mammals in the water (beluga whales most often) and land mammals on the trail (moose more often than not).

HISTORIC VALDEZ TRAIL

Location Valdez.	**Traffic level** Moderate.
Distance 8 miles.	**Facilities** Marked trailheads with parking, outhouses, and several entry points. Interpretive signs along the way point out the history of the trail.
Trail configuration End-to-end.	
Difficulty ★★	
Suitable for kids? Yes.	
Time to hike 4–5 hours.	**Maps** USGS Valdez Quads A-5, A-6 (SE).
Best time of year to hike May–Sept.	

TRAIL SUMMARY   After a steep climb, the trail follows a level, easy path locally known as the **Pack Trail** and **Goat Trail,** established by gold seekers who first passed through Keystone Canyon a century ago. Visitors like the hike because of its fantastic views of big waterfalls, tall spruce and hemlock, and great gorges carved over centuries. You will traverse the **Lowe River,** a popular rafting destination, and sometimes will see the boats splashing through the rapids. **Snowslide Gulch** is about two-thirds of the way through the trail (for those headed north); sometimes snow from earlier avalanches can be found in the chutes as late as July.

DIRECTIONS TO TRAILHEAD   From Valdez, drive to Mile 11.8 of the Richardson Highway. Turn left on the Old Richardson Highway Loop. Look for the trailhead on the left at Mile 0.3. The park is in a clearing on the other side of the road. Another access point, if you want a short hike, is at the pulloff for the Bridal Veil Falls overlook, at Mile 13.8.

LOST LAKE TRAVERSE

Location Seward.	**Best time of year to hike** June–Sept.
Distance 15 miles.	**Traffic level** Light–moderate.
Trail configuration End-to-end.	**Facilities** U.S. Forest Service cabin; Primrose Campground on the north end.
Difficulty ★★★	
Suitable for kids? Veteran kid-hikers can handle it.	
Time to hike 6–9 hours.	**Maps** USGS Quads Seward B-7, A-7.

TRAIL SUMMARY   Considered by many to be the most beautiful trail on the Kenai Peninsula, the trail quickly rises above tree line into alpine meadows. The glacier-sculpted landscape is dotted with lakes. Surrounding peaks remain snow-covered year-round.

DIRECTIONS TO TRAILHEAD   From Anchorage, take the Seward Highway south 110 miles to Primrose Landing Campground at Mile 17.1. Turn right on Primrose Road, and drive to the end of the road. Parking is in front of the campground at the lake, by the boat ramp.

TRAVELER'S TIP

▶ The Lost Lake Traverse is the site of an annual mountain race in August to raise money for the Cystic Fibrosis Foundation—don't hike it on that day, or you'll be trampled.

The trailhead is at the back of the campground near the rear outhouses. There is a sign-in kiosk and trailhead marker. To get to the southern trailhead, drive to Mile 5.3 of the Seward Highway. Turn west on Scott Way, left on Heather Lee Lane, and right on Hayden Berlin Road to the end of the road. This trailhead is not as easily recognized.

POWER CREEK–CRATER LAKE

Location Cordova.	**Best time of year to hike** June–Sept.
Distance 12.5 miles.	**Traffic level** Light.
Trail configuration End-to-end.	**Facilities** Established campsites,
Difficulty ★ ★ ★ ★	public-use cabin, and a marked
Suitable for kids? Teens.	trailhead with parking.
Time to hike 4–6 hours.	**Maps** USGS Quad Cordova C-5.

TRAIL SUMMARY   **Crater Lake** is the high point to this scenic hike outside of Cordova. The **Power Creek** side has numerous switchbacks, and the **Crater Lake Trail** is steep at the beginning as well. From either direction, you'll be doing a lot of climbing. But the reward is the scenery.

DIRECTIONS TO TRAILHEAD   From downtown Cordova, take Second Avenue to Lake Avenue and turn right. Follow Lake Avenue about 2 miles, past the airport and floatplane base to the trailhead at Crater Lake, which is on the left side of the road. You'll probably have to park on the other side of the road. To reach the Power Creek trailhead, keep driving to the end of the road, another 5.5 miles.

Southcentral Coastal Resources

▶ **Central Charters** (800-478-7847 or 907-235-7847; **centralcharter.com**) can arrange a water taxi across Kachemak Bay. Prices start at $50.

▶ Lands of the **Chugach National Forest** (3301 C St., Suite 300, Anchorage 99503; 907-743-9500; **fs.fed.us/r10/chugach**) include many great hiking trails, most of which are located in Southcentral Coastal Alaska. The Glacier District can be reached at 907-783-3242, the Seward District at 907-224-3374, and the Cordova District at 907-424-7661.

▶ **Cordova Coastal Outfitters** (800-357-5145 or 907-424-7424; **cdvcoastal.com**), located at the harbor in the brightly colored boathouse, will rent you everything you need for an impromptu day hike. Rates start at $5, and overnight gear is $40, which is a bargain, considering today's airline baggage fees.

▶ **Kachemak Bay State Park:** More information is available through Alaska State Parks, Kenai Area Office; 907-262-5581; **dnr.alaska.gov/parks/units/kbay/kbay .htm.** The **Halibut Cove Ranger Station** (907-235-6999) can answer questions in the summer.

▶ **Kenai National Wildlife Refuge** (Ski Hill Road, Soldotna 99669; 907-262-7021; **kenai.fws.gov**) affords many hiking opportunities. Check out the Web site, or stop by the visitor center in Soldotna, where a few trails leave right from the center.

▶ *Trails Illustrated* makes a Kenai Fjords National Park Map (Map 760) that outlines hikes such as Lost Lake, mentioned in this chapter, along with many other hikes worth exploring. Available at **rei.com; alaskanha.org;** and the company Web site, **trailsillustrated.com.**

▶ **U.S. Geological Survey** (**USGS**) maps are available at most sporting-goods stores, although you'll have better luck finding the ones you need in Anchorage. Or check **usgs.gov.**

Southcentral Coastal Outfitters

▶ **KODIAK TREKS** ➤ 907-487-2122; **kodiaktreks.com.** The company offers guided day hikes in one of the world's most renowned bear-viewing areas. Guide Harry Dodge has more than 30 years of experience and provides a wealth of information on the bears and their life cycles and habitat. This eco-friendly guide service offers small group tours with minimal impact on the animals, while offering an up-close experience you'll never forget. Prices start at $350 per person, per night, and include cabin lodging and bear viewing. Other activities are also offered.

▶ **PANGAEA ADVENTURES** ⟫ *Valdez* 800-660-9637 or 907-835-8442; **alaskasummer.com.** Pangaea offers day hikes on Valdez and Worthington glaciers. Prices range $99–$129 per person for 2–5 hours, with hikes accommodating various ability levels. For the novice, the Valdez Glacier hike offers easy hiking and climbing, while the trip atop Worthington Glacier is more challenging, allowing hikers to try out glacier ice climbing (with excellent instruction, of course). Crampons and ice-climbing gear are provided.

▲ Southeast Day Hikes

DEER MOUNTAIN

Location Ketchikan.	**Best time of year to hike** May–Sept.
Distance 6 miles round-trip.	**Traffic level** Heavy when cruise ships are in; moderate otherwise.
Trail configuration Out-and-back.	**Facilities** A U.S. Forest Service shelter and marked trail.
Difficulty ★ ★ ★	
Suitable for kids? Yes.	**Maps** USGS Ketchikan B-5.
Time to hike 3 hours.	

TRAIL SUMMARY   The trail begins with a muskeg-spanning boardwalk and quickly ascends toward the peak. Stay to the right when the trail forks and you'll reach the summit, which on clear days offers great views of the **Tongass Narrows** and **Prince of Wales Island.** You can keep going for a traverse to Silvis Lakes and beyond, but there are no markers and it takes more planning than a simple day hike. Deer Mountain is the most popular trail in Ketchikan, but we still recommend it because it leads to the summit of the distinctive peak that dominates the town.

DIRECTIONS TO TRAILHEAD   Take Stedman Street south through town to Deermount. Turn east and continue 0.3 miles to Fair Street. Turn right on Fair, and follow to the top of the hill. Cross Nordstrom Drive, and turn right into the parking lot at the trailhead, which is marked.

INDIAN RIVER TRAIL

Location Sitka.	**Time to hike** 2–5 hours.
Distance 8 miles round-trip.	**Best time of year to hike** May–Sept.
Trail configuration Out-and-back.	**Traffic level** Moderate.
Difficulty ★★	**Facilities** Marked trail.
Suitable for kids? Yes.	**Maps** USGS Sitka A-4.

TRAIL SUMMARY   This trail is easily accessed from downtown Sitka and has a rewarding waterfall view at the end. The path follows the **Indian River,** a popular salmon stream, to the 80-foot waterfall at the base of **Three Sisters Mountain.** Black bears, deer, and eagles are often seen along the trail, and the forested hike affords a nice contrast to all the other popular mountain climbs in Southeast Alaska.

DIRECTIONS TO TRAILHEAD   From downtown, follow Sawmill Creek Road to the intersection with Indian River Road near the State Trooper Training Academy. Follow Indian River Road to the gate. Park there and walk to the trailhead near the abandoned city water plant.

MOUNT RILEY

Location Haines.	**Best time of year to hike** May–Sept.
Distance 8 miles round-trip.	**Traffic level** Moderate.
Trail configuration Out-and-back.	**Facilities** A marked trail with three
Difficulty ★★★	access points.
Suitable for kids? Yes.	**Maps** USGS Quads Skagway A-2 (NE)
Time to hike 2–5 hours.	and A-1 (NW).

TRAIL SUMMARY   At 1,760 feet, **Mount Riley** is the highest point on the Chilkat Peninsula. There are three ways to access the trail, and you can connect those access points to make longer hikes. But we like the Beach Road access point, because in its 8-mile round-trip, you get a sampling of everything that makes the area so pretty. It faces north, though, so hike it when you know the sun will be shining, or later in the season when all the snow has melted. The trail climbs gradually, going through coastal forest that at some points overlooks **Chilkat Inlet.** The side trail to **Kelgaya Point** is also nice.

DIRECTIONS TO TRAILHEAD   Drive along the waterfront, following Haines Highway east until it becomes Beach Road. Follow Beach Road past Portage Cove Campground and up a hill to the road's end and the trailhead. You will be on the Battery Point Trail until it forks off for the Mount Riley hike.

WEST GLACIER

Location Juneau.	**Time to hike** 4 hours.
Distance 6.5 miles round-trip.	**Best time of year to hike** May–Sept.
Trail configuration Out-and-back.	**Traffic level** Moderate–high.
Difficulty ★★	**Facilities** Marked trail and established overlook.
Suitable for kids? Yes.	**Maps** USGS Quad Juneau B-2 (NW).

TRAIL SUMMARY   This scenic hike along the west side of **Mendenhall Lake** and the **Mendenhall Glacier** leads to a spectacular view of the glacier.

DIRECTIONS TO TRAILHEAD   Drive 9 miles north on the Glacier Highway to the junction with Mendenhall Loop Road. Drive 3.7 miles and turn right on Montana Creek Road. Go right on Mendenhall Lake Road past the campground; the trailhead is at the end of the road.

TRAVELER'S TIP

▶ The West Glacier Trail, though scenic, is far from a wilderness experience—be prepared for helicopter noise, as the glacier is a popular destination for cruise-ship passengers on day excursions.

Southeast Resources

▶   The **Division of Natural Resources Public Information Center** (400 Willoughby Ave., Fourth Floor, Juneau; 907-465-3400; **dnr.alaska .gov**) can answer questions about Alaska State Parks lands, including the Mount Riley Trail, which is part of Chilkat State Park.

▶   The **Southeast Alaska Discovery Center** (50 Main St., Ketchikan 99901; 907-228-6220; **alaskacenters.gov/ketchikan.cfm**) offers information on trails across Southeast Alaska, including Deer Mountain.

▶   The **Southeast Alaska Trail System,** a nonprofit organization also known as SEAtrails (in Douglas, across the bridge in Juneau; 907-364-2427;

seatrails.org), uses grant and donor money to upgrade and maintain the wealth of trails throughout Southeast Alaska.

▶ The **Tongass National Forest** (907-225-3101; **fs.fed.us/r10/tongass**) manages the Deer Mountain Trail in Ketchikan, the Indian River Trail in Sitka, and the West Glacier Trail in Juneau.

▶ **USGS** maps are available at the public-information centers in Southeast Alaska and online at **usgs.gov**.

Southeast Outfitters

▶ **ALASKA NATURE TOURS** ≫ *Haines* 907-766-2876; **alaskanaturetours.net.** Enjoy nature hikes through the rainforests of the Chilkat Valley or more-strenuous, vista-oriented treks high atop the mountain peaks that tower over Haines. Hikes are 4–8 hours and vary in difficulty; prices range $85–$130 per person, with lunch included on some trips. The 5-hour Mount Riley hike, at $95, is particularly beautiful.

▶ **GASTINEAU GUIDING** ≫ *Juneau* 907-586-8231; **stepintoalaska.com.** Gastineau offers options for the independent traveler as well as for cruise-ship passengers. You can take seaside or rainforest hikes—or combine the two into one trip—but our favorite is the guide's choice, which is suited to fit hikers who want less of a tour and more of an outdoor adventure. Rates are $89–$159. The Rainforest & Sea Coast Nature Walk, at $89, is our choice for a good cross-section of the region.

▲ Interior Day Hikes

ANGEL ROCKS– CHENA HOT SPRINGS TRAVERSE

Location The Interior.

Distance 3.5 miles, 8 miles with traverse.

Trail configuration End-to-end.

Difficulty ★★★★

Suitable for kids? No.

Time to hike 6–9 hours.

Best time of year to hike June–Sept.

Traffic level Moderate on Angel Rocks; light on traverse.

Facilities Trail shelter; marked trailheads.

Maps USGS Circle A-5.

TRAIL SUMMARY   The steep and rocky trail accesses the granite outcrop known as **Angel Rocks.** An alpine ridge traverse marked by rock cairns links up with the **Chena Hot Springs Trail,** which leads to the popular resort. The traverse is particularly nice, although challenging, passing through the saddle before turning east. Eventually it connects with the Overlook Trail, which leads to **Chena Hot Springs Resort** and eventually the **Hillside Cutoff.** When the trail dead-ends at a dirt road, turn right and follow it to the resort.

DIRECTIONS TO TRAILHEAD   Drive 5 miles north on the Steese Highway to Chena Hot Springs Road. The trailhead is on the right side of the road at Mile 49. If you do the traverse, you will come off the trail at Mile 56.5, 7.5 miles down the road.

GRANITE TORS

Location Outside Fairbanks.	**Best time of year to hike** June–Sept.
Distance 15 miles.	**Traffic level** Moderate–heavy.
Trail configuration Loop.	**Facilities** A trail shelter, campground
Difficulty ★ ★ ★ ★	at trailhead, and marked trailhead.
Suitable for kids? No.	**Maps** USGS Big Delta D-5.
Time to hike 6–8 hours.	

TRAIL SUMMARY   The trail circles the **Rock Creek** drainage accessing the **Plain of Monuments,** also known as Alaska's natural Stonehenge for its otherworldly rock-outcrop arrangement. Five miles of the trail are marked by stone cairns. It is a challenging hike, and those who want a similar yet shorter hike can tackle the **Angel Rocks** trail (see previous profile).

TRAVELER'S TIP

▶ The Granite Tors Trail is one of the few loops that start and stop in the same place, which is one of the reasons we like it.

DIRECTIONS TO TRAILHEAD   Drive north on the Steese Highway to Chena Hot Springs Road. Drive east 40 miles to the Tors Trail Campground. The trailhead is at the campground.

LANDMARK GAP TRAIL

Location The Interior–Denali Highway.	**Best time of year to hike** Mid-June– Sept.
Distance 5 miles round-trip.	
Trail configuration Out-and-back.	**Traffic level** Low but can include ATVs during hunting season.
Difficulty ★ ★ ★	
Suitable for kids? Yes.	**Facilities** Well-developed trail.
Time to hike 3 hours.	**Maps** USGS Mount Hayes A-5.

TRAIL SUMMARY   The trail is a crude dirt road that accesses its namesake lake, which fills a glacier-carved gap in the **Amphitheater Mountains.** The glaciated **Alaska Range** is visible beyond.

DIRECTIONS TO TRAILHEAD   From Paxson, off the Richardson Highway, turn west on the Denali Highway. Drive approximately 25 miles; the trailhead is on the north side, about 12 miles east of Maclaren Summit.

Interior Resources

▶   The **Alaska Public Lands Information Center** (101 Dunkel St., Suite 110, Fairbanks 99701; 907-459-3730; **alaskacenters.gov/fairbanks.cfm**) can provide information on day hikes in the Fairbanks and surrounding areas, including the Granite Tors and Angel Rocks hikes.

▶   **Department of Natural Resources Public Information Center:** 3700 Airport Way, Fairbanks 99709; 907-451-2705; **dnr.alaska.gov.** This office can answer questions about Alaska State Parks lands, which include the Granite Tors and Angel Rocks trails.

▶   *Trails Illustrated* makes a map of Wrangell–St. Elias National Park and Preserve (Map 249) that outlines hikes in the McCarthy area. Available at **rei.com; alaskageographic.org**; or the company Web site, **trailsillustrated.com.**

▶   The **U.S. Bureau of Land Management's Northern District office** (1150 University Ave., Fairbanks 99709; 907-474-2250; **ak.blm.gov**) can point you toward hikes in the White Mountain National Recreation Area. The Glennallen District office (907-822-3217) can provide more details on the Landmark Gap Trail.

▶   **USGS** maps are available at sporting-goods stores and **usgs.gov.**

Interior Outfitter

▶ **1ST ALASKA OUTDOOR SCHOOL ➳** 907-590-5900; **1stalaskaoutdoorschool
.com.** Whether it's a berry-picking trek or a wildlife-watching expedition,
these guys can guide you. The rates start at $100 and vary based on the
traveling distance. The owners offer classes in everything from canning and
preserving to remote-traveling skills.

PART NINE
SEA KAYAKING

KAYAKS—OR *BIDARKAS* or *umiaks,* as you also will hear them called in Alaska—are among the oldest modes of transportation in the Far North, used for hundreds of years by Eskimos and Aleuts to hunt seals and whales. Back then the boats were constructed of wooden frames covered by the dried skins of sea mammals such as walruses and seals. They were light and quiet on the water, and they moved swiftly, making them the perfect hunting vessel. One or two men could carry them, and maintenance involved little more than letting them dry out between uses to keep the skins from rotting. *Bidarkas,* the Aleut versions, carried one man; the *umiaks* used in the Chukchi and Bering seas were sometimes as long as 40 feet. Today, the kayaking tradition continues,

▲ alaska sea kayaking @ a glance

Glacier Bay

REGION ›› Southeast
DISTANCE ›› Varies
TRAFFIC ›› Moderate
DIFFICULTY ›› ★ ★ ★
TRIP LENGTH ›› 3–10 days
SUITABLE FOR KIDS? ›› Yes
GUIDE SUGGESTED? ›› No

Prince William Sound

REGION ›› Southcentral Coastal
DISTANCE ›› Varies
TRAFFIC ›› Moderate
DIFFICULTY ›› ★ ★ ★ ★
TRIP LENGTH ›› 3–15 days
SUITABLE FOR KIDS? ›› Varies
GUIDE SUGGESTED? ›› Recommended

Kachemak Bay

REGION ›› Southcentral Coastal
DISTANCE ›› Varies
TRAFFIC ›› Moderate–heavy
DIFFICULTY ›› ★ ★
TRIP LENGTH ›› 3–5 days
SUITABLE FOR KIDS? ›› Yes
GUIDE SUGGESTED? ›› No

Resurrection Bay

REGION ›› Southcentral Coastal
DISTANCE ›› Varies
TRAFFIC ›› Light–moderate
DIFFICULTY ›› ★ ★ ★
TRIP LENGTH ›› 3–7 days
SUITABLE FOR KIDS? ›› Varies
GUIDE SUGGESTED? ›› No

Katmai Coast

REGION ›› The Bush
DISTANCE ›› 30–50 miles
TRAFFIC ›› Light
DIFFICULTY ›› ★ ★ ★ ★
TRIP LENGTH ›› 6–10 days
SUITABLE FOR KIDS? ›› No
GUIDE SUGGESTED?
›› Highly recommended

Shuyak Island

REGION ›› Southcentral Coastal
DISTANCE ›› 35–40 miles
TRAFFIC ›› Light
DIFFICULTY ›› ★ ★ ★
TRIP LENGTH ›› 3–5 days
SUITABLE FOR KIDS? ›› Yes
GUIDE SUGGESTED? ›› No

and some native whale hunters still use their skin boats. Recreationists also enjoy the ease of kayaks, paddling into remote channels and bays to explore parts of Alaska that really aren't accessible any other way.

This chapter explores the myriad places to which a sea kayaker can travel. With more than 6,600 miles of coastline, the destinations are endless. Creating a best-of-the-best list for this sport was particularly difficult

continued on page 194

▲ sea-kayaking outfitters @ a glance

Alaska Alpine Adventures

877-525-2577 or 907-781-2253
alaskaalpineadventures.com

REGION ›› The Bush
COST ›› $$$
SUITABLE FOR KIDS? ›› No
ACTIVITY LEVEL ›› Moderate–high
TRIP LENGTH ›› 12 days

Alaska Kayak School

907-235-2090
alaskakayakschool.com

REGION ›› Southcentral Coastal
COST ›› $$
SUITABLE FOR KIDS? ›› Yes
ACTIVITY LEVEL ›› All levels
TRIP LENGTH ›› Day trip

Alaska Mountain Guides and Climbing School

800-766-3396
alaskamountainguides.com

REGION ›› Southeast
COST ›› $$
SUITABLE FOR KIDS? ›› Yes
ACTIVITY LEVEL ›› Light–moderate
TRIP LENGTH ›› 1–7 days

Alaska on the Home Shore Coastal Wilderness Adventures

800-287-7063 or 360-738-2239
homeshore.com

REGION ›› Southeast
COST ›› $$$$
SUITABLE FOR KIDS? ›› No
ACTIVITY LEVEL ›› Light–moderate
TRIP LENGTH ›› 8 days

Alaska Sea Kayakers

877-472-2534 or 907-472-2534
alaskaseakayakers.com

REGION ›› Southcentral Coastal
COST ›› $$$
SUITABLE FOR KIDS? ›› Some
ACTIVITY LEVEL ›› Moderate
TRIP LENGTH ›› 1–5 days

Anadyr Adventures

800-TO-KAYAK or 907-835-2814
anadyradventures.com

REGION ›› Southcentral Coastal
COST ›› $$$
SUITABLE FOR KIDS? ›› Yes
ACTIVITY LEVEL ›› Light–moderate
TRIP LENGTH ›› 1–7 days

Cordova Coastal Outfitters

907-424-7424
cdvcoastal.com

REGION ›› Southcentral Coastal
COST ›› $
SUITABLE FOR KIDS? ›› Yes
ACTIVITY LEVEL ›› Moderate
TRIP LENGTH ›› ½ day/custom

Exposure Alaska

800-956-6422 or 907-761-3761
exposurealaska.com

REGION ›› Southcentral Coastal
COST ›› $$$
SUITABLE FOR KIDS? ›› Yes
ACTIVITY LEVEL ›› Moderate
TRIP LENGTH ›› 7 days

Lifetime Adventures

907-952-8624
lifetimeadventures.net

REGION ›› Southcentral Coastal
COST ›› $$$
SUITABLE FOR KIDS? ›› No
ACTIVITY LEVEL ›› Moderate
TRIP LENGTH ›› 7 days

sea-kayaking outfitters @ a glance [continued]

Liquid Adventures

888-325-2925
liquid-adventures.com

REGION ›› Southcentral Coastal
COST ›› $$
SUITABLE FOR KIDS? ›› Some trips
ACTIVITY LEVEL ›› Moderate–high
TRIP LENGTH ›› 1–5 days

Miller's Landing

866-541-5739 or 907-224-5739
millerslandingak.com

REGION ›› Southcentral Coastal
COST ›› $$
SUITABLE FOR KIDS? ›› Some trips
ACTIVITY LEVEL ›› Moderate
TRIP LENGTH ›› Day trip/custom

Pangaea Adventures

800-660-9637 or 907-835-8442
alaskasummer.com

REGION ›› Southcentral Coastal
COST ›› $$$
SUITABLE FOR KIDS? ›› Some trips
ACTIVITY LEVEL ›› All levels
TRIP LENGTH ›› 1–8 days

Prince William Sound Kayak Center

877-472-2452 or 907-472-2452
pwskayakcenter.com

REGION ›› Southcentral Coastal
COST ›› $$
SUITABLE FOR KIDS? ›› Yes
ACTIVITY LEVEL ›› Light–moderate
TRIP LENGTH ›› Day trip

Southeast Exposure Alaska Sea Kayaking Adventures

907-225-8829
southeastexposure.com

REGION ›› Southeast
COST ›› $
SUITABLE FOR KIDS? ›› Some trips
ACTIVITY LEVEL ›› Light–moderate
TRIP LENGTH ›› Varies

Southeast Sea Kayaks

800-287-1607 or 907-225-1258
kayakketchikan.com

REGION ›› Southeast
COST ›› $$
SUITABLE FOR KIDS? ›› Yes
ACTIVITY LEVEL ›› Light–moderate
TRIP LENGTH ›› ½–5 days

Sunny Cove Sea Kayaking Co.

800-770-9119 or 907-224-4426
sunnycove.com

REGION ›› Southcentral Coastal
COST ›› $$
SUITABLE FOR KIDS? ›› Some trips
ACTIVITY LEVEL ›› Moderate–high
TRIP LENGTH ›› 1–10 days

True North Adventures

907-235-0708
truenorthkayak.com

REGION ›› Southcentral Coastal
COST ›› $$
SUITABLE FOR KIDS? ›› Yes
ACTIVITY LEVEL ›› Moderate
TRIP LENGTH ›› ½–3 days

Wilderness Birding Adventures

907-694-7442
wildernessbirding.com

REGION ›› Southcentral Coastal
COST ›› $$$
SUITABLE FOR KIDS? ›› Teens and older
ACTIVITY LEVEL ›› Moderate
TRIP LENGTH ›› 7 days

continued from page 191

because we have a bias. We love sea kayaking: the smell of the ocean, the sounds of the birds, the occasional sea otter playfully following alongside.

If you're here to experience the wonders of Alaska, they're easy to appreciate while paddling along at a comfortable pace and taking in the whales and glaciers and other assorted Alaska scenery.

The best places to go sea kayaking in Alaska are, predictably, the coastal regions, including Southcentral Coastal and Southeast Alaska. The communities of **Homer, Seward, Whittier, Valdez, Juneau, Ketchikan,** and **Gustavus** are particularly promising places from which to embark.

We offer a few of our favorite trips, which take in some of the most dramatic coastal landscapes in the state.

▲ Checklist for Success

✔ **KAYAK WITH AT LEAST ONE OTHER PERSON,** and stay within shouting or whistling distance. A two-person rescue is much easier than a self-rescue.

TRAVELER'S TIP

▶ Knee-high or calf-length rubber boots are a must in Alaska waters. Neoprene whitewater booties usually aren't enough to keep you comfortably dry. We can't stress this enough. If you want to fit in with the locals, **XtraTufs** are a brand that most Alaskans prefer.

✔ **RETHINK YOUR PACKING STRATEGIES.** The nice thing about sea kayaking is that you can pack more luxuries than you can on canoe trips, when portages are necessary, or on backpacking trips, when the weight is on your back. So let up a little and bring that bigger tent, that thicker book, that bottle of wine. Carry everything in waterproof stuff-sacks with double seals. Using small stuff-sacks allows you to pack into smaller compartments of the kayak's holds, and to better distribute weight.

✔ **DRESS APPROPRIATELY.** It rains a lot on the coast, so you'll be battling the wet from the sea and the rain. Wear layers and a paddling jacket that seals tightly at the wrists. On those glorious clear, sunny days, stuff extra clothes in your hold and let the summer sun bathe you in its warmth (while properly covered in sunscreen, of course). Need we mention the necessity of life jackets?

✔ **KNOW HOW TO NAVIGATE.** Topographic maps and marine charts are your best mapping sources, especially on longer trips in which you are traveling from point to point. **U.S. Geological Survey** (USGS) and **National Oceanic and Atmospheric Administration** (NOAA) maps are the most accurate for the conditions. Many outdoor travelers can read global-positioning systems (GPS) and rely on them for backcountry travel. These can be particularly useful tools for travel in areas with multiple channels and bays, but if they drop into the water (it's happened to us!), they're done for. Always have hard-copy maps on hand.

✔ **AVOID GIARDIA.** If you plan on drinking water from a natural source, boil or treat it first to avoid catching this nasty intestinal bug.

✔ **PROTECT AGAINST HYPOTHERMIA.** If you roll your kayak, an enjoyable trip can quickly turn dangerous. Get to land and find a way to get warm, whether by building a fire or changing into dry clothes or huddling with a dry partner.

✔ **CARRY BASIC FIRST-AID ITEMS,** including bandages to patch up minor cuts as well as any specific medications that may be needed for anyone in your traveling party.

✔ **BRING ALONG A CAMPSTOVE THAT CAN HEAT WATER QUICKLY.** This is a better choice than building fires, which can be hard to do in treeless areas and is more damaging to the landscape. In some places, fires are even prohibited. Also, carry waterproof matches as well as a lighter.

✔ **PACK A WHISTLE, FLARES,** or something else to use as an SOS device in case of an emergency.

✔ **CLAM WITH CAUTION.** If you plan to harvest shellfish such as clams or mussels, make sure the area in which you will be paddling is open to gathering and that what you take is safe to eat. The big risk is paralytic shellfish poisoning, or PSP, which can cause numbness, paralysis, disorientation, or even death. Microscopic algae called dinoflagellates, which some shellfish feed on, produce the toxins that cause the disorder. The state tests for the presence of these organisms often and issues warnings when dinoflagellates are detected. The **Marine Advisory Program**'s main office (907-274-9691; **uaf.edu/map**) can offer more information. Also be aware that a fishing license is required to harvest shellfish; you can buy one at most sporting-goods stores and grocery stores; fees range $10–$50 for nonresidents, depending on how long you plan to fish. You'll also need a Household Shellfish Permit (if you're searching for littleneck or butter clams), which is free but requires registration.

✔ **CHECK MARINE CONDITIONS FOR YOUR AREA** from a marine-radio forecast, by calling the local marine weather office, or by checking online with the

TRAVELER'S TIP

▶ Free tide-table booklets are available at most grocery stores and banks and some gas stations.

Alaska Marine Weather Forecast (**pafc.arh.noaa.gov/ marfcst.php**).

✔ **KNOW THE TIDES.** Tides may determine your launch site and destination. Tides also cause currents, so know the rise and ebb for the area where you are planning on paddling. In general, if the tide and wind are traveling the same direction, water conditions will be somewhat calm. Wind traveling against the tidal current creates waves. Attach your paddle to the kayak with a paddle leash to avoid losing it in these conditions.

✔ **ALWAYS CARRY FRESH WATER FOR DRINKING.** It is surprisingly easy to get dehydrated while paddling. We like to attach a looped-lidded Nalgene bottle to the top front of our kayak for easy reach. We also store easily accessible snacks in an inflatable snap-on pouch.

Travel with a Guide?

Traveling with a guide is a personal choice that should reflect exactly what you are looking for in a kayaking trip. Even seasoned paddlers sometimes choose to travel with a guide if they are visiting areas with which they are unfamiliar, so the decision is not solely based on experience level.

TRAVELER'S TIP

▶ If you choose to travel with a guide, be sure to research his or her travel habits well. Some guides do almost all the work, and your paddling days end in a fully set-up camp with food and hot beverages waiting. Others take a more primitive approach, and you may carry your own gear and help set up camp each evening. You may even help prepare meals.

Using a guide is an excellent way to eliminate the guesswork from any trip. Guides know the areas well and can predict which type of gear will work best, what the weather will be like, and how far you will be able to paddle in reality versus what you may think you can paddle by looking at a map. These are invaluable perks, but they will cost you extra.

Another reason you might choose a guide is logistics. Unless you have a folding kayak, traveling with a kayak is extremely cumbersome, and renting one can quickly get expensive. Most rental companies charge at least $45 per day, usually more, for a single kayak.

Whether you choose a leisurely approach to kayaking or want to make the experience as close to your own camping trip as possible is up to you. Neither choice is right or wrong.

Another consideration particular to water sports is the necessity of traveling in groups. Because a simple tip into the water can turn life-threatening in minutes. (Alaska's water in July, for instance, averages 48°F–58°F, depending on the location. By comparison, the water temperature in Baja California at that time of year is 80°F–86°F.) If you are a solo kayaker, you may consider traveling with a guide if for no other reason than the safety in numbers.

That said, we believe a kayaker with reasonably good skills can easily arrange his or her own trip in Alaska. Many kayaking locations here cater to these independent travelers, and locals can offer advice on specific routes and places that allow for the most enjoyment with the least amount of risk. The trips we suggest in this chapter, with the exception of the Katmai Coast trip, are all easily arranged on your own.

▲ Alaska's Best Kayaking

GLACIER BAY

Region Southeast Alaska.	**Best time of year to go** June–Sept.
Distance Infinite options.	**Traffic level** Moderate.
Difficulty ★★★.	**Facilities** Required camper orientation,
Suitable for kids? Yes.	visitor station with nautical charts,
Time to paddle 3–10 days is ideal.	and other limited book supplies.

PADDLING SUMMARY   Some of the best protected-waterway paddling in the state, with great lush forests, deep fjords, and open beaches for camping. There are also paddling opportunities among the icebergs, with proper precautions, of course. Routes can be easily accessed just a few miles from the Glacier Bay National Park visitor center or as far away as 50 or 60 miles.

DIRECTIONS   Access to Glacier Bay is by small plane, usually from Ketchikan or Juneau. **Alaska Airlines** (800-426-0333; **alaskaair.com**) provides daily jet service from Seattle via Juneau to Gustavus during the summer visitor season. The Gustavus airport is 10 miles by road from park headquarters at Bartlett Cove. Shuttles usually are available.

PADDLING DESCRIPTION   Glacier Bay is perhaps one of the best places for kayaking in Alaska, which also means that you will be sharing the land with many other kayakers enjoying this wonderful Southeast Alaska park. However, remember that Alaska is a *huge* place, and here the term *crowded* often can be translated into "We saw 10 people during our week on the water."

Actually, it's quite possible that you will encounter more than 10 people at the height of the kayaking season in Glacier Bay, but you can still have a wonderfully blissful experience. The infrastructure in Glacier Bay is such that planning your own trip is quite simple. A concessionaire within the park helps plan trips, offers shuttles, and rents kayaks (see Resources, below). With their help, your trip will be relatively hassle-free.

Be prepared for wilderness camping conditions, wildlife encounters, and finicky weather. Southeast Alaska can be rainy and foggy, making for cold, wet conditions even in summer. Temperatures in the summer range from a dry, warm 70°F to cool, wet, and windy weather in the 50s.

Glacier Bay National Park is gorgeous, with snow-capped mountain ranges rising 15,000 feet and higher and coastal beaches that offer some of the most protected kayaking in the state. There are receding glaciers, complex tide pools, deep fjords, and long valleys.

The most popular areas for kayaking are **Bartlett Cove** and the **Beardslee Islands,** which make for great two- to three-day adventures, and the **West Arm** and **Muir Inlet,** which are farther out and offer a glimpse of tidewater glaciers. These trips are in the 5- to 10-day range.

TRAVELER'S TIP

▶ Experienced Glacier Bay paddlers can handle the open water alone if they understand the conditions, but the real risk is the constant flow of cruise ships and pleasure boats. The largest ships can barely make out a kayak, so always paddle on the defensive, assuming they do not see you. We prefer taking a water taxi across because it eliminates the open-water paddle, which is just a lot of work, really!

Resources

▶ All of Glacier Bay is included in **NOAA Nautical Chart 17318** (available at **nauticalcharts.noaa.gov/mcd/ccatalogs.htm**). **U.S. Geological Survey** (USGS) maps also are helpful (check with one of the **Alaska Public Lands Information Centers** listed in Part Three on page 62, or go to **usgs.gov** and click on "Maps, Imagery, and Publications"). Tide tables are provided at no charge at the **Bartlett Cove Visitor Information Station** (907-697-2627) during the required camper orientation.

▶ The nonprofit education organization **Alaska Geographic** offers several books that focus solely on Glacier Bay National Park and Preserve. *Adventure Kayaking: Trips in Glacier Bay* by Don Skillman is worth checking out if you want to read about your route in great detail ($12.95; **alaskageographic .org**). Limited copies are available at the Bartlett Cove Information Station. The book is available locally at the **Glacier Bay Alaska Natural History Association** (907-697-2635).

▶ **Glacier Bay Sea Kayaks** (907-697-2257; **glacierbayseakayaks.com**) is the kayak-rental concessionaire in the park. They also lead the required backcountry camper orientations and can help arrange water taxis for drop-offs and pick-ups. Kayak rentals range from $45 per day for a single to $60 per day for an expedition-sized double kayak. The rates are slightly less for rentals of 10 days or longer. Rental and transportation outfits in Gustavus include **Glacier Bay Lodge and Tours** (888-229-8687; **visitglacierbay.com**), which organizes rentals for its guests and the **Whisper Marine Water Taxi** (907-697-2409 or 907-259-9205; **douglasogilvy.com/taxi.htm**).

▶ Visitor information is available at the **Gustavus Visitors Association** (907-697-2454; **gustavusak.com** or **gustavus.com**).

▶ The **Southeast Alaska Discovery Center** in Ketchikan (50 Main St., Ketchikan 99901; 907-228-6220; **alaskacenters.gov/ketchikan.cfm**) can help with trip planning in other regions of Southeast Alaska.

▶ Taxi service in and around Gustavus is available through **TLC Taxi** (907-697-2239). They can accommodate kayaks.

▶ *Trails Illustrated* has a map of Glacier Bay National Park, Number 255 ($9.95; available through **Alaska Geographic** or at the Bartlett Cove Visitor Information Station; **alaskageographic.org**).

Glacier Bay—Southeast-area Outfitters

▶ **ALASKA MOUNTAIN GUIDES AND CLIMBING SCHOOL** » *Haines* 800-766-3396; **alaskamountainguides.com**. Offers the ultimate in versatile sporting adventures. The company's experienced guides offer sea-kayaking trips up the Inside Passage, in Lynn Canal out of Haines, and in Glacier Bay. No experience is necessary for these one- to seven-day trips; prices range $85–$2,200.

▶ **ALASKA ON THE HOME SHORE COASTAL WILDERNESS ADVENTURES »** *Deming, Washington, and Glacier Bay* 800-287-7063 or 360-738-2239; **home shore.com.** Home Shore offers three memorable kayaking adventure routes in the Sitka and Petersburg areas and up the Inside Passage, giving you alternative destinations to Glacier Bay. Focusing on wildlife, especially whale watching, guides will take you gliding past lush Admiralty Island, historical Baranof Island, and scenic Chichagof Island. This option is an upscale version of kayak camping because it includes lodging in a cozy stateroom aboard Home Shore's adventure ship. The eight-day trip starts at $3,600 per person for groups of four or more.

▶ **SOUTHEAST EXPOSURE ALASKA SEA KAYAKING ADVENTURES »** *Ketchikan* 907-225-8829; **southeastexposure.com.** Since 1986, Southeast Exposure has been taking guests on some great trips in the area, from scenic no-experience-necessary trips through Clover Passage out of Ketchikan to expeditions in Misty Fjords National Monument, another kayaking jewel in Southeast Alaska. They also offer tours through the rainforest trees via zip lines and ropes, but they're mostly geared to cruise-ship passengers. Trips range from 6 hours to four days and $125–$850.

▶ **SOUTHEAST SEA KAYAKS »** *Ketchikan* 800-287-1607 or 907-225-1258; **kayak ketchikan.com.** This operation doesn't go to Glacier Bay—our favorite kayak-ing destination in Southeast—but it comes close, with trips to second-best Misty Fjords, out of Ketchikan. There are half-day, full-day, and overnight kay-ak excursions in and around Misty Fjords National Monument. Or take five days to explore Misty Fjords in depth. These trips are designed for novice and experienced paddlers and focus on the scenery and wildlife of the area. The weekend trip is $899, and the five-day Misty Fjords trip costs $1,599.

KACHEMAK BAY

Region Southcentral Coastal Alaska.	**Best time of year to go** June–Sept.
Distance You choose.	**Traffic level** Moderate–heavy.
Difficulty ★★.	**Facilities** Established campsites,
Suitable for kids? Yes.	private lodge options, public-use
Time to paddle 3–5 days.	cabins, marked trailheads.

PADDLING SUMMARY   **Kachemak Bay State Park** is one of the jewels of the Kenai Peninsula, with glaciers and snowcapped mountains dipping dramatically to coastal waters that creep into inlets, shaded coves, and wide bays. It's a great place for wildlife watching and exploring in protected waters.

DIRECTIONS   Kachemak Bay is off the coast of **Homer,** a seaside community at the tip of the Kenai Peninsula at the end of the Sterling Highway. From Anchorage, drive approximately 225 miles south on the Seward Highway, then the Sterling Highway. Park at the Homer Spit long-term parking area, which we have found to be relatively safe. You can also get there by air from Anchorage aboard **Alaska Airlines** commuter flights (800-426-0333; **alaskaair.com**).

PADDLING DESCRIPTION   Many exciting coves and bays make great kayaking destinations in Homer, including **Sadie Cove, Otter Cove,** and **Tutka Bay.** We are going to describe Tutka Bay, but pull out a map and take a look yourself; there are myriad options.

Tutka Bay is 9 miles across Kachemak Bay to the south of Homer and has only about 40 year-round residents; you will spot homes and cabins tucked in the woods as you paddle along the coves and lagoons in this bay. The area looks dramatic, with virgin forests and cascading waterfalls visible from a distance. The tidepooling is terrific, and we have enjoyed many a clam and mussel plucked from the beaches at low tide. Although people live here, no stores or facilities are in the area.

For a nice four-day paddle, get dropped off at the head of the bay, at a protected beach—appropriately called Kayak Beach, just across from **Tutka Bay Wilderness Lodge.** You can set up camp in the woods and spend the day paddling around the mouth of the bay and peeking into **Little Tutka Bay** when the tide is right.

On day two, you can paddle deeper into the bay, stopping at the privately operated Tutka fish hatchery at **Tutka Lagoon.** The best time to go into the area is at high tide, when the water is deep—get caught there at mid- to low tide when the shoals are exposed, and you'll have to wait a while to get out. The Tutka hatchery, once managed by the Cook Inlet Aquaculture Association, produced pink salmon, which returned to Tutka Creek at

TRAVELER'S TIP

▶ Camping in Tutka Bay is generally wherever you can find a clear spot, but be sure to avoid any beaches that are near homes, as you could be trespassing.

spawning time. Today it is privately operated. The bay is still the most consistent producer of pink salmon in the area, so if you want to fish on light tackle, this will be a fun endeavor. The first two weeks of July are the peak.

Several established public camping areas are in Tutka Bay, past the hatchery. One is about two-thirds into the bay, on a spit of land jutting into the water, but it has seen heavy use. If you choose to camp here, beware of bold squirrels that will filch your food, and avoid building campfires unless you can use driftwood. The trees have been scavenged. Closer to the hatchery, and marked by a small gravel beach and orange triangular trailhead sign, is a camping spot at the base of the Tutka Lake Trail, which makes a great day hike if you get socked in by high seas and can't kayak.

Alaska State Parks, through an agreement with Nomad Yurts, offers six yurts for rent at various locations in Kachemak State Park, all within 100 yards of the coastline. Each yurt has bunks, a woodstove, and a table and chairs, and each sleeps a maximum of five people. One is at Kayak Beach, another at the Tutka Lake trailhead campsite. Wood for the stove is provided (907-235-0132 or 907-299-1680; **nomadshelter.com**). Rentals are $65 per day.

On day three, leave your tent (or yurt) site intact and take a base-camp paddle to the mouth of the bay. Hop out for a walk in the woods or paddle the opposite side of the bay for a different perspective. Camp in the same spot.

On day four, return to your original location for a prearranged meeting with your water taxi. You will probably have time to explore Sadie Cove, to the north, by popping out into Eldred Passage and swinging into the next bay. Only attempt this in good weather and if you are confident in your paddling abilities, as day winds can whip up the water.

Communications, if you are traveling with a marine radio, are by VHF Channel 16, CB Channel 13. A telephone is at **Tutka Bay Wilderness Lodge** (see Resources, right), although it should be used only in emergencies. Overall, the paddling in Tutka Bay and the vicinity is easy, assuming the weather is good. Even if there are high seas, the coves and lagoons stay protected and offer paddling close to shore, but use good judgment: one flip and you can be in danger quickly.

Resources

▶ **Homer Ocean Charters** (800-426-6212 or 907-235-6212; **homerocean.com**) can get you safely across the bay, which we recommend. Even in good water, there is a lot of boat traffic, both commercial fishing and recreational, and you can get swamped easily. A round-trip is $65, with discounts for larger groups and children.

▶ Call the **Marine Advisory Program** (907-269-7640) to check on shellfish-harvesting conditions, or ask at local charter offices. Only clams on the south side of Kachemak Bay are tested for paralytic shellfish poisoning (discussed in the beginning of this chapter). Clamming in all other locations is at your own risk. Kachemak Bay is generally safe.

▶ **NOAA Nautical Chart 16645 for Tutka Bay and Tutka Bay Lagoon** is available at **nauticalcharts.noaa.gov/mcd/ccatalogs.htm.** Use the Seldovia Tide Tables for Tutka Bay.

▶ To insert some luxury into your Tutka Bay adventure, book a few nights at the posh **Tutka Bay Wilderness Lodge** (907-274-2710; **withinthewild.com/tutka-bay -lodge**), a remote four-star retreat that offers the finest in rooms, food, amenities, and overall spoiling. Kayaks are on-site, and you can paddle guided or on your own. Rates are steep, beginning at $885 per person per night, but this is a place you won't forget.

Kachemak Bay Outfitters

▶ **ALASKA KAYAK SCHOOL** ➤ 907-235-2090; **alaskakayakschool.com.** This outfit not only serves as an educational center but also offers adventures to locals and visitors alike. It can provide great advice on the proper gear to use when in Alaska, and might even have it for sale in its used-items collection. Schedules vary according to the teaching schedule.

▶ **TRUE NORTH ADVENTURES** ➤ 907-235-0708; **truenorthkayak.com.** This outfit will take you to Eldred Passage near Tutka Bay for guided kayaking. Half-day trips start at $105. All-day trips are $150. Overnighters are available for $375 or $495 for three days. This outfit is one of the most experienced in Homer, and the guides are friendly and knowledgeable about the area. They also rent kayaks for do-it-yourselfers; $45 for singles, $65 for doubles.

KATMAI COAST

Region The Bush.	**Time to paddle** 6–10 days.
Distance 30–50 miles.	**Best time of year to go** June–Sept.
Difficulty ★★★★.	**Traffic level** Light.
Suitable for kids? No.	**Facilities** None; camping on beaches, islands.

PADDLING SUMMARY   **Katmai National Park** comprises 4.7 million acres and hundreds of miles of coastline for exploration, with chances to view the more than 2,000 brown bears that frequent the area. This is one of the most unobtrusive ways to watch these creatures in their natural habitat.

DIRECTIONS   Access is by small plane from Kodiak, Homer, or King Salmon, where park headquarters is located. **Alaska Airlines** provides daily flights into these towns (800-426-0333; **alaskaair.com**). Driving to Homer and flying from there is the cheapest option because it eliminates the flight to King Salmon or Kodiak.

PADDLING DESCRIPTION   The coast of Katmai National Park is one of the most ecologically diverse areas in Alaska, and it is an especially nice place to kayak because the chances are good that you will see more bears than humans on this adventure. The beaches along Katmai are home to some of the largest concentrations of brown bears in the world, and viewing them from the comfort of a kayak that is safely out of their way is a truly unforgettable experience. Katmai also is home to hundreds of species of migratory birds such as puffins, cormorants, kittiwakes, and murres. Whales and porpoises are common too.

> **TRAVELER'S TIP**
>
> ▶ The Katmai Coast also has active volcanoes and wonderful hiking.

The mountains of Katmai provide a dramatic backdrop, with 15 active volcanoes sprouting up here and there. This is why the park also is home to a region known as the **Valley of 10,000 Smokes.** While Prince William Sound and Southeast Alaska are certainly gorgeous, the privacy that one feels in Katmai is simply unsurpassed, and that is why this trip is high in our best-of selection. Even in Alaska, it sometimes can be hard to find total solitude. Not many people come here to kayak, but a lot of them come to see bears—about 900 applied for permits to the nearby McNeil River Bear Viewing Area in 2006, but only 183 permits were issued. We say you can do both and get away from those crowds.

Katmai is a 4.7-million-acre national park and preserve, home to more than 2,000 brown bears, which congregate by the dozens during salmon-spawning season to feed on the carcasses of the nutrient-rich fish. They usually congregate in **Brooks Camp** along the Brooks River and the **Naknek Lake** and **Brooks Lake** shorelines. However, the bears' range goes beyond this region, and they can be found all along the 480-mile Katmai Coast feeding on clams, crabs, and an occasional whale carcass.

The paddling is excellent from **Kukak Bay** to **Geographic Harbor** and beyond. Plenty of camping is available along the beaches and islands on this stretch of coast. Explore the countless fjords, islands, bays, and rocky headlands; all along the way are views of the volcanoes.

Resources

▶ For more information on **Katmai National Park,** contact Field Headquarters (1 King Salmon Mall, King Salmon 99613; 907-246-3305) or Administrative Headquarters (4230 University Dr., Suite 311, Anchorage 99508-4626). The Web site is **nps.gov/katm.**

▶ **NOAA Nautical Chart 16603** covers Kukak Bay and Kukak Point; 16576 and 16580 cover Geographic Bay. Available at **nauticalcharts.noaa.gov/mcd/ ccatalogs.htm.**

Katmai Coast Outfitters

▶ **ALASKA ALPINE ADVENTURES »** 877-525-2577 or 907-781-2253; **alaskaalpine adventures.com.** The company specializes in this awesome Katmai Coast paddle, which is truly a once-in-a-lifetime opportunity. Their 12-day trip includes nine days of paddling in the remote national park. The cost is $3,995.

▶ **LIFETIME ADVENTURES »** 800-952-8624; **lifetimeadventures.net.** This company offers a guided seven-day trip kayaking the Savonoski Loop, a high-level kayak trip that will allow you to glimpse all manner of wildlife. The rate is $2,300 per person, which is a steal, but that doesn't include food, so be sure to factor in that added cost.

PRINCE WILLIAM SOUND

Region Southcentral Coastal Alaska.	**Best time of year to go** June–Sept.
Distance Infinite options.	**Traffic level** Moderate close to towns.
Difficulty ★★★★.	**Facilities** Some public-use cabins and
Suitable for kids? In some places.	camping areas; some marked trail-
Time to paddle 3–15 days is ideal;	heads onshore.
good location for expeditions.	

PADDLING SUMMARY   One of the largest areas for kayak exploration, this region of the state is a paddler's paradise. Glaciers, forested islands on inland hiking trails, excellent fishing, and flat-calm protected waterways are just some of the highlights. A particularly active place for wildlife.

DIRECTIONS   There are several ways to access Prince William Sound. By vehicle, drive from Anchorage east on the Glenn Highway and south on the Richardson Highway until you reach the town of Valdez, at the head of Prince William Sound. Or drive south from Anchorage on the Seward Highway to the Portage Valley Road through the Anton Anderson Memorial Tunnel, which spits you out at the sound in the tiny town of Whittier. You can also fly into Valdez or Cordova on **Alaska Airlines** (800-426-0333; **alaskaair.com**) or take the **Alaska Marine Highway** ferry system from points south (800-642-0066; **ferry-alaska.com**).

TRAVELER'S TIP

▶ Camping in Prince William Sound is relatively easy, although you may have to search for good sites in some locations. It's a good idea to get maps ahead of time and estimate your route before leaving. Even if you plan to travel alone, contact local outfitters for their advice.

PADDLING DESCRIPTION   If anything is synonymous with Prince William Sound, it is kayaking, and for good reason. From Valdez to Cordova to Whittier, this vast body of water at the northern tip of the Gulf of Alaska offers some of the most protected waterways in South-central Coastal Alaska.

Surrounded to the west by the **Kenai Mountains** and the east by the **Chugach Mountains,** the area is literally bounded by peaks. Its 15,000 square miles are all open to exploration. There are whales, sea otters, seals, sea lions, and more seabirds than you can imagine. On land, there are Dall sheep, foxes, mountain goats, deer, and plenty of bears (mostly black).

Prince William Sound lends itself to longer kayaking expeditions, although overnight and day trips are easily accomplished as well. It's just that there is so much to see that it is hard to resist the "just around the next corner" mentality. You could do that for days and still only scrape the surface of what this area has to offer.

The best places from which to launch a Prince William Sound trip are **Whittier** and **Valdez** because the easy road access eliminates part of the expense. However, don't overlook trips that leave from **Cordova,** the other primary Prince William Sound community, accessible only by ferry or airplane. If privacy and solitude are your goals, you might consider a Cordova-based trip.

Columbia Glacier is the most impressive of Prince William Sound's many glaciers, but paddling among the bergs near any of the glaciers is an awe-inspiring feat. (Never approach too closely, though—calving ice can flip a kayak before you can blink.)

Resources

▶ Kayak rentals are available in **Cordova, Valdez,** and **Whittier** (see Outfitters listing, next page).

▶ *Kayaking and Camping in Prince William Sound,* by Paul Twardock, features maps and sketches of many of the trips outlined in the book. Twardock is a well-respected paddler in Alaska with more than 20 years of guiding and kayaking experience. The book is $18.95 and, along with other books and maps on the region, is available through **Alaska Geographic (alaskageographic.org)**.

▶ A half-dozen public-use cabins, managed by **Chugach National Forest, Glacier Ranger District** (907-783-3242), are located throughout Prince William Sound. They cost $25–$45 per night and must be reserved in advance either over the phone or online (877-444-6777; **recreation.gov**). Reservations can be made up to 180 days (six months) in advance of the first night's stay. For details about the cabins, visit **fs.fed.us/r10/chugach/cabins/index.html.** Visit this site before making your reservations online or over the phone, because the agents at **recreation.gov** are located somewhere in the Lower 48 states and don't know much about the cabins. The **Alaska Public Lands Information Center** in Anchorage can also help (605 W. 4th Ave., Suite 105, Anchorage 99501; 866-869-6887 or 907-644-3661; **alaskacenters.gov/anchorage.cfm**).

▶ More information on the Prince William Sound communities is available through the **Cordova Chamber of Commerce** (907-424-7260; **cordovachamber .com**), the **Valdez Convention and Visitors Bureau** (800-770-5954; **valdezalaska .org**), and the **Greater Whittier Chamber of Commerce** (**whittieralaskachamber .org**). Or read up on Prince William Sound in Part Thirteen (see page 343).

Prince William Sound Outfitters

▶ **ALASKA SEA KAYAKERS »** *Whittier* 877-472-2534 or 907-472-2534; **alaskasea kayakers.com.** Offers day and multiday trips in addition to kayaking, rentals, and kayaking classes. We like this outfit because the guides take you to areas of the sound not explored by most other companies. For a group of four on a mother ship tour, the price is $3,000 per day for up to four people. Alaska Sea Kayakers also is one of the few companies that rent fiberglass doubles, if that is your preference ($130 for two days).

▶ **ANADYR ADVENTURES »** *Valdez* 800-TO-KAYAK or 907-835-2814; **anadyr adventures.com.** Anadyr has something for everyone. This Prince William Sound company offers mother ship adventures, lodge-based trips, multiday paddles, and day trips in some of the most spectacular water in Alaska. Also offered are custom trips, youth eco-tours, and theme trips focusing on natural history, ecology, and other fascinating topics. Guides will take you to a variety of bays, glaciers, islands, and waterways within Prince William Sound. Other activities are also available, and we like the company's family-friendly environment. Tours range from 3 hours to seven days. The popular "mother ship" tours start at $425 per person per day.

▶ **CORDOVA COASTAL OUTFITTERS »** *Cordova* (at the harbor, in the brightly colored boathouse). 907-424-7424; **cdvcoastal.com.** The company rents kayaks and offers guided half-day, day, and custom kayak tours to Orca Cove and beyond. Kayaks are $45 per day for singles, $65 for doubles. Guided trips start at $75.

▶ **EXPOSURE ALASKA »** *Anchorage–Prince William Sound* 800-956-6422 or 907-761-3761; **exposurealaska.com.** A Prince William Sound trip is among this company's many excursions. No paddling experience is necessary for these trips, which start at $2,275 per person and include amenities designed to make the trip comfortable and enjoyable for each paddler.

▶ **PANGAEA ADVENTURES »** *Valdez* 800-660-9637 or 907-835-8442; **alaska summer.com.** Pangaea takes paddlers on day trips and kayaking-camping trips out of Prince William Sound. A 3-hour tour costs $55 and takes in Duck Flats, one of the calmest and most unspoiled spots in the area. Wildlife viewing and scenery are phenomenal, and guides will even give you a natural-history lesson. The company's eight-day Whales and Ice Kayak Camp is $1,995 per person and includes trips to Icy Bay and Knight Island, two great areas for paddling among the whales. Pangaea also offers a plethora of other adventures, including numerous multisport trips.

▶ **PRINCE WILLIAM SOUND KAYAK CENTER »** *Whittier* 877-472-2452 or 907-472-2452; **pwskayakcenter.com.** This longtime outfit will teach classes, rent boats, and escort you on your first kayaking outing without adding guide charges—just to make sure you are comfortable. They are one of the most highly respected companies in the field, so you can't go wrong with their trips. Rentals start at $80 per day for doubles and $50 for singles, but the price goes down for added days. Day tours start at $160 and get cheaper the more people you have in your party (as low as $70 per person if six people sign up).

RESURRECTION BAY

Region Southcentral Coastal Alaska.	**Best time of year to go** June–Sept.
Distance Infinite options.	**Traffic level** Light–moderate.
Difficulty ★★★.	**Facilities** Some public-use cabins,
Suitable for kids? Some areas.	private cabins, and camping areas;
Time to paddle 3–7 days is ideal.	some marked trailheads onshore.

PADDLING SUMMARY   Resurrection Bay surrounds the coastal community of **Seward,** on the Kenai Peninsula, and is part of **Kenai Fjords National Park,** one of the most-visited parks in the state, as well as **Caines Head State Recreation Area.** This glacier-studded waterway is also home to some of the best whale watching in Alaska.

DIRECTIONS   From Anchorage, drive south on the Seward Highway approximately 127 miles until the road ends in Seward. Long-term parking is available by the boat harbor, and water taxis are easily available to take you across to the more-protected waters. Or launch from **Lowell Point,** 3.5 miles south of town, where all the kayaking outfits are located. Regular flights don't go to Seward, but a landing strip is in town for charter flights. The **Alaska Railroad** travels to Seward from Anchorage (800-544-0552 or 907-265-2494; **alaskarailroad.com**). Rates are $119 round-trip for adults; kayaks cost extra, but we recommend getting your kayak in Seward to

TRAVELER'S TIP

▶ If kayaking with whales is one of your goals, Resurrection Bay is the place to go. It is also one of the least-expensive trips on our list because of its proximity to Anchorage. Be forewarned, though. The bay can get ultra-windy, so this is an area best suited for very experienced paddlers. If you take a water taxi to more-secluded areas within the bay, the paddling will be easier.

save the hassle of loading a boat in Anchorage. The **Alaska Marine Highway** ferry system travels from points south (800-642-0066; **ferryalaska.com**).

PADDLING DESCRIPTION   The options for paddling in Resurrection Bay are about as endless as the sea feels once you're out there. Resurrection Bay— which includes **Kenai Fjords National Park, Caines Head State Recreation Area,** and **Resurrection Bay State Marine Parks**—lies on the southeast coast of Alaska's Kenai Peninsula, capped by the **Harding Ice Field,** the largest ice field within U.S. borders. Otters, puffins, bears, moose, and mountain goats are just a few of the creatures that can be spotted here. Glaciers are everywhere, and whales breach often. This is one of the best places to spot the gray whale on its annual migration from Baja California in Mexico.

You can choose protected bays and inlets or venture to the outer coast for some high seas—this is one of the best places for seasoned kayakers to visit.

Popular destinations include **Fox Island, Thumb Cove, Sunny Cove, Humpy Cove, Kayaker's Cove,** and **Kenai Fjords National Park.** State-park cabin rentals are available at **Thumb Cove State Marine Park** and **Caines Head State Recreation Area.** U.S. Forest Service cabin rentals are available in the **Aialik Bay** area of Kenai Fjords National Park.

The climate of the park is maritime, meaning it rains often and is windy most of the time. Dress in layers in gear that can protect you from ultra-wet conditions.

Resources

▸ Camping is allowed in most areas of **Kenai Fjords National Park.** Three public-use cabins at **Aialik, Holgate,** and **Northarm,** along the Kenai Fjords coast, are available on a reservation basis and accessible by boat or floatplane; kayaking trips can be launched from the cabins. For reservations, contact the **Alaska Public Lands Information Center** in Anchorage (866-869-6887 or 907-644-3661). For more information on Kenai Fjords, contact the **Seward Information Center** (1212 4th Ave.; 907-224-2132 or 907-224-7500; **nps.gov/kefj**), which offers maps, publications, videos, interpretive displays, and other helpful resources.

▸ **Caines Head State Recreation Area** and **Resurrection Bay State Marine Parks** information: 907-262-5581; **dnr.alaska.gov/parks/units/caineshd.htm.** Cabin rentals can be arranged online at **dnr.alaska.gov/parks/cabins/onlineres.htm** or in person at the **DNR Public Information Center** (550 W. 7th Ave., Suite 1260, Anchorage 99501-3557; 907-269-8400).

▸ **NOAA Nautical Chart 16682 for Resurrection Bay** is available at **nauticalcharts .noaa.gov/mcd/ccatalogs.htm.**

▸ For more details on Seward, see page 339 of Part Thirteen, Southcentral Coastal Alaska.

Resurrection Bay Outfitters

▸ **LIQUID ADVENTURES »** *Lowell Point* (3.5 miles south of Seward) 888-325-2925; **liquid-adventures.com.** Explores the waters around Seward, including Holgate Arm, Kenai Fjords, and Northwestern Lagoon. This is our first choice in guides for its laid-back demeanor and years of experience. The main guide is an expert fisherman and can help you land that fish, big or small. From 3 hours to five days, Liquid Adventures teaches paddlers about the area's landscape, wildlife, and history. The company even offers customized trips upon request. Prices range $69–$1,549 per person.

▸ **MILLER'S LANDING »** *Lowell Point* 866-541-5739 or 907-224-5739; **millers landingak.com.** Kayak rentals are $45 per day for singles, $50 for doubles. An overnight trip to Thumb Cove is $315 per person. An overnight to Kayaker's Cove (one of our favorite Resurrection Bay areas) is $335. Longer tours also are available.

▸ **SUNNY COVE SEA KAYAKING CO. »** *Lowell Point* 800-770-9119 or 907-224-4426; **sunnycove.com.** Sunny Cove takes you to Lowell Point, Fox Island, and Kenai Fjords National Park on day trips or overnight and multiday kayaking adventures. Prices range $65–$1,599 per person.

SHUYAK ISLAND

Region Southcentral Coastal Alaska.	**Time to paddle** 3–5 days.
Distance 35–40 miles.	**Best time of year to go** June–Sept.
Difficulty ★★★.	**Traffic level** Very light.
Suitable for kids? Yes.	**Facilities** Four public-use cabins, ranger station; kayak-rental facility.

PADDLING SUMMARY   Shuyak Island has the most extensive protected-waterway kayaking on all the Kodiak Archipelago. Access to the outer coast provides more-challenging kayaking for experienced paddlers and offers stunning scenery of the forested island and the Katmai Coast, across Shelikof Strait.

DIRECTIONS   Shuyak is 40 minutes north of Kodiak, accessible by boat or plane. There is also access via Homer, a 50-minute flight from the north. Access by water taxi is available from Kodiak but not from Homer.

PADDLING DESCRIPTION   Kayakers the world over recognize **Shuyak Island State Park** as one of the best kayaking destinations in Alaska. It is the northernmost of the islands that make up the Kodiak Archipelago, with the state park composing most of the island's 47,000 acres. The park provides access to an intricate maze of sheltered bays, channels, and inlets and has a limited but impressive trail system for hiking, as well as fishing opportunities in just about every lake, stream, or saltwater location (especially in August and September, when the silver salmon are spawning). There is an infinite variety of seabirds, otters, whales, harbor seals, sea lions, and Dall porpoises. Even some of Kodiak's famed brown bears wander the island.

Visitors can tent-camp nearly anywhere on the island or rent one of four $60- to $75-per-night public-use cabins. There is a ranger station at one end of the park and a place to pick up your rented kayak (rental must be arranged in advance), but other than that, there are no facilities. Groceries and other supplies must be purchased in Kodiak or Homer.

Resources

▶ For more information about **Shuyak Island State Park,** contact the Kodiak District Office (1400 Abercrombie Dr., Kodiak 99615; 907-486-6339; **dnr .alaska.gov/parks/units/kodiak/shuyak.htm**). You must reserve cabins in advance. *Important:* Because Kodiak's weather is notorious for changing quickly, work a few extra days into your itinerary in case your plane cannot pick you up as planned.

▶ **NOAA Nautical Chart 16604 for Shuyak and Afognak islands** is available at **nauticalcharts.noaa.gov/mcd/ccatalogs.htm.**

▶ The best places to get supplies in Kodiak before leaving are **Safeway** (2685 Mill Bay Rd.; 907-486-6811) and **Alaska Commercial Co.** (111 W. Rezanof Dr., 907-486-5761). In Homer, get supplies at **Safeway** (90 Sterling Hwy., 907-235-2408).

▶ Our number-one choice for an air charter from Kodiak is **SeaHawk Air** (800-770-4295 or 907-486-8282; **seahawkair.com**). From Homer, we recommend **Bald Mountain Air** (800-478-7969 or 907-235-7969; **baldmountainair.com**).

▶ For more details on planning your trip from Kodiak or Homer, see Part Thirteen, Southcentral Coastal Alaska (page 326).

Shuyak Island Outfitter

▶ **WILDERNESS BIRDING ADVENTURES »** 907-694-7442; **wildernessbirding .com.** This is the only outfit that consistently offers trips to Shuyak Island, and they combine birding with kayaking for a well-rounded adventure. Check with them first to see if Shuyak is on their current year's itinerary, as they switch up from year to year. The rate is approximately $2,600 for seven days and includes local air and ground transportation (you get to Alaska on your own), kayaks, food, cooking gear, and guide service. The trip combines cabin and tent camping.

PART TEN
RIVER RUNNING

ALASKA BOASTS MORE than 3,000 rivers, many of which are suitable for running in canoes, kayaks, or, most popularly, rafts. These adventures range from leisurely float trips to whitewater adrenaline rushes. It doesn't matter where you go in the state—from Southeast Alaska to the Far North—there are rivers to be explored.

We think all of Alaska's rivers are beautiful, but 25 are considered so spectacular that they have been named National Wild and Scenic Rivers; only Oregon has more such designations.

This chapter introduces you to just a small sampling—the best of the best—of Alaska's rivers. We've provided two sections, one for splashy day trips that can be enjoyed in a few hours or a full day, and multiday float trips that can take as long as 12 days. Our river descriptions are brief and designed to pique your interest in one or another based on a given overview. As any river runner knows, once you've selected your river of choice, it helps immensely to get detailed descriptions, topographic maps, hints from local experts, and up-to-date weather conditions so you can accurately assess the river's safety.

To that end, we offer additional resources that can help make your river-running trip a success. The more information you have before your trip, the better prepared you'll be for any possible surprises.

▲ Checklist for Success

✔ **OBTAIN CURRENT INFORMATION ON THE RIVER YOU PLAN TO PADDLE.** Water levels can change drastically, even with small amounts of rainfall or snowmelt. Bush pilots, park rangers, and local outfitters are the best sources of information because they are on the rivers regularly. Another good information source is the Anchorage-based group **Knik Canoers and Kayakers** (**kck.org**).

✔ **PROTECT AGAINST HYPOTHERMIA.** Many of Alaska's rivers are glacially fed. (Need we mention that they're cold?) Always wear a wet- or dry suit and appropriate footwear on rivers with Class III rapids or above. Your chances of falling in are higher on some rivers than others, so it's best to play it safe. Ask at your local kayak or raft-rental facility for water-wear rentals.

✔ **ALWAYS WEAR A HELMET AND A LIFE VEST** that is beefy enough to hold you up under the pressure of river water. (Lighter personal flotation devices are OK for lakes and other calm waters.)

✔ **CARRY BASIC FIRST-AID ITEMS,** including bandages to patch up minor cuts as well as any specific medications that may be needed for anyone in your traveling party.

✔ **PACK A WHISTLE, FLARES,** or something else that can be used as an SOS device in an emergency.

✔ **DON'T GO ALONE.** Always run rivers with at least one other person, and stay within shouting or whistling distance. A two-person rescue is much easier than a self-rescue.

alaska river running @ a glance

American Creek

REGION ›› The Bush
DISTANCE ›› 50 miles
TRAFFIC ›› Light
DIFFICULTY ›› Class I–III
TRIP LENGTH ›› 4–9 days
SUITABLE FOR KIDS? ›› Yes
GUIDE SUGGESTED? ›› Highly recommended

Canning River

REGION ›› The Bush
DISTANCE ›› 125 miles
TRAFFIC ›› Light
DIFFICULTY ›› Class II–III
TRIP LENGTH ›› 7–12 days
SUITABLE FOR KIDS? ›› No
GUIDE SUGGESTED? ›› Highly recommended

Chilkat River

REGION ›› Southeast
DISTANCE ›› 20 miles
TRAFFIC ›› Light–moderate
DIFFICULTY ›› Class I
TRIP LENGTH ›› Day trip
SUITABLE FOR KIDS? ›› Yes
GUIDE SUGGESTED? ›› Recommended

Copper River

REGION ›› Southcentral Coastal, Inland
DISTANCE ›› 100 miles
TRAFFIC ›› Light
DIFFICULTY ›› Class I
TRIP LENGTH ›› 6 days
SUITABLE FOR KIDS? ›› Yes
GUIDE SUGGESTED? ›› Recommended

Eagle River

REGION ›› Southcentral Inland
DISTANCE ›› 8–21 miles
TRAFFIC ›› Moderate
DIFFICULTY ›› Class II–IV
TRIP LENGTH ›› Day trip
SUITABLE FOR KIDS? ›› Some parts
GUIDE SUGGESTED? ›› Recommended

Kenai River

REGION ›› Southcentral Coastal
DISTANCE ›› 18 miles
TRAFFIC ›› Moderate–heavy
DIFFICULTY ›› Class II–III
TRIP LENGTH ›› Day trip
SUITABLE FOR KIDS? ›› Yes
GUIDE SUGGESTED? ›› Recommended

GENERAL RIVER-RUNNING RESOURCES

▶ The **Alaska Kayak School** in Homer (907-235-2090; **alaskakayakschool.com**) can offer advice on whitewater and sea kayaking.

▶ The **Alaska River Forecast Center** in Anchorage (6930 Sand Lake Rd.; 907-266-5160; **aprfc.arh.noaa.gov/data**) tracks water levels and dangers. Check with the center before departing on a trip on your own.

▶ *The Alaska River Guide* by Karen Jettmar outlines 85 waterways worth exploring throughout the state. Updated in 2008, her book is well regarded by locals and is a must-have for any in-depth river trip in Alaska. $17.95; available at **Amazon.com** and **menasharidge.com**.

▲ more alaska river running @ a glance

Lowe River

REGION ›› Southcentral Coastal
DISTANCE ›› 5–25.5 miles
TRAFFIC ›› Light–moderate
DIFFICULTY ›› Class III
TRIP LENGTH ›› Day trip
SUITABLE FOR KIDS? ›› No
GUIDE SUGGESTED? ›› Highly recommended

Matanuska River–Lion Head

REGION ›› Southcentral Inland
DISTANCE ›› 5.3 miles
TRAFFIC ›› Light–moderate
DIFFICULTY ›› Class III–IV
TRIP LENGTH ›› Day trip
SUITABLE FOR KIDS? ›› Yes
GUIDE SUGGESTED? ›› Highly recommended

Nenana River

REGION ›› The Interior
DISTANCE ›› 8–38 miles
TRAFFIC ›› Moderate–heavy
DIFFICULTY ›› Class II–IV
TRIP LENGTH ›› Day trip
SUITABLE FOR KIDS? ›› Some parts
GUIDE SUGGESTED? ›› Recommended

Nizina River

REGION ›› Southcentral Inland
DISTANCE ›› 45 miles
TRAFFIC ›› Light
DIFFICULTY ›› Class II–III
TRIP LENGTH ›› 2–3 days
SUITABLE FOR KIDS? ›› Yes
GUIDE SUGGESTED? ›› Recommended

Sixmile Creek

REGION ›› Southcentral Coastal
DISTANCE ›› 9 miles
TRAFFIC ›› Moderate
DIFFICULTY ›› Class III–V
TRIP LENGTH ›› Day trip
SUITABLE FOR KIDS? ›› No
GUIDE SUGGESTED? ›› Recommended

Tatshenshini-Alsek Rivers

REGION ›› Southeast
DISTANCE ›› 129 miles
TRAFFIC ›› Light
DIFFICULTY ›› Class I–IV
TRIP LENGTH ›› 9–12 days
SUITABLE FOR KIDS? ›› Some parts
GUIDE SUGGESTED? ›› Recommended

▸ *Fast and Cold: A Guide to Alaska Whitewater* by Andrew Embick is a great resource for any paddler intent on sampling Alaska's rivers. Embick was a well-known expert in Alaska on the most challenging whitewater in Southcentral and beyond, completing trips so difficult that some have never been duplicated. The book provides in-depth details of each of the 79 trips outlined. $27.50; available at bookstores in Alaska and on **Amazon.com.**

▸ The Web sites **riverfacts.com** and **americanwhitewater.org** are helpful for getting details on the rivers of your choice.

There are some sports that, because of their inherent risks, are best left to the experts to lead. We believe that river running is one of them. If, however, you are intent on traveling alone, do not use this chapter as your sole source of information during planning: it is meant mainly to discuss our

▲ river-running outfitters @ a glance

Alaska Outdoors

800-320-2494
alaskaoutdoorstours.com

REGION » Southcentral Inland
COST » $$$
SUITABLE FOR KIDS? » Teens
ACTIVITY LEVEL » Moderate–high
TRIP LENGTH » 6 days

Alaska Wilderness Guides

907-345-4470
akwild.com

REGION » Statewide
COST » $$$
SUITABLE FOR KIDS? » No
ACTIVITY LEVEL » Moderate–high
TRIP LENGTH » 7 days/custom

Alaska Rivers Company

888-595-1226
alaskariverscompany.com

REGION » Southcentral Coastal
COST » $$
SUITABLE FOR KIDS? » Yes
ACTIVITY LEVEL » Light–moderate
TRIP LENGTH » Day trip

Alaska Wildland Adventures

800-334-8730 or 907-783-2928
alaskawildland.com

REGION » Southcentral Coastal
COST » $$
SUITABLE FOR KIDS? » Most trips
ACTIVITY LEVEL » Light–moderate
TRIP LENGTH » Day trip

Alaska Trophy Adventures

877-801-2289
alaskatrophyadventures.com

REGION » The Bush
COST » $$$
SUITABLE FOR KIDS? » No
ACTIVITY LEVEL » Moderate–high
TRIP LENGTH » 7 days

Arctic Treks

907-455-6502
arctictreksadventures.com

REGION » The Interior, The Bush
COST » $$$$
SUITABLE FOR KIDS? » Teens
ACTIVITY LEVEL » Moderate–high
TRIP LENGTH » 10 days

Alaska Vistas

866-874-3006 or 907-874-3006
alaskavistas.com

REGION » Southeast
COST » $$$
SUITABLE FOR KIDS? » Varies
ACTIVITY LEVEL » Light–moderate
TRIP LENGTH » 1–9 days

Chilkat Guides

888-292-7789
raftalaska.com

REGION » Southeast
COST » $–$$$$
SUITABLE FOR KIDS? » Varies
ACTIVITY LEVEL » All levels
TRIP LENGTH » 1–12 days

favorite trips based on years of living and playing in Alaska, and these are samplings that just scratch the surface of what is out there. Entire books have been written about running rivers in Alaska—for starters, we suggest reading the ones listed previously before you leave.

more river-running outfitters

Chugach Outdoor Center

866-277-RAFT or 907-277-RAFT
chugachoutdoorcenter.com

REGION ›› Statewide
COST ›› $$
SUITABLE FOR KIDS? ›› Some trips
ACTIVITY LEVEL ›› Moderate–high
TRIP LENGTH ›› 1–7 days

Copper Oar Alaska Adventure Travel

800-523-4453 or 907-554-4453
copperoar.com

REGION ›› Southcentral Inland
COST ›› $$$
SUITABLE FOR KIDS? ›› Yes
ACTIVITY LEVEL ›› Light–moderate
TRIP LENGTH ›› 6 days

Cordova Coastal Outfitters

800-357-5145 or 907-424-7424
cdvcoastal.com

REGION ›› Southcentral Coastal
COST ›› $
SUITABLE FOR KIDS? ›› Yes
ACTIVITY LEVEL ›› All levels
TRIP LENGTH ›› Day trip

Keystone Raft and Kayak Adventures

907-835-2606
alaskawhitewater.com

REGION ›› Southcentral Coastal
COST ›› $–$$$$
SUITABLE FOR KIDS? ›› Varies
ACTIVITY LEVEL ›› All levels
TRIP LENGTH ›› 1–7 days

NOVA River Runners

800-746-5753
novalaska.com

REGION ›› Southcentral Inland
COST ›› $$
SUITABLE FOR KIDS? ›› Varies
ACTIVITY LEVEL ›› Light–moderate
TRIP LENGTH ›› 1–6 days

Wilderness Birding Adventures

907-694-7442
wildernessbirding.com

REGION ›› The Interior/The Bush
COST ›› $$$$
SUITABLE FOR KIDS? ›› Teens
ACTIVITY LEVEL ›› Moderate–high
TRIP LENGTH ›› 12 days

Wilderness River Outfitters

800-252-6581
wildernessriver.com

REGION ›› Southeast
COST ›› $$$
SUITABLE FOR KIDS? ›› Teens
ACTIVITY LEVEL ›› Moderate–high
TRIP LENGTH ›› 11 days

TRAVELER'S TIP

▶ Even if you're an experienced paddler, it can be difficult to read Alaska's often-silty water, and immersion in the colder-than-normal waters can lead to problems much sooner than it would in locations in the Lower 48.

▲ Day Trips

CHILKAT RIVER

Region Haines, Southeast Alaska.	**Suitable for kids?** Yes.
Distance 20 miles.	**Best time of year to go** June–Sept.
Difficulty Class I.	**Traffic level** Light–moderate.
Experience level Beginner.	**Facilities** Established put-ins and takeouts.
Time to paddle 1 day.	

PADDLING SUMMARY   An enjoyable float with little in the way of danger and a lot in the way of scenery. The river flows through the **Chilkat Bald Eagle Preserve,** and wildlife in the area is abundant. Most of the time, the water is silty and runs gray; it is also quite cold.

DIRECTIONS   The put-in for this float actually begins on the **Klehini River,** off Mile 26.3 of the Haines Highway in Southeast Alaska. Travel the first few miles on the Klehini, which eventually feeds into the Chilkat. Follow the Chilkat back toward Haines, about a mile outside of town. For a shorter version, drive to Mile 19 of the Haines Highway and put in at the Chilkat.

TRAVELER'S TIP

▶ The Chilkat River is an ideal destination for families. Swift but stable, this river takes you through pristine country, home to thousands of bald eagles, as well as moose, brown bears, and other wildlife. There are plenty of places to pull over to take a break, enjoy some lunch, and learn about the country.

PADDLING DESCRIPTION   Two rivers, the **Tsirksu** and **Klehini,** drain into the Chilkat, and both are floatable if you want to extend your trip. Many people like to put in on the Klehini River, farther up the Haines Highway, to extend the trip a few more miles, which is what we suggest. For most of the way, the river skirts alongside the highway, so you will not have a total wilderness experience. However, your possibility of viewing wildlife is just as high.

EAGLE RIVER

Region Eagle River, Southcentral Inland Alaska.	**Time to paddle** 1 day.
	Suitable for kids? Some parts.
Distance Up to 21 miles, 8 miles of good paddling.	**Best time of year to go** June–Sept.
	Traffic level Moderate.
Difficulty Class II–IV.	**Facilities** Public boat launches and parking; some signage.
Experience level Beginner–advanced, depending on the section.	

PADDLING SUMMARY   Silty and cold, this river has several hazards, including sweepers and boulders; the Eagle is popular with kayakers and rafters but is not recommended for canoeists.

DIRECTIONS   From Anchorage, drive north on the Glenn Highway to the Hiland Road exit. Veer right off the exit and follow Eagle River Loop Road to Eagle River Road (there is a stoplight and an oddly out-of-place Walmart here). Turn right and follow to Mile 7.4 of Eagle River Road. The most-often-used put-in is located here.

PADDLING DESCRIPTION   This river is popular because of its proximity to Anchorage. On many a summer day you can spot rafters and kayaks on the river, usually locals looking for a quick paddle before heading back to their homes in Anchorage. The first 11 miles are the most benign, with Class I and II rapids and sweepers for which to be on the lookout, although you will miss the first 3 miles because there is no put-in. Once you reach the area around **Briggs Bridge,** however, the water gets trickier. The rapids become Class II and III, and steep banks provide challenges for pulling out if you want to scout the exposed boulders along the river. This section lasts for about 3.5 miles, and there is a place to take out just above the **Eagle River Campground.** There will be large signs pointing this out, and we hope you see them. Unless

TRAVELER'S TIP

▶ Don't let Eagle River's somewhat-urban location fool you. There are some gnarly sweepers and tricky boulder fields that make running the river a thrill for the experienced kayaker.

you are extremely experienced, it is very wise to stop here and scout the rapids below. If you go forward, the last 6 miles get even more hairy, passing underneath the **Glenn Highway–Eagle River Bridge** and going onto military land owned by **Fort Richardson Army Base.** The rapids become Class III and IV at this section, and it's nearly impossible to take out. It leads to the **Route Bravo Bridge,** then to the **Knik Arm mudflats,** which have dangerous bore tides and quicksand. We do not recommend this section.

The best and most convenient place to take out is at the **Eagle River Day Use Area,** adjacent to the Eagle River campground, 5.8 miles shy of the 21-mile length of the river.

KENAI RIVER

Region Cooper Landing, Southcentral Coastal Alaska.

Distance 18 miles.

Difficulty Class II–III.

Experience level Beginner–intermediate depending on section.

Time to paddle Half day–full day.

Suitable for kids? Yes.

Best time of year to go May–Sept., peak flow in mid-June–July.

Traffic level Heavy in tourist season.

Facilities Established put-ins and take-outs; outhouses; some signage.

PADDLING SUMMARY   The scenic aquamarine waters of the Kenai are a pleasant float from one big lake (**Kenai**) to the next (**Skilak**). Relatively easy paddling with a high probability of spotting wildlife.

DIRECTIONS   From Anchorage, take the Seward Highway south to the turn-off for the Sterling Highway. Follow the Sterling Highway into Cooper Landing, about 8 miles. The rafting companies are located right on the river, past the Kenai Lake bridge, on the right. The best takeout, if you go all the way to Skilak Lake, is **Jim's Landing,** on Skilak Lake Road.

PADDLING DESCRIPTION   The famed Kenai River is known for its great angling, but it is also a wonderfully relaxing place to explore in a raft. You can choose a shorter float with easy waves and only a few Class II rapids, or continue on for the 18-mile trip to **Skilak Lake,** through the **Kenai National Wildlife Refuge.** Look for moose, river otters, bears, and eagles. With a guide, the shorter trip is appropriate for families.

LOWE RIVER

Region Valdez, Southcentral Coastal Alaska.	**Suitable for kids?** No.
Distance 25.5 miles (5 miles for the Keystone Canyon section).	**Best time of year to go** May–Sept., peak flow in mid-June.
Difficulty Class III.	**Traffic level** Moderate during tourist season.
Experience level Beginner–advanced.	**Facilities** Established put-ins and takeouts; some signage.
Time to paddle 1 hour or longer depending on distance.	

PADDLING SUMMARY   A scenic, steep-walled river near Valdez that offers spectacular views of waterfalls and spruce-covered forests. The most popular section, **Keystone Canyon,** is Class III, but some Class II and Class V segments also exist.

DIRECTIONS   Most people come to the Lowe River from the Prince William Sound community of Valdez, at the beginning of the Richardson Highway. The Lowe River is half an hour north of Valdez, along the Richardson Highway.

PADDLING DESCRIPTION   The Lowe River through Keystone Canyon gives you a brief (1 hour) but splashy introduction to whitewater rafting. The canyon itself is stunning, and because the rapids are not too challenging, you can actually look around to enjoy the surroundings. You can stop at **Bridal Veil Falls** to view the 900-foot-tall waterfalls right off the road. The vertical rock walls and thickly forested mountain slopes make you feel as if you're at the center of the earth.

The river can be made much more challenging and exciting in other parts. The 7.5-mile **Heiden Canyon** upstream of Keystone Canyon is Class V and should not be attempted without local experts. Downstream from Keystone Canyon is easy Class II water.

MATANUSKA RIVER–LION HEAD

Region Palmer, Southcentral Inland Alaska.	**Suitable for kids?** Yes, in rafts.
Distance 5.3 miles.	**Best time of year to go** Late May–August; best run between 5 feet and 12 feet.
Difficulty Class III–IV.	
Experience level Intermediate–advanced.	**Traffic level** Light–moderate.
Time to paddle Half day.	**Facilities** Pulloffs for put-ins and takeouts.

PADDLING SUMMARY   A challenging, wide, glacially fed river that is silty, making it difficult to detect hidden obstacles. Very experienced paddlers can manage it; paddlers with some experience should do well too, if accompanied by those who have run the river before.

DIRECTIONS   From Anchorage, drive northeast on the Glenn Highway through the town of Palmer to the Caribou Creek bridge at Mile 107. Look just past the bridge to the left—the put-in access is along a gravel road leading below the bridge. The takeout is off the Glenn Highway, at Mile 102. Follow the dirt road with steep switchbacks (a four-wheel-drive vehicle is recommended). Parking is at a clearing just before the Glacier Park Resort bridge. The resort is private property, but it is generally accepted that you can park there.

TRAVELER'S TIP

▶ The Matanuska River is frigid. Wet- or dry suits, neoprene foot covers, and a warm head covering (and helmet) are strongly advised.

PADDLING DESCRIPTION   The Matanuska River is wide, with impressive waves and open vistas for viewing the surroundings (during the rare moments when you can relax, that is).

The **Lion Head** portion of the Matanuska is some of the most scenic on this 77-plus-mile stretch of runnable river. The rapids are formed where the Matanuska Glacier pinches the Matanuska against a rock outcrop known as Lion Head. The massive stone feature stands like a gatekeeper to the upper Matanuska-Susitna Valley, and when viewed from a right angle, it does indeed look like a lion. The rapids are big-water style, with dramatic waves and more-technical challenges at low water levels.

Both kayakers and rafters tackle this section of river. From the put-in at **Caribou Creek,** beware the braids that are just enough to get rafts stuck and push kayakers to the bank where sweepers hang low. You'll reach the **East Fork of the Matanuska** in less than half an hour, and the river forms a more manageable single channel. The steep rock bank that forms Lion Head will be the first major rapid, and it is a splashy one. When the water is high, you can go for almost 4 miles from rapid to rapid, wave after wave, with little stopping. It makes for an exhilarating but slightly white-knuckle experience. At low water, things get tricky with rock outcrops, and you'll be slowed down considerably.

NENANA RIVER

Region The Interior.	**Suitable for kids?** Some parts.
Distance 38 miles (8 miles for the mellowest part of the river).	**Best time of year to go** May–Sept., peak flow in mid-June.
Difficulty Class II–IV.	**Traffic level** Moderate–heavy during tourist season.
Experience level Beginner–advanced depending on the section.	**Facilities** Established put-ins and takeouts; some signage.
Time to paddle Half day–full day.	

PADDLING SUMMARY   A scenic, steep-walled river near **Denali National Park** that can be split into four segments, depending on the challenges you seek. The first section provides opportunities for mild Class II trips. As you travel downstream, you encounter more-challenging Class IV rapids near Nenana Canyon.

DIRECTIONS   From Anchorage, take the Parks Highway north approximately 210 miles. At Cantwell, you can turn off onto the Denali Highway for a longer trip, but we're concentrating on the day trips. Keep driving to Carlo Creek.

PADDLING DESCRIPTION   The **Carlo Creek–McKinley Village** section of the Nenana River is 8 miles long and includes Class II and III rapids that are manageable by most people with intermediate to advanced skills. The challenge with the Nenana, as with many of Alaska's rivers, is its silty gray color, which makes it difficult to see obstacles under water. **McKinley Village** to **Riley Creek** provides a mostly Class III 10.5-mile section of water and is suitable for rafts and kayaks. The intriguingly named **Terror Corner** is a particularly challenging spot in this section of river.

The 9.5-mile segment from **Twin Rocks** to **Nenana Canyon** is the most challenging, with easy access off the Parks Highway, just outside the park. This section is perhaps Alaska's most popular whitewater trip, and an annual competition draws kayakers from all over for slalom and wild-water races. Several outfitters offer trips on this stretch of river, as well as milder versions upstream.

SIXMILE CREEK

Region Hope, Southcentral Coastal Alaska.	**Suitable for kids?** No.
	Best time of year to go June–August.
Distance 9 miles.	**Traffic level** Moderate.
Difficulty Class III–V.	**Facilities** Alaska River Forecast Center gauge; public boat launch and parking; some signage.
Experience level Advanced paddlers only.	
Time to paddle 1 day.	

PADDLING SUMMARY   A challenging, mostly clear-water creek that slices through some of the most dramatic landscape of the **Kenai Peninsula,** and at some points can be seen right off the Seward Highway. There are three canyons, each getting progressively harder as you travel downstream. An ideal kayaker's river, although rafters now use it regularly as well.

DIRECTIONS   From Anchorage, drive south on the Seward Highway to Mile 59, just a few miles before the turnoff to Hope. A paved parking lot is on the right side of the road. There are three takeouts, all along the Hope Road. The first is at about Mile 1 of the Hope Road, below the first canyon. A small road on the right leads to the Hope Road, and it can be easy to miss. The second takeout is at Mile 4.5, past the second canyon and also on the right and leading up a hill.

The third takeout is at Mile 7. A driveway on the right leads to the main road.

PADDLING DESCRIPTION   Sixmile is one of the best-known waters for kayaking because it is technical and gets more difficult as it flows downstream, giving kayakers an ever-increasing challenge as they travel along. It wasn't until 10–15 years ago that commercial operators started using rafts to float the river, and today it is a popular day trip for those coming from Anchorage or the Kenai Peninsula.

> **TRAVELER'S TIP**
>
> ▶ Sixmile Creek can be run at high and low levels, but it becomes more technical with less water. Many river runners also don't go out when it's at 11 feet or more, feeling it is too dangerous.

The creek has some great sections, including **Seventeen Ender, The Slot, Predator, Waterfall,** and **Pearly Gates** (the last one makes us nervous!). You can scout the river ahead of time by driving along the Hope Highway and going along the road for glimpses of certain canyons. Debris and logs often get moved into the water—we recommend scouting for such dangers.

Day-trip Resources

▶ **Alaska Raft and Kayak** (401 W. Tudor Rd., Anchorage 99503; 800-606-5950 or 907-561-7238; **alaskaraftandkayak.com**) rents rafts ($100 per day) and catamarans, which are used on the Sixmile.

▶ The Chilkat River is managed by the **Chilkat Bald Eagle Preserve** and the Juneau office of the **Alaska Division of State Parks** (907-465-4563; **dnr.alaska .gov/parks/units/eagleprv.htm**).

▶ Sixmile Creek and all its takeouts are on **Chugach National Forest** property. For more information, contact the administrative offices in Anchorage (3301 C St., Anchorage 99503; 907-743-9500; **fs.fed.us/r10/chugach**).

▶ **Chugach State Park** manages the Eagle River and surrounding land (907-345-5014; **dnr.alaska.gov/parks/units/chugach**). The **Division of Natural Resources Public Information Center** can provide details on the Eagle River as well (550 W. 7th Ave., Suite 1260; Anchorage 99501-3557; 907-269-8400; **dnr.alaska.gov/commis/pic/index.htm**).

▶ **Denali National Park** and the **U.S. Bureau of Land Management** manage most of the Nenana River. For more information on Denali National Park, call 907-683-2294 or visit **nps.gov/dena;** to get in touch with the Bureau of Land Management, call the Glennallen District office (907-822-3217) or visit **blm.gov/ak.** (Incidentally, the Glennallen office can also give you information on the Delta National Wild and Scenic River and the Gulkana National Wild River as well.)

▶ **Denali Outdoor Center** (888-303-1925 or 907-683-1925; **denalioutdoorcenter .com**) can provide information on Nenana River conditions; it also offers rentals and guided trips.

▶ **Fort Richardson Army Base** requires a paddler's permit to enter the 6-mile section of Eagle River on its property. Permits are $50; call 907-384-1476 for details.

▶ The Anchorage-based paddling club **Knik Canoers and Kayakers** has a great Sixmile Creek mile-by-mile guide written by one of its members that is an entertaining must-read for do-it-yourselfers. Access it online at **kck.org.** The club also covers other rafting and kayaking locales.

▶ For more information on the Matanuska River, contact **Matanuska-Susitna Borough** (matsugov.us).

▶ **U.S. Geological Survey maps,** available locally or through **usgs.gov,** include Chilkat–Skagway A-2, B-2, B-3, B-4; Eagle River–Anchorage A-7, B-6, and B-7; Kenai River–Seward B-8, and Kenai B-1; Matanuska-Anchorage D-2, D-3; Nenana-Fairbanks A-5, B-5, C-5; Healy B-3, B-4, C-4, D-4, D-5; Sixmile-Anchorage B-8.

▶ There are no nearby kayak- or raft-rental outfits in Valdez for the Lowe River. Check at the **Valdez Visitors and Convention Bureau** (off Fairbanks Street, between Chenega and Fidalgo; 907-835-2984; **valdezalaska.org**).

Day-trip Outfitters

▶ **ALASKA RIVERS COMPANY** » *Cooper Landing* 888-595-1226; **alaskarivers company.com.** Along with phenomenal fishing and other Alaska adventures, Alaska Rivers Company offers two options for scenic floating on the Kenai River. The 3-hour trip is suitable for all ages and takes guests on a relaxing float on the Upper Kenai. The 7-hour float explores Kenai Canyon and includes a guided nature hike. These day trips range from 3 to 7 hours and include a knowledge-able guide, a gourmet lunch, and gear. Trips are $49–$142 per person.

▶ **ALASKA VISTAS** » *Wrangell* 866-874-3006 or 907-874-3006; **alaskavistas.com.** Alaska Vistas provides custom adventures for almost any skill level and desire. Pick a trip based on your interests and where you'd like to go, and Alaska Vistas will arrange for guided or independent trips as well as equipment rentals. The company is known for its Stikine River trips and also provides a jet-boat tour and other activities on the river. Other destinations include Anan Wildlife

Observatory, Telegraph Creek, and numerous scenic areas in the Tongass National Forest and Stikine-LeConte Wilderness. A one-day guided trip to Anan is $210, and a nine-day guided trip on the Stikine is $2,600 per person.

▶ **ALASKA WILDLAND ADVENTURES** ▸▸ *Cooper Landing and Girdwood* 800-334-8730 or 907-783-2928; **alaskawildland.com.** The longest-running float-trip outfitter on the river, Alaska Wildland offers a half-day Kenai River float ($54) and the more exhilarating 7-hour Kenai Canyon Tour ($140). Both offer some nice waves but nothing too technical.

▶ **CHILKAT GUIDES** ▸▸ *Haines* 888-292-7789; **raftalaska.com.** Founded in 1978, Chilkat Guides offers day and multiday trips on the Chilkat, Kongakut, and Tatshenshini-Alsek rivers. The half-day scenic float on the Chilkat offers a chance to see the world's largest concentration of bald eagles up close at the Chilkat Bald Eagle Preserve. A 12-day trip on the Alsek offers serene floating and rugged whitewater against a backdrop of dramatic glacier and mountain scenery. More-remote trips include an eight-day excursion on the Kongakut, which cuts through Arctic National Wildlife Refuge. Trips start at $93 for the Chilkat River float and can be up to $4,495 for the Kongakut River trip.

▶ **CHUGACH OUTDOOR CENTER** ▸▸ *Hope* 866-277-RAFT or 907-277-RAFT; **chugachoutdoorcenter.com.** Leads trips on Sixmile Creek and on the Talkeetna and Tana rivers. Denali National Park trips via the Nenana River are also offered. Denali raft trips range from a couple of hours to multiple days requiring helicopter support. Whether on short day trips or weeklong camping excursions, guides lead guests through exhilarating whitewater and dramatic Alaska scenery. Rates range $80–$2,400 per person.

▶ **KEYSTONE RAFT AND KAYAK ADVENTURES** ▸▸ *Valdez* 907-835-2606; **alaskawhitewater.com.** From 1½ hours on the Lowe River to multiple days on the Tazlina, Tana, Copper, Chitina, and Talkeetna rivers, Keystone Raft and Kayak offers the opportunity to float in a variety of regions and terrains. The company also provides half- and full-day trips on the Tonsina and Tsaina rivers. These trips are for more-adventurous types, as whitewater is Keystone's specialty. Rates start at $55 for the 1½-hour trip; $1,300–$1,700 for multiday trips.

▶ **NOVA RIVER RUNNERS** ▸▸ *Chickaloon* 800-746-5753; **novalaska.com.** NOVA has been guiding Alaskans and visitors on rafting and other adventures through the wilderness since 1975. The company offers 4- to 5-hour day trips on Sixmile Creek and the Matanuska River. A favorite of NOVA's guides is the remote Kings River trip, a 5-hour tour that includes a helicopter or mountain-bike ride to the put-in. Multiday adventures are available on the Matanuska, Tana, Talkeetna, and Copper rivers and on Lake Creek. Sightseeing by air, fishing, and other activities are also part of the adventure. Rates start at $75 for day trips to $2,950 for six-day trips.

▲ Multiday Trips

HERE'S WHERE THE pickings get even more difficult to pare down. There are so many wilderness rivers in Alaska from which to choose, and each has something special to offer the person who chooses to explore them. We've selected five such rivers, and the guides we trust who can get you there.

We recommend traveling with the outfitters that follow. If, however, you are planning the trip on your own, please refer to our general resources listed at the beginning of this chapter, as well as the managing agency for each river.

AMERICAN CREEK

Region Katmai National Park, The Bush.	**Time to paddle** 4–9 days.
	Suitable for kids? Yes.
Distance 50 miles.	**Best time of year to go** June–Sept.
Difficulty Class I–III.	**Traffic level** Light.
Experience level Intermediate.	**Facilities** None; wilderness float.

TRAVELER'S TIP

▶ Expedition trips to Alaska rivers require careful planning and the ability to survive in extreme outdoor conditions. It can snow any time of the year in Alaska, and it rains often. At certain times in the summer, the mosquitoes can be horrendous and the winds fierce. This is not to dissuade the outdoor traveler who wants to experience a truly remote expedition— it's simply a fact.

PADDLING SUMMARY   This river is tucked amid the **Aleutian Range** and makes a good float from two lakes, starting at tiny **Murray Lake** and then continuing to **Lake Colville**. There is some flat-water paddling on the lakes, but there also comes excitement when at one point a narrow gorge creates a technical Class III run-through to more-open water.

American Creek Outfitters

▶ **Alaska Trophy Adventures** ›› *King Salmon* 877-801-2289; **alaskatrophyadventures.com.** This outfit combines superb fly-fishing guiding with a weeklong float down American Creek for $3,800 per person. This is a hunter's and fisherman's paradise, with meat-and-potato-style meals and as much leopard rainbow, arctic char, and grayling fishing as you can squeeze in while floating the water.

▸ **Alaska Wilderness Guides** ›› *Anchorage* 907-345-4470; **akwild.com.** Alaska Wilderness offers four multiday rafting trips throughout Alaska's remote wilderness, including its American Creek float in Katmai National Park. Trips are a mix of whitewater rafting and scenic floating, and guides will take you past the famous bears of Katmai. The trip is $3,600 and includes a week of travel and fishing. Custom trips may be available on request. (For more information on Katmai National Park, contact Field Headquarters, 1 King Salmon Mall, King Salmon 99613; or Administrative Headquarters, 4230 University Dr., Suite 311, Anchorage 99508-4626; 907-246-3305; **nps.gov/katm.**)

CANNING RIVER

Region The Bush, Arctic National Wildlife Refuge.	**Time to paddle** 7–12 days.
Distance 125 miles.	**Suitable for kids?** No.
Difficulty Class II–III.	**Best time of year to go** June–Sept.
Experience level Intermediate– advanced.	**Traffic level** Light.
	Facilities None; a wilderness area.

PADDLING SUMMARY   The Canning River skirts the western boundary of the **Arctic National Wildlife Refuge,** weaving between the mountains as it makes its way to the Arctic Ocean. The Canning's unusual beauty and gentle water make it an often-overlooked but special place to experience. The water runs clear, and from your boat you can look for musk oxen, wolves, bears, nesting falcons, hawks, and eagles. Also, be sure to get out and explore for fossils on the nearby gravel bars.

Canning River Outfitters

▸ **ARCTIC TREKS** ›› *Fairbanks–Brooks Range* 907-455-6502; **arctictreks adventures.com.** In business for more than 25 years, Arctic Treks provides visitors with a once-in-a-lifetime adventure through Alaska's great Arctic. Leading more than seven different trips through the Arctic's parks and wildlife refuges, the company also includes the Canning River on its itinerary. The trip is $4,250 and includes 10 days of river rafting. Other rivers include the Kongakut, Nigu, Hulahula, and Sheenjek. Arctic Treks also offers other guided activities along the way, and there are options for special trips each year.

▸ **WILDERNESS BIRDING ADVENTURES** ›› 907-694-7442; **wildernessbirding .com.** This outfit is one of the best in the state, and the only one offering rafting-birding combination tours. The price is $4,200 for 12 days on the Canning River–Marsh Fork. The Canning River delta features variety in its upriver species, with more chances to see more birds. Wilderness Birding also explores unique birding options on the Kongakut, in the Pribilofs, and in Nome and Gambell.

COPPER RIVER

Region Southcentral Inland–Southcentral Coastal Alaska.	**Time to paddle** 6 days.
	Suitable for kids? Yes.
Distance 100 miles.	**Best time of year to go** July–August.
Difficulty Class I.	**Traffic level** Light.
Experience level Beginner (with guide).	**Facilities** Established put-ins and takeouts, camping on beaches.

PADDLING SUMMARY   The river is wide, flat, and swift, but there are no huge rapids to worry about. Calved pieces of glacier in some spots punctuate the gray, silty water. Stay away from the glaciers when they are calving—the waves produced by their weight are surprisingly powerful.

Copper River Outfitters

▶ **COPPER OAR ALASKA ADVENTURE TRAVEL »** *McCarthy* 800-523-4453 or 907-554-4453; **copperoar.com.** Copper Oar offers a six-day Copper River floating and camping expedition that takes in wildlife, cascading waterfalls, glaciers that often calve right into the river, and mild whitewater. The voyage ends in Cordova, in Prince William Sound, where you can fly out to Anchorage or take the Alaska Marine Highway ferry for an added water-based trip back to the mainland. The price is $2,350–$2,600 for adults, depending on group size.

> **TRAVELER'S TIP**
>
> ▶ Native corporations own much of the land along the right-hand bank of the Copper River, and you'll need a permit to camp there. Traveling with an outfitter eliminates the need to obtain permission on your own.

▶ **CORDOVA COASTAL OUTFITTERS »** *Cordova* (at the harbor, in the brightly colored boathouse) 800-357-5145 or 907-424-7424; **cdvcoastal.com.** For those planning to do the trip on their own, this outfit can arrange a shuttle. They also rent kayaks, which are suitable for travel on Copper River. Kayaks are $45 per day for singles, $65 for doubles. Guided day trips start at $75, but no overnight trips are operated through the company.

NIZINA RIVER

Region McCarthy, Southcentral Inland Alaska.	**Time to paddle** 2–3 days.
	Suitable for kids? Yes.
Distance 45 miles.	**Best time of year to go** June–Sept.
Difficulty Class II–III.	**Traffic level** Light.
Experience level Beginner–intermediate.	**Facilities** Established put-ins and takeouts.

PADDLING SUMMARY   A float along the Nizina combines fast water with glacial runoff and the chance to see much wildlife. The river has several difficult sections on the upper portion. Side trips include the **Kennicott River,** which can be launched from the end of McCarthy Road and accompanied by a side trip to the historic town. In low water, the Kennicott can become braided and shallow.

Nizina River Outfitter

▸ **ALASKA OUTDOORS** ⟫ *Wasilla* 800-320-2494; **alaskaoutdoorstours.com.** Offers a custom rafting adventure in Wrangell–St. Elias National Park. This six-day excursion starts with a guided tour of the park, including a pick-your-own-adventure day that may take you glacier hiking, sightseeing by air, touring, or rafting. The rest of the trip is spent rafting and camping on the Kennicott, Nizina, and Chitina rivers. The price is $1,245 per person.

TATSHENSHINI AND ALSEK RIVERS

Region Haines, Southeast Alaska.	**Time to paddle** 9–12 days.
Distance 129 miles.	**Suitable for kids?** Some parts.
Difficulty Class I–IV.	**Best time of year to go** June–August.
Experience level Advanced paddlers only.	**Traffic level** Light.
	Facilities None; very remote.

PADDLING SUMMARY   These rivers, which merge into one along the way, make for a challenging route that attracts paddlers from around the world. The heat and bugs in the upper reaches of the river usually contrast with the fog and glacial chill of the lower half, so be prepared for a variety of weather conditions.

The **Tatshenshini** starts in Canada and the **Alsek** dumps into the United States; thus, many people fly into Alaska, shuttle to Canada for the put-in at **Dalton Post,** and float the 129 miles to **Dry Bay,** back in Alaska. The Tatshenshini and Alsek are completely protected from headwater to source, creating the only large river drainage in North America that is completely safeguarded. The whitewater on the Tatshenshini is impressive, but when it joins with the Alsek River 77 miles into the trip, the river makes a dramatic jump in size and power.

Tatshenshini-Alsek Outfitter

▶   **WILDERNESS RIVER OUTFITTERS »** 800-252-6581; **wildernessriver.com;** based in *Lemhi, Idaho.* Offers an awesome 11-day trip on the Tatshenshini for $3,300. Bring your own gear and get a $75 discount.

IT GOES WITHOUT saying that Alaska is a wintertime paradise. There is no shortage of things to do when the snow begins to fall—and it falls often. For Alaskans, snow can come as early as late September and cling to the mountains and trails until well into May. The winters can be long—and cold—but it's also one of the best times to visit, because you get to see how life in the Far North really is for the locals.

Among the wintertime activities to be enjoyed in Alaska are skiing, snowmobiling, mountaineering (including ice climbing), dog mushing, and snowshoeing. Outfitters here can help plan trips ranging from beginner ice climbing to advanced mountaineering on some of Alaska's tallest peaks. Alaska's experienced dog mushers can teach newbies how to run their own team of huskies, and the state's well-equipped ski resorts and guide companies can lead you to some of the best powder to be had.

This chapter will briefly profile our favored winter pastimes: skiing, mountaineering and ice climbing, and dog mushing. Skiing can be accomplished individually, but we recommend a guide for dog mushing and climbing.

▲ Skiing

In Alaska, you can ski year-round. You can ski on a glacier. You can jump out of a helicopter and ski down a mountain. You can ski on a groomed trail. You can ski at a resort. Simply put, there is no shortage of skiing in Alaska.

However, skiing in Alaska is not the resort-packed winter wonderland you might think, but rather an outdoor adventure that usually requires climbing mountains on your own and gliding back down in fluid motion. In the entire state, there is only one ski area that qualifies as a resort (that is, with a fancy hotel, multiple lifts, and an array of fine-dining and entertainment options), not to mention less than a half-dozen local downhill-skiing areas. Considering that Alaska is so vast and covered in snow for so much of the year, this may come as a surprise.

In the Lower 48 states, downhill skiing catches most of the spotlight. Resorts from Utah to Colorado to Vermont cater to the thrill of flying down mountains at high speeds. And it is great fun. But the truth is, Nordic skiing reigns supreme in Alaska. And

TRAVELER'S TIP

▶ Late winter and early spring are the best times to visit Alaska for a skiing vacation. The first part of March brings with it warmer temperatures and longer days. It is not uncommon to see sunny, clear afternoons with temperatures in the high 30s, a far cry from the 15° days most common during January and February. (In the Interior and the Bush, the average winter temperatures are even lower, often in the negative digits.)

▲ alaska skiing @ a glance

Anchorage

REGION ›› Southcentral Inland
SKIING TYPES ›› All
TRAFFIC ›› Moderate–heavy
DIFFICULTY ›› ★–★★★★★
ROAD ACCESS? ›› Yes
SUITABLE FOR KIDS? ›› Yes
GUIDE SUGGESTED? ›› No

Fairbanks and Beyond

REGION ›› The Interior
SKIING TYPES ›› All
TRAFFIC ›› Light–moderate
DIFFICULTY ›› 1–★★★
ROAD ACCESS? ›› Yes
SUITABLE FOR KIDS? ›› Yes
GUIDE SUGGESTED? ›› No

Haines

REGION ›› Southeast
SKIING TYPES ›› Heli-skiing, downhill, cross-country, telemark
TRAFFIC ›› Light
DIFFICULTY ›› ★★★★★
ROAD ACCESS? ›› No
SUITABLE FOR KIDS? ›› No
GUIDE SUGGESTED? ›› Yes

Hatcher Pass–Mat-Su Borough

REGION ›› Southcentral Inland
SKIING TYPES ›› All
TRAFFIC ›› Light–moderate
DIFFICULTY ›› ★★–★★★★
ROAD ACCESS? ›› Yes
SUITABLE FOR KIDS? ›› Yes
GUIDE SUGGESTED? ›› Recommended

Juneau

REGION ›› Southeast
SKIING TYPES ›› Downhill, cross-country
TRAFFIC ›› Moderate
DIFFICULTY ›› ★★★
ROAD ACCESS? ›› Yes
SUITABLE FOR KIDS? ›› Yes
GUIDE SUGGESTED? ›› No

Valdez

REGION ›› Southcentral Coastal
SKIING TYPES ›› Heli-skiing, downhill, cross-country, telemark
TRAFFIC ›› Light
DIFFICULTY ›› ★★★★★
ROAD ACCESS? ›› No
SUITABLE FOR KIDS? ›› No
GUIDE SUGGESTED? ›› Yes

while there are many downhill skiers and some excellent places at which to Alpine-ski here, in Alaska you can access cross-country ski trails from just about anywhere.

First, a short primer on skiing. There are many variations on the activity, but we generally group them in three categories: downhill (or Alpine), cross-country (or Nordic), and backcountry (telemarking, for example). There is also snowboarding, which can be accomplished in the backcountry and on established ski slopes.

skiing outfitters @ a glance

Alaska Alpine Adventures

877-525-2577
alaskaalpineadventures.com

REGION ▸▸ The Bush
COST ▸▸ $$$
SUITABLE FOR KIDS? ▸▸ No
ACTIVITY LEVEL ▸▸ High
TRIP LENGTH ▸▸ 7–14 days

Alaska Heliskiing

877-SKI-HAINES or 907-767-5745
alaskaheliskiing.com

REGION ▸▸ Southeast
COST ▸▸ $$$$
SUITABLE FOR KIDS? ▸▸ No
ACTIVITY LEVEL ▸▸ High
TRIP LENGTH ▸▸ 1–6 days

Chugach Powder Guides

907-783-4354
chugachpowderguides.com

REGION ▸▸ Southcentral Inland
COST ▸▸ $$$
SUITABLE FOR KIDS? ▸▸ Teens
ACTIVITY LEVEL ▸▸ High
TRIP LENGTH ▸▸ 1–7 days

Points North Heli-Adventures

877-787-6784
alaskaheliski.com

REGION ▸▸ Southcentral Coastal
COST ▸▸ $$$
SUITABLE FOR KIDS? ▸▸ No
ACTIVITY LEVEL ▸▸ High
TRIP LENGTH ▸▸ 6 days

St. Elias Alpine Guides

888-933-5427 or 907-345-9048
steliasguides.com

REGION ▸▸ Southcentral Inland
COST ▸▸ $$$
SUITABLE FOR KIDS? ▸▸ Teens
ACTIVITY LEVEL ▸▸ High
TRIP LENGTH ▸▸ 1–6 days

Valdez Heli-Camps

907-783-3513 or 907-783-3243
valdezhelicamps.com

REGION ▸▸ Southcentral Coastal
COST ▸▸ $$$$
SUITABLE FOR KIDS? ▸▸ Teens
ACTIVITY LEVEL ▸▸ High
TRIP LENGTH ▸▸ 1–6 days

Valdez Heli-Ski Guides

907-835-4528
valdezheliskiguides.com

REGION ▸▸ Southcentral Coastal, Inland
COST ▸▸ $$$$$
SUITABLE FOR KIDS? ▸▸ No
ACTIVITY LEVEL ▸▸ High
TRIP LENGTH ▸▸ 6 days

SKIING RESOURCES

ANCHORAGE

Region Southcentral Inland Alaska. **Types of skiing** Downhill, cross-country, randonnée, telemarking. **Difficulty** ★–★★★★★. **Road access?** Yes. **Suitable for kids?** Yes. **Traffic** Moderate–heavy.	**Contact** Anchorage Convention and Visitors Bureau, 524 W. 4th Ave., Anchorage 99501-2212; 907-276-4118; **anchorage.net.** Look for the sod-roofed Log Cabin and Downtown Visitor Information Center at the corner of F Street and Fourth Avenue.

DESTINATION SUMMARY   Anchorage has three ski areas close by and offers several options for Alpine skiing. However, cross-country skiing on groomed municipal trails and in **Chugach State Park** are the main attractions. Anchorage has hundreds of miles of trails, many of them groomed and lighted, or at least well established, during the winter months. It is one of the best urban trail systems in the country, and winter travelers will be surprised by how much is available. The most popular areas for Nordic skiing are **Kincaid Park,** the local greenbelt trails, and **Russian Jack Springs Park.** Check with the **Anchorage Parks and Recreation** office (907-343-4355; **muni. org/departments/parks/pages/default.aspx**) and the **Alaska Public Lands Information Center** (605 W. 4th Ave., Suite 105, Anchorage 99501; 866-869-6887 or 907-644-3661; **alaskacenters.gov/anchorage.cfm**) for more information about trails and skiing options.

FAIRBANKS AND BEYOND

Region The Interior. **Types of skiing** Downhill, cross-country, randonnée, telemarking. **Difficulty** ★–★★★. **Road access?** Yes.	**Suitable for kids?** Yes. **Traffic** Light–moderate. **Contact** Fairbanks Convention and Visitors Bureau (101 Dunkel St., Suite 111, Fairbanks 99701; 800-327-5774; **explorefairbanks.com**).

DESTINATION SUMMARY   Cross-country skiing opportunities abound in the Interior. Winter trails maintained by the U.S. Bureau of Land Management and other public agencies provide excellent access to open valleys and high traverses. Established trails are also around some communities, as well as at most high schools and the University of Alaska. These trails are multiple-use, however, so beware of snowmobiles and dog teams. Some Alpine skiing is also available. Two ski areas in Fairbanks provide some good local downhill action for Alpine skiers and snowboarders, and are affordable for just about anyone (see "Ski Resorts," page 242).

HAINES

Region Southeast Alaska.	**Suitable for kids?** No.
Types of skiing Heli-skiing, downhill, cross-country, telemarking.	**Traffic** Light.
Difficulty ★ ★ ★ ★ ★.	**Contact** Haines Convention and Visitors Bureau, 907-766-2234 or
Road access? No.	800-458-3579; **visithaines.net.**

DESTINATION SUMMARY   Haines offers plenty of opportunities for Alpine and cross-country skiing, telemarking, and snowboarding. Spring skiing in the area in March and April is unsurpassed. **Haines Summit** and **Chilkat Pass** are the most popular skiing areas, and numerous maintained cross-country trails are also near town. Lodging is available at hotels and bed-and-breakfasts in and around Haines.

HATCHER PASS–MAT-SU BOROUGH

Region Southcentral Inland Alaska.	**Traffic** Light–moderate.
Types of skiing Downhill, cross-country, randonnée, telemarking.	**Contact** Mat-Su Convention and Visitors Bureau (7744 E. Visitors View Ct., Palmer 99645;
Difficulty ★ ★–★ ★ ★ ★.	907-746-5000; **alaskavisit.com**). The visitor center is at Mile
Road access? Yes.	35.5 Parks Hwy. (take the Trunk
Suitable for kids? Yes.	Road Exit).

DESTINATION SUMMARY This immense area offers Alpine and cross-country skiing and snowboarding. There are no established ski areas here currently, and hike-in and backcountry skiing are most common. The wide glacial valleys and scenic landscapes make for great touring, and the surrounding mountains provide some opportunities for Alpine and telemark skiing and randonnée as well.

One of the best and most popular areas for skiing and other winter recreation is **Hatcher Pass,** about 15 miles outside of Palmer. This area includes **Independence Mine State Historical Park** and gets an abundance of snow during winter months. Hike-in skiing and snowboarding are popular here, and there are also established Nordic trails. Some of the most-used trails include those near Independence Mine and multiuse trails such as the **Gold Mint Glacier** trail. The **Hatcher Pass Recreation Area** is relatively easy to reach, and visitors can drive up, park in an established lot, and hike a short distance for untracked Alaska powder. Lodging and services in the area are limited to the **Hatcher Pass Lodge.** A small ski area and a groomed and lighted Nordic trail system also are planned for the area, but those plans have been in the works for years to no avail.

JUNEAU

Region Southeast Alaska.	**Suitable for kids?** Yes.
Types of skiing Downhill, cross-country.	**Traffic** Moderate.
Difficulty ★★★.	**Contact** Juneau Convention and Visitors Bureau, 1 Sealaska Plaza, Suite 305, Juneau 99801-1245; 907-586-1737; **traveljuneau.com.**
Road access? Yes.	

DESTINATION SUMMARY The expansive valleys of the Juneau area offer great cross-country skiing. The most popular sites are the **Juneau Ice Field** and **Mendenhall Glacier.** The area offers mainly Nordic skiing, but there are some opportunities for Alpine skiing and snowboarding as well as backcountry touring. Juneau also has an established ski area.

VALDEZ

Region Southcentral Coastal Alaska.	**Suitable for kids?** No.
Types of skiing Heli-skiing, downhill, cross-country, telemarking, randonnée.	**Traffic** Light.
	Contact Valdez Convention and Visitors Bureau, 200 Fairbanks Dr.,
Difficulty ★★★★★.	Valdez 99686; 800-770-5954;
Road access? No.	**valdezalaska.org.**

DESTINATION SUMMARY   With the **Chugach Range** and the mountains in Thompson Pass and around Valdez being some of the most snow-rich areas in the state, Valdez is a popular destination for all skiers. The area offers endless backcountry and front-country opportunities for Alpine skiing, snowboarding, telemarking, randonnée, and cross-country touring. Heli-skiing and snowcat skiing atop some of the highest peaks in the Chugach are ideal. There are several guides in the area and from out of state. Lodging is at wilderness lodges, hotels, and bed-and-breakfasts in and around Valdez.

SKI RESORTS

OK, we're using the term *resort* loosely. In Alaska, any ski area that has a chairlift or towrope is close enough because such things are luxuries. Alaskans generally are hardy folk who won't scoff at climbing a mountain to get in their ski or snowboard run. But when they want a little pampering, they can visit one of these ski areas for a lift.

ALYESKA RESORT

Region Girdwood, Southcentral Inland Alaska.
Types of skiing Mostly downhill, terrain park, some cross-country, telemarking.
Contact 800-880-3880 or 907-754-2111; **alyeskaresort.com.**

DESTINATION SUMMARY   The only true resort in the state, with a luxury hotel, nearby shops and restaurants, and lively nightlife. *Tickets:* $60; *terrain:*

2,500 vertical feet; *lifts:* one high-speed detachable quad, two fixed quads, three double chairs, two pony lifts, a magic carpet, one 60-passenger tram; *level:* 52% intermediate, 37% advanced, 11% beginner; *location:* about 3 miles up the Alyeska Highway off the Seward Highway, 40 miles south of Anchorage.

ALPENGLOW AT ARCTIC VALLEY

Region Anchorage, Southcentral Inland Alaska.
Types of skiing Mostly downhill, some cross-country, telemarking.
Contact 907-428-1208; **skiarctic.net.**

DESTINATION SUMMARY   Longtime Anchorage facilities run completely by volunteers. *Tickets:* $15–$28 (children under age 7 and guests over age 70 ski free); *terrain:* 1,214 vertical feet; *lifts:* one T-bar/platter, two double chairs, one rope tow; *level:* easiest to more difficult; *location:* just outside Anchorage, Mile 7, Arctic Valley Road.

EAGLECREST

Region Juneau, Southeast Alaska.
Types of skiing Downhill, cross-country, telemarking.
Contact 907-790-2000; **juneau.org/ecrestftp.**

DESTINATION SUMMARY   *Tickets:* $40, Nordic trails $5–$10; *terrain:* 1,400 vertical feet; *lifts:* two double, one surface; *level:* 40% intermediate, 40% expert, 20% novice; *location:* 18 miles from Juneau off Juneau-Douglas Memorial Highway.

HILLBERG SKI AREA

Region Elmendorf Air Force Base, Anchorage, Southcentral Inland Alaska.
Types of skiing Mostly downhill, some cross-country, telemarking, snow tubing.
Contact 907-552-4838 or 907-552-3472; **elmendorf-richardson.com** (click on "Travel & Recreation").

DESTINATION SUMMARY You must have military privileges to get to this recreational ski area. *Tickets:* $17 to ski, $27 for skiing and tubing; *terrain:* 236 vertical feet; *lifts:* one chair lift, two surface lifts; *location:* 4 miles off the main road on Elmendorf Air Force Base, just outside of Anchorage.

HILLTOP SKI AREA

> **Region** Anchorage, Southcentral Inland Alaska.
> **Types of skiing** Downhill (popular for snowboarding), cross-country.
> **Contact** 907-346-1407; **hilltopskiarea.org.**

DESTINATION SUMMARY *Tickets:* $28, Nordic trails free (maintained by municipality of Anchorage); *terrain:* 294 vertical feet, 2,090 feet in all; *lifts:* one triple chair, one rope tow, one platter lift; *level:* 80% easiest, 10% more difficult, 10% most difficult; *location:* about 15 minutes southeast of downtown Anchorage off Abbott Loop.

KINCAID PARK OUTDOOR CENTER

> **Region** Anchorage, Southcentral Inland Alaska.
> **Type of skiing** Cross-country.
> **Contact** 907-343-6397; **muni.org/parks/parkdistrictsw.cfm.**

DESTINATION SUMMARY The best cross-country trails in Southcentral Alaska are in this 1,400-acre park. Skiing is free. Open daily. The sledding hill in front of the chalet is popular with kids. Because this is cross-country skiing, there are no lifts or terrain parks, just a spiderweb maze of beautiful wooded trails.

MOOSE MOUNTAIN SKI RESORT

> **Region** Fairbanks, the Interior.
> **Types of skiing** Downhill, telemarking.
> **Contact** 907-479-4732; **shredthemoose.com.**

DESTINATION SUMMARY   *Tickets:* $35; *terrain:* more than 1,250 vertical feet; *lifts:* buses with ski racks; *level:* all levels, all ages; *location:* 10 miles west of Fairbanks off Sheep Creek Road.

MOUNT AURORA SKILAND

Region Fairbanks, the Interior.
Types of skiing Downhill, cross-country, telemarking.
Contact 907-389-2314; **skiland.org.**

DESTINATION SUMMARY   *Tickets:* $30; *lifts:* one double chair (farthest north ski lift); *level:* mostly beginner to intermediate with some advanced slopes; *location:* off Steese Highway north of Fairbanks.

MOUNT EYAK

Region Cordova, Southcentral Coastal Alaska.
Types of skiing Mostly downhill, some cross-country, telemarking.
Contact 907-424-7766; **mteyak.com.**

DESTINATION SUMMARY   *Tickets:* $25 and up; *terrain:* 800 vertical feet; *lifts:* one single chair; *level:* 60% more difficult, 20% most difficult, 20% easiest; *location:* Cordova (take Sixth Avenue off Council Road).

SKIING OUTFITTERS

In Alaska there are skiing adventures for every budget. As the prices at the ski areas listed previously demonstrate, a day of fun on the slopes can come pretty cheap, even free. The outfitters here provide adventures that are considerably pricier, but the excitement they deliver is worth every penny. Many specialize in heli-skiing, the extreme sport of which many a high-decibel action movie is made, and a popular pastime in Alaska.

▸ **Alaska Alpine Adventures:** 877-525-2577; **alaskaalpineadventures.com;**
   Port Alsworth, the Bush. In conjunction with All-Mountain Ski Pros, Alaska

Alpine offers one- and two-week ski-plane trips to the jagged peaks of the Neacolas in Lake Clark National Park and Preserve. You'll camp at the glacier terminus and practice backcountry and glacier-climbing techniques on this ski-mountaineering trip dedicated to first ascents and descents. Trips are $3,800–$4,800 per person.

▸ **Alaska Heliskiing:** 877-SKI-HAINES or 907-767-5745; **alaskaheliskiing.com;** *Haines, Southeast Alaska.* Offers heli-skiing, ski-plane trips, and guiding school. Ski trips are from one to six days; guiding school is 10 days. Helicopter skiing is $600 per person per day (six runs). Packages start at $4,250 and include lodging, five days of skiing, and gear. Private trips and charters are also available.

▸ **Chugach Powder Guides:** 907-783-4354; **chugachpowderguides.com;** *Girdwood, Southcentral Inland Alaska.* Combines luxury with unsurpassed backcountry skiing and snowboarding on its guided heli-skiing and snowcat trips. Chugach Powder Guides holds a permit from the Chugach National Forest and has access to terrain inaccessible to any other company and the majority of travelers. The company offers day trips ($1,075 per person) and weeklong packages (starting at $4,950 per person and as high as $8,900 per week). Other adventures are also available, including the wildly popular spring Kings and Corn fishing and skiing package ($8,650).

▸ **Points North Heli-Adventures:** 877-787-6784; **alaskaheliski.com;** *Cordova, Southcentral Coastal Alaska.* This company offers six-day trips in the Chugach. They provide custom trips as needed, but those fill up fast. An average day of skiing or snowboarding consists of 20,000–25,000 feet of vertical per day. The price averages about $850–$950 per day, with about 6–10 helicopter runs in a given area.

▸ **St. Elias Alpine Guides:** 888-933-5427 or 907-345-9048; **steliasguides.com;** *Anchorage/Wrangell–St. Elias, Southcentral Inland Alaska.* Takes guests on ski-mountaineering excursions in the Chugach Mountains during the spring and summer seasons. The guides also give ski-mountaineering and avalanche instruction. Unique to St. Elias Alpine Guides is the kite-skiing trip to Bagley Icefield. An awe-inspiring flight through Wrangell–St. Elias starts off the adventure, and an experience like no other follows. The mountaineering classes range from $1,250 for a five-day glacier travel course to $3,750 for a weeklong First Ascents course; the kite-skiing trip starts at $5,250.

▸ **Valdez Heli-Camps:** 907-783-3513 or 907-783-3243; **valdezhelicamps.com;** *Valdez, Southcentral Coastal Alaska.* This company's Web site dubs its trips "skiing that will change your life." And they may very well do so, as you spend one to six days floating through virgin powder on some of the Chugach's tallest peaks. Alpine heli-skiing and snowcat skiing and boarding are offered. The company's most popular trips are all-inclusive, with deluxe accommodations and gourmet food. Valdez Heli-Camps also offers a Sound to Summit adventure that includes some of the world's best fishing coupled with some of the world's best skiing. One overnight of snowcat skiing costs $1,049 (double occupancy), and three-day heli-trips start at $4,149.

TRAVELER'S TIP

▶ The most popular time of year for heli-skiing is February to May; if you'd like to try it, plan your trip for spring. You won't be disappointed.

▶ **Valdez Heli-Ski Guides:** 907-835-4528; **valdezheliskiguides.com;** *Girdwood, Southcentral Inland Alaska.* Valdez Heli-Ski is synonymous with endless powder and phenomenal adventure. Individual and private ski packages are available out of Valdez and renowned Thompson Pass, billed as one of the snowiest places in Alaska. On no-fly days, the company offers alternate activities—ice climbing, sea kayaking, snow machining, and fishing. Rates start at $7,831 per person for six days of skiing (30–36 runs), including lodging and meals; private trips are $67,142 per party—and that's not a typo!

▲ Ice Climbing and Mountaineering

WITH 3 OF the 10 highest peaks in North America and 20 peaks of more than 14,000 feet within our borders, it's no wonder Alaska is a Mecca for mountaineers the world over. Each year more than 1,000 people attempt to summit **Denali,** and, on average, 2 die trying. Others head for lesser-known peaks such as **Hunter** or **St. Elias** because the climbs are more challenging and provide more solitude.

Whether you're joining the crowds on Denali or you've set your sights on one of the lesser-known neighboring peaks or a mountain tucked away in the coastal range of the Southeast, there are enough mountains here for a lifetime of climbing.

If you prefer smaller climbs, there are even more options. For a day of bouldering while visiting the Interior town of Fairbanks, head for the unearthly landscape of the **Granite Tors,** a short hike from Chena Hot Springs Road, northeast of the city. Looking for something with a shorter approach?

▲ alaska climbing & mountaineering @ a glance

Denali (Mount McKinley)

REGION ›› The Interior
ELEVATION ›› 20,320 feet
DIFFICULTY ›› ★ ★ ★ ★ ★
TIME NEEDED ›› 20–30 days
SUITABLE FOR KIDS? ›› No
GUIDE SUGGESTED?
›› Highly recommended

Mount Blackburn

REGION ›› Southcentral Inland
ELEVATION ›› 16,390 feet
DIFFICULTY ›› ★ ★ ★ ★
TIME NEEDED ›› 12–20 days
SUITABLE FOR KIDS? ›› No
GUIDE SUGGESTED?
›› Highly recommended

Mount Bona

REGION ›› Southcentral Inland
ELEVATION ›› 16,550 feet
DIFFICULTY ›› ★ ★ ★ ★
TIME NEEDED ›› 9–15 days
SUITABLE FOR KIDS? ›› No
GUIDE SUGGESTED?
›› Highly recommended

Mount Foraker

REGION ›› The Interior
ELEVATION ›› 17,400 feet
DIFFICULTY ›› ★ ★ ★ ★ ★

TIME NEEDED ›› 10–15 days
SUITABLE FOR KIDS? ›› No
GUIDE SUGGESTED?
›› Highly recommended

Mount Hunter

REGION ›› The Interior
ELEVATION ›› 14,573 feet
DIFFICULTY ›› ★ ★ ★ ★ ★
TIME NEEDED ›› 12–18 days
SUITABLE FOR KIDS? ›› No
GUIDE SUGGESTED?
›› Highly recommended

Mount St. Elias

REGION ›› Southcentral Inland
ELEVATION ›› 18,008 feet
DIFFICULTY ›› ★ ★ ★ ★ ★
TIME NEEDED ›› 15–30 days
SUITABLE FOR KIDS? ›› No
GUIDE SUGGESTED?
›› Highly recommended

Mount Sanford

REGION ›› Southcentral Inland
ELEVATION ›› 16,237 feet
DIFFICULTY ›› ★ ★ ★ ★
TIME NEEDED ›› 9–15 days
SUITABLE FOR KIDS? ›› No
GUIDE SUGGESTED?
›› Highly recommended

Try the single-pitch routes along the **Seward Highway** that begin just a few feet from the blacktop.

Come winter, the rock-climbing options turn to ice. The high mountains are forbidding to all but the most hard-bitten adventurers, but closer to sea level, an altogether different type of climbing presents itself as waterfalls solidify into fantastic cascades of ice. From **Bridal Veil Falls** on the Richardson Highway to **Ripple** and **Boone's Farm** deep in the Eklutna Gorge,

▲ climbing outfitters @ a glance

Alaska Mountain Guides and Climbing School

800-766-3396
alaskamountainguides.com

REGION » Statewide
COST » $$$
SUITABLE FOR KIDS? » No
ACTIVITY LEVEL » High
TRIP LENGTH » Varies

Alaska Mountaineering School– Alaska Denali Guiding

907-733-1016
climbalaska.org

REGION » The Interior
COST » $$$$
SUITABLE FOR KIDS? » No
ACTIVITY LEVEL » High
TRIP LENGTH » 10–24 days

Alaska Rock Gym

907-562-7265
alaskarockgym.com

REGION » Southcentral Inland
COST » $$
SUITABLE FOR KIDS? » Age 6 and older
ACTIVITY LEVEL » Light–moderate
TRIP LENGTH » Day trip

Alpine Ascents International

206-378-1927
alpineascents.com

REGION » The Interior
COST » $$$$
SUITABLE FOR KIDS? » No
ACTIVITY LEVEL » High
TRIP LENGTH » 8–20 days

The Ascending Path

877-783-0505 or 907-783-0505
theascendingpath.com

REGION » Southcentral Inland
COST » $$
SUITABLE FOR KIDS? » Varies
ACTIVITY LEVEL » Moderate–high
TRIP LENGTH » Day trip

Exposure Alaska

907-761-3761
exposurealaska.com

REGION » Southcentral Inland
COST » $$
SUITABLE FOR KIDS? » No
ACTIVITY LEVEL » Moderate–high
TRIP LENGTH » Day trips–expeditions

MICA Guides

800-956-6422
micaguides.com

REGION » Southcentral Inland
COST » $
SUITABLE FOR KIDS? » Age 6 and older
ACTIVITY LEVEL » Moderate
TRIP LENGTH » Day trip

Mountain Trip International

866-886-8747 or 970-369-1153
mountaintrip.com

REGION » The Interior
COST » $$$
SUITABLE FOR KIDS? » No
ACTIVITY LEVEL » High
TRIP LENGTH » 14–30 days

there is plenty of ice for climbing. Glacier climbing is another popular way to explore the landscape, whether it's in the winter or summer. Some of it doesn't require the technical skills of climbing vertical ice, but you shouldn't venture out alone, either.

▲ more climbing outfitters @ a glance

North Star Trekking

866-590-4530 or 907-790-4530
northstartrekking.com

REGION ›› Southeast
COST ›› $$
SUITABLE FOR KIDS? ›› Some trips
ACTIVITY LEVEL ›› Moderate
TRIP LENGTH ›› Day trip

NOVA River Runners

800-746-5753
novalaska.com

REGION ›› Southcentral Inland
COST ›› $

SUITABLE FOR KIDS? ›› Teens
ACTIVITY LEVEL ›› Moderate
TRIP LENGTH ›› Day trip

St. Elias Alpine Guides

888-933-5427 or 907-345-9048
steliasguides.com

REGION ›› Southcentral Inland
COST ›› $$$
SUITABLE FOR KIDS? ›› No
ACTIVITY LEVEL ›› High
TRIP LENGTH ›› 8–21 days

Unlike other special-interest sections in this book, this one will not outline do-it-yourself trips and related information. Mountaineering and climbing is a specialized sport that requires experience and thorough knowledge of the conditions before you head out. All mountaineers should understand the science behind the behavior of snow—how it lies, when it falls, and under what conditions it is most likely to cause an avalanche. Even if you are a novice, it is important to go with someone who has experience and can show you the ropes—literally.

The sport also requires specific tools such as ropes, axes, crampons, and hardware, none of which are cheap. While this gear is readily available, it helps to get on the ice a few times before going out and purchasing the gear on the spot.

We will, however, whet your appetite to learn more. Several regions of the state are popular for climbing, and there are many resources to help you plan your adventure. This section offers a description of the best climbing locations, a list of resources for planning, and outfitters that lead guided trips up big mountains.

If big-mountain climbing is something you are considering for the future, we also suggest a few outfitters and locations that offer day trips at area ice-climbing and trekking locales. Think of these outfitters' trips as samplings of what could be. While trekking along Matanuska Glacier with a guide, you can get a small idea of what it would be like to do the same thing for weeks on a remote peak in Alaska. The major difference: you get to sleep in a warm bed come nighttime!

GENERAL CLIMBING RESOURCES

No matter which Alaska peak you decide to pursue, these resources can help prepare you for the journey and give you an idea of what resources are available once you land in Alaska. These are general tips; resources for specific climbing areas—such as area air taxis, books on the mountains themselves, and rental companies that cater to just one area—are listed later in this section.

International Climbers

Go to **cbp.gov/xp/cgov/travel/id_visa** for details on getting through U.S. Customs with the equipment you need. Keep required traveling documents in a safe place during your expedition. Several years ago, an Italian climber cached his paperwork on Denali and a snowstorm buried his marker. It was not a wise move. The site outlines visa and passport requirements; another option is to contact your nation's embassy or consulate.

Reading

These references can help you learn about important safety issues such as wilderness first aid and avalanche dangers.

▸ *Alaska: A Climbing Guide* by Mike Wood and Colby Coombs.

▸ *American Alpine Journal,* various issues. Go to the library or do an Internet search for journal issues that have information on climbing Denali. An excellent resource, and the accepted journal of choice for serious climbers. The journal is a publication of the **American Alpine Club (americanalpineclub.org)**, which has an Alaska section based in Anchorage (visit **mcak.org/aac**).

▶ *The Illustrated Guide to Glacier Travel and Crevasse Rescue* by Andy Tyson and Mike Clelland.

▶ *Medicine for Mountaineering,* edited by James A. Wilkerson, MD. A reality in climbing is the possibility of everything from altitude sickness to high-altitude pulmonary edema.

▶ *Snow Sense: A Guide to Evaluating Snow Avalanche Hazard* by Jill Fredston and Doug Fesler. These Alaska residents are experts worldwide in avalanche safety. A must-read for mountaineers.

Gear, Etc.

▶ Some rental gear is available in Anchorage at **Alaska Mountaineering and Hiking** (2633 Spenard Rd., Anchorage 99503; 907-272-1811; **alaska mountaineering.com**) and **REI** (1200 W. Northern Lights Blvd., Anchorage 99503; 907-272-4565; **rei.com**).

▶ **Exposure Alaska** (907-761-3761; **exposurealaska.com**), an Anchorage-based outfit, provides support for climbing ascents, including van support and food. The company also offers a seven-night fly-in trip to Wrangell–St. Elias National Park for ice climbing, backpacking, and remote camping. Prices range from $425 for support packages to $2,790 for fly-in expeditions.

DENALI NATIONAL PARK AND PRESERVE

The granddaddy of all mountains lies in the midst of Denali National Park and Preserve, the tallest peak in all of North America: **Denali,** or as it is known to many, **Mount McKinley.** Denali is 20,320 feet high, and on a clear day it looms so high over the horizon that it looks unreal.

The mountain lures climbers by the hundreds, sometimes as many as 1,000 attempting to reach its summit per season. Equally alluring is neighboring **Mount Foraker,** which, because of its technical aspects, is considered just as challenging and sometimes more enjoyable because of the smaller crowds.

By nature of its largest-mountain status, Denali is the most popular mountain scale attempted each year, and as a result can get crowded at the base camp. Where Wrangell–St. Elias is practically deserted, Denali National Park is a veritable party. Both have their advantages; it is up to you as the climber to decide which appeals to you more.

All climbers attempting Mounts Denali and Foraker must register with **Denali National Park and Preserve (nps.gov/dena/planyourvisit/mountaineering .htm)** and pay a special-use charge of $200 per climber, in addition to the park-entrance fee of $10 per person or $20 per family. The fee helps pay for the high-altitude base camp at **Kahiltna Glacier,** which has a manned ranger station and rescue team available. Each year, injured climbers are hoisted off the mountain, at great expense and often risking the lives of the rescuers. Climbers die on the mountain regularly.

In addition to the special-use fee, a 60-day preregistration regulation allows mountaineering rangers to contact climbers before they arrive in Talkeetna, which is the launching point for most expeditions. Rangers are able to evaluate the would-be climbers and suggest appropriate routes for different levels of expertise.

The **Talkeetna Ranger Station** (907-733-2231), the contact point for climbers, will send its informative mountaineering booklet (written in eight languages) for review ahead of time. Its stark introduction, written by South District Ranger Daryl Miller, sets forth the life-or-death realities of climbing in Alaska, without any sugarcoating or romanticizing. It is a must-have for anyone considering climbing the "high one." The booklet can be ordered or downloaded at no charge at **nps.gov/archive/dena/home/mountaineering/booklet.htm.** See our listings on the next page for other climbing resources in Denali.

DENALI (MOUNT McKINLEY)

Region The Interior.	**Best suited for** Experienced moun-
Type of climbing Mountaineering.	taineers; West Buttress is Grade II.
Elevation 20,320 feet.	**Maps** U.S. Geological Survey (USGS)
Difficulty ★★★★★.	Mount McKinley A-1 and A-3
Suitable for kids? No.	(1-inch/mile scale recommended);
Best time of year to go May–July.	24 maps within this region; to
Time commitment 20–30 days.	order or download, visit **usgs.gov.**

DESTINATION SUMMARY   Even the easiest of the 30-plus routes to reach Denali's summit, the West Buttress route, is not easy. No matter how you approach it, Denali is a challenging climb, as much for the extreme weather as anything else. There are only a handful of licensed guides with whom to travel, and we suggest three in our outfitters section on the next page. Be prepared for a logjam of travelers at the Kahiltna Base Camp. This is far from a wilderness experience.

MOUNT FORAKER

Region The Interior.	**Best time of year to go** May–July.
Type of climbing Mountaineering.	**Time commitment** 10–15 days.
Elevation 17,400 feet.	**Best suited for** Experienced
Difficulty ★★★★.	mountaineers.
Suitable for kids? No.	**Maps** USGS Talkeetna D-3 Quad.

DESTINATION SUMMARY   The less-traveled Mount Foraker is a challenging hike from whichever direction you choose to approach it. Many accomplished Denali climbers also attempt this peak. The mountain's current name is English, but its native names were *Sultana* and *Menlale*, meaning "Denali's wife."

MOUNT HUNTER

Region The Interior.	**Best time of year to go** May–July.
Type of climbing Mountaineering.	**Time commitment** 12–18 days.
Elevation 14,573 feet.	**Best suited for** Experienced
Difficulty ★★★★.	mountaineers; Grade III.
Suitable for kids? No.	**Maps** Visit **topographicalmaps.com**.

DESTINATION SUMMARY   Athabascans called Hunter *Begguya*, which means "Denali's child." It is the steepest and most technical of the three great peaks in Denali National Park. It has a north and south summit and is considered the hardest-to-climb 14,000-foot mountain in North America. Those who climb all these peaks will round out the entire Denali family.

Resources

▶ **"Mountaineering in Denali National Park and Preserve"** is required reading (see the Denali National Park and Preserve introduction for details on ordering).

But there are many other excellent books on climbing Denali and other peaks. For example, ***Denali's West Buttress: A Climber's Guide to Mount McKinley's Classic Route*** by Colby Coombs outlines the most popular route taken by climbers and will help prepare you mentally. And ***The Ascent of Denali*** by Hudson Stuck is a classic story of climbing the mountain.

▶ Several air-taxi operators in Talkeetna can get climbers to the base camp at Kahiltna Glacier. We know and recommend **K-2 Aviation** (800-764-2291 or 907-733-2291; **flyk2.com**), but climbers also use **Fly Denali** (866-733-7768 or 907-733-7768; **flydenali.com**) and **Talkeetna Air Taxi** (800-533-2219 or 907-733-2218; **talkeetnaair.com**). These companies also can take you sightseeing at the glacier to see the climbers in action, if they have space and time during the climbing season. It's a great way to get a feel for the real thing.

▶ **The Park Connection** (800-266-8625; **alaskacoach.com**) and **Talkeetna Shuttle Service** (800-288-6008 or 907-733-1725) can get you from Anchorage to Talkeetna and back if you don't have your own transportation. Most climbers use **Denali Overland Transportation** (800-651-5221 or 907-733-2384; **denali overland.com**).

Denali National Park Outfitters

▶ **ALASKA MOUNTAINEERING SCHOOL–ALASKA DENALI GUIDING** ›› *Talkeetna– Mount McKinley* 907-733-1016; **climbalaska.org.** This goal-oriented educational institution and guiding service is dedicated to providing safe and successful Denali ascents while also focusing on improving your mountaineering skills. They've led more than 100 expeditions around the world, most within the Alaska Range. AMS provides instruction in general mountaineering, wilderness expeditions, and medicine and other custom courses. Expeditions include the West Buttress ($6,000) and West Rib ($7,400).

▶ **ALPINE ASCENTS INTERNATIONAL** ›› *Seattle–Mount McKinley* 206-378-1927; **alpineascents.com.** Alpine Ascents begins its ascents with an eight-day Denali Prep Course designed to give all climbers the tools necessary for a safe and rewarding expedition. Climbers are carefully screened to ensure the enjoyment and safety of the entire group. With a maximum of six climbers, the guides offer an intimate mountain experience on a 20-day climb up McKinley's West Buttress. The $6,300 fee includes an air taxi to the base camp on Kahiltna Glacier, group gear, guide fees, and meals during the expedition. The company also offers private climbs in Alaska and around the globe.

▶ **MOUNTAIN TRIP INTERNATIONAL** ›› *Ophir, Colorado–Mount McKinley* 866-886-8747 or 970-369-1153; **mountaintrip.com.** This company, which has been guiding in Denali since 1976, leads trips up the West Buttress and the West Rib. Its experience and summit success rate are its claims to fame; mountain experiences are available for a variety of ability levels and interests. Trips range 14–30 days and start at $5,800, including air taxi and group gear. Mountain Trip also offers private climbs, ski mountaineering, rock climbing, and other climbing and mountaineering seminars, as well as shorter expeditions to such peaks as Foraker and Hunter.

WRANGELL–ST. ELIAS NATIONAL PARK AND PRESERVE

This remote park shares borders with Canada's **Kluane National Park** and features some of the most remote and least-climbed mountains in the world, all part of the Chugach and St. Elias mountain ranges. Many of them are higher than 15,000 feet. There are so many mountains here, in fact, that often they don't even have names.

Because the park is so remote and the climbing community so small and elite, there is no high-altitude rescue team here such as you will find at Denali National Park and Preserve. Climbers should know how to navigate not only with GPS units but also with topographical maps and a compass.

Extreme physical fitness is a must here, as are knowledge of avalanche dangers, glacier travel, and self-arrest techniques, as well as the ability to read the ice for crevasse dangers.

Access to the most remote and highest mountains is usually by chartered plane from Yakutat or other points within the park. Because the park borders Canada, all climbing expeditions that enter Kluane National Park must secure a permit before heading out (contact Superintendent, Kluane National Park; 867-634-7208). On the American side, climbers are encouraged to fill out a trip itinerary at park headquarters or one of the outlying ranger stations. Contact Wrangell–St. Elias National Park and Preserve, Mile 106.8 Richardson Hwy., Copper Center 99573; 907-822-5234; or the Yakutat District Ranger, 907-784-3295; **nps.gov/wrst.**

MOUNT BLACKBURN

Region Southcentral Inland Alaska.	**Time commitment** 12–20 days.
Type of climbing Mountaineering.	**Best suited for** Experienced
Elevation 16,390 feet.	mountaineers.
Difficulty ★★★★.	**Maps** USGS McCarthy Quad C-7 and
Suitable for kids? No.	D-7 (1:63,360 scale), McCarthy
Best time of year to go April–July.	(1:250,000 scale).

DESTINATION SUMMARY   Four potential routes along the North, East, Southeast, and South/Southwest ridges. The South/Southwest ridge has been attempted numerous times without success. Avalanche danger is high throughout.

MOUNT BONA

Region Southcentral Inland Alaska.	**Best time of year to go** April–June.
Type of climbing Mountaineering.	**Time commitment** 9–15 days.
Elevation 16,550 feet.	**Best suited for** Experienced
Difficulty ★★★★.	mountaineers.
Suitable for kids? No.	**Maps** USGS McCarthy B-2 Quad.

DESTINATION SUMMARY   Located in the Wrangell Mountains, this challenging peak also is one of the more doable treks within the park. It gets less traffic too. It is the 4th-highest peak in Alaska and the 11th-highest peak in North America.

MOUNT SANFORD

Region Southcentral Inland Alaska.	**Time commitment** 9–15 days.
Type of climbing Mountaineering.	**Best suited for** Experienced
Elevation 16,237 feet.	mountaineers.
Difficulty ★★★★.	**Maps** USGS Gulkana Quad, A-1
Suitable for kids? No.	(1:63,360 scale), Gulkana, B-1
Best time of year to go April–July.	(1:250,000 scale).

DESTINATION SUMMARY   This trip requires travel across tundra and along Sheep Glacier to reach the summit. Riddled with crevasses and buffeted by excessively strong winds, it is not the romanticized trip it has been made out to be in written accounts.

MOUNT ST. ELIAS

Region Southcentral Inland Alaska.	**Time commitment** 15–30 days.
Type of climbing Mountaineering.	**Best suited for** Experienced mountaineers.
Elevation 18,008 feet.	
Difficulty ★★★★★.	**Maps** Purchase the 1:250K USGS map of Mount St. Elias, or zoom in on the 11 15-minute Alaska maps, depending on the route.
Suitable for kids? No.	
Best time of year to go April–June.	

DESTINATION SUMMARY   Stormy weather patterns and a lack of high-altitude rescue teams in Wrangell–St. Elias make this a trek for only the most advanced of mountaineers. St. Elias and the other many unnamed peaks in the park are rarely traveled, providing amazing solitude but requiring advanced outdoor-survival skills. Mount St. Elias was the first of the Alaska mountains to be discovered and the first to be climbed. It long was thought to be the highest peak in North America but ranks at number three.

Resources

▸ *A Most Hostile Mountain* by Jonathan Waterman. This engaging tale deals in part with Waterman's time in Wrangell–St. Elias while also re-creating the steps of the Italian explorer who first discovered the mountain.

▸ *Hiking in Wrangell–St. Elias National Park* by Danny Kost. This is a hiking guidebook, but Kost, also an accomplished climber, knows the area *better than most.*

▸ *Mountain Wilderness: An Illustrated History of the Wrangell–St. Elias National Park and Preserve* by William R. Hunt. A good overview of the Wrangell–St. Elias region.

▸ *National Geographic–Trails Illustrated* has produced a 1:375,000-scale map of Wrangell–St. Elias that is good for pretrip planning. It covers the entire park, including detailed inserts of the Nabesna Road and McCarthy-Kennicott areas. It is available at the ranger stations or online through **Alaska Geographic** ($11.95; **alaskageographic.org**).

▶ Air taxis serving the area include **Alsek Air Service** (907-784-3231; **alsekair .com**) out of Yakutat; **McCarthy Air** (907-554-4440; **mccarthyair.com**) in McCarthy; **Ultima Thule Outfitters and Lodge** (907-854-4500; **ultimathule lodge.com**) out of Chitina; and **Wrangell Mountain Air** (800-478-1160; **wrangellmountainair.com**) in Glennallen.

Wrangell–St. Elias Outfitters

▶ **ALASKA MOUNTAIN GUIDES AND CLIMBING SCHOOL ▸▸** *Haines* 800-766-3396; **alaskamountainguides.com.** Leads several expeditions around the state, mostly in Denali and Wrangell–St. Elias National Park. Mountaineering, expedition, and rock- and ice-climbing classes are also offered through the climbing school. The company also guides skiing, hiking, sea-kayaking, rafting, and multisport adventures around the state and the country. Prices range from $160 for a one-day rock-climbing course to $5,500 for a 22-day Denali ascent.

▶ **ST. ELIAS ALPINE GUIDES LLC ▸▸** *Anchorage/Wrangell–St. Elias* 888-933-5427 or 907-345-9048; **steliasguides.com.** One of Alaska's most experienced and trusted guiding services, St. Elias offers expeditions to Mounts Bona, Blackburn, St. Elias, and Drum and other well-known peaks. Trips range 8–21 days and from $1,280 for a glacier- and ice-climbing excursion to $3,750 for mountaineering expeditions, including transportation to remote areas. Also offers ski mountaineering and other adventure trips in Alaska's wild country.

DAY TRIPS

After scanning the previous listings, you may be encouraged to see what all this talk of climbing is really about. The following trips are offered by experienced guide companies that can give you a sampling of ice and glacier climbing. No experience is necessary, although it helps to be in good shape.

ALASKA ROCK GYM

Region Southcentral Inland Alaska.	**Best time of year to go** Year-round.
Type of climbing Indoor.	**Traffic level** Moderate–heavy.
Cost $$.	**Contact** 4840 Fairbanks St., Anchorage 99503; 907-562-7265; **alaska rockgym.com.**
Activity level Light–moderate.	
Suitable for kids? Age 6 and up.	

DESTINATION SUMMARY   This 6,000-square-foot facility is an excellent way to practice skills if you're in town and rained out. The gym features bouldering and climbing walls and experts who can help belay or teach, either in classes or individually. Day passes are $7 for kids age 13 and younger, $15 for adults and kids age 14 and up (gear and instruction cost $14 and $21 for these respective age groups). There are Monday and Friday classes and a Thursday women's climbing class too.

THE ASCENDING PATH

Region Southcentral Inland Alaska.	**Best time of year to go** Mid-June–Sept.
Type of climbing Glacier trekking, ice climbing, rock climbing.	**Traffic level** Moderate.
Cost $$.	**Contact** At the yurt at Alyeska Resort; 907-783-0505; **theascendingpath.com.**
Activity level Moderate–high.	
Suitable for kids? Some trips.	

DESTINATION SUMMARY   This experienced guide company can introduce the budding climber to ice or rock climbing and glacier trekking in summer. The 3-hour $139 glacier trek includes interpretive glaciology discussions, great views of the seven glaciers in the Girdwood bowl, a round-trip ticket up the mountain on the Tramway, trekking poles, and overboot rentals. Learn about moats; lateral, medial, and terminal moraine; firn line; and nunataks, among other topics. The 3-hour rock-climbing and 5-hour ice-climbing programs are $129 and $220, respectively.

MICA GUIDES

Region Southcentral Inland Alaska.	**Best time of year to go** Mid-June–Sept.
Type of climbing Glacier trekking, ice climbing.	**Traffic level** Light.
Cost $.	**Contact** Based in Chickaloon, north of Palmer; 800-956-6422; **mica guides.com.**
Activity level Moderate.	
Suitable for kids? Age 6 and up.	

DESTINATION SUMMARY   *MICA* stands for Matanuska Ice Climbing Adventures, and that's what you get with this family-friendly outfit. It offers 1½-hour glacier treks on Matanuska Glacier for an extremely affordable $45 per person. The 1½-hour trek isn't as educational as the 3-hour trek, which takes in natural ice formations and costs $70 per person. MICA's 6-hour ice-climbing course is another bargain at $130 per person. At the same Matanuska Glacier location, participants can learn about the technical aspects of climbing and hit the ice themselves. MICA allows younger kids on the glacier, while their ice-climbing trips are for folks age 12 and older.

NORTH STAR TREKKING

Region Southeast Alaska.	**Suitable for kids?** Some trips.
Type of climbing Glacier trekking, ice climbing.	**Best time of year to go** June–Sept.
	Traffic level Moderate.
Cost $$.	**Contact** Based in Juneau; 866-590-4530 or 907-790-4530; **northstar**
Activity level Moderate.	**trekking.com.**

DESTINATION SUMMARY   These glacier treks are combined with a helicopter ride to reach Mendenhall Glacier, so the price is a bit higher than the walk-to locations in Southcentral Inland. Still, the helicopter flight is an adventure in itself. The Level 1 Walkabout ($295) is the cheapest, but it's sort of boring. The 2-hour Level 2 Glacier Trek ($359) emphasizes proper use of gear and learning glacier features. The Level 3 X-Trek ($459) is an extended outing that includes 4 hours of trekking, ice climbing, and learning how to use ropes. We recommend getting the most for your helicopter-riding hours by tackling this one. The price is only $100 more for twice as much learning.

NOVA RIVER RUNNERS

Region Southcentral Inland Alaska.	**Best time of year to go** Mid-June–Sept.
Type of climbing Glacier trekking.	
Cost $.	**Traffic level** Light.
Activity level Moderate.	**Contact** Based in Chickaloon, north of Palmer; 800-746-5753;
Suitable for kids? Preteens and up.	**novalaska.com.**

DESTINATION SUMMARY   NOVA is a longtime outdoor-adventure company, and as its name implies, rivers are what it does. However, the Chickaloon-based outfitter also offers an exciting 3½-hour Matanuska Glacier trek in which guests can walk on the glacier and experience the ice up close while wearing crampons. View crevasses, caves, and surface ponds, among other naturally occurring formations. The hike is $85 per person, unless you choose the $155 raft trip to Lion Head, a local point of interest (hike included in price).

▲ Dog Mushing

DOGSLEDDING IS TO Alaska what surfing is to Hawaii or rodeo is to Wyoming: it is a way of being for the many, many dog lovers here who also happen to enjoy spending time outdoors. In fact, dog mushing is considered the state sport, and every March spectators locally and from the world over arrive in Alaska by the thousands to watch the start of the **Iditarod Trail Sled Dog Race,** in which teams and their drivers run more than 1,000 miles from Anchorage to Nome, in western Alaska.

The Iditarod commemorates the feats of sled dogs in 1925, when an outbreak of diphtheria struck the town of Nome and poor weather prevented the delivery of the life-saving serum needed to treat those afflicted. Quick-thinking mushers suggested a relay in which they could bring the medicine to Nome by dogsled. (The train carrying the serum made it to Nenana, a small Interior village, before getting stuck, so the actual relay began there. Today's race covers the entire route, however.) Twenty-one teams took part in the relay, traveling as fast as they could go. The trip that the Nome doctor thought would take 15 days took fewer than 6, amazing not only the doctor but the mushers and townspeople as well. The dogs' bravery saved the town from the deadly epidemic and gave Alaskans a renewed appreciation for the working canines of Alaska.

Today, the Iditarod attracts racers from all over the world, and the prize is hefty—usually more than $50,000 in cash and a brand-new pickup truck. Critics of the race claim that the dogs are asked to go beyond their abilities, pushed for the prize, and treated as objects to help their owners win that ultimate reward. Supporters say that the dogs are born to run, happiest when in harness leading a team through a wilderness path, and healthiest by staying so active.

TRAVELER'S TIP

▸ *Many mushers make a living sharing their sport with those who don't know much about it. They teach people how to harness a dog to a team and how to drive a sled; many also let their clients share in chores such as feeding and cleaning up after the animals.*

Whatever your opinion, we say come to Alaska and find out for yourself. The sport of dog mushing extends far beyond the high profile of the Iditarod. There are hundreds of recreational dog mushers throughout the state—ordinary people who enjoy working with dogs and getting into the backcountry during winter. Some take part in local sprint or distance races, or they meet on weekends to run their teams together.

The center of dog mushing is, without a doubt, the Fairbanks area, especially the outlying communities of **Two Rivers** and **Chena Hot Springs.** Here the land is vast, the trail system endless, and the snow season longer than anywhere else in the state. In Southcentral Inland Alaska, **Chugiak** and the **Matanuska-Susitna Valley** are dog-mushing hot spots. In Southcentral Coastal Alaska, the **Caribou Hills** of the Kenai Peninsula draw mushers from such communities as Kasilof, Clam Gulch, and Ninilchik, among other locales. Southeast has a few mushers, but the snow season is short and inconsistent. In the Bush, dog mushing is still an accepted mode of transportation, and dog teams are as common as snowmobiles and pickup trucks.

This section spotlights a handful of outfitters that can guide you on a backcountry dog-mushing expedition. This is a sport for which we can say, definitively, that you must travel with a guide. Mushers understand and recognize safety issues that can affect their dogs—tangled lines, wildlife encounters, ice overflow, and other concerns. They understand their dogs well enough to know if one of the pack is getting tired or is not running quite right due to an injury or fatigue. These skills are the mushers' responsibility, so they will not and should not let inexperienced people loose with their dogs without first knowing for sure that they can handle it. But while dog mushing requires specialized gear and some dog-handling knowledge, even someone who has

dog-mushing outfitters @ a glance

Chena Dog Sled Adventures

907-488-5845
ptialaska.net/~sleddogs

REGION » The Interior
COST » $$
SUITABLE FOR KIDS? » Yes
ACTIVITY LEVEL » Light–moderate
TRIP LENGTH » 1–2 days

Chugach Express Dog Sled Tours

907-783-2266
chugachexpress.com

REGION » Southcentral Inland
COST » $
SUITABLE FOR KIDS? » Yes
ACTIVITY LEVEL » Light
TRIP LENGTH » Day trip

Earthsong Lodge and Denali Dogsled Expeditions

907-683-2863
earthsonglodge.com

REGION » The Interior
COST » $$$
SUITABLE FOR KIDS? » Teens
ACTIVITY LEVEL » Moderate
TRIP LENGTH » 1–10 days

1st Alaska Outdoor School

907-590-5900
1stalaskaoutdoorschool.com

REGION » The Interior
COST » $
SUITABLE FOR KIDS? » Some
ACTIVITY LEVEL » Moderate–high
TRIP LENGTH » Day trip

Jeff King's Husky Homestead Tours

907-683-2904
huskyhomestead.com

REGION » The Interior
COST » $
SUITABLE FOR KIDS? » Age 7 and older
ACTIVITY LEVEL » Light
TRIP LENGTH » Day trip

Jerry Austin's Alaska Adventures

877-923-2419
alaskadogsledding.com or
alaskaadventures.net

REGION » The Bush
COST » $$$
SUITABLE FOR KIDS? » Teens
ACTIVITY LEVEL » Moderate–high
TRIP LENGTH » 6 days

Seavey's IdidaRide Sled Dog Tours

907-224-8607
ididaride.com

REGION » Southcentral Coastal
COST » $
SUITABLE FOR KIDS? » Yes
ACTIVITY LEVEL » Light
TRIP LENGTH » Day trip/custom

Sky Trekking Alaska

907-315-6098
skytrekkingalaska.com

REGION » Statewide
COST » $$$$
SUITABLE FOR KIDS? » No
ACTIVITY LEVEL » Light
TRIP LENGTH » 4–12 days

never driven a sled can become a musher for a day or a week or even two weeks with a little guidance.

Dog-mushing trips can range from 1 hour to two weeks, from a kennel tour to an interpretive program on the history of sled dogs in Alaska. We offer all of this to you and encourage you to get a little education while you're here in Alaska. Learn about our state sport and gain a better understanding of these amazing animals we call sled dogs.

GENERAL DOG-MUSHING RESOURCES

Want to learn a little more about dog mushing ahead of time? Here are a few resources that you can look up before landing in Alaska.

▸ The **Alaska Dog Mushers Association** in Fairbanks (907-457-6874; **sleddog.org**) and the **Chugiak Dog Mushers Association** in Chugiak (907-689-7899; **chugiak dogmushers.com**) are local clubs in their communities that help support the sport. For statewide information, contact Fairbanks-based **Mush with PRIDE** (Providing Responsible Information on a Dog's Environment; 800-507-7433 or 907-490-6874; **mushwithpride.org**), which promotes responsible care and humane treatment of all dogs. The **Alaskan Sled Dog and Racing Association** in Anchorage (**asdra.org**) concentrates on sprint racing and racing regulations.

▸ The annual **Iditarod Trail Sled Dog Race** (visit **iditarod.com** for details) takes place the first weekend in March. Watch as up to 80 teams take off from downtown Anchorage, then restart the next day in the Matanuska-Susitna Valley. Iditarod Headquarters, at Mile 2.2 Knik Goose Bay Rd. in Wasilla, has an office and gift shop that are open weekdays 8 a.m.–5 p.m. Some outfitters allow armchair mushers to follow the race via small plane; see listings following for details.

▸ *Mushing* magazine (917-929-6118; **mushing.com**) has been published in Interior Alaska for nearly 20 years. Back issues are available for a fee. Another resource is *Sled Dog Sports* magazine (online at the same address). The Web site features a listing of sled-dog tours.

DOG-MUSHING OUTFITTERS

Bettles

1ST ALASKA OUTDOOR SCHOOL

Region The Interior.
Type of mushing Day or multiday.
Cost $.
Activity level Moderate–high.
Suitable for kids? Sometimes.
Best time of year to go Jan.–March.

Summer activities Hiking, canoeing, backpacking, remote lodging, camping, and other educational programs.

Contact 907-590-5900; **1stalaskaoutdoorschool.com**.

OUTFITTER SUMMARY   1st **Alaska Outdoor School** not only can teach you how to run dogs in a day program, but it also helps coordinate and guide multi-day treks in the Interior backcountry by dogsled.

These trips explore some of the most serene, untraveled country in the world. They are designed for those who want to be part of the team, helping with the dogs and camp chores at the end of the day and enjoying the ride during the day. Some winter trips require you to wear a headlamp, as sunlight is scarce, but the northern lights and an immense blanket of stars are your reward. Prices are dependent on the length of trip—$75 for a short tour to $125 for a daylong expedition—but we have found this outfit to be one of the most reasonably and inexpensively priced offerings in the market—and they're friendly to boot.

Denali

JEFF KING'S HUSKY HOMESTEAD TOURS

Region The Interior.	**Best time of year to go** June–August.
Type of mushing Day tours.	**Summer activities** Summer-only kennel tours.
Cost $.	
Activity level Light.	**Contact** 907-683-2904;
Suitable for kids? Age 7 and up.	huskyhomestead.com.

OUTFITTER SUMMARY   Jeff King, a four-time Iditarod champion and long-time Denali Park musher, offers 1½-hour kennel tours during which guests are shuttled to his scenic log home at Goose Lake and immediately greeted with tiny puppies to pet and hold. Learn about the training, equipment, and tenacity needed to become a successful competitive dog musher. Tours are $49 for adults.

Girdwood

CHUGACH EXPRESS DOG SLED TOURS

Region Southcentral Inland.	**Suitable for kids?** Yes.
Type of mushing Hourly and day trips.	**Best time of year to go** Jan.–March.
	Summer activities Camp tour in summer via helicopter flight to glacier.
Cost $.	**Contact** 907-783-2266;
Activity level Light.	**chugachexpress.com.**

OUTFITTER SUMMARY   For the sampler in you, this outfitter offers short dogsled rides in the winter at the base of Mount Alyeska in Girdwood. In the summer, however, you can take part in dogsledding tours atop a glacier. Your guide, a longtime Alaska musher, handles both. His summer tour costs $400 and comprises a 1½-hour Iditarod training camp, including a scenic helicopter flight to the site. During the fall season, you can take a wheeled cart ride behind the dogs for $65. A 1-hour training and educational program is offered at Alyeska Resort for $155; a half-day program on a nearby snowfield costs $405 and includes instruction, lunch, gear, and the opportunity to drive your own dog team on a guided run. Make sure to call and confirm ahead of time, because business is come-and-go depending on how busy the guide is. If you can catch him, it's well worth the trip.

Healy

EARTHSONG LODGE AND DENALI DOGSLED EXPEDITIONS

Region The Interior.	**Suitable for kids?** Preteens and older.
Type of mushing Day trips, overnighters, expeditions, interpretive programs.	**Best time of year to go** Nov.–Jan.
	Summer activities Dogsled training via cart; kennel tours.
Cost $$$.	**Contact** 907-683-2863;
Activity level Moderate.	**earthsonglodge.com.**

OUTFITTER SUMMARY   The lodge owners are Denali National Park conces-
sionaires who can get you closer to Denali (Mount McKinley) than any other
guides around. The retreat is open all winter, providing dogsled adventures
ranging from lodge-based to multiday expeditions in the park. Very small
groups (no more than four people) make this an exceptionally enjoyable trip.
Prices start at $125 for day trips and go up to $6,700 for 10-day expeditions.
This is our highest-recommended location for accessible dog mushing. Owner
Jon Nierenberg is a former Denali park ranger and an experienced musher; the
lodge is an exceptionally nice spot to relax pre- and post-mush.

Iditarod Trail

SKY TREKKING ALASKA

Region Along the trail.	**Best time of year to go** March.
Type of mushing Armchair mushing.	**Summer activities** Other non-
Cost $$$$.	dog-related tours available.
Activity level Light.	**Contact** 907-315-6098;
Suitable for kids? No.	skytrekkingalaska.com.

OUTFITTER SUMMARY   This Wasilla-based outfit offers three itineraries for
4–12 days. All trips are centered on the Iditarod; you'll see the sights, hear
the sounds, and experience the exhilaration of the race as you follow the trail
from start to finish via small plane. Sky Trekking caters to those who prefer a
restaurant-style meal and a warm cabin to camping food and a trailside tent.
Prices range $4,500–$13,775 per person—that's 4 days up to 12 days.

Nome–St. Michael

JERRY AUSTIN'S ALASKA ADVENTURES

Region The Bush.	**Best time of year to go** Jan.–March.
Type of mushing Overnighters and expeditions.	**Summer activities** Fishing lodge, fishing packages available.
Cost $$$.	**Contact** 877-923-2419;
Activity level Moderate–high.	alaskadogsledding.com or
Suitable for kids? Teens.	alaskaadventures.net.

OUTFITTER SUMMARY   Iditarod Hall of Fame inductee Jerry Austin (he has run the race an incredible 18 times) and his friendly wife, Clara, a Yup'ik Eskimo from St. Michael, have been leading small groups on dogsled eco-tours since 1976. Not only does Jerry cater to the average outdoors enthusiast, but he also offers corporate retreats, women-only trips, and even family-reunion packages. You'll travel on frozen tundra and can even time your trip during the Iditarod to meet the mushers as they cross the finish line in Nome. Prices range $2,500–$3,500 per person for a six-day trip, which includes lodging, home-cooked meals, and winter gear. While getting to Austin's place is more complicated than, say, going to Girdwood for a day trip or up to Earthsong Lodge for a guided trek, there is no question these trips are more like the "real" mushing than you will get anywhere else in the state—a little more rustic, a lot more sparse, but truly authentic.

Seward

SEAVEY'S IDIDARIDE SLED DOG TOURS

Region Southcentral Coastal.	short tours; winter for extended tours.
Type of mushing Day tours.	
Cost $.	**Summer activities** Cart rides, kennel tours.
Activity level Light.	
Suitable for kids? Yes.	**Contact** 907-561-6874 (Wild Ride Show) or 907-224-8607;
Best time of year to go Summer for	**ididaride.com.**

OUTFITTER SUMMARY   This operation is probably the most commercial of the mushing outfits out there, and their presentations can seem a little touristy, but if you're limited for time, you can learn a lot about dog mushing here. Three generations of Seaveys have run the Iditarod—most recently, in 2004, second-generation musher Mitch Seavey won the race. The tour includes a summer cart ride (2-mile and 1½-hour options) and kennel visit, plus a full-day tour including Exit Glacier, or a Sterling-based presentation. The Seaveys also have begun offering winter tours in which you can join the family during their training and preparation for the Iditarod. Summer tours range $59–$130 per adult; winter tours start at $249 for a 3-hour dog mushing experience, but custom tours also are an option. A popular addition in 2007 is the Anchorage-based Wild Ride Sled Dog Show, in which Seavey's dogs perform and educate visitors in an entertaining and sometimes hilarious manner. That tour is daily in the summer and costs $24 ($12 for children). There also is a 2-hour dinner and Iditarod combination for $59.

Two Rivers

CHENA DOG SLED ADVENTURES

Region The Interior.	**Best time of year to go** Dec.–April.
Type of mushing Day, overnight, and multiday expeditions.	For snowshoeing, ice fishing, and dog mushing.
Cost $$.	**Summer activities** None.
Activity level Light–moderate.	**Contact** 907-488-5845;
Suitable for kids? Yes.	ptialaska.net/~sleddogs.

OUTFITTER SUMMARY   This outfitter offers trips ranging from 1 hour to two days in Chena River State Recreation Area. Trips include a dog-handler training course, short dog-team rides, multisport adventures, and overnight mushing expeditions. In addition, you'll have the choice to visit Chena Hot Springs and try your hand at ice fishing or snowshoeing. Prices range from $35 for a 2-mile dogsled ride to $700 for a musher-training course.

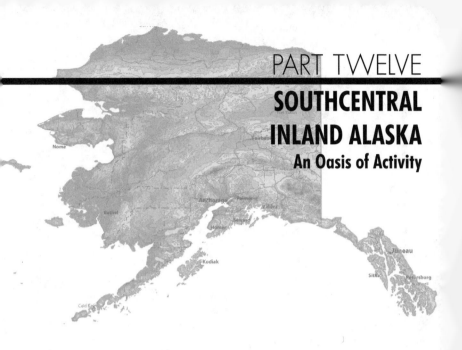

PART TWELVE

SOUTHCENTRAL INLAND ALASKA
An Oasis of Activity

▲ An Overview of the State's Liveliest Region

TAKE ALASKA AS a whole, and it can be quite overwhelming, with all there is to do and see. From the windblown tundra of Barrow to the rainforest lushness of Southeast Alaska, this is a land of diversity and unparalleled natural beauty. But there is one corner of Alaska, flanked by snowy mountain ranges along the northern end and rimmed by sandy, sea-lapped beaches along the southern end, where all of Alaska's best features can be found in one condensed package.

continued on page 278

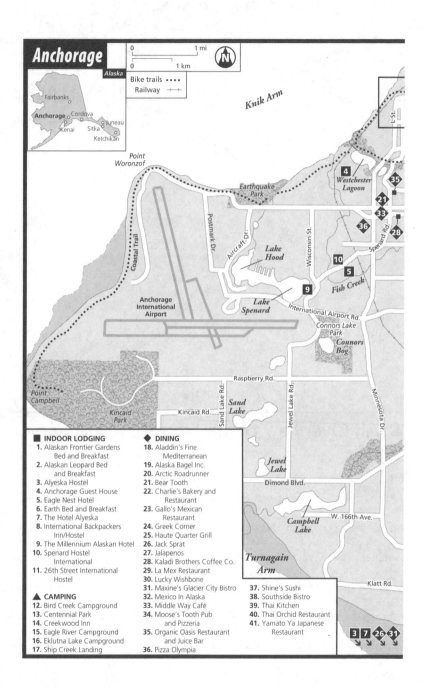

Anchorage

Alaska

0 ——————— 1 mi
0 ——————— 1 km

Bike trails ••••
Railway ┼┼┼

Fairbanks

Anchorage   Cordova
Kenai   Sitka   Juneau
Ketchikan

Knik Arm

Point Woronzof

Earthquake Park

Westchester Lagoon

L St.

4   **35**
21
33
36   Spenard Rd.
28

Postmark Dr.

Aircraft Dr.

Wisconsin St.

Lake Hood

10
5

Coastal Trail

Anchorage International Airport

Lake Spenard

9   Fish Creek

International Airport Rd.

Connors Lake Park

Connors Bog

Raspberry Rd.

Point Campbell

Kincaid Park

Kincaid Rd.   Sand Lake Rd.   Sand Lake

Jewel Lake Rd.

Minnesota Dr.

Jewel Lake

Dimond Blvd.

Campbell Lake   W. 166th Ave.

Turnagain Arm

Klatt Rd.

3 **7** **26** **31**

■ **INDOOR LODGING**
1. Alaskan Frontier Gardens Bed and Breakfast
2. Alaskan Leopard Bed and Breakfast
3. Alyeska Hostel
4. Anchorage Guest House
5. Eagle Nest Hotel
6. Earth Bed and Breakfast
7. The Hotel Alyeska
8. International Backpackers Inn/Hostel
9. The Millennium Alaskan Hotel
10. Spenard Hostel International
11. 26th Street International Hostel

▲ **CAMPING**
12. Bird Creek Campground
13. Centennial Park
14. Creekwood Inn
15. Eagle River Campground
16. Eklutna Lake Campground
17. Ship Creek Landing

◆ **DINING**
18. Aladdin's Fine Mediterranean
19. Alaska Bagel Inc.
20. Arctic Roadrunner
21. Bear Tooth
22. Charlie's Bakery and Restaurant
23. Gallo's Mexican Restaurant
24. Greek Corner
25. Haute Quarter Grill
26. Jack Sprat
27. Jalapenos
28. Kaladi Brothers Coffee Co.
29. La Mex Restaurant
30. Lucky Wishbone
31. Maxine's Glacier City Bistro
32. Mexico In Alaska
33. Middle Way Café
34. Moose's Tooth Pub and Pizzeria
35. Organic Oasis Restaurant and Juice Bar
36. Pizza Olympia
37. Shine's Sushi
38. Southside Bistro
39. Thai Kitchen
40. Thai Orchid Restaurant
41. Yamato Ya Japanese Restaurant

Downtown Anchorage

■ **INDOOR LODGING**

1. Anchorage Downtown Bed and Breakfast at Raspberry Meadows
2. Anchorage International Hostel
3. City Garden Bed and Breakfast
4. Copper Whale Inn
5. Hilton Anchorage
6. Hotel Captain Cook
7. Parkside Guest House
8. Voyager Rodeway Inn Hotel

◆ **DINING**

9. Club Paris
10. Crow's Nest at the Hotel Captain Cook
11. Fletcher's at the Hotel Captain Cook
12. Glacier BrewHouse
13. Humpy's Great Alaskan Alehouse
14. La Cabana Mexican Restaurant
15. Marx Bros. Café
16. Orso
17. Sacks Cafe & Restaurant
18. Side Street Espresso
19. Snow City Cafe
20. Snow Goose Restaurant
21. Sweet Basil Cafe
22. White Spot Cafe

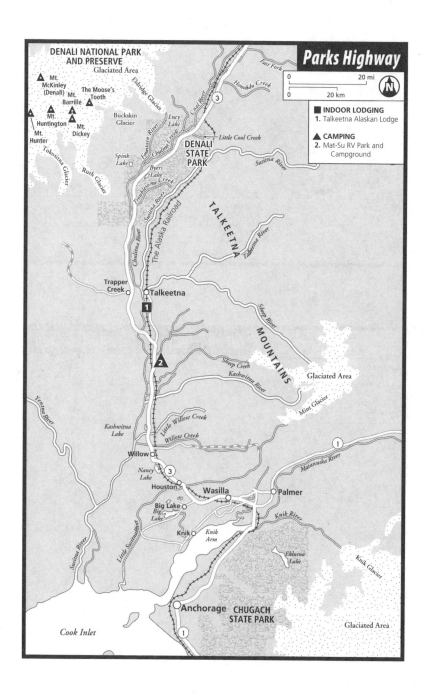

DENALI NATIONAL PARK
AND PRESERVE
Glaciated Area

Mt.
McKinley
(Denali)   Mt.   The Moose's
Barrille   Tooth
Mt.
Huntington   Mt.
Mt.   Dickey
Hunter

Buckskin
Glacier

Eldridge Glacier

Lucy
Lake

Cool River

Little Cool Creek

East Fork

Honobulu Creek

Fountain River

Chulitna Creek

DENALI
STATE
PARK

Spink
Lake

Byers
Lake

Tokositna Glacier

Ruth Glacier

Troublesome Creek

Susitna River

Susitna River

Susitna River

Chulitna River

The Alaska Railroad

Parks Highway

0   20 mi
0   20 km

N

INDOOR LODGING
1. Talkeetna Alaskan Lodge

CAMPING
2. Mat-Su RV Park and
Campground

T
A
L
K
E
E
T
N
A

Talkeetna River

Trapper
Creek   **1** Talkeetna

2

M
O
U
N
T
A
I
N
S

Sheep River

Sheep Creek

Kashwitna River

Glaciated Area

Mint Glacier

Yentna River

Kashwitna
Lake

Little Willow Creek

Willow Creek

1

Matanuska River

Willow

Nancy
Lake   **3**

Houston

Wasilla

Palmer

Big Lake

Big
Lake

Knik   Knik
Arm

Knik River

Eklutna
Lake

Knik Glacier

Little Susitna River

Susitna River

Cook Inlet

1

Anchorage   CHUGACH
STATE
PARK

Glaciated Area

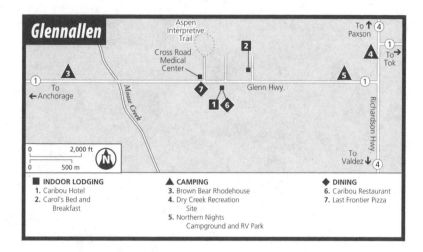

Glennallen

Aspen Interpretive Trail

Cross Road Medical Center

To Paxson
To Tok
To ←Anchorage
To Valdez ↓

Glenn Hwy.

Moose Creek

Richardson Hwy.

| 0 | 2,000 ft |
| 0 | 500 m |

■ INDOOR LODGING
1. Caribou Hotel
2. Carol's Bed and Breakfast

▲ CAMPING
3. Brown Bear Rhodehouse
4. Dry Creek Recreation Site
5. Northern Nights Campground and RV Park

◆ DINING
6. Caribou Restaurant
7. Last Frontier Pizza

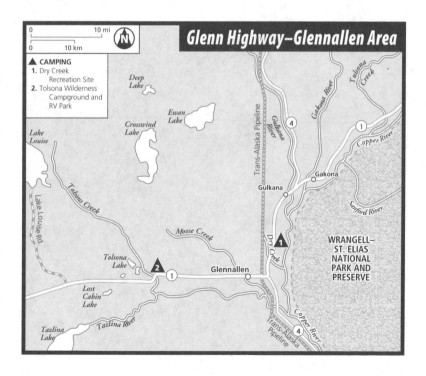

Glenn Highway–Glennallen Area

| 0 | 10 mi |
| 0 | 10 km |

▲ CAMPING
1. Dry Creek Recreation Site
2. Tolsona Wilderness Campground and RV Park

Deep Lake

Ewan Lake

Crosswind Lake

Lake Louise

Lake Louise Rd

Tolsona Creek

Moose Creek

Tolsona Lake

Lost Cabin Lake

Tazlina Lake

Tazlina River

Glennallen

Trans-Alaska Pipeline

Gulkana River

Gakona River

Tulsona Creek

Copper River

Gakona

Gulkana

Sanford River

Dry Creek

WRANGELL–ST. ELIAS NATIONAL PARK AND PRESERVE

Copper River

Trans-Alaska Pipeline

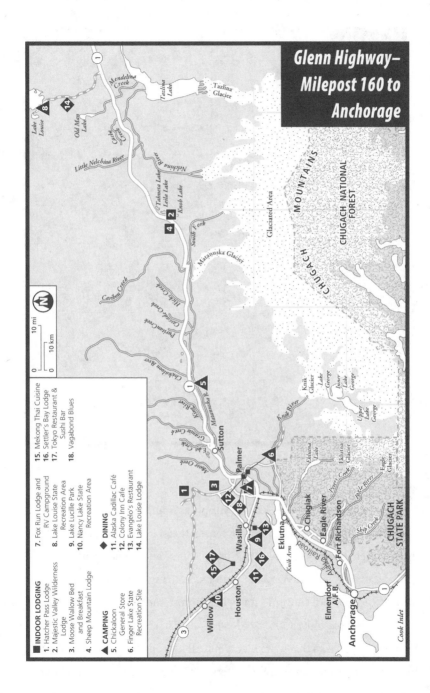

Glenn Highway– Milepost 160 to Anchorage

■ **INDOOR LODGING**
1. Hatcher Pass Lodge
2. Majestic Valley Wilderness Lodge
3. Moose Wallow Bed and Breakfast
4. Sheep Mountain Lodge

▲ **CAMPING**
5. Chickaloon General Store
6. Finger Lake State Recreation Site

7. Fox Run Lodge and RV Campground
8. Lake Louise State Recreation Area
9. Lake Lucille Park
10. Nancy Lake State Recreation Area

◆ **DINING**
11. Alaska Cadillac Café
12. Colony Inn Cafe
13. Evangelo's Restaurant
14. Lake Louise Lodge

15. Mekong Thai Cuisine
16. Settler's Bay Lodge
17. Tokyo Restaurant & Sushi Bar
18. Vagabond Blues

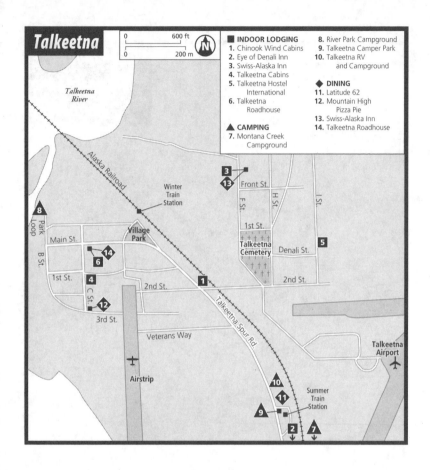

Talkeetna

| 0 | 600 ft |
| 0 | 200 m |

■ INDOOR LODGING
1. Chinook Wind Cabins
2. Eye of Denali Inn
3. Swiss-Alaska Inn
4. Talkeetna Cabins
5. Talkeetna Hostel International
6. Talkeetna Roadhouse

▲ CAMPING
7. Montana Creek Campground

8. River Park Campground
9. Talkeetna Camper Park
10. Talkeetna RV and Campground

◆ DINING
11. Latitude 62
12. Mountain High Pizza Pie
13. Swiss-Alaska Inn
14. Talkeetna Roadhouse

continued from page 271

This section of the state, known simply as Southcentral (which Alaskans typically spell as one word), encompasses the state's largest city, one of its most famed rivers, its most striking glaciers, and some of its finest and most accessible wildlife-viewing options. Touring the Southcentral region is an affordable and convenient way to glimpse the best of Alaska.

We at *Alaska Adventure Guide* realize that so much is happening in Southcentral Alaska that we can't cram it all into one chapter. So you'll notice that we have two Southcentral chapters: This one focuses on inland outdoor adventure, and the other (page 326) concentrates on coastal activities. The rationale behind this division is that many of the outdoor adventures that travelers seek can be found more predominantly in one region over the other. Southcentral Inland Alaska, for example, is a paradise for backpackers and mountaineers. It features mountains and valleys perfect for exploration. Southcentral Coastal Alaska, on the other hand, is the place to go if you are a kayaker or river runner.

Think of Southcentral Inland Alaska as a giant triangle. Starting north of Valdez on the Richardson Highway, the first communities of the Inland area are **McCarthy** and **Kennicott,** on the edge of the Copper River Basin (the coastal communities of the Copper River Basin are covered in the South-central Coastal chapter, which follows this one). Continue north until you reach the Glenn Highway, which heads west toward the Matanuska-Susitna Valley and Anchorage. The community of **Glennallen** is situated at the cross-roads and is thus included in this chapter. (See Part One, page 6, for a map of the Southcentral Inland region.)

This chapter covers areas as far north as **Talkeetna,** off the Parks Highway as travelers head north to the Interior. While it borders on being considered the Interior, we have included Talkeetna as part of Southcentral Inland Alaska because it is part of the Matanuska-Susitna Borough and a common day-trip destination for those basing their vacations out of Anchorage.

Back on the Glenn Highway, the Inland region travels through the **Matanuska-Susitna Valley** and its outlying communities. Then it continues southward toward **Anchorage,** the most populous city in the state, with nearly 300,000 residents.

No matter where your outdoor adventure takes you in Alaska, you'll likely pass through the Southcentral Inland region at one time or another. It is the major supply point for the rest of the state and home to Ted Stevens Anchor-age International Airport, a bustling, newly renovated facility serving all of the major airlines, both nationally and internationally.

So start here, and let your planning begin.

▲ Anchorage

ANCHORAGE CONVENTION AND VISITORS BUREAU

524 W. 4th Ave.

Anchorage 99501-2212

907-276-4118 or 800-478-1255

anchorage.net

Look for the sod-roofed Log Cabin and Downtown Visitor Information Center at the corner of F Street and Fourth Avenue.

ALASKANS WHO DON'T LIVE IN ANCHORAGE sometimes refer to the state's largest city as Los Anchorage, as if it were a huge metropolis. They prefer their small towns and isolated communities to the hustle and bustle of city life.

But as cities go, Anchorage is welcoming indeed. And while it may seem big to those in tiny, remote villages, in reality it is one of the friendliest mid-size cities in the country, with the added benefit of having the wilderness right at its back door. Consider this: where can you jump in a dogsled and mush along a snow-covered trail, hop on a plane and fly over a glacier, and then still have time to change into fancy clothes and enjoy a night of fine dining and theater? In Anchorage, of course. This city of nearly 300,000 is a modern gem in the roughs of Alaska, surrounded partly by the **Chugach Mountains** and partly by the waters of **Cook Inlet.** It encompasses some 1,955 square miles. Its boundaries extend from the **Eklutna region,** about 25 miles to the north, to the laid-back ski town of **Girdwood,** 37 miles to the south.

In the late 1700s, when Captain James Cook arrived in this spruce-tree-covered region, he saw little more than boggy areas with no inhabitants, despite the presence of many native settlements nearby. But soon after, Anchorage developed a small port for incoming ships, and the city grew. A railroad was built, and it grew even more. By the 1930s, Anchorage was well on its way to becoming a thriving city.

Today, Anchorage has all the amenities of Lower 48 cities. It boasts a community opera, a civic orchestra, a concert association, and several theater companies. Movie theaters are scattered throughout town, and major musicians, bands, and sports teams play at the city's civic center and performing arts center throughout the year. It has a bustling international airport that services passengers and cargo from all over the world. The **Alaska Railroad** still travels to points north and south. And two main highways access the Interior and Kenai Peninsula.

There are a variety of places to eat too. From a simple meal of Chinese stir-fry to elegant French cuisine with an Alaskan twist, the city has it all. Choose your pleasure: Thai, Korean, Mexican, or Greek. Italian, Vietnamese, Japanese, or Cajun. Chefs from around the globe, lured by Alaska's beauty, have established their own niches in Anchorage, surprising even the savviest traveler with their culinary skills out here on the Last Frontier.

Lodging in Anchorage runs from a simple bed in a hostel to the lavish multiroom suites for rent in some of Anchorage's finest hotels. Bed-and-breakfasts, too, run a thriving business in the summer, attracting visitors who prefer a more intimate view of the city as seen in area neighborhoods. Even campers can find a place to sleep in Anchorage.

▲ Matanuska-Susitna Valley

MAT-SU CONVENTION AND VISITORS BUREAU
7744 E. Visitors View Ct.
Palmer 99645
907-746-5000; **alaskavisit.com**
Visitor center is at Mile 35.5 Parks Hwy. (Trunk Road Exit).

ABOUT 35 MILES north of Anchorage is a place that most locals simply call "the Valley." In fact, they are talking about a vast expanse of land, part of the Matanuska-Susitna Borough, which stretches from the northern end of **Eklutna** to just beyond **Talkeetna** and east to **Lake Louise.**

The Valley is a sportsman's paradise. Easily accessible lakes and rivers offer several species of salmon, trout, and grayling. There are great trails for hiking and mountain biking, and several rafting and ice-climbing options for those who like their outdoors adventures with a bit of an adrenaline rush.

The Hatcher Pass area is one of the highlights of the Valley. In the summer, it offers excellent biking, hiking, and birding. In the winter, skiers, dog mushers, and snowmobilers flock there because it is one of the first areas to get snow. For more on Hatcher Pass, see our listing in this chapter under "Wild Lands" (page 290).

If Alaska has a breadbasket, the Valley is it. This was no-man's-land until 1935 when, at the height of the Great Depression, the Federal Relief Administration sent struggling Midwesterners to Palmer to build new lives. The land was theirs, the government said, as long as they could make a living off of it. Today, some of those same farms still thrive, and the Palmer-Wasilla area bears some of the richest produce in the state.

Driving into the town of **Palmer** may remind you of Small Town, U.S.A.— and it is. This close-knit community is home to the annual **Alaska State Fair,** which attracts thousands of carnival-goers at summer's end. Giant vegetables that grow fast under Alaska's constant summertime sun are heaved out of area gardens, weighed, and then judged. Hundred-pound cabbages, zucchinis, and squash are among the contestants. Agricultural exhibits, including milking cows, nursing sow pigs, and dog-handling competitions, keep the youngsters thrilled. And adults can join in the fun by entering any number of pie-baking, model-car building, or quilt-making contests.

Neighboring **Wasilla** is a community gone to the dogs. Billing itself as "Home of the Iditarod," it is the official restarting point of the **Iditarod Trail Sled Dog Race** (the ceremonial start is in downtown Anchorage). Although the original Iditarod Trail started down in Seward, Congress has officially recognized the current route as a Millennium Trail. Race headquarters, just down Knik–Goose Bay Road, proudly displays videos and photographs of this 1,000-mile dogsled route to Nome, as well as a mount of beloved lead dog Togo. While Balto may be the lead dog who claimed most of the fame of the lifesaving diphtheria-medication run to Nome in 1925, it was faithful Togo whom musher Leonard Seppala loved most.

▲ Talkeetna

TALKEETNA CHAMBER OF COMMERCE
907-733-2330 | talkeetnachamber.org

WHILE STILL PART of the Matanuska-Susitna Borough, this independent community of about 850 considers itself its own destination. Talkeetna serves as the starting point for the hundreds of mountaineers who attempt to climb **Mount McKinley** (called **Denali** locally) each year. Come late spring, Talkeetna changes from a sleepy little outpost of locals to a melting pot of international guests from all over the world, and their accents and languages can be heard from the local saloon to the community mercantile.

The town is at the junction of the Talkeetna and Susitna rivers, 99 miles north of Anchorage via the Parks Highway (the 14-mile Talkeetna Spur Road gets you to the center of town). It is also accessible by Alaska Railroad from Fairbanks or Anchorage, or by small aircraft. Within its 43 square miles are rivers, mountains, valleys, and lakes. Its location at the base of Denali (and other surrounding and equally impressive mountains) means Talkeetna gets a lot of snow, too, attracting skiers and dog mushers in the winter with its average 70-inch snowfall each year.

In the summer, it can get as warm as 83°F, but it also can get buggy. The lakes and rivers attract pests by the millions, and they can drive one to distraction.

Talkeetna (pronounced Tall-**KEET**-nah) is a Dena'ina Indian word meaning "river of plenty." The area was settled as a mining town and Alaska Commercial company trading post in 1896. Gold prospectors came to the area, and by 1910, Talkeetna was a riverboat-steamer station. In 1915, Talkeetna was chosen as the headquarters for the Alaska Engineering Commission, which built the Alaska Railroad, and the community population peaked near 1,000. When World War I began and the railroad was completed, however, many people left. The community has maintained many of its historical buildings, though, and today Talkeetna is listed on the National Register of Historic Places.

One of Talkeetna's largest economic mainstays is the local fleet of air-taxi operators that help climbers reach their destinations. Local businesses also provide helicopters, guiding, and related services.

▲ Glennallen

GREATER COPPER VALLEY CHAMBER OF COMMERCE
907-822-5558 | coppervalleychamber.com

GLENNALLEN IS THE supply hub for the surrounding Copper River Basin region, with a centralized location and most agencies that serve the people of this part of the state. Police, government, and federal land offices are in Glennallen, as well as transportation-department facilities.

The 550-person community is not so spectacular to look at as you drive along the Glenn Highway, but if you get out and beyond the road system, you can truly appreciate its outdoor beauty. Most people come to Glennallen as they are passing through to other destinations, but some people choose to stop and explore. Off-road adventures, dog mushing, and fishing are some of the more popular pastimes.

Glennallen is located along the Glenn Highway at its junction with the Richardson Highway, 189 road miles east of Anchorage. It is just outside the western boundary of **Wrangell–St. Elias National Park and Preserve,** the country's largest national park. It is bordered by four mountain ranges, which attract climbers during the season. There are dozens of rivers from which to fish.

The mean temperature in January is –10°F; in July, it is 56°F. It's a relatively dry area, though, with snowfall averaging 39 inches, with total precipitation (including melted snow and rain) of 9 inches per year.

Glennallen's name is derived from Major Edwin Glenn and Lieutenant Henry Allen, both leaders in the early explorations of the Copper River region. It is one of the few communities in the region that was not built on the site of a native village.

▲ Copper Valley

GREATER COPPER VALLEY CHAMBER OF COMMERCE

907-822-5558 | coppervalleychamber.com

Stretching along either side of the Copper River and spreading 3.5 million acres in either direction is the Copper Valley, a region of the state that offers just about any outdoor adventure you can imagine, whether on a river, glacier, or mountain. The Copper Valley, which includes **Wrangell–St. Elias National Park and Preserve,** is located 189 miles northwest of Anchorage, 250 miles south of Fairbanks, and 115 miles north of Valdez. It is only 200 miles from Canada and is accessed by two main roads, the Richardson and Glenn highways.

Summer recreational activities in the Copper Valley include rafting, hiking, and excellent fishing for king and red salmon in the rivers, as well as trout and grayling in the lakes and streams. The **Copper, Klutina, and Gulkana rivers** are major fishing destinations that offer excellent angling without the crowds of some of the state's other rivers.

In the winter, Copper River visitors can enjoy snowmobiling, skiing, ice fishing, snowboarding, and the **Copper Basin** 300 sled-dog race, which has become a qualifying race for the Iditarod.

The largest Southcentral Inland community in the Copper Valley is **Glenn-allen,** outlined in the previous section. But other smaller communities that fall within the Southcentral Inland–Copper Valley region include **Copper Center, Kenny Lake,** and **McCarthy.**

The 61-mile **McCarthy Road** offers access directly into Wrangell–St. Elias National Park and Preserve. Driving this road is an adventure, with its gravel-and-dirt surface making for slow travel. It can take as long as 3 hours to cover the 60 miles, and flat tires are not uncommon. At the end of the road, you will find parking areas and two footbridges that cross the Kennicott River and lead to the historical communities of **McCarthy** and **Kennicott.** Access to McCarthy is by foot, bike, or shuttle. Traveling the McCarthy Road provides access to some incredible hiking, fishing, and camping.

▲ Wild Lands

CHUGACH STATE PARK

CHUGACH STATE PARK Potter Section House Mile 115 Seward Hwy. Indian 99540 907-345-5014 dnr.alaska.gov/parks/units/chugach	**DIVISION OF NATURAL RESOURCES** **PUBLIC INFORMATION CENTER** Robert Atwood Building 550 W. 7th Ave., Suite 1260 Anchorage 99501-3557 907-269-8400 dnr.alaska.gov/pic/index.htm

Primary activities: *backpacking, hiking, mountain biking, birding, mountaineering, off-road travel, kayaking, fishing, skiing, rafting*

There's really not much you *can't* do in the great outdoor playground that is Chugach State Park. The park's 500,000 acres of glaciers, mountains, and valleys are right in Anchorage's backyard, surrounding the city like a comfortable blanket. Grizzly bears, wolves, moose, and even the occasional lynx will sometimes wander into town, reminding Alaskans of just how close the wilderness is to our civilization.

Chugach State Park is the third-largest state park in America—a half-million acres of some of the most accessible outdoor activity on the planet. For many people who live in Anchorage, reaching the park is simply a matter of slipping on their skis and heading out their front doors, or lacing up their boots and climbing the mountain directly behind their homes.

Access to the park is amazingly simple—you can even take a taxi to local trailheads. But first you must get to Anchorage, which is accessible by daily jet service from most major airlines, or the Glenn Highway, which is the sole feeder highway from all points north.

Several highlights of Chugach State Park include the **Flattop Trail,** which overlooks the city and is perhaps the most-hiked trail in all of Alaska; the **Eagle River Nature Center,** run by a nonprofit park-supporter and offering dozens of interpretive programs year-round; and **Eklutna Lake,** an aquamarine lake at the northern edge of Alaska with everything from kayaking to mountaineering to fishing.

WRANGELL–ST. ELIAS NATIONAL PARK AND PRESERVE

WRANGELL–ST. ELIAS NATIONAL PARK AND PRESERVE
Mile 106.8 Richardson Hwy.
Copper Center 99573
907-822-5234 | nps.gov/wrst

Primary activities:
backpacking, hiking, mountaineering, skiing, dog mushing, kayaking, fishing, rafting

Many superlatives are associated with Wrangell–St. Elias National Park and Preserve. At 13 million acres, it is the nation's largest national park. It includes the continent's largest assemblage of glaciers and the greatest collection of peaks above 16,000 feet—**Mount Sanford** (16,237 feet), and **Mount Blackburn** (16,390 feet), to name just a few. **Mount St. Elias,** at 18,008 feet, is the second-highest peak in the United States, after Denali, a few hundred miles to the northwest.

Here's another way to think about it, as National Park Service rangers often do when trying to convey the region's vastness: Wrangell–St. Elias is as big as six Yellowstones!

Wrangell–St. Elias became a national park and preserve in 1980, and ever since has maintained its rugged remoteness. Most people access the area by the Richardson Highway, to the Edgerton Highway, which goes to the in-park community of **McCarthy**. You can also take the less-traveled Nabesna Road, north of Glennallen, in what we consider to be part of the Interior. Or you can fly in. There are several charter operators that can fly guests into areas of the park ranging from glacier landings to river drop-offs.

Wildlife is abundant in the area. The park has the largest concentration of Dall sheep in North America. Other large-animal species include goats, caribou, moose, grizzly bears, black bears, and bison. The more-elusive lynx, wolverines, martens, foxes, and wolves also prowl the landscape.

Most travelers into Wrangell–St. Elias choose to tent-camp, but this park is unique in that it also has 13 public-use cabins, most of which were old mining, trapping, or hunting cabins. The National Park Service has restored them all, and all but two of them are free and available on a first-come, first-served basis. They have woodstoves and bunks, but you have to supply the rest. Replenish any firewood stored in the cabins for the next user.

MUNICIPALITY OF ANCHORAGE

ANCHORAGE PARKS AND RECREATION	*To get an Anchorage Parks and Trails Map:*
907-343-4474	Anchorage Parks and Recreation
EAGLE RIVER–CHUGIAK PARKS AND RECREATION	120 S. Bragaw St.
	Anchorage 99519
907-694-2011	
muni.org/parks/parks.cfm	

Primary activities:
hiking, mountain biking, skiing, dog mushing

The Anchorage Parks and Recreation department maintains a surprising number of parks from Eagle River to Girdwood and points between. Of the 200-plus locations, a select few are perennial favorites among outdoors-lovers. These locations are perfect day-outings for those based in Anchorage.

Dog mushers go to the **Beach Lake Trails** in **Chugiak,** about 20 miles north of Anchorage and considered the center of dog mushing for Anchorage-area residents. The extensive trail system there is managed by the Chugiak Dog Mushers Association, an involved group of folks dedicated to providing access for dog mushing in their community.

In **Anchorage,** skiers like **Hillside Park** and **Hilltop Ski Area** off Abbott Loop Road (from the Seward Highway, turn east toward the mountains at the Abbott Lake–Dimond exit) or 1,400-acre **Kincaid Park** (take Minnesota Boulevard to Raspberry Road and follow it to its end). **Russian Jack Springs Park** is another favorite for those just getting started in cross-country skiing, with beginner trails (take DeBarr Road east to the turnoff on the right).

Mountain bikers are drawn to Hillside, Kincaid, and Russian Jack Springs for its extensive trail system, as well. Beach Lake Trails are mushing-only trails, however, and too wet to ride in the summer.

A number of other leisure areas, ranging from covered picnic spots to playgrounds to athletic and sports fields, are maintained by Anchorage Parks and Recreation. Purchasing a park map is a great idea for anyone spending time in Anchorage. It's amazing how far out you can feel when just minutes from the highway.

U.S. BUREAU OF LAND MANAGEMENT

BLM–ALASKA STATE OFFICE 222 W. 7th Ave., Suite 13 Anchorage 99513 907-271-5960 blm.gov/ak/st/en.html	**CAMPBELL CREEK SCIENCE CENTER** 6865 Abbott Loop Rd. Anchorage, Alaska 99507-2599 907-267-1247

Primary activities:
hiking, mountain biking, skiing, dog mushing

The Bureau of Land Management in Alaska manages 85.5 million acres of land across the state, and the **Anchorage Field Office,** including 700 acres right in the city, manages 16 million acres. A popular jumping-off point for day-trip adventures within the park is at the **Campbell Creek Science Center,** which is run by BLM employees and serves as an educational and interpretive center for Anchorage residents and visitors.

The **Campbell Tract** area surrounding the Science Center has a series of trails used by dog mushers, skijorers (skiers who are pulled by sled dogs), hikers, mountain bikers, and horsemen. The BLM office works with different user groups to provide multiuse trails and to offer other programs for those who want to explore nature within the city limits.

HATCHER PASS–SUMMIT LAKE STATE RECREATION-SITE

MAT-SU AREA PARK OFFICE
Mile 0.7 Bogard Rd.
Wasilla 99654
907-745-3975 | dnr.alaska.gov/parks/units/summit.htm

Primary activities:
hiking, skiing, dog mushing, mountain biking

As you climb the Hatcher Pass Road that winds up, up, and up toward Summit Lake, it feels as if you're in Switzerland. The rugged peaks get taller and closer, and the small A-frame chalets near the pass add a winter-resort feel to this gem in the Matanuska-Susitna Borough.

TRAVELER'S TIP

▶ A trail around Summit Lake is great for family hiking, and the views are incredible. Sometimes paragliders launch from here, which is fun to watch on nice days.

The Hatcher Pass area is managed by **Alaska State Parks,** but the Summit Lake State Recreation-site, located at Mile 19 of Hatcher Pass Road, and about 2 miles past the historic Independence Mine State Historic Park, is the highlight. Hatcher Pass Summit is in the park at an elevation of 3,886 feet, and it is here that the first snows of the season usually arrive.

There is road access to the Summit Lake area, but it is closed as soon as the snow conditions make it not drivable. You can, however, reach as far as Hatcher Pass Lodge and Independence Mine, 17 miles in, year-round.

The Summit Lake recreation-site encompasses **Summit Lake,** a small, steep-banked lake, or tarn, that is about 20 feet deep at its deepest point. It is the remains of an old glacier, and it is easy to imagine that it was once a snow-covered area year-round.

Above Summit Lake is **April Bowl,** a favorite among skiers and snowboarders who flock to the area as soon as there is enough snow to cover the rocks. On weekend days, it isn't uncommon to see these winter alpinists climbing up and boarding or skiing down the bowl over and over.

However, avalanches occur regularly on the steep slopes in the area. Use extreme caution when doing any wintertime activities in the park, and know how to read the snow.

NANCY LAKE STATE RECREATION AREA

NANCY LAKE RANGER STATION
Mile 1.3 Nancy Lake Pkwy.
Willow 99688
907-495-6273 | dnr.alaska.gov/parks/units/nancylk/nancylk.htm

Primary activities:
canoeing, camping, fishing, dog mushing, skiing

Just outside of Wasilla and 67 miles north of Anchorage is one of Valley residents' favorite places to play: the Nancy Lake State Recreation Area. This 22,685-acre park has canoe trails, ski trails, cabins, and more.

To get there, turn west onto Nancy Lake Parkway at Mile 67.3 of the Parks Highway. In the summer, the road is open to Mile 6.5, at the South Rolly Lake Campground. In the winter it is not plowed and is closed from Mile 2.2 at the Winter Trailhead.

Through the years, most of the Nancy Lake area has remained wild and natural. The area is too wet for ideal cultivation and is not mineral-rich, so it has escaped large-scale human settlement. The weather in the summer stays in the 70°F range, but in the winter it can fall to −40°F and seldom rises above freezing until mid-March. The first snow usually arrives by late October, about the same time the lakes freeze over. Snow depth in late winter averages 3–4 feet. Lakes are usually free of ice by late May.

Among the great things about this recreation area are the public-use cabins located on **Red Shirt, Lynx, Nancy, James,** and **Bald lakes.** They're insulated and equipped with wooden bunks, counters, and wood-burning stoves. Each cabin has an outhouse and an outdoor fire ring. The cabins rent for $25–$60 per night depending on which one is reserved.

Birding in the area is another favorite pastime, and canoeists can enjoy hearing the call of the common loon and, occasionally, their smaller, grey-headed relative, the Pacific loon.

Other wildlife in the area include moose, which love to munch on the sludge from shallow ponds or the brushy areas surrounding the lakes. Black bears also are common, and grizzlies are spotted now and then.

▲ Getting around Southcentral Inland Alaska

ANCHORAGE

Access by air is through **Alaska Airlines** (800-252-7522; **alaskaair.com**). You can also drive to Fairbanks from the Richardson or Parks highways.

More than a dozen car-rental options are available in the Anchorage area, but we have found **Budget** (800-527-0700; **budgetrentacar.com**), **Enterprise** (800-261-7331; **enterprise.com**), **Hertz** (800-654-3131; **hertz.com**), and **Denali Used Car Rental** (907-276-1230; **denalicarrentalak.com**) to be the best.

Anchorage has fair bus service, called the **People Mover** (700 W. 6th Ave., at the transit center; 907-343-6543; **peoplemover.org**). The system has 14 regular routes that travel to specified areas as reserved. Fares are $1.75 for adults, one-way. Day passes are available for $4, and you can travel all routes. The bus runs 5:45 a.m.–11:55 p.m. weekdays and 7:45 a.m.–9:15 p.m. Saturdays. On Sundays it operates 9:30 a.m.–7 p.m.

The **Ship Creek Shuttle,** also affiliated with People Mover, offers free transportation in the downtown and Ship Creek areas.

▶ **ABC Motorhome and Car Rentals**   800-421-7456, **abcmotorhome.com.** This company has a range of RVs, as well as a luxury van for large groups and camper rentals for smaller parties. No-smoking vehicles. No pets allowed. Rates in the $220–$250 range.

▶ **Alaska Affordable Motor Home Rental**   907-349-4878 or 360-624-6507; **alaska-rv-rental.com.** Much less expensive than its competitors, with rates at $175 per day with free, unlimited miles in Alaska. No smoking or pets allowed.

▶ **Alaska Best RV Rentals**   866-544-4981 or 907-344-4981; **alaskabestrvrentals. com.** With rates lower than the large-company averages—$160–$175. No smoking or pets allowed.

▶ **Alaska Railroad**   327 W. Ship Creek Ave.; 907-265-2494 or 800-544-0552; **alaskarailroad.com.** The railroad has daily routes serving Anchorage, the Valley, and Talkeetna, among other regions. One-way rates from Anchorage are $54 to the Valley, $89 to Talkeetna.

▶ **Magic Bus**   907-268-6311; **themagicbus.com.** If you have a group and want to travel anywhere within Southcentral Coastal Alaska to the southern edge of the Interior and all points between, you can rent these private motor coaches and vans, complete with a driver.

▶ **Park Connection**   800-266-8625; **alaskacoach.com.** This driver-supplied option offers twice-daily coach service between Anchorage and Seward, including connecting service between Denali Park and Talkeetna, Anchorage, and Seward.

MATANUSKA-SUSITNA VALLEY

▶ **Valley Car Rentals**   435 S. Knik St., Wasilla; 888-719-2880 or 907-775-2880; **valleycarrental.com.** Cars, RVs, and SUVs, free miles, and delivery/pickup. Also offers an airport shuttle to and from Anchorage.

TALKEETNA/GLENNALLEN/COPPER VALLEY

▶ **Alaska Railroad**   327 W. Ship Creek Ave.; 907-265-2494 or 800-544-0552; **alaskarailroad.com**. The railroad has daily routes serving Anchorage and Talkeetna. The cost is $89.

▶ **Kennicott Shuttle and Alaska Charters**   907-822-5292; **kennicottshuttle.com**. Kennicott Shuttle offers one-way and round-trip transportation to Wrangell–St. Elias National Park and Preserve to the McCarthy footbridge from Glennallen, Copper Center, Kenny Lake, and Chitina, picking up at hotels, bed-and-breakfasts, campgrounds, and RV parks. They link up with the Wrangell Mountain Bus for transport to Kennicott. Rates are $79 one-way, $99 round-trip same day, and $139 round-trip on separate days; fly-drive is $194.

▶ **Sparks General Store and Automotive**   Mile 188.5 Glenn Hwy.; 907-822-5990 or 907-822-5991; **sparksgeneralstore.com**. They carry everything from groceries to auto-supply parts and cell phones, and they also rent vehicles. We're not making this up—we promise.

▶ **Wrangell Mountain Air**   800-478-1160 or 907-554-4411; **wrangellmountainair .com**. This company is the one to use if you want to be dropped off in the wilderness. They know Wrangell–St. Elias National Park and Preserve intimately and can land safely. Additional companies that provide air service into the park and other locations throughout the Copper Valley include **Copper Valley Air Service** (866-570-4200 or 907-822-4200; **coppervalleyair.com**) and **Lee's Air Taxi** (907-822-5030; **leesairtaxi.com**).

▶ **Wrangell–St. Elias Lodging and Tours**   Mile 7.5 Edgerton Hwy., between Kenny Lake and Copper Center; 907-822-5978; **alaskayukontravel.com**. The company does tours but also offers shuttle service for backpackers and anglers traveling in the area.

▲ Gearing Up

SOUTHCENTRAL INLAND ALASKA is the place to gear up to go anywhere in the state. This region boasts more stores, more selection, and, in most cases, better prices than anywhere else in the state.

The majority of choices are in the Anchorage area, with a few good retailers in the Matanuska-Susitna Valley. The nice thing about buying some of your supplies in these communities instead of purchasing them ahead of time is that most shops have experience in the places to which you will be traveling, and they can recommend the most appropriate gear. Stores such as **REI** and

Alaska Mountaineering and Hiking, both in Anchorage, offer prices that are just as good as what you will find in Lower 48 cities, although not always as low as discounts you may be able to find online. We still think shopping locally is the way to go, though, because unless you know exactly which product you want, online discounts won't help much if the gear you've selected turns out to be wrong for Alaska conditions.

This section of the book is broken down by the main communities in Southcentral Inland Alaska with shops that will help you find what you are looking for. We list sporting goods/camping supplies and groceries separately, but many stores in the communities along the Copper River Basin carry a little of everything in one stop.

> **TRAVELER'S TIP**
>
> ▶ As you would when traveling elsewhere in the state, check with the air carriers on which you will be flying for regulations on carrying items such as knives, guns, campstoves, and camp fuel. You may need to purchase certain items at your final destination and leave them behind when you fly home.

SPORTING GOODS AND CAMPING SUPPLIES

Anchorage

▶ **Alaska Mountaineering and Hiking**   2633 Spenard Rd.; 907-272-1811; **alaska mountaineering.com.** An Anchorage favorite, featuring skiing, mountaineering, and other outdoors clothing and gear. Locally owned.

▶ **Barney's Sports Chalet**   906 W. Northern Lights Blvd.; 907-561-5242. A longtime Anchorage business that offers high-quality camping and skiing gear at competitive prices.

▶ **The Bicycle Shop**   1035 W. Northern Lights Blvd.; 907-272-5219; and 1801 W. Dimond Blvd.; 907-222-9953. These guys carry Cannondale, Rocky Mountain, Specialized, Trek, and other popular brands; they no longer rent bikes, though.

▶ **Chain Reaction Cycles**   12201 Industry Way, Unit 2, South Anchorage; 907-336-0383; **chainreactioncycles.us.** It carries Litespeed, Orbea, Cervelo, Jamis, Serotta, and other high-end brands, and it's the bike shop of choice for elite riders and triathletes.

▶ **Mountain View Sports**   3838 Old Seward Hwy.; 907-563-8600. This longtime sporting-goods store has everything for outdoor adventures, especially fishing and other water sports.

▶ **Paramount Cycles**   1320 Huffman Park Dr., South Anchorage; 907-336-2453. They carry Raleigh, Gary Fisher, Giant, LeMond, and a few other brands.

▶ **Peter Glenn of Alaska**   8840 Old Seward Hwy.; 907-349-2929. The shop, in front of a Walmart, has a great selection of snowboards and skis.

▶ **Recreational Equipment Inc.** (REI)   1200 W. Northern Lights Blvd.; 907-272-4565; **rei.com/stores/anchorage.** The store, expanded to almost double its original size in 2007, is massive, with virtually any type of gear you'll ever need.

▶ **Skinny Raven Sports**   800 H St., downtown; 907-274-7222. Plenty of outdoor gear, including the hottest in local sports such as Frisbee golf and handball.

▶ **The Sport Shop**   570 E. Benson Blvd.; 907-272-7755. A great choice for women's outdoor apparel. Not much in the way of technical gear, though.

Glennallen–Copper River Basin

▶ **The Hub of Alaska**   Mile 114 Richardson Hwy.; 907-822-3555. They carry limited sporting goods and sell hunting and fishing licenses.

▶ **Tolsona Lake Resort**   Mile 170.5 Glenn Hwy.; 907-822-3433 or 800-245-3342. They sell hunting and fishing licenses.

GROCERY

Anchorage

▶ **Carrs/Safeway**   Locations throughout Anchorage and in Eagle River. This full-service grocery store has a very limited supply of sporting goods, mostly fishing tackle. They all sell fishing and hunting licenses.

▶ **Fred Meyer**   Locations at Abbott Road, Dimond Boulevard, Muldoon Road, Northern Lights Boulevard, and Eagle River. Locations are spread across town, and this is the best choice for one-stop shopping, including sporting goods, fishing licenses, and full-service groceries.

▶ **Natural Pantry**   3801 Old Seward Hwy.; 907-770-1444. All-organic and health foods are offered, as well as a tasty cafe for lunches.

▶ **New Sagaya**   900 W. 13th Ave.; 907-274-6173; and 3700 Old Seward Hwy.; 907-561-5173. Organic and hard-to-find foods with cafes in both locations.

Matanuska-Susitna Valley

▶ **Carrs/Safeway**   595 E. Parks Hwy., Wasilla; 907-352-1100 and at Palmer Square Mall, Palmer; 907-761-1400. Both locations offer a full line of groceries. Fishing licenses available.

▶ **Chickaloon General Store**   Mile 76.3 Glenn Hwy.; 907-746-4520. If you forgot something in Palmer, here's another chance to find it. Groceries, gas, and liquor, as well as fishing licenses, are available. Camping also is allowed by the river.

▶ **Fred Meyer**   1601 E. Parks Hwy., Wasilla; 907-352-5000 and at the intersection of Palmer-Wasilla Highway, 650 S. Cobb St., Palmer; 907-761-4200. Both locations offer a full line of groceries and sporting goods. Fishing licenses available.

Talkeetna

▶ **Nagley's General Store**   907-733-3663. General groceries, household supplies, and ice cream, plus a gift shop upstairs.

Glennallen–Copper River Basin

▶ **Glennallen Chiropractic Organic Garden**   Mile 187.5 Glenn Hwy.; 907-822-3353. Get your back adjusted while enjoying fresh smoothies and stocking up on health-food supplies.

▶ **Park's Place**   Mile 188 Glenn Hwy.; 907-822-3334. Full-service grocery and hand-packed meats. Also serves espresso and deli sandwiches to order.

▶ **Sparks General Store and Automotive**   Mile 188.5 Glenn Hwy., Glennallen; 907-822-5990 or 907-822-5970. They carry everything groceries to auto parts.

▲ Where to Stay

WHERE THERE ARE more people, there also are more lodging opportunities. In Southcentral Inland Alaska, the offerings range from fine hotels housing restaurants that serve foie gras to one-room cabins with no running water or electricity. Each option has a charm all its own—it just depends on what kind of adventure you envision.

In this section, we offer our favorite choices, places that we've tried ourselves and found to be memorable.

ANCHORAGE

Indoor Lodging

▶ **Alaskan Frontier Gardens Bed and Breakfast**   7440 Alatna Ave., on the Anchorage Hillside; 907-345-6556; **alaskafrontiergardens.com.**

QUALITY ★★★★ | VALUE ★★★ | $150–$225

This award-winning bed-and-breakfast is beautiful inside and out. The breakfasts are elegant, and on-site spa services are available.

▲ southcentral inland alaska indoor lodging

NAME	LODGING TYPE	QUALITY RATING	VALUE RATING	COST
ANCHORAGE				
Alaskan Frontier Gardens B&B	B&B	★★★★	★★★	$150–$225
Alaskan Leopard B&B	B&B	★★★★★	★★★★★	$129–$159
Alyeska Hostel	Hostel	★★★	★★★★★	$20–$85
Anchorage Downtown B&B at Raspberry Meadows	B&B	★★★★	★★★★★	$85–$145
Anchorage Guest House	Hostel	★★★★★	★★★★★	$30–$140
Anchorage International Hostel	Hostel	★★★	★★★★	$25–$65
City Garden Bed and Breakfast	B&B	★★★★	★★★★	$100–$150
Copper Whale Inn	B&B	★★★★★	★★★★	$185–$210
Eagle Nest Hotel	Hotel	★★★	★★★	$110–$150
Earth Bed and Breakfast	B&B	★★★	★★★★★	$110–$130
Hilton Anchorage	Hotel	★★★★★	★★★	$270–$975
The Hotel Aleyska	Hotel	★★★★★	★★★★	$199–$2,200
Hotel Captain Cook	Hotel	★★★★★	★★★	$255–$1,500
International Backpackers Inn/ Hostel	Hostel	★★	★★★	$22.40
The Millennium Alaskan Hotel Anchorage	Hotel	★★★★	★★★	$239–$339
Parkside Guest House	B&B	★★★★★	★★★	$165–$195
Spenard Hostel International	Hostel	★★★★	★★★★★	$25–$27
26th Street International Hostel	Hostel	★★	★★★★	$25–$67.25
Voyager Rodeway Inn Hotel	Hotel	★★★★	★★★★	$170–$190
MATANUSKA-SUSITNA VALLEY				
Hatcher Pass Lodge	Cabins/ lodge	★★★★	★★★★★	$95–$165
Majestic Valley Wilderness Lodge	Lodge	★★★★	★★★★★	$120–$165
Moose Wallow Bed and Breakfast	B&B/ cabins	★★★	★★★★	$110–$145
Sheep Mountain Lodge	Cabins/ hostel	★★★★	★★★★	$60–$189

▲ southcentral inland alaska indoor lodging [continued]

NAME	LODGING TYPE	QUALITY RATING	VALUE RATING	COST
TALKEETNA				
Chinook Wind Cabins	B&B/cabins	★★★	★★	$90–$165
Eye of Denali Inn	B&B	★★★★	★★★★★	$89–$275
Swiss-Alaska Inn	Hotel	★★★	★★★	$95–$140
Talkeetna Alaskan Lodge	Lodge/hotel	★★★★★	★★★★	$145–$555
Talkeetna Cabins	Cabins	★★★★	★★	$175
Talkeetna Hostel International	Hostel	★★	★★★★	$22–$65
Talkeetna Roadhouse	Hotel/hostel	★★★	★★★	$21–$141
GLENNALLEN				
Caribou Hotel	Hotel	★★★	★★★★	$69–$175
Carol's Bed and Breakfast	B&B	★★★	★★★	$100
COPPER RIVER BASIN				
Copper Center Lodge	Inn	★★★	★★★	$125
Copper Moose B&B	B&B	★★★★	★★★★	$125
Copper River Princess Wilderness Lodge	Hotel	★★★★★	★★★★	$179–$240
Kennicott Glacier Lodge	Motel	★★★★★	★★★★	$165–$375
Kennicott River Lodge and Hostel	Hostel/cabins	★★★	★★★★	$30–$150
Kenny Lake Hotel	Motel-style	★★	★★★	$70–$90
McCarthy Lodge–Lancaster's Backpackers Hotel	Lodge/hotel	★★★	★★★	$68–$259
Pippin Lake Bed and Breakfast	Cabin	★★★★	★★★★	$150

▶ **Alaskan Leopard Bed and Breakfast**   16136 Sandpiper Dr.; 907-868-1594 or 877-454-3046; **alaskanleopard.com.**

QUALITY ★★★★★ | VALUE ★★★★★ | $129–$159

With outstanding views from its Upper Hillside location, this little-known but excellent bed-and-breakfast is a true treat. The chefs' food rivals that of the fine restaurants in town.

▶ **Alyeska Hostel**   Alpina Way, Girdwood, 35 miles south of Anchorage; 907-783-2222; **alyeskahostel.com.**

QUALITY ★★★ | VALUE ★★★★★ | $20–$85

Accommodations consist of bunks and private rooms, and also a cabin, great for families.

▶ **Anchorage Downtown Bed and Breakfast at Raspberry Meadows** 1401 W. 13th Ave.; 907-278-9275; **anchoragedowntown.com.**

QUALITY ★★★★ | VALUE ★★★★★ | $85–$145

This historical downtown bed-and-breakfast is within walking distance of all downtown shops, hotels, tourist attractions, and outdoor activities. It's a favorite lodging choice among active travelers, with two private suites and one room in the house. A guesthouse is available for extended stays.

▶ **Anchorage Guest House**   2001 Hillcrest Dr. off L Street; 907-274-0408; **alaska.net/~house/index.html.**

QUALITY ★★★★★ | VALUE ★★★★★ | $30–$140

This is probably the nicest hostel in Anchorage, in a good section of town. The guesthouse is located right off the Tony Knowles Coastal Trail, which is a great link to the rest of the city. Private rooms and bunks are available.

▶ **Anchorage International Hostel**   Seventh Avenue and H Street; 907-276-3635; **anchorageinternationalhostel.org.**

QUALITY ★★★ | VALUE ★★★★ | $25–$65

Practically downtown, this convenient hostel has 95 beds that fill up fast. There's a 1 a.m. curfew, and the only parking is metered parking on the street. A $3 discount is available for Hostelling International members. Private rooms are available at a higher rate, but they must be reserved in advance by phone.

▶ **City Garden Bed and Breakfast**   1352 W. 10th Ave.; 907-276-8686; **citygarden.biz.**

QUALITY ★★★★ | VALUE ★★★★ | $100–$150

The rooms are bright and sunny, with beautiful artwork.

▶ **Copper Whale Inn**   440 L St.; 907-258-7999; **copperwhale.com.**

QUALITY ★★★★★ | VALUE ★★★★ | $185–$210

The excellent location is reason enough to stay here, with great views of the inlet and easy access to downtown or the Tony Knowles Coastal Trail.

▶ **Eagle Nest Hotel**   4110 Spenard Rd.; 907-243-3433 or 866-344-6835; **alaskabestinn.com.**

QUALITY ★★★	VALUE ★★★	$110–$150

A basic hotel that looks better inside than out. But it is close to the airport— and cheap if you book online and take advantage of the often-found discounts.

▶ **Earth Bed and Breakfast**   1001 W. 12th Ave.; 907-279-9907; **earthbb.com**

QUALITY ★★★	VALUE ★★★★★	$110–$130

This wonderful B&B has gained a reputation among mountaineers who choose it as their lodging while in Anchorage. Rates are based on shared versus private baths.

▶ **Hilton Anchorage**   907-272-7411 or 800-445-8667; **hilton.com.**

QUALITY ★★★★★	VALUE ★★★	$270–$975

If you prefer the swankiness of major chain hotels, we suggest the Hilton over the Sheraton. While the latter is quite nice, it's not as centrally located as the Hilton, and it overlooks a cemetery instead of Cook Inlet. In the summer, rates are outrageously expensive, but you will notice this at all the larger hotels.

▶ **The Hotel Alyeska**   In Girdwood, 35 miles southeast of Anchorage on the Seward Highway; 907-754-2111 or 800-880-3880; **alyeskaresort.com.**

QUALITY ★★★★★	VALUE ★★★★	$199–$2,200

This luxurious year-round hotel, in the ski town of Girdwood, at the base of the ski resort of the same name, is a favorite getaway for Southcentral Alaskans. Enjoy the fine dining at the top of the mountain via the scenic tram, or indulge in the giant hot tub with a view of the mountains. Lodging/ski packages are available. New ownership in 2007 has pointed to seriously posh upgrades—now you can get hot-stone massages and facials.

▶ **Hotel Captain Cook**   Fourth Avenue and K Street; 907-276-6000 or 800-843-1950; **captaincook.com.**

QUALITY ★★★★★	VALUE ★★★	$255–$1,500

Perhaps Anchorage's finest hotel, with valet parking, an outstanding athletic club, and some of the best food in the city. The rooms are nice too, and expensive. But the hotel's Web site often offers specials that drastically cut the rate, so check online while planning your trip to see if you can get a deal.

▶ **International Backpackers Inn/Hostel**   3601 Peterkin Ave.; 907-274-3870.

QUALITY ★★	VALUE ★★★	$22.40

The hostel itself is OK, but the section of town is a bit rough. And we say that kindly. But it's literally the cheapest alternative you'll find to sleeping in the streets.

▶ **Millennium Alaskan Hotel Anchorage**   4800 Spenard Rd.; 907-243-2300 or 800-544-0553; **millenniumhotels.com**

QUALITY ★★★★ | VALUE ★★★ | $239–$339

A very Alaska-looking hotel that serves as headquarters during the Iditarod each March. In the summer, its adjoining restaurant is a great place to sit outside on the patio and watch floatplanes land on nearby Lakes Hood and Spenard. The rooms, compared with those at places like the Captain Cook, are overpriced.

▶ **Parkside Guest House**   Downtown off the Delaney Park Strip; 907-683-2290; **parksideanchorage.com.**

QUALITY ★★★★★ | VALUE ★★★ | $165–$195

Those who appreciate fine architecture and decorating will immediately notice the quality that infuses this Arts and Crafts–inspired home. Mission-style furniture complements the decor and design. Rates are based on shared baths versus private baths. Discounts available for guests of Camp Denali and North Face Lodge in Denali National Park.

▶ **Spenard Hostel International**   2845 W. 42nd Ave.; 907-248-5036; **alaskahostel.org**

QUALITY ★★★★ | VALUE ★★★★★ | $25 cash, $27 credit card

This one fills up fast, so it helps to make reservations in advance. There is Wi-Fi and no curfew, and some coed rooms are available. Occasional potluck dinners and mountain-bike rentals. Our hostel of choice because of the friendly staff.

▶ **26th Street International Hostel**   1037 26th St., Spenard; 907-274-1252; **26streethostel.com.**

QUALITY ★★ | VALUE ★★★★ | $25–$67.25

Basic hostel in a quiet neighborhood. Bunks and private rooms are available.

▶ **Voyager Rodeway Inn Hotel**   501 K St., at Fifth Avenue; 907-277-9501 or 800-247-9070; **rodewayinn.com.**

QUALITY ★★★★ | VALUE ★★★★ | $170–$190

Step into this small hotel and you might feel as if you're in Europe. The decor and feel of the building are unique to Anchorage, and a wonderfully different place to stay. Unlike many European hotels, this one has spacious rooms.

Camping

Within the city limits are three Alaska State Parks campgrounds—**Bird Creek, Eklutna Lake,** and **Eagle River**—where nature can be enjoyed just a short drive from town. For more information, visit **dnr.alaska.gov/parks/ units/chugach** or **lifetimeadventures.net,** the company that manages two of the campgrounds.

▶ **Bird Creek Campground**   20 miles south of Anchorage at Mile 101 on the Seward Highway; 907-345-5014.

| QUALITY ★★★★ | VALUE ★★★★ | $15 |

Twenty-eight sites, some overlooking the inlet. Overflow-camping area. Fishing, walking, birding, and cycling are among the recreational options.

▶ **Centennial Park**   Off the Muldoon Road exit, Anchorage; 907-343-6986; **muni.org/parks/camping.cfm.**

| QUALITY ★★★ | VALUE ★★★ | $20 |

Nice enough, but theft can be a problem. Showers are available for $3.

▶ **Creekwood Inn**   Off Gambell Street, Anchorage; 907-258-6006; **creekwoodinn-alaska.com.**

| QUALITY ★★★ | VALUE ★★★★ | $22–$28 |

It's off the Chester Creek Greenbelt and bike trail, and it's more secure than Centennial Park and Ship Creek Landing. But it's also right off a busy road. No tent camping is available.

▶ **Eagle River Campground**   12 miles north of Anchorage, off the Hiland Road exit; 907-694-7982.

| QUALITY ★★★★ | VALUE ★★★★★ | $15 |

Fifty-seven sites, some on the river. Overflow-camping area of 10 sites. Fishing, whitewater rafting or kayaking, and hiking are popular. Right off the highway, so expect traffic noise. *Note:* Half of the sites are available by reservation.

▶ **Eklutna Lake Campground**   45 minutes north of Anchorage; 907-345-5014.

| QUALITY ★★★★★ | VALUE ★★★★★ | $10 |

Offering 50 sites, some of which are walk-in tent sites. Overflow-camping area of 15 sites. Fishing, hiking, mountain biking, mountaineering, and off-roading are popular. Best during weekdays when the local crowd hasn't shown up.

▶ **Ship Creek Landing**   In the downtown industrial area, Anchorage; 907-277-0877 or 888-778-7700.

| QUALITY ★★ | VALUE ★★★ | $26–$55 |

Adequate facilities, but theft can be a problem and homeless people hang out nearby. Tent sites.

▲ southcentral inland alaska camping

NAME	CAMPING TYPE	QUALITY RATING	VALUE RATING	COST
ANCHORAGE				
Bird Creek Campground	RV/tent	★★★★	★★★★	$15
Centennial Park	RV/tent	★★★	★★★	$20
Creekwood Inn	RV only	★★★	★★★★	$22–$28
Eagle River Campground	RV/tent	★★★★	★★★★★	$15
Eklutna Lake Campground	RV/tent	★★★★★	★★★★★	$10
Ship Creek Landing	RV/tent	★★	★★★	$26–$55
MATANUSKA-SUSITNA VALLEY				
Chickaloon General Store	Tent	★★★	★★★	$15
Finger Lake State Recreation-site	RV/tent	★★★★	★★★★	$15
Fox Run Lodge and RV Campground	RV/tent	★★★	★★★★	$20–$169
Lake Louise State Recreation Area	RV/tent	★★★	★★★★	$5–$15
Lake Lucille Park	RV/tent	★★★	★★★★★	$10
Mat-Su RV Park and Campground	RV/tent	★★★	★★★	$17–$35
Nancy Lake State Recreation Area	RV/tent	★★★★	★★★★	$10
Montana Creek Campground	RV/tent	★★★★	★★★	$28–$45

MATANUSKA-SUSITNA VALLEY

Indoor Lodging

▶ **Hatcher Pass Lodge**   Mile 17 Hatcher Pass Rd.; 907-745-1200; **hatcherpasslodge.com.**

QUALITY ★★★★ | VALUE ★★★★★ | $95–$165

Our favorite destination in the Valley, with Swiss-looking A-frame chalets and cabins for wintertime and summertime fun. Pets are allowed for an extra $15.

▲ southcentral inland camping [continued]

NAME	CAMPING TYPE	QUALITY RATING	VALUE RATING	COST
TALKEETNA				
River Park Campground	Tent	★★★	★★★	$13+
Talkeetna Camper Park	RV	★★★★	★★★	$20+
Talkeetna RV and Campground	RV/tent	★★★★	★★★★	$15+
GLENNALLEN				
Brown Bear Rhodehouse	Tent	★★★	★★★	$8
Dry Creek State Recreation-site	RV/tent	★★★★	★★★★	$10
Northern Nights Campground and RV Park	RV/tent	★★★★	★★★★★	$12–$22
Tolsona Wilderness Campground and RV Park	RV/tent	★★★	★★★★	$25–$45
COPPER RIVER BASIN				
End of the Road Camping	Tent	★★★★	★★★★	$10–$15
Glacier View Campground	Tent	★★★	★★★★	$22–$85
Kenny Lake Mercantile/ RV Park	RV/tent	★★★	★★★★	$12–$20

▶ **Majestic Valley Wilderness Lodge**   Mile 115 Glenn Hwy., north of Palmer; 907-746-2930; **majesticvalleylodge.com.**

QUALITY ★★★★ | VALUE ★★★★★ | $120–$165

This beautiful log lodge on 10 acres offers comfortable lodging, with meals provided when you reserve ahead of time. Access to skiing, hiking, and other activities is right outside the door.

▶ **Moose Wallow Bed and Breakfast**   Off Mile 53 Glenn Hwy., near Sutton; 907-745-7777; **moosewallow.com.**

QUALITY ★★★ | VALUE ★★★★ | $110–$145

An off-the-beaten path location for private lodging; walking trails are nearby.

▶ **Sheep Mountain Lodge**   Mile 113.5 Glenn Hwy., north of Palmer; 877-645-5121; **sheepmountain.com.**

QUALITY ★★★★ | VALUE ★★★★ | $60–$189

This lodge in the shadow of Sheep Mountain is popular among skiers and dog mushers. There are 11 cabins, plus a bunkhouse in the summer. One of our favorite destinations.

Camping

▶ **Chickaloon General Store**   Mile 76.3 Glenn Hwy.; 907-746-1801.

QUALITY ★★★ | VALUE ★★★ | $15

Camping is allowed by the river. Showers ($3.50) and laundry facilities on-site.

▶ **Finger Lake State Recreation-site**   Mile 0.7 Bogard Rd.; 907-745-2827.

QUALITY ★★★★ | VALUE ★★★★ | $15

Thirty-six campsites.

▶ **Fox Run Lodge and RV Campground**   Mile 36.3 Glenn Hwy.; 877-745-6120 or 907-745-6120; **foxrun.freeservers.com.**

QUALITY ★★★ | VALUE ★★★★ | $20–$169

Right off the highway near Kepler-Bradley State Recreation Area, which is great for fishing and hiking but can get pretty buggy in the summer. Camping fees include your shower. You can also rent a rowboat, canoe, or kayak by the hour.

▶ **Lake Louise State Recreation Area**   At Lake Louise, off Mile 159.8 Glenn Hwy.; 907-441-7575 or 907-278-7575; **dnr.alaska.gov/parks/aspunits/matsu/lklouisesra.htm.**

QUALITY ★★★ | VALUE ★★★★ | $5–$15

Primitive RV and tent sites; offers some of the best lake fishing in the state.

▶ **Lake Lucille Park**   Mile 2.2 Knik-Goose Bay Rd.; 907-745-9690; **cityofwasilla.com/index.aspx?page=612**

QUALITY ★★★ | VALUE ★★★★★ | $10

This park is about the closest place to town that you can camp, with 57 sites for tents and RVs. There are some nice trails in the area, as well as good fishing in the lake.

▶ **Mat-Su RV Park and Campground**   Outside of Willow, Mile 90.8 Parks Hwy.; 907-495-6300; **matsurvpark.com.**

QUALITY ★★★ | VALUE ★★★ | $17–$35

The park is right off the road but convenient. A small store sells snacks.

▶ **Nancy Lake State Recreation Area**   Off Nancy Lake Parkway; 907-745-3975; dnr.alaska.gov/parks/units/nancylk/nancylk.htm.

QUALITY ★★★★ | VALUE ★★★★ | $10

The South Rolly Campground and Nancy Lake Campground are both available for summer camping, and public-use cabins are for rent as well.

▶ **Montana Creek Campground**   On Montana Creek, between Willow and Talkeetna; 907-733-5267 or 877-475-2267; **montanacreekcampground.com.**

QUALITY ★★★★ | VALUE ★★★ | $28–$45

This is a great spot for anglers. Tent and RV camping are in a pretty, tree-shaded area just by the creek. The campground is spotless but can get crowded.

TALKEETNA

Indoor Lodging

▶ **Chinook Wind Cabins**   Within walking distance of downtown; 907-733-1899 or 800-643-1899; **chinookwindcabins.com.**

QUALITY ★★★ | VALUE ★★ | $90–$165

The six well-built cabins are side-by-side but still very private. Rates are higher than average in the area, but for those without a vehicle, the convenience of being in town is worth it.

▶ **Eye of Denali Inn**   Within walking distance of town; 907-733-8728; eyeofdenali.com.

QUALITY ★★★★ | VALUE ★★★★★ | $89–$275

This place bills itself as a no-host bed-and-breakfast, which we find delightful because we get the perk of a hot breakfast but the privacy to do what we want at our own pace.

▶ **Swiss-Alaska Inn**   F Street, off Talkeetna Spur Road (visit Web site for full directions and map); 907-733-2424; **swissalaska.com.**

QUALITY ★★★ | VALUE ★★★ | $95–$140

This longtime inn features a casual dining room with a full menu. It's an aging but well-kept facility.

▶ **Talkeetna Alaskan Lodge**   907-733-9500 or 877-777-4067; **talkeetnalodge.com.**

QUALITY ★★★★★ | VALUE ★★★★ | $145–$555

A very nice native-owned lodge that tends to attract tour and cruise-ship travelers. Rooms are elegant but still maintain an Alaska feel. The restaurant is a fine-dining experience, and the wine list is extensive. Easily the fanciest place in town.

▶ **Talkeetna Cabins**   Another option close to downtown; 907-733-2227 or 888-733-9933; **talkeetnacabins.org.**

QUALITY ★★★★ | VALUE ★★ | $175

These small log cabins, just a 5-minute walk from town, are well built and comfortable.

▶ **Talkeetna Hostel International**   On I Street, just east of the town site; 907-733-4678; **talkeetnahostel.com.**

QUALITY ★★ | VALUE ★★★★ | $22–$65

No lockouts or curfews, and they have a book exchange and bike rentals for getting around town. We love the VW minibus you can sleep in.

▶ **Talkeetna Roadhouse**   907-733-1351; **talkeetnaroadhouse.com.**

QUALITY ★★★ | VALUE ★★★ | $21–$141

This locally famous roadhouse is in the middle of downtown—another favorite among climbers for lodging. All the rooms come with shared baths. The rates are affordable, but this is definitely for the traveler who doesn't mind mingling with strangers. Free Internet access is a plus. Cabins also are available.

Camping

▶ **River Park Campground**   At the end of Main Street; 907-745-9690 or 907-745-2856.

QUALITY ★★★ | VALUE ★★★ | $13+

Informal camping close to the activity of downtown.

▶ **Talkeetna Camper Park**   907-733-2693; **talkeetnacamper.com.**

QUALITY ★★★★ | VALUE ★★★ | $20+

The campground has 35 sites near the popular Latitude 62 restaurant, with showers, full and partial hookups, and a small store.

▶ **Talkeetna RV and Campground**   907-733-2604.

QUALITY ★★★★ | VALUE ★★★★ | $15+

The campground has 60 wooded sites right off the boat launch, with showers and bathrooms. Talkeetna River Guides manages it (800-353-2677; **talkeetna riverguides.com**).

GLENNALLEN

Indoor Lodging

▶ **Caribou Hotel**   In Glennallen; 907-822-3302; **caribouhotel.com.**

QUALITY ★★★ | VALUE ★★★★ | $69–$175

This modern hotel offers two-room suites with kitchens available. An adjoining annex where pipeline workers once stayed has less-expensive rooms, and they have a pair of cabins and a pair of apartments.

▶ **Carol's Bed and Breakfast**   Mile 187 Glenn Hwy., Glennallen; 907-822-3594; **alaska.net/~neeley.**

QUALITY ★★★	VALUE ★★★	$100

Carol's breakfast includes homemade wild-berry jams and jellies, sourdough hotcakes, and reindeer sausage.

Camping

▶ **Brown Bear Rhodehouse**   Mile 183.5 Glenn Hwy.; 907-822-3663.

QUALITY ★★★	VALUE ★★★	$8

A restaurant and cocktail lounge that also offers camping.

▶ **Dry Creek State Recreation-site**   Mile 117 Richardson Hwy.; 907-259-5558 or 907-822-5208.

QUALITY ★★★★	VALUE ★★★★	$10

This site has 50 campsites and four walk-in wilderness sites; the latter are our favorites.

▶ **Northern Nights Campground and RV Park**   Mile 188.7 Glenn Hwy.; 907-822-3199; **northern-nights-rv.com.**

QUALITY ★★★★	VALUE ★★★★★	$12–$22

Tent-camping sites are shaded and have tent platforms, but this place mostly attracts the RV crowd. Showers cost extra.

▶ **Tolsona Wilderness Campground and RV Park**   Mile 173 Glenn Hwy., about 14 miles west of Glennallen; 907-822-3865; **tolsona.com.**

QUALITY ★★★	VALUE ★★★★	$25–$45

This full-service campground has tent sites, restrooms, a dump station, showers, laundry facilities, free Wi-Fi, and a mini-store. Trails and fishing nearby.

COPPER RIVER BASIN

Indoor Lodging

▶ **Copper Center Lodge**   Mile 101 Old Richardson Hwy. Loop; 866-330-3245 or 907-822-3245; **coppercenterlodge.com.**

QUALITY ★★★	VALUE ★★★	$125

This aging but historical lodge has private or shared baths. The rooms are small to accommodate the plumbing that was added years after the lodge was built, but they are cozy and comfortable.

▶ **Copper Moose Bed and Breakfast**   Mile 5.8 Edgerton Hwy., toward McCarthy; 907-822-4244 or 866-922-4244; **coppermoosebb.com.**

QUALITY ★★★★ | VALUE ★★★★ | $125

This gorgeous log structure, built by the owner himself, makes a splendid home away from home when you're staying in the area. The friendly owners are a real treat. Guests are invited to eat with the family at all meals due to the scarcity of restaurants in the area.

▶ **Copper River Princess Wilderness Lodge**   Mile 102 Richardson Hwy.; 907-822-4000; **princesslodges.com.**

QUALITY ★★★★★ | VALUE ★★★★ | $179–$240

This is a newer and more luxurious alternative to the Copper Center Lodge (see first profile in this section), but the prices are higher and the atmosphere more corporate and not as personalized.

▶ **Kennicott Glacier Lodge**   On Main Street, Kennicott, Wrangell–St. Elias National Park; 800-582-5128; **kennicottlodge.com.**

QUALITY ★★★★★ | VALUE ★★★★ | $169–$375

This is a rustic, historical renovated lodge in the heart of the nation's largest national park. The rooms are simple, but that's part of the charm—no TVs or phones to interrupt the tranquility. The restaurant serves outstanding gourmet meals. The package prices, which include all meals, are the best deals.

▶ **Kennicott River Lodge and Hostel**   907-554-4441; **kennicottriverlodge.com.**

QUALITY ★★★ | VALUE ★★★★ | $30–$150

Private cabins, hostel bunks, and a six-person suite available. Within walking distance to McCarthy and the Kennicott River.

▶ **Kenny Lake Hotel**   Mile 7.2 Edgerton Hwy., toward McCarthy; 907-822-3313; **kennylake.com/hotel.html.**

QUALITY ★★ | VALUE ★★★ | $70–$90

Large rooms, all with gorgeous views of the surrounding mountains.

▶ **McCarthy Lodge–Lancaster's Backpackers Hotel**   In downtown McCarthy; 907-554-4402; **mccarthylodge.com.**

QUALITY ★★★ | VALUE ★★★ | $68–$259

This historical hotel includes Ma Johnson's Hotel, with great food and drinks. Lodging options include traditional rooms and economical accommodations in the very simple Lancaster Hotel, designed for backpackers.

▶ **Pippin Lake Bed and Breakfast**   Mile 82.2 Richardson Hwy.; 907-822-3046 or 907-320-0435; **pippinlakebnb.com.**

QUALITY ★★★★ | VALUE ★★★★ | $150

The closest community to this quaint B&B in the woods is Copper Center, 20 miles away. The cabins sleep up to five comfortably; rates include breakfast fixings. Located right on the lake, where you can use the paddleboat or canoe and explore or go fishing.

Camping

▶ **End of the Road Camping**   Right at the end of McCarthy Road, near the footbridge.

QUALITY ★★★★ | VALUE ★★★★ | $10–$15

The river breeze keeps bugs to a minimum, but the sites are not as nice as those at Glacier View Campground. There's no phone, so you can just show up. Spaces are always available.

▶ **Glacier View Campground**   Less than a mile from the Kennicott River footbridge, near the end of McCarthy Road; 907-554-4490; **glacierviewcampground.com.**

QUALITY ★★★ | VALUE ★★★★ | $22–85

There are always spaces open; also has a cabin available and bike rentals.

▶ **Kenny Lake Mercantile/RV Park**   Mile 7.2 Edgerton Hwy., toward McCarthy; 907-822-3313; **kennylake.com.**

QUALITY ★★★ | VALUE ★★★★ | $12–$20

Camping for RVs and tents, as well as showers, laundry facilities, and assistance with planning tours.

▲ Where to Eat

ANCHORAGE

BECAUSE THERE ARE so many places in Anchorage from which to choose, we've arranged the food into categories, giving you simple listings and locations. We've eaten at every one of these restaurants and recommend any of them.

Burgers

▶ **Arctic Roadrunner**   5300 Old Seward Hwy.; 907-561-1245; and 2477 Arctic Blvd.; 907-279-7311.

BURGERS | QUALITY ★★★★ | $5–$9 | SUITABLE FOR KIDS? Y

Consistently voted Anchorage's best burger joint.

▲ southcentral inland alaska dining

NAME	CUISINE	FOOD QUALITY	COST
ANCHORAGE			
Aladdin's Fine Mediterranean	Mediterranean	★★★★	$8–$25
Alaska Bagel Inc.	Sandwiches	★★★★	$5–$9
Arctic Roadrunner	Burgers	★★★★	$5–$9
Bear Tooth	Fusion	★★★★	$9–$25
La Cabana Mexican Restaurant	Mexican	★★★★	$6–$14
Charlie's Bakery and Restaurant	Chinese	★★★★	$5–$15
Club Paris	Steaks	★★★★	$9–$40
Crow's Nest at the Hotel Captain Cook	Fusion	★★★★★	$12–$40
Fletcher's at the Hotel Captain Cook	Fusion	★★★★★	$7–$21
Gallo's Mexican Restaurant	Mexican	★★★	$6–$16
Glacier BrewHouse	Fusion	★★★★	$9–$30
Greek Corner	Greek	★★★	$5–$12
Haute Quarter Grill	Fusion	★★★★	$11–$28
Humpy's Great Alaskan Alehouse	Casual/bar	★★★	$5–$12
Jack Sprat	Fusion	★★★★★	$8–$31
Jalapenos	Mexican	★★★★	$8–$15
Kaladi Brothers Coffee Co.	Neighborhood	★★★	$2–$5
Lucky Wishbone	American	★★	$6–$12
Marx Bros. Café	Fusion	★★★★★	$12–$39
Maxine's Glacier City Bistro	Fusion	★★★★	$8–$24
Mexico in Alaska	Mexican	★★★★★	$9–$18
La Mex Restaurant	Mexican	★★★	$5–$12
Middle Way Café	Neighborhood	★★★★	$5–$9
Moose's Tooth Pub and Pizzeria	Pizza	★★★★★	$8–$26
Organic Oasis Restaurant and Juice Bar	Vegetarian	★★★	$7.50–$15

▲ more southcentral inland alaska dining

NAME	CUISINE	FOOD QUALITY	COST
ANCHORAGE [CONTINUED]			
Orso	Italian	★★★★★	$7–$40
Pizza Olympia	Pizza	★★★	$5–$21
Sacks Cafe & Restaurant	Fusion	★★★★★	$10–$34
Shine's Sushi	Japanese	★★★★★	$9–$24
Side Street Espresso	Baked Goods	★★★★	$2–$5
Snow City Café	American	★★★★	$7–$12
Snow Goose Restaurant	Fusion	★★★	$8–$39
Southside Bistro	Fusion	★★★★★	$12–$36
Sweet Basil Cafe	Neighborhood	★★★★	$6–$13
Thai Kitchen	Thai	★★★★	$6–$14
Thai Orchid Restaurant	Thai	★★★	$6–$20
White Spot Cafe	American	★★★	$4–$8
Yamato Ya Japanese Restaurant	Japanese	★★★★	$6–$26
MATANUSKA-SUSITNA VALLEY			
Alaska Cadillac Café	American	★★★	$5–$12
Colony Inn Café	American	★★★	$8–$20
Evangelo's Restaurant	Italian/pizza	★★★	$8–$21
Mekong Thai Cuisine	Thai	★★★★	$7–$16
Settler's Bay Lodge	American	★★★★	$9–$34
Tokyo Restaurant & Sushi Bar	Japanese	★★★	$6–$23
Vagabond Blues	Neighborhood	★★★★★	$3–$7
TALKEETNA			
Latitude 62	American	★★★	$8–$25
Mountain High Pizza Pie	Pizza	★★★★	$7–$19
Swiss-Alaska Inn	American	★★	$8–$15
Talkeetna Roadhouse	American	★★★	$6–$16

▲ more southcentral inland dining

GLENNALLEN

Caribou Restaurant	American	★★★	$7–$19
Lake Louise Lodge	American	★★★	$8–$24
Last Frontier Pizza	Pizza	★★★	$9–$17

COPPER RIVER BASIN

Copper Center Lodge	Fusion	★★★	$7–$27
Copper River Princess Wilderness Lodge	Upscale Regional	★★★★★	$9–$29
Kennicott Glacier Lodge	Fusion	★★★★★	$9–$25
Kenny Lake Diner & Bakery	American	★★	$5–$7
McCarthy Lodge	American	★★★	$8–$25

Cafes

▶ **Alaska Bagel Inc.** 113 W. Northern Lights Blvd.; 907-276-3900.

SANDWICHES | QUALITY ★★★★ | $5–$9 | SUITABLE FOR KIDS? Y

Bagel sandwiches in just about any variety you can imagine. Cream cheeses and other toppings make for a filling meal.

▶ **Kaladi Brothers Coffee Co.** 6921 Brayton Dr.; 907-344-5483.

NEIGHBORHOOD | QUALITY ★★★ | $2–$5 | SUITABLE FOR KIDS? Y

The "it" cafe in town, whether it's this one or the one on Tudor Road or downtown or Northern Lights Boulevard.

▶ **Middle Way Café** 1200 W. Northern Lights Blvd.; 907-272-6433.

NEIGHBORHOOD | QUALITY ★★★★ | $5–$9 | SUITABLE FOR KIDS? Y

A trendy coffee shop that gets slammed at lunchtime because of its excellent organic and vegetarian selections.

▶ **Organic Oasis Restaurant and Juice Bar** 2610 Spenard Rd.; 907-277-7882.

VEGETARIAN | QUALITY ★★★ | $7.50–$15 | SUITABLE FOR KIDS? Y

A good choice for those on strict vegetarian diets. Espresso and teas available too.

▶ **Side Street Espresso**   412 G St.; 907-258-9055.

BAKED GOODS	QUALITY ★★★★	$2–$5	SUITABLE FOR KIDS? Y

Yummy sweets and other snacks in a very casual atmosphere.

▶ **Snow City Cafe**   1034 W. 4th Ave.; 907-272-2489.

AMERICAN	QUALITY ★★★★	$7–$12	SUITABLE FOR KIDS? Y

Breakfast is their strong suit. The egg dishes are imaginative, and there are plenty of options for vegetarians.

▶ **Sweet Basil Cafe**   1021 W. Northern Lights Blvd.; 907-274-0070.

NEIGHBORHOOD	QUALITY ★★★★	$6–$13	SUITABLE FOR KIDS? Y

Has inexpensive, healthy meals, including lunch and dinner to go until 5 p.m.; espresso; and a bountiful juice bar. Delicious desserts too.

Casual and Innovative
(our favorite category after sushi)

▶ **Bear Tooth**   1230 W. 27th Ave.; 907-276-4200.

FUSION	QUALITY ★★★★	$9–$25	SUITABLE FOR KIDS? Y

The same folks who own Moose's Tooth Pub (page 318) own and operate this eatery, which is next to a second-run-movie theater. You can dine in or have your order delivered to you in the theater.

▶ **Fletcher's at the Hotel Captain Cook**   Fourth Avenue at K Street; 907-276-6000.

FUSION	QUALITY ★★★★★	$7–$21	SUITABLE FOR KIDS? N

The food is just as good as what you'll find up in the Crow's Nest (see page 317), only at half the price and in a swank mahogany-colored bar. Located on the floor level of the hotel.

▶ **Glacier BrewHouse**   737 W. 5th Ave., Suite 110; 907-274-2739.

FUSION	QUALITY ★★★★	$9–$30	SUITABLE FOR KIDS? Y

We've always enjoyed the food, but the prices are kind of high. Ask for a table near the fireplace.

▶ **Humpy's Great Alaskan Alehouse**   610 W. 6th Ave.; 907-276-2337.

CASUAL/BAR	QUALITY ★★★	$5–$12	SUITABLE FOR KIDS? N

Great bar, great food. The halibut tacos are a local favorite.

▶ **Jack Sprat**   Olympic Mountain Loop in Girdwood, 35 miles south of Anchorage; 907-783-5225.

FUSION | QUALITY ★★★★★ | $8–$31 | SUITABLE FOR KIDS? N

Some of the most creative food in all of Anchorage, but without the large prices. The granola atmosphere fits in well with the entire laid-back-town attitude in Girdwood. Our favorite restaurant here.

▶ **Maxine's Glacier City Bistro**   On Crow Creek Road in Girdwood; 907-783-1234.

FUSION | QUALITY ★★★★ | $8–$24 | SUITABLE FOR KIDS? Y

Another Girdwood favorite, with an exceptionally creative menu. The downside: sometimes you have to wait a long, long time for your food.

▶ **Sacks Cafe & Restaurant**   328 G Street; 907-276-3546.

FUSION | QUALITY ★★★★★ | $10–$34 | SUITABLE FOR KIDS? N

On the upper end of casual, serving tasty seafood dishes and pastas, among other selections. Known for its outstanding wine list.

▶ **Snow Goose Restaurant**   717 W. 3rd Ave.; 907-277-7727.

FUSION | QUALITY ★★★ | $8–$39 | SUITABLE FOR KIDS? Y

The food is imaginative and ranges from basic burgers to flavorful salmon and halibut dishes. We really like this place, though, for its picturesque deck dining, with prime views of the Inlet.

Chinese

▶ **Charlie's Bakery and Restaurant**   2729 C St.; 907-677-7777.

CHINESE | QUALITY ★★★★ | $5–$15 | SUITABLE FOR KIDS? Y

This tucked-away strip-mall spot is the only one in town that serves dim sum. It's our only choice for Chinese in a city packed with Chinese restaurants.

Diners

▶ **Lucky Wishbone**   1033 E. 5th Ave.; 907-272-3454.

AMERICAN | QUALITY ★★ | $6–$12 | SUITABLE FOR KIDS? Y

They've been in business forever; you'll feel like you're stepping back in time when you enter the place. Gets crowded with locals at lunchtime. The French fries are excellent.

▶ **White Spot Cafe**   109 W. 4th Ave.; 907-279-3954.

AMERICAN | QUALITY ★★★ | $4–$8 | SUITABLE FOR KIDS? Y

A true corner diner with lots of plastic, lots of burgers being flipped, and lots of baskets o' fries. Has a following among locals and downtown workers.

Fine Dining

▶ **Club Paris**   417 W. 5th Ave.; 907-277-6332.

STEAKS | QUALITY ★★★★ | $9–$40 | SUITABLE FOR KIDS? N

An Anchorage institution specializing in tender steaks and gourmet burgers; the salads are a disappointment, though.

▶ **Crow's Nest at the Hotel Captain Cook**   Fourth Avenue at K Street; 907-276-6000.

FUSION | QUALITY ★★★★★ | $12–$40 | SUITABLE FOR KIDS? N

Where Anchorage couples go to celebrate very special occasions; one of the best and most romantic places in town.

▶ **Haute Quarter Grill**   11221 Old Glenn Hwy.; 907-622-4745.

FUSION | QUALITY ★★★★ | $11–$28 | SUITABLE FOR KIDS? N

This will require a drive to Eagle River, but the food is excellent, and chef-owner Alex Perez has experience at some of the finest restaurants in the state. The ahi tuna is wonderful. Open for dinner only.

▶ **Marx Bros. Café**   627 W. 3rd Ave.; 907-278-2133.

FUSION | QUALITY ★★★★★ | $12–$39 | SUITABLE FOR KIDS? N

A true dinner house, open only at night and serving top-notch meals in an elegant atmosphere.

▶ **Southside Bistro**   1320 Huffman Park Dr.; 907-348-0088.

FUSION | QUALITY ★★★★★ | $12–$36 | SUITABLE FOR KIDS? N

The food looks as good as it tastes, with artful presentation and interesting taste combinations. Our favorite special-occasion restaurant after Crow's Nest.

International

▶ **Aladdin's Fine Mediterranean**   4240 Old Seward Hwy., Suite 20; 907-561-2373.

MEDITERRANEAN | QUALITY ★★★★ | $8–$25 | SUITABLE FOR KIDS? N

A wide range of Mediterranean favorites at reasonable prices.

▶ **Greek Corner**   201 E. Northern Lights Blvd.; 907-276-2820.

GREEK | QUALITY ★★★ | $5–$12 | SUITABLE FOR KIDS? Y

A restaurant that serves great Greek food, including moussaka and baklava. Not the best, but if you're craving a gyro, here's where to get it.

▶ **Orso**   737 W. 5th Ave.; 907-222-3232.

ITALIAN	QUALITY ★★★★★	$7–$40	SUITABLE FOR KIDS? N

This Mediterranean restaurant has taken over the fine-dining scene for those who like Tuscan-influenced meals. They also have some fine fusion items on the menu and an extensive wine list.

Mexican

▶ **La Cabana Mexican Restaurant**   312 E. 5th Ave.; 907-272-0135.

MEXICAN	QUALITY ★★★★	$6–$14	SUITABLE FOR KIDS? Y

The location leaves a bit to be desired, but the food is truly authentic.

▶ **Gallo's Mexican Restaurant**   8311 Arctic Blvd.; 907-344-6735.

MEXICAN	QUALITY ★★★	$6–$16	SUITABLE FOR KIDS? Y

The building and atmosphere are older and more authentic than the other Gallo's locations in town.

▶ **Jalapenos**   11823 Old Glenn Hwy., Eagle River, 15 miles north of Anchorage; 907-694-1888.

MEXICAN	QUALITY ★★★★	$8–$15	SUITABLE FOR KIDS? Y

This Eagle River restaurant does a good job with its Mexican seafood dishes, and the homemade salsa is just right. Try the sopaipillas if you have room left for dessert.

▶ **Mexico in Alaska**   7305 Old Seward Hwy.; 907-349-1528.

MEXICAN	QUALITY ★★★★★	$9–$18	SUITABLE FOR KIDS? Y

Nobody makes mole like the folks at this longtime Anchorage restaurant.

▶ **La Mex Restaurant**   8330 King St.; 907-344-6399.

MEXICAN	QUALITY ★★★	$5–$12	SUITABLE FOR KIDS? Y

With several locations throughout town, this is the widely accepted Mexican restaurant among locals.

Pizza

▶ **Moose's Tooth Pub and Pizzeria**   3300 Old Seward Hwy.; 907-258-2537.

PIZZA	QUALITY ★★★★★	$8–$26	SUITABLE FOR KIDS? Y

Very popular hangout. They make more than 15 of their own microbrews, and the 39-plus topping choices on the pizza menu range from halibut to pepperoni to eggplant. *Warning:* It's busy all the time, so try to go at nonpeak hours.

▶ **Pizza Olympia**   2809 Spenard Rd.; 907-561-5464.

PIZZA | QUALITY ★★★ | $5–$21 | SUITABLE FOR KIDS? Y

A longtime pizza shop that also has some good salads and Italian and Greek dishes. It's never as busy as Moose's Tooth.

Sushi

▶ **Shine's Sushi**   11401 Old Glenn Hwy. in Eagle River; 907-622-8889.

JAPANESE | QUALITY ★★★★★ | $9–$24 | SUITABLE FOR KIDS? Y

You have to drive all the way to Eagle River, but when it comes to sushi, Shine's is the best of the best.

▶ **Yamato Ya Japanese Restaurant**   3700 Old Seward Hwy.; 907-561-2128.

JAPANESE | QUALITY ★★★★ | $6–$26 | SUITABLE FOR KIDS? Y

In the City Market building; not fancy but the most authentic.

Thai

▶ **Thai Kitchen**   3405 E. Tudor Rd.; 907-561-0082.

THAI | QUALITY ★★★★ | $6–$14 | SUITABLE FOR KIDS? Y

The wraps and fresh rolls are fabulous. Good choices for vegetarians too. Service can be slow, so don't go if you're in a hurry.

▶ **Thai Orchid Restaurant**   219 E. Dimond Blvd.; 907-868-5226.

THAI | QUALITY ★★★ | $6–$20 | SUITABLE FOR KIDS? Y

A local favorite with very reasonable prices.

MATANUSKA-SUSITNA VALLEY

▶ **Alaska Cadillac Café**   Mile 49 Parks Hwy. just outside of Wasilla; 907-376-5833.

AMERICAN | QUALITY ★★★ | $5–$12 | SUITABLE FOR KIDS? Y

It's a gas station on one side and an impressively well-managed restaurant on the other. The service and ambience are good, though the pizzas have gotten mixed reviews. We go for their sandwiches and burgers.

▶ **Colony Inn Café**   325 E. Elmwood, Palmer; 907-745-3330.

AMERICAN | QUALITY ★★★ | $8–$20 | SUITABLE FOR KIDS? Y

The dining room is cozy and comfortable, and the meals are some of the nicer ones you'll find in town.

▶ **Evangelo's Restaurant**   At 301 Parks Hwy., Wasilla; 907-376-1249.

ITALIAN/PIZZA | QUALITY ★★★ | $8–$21 | SUITABLE FOR KIDS? N

This very large restaurant can serve many people at a time and is a favorite among Valley folks for banquets and special events. They have Italian food and pizza, both of which are popular.

▶ **Mekong Thai Cuisine** 473 W. Parks Hwy., Wasilla; 907-373-7690.

THAI	QUALITY ★★★★	$7–$16	SUITABLE FOR KIDS? Y

Very reasonable prices, and they know how to prepare tofu just right.

▶ **Settler's Bay Lodge** Mile 8 Knik–Goose Bay Rd., outside of Wasilla; 907-357-5678.

AMERICAN	QUALITY ★★★★	$9–$34	SUITABLE FOR KIDS? N

Experience fine dining in a rural setting. Lovely views and lots of warm wood and stonework throughout.

▶ **Tokyo Restaurant & Sushi Bar** 735 W. Parks Hwy., Wasilla; 907-357-8888.

JAPANESE	QUALITY ★★★	$6–$23	SUITABLE FOR KIDS? Y

The tempura is a local favorite, but we like the fish bait. It's fresh, and the chefs create edible art.

▶ **Vagabond Blues** 642 S. Alaska St., Palmer; 907-745-2233.

NEIGHBORHOOD	QUALITY ★★★★★	$3–$7	SUITABLE FOR KIDS? Y

The soups are delicious, and the atmosphere is hip and relaxed. Mellow live entertainment some nights. This is our favorite hangout in Palmer.

TALKEETNA

▶ **Latitude 62** Just before the Main Street area on your right; 907-733-2262.

AMERICAN	QUALITY ★★★	$8–$25	SUITABLE FOR KIDS? Y

Locals love the tasty burgers and steaks.

▶ **Mountain High Pizza Pie** 907-733-1234.

PIZZA	QUALITY ★★★★	$7–$19	SUITABLE FOR KIDS? Y

A favorite among locals and guests, with outdoor picnic-table seating in the summer. They serve salads, sandwiches, beer, and wine as well.

▶ **Swiss-Alaska Inn** 907-733-2424; **swissalaska.com**.

AMERICAN	QUALITY ★★	$8–$15	SUITABLE FOR KIDS? Y

Casual dining with breakfast, lunch, and dinner menu.

▶ **Talkeetna Roadhouse** On Main Street; 907-733-1351; **talkeetnaroadhouse.com**.

AMERICAN	QUALITY ★★	$6–$16	SUITABLE FOR KIDS? N

Their breakfasts, especially the huge cinnamon rolls, are delicious. Bakery on-site.

GLENNALLEN

▶ **Caribou Restaurant**   In Glennallen; 907-822-3149; **caribouhotel.com.**

| AMERICAN | QUALITY ★★★ | $7–$19 | SUITABLE FOR KIDS? Y |

Basic food and filling breakfasts in a family-style atmosphere.

▶ **Lake Louise Lodge**   Mile 16 Lake Louise Rd., outside of Glennallen; 907-822-3311.

| AMERICAN | QUALITY ★★★ | $8–$24 | SUITABLE FOR KIDS? Y |

Full restaurant and bar. They make their bread from scratch.

▶ **Last Frontier Pizza**   907-822-3030.

| PIZZA | QUALITY ★★★ | $9–$17 | SUITABLE FOR KIDS? Y |

All-you-can-eat pizza that the locals favor.

COPPER RIVER BASIN

▶ **Copper Center Lodge**   Mile 101 Old Richardson Hwy. Loop; 866-330-3245 or 907-822-3245; **coppercenterlodge.com.**

| FUSION | QUALITY ★★★ | $7–$27 | SUITABLE FOR KIDS? Y |

This aging but historical lodge has a nice dining room with full meals available.

▶ **Copper River Princess Wilderness Lodge**   Mile 102 Richardson Hwy.; 800-426-0500 or 907-822-4000; **princesslodges.com.**

| UPSCALE REGIONAL | QUALITY ★★★★★ | $9–$29 | SUITABLE FOR KIDS? N |

This is a luxurious hotel with excellent food in a beautiful dining room.

▶ **Kennicott Glacier Lodge**   On Main Street, Kennicott, Wrangell–St. Elias National Park; 800-582-5128 or 907-258-2350; **kennicottlodge.com.**

| FUSION | QUALITY ★★★★★ | $9–$25 | SUITABLE FOR KIDS? Y |

This first-class, historical renovated lodge serves outstanding gourmet meals.

▶ **Kenny Lake Diner & Bakery**   Mile 7.2 Edgerton Hwy., toward McCarthy; 907-822-3355; **kennylake.com.**

| AMERICAN | QUALITY ★★ | $5–$7 | SUITABLE FOR KIDS? Y |

Home-style cooking with burgers, pies, breakfasts, soups, and sandwiches. Those staying in the nearby RV park or hotel get a 10% discount.

▶ **McCarthy Lodge**   In downtown McCarthy; 907-554-4402; **mccarthylodge.com**

AMERICAN | QUALITY ★★★ | $8–$25 | SUITABLE FOR KIDS? Y

Also called Ma Johnson's Hotel, this renovated lodge offers nice dining.

▲ On the Town:
What to Do after the Outdoor Adventure

ANCHORAGE HAS NO shortage of places to hang out in the evenings, as well as many daytime activities that will keep you busy. The pickings get a bit slim in outlying communities, though.

This section offers our suggestions for museums, nightclubs, and other points of interest in each region of Southcentral Inland Alaska.

ANCHORAGE

Attractions

▶ **Alaska Botanical Garden**   Tudor and Campbell Airstrip roads; 907-770-3692; **alaskabg.org.** Wander through 110 acres of immaculate grounds, featuring an herb garden, a wildflower trail, perennial gardens, and a rock garden dotted with dozens of fabulous plants. Admission is free, but donations are encouraged.

▶ **Alaska Heritage Library Museum**   301 W. Northern Lights Blvd., in the Wells Fargo bank building; 907-265-2834. This is an easily overlooked destination, but stop by the bank and take a look. There are native artifacts and baskets that date back hundreds of years, and artwork by such famous Alaska artists as Sydney Laurence and Fred Machetanz. Free admission.

▶ **Alaska Native Heritage Center**   8800 Heritage Center Dr.; 907-330-8000 or 800-315-6608; **alaskanative.net.** Learn about Alaska's indigenous peoples at this comprehensive living museum dedicated to preserving native history and culture. Admission is a little steep—$24.95 for adults—but it can be an all-day experience, and if there are dance performances scheduled, it's well worth it.

▶ **The Alaska Zoo**   4731 O'Malley Rd.; 907-346-2133; **alaskazoo.org.** For the size of Alaska, the zoo here is pretty impressive. It somehow manages to maintain a natural feel, with trails meandering through the woods and cages scattered throughout. Most of the residents are animals that are accustomed to cold climates such as Alaska's; many have also been rehabilitated after being brought in orphaned or injured. The grizzly bears, Jake and Oreo, and the polar bears, Ahpun and Louie, are the highlights, but we like the snow leopard the best. Admission is $12 for adults, $9 for seniors over 65, $6 for children ages 3–17, and free for children age 2 and under. The zoo is open daily except Christmas and Thanksgiving.

▶ **Anchorage Market and Festival**   Third Avenue and E Street; 907-272-5634; **anchoragemarkets.com.** Arts, crafts, fresh Valley produce, and an assortment of food and entertainment are available at this open-air market, held weekends during the summer. More than 300 vendors and a chance to meet talented local artists in person.

▶ **Anchorage Museum at Rasmuson Center**   121 W. 7th Ave.; 907-343-4326; **anchoragemuseum.org.** This is the state's largest museum, and a place you could spend an entire day browsing. We like the special native-dance performances that are scheduled during the summer, as well as the gallery featuring works by some of the state's most renowned artists. Admission is $10 for adults and $7 for ages 3–12. Planetarium admission is $5–$8 extra.

▶ **Title Wave Book Co.**   1360 W. Northern Lights Blvd.; 907-278-9283; and 415 W. 5th Ave.; 907-258-7323; **wavebooks.com.** Entering this bookstore is like getting a history lesson in Alaska. All things and subjects Alaskan can be found in this great downtown bookstore. Its other location, at 1360 W. Northern Lights Blvd., is even bigger and better, although not as convenient for downtown visitors.

Entertainment

▶ **Bear Tooth Theatrepub and Grill**   1230 W. 27th Ave.; 907-276-4200; **beartooth theatre.net.** This awesome movie-and-lunch/dinner house shows alternative, second-run, and independent films, and serves delicious Tex-Mex food and pizza from the locally famous Moose's Tooth Pub (page 318). They also serve a fine selection of microbrews that you can enjoy while watching the movie.

▶ **Cyrano's Off-Center Playhouse**   413 D St.; 907-274-2599; **cyranos.org.** Hours vary, but plays are 7 p.m. Thursday–Saturday and 3 p.m. Sundays. The theater-cafe-bookstore has goodies, and the monthly performances range from Alaska favorites to contemporary offbeat productions. Other attractions include a house jazz band, a comedy improv troupe, poetry readings, and special events. $15 for adults (not suitable for children most of the time).

▶ **The Great Alaskan Bush Co.** 631 E. International Airport Rd.; 907-561-2609; **akbushcompany.com.** Want to see Alaskan women without their clothes on? A perennial favorite among the guys (and gals) who like strip joints. No cover.

▶ **Summer in the City**   Peratrovich Park, Fourth Avenue and E Street, downtown; 907-279-5650; **ancdp.com** or **anchoragedowntown.org.** Concert and theatre programs spread through the summer include Music in the Park, Music for Little Ones, and Cultural Saturdays as well as special events such as Galway Days. Music in the Park is noon–1 p.m. Wednesdays, Thursdays, and Fridays. All events are free.

Bars

▶ **Bernie's Bungalow**   626 D St.; 907-276-8808. This house-in-the-city bar features primo martinis and outside patio partying for some of Anchorage's hippest. Definitely the happening spot of the past few years.

▶ **Chilkoot Charlie's**   2435 Spenard Rd.; 907-272-1010; **koots.com.** The rambling log-facade building, perennially voted a favorite by Anchorage folks, has three dance floors and 11 bars. Even national magazines have rated it a number-one bar. Live entertainment and plenty of hook-up opportunities.

▶ **Club Soraya**   333 W. 4th Ave.; 907-563-6940. A very popular place for Latin dance; watching the experts on the floor will blow you away. The Latin gentlemen aren't shy, either: they'll ask you to dance, so be prepared. If you don't know how, they *will* show you.

▶ **Darwin's Theory**   426 G St.; 907-277-5322; **alaska.net/~thndrths.** Very small and smoky—despite the citywide smoking ban—this bar is an Anchorage institution. It's the kind of place where everyone feels truly welcome, no matter their age, size, color, or sexual orientation.

▶ **F Street Station**   325 F St.; 907-272-5196. Well-loved by locals and visitors alike, including regular visitors such as traveling pilots and flight attendants. The "cheese wheel" story is so old that we refuse to tell it, but if you happen into the bar and see it sitting there, ask anyone and they'll be glad to regale you.

▶ **Humpy's Great Alaskan Alehouse**   610 6th Ave.; 907-276-2337. Live music is featured just about every night. Paired with the excellent bar food (probably the best bar food in Anchorage) and the great beer selection, Humpy's is a home run.

▶ **The Peanut Farm**   Old Seward Highway and International Airport Road; 907-563-3283; **wemustbenuts.com.** Favored by sports fanatics because of its multiple TV screens—even little ones at many of the tables, so you can watch what you want while you imbibe.

MATANUSKA-SUSITNA VALLEY

▶ **Alaska State Fair**   Palmer State Fairgrounds off the Glenn Highway; 907-745-4827; **alaskastatefair.org.** If you happen to be in Southcentral during the week before Labor Day, you should stop by this huge fair, which features everything from a rodeo to arts-and-crafts booths to monster trucks, monster vegetables, and the famed lumberjack show.

▶ **Iditarod Trail Headquarters**   Mile 2.2 Knik–Goose Bay Rd.; 907-376-5155. Learn more about the most famous dog-mushing race in history, as well as the story behind this great battle of canine athletes. For more musher and dog history, keep traveling to Mile 13.9 Knik–Goose Bay Rd. to the **Knik Museum and Mushers Hall of Fame** (907-376-7755).

▶ **Independence Mine State Historical Park Visitor Center**   907-745-2827; **dnr.alaska
.gov/parks/units/summit.htm.** This old abandoned gold mine is spectacular to
visit on a clear day. Recently refurbished, it tells the tale of Southcentral Alaska's
gold-rush past. Daily tours, temporarily (we hope) cut in 2010 for budgetary
reasons, take place during the summer. For more information, contact the Mat-
Su Area Park Office, Mile 0.7 Bogard Rd., Wasilla 99654; 907-745-3975.

▶ **Musk Ox Farm**   Mile 50.1 Glenn Hwy., past the Palmer–Wasilla Highway stoplight
on the left; 907-745-4151; **muskoxfarm.org.** See these ancient creatures up close
and learn about their excellent wool, called *quviut,* used in hats and mittens.

▶ **Reindeer Farm**   Off Bodenburg Loop Road in Butte; 907-745-4000; **reindeer
farm.com.** Take tours of this reindeer farm and learn about the differences
between the domesticated version of caribou and Rudolph.

TALKEETNA

▶ **Fairview Inn**   On Main Street; 907-733-2423; **denali-fairview.com.** Features
music sometimes, alcohol all the time. Or wander in and out while exploring
the historical buildings along Main Street. Walking the street takes all of
5 minutes, even if your faculties aren't at their sharpest.

▶ **Latitude 62**   Just before the downtown area; 907-733-2262. The lodge offers a
wide range of food and cocktails, and is a favorite for socializing and listening
to music.

▶ **Museum of Northern Adventure**   Downtown; 907-733-3999. This gift shop–
museum highlights Alaska's history in 24 dioramas, including homesteading,
prospecting, wildlife, mushing, Bush pilots, and more.

▶ **Talkeetna Historical Society Museum**   On the village airstrip, just before
the heart of town; 907-733-2487. Contains displays and information from its
gold-mining past as well as items commemorating the life of Bush pilot
Don Sheldon, a longtime Talkeetnan who died in 1975. Admission is $3.

PART THIRTEEN

SOUTHCENTRAL COASTAL ALASKA
Where Mountains and Sea Meet

▲ An Overview of the State's Playground

EVERY SUMMER, TRAFFIC on the Seward Highway heading south to the Kenai Peninsula gets unbelievably busy. On the weekends, it is not uncommon to slow down to 50 miles per hour on a highway that's easily traveled at faster speeds under normal conditions.

That's because the secret is out: Southcentral Coastal Alaska is the place to be. Folks from Southcentral Inland communities such as Anchorage and the Matanuska-Susitna Valley head south almost every weekend to have fun and unwind. With the region's fish-rich rivers and bays, protected paddling locations, and world-class hiking trails, it's no wonder. It is a given that this region in Alaska is beautiful—to be honest, that adjective can be applied to most of the state. The advantage of the Southcentral Coastal region, however, is that it is easily accessible. While reaching paradise in the Bush may require two, three, or sometimes even four airplane flights, getting to most of Southcentral Coastal Alaska requires only a few hours in a car.

This section of the state is part of what most Alaskans collectively call Southcentral—with the exception of **Kodiak Island,** which is part of Southwest Alaska in many guidebooks. But we at *Alaska Adventure Guide* are thinking as an outdoors person would. Many of the same outdoor activities popular in Southcentral communities on the **Kenai Peninsula** and **Prince William Sound** are also popular on Kodiak Island. Kodiak Island has much more in common with these places than some of the farther-flung communities of the Bush. Like the Bush, though, it is remote, accessible only by plane or ferry. Still, flights leaving for Kodiak are easily arranged, and most take off from Anchorage. Those taking the **Alaska Marine Highway ferry** system to Kodiak must first drive clear through the Kenai Peninsula to board at the ferry dock in Homer, thus getting a tour of this region anyway.

True to its name, Southcentral Coastal Alaska is made up of the southernmost lands in the central part of Alaska that are bordered by or close to, coastal waters (see Part One, page 7, for a map of the region). For our purposes, that area begins at **Turnagain Arm,** just south of Girdwood, and continues along the Seward Highway through the small community of **Moose Pass** and then into the coastal fishing town of **Seward.** It also extends from the Seward Highway–Sterling Highway cutoff as it heads west through **Cooper Landing** and **Sterling** and then reaches **Soldotna.** Keep going south on the Sterling Highway, through the communities of **Kasilof, Clam Gulch, Ninilchik,** and **Anchor Point,** and the road eventually will end at a tiny spit of land in the picturesque town of **Homer.** Other communities that can be reached by turning left here or right there (it's amazing how easy it is to

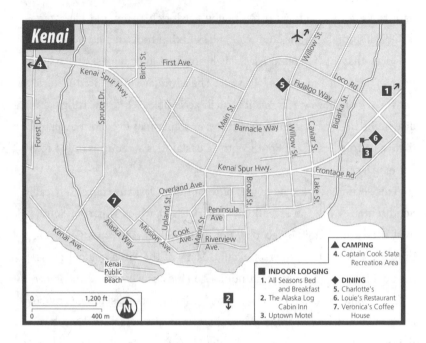

Kenai

First Ave.
Kenai Spur Hwy.
Birch St.
Spruce Dr.
Forest Dr.
Willow St.
Loco Rd.
Fidalgo Way
5
Bidarka St.
1
Main St.
Barnacle Way
Willow St.
Caviar St.
6
3
Kenai Spur Hwy.
Frontage Rd.
Overland Ave.
Broad St.
Lake St.
7
Peninsula Ave.
Upland St.
Alaska Way
Mission Ave.
Cook Ave.
Mann St.
Riverview Ave.
Kenai Ave.
Kenai Public Beach

| ▲ CAMPING |
| 4. Captain Cook State Recreation Area |

■ INDOOR LODGING	◆ DINING
1. All Seasons Bed and Breakfast	5. Charlotte's
2. The Alaska Log Cabin Inn	6. Louie's Restaurant
3. Uptown Motel	7. Veronica's Coffee House

0   1,200 ft
0   400 m

get around in such a vast land!) include **Hope,** off the Seward Highway on the Hope Highway, and **Kenai** and **Nikiski,** accessed at the Y in Soldotna, where the Kenai Spur Highway heads northwest, then north.

Southcentral Coastal Alaska also includes Prince William Sound, which can be reached by road by turning onto the Portage Glacier Road, which leads to **Whittier,** on the west side of the sound. A fun drive through the longest tunnel in North America will get you to Whittier, where you can then embark on a ferry or boat trip across the entire Prince William Sound to reach **Valdez** or **Cordova.** Both communities are beautiful waterfront fishing villages that offer endless outdoor-recreation opportunities. Cordova is one of the best birding spots in the state. Valdez is where you want to go for sea kayaking. Both areas offer excellent fishing, especially from the deck of a charter boat, while jigging for giant halibut deep in the ocean.

Prince William Sound is a spectacular maritime habitat and one of the highlights of any Alaska vacation. It also is the site of one of the nation's most devastating oil spills in history, which occurred in 1989 when the *Exxon*

INDOOR LODGING
1. Aspen Hotel Soldotna
2. Jana House Hostel
3. Kenai River Lodge
4. Longmere Lake Lodge
   Bed and Breakfast
5. Soldotna Bed and
   Breakfast Lodge

CAMPING
6. Centennial Campground
7. Kenai National Wildlife
   Refuge
8. Swiftwater Park

DINING
9. Jersey Subs
10. Kaladi Brothers
    Coffee Co.
11. The Moose Is Loose
12. Mykel's Restaurant
13. River City Books
14. Sal's Klondike Diner
15. St. Elias Brewing Co.

Soldotna

Valdez oil tanker ran aground on Bligh Reef and dumped 11.3 million gallons of North Slope crude oil into the sound. More than 1,500 miles of coastline were affected, killing plants by the millions and birds and sea mammals by the thousands. Fisheries were devastated. Fishermen went broke. Today, after more than 15 years of rehabilitation, the recovery process is basically over, but the effects of the spill remain in untold ways.

Prince William Sound is the ideal recreation destination, although it can be rainier than other areas of the region. It offers fishing, kayaking, hiking, backpacking, ice climbing, and mountain biking. There are cabins tucked in the woods for camping, or you can choose an open beach and pitch a tent. The people in the communities are friendly and will help you plan the perfect trip to suit your needs—in fact, that's an advantage of working with the smaller, family-owned businesses: they tend to cater each trip to the clients they are serving.

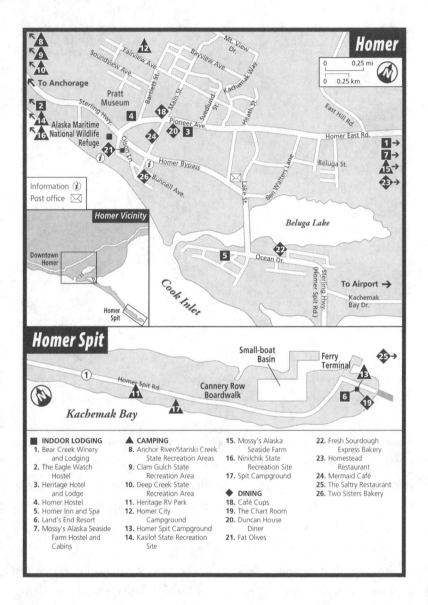

Homer

To Anchorage

Pratt Museum

Alaska Maritime National Wildlife Refuge

Information ⓘ
Post office ✉

Homer Vicinity

Downtown Homer

Homer Spit

Cook Inlet

Beluga Lake

To Airport →
Kachemak Bay Dr.

Homer Spit

Small-boat Basin

Ferry Terminal

Homer Spit Rd.

Cannery Row Boardwalk

Kachemak Bay

■ INDOOR LODGING	▲ CAMPING	15. Mossy's Alaska	22. Fresh Sourdough
1. Bear Creek Winery and Lodging	8. Anchor River/Stariski Creek State Recreation Areas	Seaside Farm	Express Bakery
		16. Ninilchik State	23. Homestead
2. The Eagle Watch Hostel	9. Clam Gulch State Recreation Area	Recreation Site	Restaurant
		17. Spit Campground	24. Mermaid Café
3. Heritage Hotel and Lodge	10. Deep Creek State Recreation Area		25. The Saltry Restaurant
4. Homer Hostel	11. Heritage RV Park	◆ DINING	26. Two Sisters Bakery
5. Homer Inn and Spa	12. Homer City Campground	18. Café Cups	
6. Land's End Resort	13. Homer Spit Campground	19. The Chart Room	
7. Mossy's Alaska Seaside Farm Hostel and Cabins	14. Kasilof State Recreation Site	20. Duncan House Diner	
		21. Fat Olives	

Lastly, there is Kodiak Island, one of our favorite destinations. Dubbed the Emerald Isle (though we beg to differ; Kodiak is beautiful, but the term "Emerald Isle" rightly belongs to Ireland), Kodiak Island is home to more than 13,000 people, stretching from **Akhiok** to the south to **Ouzinkie** to the north. It is popular among fishermen, birders, and wildlife watchers.

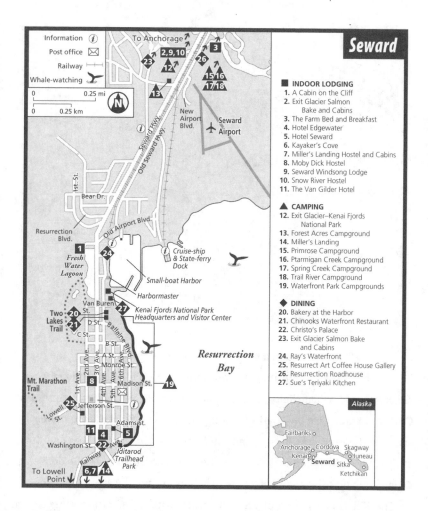

Seward

Information ⓘ
Post office ✉
Railway ┝━┥
Whale-watching

0   0.25 mi
0   0.25 km

To Anchorage

New Airport Blvd.
Seward Airport

Seward Hwy
Old Seward Hwy

1st St.
Bear Dr.
Resurrection Blvd.
Old Airport Blvd.
Fresh Water Lagoon
Cruise-ship & State-ferry Dock
Small-boat Harbor
Harbormaster
Kenai Fjords National Park Headquarters and Visitor Center

Two Lakes Trail
Van Buren St.
D St.
C St.
B St.
A St.
Ballaine Blvd.
1st Ave.
2nd Ave.
3rd Ave.
4th Ave.
5th Ave.
6th Ave.
Monroe St.
Madison St.
Jefferson St.
Adams St.
Washington St.
Railway Ave.

Mt. Marathon Trail
Lowell St.

Iditarod Trailhead Park

To Lowell Point

Resurrection Bay

■ INDOOR LODGING
1. A Cabin on the Cliff
2. Exit Glacier Salmon Bake and Cabins
3. The Farm Bed and Breakfast
4. Hotel Edgewater
5. Hotel Seward
6. Kayaker's Cove
7. Miller's Landing Hostel and Cabins
8. Moby Dick Hostel
9. Seward Windsong Lodge
10. Snow River Hostel
11. The Van Gilder Hotel

▲ CAMPING
12. Exit Glacier–Kenai Fjords National Park
13. Forest Acres Campground
14. Miller's Landing
15. Primrose Campground
16. Ptarmigan Creek Campground
17. Spring Creek Campground
18. Trail River Campground
19. Waterfront Park Campgrounds

◆ DINING
20. Bakery at the Harbor
21. Chinooks Waterfront Restaurant
22. Christo's Palace
23. Exit Glacier Salmon Bake and Cabins
24. Ray's Waterfront
25. Resurrect Art Coffee House Gallery
26. Resurrection Roadhouse
27. Sue's Teriyaki Kitchen

Alaska
Fairbanks
Anchorage Cordova Skagway
Kenai Juneau
Seward Sitka
Ketchikan

▲ Kenai Peninsula

LOOK AT THE word *Kenai* and you might be tempted to pronounce it "Keh-NIGH." Don't feel bad: a lot of people do it. In fact, it is "KEY-nigh," a peninsula that offers open valleys, high mountain passes, glaciers, oceans, and even a little bit of sophistication amid all that wilderness. It truly is one of the most diverse areas of the state.

About 53,400 people live in the Kenai Peninsula Borough, and the area continues to grow. The Kenai Peninsula Borough is composed of the Kenai

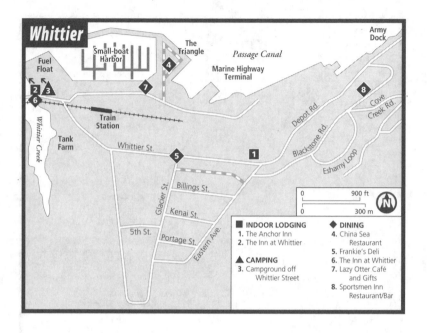

Peninsula, Cook Inlet, and a large, unpopulated area northeast of the Alaska Peninsula. The borough includes portions of the **Chugach National Forest, Kenai National Wildlife Refuge, Kenai Fjords National Park,** and portions of **Lake Clark** and **Katmai national parks** (although those last two parks are more associated with Southwest Alaska, and thus discussed in the Bush chapter [page 471]). The most populated areas of the Kenai Peninsula are **Soldotna** and **Kenai,** known as the Twin Cities because they are side-by-side.

The Kenai is a region of varied weather, with temperature ranges from 4°F in January to as warm as 65°F in July. Often it will get much colder or warmer, depending on the weather patterns, so it's not uncommon to get winter lows of –20°F and summer highs in the 70s. It is dominated by the Kenai Mountains, Harding Ice Field, four active volcanoes, and the protected lands of Kachemak Bay State Park, Kenai Fjords National Park, and the Kenai National Wildlife Refuge.

The larger communities that make up the Kenai Peninsula include Seward, Homer, Soldotna, and Kenai. We discuss each community in depth on the following pages. Several outlying communities include **Hope, Moose**

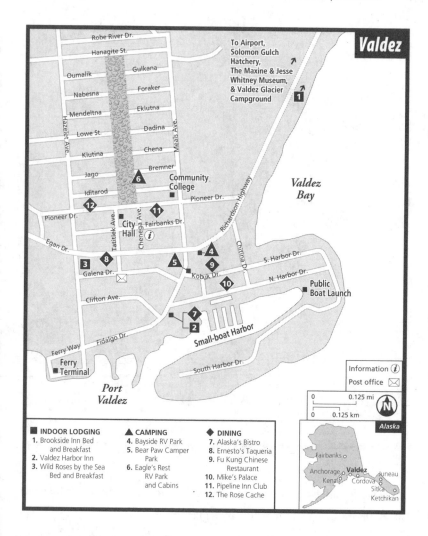

Pass, Cooper Landing, Sterling, Ninilchik, and Anchor Point. We provide limited information on these towns under "Surrounding Areas" (page 341).

While most people think of the North Slope when they think of Alaska's oil reserves, it actually was on the Kenai Peninsula that the first oil was discovered, in 1957. It has been a center for exploration and production ever since.

One of the Kenai Peninsula's most famed attributes is the **Kenai River,** a major sportfishing location for Anchorage residents and tourists alike. The

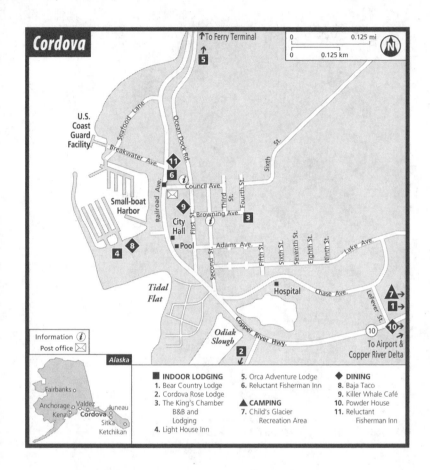

Cordova

To Ferry Terminal

0 — 0.125 mi
0 — 0.125 km

U.S. Coast Guard Facility

Seafood Lane
Breakwater Ave.
Ocean Dock Rd.
Sixth St.

Small-boat Harbor

Railroad Ave.
Council Ave.
Third St.
Fourth St.

City Hall
Browning Ave.
First St.

Pool
Adams Ave.
Second St.
Fifth St.
Sixth St.
Seventh St.
Eighth St.
Ninth St.
Lake Ave.

Tidal Flat

Hospital
Chase Ave.
Lefever St.

Odiak Slough
Copper River Hwy.

To Airport & Copper River Delta

Information (i)
Post office ✉

Alaska

Fairbanks
Anchorage   Valdez   Juneau
Kenai   Cordova
Sitka
Ketchikan

■ INDOOR LODGING
1. Bear Country Lodge
2. Cordova Rose Lodge
3. The King's Chamber B&B and Lodging
4. Light House Inn

5. Orca Adventure Lodge
6. Reluctant Fisherman Inn

▲ CAMPING
7. Child's Glacier Recreation Area

◆ DINING
8. Baja Taco
9. Killer Whale Café
10. Powder House
11. Reluctant Fisherman Inn

river is world-renowned for trophy king, silver, and red salmon, so it attracts visitors whose sole purpose is to land a giant fish.

The community has grown to accommodate these visitors, and there is a small (albeit busy) airport, along with roads, plenty of guides, and tackle shops to outfit even the newest of anglers. Still, the economy of the borough consists of industries such as commercial fishing, mining, and timber, as well as petroleum-industry activities. While the natural beauty and recreational activities have led to a growing tourism industry, the area maintains a certain remoteness that still allows the visitor to feel like he or she is getting away from it all.

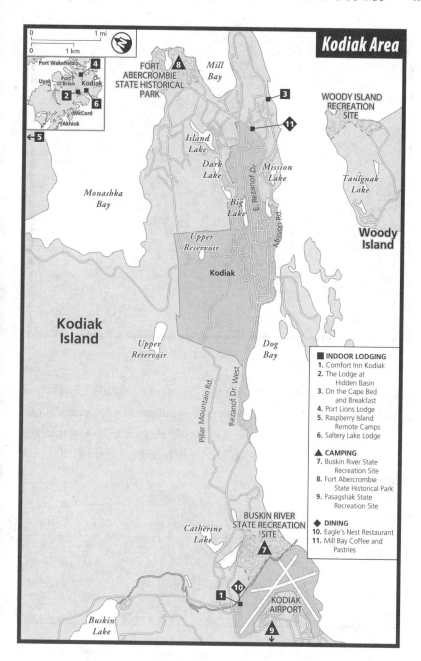

Kodiak Area

0 — 1 mi
0 — 1 km

Port Wakefield
Uyak
Port O'Brien
Kodiak
McCord
Akhiok

4
2
6
5

FORT ABERCROMBIE STATE HISTORICAL PARK

8

Mill Bay

3

WOODY ISLAND RECREATION SITE

Island Lake

11

Dark Lake

Mission Lake

Tanignak Lake

Monashka Bay

Big Lake

E. Rezanof Dr.

Mission Rd.

Woody Island

Upper Reservoir

Kodiak

Kodiak Island

Upper Reservoir

Dog Bay

Pillar Mountain Rd.

Rezanof Dr. West

Catherine Lake

BUSKIN RIVER STATE RECREATION SITE

7

1

10

KODIAK AIRPORT

9

Buskin Lake

■ INDOOR LODGING
1. Comfort Inn Kodiak
2. The Lodge at Hidden Basin
3. On the Cape Bed and Breakfast
4. Port Lions Lodge
5. Raspberry Island Remote Camps
6. Saltery Lake Lodge

▲ CAMPING
7. Buskin River State Recreation Site
8. Fort Abercrombie State Historical Park
9. Pasagshak State Recreation Site

◆ DINING
10. Eagle's Nest Restaurant
11. Mill Bay Coffee and Pastries

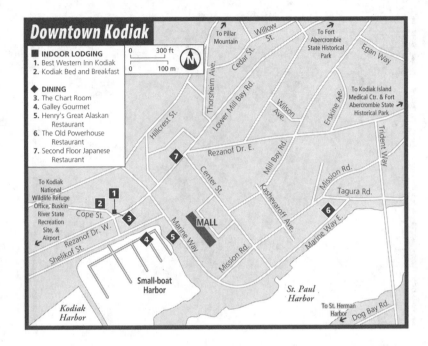

Access to the Kenai Peninsula is by the Sterling and Seward highways from the north, the Alaska Marine ferry from the south, and by scheduled flights from varying directions, mostly Anchorage. When driving from Anchorage, allow at least 3 hours to reach Soldotna, more if you want to stop often and take photos. The drive is stunning.

KENAI

KENAI VISITORS AND CULTURAL CENTER
11471 Kenai Spur Hwy.
Kenai 99611
907-283-1991; **visitkenai.com**

The city of Kenai was founded in 1791 as a Russian fur-trading post, and in the early 1900s cannery operations started to crop up, providing jobs and allowing the community to grow. Today, nearly 6,800 people live in the area for which the peninsula was named, specifically on the western coast of the Kenai Peninsula, fronting **Cook Inlet.** Kenai is approximately 65 air miles and 158 highway miles southwest of Anchorage via the Sterling Highway. The central airport for the peninsula is located in Kenai, and this is where many an adventure begins.

As you walk through the original Kenai town site, it is easy to imagine its historical past. The log buildings tell of a simpler time, and the onion-domed church is evidence of the Russian Orthodox influence, which remains in many Kenai Peninsula communities today. When Russians settled the area in 1791, they first named it Fort St. Nicholas. It was the second permanent Russian settlement in Alaska (the first was in Kodiak). In 1849, the Holy Assumption Russian Orthodox Church was established, and in 1869 the U.S. military established a post for the Dena'ina Indians in the area, called Fort Kenay. The area was abandoned in 1870 after the United States purchased Alaska. Still, residents continued to live there, developing commercial fishing and settling the wild lands first by clearing the spruce trees away and planting crops and farms. The first dirt road from Anchorage was constructed in 1951, and the discovery of oil in 1957 along the Swanson River, 20 miles northeast of Kenai, prompted a flurry of activity and rapid development. Kenai has been a growing center for oil exploration, production, and services ever since.

The Kenaitze (Tanaina Athabascans) are the primary indigenous population in the area, although the city is predominantly nonnative.

SOLDOTNA

GREATER SOLDOTNA CHAMBER OF COMMERCE
44790 Sterling Hwy.
Soldotna 99669
907-262-9814; **soldotnachamber.com**

Kenai's sister city is Soldotna, population about 4,000—although locals seem to have an unspoken rivalry more than a sisterhood. The famed **Kenai River** flows through Soldotna, which is on the main road system as you drive south. Kenai, the town for which the peninsula got its name, however, is off on a spur road, offering governmental and air support for travelers who fly in and immediately head for Soldotna.

Soldotna is 147 miles south of Anchorage, at the junction of the Sterling and Kenai Spur highways. It has a similar climate and temperature range to Kenai's and was historically home to the Kenaitze Indians, then developed by nonnatives for such resources as fish, timber, and oil.

The city got its name for a nearby stream, which in Russian means "soldier"—at least that's what some locals proclaim. Like Kenai, the area grew quickly with the discovery of oil in the Swanson River in 1957. By 1960, the area was named a city.

The Kenai River is Soldotna's greatest asset, and it offers trophy king-salmon fishing during June and July. In 1985, a local fisherman hoisted a 97-pound, 4-ounce world-record king salmon from the river. Catching a king that tops the scales at 65 pounds is not unusual.

Access to Soldotna is mostly via the Sterling Highway from the north, although there is a municipal airport for charter service. Regularly scheduled flights to the peninsula land at the larger **Kenai Municipal Airport,** 10 miles away.

HOMER

HOMER CHAMBER OF COMMERCE
201 Sterling Hwy.
Homer 99603
907-235-7740; **homeralaska.org**

This community of 5,400 friendly, sometimes funky, and always interesting people is our favorite location in Alaska. Unfortunately, it has grown tremendously in the past decade, and we hope that it will not lose its small-town charm over the next 10 years. Still, it is a beautiful place, located on the north shore of **Kachemak Bay** on the southwestern edge of the Kenai Peninsula, where the mountains meet the ocean in stark and beautiful contrast. **Homer**

Spit, a 4.5-mile-long bar of gravel, extends out from the Homer shoreline.

Homer is 227 road miles south of Anchorage, at the southernmost point of the Sterling Highway, so it's more than a day trip for travelers based in the big city. And it should be. There is so much to do in Homer, from kayaking to fishing to hiking, that it's hard to limit your stay to just a day.

The community is in a maritime climate zone, which means that winter temperatures are slightly higher (14°F–27°F is the average range) and summer temperatures tend to be cooler than inland towns (45°F–65°F in the summer).

The name came from Homer Pennock, a gold-mining-company promoter, who arrived in 1896 and built living quarters for his crew of 50 on the spit. But today, the name most associated with Homer is Jewel, the pop-singer-turned-poet who grew up there, riding horses on the Kilcher family homestead.

While commercial and sportfishing are the center of the economic activity, Homer has a large community of artists. The **Homer Jackpot Halibut Derby** runs from May 1 through Labor Day each year, bringing in halibut anglers from all over the country. The visitor industry also is growing as people discover Homer's beauty. About 10 cruise ships dock each summer, and during the summer, the population swells with students and others seeking cannery or fishery employment.

Homer is accessible by the Sterling Highway, which links to Anchorage and the rest of the Lower 48 states. It is often referred to as the end of the road because it lies at the terminus of the Sterling Highway. The **Homer Airport** also provides daily air service to Anchorage and connecting communities. The **Alaska Marine Highway** and local ferry services provide water transportation.

SEWARD

SEWARD CHAMBER OF COMMERCE
907-224-8051; seward.com

On the eastern tip of the Kenai Peninsula is another water-meets-mountains community called Seward, population 3,000. This small city is only a 2½-hour drive from Anchorage and makes a pleasant day trip, although it, too, is worth exploring more in-depth.

Looming over the city is **Mount Marathon,** a peak that attracts mountain runners worldwide every July 4 for the annual Mount Marathon race. Spreading out on the other end of town are **Kenai Fjords National Park** and **Resurrection Bay,** an oceanfront playground that affords wonderful sea kayaking, fishing, and exploring. **Bear Creek** and **Lowell Point** are adjacent to Seward and offer wilderness access as well.

Like Homer, Seward has a maritime climate that brings lots of rain and temperatures that are a bit milder in the winter. It does, however, tend to get more snow than Homer, about 80 inches per year versus 50 in Homer.

The name Seward is heard often in Alaska. From 1861 to 1869, the then–U.S. Secretary of State William Seward was responsible for the U.S. purchase of Alaska from the Russians during the Lincoln administration. Naysayers thought it was a huge mistake to buy a frozen wasteland, and they called the deal Seward's Folly or Seward's Icebox.

It turns out that Seward was a very wise man because Alaska's natural resources have brought trillions of dollars to the United States. The last Monday in March, Alaskans celebrate Seward's Day to honor the man's accomplishment. The town of Seward is especially proud of the name for that reason.

As the southern terminus for the **Alaska Railroad** and a road link to Anchorage and the Interior, Seward has long been a transportation center. The economy has diversified with tourism, commercial fishing and processing, ship services, and other natural resource endeavors. As an ice-free harbor, Seward has become an important supply center for Interior Alaska.

Cruise ships flock to Seward in the summer, justifying such state-of-the-art visitor attractions as the **Alaska SeaLife Center,** a marine-animal research and education facility. More than 320,000 cruise-ship passengers visit Seward annually, spending hundreds of thousands of dollars as they come.

Access to the area includes driving your own vehicle, as well as bus service to and from Anchorage daily and the railroad. Air service and charters are available at the state-owned airport. The **Alaska Marine Highway ferry** also brings passengers from the Lower 48 and other Alaska communities.

SURROUNDING AREAS

There are many, many small communities along the roads and even off the road system that compose the whole of the Kenai Peninsula. There are so many, in fact, that each one, with its own unique characteristics, could be a visitor destination.

In this section, we share just a few of the larger ones. If you have time, stop by these tiny villages. They could be the most interesting part of your visit. Check out the gift shop in Ninilchik. Eat lunch at the local diner in Hope. Take a hike in Cooper Landing. Sometimes, it is the small things you do in an epic adventure-based vacation that have the most impact. These communities can provide such moments.

HOPE (*population 140*) lies on the northern end of Kenai Peninsula, on the south shore of the Turnagain Arm of Cook Inlet. Access it by driving south on the Seward Highway and turning right on 17-mile-long Hope Highway, near the mouth of Resurrection Creek. Hope City was a mining camp for Resurrection Creek, established in 1896. Portions of the town were destroyed in the 1964 earthquake, but several old and historical buildings remain. Hiking, backpacking, mountain biking, and rafting are popular sports here.

MOOSE PASS (*population 220*) is 26 miles north of Seward on the Kenai Peninsula. It is on the southwest shore of Upper Trail Lake, off the Seward Highway. The community was first named in 1912 as a station on the Alaska Railroad. The name is reportedly derived from a mail carrier's team of dogs that in 1903 had a moose–dog misunderstanding: the moose would not move out of the way, and the dogs would not take no for an answer. Kayaking, fishing, and canoeing are popular sports here.

COOPER LANDING (*population 370*) is at the west end of Kenai Lake on a stretch of the Sterling Highway, 30 miles northwest of Seward in the

Chugach Mountains. Cooper Landing was named for Joseph Cooper, a miner who discovered gold here in 1884. In 1948 a road to Kenai provided vehicle access to Cooper Landing. By 1951 a road to Anchorage completed the link. The population of the area nearly doubles each summer to support tourism businesses and activities. Fishing, backpacking, canoeing, kayaking, skiing, hiking, rafting, and mountain biking are popular sports here.

STERLING (*population 5,000*) is located on the Sterling Highway at the junction of the Moose and Kenai rivers, just north of Soldotna. Sterling became the name of this collection of homes when in 1954, the first post office was established. The community caters to the sportfishing industry and summer influx of recreation enthusiasts. Fishing, canoeing, skiing, kayaking, and rafting are popular sports here.

KASILOF (*population 780*) is on the east shore of Cook Inlet on the Kenai Peninsula. It is accessed via the Sterling Highway, just south of Soldotna. Unlike many fishing-based communities, Kasilof was an agricultural settlement of Kenaitze Indians. Today, however, fishing is an integral part of the community. More than 155 Kasilof residents hold commercial-fishing permits, and sportfishing is also very popular in the Kasilof River. Fishing, canoeing, skiing, hiking, and dog mushing are popular sports here.

NINILCHIK CHAMBER OF COMMERCE
907-567-3571; ninilchikchamber.com

NINILCHIK (*population 780*) lies on the western coast of the Kenai Peninsula along the Sterling Highway, 188 road miles from Anchorage. The **Ninilchik River, Deep Creek,** and **Cook Inlet** are the reasons the community exists, and sportfishing is one of the most popular summertime endeavors pursued here today. The community's history is steeped in Dena'ina Indian tradition. The Dena'ina word *niqnilchint* means "lodge by the river," which is how the name *Ninilchik* came to be. The Russian influence also is found here, and the Russian Orthodox Church, constructed in 1901, is still a stunning sight to see when you drive into town. Fishing, retail businesses, tourism, and logging make up the majority of private-sector activities in Ninilchik. Fishing, hiking, camping, and dog mushing are popular sports here.

> **ANCHOR POINT CHAMBER OF COMMERCE**
> 907-235-2600; **anchorpointchamber.org**

ANCHOR POINT (*population 1,845*) is on the Kenai Peninsula at the junction of the Anchor River and its north fork, 14 miles northwest of Homer. It lies at Mile 156 of the Sterling Highway. The community got its name when, in the summer of 1778, Captain James Cook and his crews sailed into the inlet looking for a northwest passage and lost an anchor to the strong tides there. Many residents work in nearby Homer or in town catering to the sportfishing industry. Fishing is the primary pastime here.

> **SELDOVIA CHAMBER OF COMMERCE**
> 907-234-7612; **xyz.net/~seldovia**

SELDOVIA (*population 280*) is on the Kenai Peninsula across from Homer, on the south shore of Kachemak Bay. It is a 15-minute flight from Homer, or 45 minutes from Anchorage. Many people take a water taxi to get there, and the **Alaska Marine Highway ferry** also stops there. The name Seldovia comes from *seldevoy,* a Russian word meaning "herring bay." In the mid- to late 1800s, a trading post was established, and commercial fishing and fish processing were the major industries. Today, Seldovia remains a commercial-fishing center. It's also a fun place to be for its annual Fourth of July parade.

▲ Prince William Sound

THE 70-MILE-WIDE Prince William Sound is a kayaker's dream, and as you ply the waters of this protected coastal region in Southcentral Alaska, you'll notice the small boats everywhere, usually close to shoreline exploring the nooks and crannies that make this area so interesting.

The sound is at the northern end of the Gulf of Alaska and is dominated by high cliffs, protected inlets, and many glaciers and mountains to be enjoyed at a distance or up close. Dall sheep, mountain goats, sea lions, seals, and otters, as well as thousands of shorebird and seabird species and plenty of salmon and halibut, can be found in this area.

Among the large sightseeing destinations in Prince William Sound is **Columbia Glacier,** one of the largest tidewater glaciers on the Alaska coast. It got its name in 1899, during the Harriman expedition to Alaska, and is named for the university of the same name in New York City.

The sound has 3,000 miles of shoreline and is surrounded by the **Chugach Mountains** to the east, west, and north. Fifty-mile-long **Montague Island** and several smaller islands form natural breakwaters between the sound and the Gulf of Alaska, calming the swells and providing protected boating.

Fewer than 10,000 people live in all of Prince William Sound's three main and several outlying communities. In fact, more visitors come to the area each year than there are year-round residents.

This section tells you a little more about the three largest communities— **Valdez, Cordova,** and **Whittier.** Even though the best of Prince William Sound is out in the wild, you'll likely embark on your trip from one of these towns.

WHITTIER

GREATER WHITTIER CHAMBER OF COMMERCE
whittieralaskachamber.org

Of the three main communities in Prince William Sound, Whittier has the fewest people—only about 180 live here year-round—but it is in a geographically significant location. Accessible by road from Anchorage, the community is a launching point for many an outdoor adventure. Located on the northeast shore of the Kenai Peninsula, at the head of Passage Canal, it is also on the west side of Prince William Sound, 75 miles southeast of Anchorage.

Whittier is, to say the least, a funky community, featured once in *Outside* magazine as the ugliest town on the planet. Of course, that isn't true:

the natural beauty surrounding Whittier is astounding, and it literally takes 5 minutes to reach it.

But the town itself? There's not much to be said for the collection of boxy, run-down-looking high-rises that scar the landscape. But there is a reason. Let us explain.

The town started as an entrance point for U.S. troops during World War II, and the buildings were constructed as purely functional living quarters for troops. The 14-story **Hodge Building** (now called **Begich Towers**) had 198 apartments and housed families and bachelors. The nearby **Buckner Building,** completed in 1953, had 1,000 apartments and was once the largest building in Alaska. It was called the "city under one roof," and boasted a bowling alley, theater, swimming pool, and shops for Army personnel. The hospital also was housed there. **Whittier Manor** was built in the early 1950s as rental units for civilians. During this time, more than 1,000 people were living there, while the facility remained active. But once the Army closed the port in 1960, the population quickly dived, leaving the behemoth buildings behind. Whittier Manor was converted to condominiums in 1964, and Begich Towers now is home to the majority of the residents. The Buckner building is no longer occupied, although there has been talk of refurbishing it.

The weather in Whittier is blustery and often wet. Winter temperatures range 17°F–28°F; summer temperatures average 49°F–63°F. Average annual precipitation includes 66 inches of rain and 80 inches of snow. Summer tourism is the primary economic driver in Whittier, and the summer stays busy with boaters and fishermen loading up and heading out to the sound. Charter tours, glacier sightseeing tours, and other activities are available in the area.

Whittier has become even more attractive to travelers now that it is more easily accessible. A $70 million road connection was completed in the summer of 2000, creating the **Anton Anderson Memorial Tunnel.** The tunnel allows access to Whittier via Anchorage, and can accommodate vehicles and trains. The railway carries passengers, vehicles, and cargo 12 miles from the Portage Station, east of Girdwood.

VALDEZ

VALDEZ CONVENTION AND VISITORS BUREAU
200 Chenega St.
Valdez 99686
907-835-INFO; **valdezalaska.org**

Here is a community that can be downright intimidating when the weather socks in and the rain goes on for days. But come the first sunshiny day, the views open up and the mountains surrounding this seaside community make one understand what is so great about Valdez: it's gorgeous.

About 4,000 people live in Valdez (pronounced Val-**DEEZ,** even though it is a Spanish word that is supposed to be pronounced Val-**DEHZ**), promoting their area through tourism, fishing, or oil development. Valdez is the southern terminus to the **Trans-Alaska Pipeline System,** which feeds crude oil from the North Slope clear to the port for passage south.

Port Valdez is a deep-water fjord located 305 miles east of Anchorage and 364 miles south of Fairbanks. Even though it is right on the water and many coastal communities do not get much snow, Valdez is different. January temperatures range 21°F–30°F, and July temperatures are in the 46°F–61°F range. Annual precipitation is 62 inches, but average snowfall—and this is not a typo—is 325 inches, or 27 feet!

Naturally, snow sports are popular here. Valdez is the heli-skiing capital of the state, and any skiing extremist will be floored by the skiing and snowboarding possibilities. Valdez is where those insane scenes from extreme-ski movies are often shot: skiers flipping upside down and landing backward, skiing down sheer cliffs—that sort of thing.

Ice climbers and mountaineers are drawn by the great ice and numerous glaciers. On the Richardson Highway, one scenic spot along the road is a rushing waterfall during the summer: **Bridal Veil Falls.** But come winter, you'll see hardy ice climbers making their way up the steep pitch of ice.

Farther north is Valdez's famed **Thompson Pass,** almost 2,800 feet above sea level and owning the coveted superlative of being the location in Alaska that gets more snow than anywhere else in the state. The record 24-hour snowfall there is 5 feet.

Valdez began as yet another point of entry for gold seekers in 1898 (although it had been discovered and named by Spanish explorers back in 1790). It became incorporated as a city in 1901, and in the 1920s the Alaska Road Commission further developed a road for travel to Fairbanks. The original waterfront community was destroyed by the 1964 Good Friday earthquake, which also killed several residents. Today, the community is rebuilt on a more stable bedrock foundation 4 miles to the west.

In March 1989, Valdez was the center for the massive oil-spill cleanup after the *Exxon Valdez* catastrophe. In a few short days following the spill, the population of the town tripled. Today, the town is recovering, but effects of the spill are long-lasting, and watchdog groups constantly monitor the safety of fuel transportation in the area.

For those looking for summer activities in Valdez, there are also some great hiking trails (see our Day Hiking chapter, page 167, for details), excellent road and mountain biking, fishing, kayaking, rafting, and birding.

CORDOVA

> **CORDOVA CHAMBER OF COMMERCE AND VISITORS CENTER**
> 907-424-7260; **cordovachamber.com**

Cordova is located at the southeastern end of Prince William Sound in the Gulf of Alaska and is home to about 2,400 Alaskans. The community was built on **Orca Inlet,** at the base of **Eyak Mountain,** 52 air miles southeast of Valdez and 150 miles southeast of Anchorage.

Cordova has many beautiful aspects, but one of its biggest outdoor draws is the excellent birding. The area is home to one of the largest shorebird migrations in the world, and each spring, bird enthusiasts congregate to watch.

The area has average winters, with temperatures in the 17°F–28°F range. Summer temperatures average 49°F–63°F. Annual precipitation is 167 inches, and average snowfall is 80 inches.

Cordova originally was named Puerto Cordova, by the same Spanish explorers who named Valdez, but the *Puerto* was dropped (no one really knows when) and the city was formed in 1909. Cordova became the railroad terminus and ocean-shipping port for copper ore from the Kennicott Mine up the Copper River.

Today, Cordova supports a large fishing fleet for Prince William Sound and several fish-processing plants. Copper River red salmon, pink salmon, herring, halibut, bottom fish, and other fish are harvested and sent to fancy restaurants in the Lower 48 to be consumed within 48 hours. Copper River reds have gained a reputation worldwide, and their journey to outside markets often begins in Cordova.

Other outdoor activities popular in Cordova include mountain biking, hiking, fishing, and rafting.

▲ Kodiak Island

KODIAK ISLAND CONVENTION AND VISITORS BUREAU
100 Marine Way, Suite 200
Kodiak 99615
800-789-4782 or 907-486-4782; **kodiak.org**

At 3,588 square miles, Kodiak Island is the second-largest island in the United States, following the Big Island of Hawaii (the archipelago—all the islands that make up the entire Kodiak Island Borough—is 6,559 square miles). It is located on the eastern side of the Gulf of Alaska, 252 air miles south of Anchorage, which is about a 50-minute flight, and 3 hours from Seattle. It takes 9½ hours to travel to Kodiak from Homer via the **Alaska Marine Highway ferry** system. About 13,000 people populate the island, about 6,300 of them living in the small city of Kodiak.

Kodiak's climate is dominated by a strong marine influence, which means that it rains or is foggy much of the time. But the temperature rarely dips below freezing, even in the winter, and summer days, when they are sunny, can be glorious. Annual precipitation is 60 inches on the windward side of the island and 40 inches on the leeward side.

Kodiak has maintained its workingman feel while still offering plenty of amenities to the visitor. It's not uncommon to see commercial fishermen swabbing the decks of their fishing vessels or repairing their nets, but it's also not difficult to find a hotel or bed-and-breakfast that can meet your every need. Hardware stores are next to gift shops, and the visitor center can accommodate cannery workers or cruise-ship passengers. It's a place without pretensions, comfortable the moment you step off the plane or boat.

The halibut and silver-salmon fishing here are spectacular, and that's what most people come for. There is no shortage of charter-boat operators, remote lodge owners, and air taxis eager to take you to uncharted territory not only to catch a big fish but also to catch it in a gorgeous setting.

But it's not all about fishing. The wildlife is worth seeing too. The island is home to the largest of the three brown-bear subspecies, *Ursus arctos middendorffi*, also known as the Kodiak brown bear. In general, Alaska brown bears live along the coast, grizzlies live in the Interior, and Kodiaks live only on the island for which they are named.

Other recreation opportunities include kayaking (**Shuyak Island State Park** is a particular favorite place to do it), mountain biking, hiking, and birding.

The area has a rich history, too, having been inhabited since 8,000 BC, according to archeological evidence. Russian fur trappers settled in the area in 1792, and Kodiak was actually the capital of Russian Alaska before it was moved to Sitka in 1867. Several branches of the military have maintained a presence in Kodiak since World War II, and today the Coast Guard has the largest facility in the world based there. "Coasties," as they are called, add great cultural diversity to Kodiak, coming from all over the country and sharing their experiences.

Commercial and subsistence fishing still prevail in Kodiak, as close to 20% of its residents are Alaska native or part-native. Their culture is still strong in the community and is celebrated through several museums and presentations offered to the public on a regular basis. (See the Kodiak section of "On the Town," page 401, for more.)

▲ Wild Lands

CHUGACH NATIONAL FOREST

CHUGACH NATIONAL FOREST
3301 C St., Suite 300
Anchorage 99503
907-743-9500; **fs.fed.us/r10/chugach**

Primary activities: *fishing, hiking, backpacking, mountaineering, mountain biking, kayaking, rafting*

Chugach National Forest surrounds Southcentral Coastal, beckoning outdoor travelers with all of its recreation opportunities. The forest consists of three ranger districts—**Glacier, Cordova,** and **Seward**—and 5 million acres of federal land. That's about the size of Maryland.

More than 40 public-use cabins are available for rent, ranging $25–$45 per night, depending on the location. Public campgrounds are also available, with reasonable $14-per-night camping fees.

For Southcentral Coastal residents, the Chugach is the place to play. It's where most of the maintained trails can be found, and it has easy road access from just about anywhere along the Seward and Sterling highways and all along Prince William Sound.

The best place for information on the Chugach National Forest is at the informative **Begich, Boggs Visitor Center,** at the end of Portage Valley Road, about 50 miles south of Anchorage on the Seward Highway. The center is located at what used to be the face of **Portage Glacier.** Today, that glacier has retreated, and an iceberg-studded lake greets visitors. Several interpretive programs showcase the special qualities of the Chugach. Call 907-783-3242 or 907-783-2326 for hours of operation.

KENAI NATIONAL WILDLIFE REFUGE

KENAI NATIONAL WILDLIFE REFUGE
Ski Hill Road
907-262-7021; **kenai.fws.gov**

Primary activities: *backpacking, hiking, skiing, dog mushing, canoeing, fishing*

The Kenai National Wildlife Refuge is Alaska's most-visited refuge, partly because it is 1 of 2 Alaska refuges (out of 16) that are accessible by road. But this place is also special, and outdoors travelers can easily recognize the appeal in its numerous possibilities. Canoe the Mini–Boundary Waters system on the **Kenai Canoe Trails.** Run a dog team across frozen **Tustumena Lake.** Hike into the backcountry and set up a remote camp from which to explore. The possibilities are endless.

Today, the Kenai National Wildlife Refuge is a good sampling of all of Alaska's habitats and often is referred to as a mini-Alaska. You can see glaciers, valleys, mountains, and everything in between.

Sportfishing is the top activity in the refuge, and hundreds of thousands of visitors come here each year, searching for king, red, and silver salmon as well as Dolly Varden, rainbow trout, and arctic grayling.

The refuge was established in 1941 to protect the many moose you'll see there today. The lanky ungulates share the refuge with brown and black bears, caribou, Dall sheep, mountain goats, wolves, wolverines, and countless bird species.

Accessing the refuge is easy. From Anchorage, take the Seward Highway south to the Sterling Highway. The eastern refuge boundary is at Mile 55 of the

Sterling Highway. The west entrance to the Skilak Wildlife Recreation Area is 5 miles farther down the road. The refuge visitor center is based in Soldotna.

KENAI FJORDS NATIONAL PARK

SEWARD INFORMATION CENTER
1212 4th Ave.
Seward 99664
907-224-2132 or 907-224-7500; **nps.gov/kefj**

Primary activities:
hiking, kayaking, birding, mountaineering

By Alaska standards, Kenai Fjords National Park is not all that big—607,805 acres. That's a laughable thought, actually, because it's a huge span of land. The vastness of the area strikes you as soon as you take a gander at a calving glacier or snow-covered mountain.

The park is located on the southeast coast of Alaska's Kenai Peninsula, capped by the **Harding Ice Field,** the largest ice field within U.S. borders. Otters, puffins, bears, moose, and mountain goats are just a few of the creatures that can be spotted here. Glaciers are everywhere, and whales breach often.

Access to this park is relatively easy compared with other national parks in Alaska. Take the Seward Highway south to its terminus in Seward (or the train or bus). Board a day cruise for as little as $59, and watch for whales and other wildlife for an entire afternoon. Or go with a guide. Commercial outfitters provide camping, fishing, and kayaking services. Air charters fly over the coast for access to the fjords.

The climate of the park is maritime, meaning that it rains often and is windy most of the time. Dress in layers in gear that can get ultra-wet without getting

TRAVELER'S TIP

▶ Kenai Fjords National Park is one of the best places to spot the gray whale on its annual migration from Baja California.

you wet. Camping is allowed in most areas of the park, and four public-use cabins are available on a reservation basis. They are at **Aialik, Holgate,** and **Northarm,** along the Kenai Fjords coast, and are accessible by boat or float-plane. For reservations, contact the **Alaska Public Lands Information Center** in Anchorage at 907-644-3661. **Willow Cabin** at Exit Glacier is available for winter use from mid- to late fall through early April. Contact the park at 907-422-0500 for reservations.

ALASKA MARITIME NATIONAL WILDLIFE REFUGE

ALASKA MARITIME NATIONAL WILDLIFE REFUGE
95 Sterling Hwy., Suite 1
Homer 99603
907-235-6546; alaskamaritime.fws.gov

Primary activities: *birding, kayaking, fishing*

The Alaska Maritime National Wildlife Refuge encompasses a tremendous 4.9 million acres and stretches along Alaska's coast from the Southeast panhandle west to the tip of the **Aleutian Chain,** and then heads north all the way to the Bering Sea and above the Arctic Circle. It is the most extensive public land in all of the National Wildlife Refuge System and exists to protect marine mammals and birds throughout Alaska.

More than 2,500 islands, spires, rocks, and coastal headlands provide a habitat for the 40 million marine birds and mammals that live in the refuge. Seabirds, sea lions, fur seals, and whales are just part of the overall diversity found here. In fact, new species of marine life are yet to be discovered in the area, researchers speculate.

Getting to the refuge can be expensive, as so much of it is so remote. Even though we have listed the refuge in this chapter, its territory extends into the Bush and Southeast as well, and it is not accessible by road. You'll need a boat to get to most areas, a plane to get to others.

There are no campgrounds, although camping is allowed on most of the refuge. Recreation facilities on the refuge are limited to a few first-come, first-served public-use cabins on Adak.

KACHEMAK BAY STATE PARK AND STATE WILDERNESS PARK

KACHEMAK BAY STATE PARK AND STATE WILDERNESS PARK
Kenai Area Office
907-262-5581; **dnr.alaska.gov/parks/units/kbay/kbay.htm**

Primary activities: *hiking, birding, mountaineering, skiing, kayaking, fishing*

Nine Alaska state parks, each of which offers great outdoor opportunities, are on the Kenai Peninsula. But our favorite is Kachemak Bay State Park (and Wilderness Park, which technically makes the total number of parks 10).

Kachemak Bay is Alaska's first state park and its only wilderness park, composed of roughly 400,000 acres of mountains, glaciers, forests, and ocean. There are roughly 80 miles of developed trails and unlimited kayaking opportunities in the park. The wildlife in the park is both fun and fascinating to watch. Sea otters bob on the water, seals haul out on the beaches, and porpoises and whales surface occasionally, as if to say hello. Even the less-noticeable marine life is noticeable: the tidepools are home to an amazing array of sea stars, anemones, and other intertidal species. Land mammals include moose, black bears, mountain goats, coyotes, and wolves, although even the moose seem to avoid humans.

Hiking and camping along the shoreline and in the surrounding forests and mountains is excellent. Above tree line, skiers and hikers will find glaciers and snowfields stretching for miles. Access to the park is by boat or airplane only—no roads lead to this special place. There are several camping areas that have been developed that may include fireplaces, picnic tables, tent platforms, outhouses, or food caches. Five public-use cabins are available at

Halibut Cove Lagoon, Leisure Lake, Moose Valley, and **Tutka Bay.** The $65-per-night getaways can be reserved up to six months in advance (seven months for Alaskans), and should be. They fill up fast, so start planning early.

The **Halibut Cove Ranger Station** (907-235-6999) can answer questions in the summer.

SHUYAK ISLAND STATE PARK

ALASKA STATE PARKS
Kodiak District Office
1400 Abercrombie Dr.
Kodiak 99615
907-486-6339; dnr.alaska.gov/parks/units/kodiak/shuyak.htm

Primary activities:
kayaking, birding, hiking, fishing

Shuyak Island State Park is one of six state parks managed by the Kodiak area and, in our opinion, is the most beautiful and diverse for outdoor recreation. Shuyak Island is the northernmost of the islands that make up the Kodiak Archipelago, and the state park makes up most of the island's 47,000 acres. The park encompasses part of a coastal forest system unique to the archipelago: it has only one tree species, the Sitka spruce. Shuyak Island provides access to an intricate maze of sheltered bays, channels, and inlets, making it a paddler's paradise.

The park is 54 air miles north of Kodiak and accessible by boat or plane. It is a relatively small place, only 12 miles long and 11 miles wide, but it contains miles of coastal waterway for kayaking, a limited but impressive trail system for hiking, and fishing opportunities in just about every lake, stream, or saltwater location (especially in August and September when the silver salmon are spawning). There is an infinite variety of seabirds, otters, whales, harbor seals, sea lions, and Dall porpoises. Even some of Kodiak's famed brown bears wander the island.

Visitors to Shuyak can choose from tent camping just about anywhere on the island, or renting one of four $65-per-night public-use cabins, which are wonderful retreats when it is raining—and it rains often. A ranger station is at one end of the park, but other than that there are no facilities, and groceries and other supplies must be purchased in Kodiak (or Homer, as some people fly in from that direction).

KODIAK NATIONAL WILDLIFE REFUGE

KODIAK NATIONAL WILDLIFE REFUGE
1390 Buskin River Rd.
Kodiak 99615
888-408-3514 or 907-487-2600; **kodiak.fws.gov**

Primary activities:
fishing, kayaking, birding, hiking, camping

Famous for its Kodiak brown bears, the Kodiak National Wildlife Refuge is also home to a diverse ecosystem of other plants, animals, and fish that make it a wonderful outdoor destination. Bears, bald eagles, salmon, and a host of other wildlife are numerous on the 1.9 million acres of upland and waters. The terrain is not easily traveled, is dotted with fjords, and is soggy in many places. It is the perfect habitat for the Kodiak brownies—about 2,300 of them live on the refuge and can be found wandering the land or feeding on fish in the rivers and streams.

The refuge boundary is about 20 miles from the city of Kodiak and can be accessed only by floatplane or boat. Kodiak National Wildlife Refuge offers seven public-use cabins—rarities in the refuge system—to make camping in the more remote areas more enjoyable.

The plentiful salmon streams on the refuge—117 of them, to be exact—

offer food for other species besides just the brown bear. Bald eagles thrive on the refuge thanks to all the fish, and 600 breeding pairs of eagles live there.

Despite its rugged beauty and recreation opportunities, the Kodiak refuge does not get too many visitors, only 8,000–10,000 a year. This is good for the ecosystem, and good for travelers who want the place to themselves. Reserving the public-use cabins is generally not difficult and can be done in advance. Be prepared for a maritime climate, with wet conditions and lots of fog. Generally, the west side of the refuge receives less rain due to weather patterns.

▲ Getting around Southcentral Coastal Alaska

KENAI PENINSULA

From Anchorage

Access to Anchorage, in Southcentral Inland Alaska, by air is through **Alaska Airlines** (800-252-7522; **alaskaair.com**). We suggest that anyone arriving in Anchorage but headed to the Kenai Peninsula rent transportation in the city. The rates are lower, the limits fewer, and the selection larger. Plus, the drive to the Kenai Peninsula is worth doing on your own. Most of our rental suggestions originate in Anchorage, but we've listed a few options at the end that are available on the Kenai.

More than a dozen rental options are available in the Anchorage area, but we've found **Budget** (800-527-0700; **budgetrentacar.com**), **Enterprise** (800-261-7331; **enterprise.com**), **Hertz** (800-654-3131; **hertz.com**), and **Denali Car Rental** (907-276-1230) to be the best.

▶ **ABC Motorhome and Car Rentals**   800-421-7456; **abcmotorhome.com.** This company has a range of RVs, as well as a luxury van for large groups and camper rentals for smaller parties. No-smoking vehicles. No pets allowed.

▶ **Alaska Affordable Motor Home Rental**   907-349-4878 or 907-227-6463; **alaska-rv-rental.com.** Much less expensive than its competitors, with rates at $175 per day with free, unlimited miles in Alaska. Vehicles are not as fancy but are quite functional. No smoking or pets allowed.

▶ **Alaska Best RV Rentals** 866-544-4981 or 907-344-4981; **alaskabestrvrentals .com.** With rates lower than the large-company averages—$160–$175. No smoking or pets allowed.

▶ **Alaska Railroad** 327 W. Ship Creek Ave.; 800-544-0552 or 907-265-2494; **alaskarailroad.com.** The railroad has daily routes serving Anchorage to Seward. The round-trip fare is $119 for adults.

▶ **Magic Bus** 907-268-5311; **themagicbus.com.** If you have a group and want to travel anywhere within Southcentral Coastal Alaska to the southern edge of the Interior and all points in between, you can rent these private motor coaches and vans, complete with a driver.

Options on the Kenai

The **Alaska Marine Highway** ferry system serves Homer and Seward on the Kenai Peninsula, with service from southern and southwestern ports. The ferry, the **M/V Tustumena,** has a regular schedule, and reservations can be made online (800-526-6731 or 800-642-0066; **ferryalaska.com**).

Era Aviation (800-866-8394; **flyera.com**) and **Alaska Airlines** (800-252-7522; **alaskaair.com**) travel to the Kenai Peninsula on regularly scheduled flights.

Car rentals are available at **Hertz** in Kenai (352 Airport Way; 907-283-8080; **hertz.com**) and **Best Wheels 4 Rent 4 Less** in Soldotna (224 Kenai Ave.; 907-262-6102); rates begin at about $65 per day.

The **Hertz** in Homer, located at the Homer Airport (907-235-0734), rents vehicles starting at $83 per day. Other Homer rental-car companies include **Adventure Alaska Car Rentals** (1368 Ocean Dr.; 800-882-2808 or 907-235-4022) and **Polar Car Rental** (800-876-6417 or 907-235-5998, at the airport).

Seward car rentals also are available through **Hertz.** Rates begin at $83 (600 Port Ave.; 800-654-3131 or 907-224-4378).

Taxis in Homer include **Chux Cab** (907-235-2489), **Kachecab** (907-235-1950), and **Kostas Taxi Service** (907-399-8008 or 907-399-8115).

Taxi service is available in Kenai-Soldotna through **Alaska Cab** (in Soldotna; 907-262-5050 or 907-262-1555; and in Kenai; 907-283-6000) and **Yellow Cab of the Kenai** (in Soldotna; 907-260-1900; or 907-283-1900 in Kenai).

Seward taxis include **PJ's Taxi** (907-224-5555) and **Seward Independent Cab Co.** (907-224-8463).

The Stage Line provides motor coach connection between Homer and Seward or Homer and Anchorage (907-235-2252; **thestageline.net**).

Recreational vehicles are available through **Kenai Riverfront RV Rentals** in Soldotna (907-262-1717; **kenairiverfront.com**) or **Wilson's RV Rentals,** near the Kenai Airport (907-283-4370; **wilsonsrvrentals.com**). **Best Wheels 4 Rent 4 Less** in Soldotna (224 Kenai Ave.; 907-262-6102) also rents RVs.

Seward bus-and-trolley service allows you to get around town on a day pass. Contact **Seward Trolley Company** (907-224-4378; **sewardtrolley.com**).

PRINCE WILLIAM SOUND

The **Alaska Marine Highway ferry** system serves all the communities of Prince William Sound. The ferry **M/V** *Kennicott* has a regular schedule, and reservations can be made online. The newer fast ferry, the **M/V** *Chenega,* also serves the sound. The one-way adult fare is $89 for passage from Whittier to Valdez (800-526-6731 or 800-642-0066; **ferryalaska.com**).

Whittier

For road access to Whittier, use the **Anton Anderson Memorial Tunnel (tunnel .alaska.gov**). The price is $12 for a round-trip.

Avis Alaska (4900 Aircraft Dr., Anchorage; 907-243-4300 or 907-472-2277; **avisalaska.com**) rents cars in Anchorage and now in Whittier. This is a good option if you're on a cruise ship and want to explore inland for the day.

The **Magic Bus** is a better deal if you can get a seat. The rate is $54 for adults, one-way (907-268-6311; **themagicbus.com**). If you're coming from Seward, **Two Dogs Truckin' and Transportation** can get you to Whittier for $225 with a four-person minimum, which includes the $12 tunnel fare (907-224-2746 or 907-362-2209; **home.gci.net/~twodogs**).

Cordova

Access to Cordova by air is available from **Alaska Airlines** (800-252-7522; **alaska air.com**) via Seattle and Anchorage, and **Era Aviation** (800-866-8394; **flyera .com**) via Anchorage.

The **Cordova Shuttle Van** meets most flights and runs into town for $12 (907-424-3272).

Auto rentals are available at **Cordova Auto Rentals** (907-424-5982) and **Wild Hare Taxi Service** (907-424-3939). Prices start at $70 per day.

Valdez

Rental cars are available at **Valdez U-Drive,** at the Valdez airport (800-478-4402 or 907-835-4402; **valdezudrive.com**).

You can fly into Valdez on **Era Aviation** (6160 Carl Brady Dr.; 800-478-1947 or 907-248-4422; **flyera.com**); or **Alaska Airlines** (800-252-7522; **alaskaair .com**) via Seattle and Anchorage.

Valdez Yellow Cab (907-835-2500) is 4 miles east of Valdez. A one-way fare to town from the airport is approximately $10.

KODIAK ISLAND

Car rentals are available at **Avis Rent a Car** (800-331-1212 or 907-487-2264; **avis.com**), **Budget Rent A Car** (907-487-2220), and **Rent-a-Heap** (907-487-4001).

Taxi service is available through **Bay Shuttle** (907-486-2345), **Garrett's Taxi Service** (907-654-3535), **Alaska Cab Co.** (907-481-3400), and **A and B Taxicab** (907-486-4343).

The **Alaska Marine Highway** offers ferry passage to Kodiak. The one-way adult fare is $72 (100 Marine Way; 800-526-6731 or 907-486-3800; **ferry alaska.com**).

Alaska Airlines provides daily jet service to Kodiak (1200 Airport Way; 800-252-7522 or 907-487-4000; **alaskaair.com**).

Era Aviation also provides service from Anchorage and other locations (800-866-8394 or 907-487-4000; **flyera.com**).

▲ Gearing Up

SOUTHCENTRAL COASTAL ALASKA has some surprisingly well-stocked sporting-goods and camping-supply stores, even in some of the smaller communities. You may pay higher prices than in Southcentral Inland. (A bonus to buying in Anchorage is that there is no sales tax. In most of Alaska's smaller communities, there is a sales tax.)

As with any travel in the state, check with the air carriers on which you will be traveling for regulations on carrying items such as knives, guns, campstoves, and camp fuel. Some items, such as fuel, you may need to purchase at your final destination and leave behind when flying home.

This section of the book is broken down by the main communities in Southcentral Coastal Alaska with shops that will help you find what you are looking for. We generally list sporting goods/camping supplies and groceries separately, but many stores in smaller communities such as Whittier and Cordova are one-stop-shopping destinations.

SPORTING GOODS AND CAMPING SUPPLIES

Kenai Peninsula

▶ **Alaska Canoe and Campground**   35292 Sterling Hwy., Soldotna; 907-262-2331; **alaskacanoetrips.com.** Canoes start at $27.50 for a half day; sea kayaks start at $42.50 per day. Unique to this company is its gear rental—everything from hip waders to tents and fishing poles.

▶ **Sweeney's Clothing**   35081 Kenai Spur Hwy., Soldotna; 907-262-5916. This longtime outfitter (look for the green shamrock sign) carries Alaska Wear, a favorite local alternative to Carhartt, as well as Grundens rainwear and other must-have gear.

▶ **Weigner's Backcountry Guiding**   Sterling; 907-262-7840; **alaskanet/~weigner.** Canoe rentals and shuttle services are available through this outfit.

▶ **Wilderness Way**   44370 Sterling Hwy., Soldotna; 907-262-3880; **wildernessway .com.** A great place to find quality outdoor gear, skis, kayaks, and camping equipment.

Homer

▶ **Eagle Enterprises**   1067 Ocean Dr., Homer; 907-235-7907. Mostly a marine-safety shop, but it also sells clothing and outdoor wear.

▶ **Kachemak Gear Shed**   3625 East End Rd., Homer; 800-478-8612 or 907-235-8612. Our favorite outdoor shop on the peninsula, with functional gear for fishing and outdoor treks, as well as clothing and gift items.

▶ **Main Street Mercantile**   104 E. Pioneer Ave., Homer; 907-235-9102. Offering basic sporting-goods supplies and fishing licenses.

▶ **NOMAR**   104 E. Pioneer Ave., Homer; 907-235-8363. The fleece clothing and travel bags are Alaska-made and developed from fishing-industry technology.

Seward

▶ **Bay Traders True Value**   1301 4th Ave.; 800-257-7760 or 907-224-3674. This hardware store is where the locals get their waders and duct tape.

▶ **Helly Hansen**   1304 4th Ave., at the small-boat harbor; 888-414-3559 or 907-224-3041; **hellyalaska.com.** Offering the best in wet-weather gear in a town where you'll need it often.

▶ **Miller's Landing**   At Lowell Point, 3.5 miles south of Seward; 866-541-5739 or 907-224-5739; **millerslandingak.com.** Boat and motor rentals are available for $100 for 4 hours. Rod and reel rentals are $15 for a half day, $25 for 8–16 hours. Kayak rentals are $40 for singles, $50 for doubles, per day.

▶ **Seward Bike Shop**   411 Port Ave.; 907-224-2448. Offering bike rentals starting at $13. This is also the place to visit if you want updated information on mountain-bike-trail conditions.

Whittier

▶ **The Anchor Inn**   Off the waterfront, near the residential area; 907-472-2354 or 877-870-8787; **anchorinnwhittier.com.** It has an attached store with everything from clothing to camping gear to groceries. It's a limited supply, but it could be a lifesaver if you left the big city without some important item.

▶ **The Outpost/RC's Dock & Harbor Store**   in Whittier; 907-529-5635. They sell everything from liquor to hardware to dock services and some groceries; mostly fishing tackle and bait.

Valdez

▶ **Acres Kwik Trip**   At Richardson Highway and Airport Way; 907-835-3278. A good place to get a fishing license and a few supplies fast. No lines.

▶ **Anadyr Adventures**   225 N. Harbor Dr.; 800-865-2925 or 907-835-2814; **anadyradventures.com.** Offering kayak rentals to experienced kayakers only.

They can provide water taxis to more-remote destinations too. Rentals are $45 per day for singles, $65 for doubles, with discounts for multiple days.

▶ **Fish Central**   888-835-5002 or 907-835-5090; **fishcentral.net.** For bait-and-tackle supplies, fish licenses, and kayak and boat rentals starting at $250 per day for an 18-foot skiff.

▶ **Hook, Line and Sinker**   200 Chitina St.; 907-835-4410. Sells fishing tackle, licenses, and other accessories, as well as sporting goods.

▶ **The Prospector**   141 Galena St.; 907-835-3858. Sporting goods, camping gear, and a wide selection of outdoor clothing.

Cordova

▶ **Cordova Coastal Outfitters**   At the harbor in the brightly colored boathouse; 907-424-7424; **cdvcoastal.com.** The company rents kayaks, canoes, small boats with outboards, bikes, and fishing and camping gear. They also offer guided boat and bike tours. Kayaks are $35 per day for singles, $50 for doubles. Canoes are $30 per day. Bikes are $18 a day. Camping gear ranges $5–$15 per day for everything you can think of.

▶ **Whiskey Ridge Trading Co.**   201 Whiskey Ridge Rd.; 907-424-3354. Sporting-goods supplier of high-quality outdoors gear.

Kodiak Island

▶ **Cy's Sporting Goods**   117 Lower Mill Bay Rd.; 907-486-3900; **kodiak-outfitters .com.** Fishing licenses available here. Locals go here often, as it's not as tourist-oriented.

▶ **58 Degrees North**   1231 Mill Bay Rd.; 907-486-6249. They can rent bikes by the hour, day, or week, and repair your bike if you end up crashing; $25 per day.

▶ **Mack's Sport Shop & Alaskan Gifts**   212 Lower Mill Bay Rd.; 907-486-4276; **mackssportshop.com.** Everyone who works here, down to the teenager with the nose piercing, knows their stuff and can suggest just the right lure for the fish you're trying to catch or just the right jacket for the conditions you'll be in. Our favorite sporting-goods shop in Kodiak. Plus, the local T-shirts are cool. Fishing licenses are available.

▶ **Mythos Expeditions**   907-486-5536; **thewildcoast.com.** This outfitter is the only company with a permit to lease kayaks out of Shuyak Island State Park. If you don't have your own kayak or don't want to pay to have it shipped to Shuyak, this is the only other option. The rate is $175 for three days, which is the minimum, for a double; $141 for singles.

▶ **Orion's Sports**   1247 Mill Bay Rd.; 907-486-8380. Carrying kayaking and climbing/backing supplies; the best in outdoor gear.

▶ **Sutliff's Hardware**   210 Shelikof Ave.; 888-848-5579 or 907-486-5797. This hardware store carries outdoor gear for any situation, including U.S. Geological Survey maps, which are essential for any travel in Kodiak. The employees are really friendly too.

GROCERIES

Kenai Peninsula

▶ **Carrs**   10480 Kenai Spur Hwy., Kenai; 907-283-6300.

▶ **Central Kenai Peninsula Farmers' Market**   At the intersection of East Corral Avenue and the Kenai Spur Highway, Soldotna; 907-262-5463 or 907-262-7502. Held 10 a.m.–2 p.m. Saturdays in summer. Features locally grown produce, herbs, flowers, and plants.

Country Foods IGA   140 S. Willow St., Kenai; 907-283-4834.

▶ **Fred Meyer**   43843 Sterling Hwy., Soldotna; 907-260-2200. Also sells sporting goods and camping equipment. But be warned: it's frustratingly busy here in the summer.

▶ **Safeway**   44428 Sterling Hwy., Soldotna; 907-714-5400.

▶ **Three Bears**   10575 Kenai Spur Hwy., Kenai; 907-283-6577; **threebearsalaska .com.** Buy in bulk and save a bundle here; the sporting goods section also is extensive for the hunting and fishing crowd.

Homer

▶ **The Grog Shop**   369 E. Pioneer Ave., Homer; 907-235-5601. We just love the name. The shop stays busy and has a great selection of spirits.

▶ **Safeway**   90 Sterling Hwy., Homer; 907-235-2408. The largest selection of foods; limited outdoor and sporting-goods items.

▶ **Save-U-More**   3611 Greatland St., Homer; 907-235-8661. If you're on a budget, this is the place to pinch pennies.

▶ **Smoky Bay Natural Foods**   248 W. Pioneer Ave., Homer; 907-235-7252. This is a natural-food lover's paradise, with more products and gourmet food items than you can find in some big-city stores. Bulk foods are available, as well as fresh veggies and household items—all good for you and all nice to the environment.

Seward

▶ **Safeway**   Mile 1.5 Seward Hwy.; 907-224-3698. Full-service grocery store, with espresso stand, outdoor/sporting-goods section, and of course, lots of groceries.

▶ **Three Bears**   1711 Seward Hwy.; 907-224-2081; **threebearsalaska.com.** Larger than a convenience store but smaller than a full-service store. Usually it's not as crowded as Safeway.

Valdez

▶ **Carrs/Eagle**   185 Meals Ave.; 907-835-2100. This is a full-service grocery store with some sporting goods, mostly fishing tackle. The salad bar is cheap and fresh.

▶ **Three Bears**   103 Egan St.; 907-835-5480; **threebearsalaska.com.**

Cordova

▶ **Alaska Commercial Co.**   106 Nicholoff Way; 907-424-7141. Close to the small-boat harbor. Featuring groceries, spirits, fishing licenses, and some camping and sporting-goods supplies.

▶ **Laura's Liquor Shoppe**   Downtown; 907-424-3144. The shop sells delicious espresso from Kaladi Brothers (an Alaskan-grown company that is well loved statewide), as well as liquor, limited groceries, and other goodies.

▶ **Serendipi Tea**   412 1st St.; 907-424-8327 or 907-424-8328. This is an offbeat option featuring organic vegetables, meat, and other foods. The tea selection is wonderful.

Kodiak Island

▶ **Alaska Commercial Co.**   In downtown Kodiak at 111 W. Rezanof Dr., but don't pay attention to the address because it gets confusing at the intersection; 907-486-5761. Full-service grocery store, with a clothing, household, and sporting-goods section in the back. You can get just about anything there, although you're still better off going to the sporting-goods store for specific gear.

▶ **Safeway**   2685 Mill Bay Rd.; 907-486-6811. Full-service grocery store with the best prices and produce. Not within walking distance of town, though.

▲ Where to Stay

BECAUSE THIS IS such a popular place to play, Southcentral Coastal Alaska's residents and business owners have learned that there's rarely a shortage of customers. On the weekends especially, people unwind, pull out their fishing poles, and enjoy the beauty of the area. There is a multitude of bed-and-breakfasts, small motels and inns, and even a few large, fancy hotels. Camping options are abundant too. Most federal and state land agencies have at least one campground in every town—some of them have several places at which to pitch a tent.

In this section, we offer you our favorite choices, places that we've tried ourselves and found to be memorable.

KENAI

Indoor Lodging

▶ **All Seasons Bed and Breakfast**   907-283-7050; **allseasonsbnb.com**

QUALITY ★★★★ | VALUE ★★★★ | $105

From the outside, this place doesn't have the charm you might expect in a bed-and-breakfast, but the inside is meticulously clean and spacious (2,000 square feet), and the price is absolutely right. You get two bedrooms, a fully equipped kitchen, and all the other amenities you need. Plus, it's on a quiet street, away from tourists.

▶ **The Alaska Log Cabin Inn**   49860 Eider Dr., Kenai; 907-283-3653 or 877-834-2912; **alaskalogcabininn.com.**

QUALITY ★★★★ | VALUE ★★★ | $130–$160

This expansive lodge includes cabins or rooms and a spacious area for relaxation, near the mouth of the Kenai River.

▶ **Uptown Motel**   47 Spur View Dr.; 800-777-3650 or 907-283-3660; **uptownmotel.com.**

QUALITY ★★★ | VALUE ★★★ | $135–$185

It's not much to look at from the outside, but the rooms are actually quite clean and comfortable, and the downstairs restaurant and bar give a good sampling of what life is like for Kenai locals. Nonsmoking rooms available.

Camping

▶ **Captain Cook State Recreation Area**   End of North Road, Nikiski; 907-262-5581; **dnr.alaska.gov/parks/units/captcook.htm.**

QUALITY ★★★★ | VALUE ★★★★ | $10

This beautiful campground is out of the way but quite worth the 25-minute drive into north Kenai. Named after the British explorer Captain James Cook, who discovered the inlet in 1778, this area offers great fishing, canoeing, and skiing in the winter, and it has excellent water views. Two campgrounds are within the area—Bishop Creek and Discovery.

SOLDOTNA

Indoor Lodging

▶ **Aspen Hotel Soldotna**   326 Binkley Cir.; 866-483-7848; **aspenhotelsak.com.**

QUALITY ★★★★ | VALUE ★★★★ | $130–$170

This is where you stay if you like creature comforts such as a pool, in-room hair dryers, and such. It's fairly new, and the rooms are very nice, although not very "Alaska" at all.

▶ **Jana House Hostel**   38670 Swanson River Rd., Sterling, off Mile 83.6 Sterling Hwy.; 907-260-4151.

QUALITY ★★★ | VALUE ★★★★ | $30–$50

This hostel just north of Sterling offers dorm-style bunks, tent and RV camping, and private rooms on 19 acres. The 8,900-square-foot building looks more like a hotel than a hostel, but the rates are right.

▶ **Kenai River Lodge**   800-977-4292 or 907-262-4292; **kenairiverlodge.com.**

QUALITY ★★★★ | VALUE ★★★ | $150–$190

On the banks of the Kenai River in Soldotna, the lodge has river-view rooms and barbecuing right on-site, so you can cook what you catch. Rates include breakfast in the summer.

▶ **Longmere Lake Lodge Bed and Breakfast**   35955 Ryan Lane; 907-262-9799; **longmerelakelodge.com.**

QUALITY ★★★★ | VALUE ★★★ | $250–$300

It's about 6 miles out of Soldotna but worth the drive for the peace and quiet you will enjoy. The rooms are spacious, with lots of windows overlooking the lake. It's best suited to groups of four or six, to justify the cost of the room.

▶ **Soldotna Bed and Breakfast Lodge**   399 Lovers Lane; 877-262-4779 or 907-262-4779; **soldotnalodge.com.**

QUALITY ★★★★ | VALUE ★★★ | $119–$380

People love the owners of this bed-and-breakfast, which also offers guided fishing, canoeing, and other activities. Rooms start at $119, but your best bet is to go with one of the package deals that include fishing.

continued on page 370

▲ southcentral coastal alaska indoor lodging

NAME	LODGING TYPE	QUALITY RATING	VALUE RATING	COST
KENAI				
All Seasons B&B	B&B	★★★★	★★★★	$105
The Alaska Log Cabin Inn	B&B/ cabins	★★★★	★★★	$130–$160
Uptown Motel	Motel	★★★	★★★	$135–$185
SOLDOTNA				
Aspen Hotel Soldotna	Hotel	★★★★	★★★★	$130–$170
Jana House Hostel	Hostel	★★★	★★★★	$30–$50
Kenai River Lodge	Hotel	★★★★	★★★	$150–$190
Longmere Lake Lodge B&B	B&B	★★★★	★★★	$250–$300
Soldotna B&B Lodge	B&B	★★★★	★★★	$119–$380
HOMER				
Bear Creek Winery and Lodging	Suites/B&B	★★★★★	★★★	$150–$260
The Eagle Watch Hostel	Hostel	★★★	★★★★	$15–$40
Heritage Hotel and Lodge	Hotel	★★★	★★★	$119–$165
Homer Hostel	Hostel	★★★	★★★	$27–$85
Homer Inn and Spa	Spa	★★★★★	★★★★	$159–$229
Land's End Resort	Hotel	★★★★	★★★	$115–$275
Mossy's Alaska Seaside Farm Hostel and Cabins	Hostel/ cabins	★★★	★★★★	$10–$60
SEWARD				
A Cabin on the Cliff	Cabin	★★★★★	★★★	$125–$389
Exit Glacier Salmon Bake and Cabins	Cabins	★★★	★★★★	$120
The Farm B&B	B&B	★★★	★★★★★	$88–$115
Hotel Edgewater	Hotel	★★★★	★★★	$155–$275
Hotel Seward	Hotel	★★★★	★★★	$250–$279
Kayaker's Cove	Hostel/cabins	★★★	★★★★★	$20–$60

▲ more southcentral coastal alaska indoor lodging

NAME	LODGING TYPE	QUALITY RATING	VALUE RATING	COST
KENAI [CONTINUED]				
Miller's Landing Hostel and Cabins	Hostel/cabins	★★	★★★	$50–$250
Moby Dick Hostel	Hostel	★★	★★	$22–$84
Seward Windsong Lodge	Hotel	★★★★★	★★★	$139–$289
Snow River Hostel	Hostel	★★★★	★★★★	$15–$40
The Van Gilder Hotel	Hotel	★★★★	★★★	$105–$185
SURROUNDING AREAS				
Kenai Backcountry Lodge	Wilderness lodge	★★★★★	★★★★	$975/2 nights
Kenai Princess Lodge	Hotel/lodge	★★★★★	★★★	$239–$329
Trail Lake Lodge	Motel	★★	★★★	$99–$135
WHITTIER				
The Anchor Inn	Inn	★★	★★★	$80–$100
The Inn at Whittier	Hotel	★★★★	★★★	$169–$325
VALDEZ				
Brookside Inn B&B	B&B/cabins	★★★	★★★	$135–$170
Valdez Harbor Inn	Hotel	★★★★	★★★	$139–$175
Wild Roses by the Sea B&B	B&B	★★★★	★★★	$134–$173
CORDOVA				
Bear Country Lodge	Cabins	★★★	★★★	$125
Cordova Rose Lodge	Lodge	★★★	★★★	$115–$145
The King's Chamber B&B and Lodging	B&B/apartments	★★★	★★★	$135
Light House Inn	Inn	★★★★	★★★	$145–$350
Orca Adventure Lodge	Lodge	★★★	★★★	$155–$190
Reluctant Fisherman Inn	Inn	★★★	★★★	$130–$160

▲ more southcentral coastal alaska indoor lodging

NAME	LODGING TYPE	QUALITY RATING	VALUE RATING	COST
KODIAK ISLAND				
Best Western Inn Kodiak	Hotel	★★★	★★★	$149–$209
Comfort Inn Kodiak	Hotel	★★★★	★★★	$145–$175
Kodiak Bed and Breakfast	B&B	★★★★	★★★★	$148
The Lodge at Hidden Basin	Wilderness lodge	★★★	★★★	$3,995/ 6 days
On the Cape B&B	B&B	★★★★	★★★★	$195–$325
Port Lions Lodge	Wilderness lodge	★★★	★★★	$3,695/ 5 days
Raspberry Island Remote Camps	Wilderness lodge	★★★★	★★★★	$2,600/ 4 days
Saltery Lake Lodge	Wilderness lodge	★★★★	★★★★	$2,550/ 6 days

[continued from page 367]

Camping

▶ **Centennial Campground**   Right by the river off Kalifornsky Beach Road; 907-262-3151; **ci.soldotna.ak.us/parks_rec.html.**

QUALITY ★★★ | VALUE ★★★★ | $14.70

Run by the city of Soldotna; the sites are first-come, first-served.

▶ **Kenai National Wildlife Refuge**   907-262-7021; **kenai.fws.gov.**

QUALITY ★★★ | VALUE ★★★★ | FREE–$10

The refuge maintains 13 campgrounds, located along Skilak Lake Wildlife Recreation Area and Swanson River Road. **Hidden Lake Campground** is the largest and most developed site ($10 fee). **Lower Skilak Lake Campground** has a boat launch for Skilak Lake and Kenai River fishing activities ($10 fee). All of the others, with the exception of the $10 **Kenai–Russian River Campground,** are free. All sites are first-come, first-served. No reservations.

▶ **Swiftwater Park**   On the river; 907-262-3151; **ci.soldotna.ak.us/parks_rec.html.**

QUALITY ★★★ | VALUE ★★★★ | $14.70

Small campground run by the city of Soldotna; sites are first-come, first-served.

HOMER

Indoor Lodging

▶ **Bear Creek Winery and Lodging**   Bear Creek Drive, out East End Road; 907-235-8484; **bearcreekwinery.com.**

QUALITY ★★★★★ | VALUE ★★★ | $150–$260

This Alaskan winery also features wonderful suites for rent. Everything is first-class, down to the bath towels and bedding. A splurge for sure. The winery also offers daily tastings in the summer.

▶ **The Eagle Watch Hostel**   Mile 3 Oilwell Rd. in Ninilchik; 907-567-3905; **home.gci.net/~theeaglewatch.**

QUALITY ★★★ | VALUE ★★★★ | $15–$40

Offers dorm-style bunks and private rooms.

▶ **Heritage Hotel and Lodge**   147 E. Pioneer Ave., Homer; 800-380-7787 or 907-235-7787; **alaskaheritagehotel.com.**

QUALITY ★★★ | VALUE ★★★ | $119–$165

A log hotel right in the center of the business part of town. The rooms are nice and clean, but some are better than others when it comes to location. Pet-friendly.

▶ **Homer Hostel**   304 W. Pioneer Ave.; 907-235-1463; **homerhostel.com.**

QUALITY ★★★ | VALUE ★★★ | $27–$85

Located conveniently at the business end of town, with access to local museums and shops. Be warned, though: they don't take credit cards.

▶ **Homer Inn and Spa**   895 Ocean Dr.; 800-294-7823 or 907-235-2501; **homerinn.com.**

QUALITY ★★★★★ | VALUE ★★★★ | $159–$229

This luxurious getaway is a great reward after a long kayaking or backpacking trip. Complete massage services are available, and an outdoor hot tub overlooks the water. Rates are surprisingly competitive with the cheaper places. Of course, the full-body massage will cost extra.

▲ southcentral coastal alaska camping

NAME	CAMPING TYPE	QUALITY RATING	VALUE RATING	COST
KENAI				
Captain Cook State Recreation Area	RV/tent	★★★★	★★★★	$10
SOLDOTNA				
Centennial Campground	RV/tent	★★★	★★★★	$14.70
Kenai National Wildlife Refuge	RV/tent	★★★	★★★★	Free–$10
Swiftwater Park	RV/tent	★★★	★★★★	$14.70
HOMER				
Anchor River/Stariski Creek State Recreation Areas	RV/tent	★★★★	★★★★	$10
Clam Gulch State Recreation Area	RV/tent	★★★★	★★★	$10
Deep Creek State Recreation Area	RV/tent	★★★★	★★★	$10
Heritage RV Park	RV	★★★	★★	$55
Homer City Campground	Tent	★★★	★★★★	$8
Homer Spit Campground	RV/tent	★★★	★★★	$22–$32
Kasilof State Recreation-site	RV/tent	★★★	★★★	$10
Mossy's Alaska Seaside Farm	Tent	★★★	★★★★	$10
Ninilchik State Recreation-site	Tent	★★★	★★★	$10
Spit Campground	Tent	★★★★	★★★★★	$8
SEWARD				
Exit Glacier–Kenai Fjords National Park	Tent	★★★★	★★★★★	free
Forest Acres Campground	Tent	★★★★	★★★★	$10
Miller's Landing	RV/tent	★★★★	★★★	$25–$35
Spring Creek Campground	Tent	★★★	★★★	$10
USDA Forest Service—Trail River, Ptarmigan Creek, Primrose	RV/tent	★★★★	★★★★	$10
Waterfront Park Campgrounds	RV/tent	★★★	★★★★	$10–$15

▲ more southcentral coastal camping

NAME	CAMPING TYPE	QUALITY RATING	VALUE RATING	COST
SURROUNDING AREAS				
USDA Forest Service Glacier Ranger District Campgrounds	RV/tent	★★★★	★★★★	$10
USDA Forest Service Seward Ranger District Campgrounds	RV/tent	★★★	★★★★	$10
WHITTIER				
Campground off Whittier Street	Tent	★★	★★★★	$20
USDA Forest Service Chugach Glacier Ranger District Campgrounds	cabins	★★★	★★★★	$35
VALDEZ				
Bayside RV Park	RV/tent	★★	★★★	$23–$35
Bear Paw Camper Park	RV/tent	★★★	★★★	$25–$45
Eagle's Rest RV Park and Cabins	RV/tent/cabins	★★	★★★	$27–$155
CORDOVA				
Alaska State Parks Campgrounds	Tent	★★★★	★★	Free
Child's Glacier Recreation Area	Tent	★★★★★	★★★★	$5
KODIAK ISLAND				
Buskin River State Recreation-site	Tent	★★★	★★★★	$15
Fort Abercrombie State Historical Park	Tent	★★★	★★★	$15
Pasagshak State Recreation-site	Tent	★★★★	★★★★★	Free

▶ **Land's End Resort**   At the end of Homer Spit Road; 800-478-0400 or 907-235-0400; **lands-end-resort.com.**

QUALITY ★★★★ | VALUE ★★★ | $115–$275

This is the getaway of choice for many an Alaskan who wants to go to Homer for a weekend. The food in the restaurants is delicious, the lodging is beautiful albeit a bit generic, and the view of the bay is unsurpassed.

▶ **Mossy's Alaska Seaside Farm Hostel and Cabins** 40904 Seaside Farm Rd., just outside of town; 907-235-7850; **xyz.net/~seaside/home.htm.**

QUALITY ★★★ | VALUE ★★★★ | $10–$60

A nontouristy option on a sprawling all-organic farm with animals wandering all over; very granola atmosphere. Tent camping, hostel, and cabins available.

Camping

There are several good camping choices in and around Homer.

▶ **Anchor River State Recreation Area/Stariski State Recreation-site** About 15 miles from Homer; 907-262-5581; **dnr.alaska.gov/parks/units/anchoriv.htm.**

QUALITY ★★★★ | VALUE ★★★★ | $10

A nice and private place to camp, located on a high bluff tucked in the woods overlooking the water. Geography buffs will appreciate that the campground also happens to be at the most westerly point on the U.S. highway system.

▶ **Clam Gulch State Recreation Area** Mile 117.5 Sterling Hwy.; 907-262-5581; **dnr.alaska.gov/parks/units/clamglch.htm.**

QUALITY ★★★★ | VALUE ★★★ | $10

Offers some of the best clam digging in the state, at a campground high on the bluff overlooking Cook Inlet.

▶ **Deep Creek State Recreation Area** Mile 137 Sterling Hwy.; 907-262-5581; **dnr.alaska.gov/parks/units/deepck.htm.**

QUALITY ★★★★ | VALUE ★★★ | $10

There are three campgrounds from which to choose.

▶ **Heritage RV Park** On Homer Spit Road, across from Spit Campground; 800-380-7787 or 907-226-4500; **alaskaheritagervpark.com.**

QUALITY ★★★ | VALUE ★★ | $55

This park catering to RVers shares an incredible view with Spit Campground. It can get rowdy on weekends, but no one seems to mind.

▶ **Homer City Campground** At the top of Bartlett Street (follow the signs to the left); 907-235-3170.

QUALITY ★★★ | VALUE ★★★★ | $8

Facilities at this quiet campground include restrooms, a picnic area, and playground equipment. It's a little out of the way, which is a plus, but there are also signs that longtime campers—living there—have put down roots.

▶ **Homer Spit Campground**   At the end of Homer Spit Road; 907-235-8206;
alaskacampgrounds.net/members/HomerSpitCampground/HomerSpit
Campground.htm.

QUALITY ★★★ | VALUE ★★★ | $22–$32

This privately run campground is locally—and nationally—famous, and the
resident "Eagle Lady" has been featured in numerous news articles. She feeds
the eagles fish scraps daily; thus, they congregate here. Ten tent sites and
plenty of RV sites.

▶ **Kasilof State Recreation-site**   About 15 miles south of Soldotna on the way to
Homer; 907-262-5581; **dnr.alaska.gov/parks/units/kasilof.htm.**

QUALITY ★★★ | VALUE ★★★ | $10

Three campground options at Crooked Creek, Johnson Lake, and Kasilof River
state recreation areas. *Note:* The Kasilof River site fills up fast.

▶ **Mossy's Alaska Seaside Farm Hostel and Cabins**   40904 Seaside Farm Rd., just
outside of town; 907-235-7850; **xyz.net/~seaside/home.htm.**

QUALITY ★★★ | VALUE ★★★★ | $10

The tent camping here has a great view and is absolutely nontouristy—set
among an all-organic farm with animals wandering free. Kids under age 12
stay free.

▶ **Ninilchik State Recreation-site**   Mile 135 Sterling Hwy.

QUALITY ★★★ | VALUE ★★★ | $10

Three camping areas, one right on the beach.

▶ **Spit Campground**   On Homer Spit Road, Homer; 907-235-3170.

QUALITY ★★★★ | VALUE ★★★★★ | $8

If you're going to be in a tent, we suggest enjoying the ocean sounds at this
informal city-run site with camping on the right-hand side of the road.

SEWARD

Indoor Lodging

▶ **A Cabin on the Cliff**   309 3rd Ave.; 888-227-2424 or 907-224-2411;
acabinonthecliff.com.

QUALITY ★★★★★ | VALUE ★★★ | $125–$389

One of the most notable lodging options in town, perched at the base of

Mount Marathon with a commanding view across the road and toward the harbor. The hot tub alone is worth it, but the price is crazy high.

▶ **Exit Glacier Salmon Bake and Cabins**   Mile 0.25 Exit Glacier Rd. (*note:* sign says Mile Zero); 907-224-6040; **sewardalaskacabins.com.**

QUALITY ★★★ | VALUE ★★★★ | $120

We haven't stayed here ourselves, but we can tell you that these newer cabins come highly recommended from several local outdoors outfitters, who say the salmon bake is delicious too. The cabins—tucked into the woods, tiny but cozy—sleep four, and pets are welcome. Sounds like our kind of place.

▶ **The Farm Bed and Breakfast**   3 miles from Seward on Salmon Creek Road; 907-224-5691; **thefarmbedandbreakfast.com.**

QUALITY ★★★ | VALUE ★★★★★ | $88–$115

This old but remodeled farm is in a nice, quiet area. We like this spot because the longtime owners are superfriendly, and the grassy field on their 10-acre spread is a great place to wander. You'll want a vehicle if staying here because it's a bit out of town.

▶ **Hotel Edgewater**   200 5th Ave.; 888-793-6800 or 907-224-2700; **hoteledgewater.com.**

QUALITY ★★★★ | VALUE ★★★ | $155–$275

It has a bit of a corporate feel, but you have to admit that the rooms are nice, and the view is superb. One of the better hotels in town if you don't like surprises; underwent renovations in the winter of 2007.

▶ **Hotel Seward**   221 5th Ave.; 800-440-2444 or 907-224-8001; **hotelsewardalaska.com.**

QUALITY ★★★★ | VALUE ★★★ | $250–$279

Popular downtown historical hotel specializing in rooms with a view. Rates are steep, but oh, what a view it is!

▶ **Kayaker's Cove**   On Resurrection Bay; 907-224-8662; **kayakerscove.com.**

QUALITY ★★★ | VALUE ★★★★★ | $20–$60

This is one of our favorite places to stay in Seward: a rustic wilderness lodge across the bay, with kayaks for paddling (for a small fee, of course). The main lodge is a hostel setup; private cabins are available for up to three people. A kayak rental will cost you $20 per day, and a water taxi to get there (contact Miller's Landing, below, to arrange that) is $55 round-trip.

▶ **Miller's Landing Hostel and Cabins**   Located at Lowell Point; 866-541-5739 or 907-224-5739; **millerslandingak.com.**

QUALITY ★★ | VALUE ★★★ | $50–$250

Lodging options range from two-person hostel rooms to a fancy six-person cabin and a nice wooded campground.

▶ **Moby Dick Hostel**   432 3rd Ave.; 907-224-7072; **mobydickhostel.com.**

QUALITY ★★ | VALUE ★★ | $22–$84

Offers dorm-style rooms right in town, albeit a good walk from the harbor. The owners are friendly, which makes up for the very used beds.

▶ **Seward Windsong Lodge**   0.5 Exit Glacier Road; 877-777-4079 or 907-224-7116; **sewardwindsong.com.**

QUALITY ★★★★★ | VALUE ★★★ | $139–$289

A true lodge feel but only minutes from town. It's owned by Alaska Heritage Tours, an Alaska-native-run company that has begun building high-quality lodges throughout the state.

▶ **Snow River Hostel**   Mile 16 Seward Hwy.; 907-440-1907.

QUALITY ★★★★ | VALUE ★★★★ | $15–$40

A stone building off the highway offering very clean hostel facilities. Separate men's and women's bunks; a private room is also available.

▶ **The Van Gilder Hotel**   308 Adams St.; 800-478-0400 or 907-224-3079; **vangilderhotel.com.**

QUALITY ★★★★ | VALUE ★★★ | $105–$185

A time-honored alternative to today's hotels, with a lovely antiques collection and historical displays to boot. Built in 1916, the renovated Van Gilder offers several small rooms, each of them unique.

Camping

▶ **Exit Glacier–Kenai Fjords National Park**   907-224-2132 or 907-224-7500; **nps.gov/kefj.**

QUALITY ★★★★ | VALUE ★★★★★ | FREE

This drive-to site, off Exit Glacier Road, has a 12-site walk-in tent campground. Sites are available on a first-come, first-served basis. There are no reservations or camping fees; stays are limited to 14 days. *Warning:* It fills fast in July and August. Pets are not allowed.

▶ **Forest Acres Campground**   Off Hemlock Street, away from the harbor area; **cityofseward.net/parksRec/parks.htm.**

QUALITY ★★★★ | VALUE ★★★★ | $10

One of our favorite city-run tenting options. You're on the honor system—you self-register on-site.

▶ **Miller's Landing**   At Lowell Point; 866-541-5739 or 907-224-5739; millerslandingak.com.

QUALITY ★★★★ | VALUE ★★★ | $25–$35

A nice wooded campground 3 miles outside of Seward, on the water. If you're kayaking, this is a great launching point.

▶ **Spring Creek Campground**   Off Nash Road, at the edge of town (go 5 miles and turn right, toward the water and the primitive campground); **cityofseward.net/ parksRec/parks.htm.**

QUALITY ★★★ | VALUE ★★★ | $10

Another good city-run camping choice. Self-registering on-site.

▶ **USDA Forest Service Seward Ranger District Campgrounds**   Seward Ranger District, 334 4th Ave.; 907-224-3374; National Recreation Reservation System, 877-444-6777 or **recreation.gov.**

QUALITY ★★★ | VALUE ★★★★ | $10

Three campgrounds are available along the Seward Highway. Within 25 miles of Seward is **Trail River,** at Mile 24.2 (63 sites, no hookups); **Ptarmigan Creek,** at Mile 23.1 (16 sites, no hookups); and **Primrose,** at Mile 17 (10 sites, no hookups).

▶ **Waterfront Park Campgrounds**   Near the water at Ballaine Boulevard, from Railway Avenue to D Street; **cityofseward.net/parksRec/campgrounds.htm.**

QUALITY ★★★ | VALUE ★★★★ | $10–$15

The Seward Parks and Recreation Department runs five campgrounds within Waterfront Park. Here again, the honor system is the rule, with self-registration on-site. Not the quietest choice, but the view is to die for.

SURROUNDING AREAS

Indoor Lodging

▶ **Kenai Backcountry Lodge**   In Cooper Landing; 800-334-8730 or 907-783-2928; alaskawildland.com/kenaibackcountrylodge.htm.

QUALITY ★★★★★ | VALUE ★★★★ | $975/2 NIGHTS

To stay here you have to purchase a package trip, with a minimum two-night stay, and the prices are high. But the lodge's owner, Alaska Wildland Adventures, was voted one of the best eco-tour businesses in the world by *Condé Nast Traveler* in 2005, and its environmentally aware way of doing business is noticeable. We're talking high quality. All meals and activities are covered.

▶ **Kenai Princess Lodge**   In Cooper Landing; 800-426-0500; princesslodges.com/kenai_lodge.cfm.

QUALITY ★★★★★ | VALUE ★★★ | $239–$329

This beautiful log lodge, off a back road in Cooper Landing, combines comfort with ruggedness. The rooms are like mini-cabins, although they are attached to each other. The communal hot tub is nice when you can get it to yourself. Dinner at the Eagle's Crest Restaurant is memorable.

▶ **Trail Lake Lodge**   Mile 29.5 Seward Hwy., Moose Pass; 888-395-3624; traillakelodge.com.

QUALITY ★★ | VALUE ★★★ | $99–$135

Nice enough, right on the water, and an alternative to staying in Seward. If you're craving complete isolation, however, you won't find it here: the lodge is right off the two-lane highway.

Camping

▶ **USDA Forest Service Glacier Ranger District Campgrounds**   Glacier Ranger District; 907-783-3242; National Recreation Reservation System, 877-444-6777 or **recreation.gov.**

QUALITY ★★★★ | VALUE ★★★★ | $10

Camping on the Seward Highway from Girdwood to Hope at **Bertha Creek, Black Bear, Granite Creek,** and **Williwaw** campgrounds.

▶ **USDA Forest Service Seward Ranger District Campgrounds**   Seward Ranger District; 334 4th Ave.; 907-224-3374; National Recreation Reservation System, 877-444-6777 or **recreation.gov.**

QUALITY ★★–★★★★ | VALUE ★★–★★★ | $10

Camping in Hope, Cooper Landing, and all along the Seward and Sterling highways within Seward Ranger District boundaries.

WHITTIER

Indoor Lodging

▶ **The Anchor Inn**   Off the waterfront, near the residential area in Whittier; 877-870-8787 or 907-472-2354; **anchorinnwhittier.com.**

QUALITY ★★ | VALUE ★★★ | $80–$100

The building isn't much to look at, but each room is different. A restaurant-bar and store are attached to the inn.

▶ **The Inn at Whittier**   866-472-5757 or 907-472-7000; **innatwhittier.com.**

| QUALITY ★★★★ | VALUE ★★★★ | $169–$325 |

The newest—and really the only—fine-lodging option in this tiny community. The rooms range from mountain view (least costly) to townhouse suites with fireplace, whirlpool tub, and two floors of luxury and views.

Camping

▶ **Campground off Whittier Street**   101 Whittier St., near the public parking area; 907-472-2670.

| QUALITY ★★ | VALUE ★★★★ | $20 |

The campground is little more than a parking lot itself, but it's the cheapest way to sleep in Whittier.

▶ **USDA Forest Service Chugach Glacier Ranger District Campgrounds**
National Recreation Reservation System, 877-444-6777 or **recreation.gov.**

| QUALITY ★★★ | VALUE ★★★★ | $35 |

Public-use cabins are available throughout the sound outside of Whittier-Pigot Bay, Paulsen Bay, Shrode Lake, Coghill Lake, Harrison Lagoon, and South Culross Passage. You'll need a boat—or someone with a boat who can take you— to get to them, but they offer some affordable lodging in a gorgeous setting.

VALDEZ

Indoor Lodging

▶ **Brookside Inn Bed and Breakfast**   1465 Richardson Hwy.; 866-316-9130 or 907-835-9130; **brooksideinnbb.com.**

| QUALITY ★★★ | VALUE ★★★ | $135–$170 |

The owners have a friendly dog, and the breakfast area is a lovely covered and heated patio. The rooms are spacious, especially the suite. You're right off the road, though, and some might not like the occasional highway noise.

▶ **Valdez Harbor Inn**   100 Harbor Dr.; 888-222-3440 or 907-835-2308; **valdezharborinn.com.**

| QUALITY ★★★★ | VALUE ★★★ | $139–$175 |

One of the nicest hotels in town, this inn also boasts one of the best views. Plus, the bar is a nice place to hang out after a day of hiking.

▶ **Wild Roses by the Sea Bed and Breakfast**   629 Fiddlehead Lane; 907-835-2930; **alaskabytheseabnb.com.**

| QUALITY ★★★★ | VALUE ★★★ | $134–$173 |

Close to the beach and town. Private whirlpool tub is a plus.

Camping

▶ **Bayside RV Park**   888-835-4425; baysiderv.com.

QUALITY ★★ | VALUE ★★★ | $23–$35

It's basically a cleared parking lot, but you can't get much better than a Valdez view on a clear day, so it doesn't seem to matter.

▶ **Bear Paw Camper Park**   On the small-boat harbor; 907-835-2530; bearpawrvpark.com.

QUALITY ★★★ | VALUE ★★★ | $25–$45

The in-town location makes this convenient, though not necessarily wilderness-like. The owners have two parks—one for families and an adults-only establishment for those who don't want to deal with crying or rambunctious children. The tent camping is in a wooded area, which is nice.

▶ **Eagle's Rest RV Park and Cabins**   139 E. Pioneer Dr.; 800-553-7275 or 907-835-2373; eaglesrestrv.com.

QUALITY ★★ | VALUE ★★★ | $27–$155

If you're interested only in a convenient location, this is the place for you: a big cleared area for RVers, tenters, and cabin dwellers right in town; the cabins are $125–$155.

CORDOVA

Indoor Lodging

▶ **Bear Country Lodge**   On the shore of Lake Eyak; 907-424-5901; bearcountrylodge.net.

QUALITY ★★★ | VALUE ★★★ | $125

This quiet lakefront lodge is perfect for families or small groups seeking solitude. Two cabins from which to choose.

▶ **Cordova Rose Lodge**   1315 Whitshed, on the waterfront; 907-424-7673; cordovarose.com.

QUALITY ★★★ | VALUE ★★★ | $115–$145

Birders like this scenic little lodge and stay here often; the owners can fill you in on the rich birdlife in the area. Choose from rooms with shared or private baths; breakfast is included in the rate for the latter.

▶ **The King's Chamber B&B and Lodging**   511 4th St.; 907-424-3373; thekingschamber.com.

QUALITY ★★★ | VALUE ★★★ | $135

This historical building was moved into town almost a decade ago and now can house guests in bed-and-breakfast rooms, efficiency apartments, or three- and four-bedroom apartments for extended stays. Discounts for extended stays.

▶ **Light House Inn**   212 Nicholoff Way, at the Cordova Boat Harbor; 907-424-7080 or 907-424-7673; **cordovalighthouseinn.com.**

| QUALITY ★★★★ | VALUE ★★★ | $145–$350 |

A good lodging choice because of its convenient location to shops and dining. The comfy rooms have Internet access.

▶ **Orca Adventure Lodge**   866-424-6722 or 907-424-7249; orcaadventurelodge.com.

| QUALITY ★★★ | VALUE ★★★ | $155–$190 |

This lodge is out of town and housed in a refurbished cannery. The rooms are basic, as is the food (meat or fish and potatoes), but the owner knows the area well and can accommodate just about anyone's needs.

▶ **Reluctant Fisherman Inn**   407 Railroad Ave.; 907-424-3272; reluctantfisherman.com.

| QUALITY ★★★ | VALUE ★★★ | $130–$160 |

The starting rate gets you a room by the bay.

Camping

▶ **Alaska State Parks Campgrounds**   907-262-5581.

| QUALITY ★★★★ | VALUE ★★ | FREE |

Convenient in-town or nearby camping is hard to find in Cordova (the only RV/tent park is basically a gravel lot in town), but the rest of the surrounding city is wide-open wilderness. Alaska State Parks has three beautiful recreation areas that allow camping: **Boswell Bay, Canoe Passage,** and **Kayak Island** state marine parks. There are no fees, but the campgrounds are accessible only by water taxi or floatplane—which gets expensive (thus our relatively low value rating).

▶ **Child's Glacier Recreation Area**   48 miles out the Copper River Highway.

| QUALITY ★★★★★ | VALUE ★★★★ | $5 |

There are 15 wooded tent sites here.

KODIAK ISLAND

Kodiak Island has some of the best remote lodges in the state. If you're staying in town, we have several hotel/B&B recommendations. But if you have a chance, hit one of the lodges we suggest, where you can fish, hike, or relax to your heart's content.

Indoor Lodging

▶ **Best Western Inn Kodiak**   236 W. Rezanof Dr.; 888-563-4254 or 907-486-5712; **kodiakinn.com.**

| QUALITY ★★★ | VALUE ★★★ | $149–$209 |

Right downtown; some rooms are small, but all are clean and comfortable.

▶ **Comfort Inn Kodiak**   1395 Airport Way; 800-544-2202 or 907-487-2700; **choicehotels.com.**

| QUALITY ★★★★ | VALUE ★★★ | $145–$175 |

Now part of the Choice chain, the popular hotel formerly known as the Buskin River Inn still seems to be drawing clients. The Comfort Inn has excellent rooms and dining. The drawback is that it's a few miles out of town by the airport, so getting downtown is kind of inconvenient if you're without wheels.

▶ **Kodiak Bed and Breakfast**   308 Cope St.; 907-486-5367; **home.gci.net/~mmonroe.**

| QUALITY ★★★★ | VALUE ★★★★ | $148 |

Located one block back from the harbor and within walking distance of most downtown attractions, this is our top pick among the bed-and-breakfasts in Kodiak. There are two comfortable rooms plus your own private living room.

▶ **The Lodge at Hidden Basin**   907-345-7017; **hiddenbasinalaska.com.**

| QUALITY ★★★ | VALUE ★★★ | $3,995/6 DAYS |

This intimate lodge hosts a maximum of six people at a time in a rough-cut-spruce building that is simple and comfortable. We like the homey feel of the place, complete with mismatched furniture.

▶ **On the Cape Bed and Breakfast**   3476 Spruce Cape Rd., 3 minutes from downtown; 907-942-0461; **onthecape.net.**

| QUALITY ★★★★ | VALUE ★★★★ | $195–$325 |

This home features beautiful rooms with their own bathrooms and ocean views. One of the nicest places in town.

▶ **Port Lions Lodge**   In the village of Port Lions, on the northwest end of Kodiak Island, accessible by ferry or small plane; 800-808-8447 or 907-454-2264; **portlionslodge.com.**

| QUALITY ★★★ | VALUE ★★★ | $3,695/5 DAYS |

This remote, beautiful lodge offers weeklong packages that include air transport from Kodiak, five days of guided fishing, lodging, and meals. They even clean, package, and ship your fish home. The price may seem steep, but all the details are taken care of, so you can simply relax.

▶ **Raspberry Island Remote Camps**   Raspberry Island; 701-526-1677; raspberryisland.com.

QUALITY ★★★★	VALUE ★★★★	$2,600/4 DAYS, $3,800/6 DAYS

A truly secluded lodge that concentrates equally on activities other than fishing. While most lodges can accommodate just about any interest, Raspberry owners encourage it all—hiking, kayaking, and canoeing pack trips, as well as opportunities for relaxing back at the lodge.

▶ **Saltery Lake Lodge**   Near Ugak Bay, on the eastern side of Kodiak Island; 800-770-5037 or 907-486-7083; **salterylake.com.**

QUALITY ★★★★	VALUE ★★★★	$2,550/6 DAYS OR $465/1–3 DAYS

Another fishing destination; packages include six days of fishing, lodging, meals, and transportation from Kodiak. Not as nice as Port Lions, but the fishing is excellent.

Camping

You won't see many recreational vehicles in Kodiak, thus the lack of campgrounds on every corner. This is a good thing, though: as a result, most camping areas maintain a very natural feel. The three best camping areas are all managed by the **Alaska State Parks** system, Division of Parks and Outdoor Recreation. For more information, contact Alaska State Parks, Kodiak District Office, 1400 Abercrombie Dr., Kodiak 99615; 907-486-6339; **dnr.alaska .gov/parks/units/kodiak/index.htm.**

▶ **Buskin River State Recreation-site**   Mile 4.1 W. Rezanof Dr.

QUALITY ★★★	VALUE ★★★★	$15

This 15-site camping area is conveniently located only 4.1 miles from downtown and is close to one of the most productive salmon-fishing rivers on Kodiak Island. The **Alaska Department of Fish and Game** operates a weir just outside the park. From downtown, follow Rezanof Drive west for 4.1 miles, and then turn left at the park sign at Mile 4.5 W. Rezanof Dr. *Warning:* The campground is right by the airport, thus airplane noise is directly overhead.

▶ **Fort Abercrombie State Historical Park**   Mile 3.7 E. Rezanof Dr.

QUALITY ★★★	VALUE ★★★	$15

This is a hiker's campground, with 13 sites and great hiking trails leading to a rugged coastline, in addition to a lake stocked with rainbow trout and arctic grayling. This is our favorite location because the sites are also designed with tent campers in mind, although RVers can use the overflow area. Remnants of a World War II military installation are scattered all over, giving the area a sort of deserted feel. From downtown, head east on Rezanof Drive and drive 3.7 miles; turn right onto Abercrombie Drive, which goes into the park.

▶ **Pasagshak State Recreation-site**   40 Pasagshak River Rd.

QUALITY ★★★★ | VALUE ★★★★★ | FREE

This small riverside park on the mouth of the Pasagshak River is a popular fishing area; the species found here include silver and king salmon and Dolly Varden. Take Rezanof Drive west out of town and drive 30 miles; then turn right onto Pasagshak Road just past the Kalsin River, and continue 9 miles.

▲ Where to Eat

KENAI PENINSULA

Dining on the Kenai Peninsula is an interesting experience. Figuratively speaking, if you attached weights to the best restaurants on the peninsula, the southern tip near Homer and Kachemak Bay would sink right into the ocean there. Seward, on the east side, might sag a bit, but Kenai and Soldotna, to the west, would barely move.

The truth is that the best dining options exist in the smaller Alaska communities, in Seward or Homer; Kenai and Soldotna tend to cater to the McDonald's-and-Subway crowd. We like dining options that say something about the communities in which they are located; they either step it up a notch with fine ingredients and creative presentation or offer casual confidence and a $1 cookie that melts in your mouth.

Because Kenai and Soldotna are so close to each other, we've combined their dining listings. Seward and Homer have separate listings; we also have a couple of suggestions for the drive there, in the outlying communities.

Kenai and Soldotna

▶ **Charlotte's**   115 S. Willow St., Kenai; 907-283-2777.

CASUAL | QUALITY ★★★★ | $8–$18 | SUITABLE FOR KIDS? N

Homemade bread, salad from their garden, and wonderful desserts make this one of the most charming lunchtime eateries in Kenai.

▶ **Jersey Subs**   At the North Cohoe turnoff, Kasilof; 907-260-3343.

SUBS	QUALITY ★★★	$8–$12	SUITABLE FOR KIDS? Y

It's just a shack set up by the side of the road, but the subs satisfy.

▶ **Kaladi Brothers Coffee Co.**   315 S. Kobuk Suite C, Soldotna; 907-262-5980; and 44350 Sterling Hwy., Soldotna; 907-262-3157.

ESPRESSO	QUALITY ★★★★	$2–$7	SUITABLE FOR KIDS? N

Kaladi Brothers sells the best coffee in Alaska, in our opinion. The Soldotna location on Kobuk is one of the original stores and isn't as spacious as the newer one on the Sterling.

▶ **Louie's Restaurant**   In the Uptown Motel, 47 Spur View Dr., Kenai; 800-777-3650 or 907-283-3660.

SEAFOOD	QUALITY ★★★	$8–$29	SUITABLE FOR KIDS? Y

A family-friendly restaurant that has a long and varied seafood menu. Plenty of red-meat options, very few vegetarian-friendly items.

▶ **The Moose Is Loose**   On the Sterling Highway, just past the Y in Soldotna; 907-260-3036.

BAKERY	QUALITY ★★★	$3–$8	SUITABLE FOR KIDS? Y

This is a good place to pick up some fresh baked goods on your way to wherever.

▶ **Mykel's Restaurant**   In the Soldotna Inn, 35041 Kenai Spur Hwy.; 866-262-9169 or 907-262-4305; **mykels.com**.

AMERICAN	QUALITY ★★★	$6–$27	SUITABLE FOR KIDS? Y

Family-style meals and something to please everyone. We like Mykel's because it's so clean, but it's a bit overpriced for what it offers.

▶ **River City Books**   43977 Sterling Hwy., Suite A, Soldotna; 907-260-7722.

ESPRESSO	QUALITY ★★★★	$2–$6	SUITABLE FOR KIDS? N

Enjoy some espresso and a muffin, or an inventive lunch dish made from organic and local foods. Then spend hours browsing the great book selection in this much-needed bookstore.

▶ **Sal's Klondike Diner**   44619 Sterling Hwy., Soldotna; 907-262-2220.

BURGERS	QUALITY ★★★	$4–$19	SUITABLE FOR KIDS? Y

It is what it says: a diner. And it's fast, friendly, and affordable. A family of four can eat for $30. Featuring burgers, fish-and-chips, and sandwiches. Open 24 hours for those on weird schedules or with hangovers to feed.

▶ **St. Elias Brewing Company**   434 Sharkathmi Ave, Soldotna; 907-260-7837;
steliasbrewingco.com.

AMERICAN | QUALITY ★★★★ | $10–$24 | SUITABLE FOR KIDS? Y

This is simply the best place to eat in Soldotna, with inventive one-plate pizzas and microbrew beer that is to die for. It's busy all the time, and live music
is common in the summer.

▶ **Veronica's Coffee House**   In Historic Old Town Kenai, across from the Russian
Orthodox Church; 907-283-2725.

CASUAL | QUALITY ★★★★ | $4–$14 | SUITABLE FOR KIDS? Y

This funky cafe serves breakfast, lunch, and dinner; it features homemade
soups, sandwiches, quiches, desserts, and daily specials. The outside dining
on a sunny day is beautiful.

Homer

▶ **Café Cups**   162 W. Pioneer Ave.; 907-235-8330; **cafecupshomer.com.**

FUSION | QUALITY ★★★★ | $8–$24 | SUITABLE FOR KIDS? N

With its funky giant teacups hanging off the eaves, you can't really miss the
place. The Caesar salad is delicious, and the dressings are made in-house.

▶ **The Chart Room**   At the end of Homer Spit Road, at Land's End Resort;
907-235-0400 or 800-478-0400; **lands-end-resort.com.**

FUSION | QUALITY ★★★★ | $9–$35 | SUITABLE FOR KIDS? Y

The Land's End resort is a top destination for Alaskans who want to get away
to Homer for the weekend. The food at the Chart Room is delicious (the
Sunday brunch will fill you up for the entire day), and an extensive wine list
accompanies the dinner menu.

▶ **Duncan House Diner**   125 E. Pioneer Ave.; 907-235-5344.

DINER | QUALITY ★★★ | $4–$9 | SUITABLE FOR KIDS? Y

The best place to go for diner food or a filling breakfast. The service is fast,
the food is good, and the place is packed with locals.

▶ **Fat Olives**   276 Ohlson Lane; 907-235-8488.

CASUAL | QUALITY ★★★★ | $8–$18 | SUITABLE FOR KIDS? Y

The place has awesome wines and beers, and although the pizzas are
popular, don't overlook the other offerings, including pasta.

continued on page 390

▲ southcentral coastal alaska dining

NAME	CUISINE	FOOD QUALITY	COST
KENAI AND SOLDOTNA			
Charlotte's	Casual	★★★★	$8–$18
Jersey Subs	Subs	★★★	$8–$12
Kaladi Brothers Coffee Co.	Espresso	★★★★	$2–$7
Louie's Restaurant	Seafood	★★★	$8–$29
The Moose Is Loose	Bakery	★★★	$3–$8
Mykel's Restaurant	American	★★★	$6–$27
River City Books	Espresso	★★★★	$2–$6
Sal's Klondike Diner	Burgers	★★★	$4–$19
St. Elias Brewing Company	American	★★★★	$10–$24
Veronica's Coffee House	Casual	★★★★	$4–$14
HOMER			
Café Cups	Fusion	★★★★	$8–$24
The Chart Room	Fusion	★★★★	$9–$35
Duncan House Diner	Diner	★★★	$4–$9
Fat Olives	Casual	★★★★	$8–$18
Fresh Sourdough Express Bakery	Casual	★★★★	$8–$15
Homestead Restaurant	Fusion	★★★★	$13–39
Mermaid Café	Casual	★★★	$4–$10
The Saltry Restaurant	Fusion	★★★★★	$8–$24
Two Sisters Bakery	Bakery	★★★	$4–$12
SEWARD			
Bakery at the Harbor	Bakery	★★★	$2–$7
Chinooks Waterfront Restaurant	Fusion/seafood	★★★	$7–$32
Christo's Palace	Greek/pizza	★★★	$8–$25
Exit Glacier Salmon Bake	Seafood	★★★	$9–$19

▲ more southcentral coastal dining

NAME	CUISINE	FOOD QUALITY	COST
SEWARD [CONTINUED]			
Ray's Waterfront	Fusion/seafood	★★★★	$9–$34
Resurrect Art Coffee House Gallery	Espresso	★★★	$2–$6
Resurrection Roadhouse	Fusion/pizza	★★★★	$6–$19
Sue's Teriyaki Kitchen	Asian	★★★	$5–$16
SURROUNDING AREAS			
Eagle's Crest/Kenai Princess Lodge	Fusion	★★★★	$9–$31
Tito's Discovery Café	American	★★★	$6–$15
WHITTIER			
China Sea Restaurant	Chinese/Korean	★★	$5–$14
Frankie's Deli	Sandwiches	★★	$5–$10
The Inn at Whittier	Fusion	★★★★	$8–$29
Lazy Otter Café and Gifts	American	★★★	$5–$9
Sportsmen Inn Restaurant/Bar	American/diner	★★	$4–$21
VALDEZ			
Alaska's Bistro	Mediterranean	★★★★	$7–$34
Ernesto's Taqueria	Mexican	★★★	$5–$17
Fu Kung Chinese Restaurant	Chinese	★★	$7–$15
Mike's Palace	Greek/Italian/Mex.	★★	$6–$24
Pipeline Inn Club	Steaks/seafood	★★★	$8–$28
The Rose Cache	American	★★★★	$9–$16
CORDOVA			
Baja Taco	Tex-Mex	★★★	$5–$12
Killer Whale Café	Casual	★★★	$5–$10
Powder House	American/sushi	★★★★	$6–$19
Reluctant Fisherman Inn	Casual	★★★★	$6–$18

▲ more southcentral coastal dining

NAME	CUISINE	FOOD QUALITY	COST
KODIAK ISLAND			
The Chart Room	Fusion	★★★★	$9–$29
Eagle's Nest Restaurant	Fusion	★★★★	$9–$29
Galley Gourmet	Cruise	★★★★	$95–$120
Henry's Great Alaskan Restaurant	American/seafood	★★★	$5–$19
Mill Bay Coffee and Pastries	Bakery	★★★★	$2–$9
The Old Powerhouse Restaurant	Japanese	★★★★	$7–$29
Second Floor Japanese Restaurant	Japanese	★★★	$7–$26

continued from page 387

▶ **Fresh Sourdough Express Bakery**   1316 Ocean Dr.; 907-235-7571.

CASUAL | QUALITY ★★★★ | $8–$15 | SUITABLE FOR KIDS? Y

The place attracts tourists, but even locals will admit that the food is incredible, perfectly balancing healthful, delicious, and affordable. The salad and soup selections are diverse, and the spinach-and-cheese croissant is something to return for over and over. The prices are outstanding, considering what other restaurants charge for similar meals.

▶ **Homestead Restaurant**   Mile 8.2 East End Rd.; 907-235-8723; **homesteadrestaurant.net.**

FUSION | QUALITY ★★★★ | $13–$39 | SUITABLE FOR KIDS? N

This restaurant has withstood the test of time, which shows that quality works. It has been a mainstay in Homer for more than 10 years and has a faithful following of folks who appreciate fine food and are willing to drive out East End Road to get it. Everything in Homer is casual, and if you walk in after a week of backpacking in most places, no one will bat an eye. Here, though, we'd suggest you at least shower first. Nationally recognized for its wine selection.

▶ **Mermaid Café**   At the Old Inlet Bookshop, 3487 Main St.; 907-235-7984.

CASUAL | QUALITY ★★★ | $4–$10 | SUITABLE FOR KIDS? Y

Offering used, rare, and out-of-print books, this is a place in which you can get lost. The cafe is attached, and a bed-and-breakfast is upstairs for those who can't pull themselves away from the books or food.

▶ **The Saltry Restaurant**   On the boardwalk in Halibut Cove, across Kachemak Bay; 907-296-2223 or 907-235-7487.

| FUSION | QUALITY ★★★★★ | $8–$24 | SUITABLE FOR KIDS? N |

The food is as fresh as possible, the fish is pulled from local waters, and the vegetables come from the garden patch behind the restaurant. Take the *Danny J Dinner Cruise* across the bay and make a night of it (the rate is cheaper than the day cruise). Central Charters does the booking (800-478-7847 or 907-235-7847; **centralcharter.com**). The round-trip boat ride is $30. Meals are extra; about $75 for a couple is average.

▶ **Two Sisters Bakery**   106 W. Bunnell St.; 907-235-2280.

| BAKERY | QUALITY ★★★ | $4–$12 | SUITABLE FOR KIDS? N |

A very hip, very small cafe and bakery offering creative meals for a lot less than the more-touristy spots on the spit.

Seward

▶ **Bakery at the Harbor**   1210 4th Ave.; 907-224-6091.

| BAKERY | QUALITY ★★★ | $2–$7 | SUITABLE FOR KIDS? Y |

Featuring basic but tasty baked goods. Caters to tourists.

▶ **Chinooks Waterfront Restaurant**   1404 4th Ave., on the waterfront; 907-224-2207; **chinookswaterfront.com.**

| FUSION/SEAFOOD | QUALITY ★★★ | $7–$32 | SUITABLE FOR KIDS? Y |

A direct competitor to longtime favorite Ray's Waterfront (below). Menu features seafood, steaks, and pastas, all innovatively prepared.

▶ **Christo's Palace**   133 4th Ave., across from the Sealife Center; 907-224-5255.

| GREEK/PIZZA | QUALITY ★★★ | $8–$25 | SUITABLE FOR KIDS? N |

This is one we haven't been to but have heard only good things about. The dining room is quite beautiful and richly decorated, and the antique bar is a local conversation piece. The pizzas are a favorite.

▶ **Exit Glacier Salmon Bake and Cabins**   Mile 0.25 Exit Glacier Rd. (*note:* sign says Mile Zero); 907-224-2204; **sewardalaskacabins.com.**

| SEAFOOD | QUALITY ★★★ | $9–$19 | SUITABLE FOR KIDS? Y |

A local outfitter turned us on to this eatery, featuring delicious halibut, snapper, and salmon, as well as meats and veggies. The microbrew selection from Alaska's best breweries is much appreciated.

▶ **Ray's Waterfront**   1316 4th Ave., on the waterfront; 907-224-5606.

FUSION/SEAFOOD	QUALITY ★★★★	$9–$34	SUITABLE FOR KIDS? Y

A perennial favorite featuring seafood, steaks, and a nice wine-and-beer list. It gets packed in the summer, and for good reason.

▶ **Resurrect Art Coffee House Gallery**   320 3rd Ave.; 907-224-7161.

ESPRESSO	QUALITY ★★★	$2–$6	SUITABLE FOR KIDS? Y

The name is a mouthful, but the coffee and snacks in this renovated church are wonderful, and the antique tables are fun for just sitting and relaxing. Local artwork is on display here, and local performances are often held (call ahead to find out their schedule).

▶ **Resurrection Roadhouse**   Mile 0.5 Exit Glacier Rd.; 907-224-7116.

FUSION/PIZZA	QUALITY ★★★★	$6–$19	SUITABLE FOR KIDS? Y

The hand-tossed gourmet pizzas are the locals' favorite here, but the restaurant is only open seasonally. The view out the windows and the big, chunky tables and chairs make for a nice dining experience. They also carry a good selection of Alaskan microbrewed beer.

▶ **Sue's Teriyaki Kitchen**   303 S. Harbor; 907-224-4593.

ASIAN	QUALITY ★★★	$5–$16	SUITABLE FOR KIDS? Y

From the outside, the place doesn't look all that remarkable, but Sue's does a good job with basic Asian food, and the limited sushi menu is surprisingly yummy.

Surrounding Areas

▶ **Eagle's Crest/Kenai Princess Lodge**   In Cooper Landing; 800-426-0500; princesslodges.com/kenai_lodge.cfm.

FUSION	QUALITY ★★★★	$9–$31	SUITABLE FOR KIDS? N

This beautiful log lodge also features Eagle's Crest Restaurant, which offers fine dining in a setting of wooded trees and the Kenai River. There's also an espresso bar in the hotel for those needing a midday pick-me-up.

▶ **Tito's Discovery Café**   In Hope at the end of the Hope Highway; 907-782-3274.

AMERICAN	QUALITY ★★★	$6–$15	SUITABLE FOR KIDS? N

The new rebuilt Tito's features the same great food that Alaskans loved at the old, historical Tito's that burned down in 1999. Featuring pies, soups, and chili—all homemade, of course.

PRINCE WILLIAM SOUND

Whittier

▶ **China Sea Restaurant**   907-472-2222.

CHINESE/KOREAN	QUALITY ★★	$5–$14	SUITABLE FOR KIDS? Y

Basic Chinese and Korean food, served in plain but clean surroundings on the water in Whittier.

▶ **Frankie's Deli**   907-472-2477.

SANDWICHES	QUALITY ★★	$5–$10	SUITABLE FOR KIDS? Y

A good place to stop for a quick lunch. Serves sandwiches and other fast fare in Whittier.

▶ **The Inn at Whittier**   907-472-7000; **innatwhittier.com.**

FUSION	QUALITY ★★★★	$8–$29	SUITABLE FOR KIDS? N

The newest and really the only fine-dining option in this tiny community. The menu ranges from stuffed halibut to sesame-crusted salmon to filet mignon.

▶ **Lazy Otter Café and Gifts**   800-587-6887, 907-472-6887, or 907-694-6887; **lazyotter.com.**

AMERICAN	QUALITY ★★★	$5–$9	SUITABLE FOR KIDS? Y

Our fave snack place in Whittier, serving espresso and baked goods.

▶ **Sportsmen Inn Restaurant/Bar**   In the Anchor Inn, off the waterfront, near the residential area; 877-870-8787 or 907-472-2354; **anchorinnwhittier.com.**

AMERICAN/DINER	QUALITY ★★	$4–$21	SUITABLE FOR KIDS? Y

The building's not much to look at, and the inside isn't that fancy either, with Formica tables and vinyl-covered chairs. But it's a local hangout where you can learn more about this tiny community. They serve breakfast, lunch, and dinner, with a diner-style menu ranging from eggs to halibut fish-and-chips to burgers to steaks.

Valdez

▶ **Alaska's Bistro**   At the Valdez Harbor Inn, 100 Fidalgo Dr.; 907-835-5688.

MEDITERRANEAN	QUALITY ★★★★	$7–$34	SUITABLE FOR KIDS? N

A fine-dining experience overlooking the water. A blend of Mediterranean and American dishes and an impressive wine list. Meals range from seafood paella to shrimp and scallops livornese.

▶ **Ernesto's Taqueria**   328 Egan Dr.; 877-835-2800 or 907-835-2519.

MEXICAN	QUALITY ★★★	$5–$17	SUITABLE FOR KIDS? Y

Delicious fresh guacamole and even Mexican-inspired breakfasts. The prices are reasonable too.

▶ **Fu Kung Chinese Restaurant**   207 Kobuk Ave.; 907-835-5255.

CHINESE	QUALITY ★★	$7–$15	SUITABLE FOR KIDS? Y

This Chinese restaurant also dabbles in sushi and other Asian dishes. Apparently, they do it successfully because the restaurant is large and always bustling.

▶ **Mike's Palace**   201 N. Harbor Dr.; 907-835-2365.

GREEK/ITALIAN/TEX-MEX	QUALITY ★★	$6–$24	SUITABLE FOR KIDS? Y

Restaurants that serve wildly different types of ethnic food on the same menu are something you'll see a lot of in small-town Alaska. Take Mike's Palace, which offers an interesting combo of Greek, Italian, and south-of-the-border fare. The menu offers basic burgers, calzones, and pizza. You also can get quesadillas, burritos, or a full steak dinner.

▶ **Pipeline Inn Club**   112 Egan Dr.; 907-835-4444.

STEAKS/SEAFOOD	QUALITY ★★★	$8–$28	SUITABLE FOR KIDS? N

An exclusive and dimly lit restaurant that specializes in steak and seafood. You feel like you should be in the Mafia when you enter the place, but the service and food are excellent.

▶ **The Rose Cache**   321 Egan Dr., in the Main Street Plaza; 907-835-8383.

AMERICAN	QUALITY ★★★★	$9–$16	SUITABLE FOR KIDS? N

Another fine-dining option in town, although this one is open for lunch only. The ornately decorated restaurant serves such specialties as spicy chicken salad, quiche, a soup of the day, and baked macaroni and cheese the way your mother made it. Seatings 11 a.m.–1 p.m. only, and reservations are recommended.

Cordova

▶ **Baja Taco**   At New Harbor, downtown; 907-424-5599 or 907-424-7141; bajatacoak.com.

TEX-MEX	QUALITY ★★★	$5–$12	SUITABLE FOR KIDS? Y

Offering local seafood with Mexican style served out of a red bus, with the menu scrawled on a surfboard. Because it's so close to the harbor and ocean and you can eat outside, the fish tacos seem to taste even better!

▶ **Killer Whale Café**   507 1st Ave., in the back of Orca Book and Sound Co.; 907-424-7733.

CASUAL | QUALITY ★★★ | $5–$10 | SUITABLE FOR KIDS? N

This bookstore-cafe features organic foods, lots of vegetarian choices, and wonderful espresso. It can get busy, and the prices are higher than other choices in town. But you get what you pay for, right?

▶ **Powder House**   Mile 2.1 Copper River Hwy.; 907-424-3529.

AMERICAN/SUSHI | QUALITY ★★★★ | $6–$19 | SUITABLE FOR KIDS? Y

The restaurant features homemade soups, sandwiches, and sushi, as well as fresh fish in season. Dining on the deck is delicious.

▶ **Reluctant Fisherman Inn**   407 Railroad Ave.; 907-424-3272; reluctantfisherman.com.

CASUAL | QUALITY ★★★★ | $6–$18 | SUITABLE FOR KIDS? Y

Our favorite choice for eating because the atmosphere is nice, and the prawns and fish-and-chips are made spot-on every time.

Kodiak Island

Kodiak has several wonderful eating options, including fresh organic food, island-roasted coffee, sushi, fine dining, and local favorites such as beer-battered halibut and pizza. Here are our favorites.

▶ **The Chart Room**   In the Best Western Kodiak Inn; 888-563-4254 or 907-486-5712.

FUSION | QUALITY ★★★★ | $9–$29 | SUITABLE FOR KIDS? Y

The food is well prepared, with a wide selection of modern, innovative seafood and meat dishes, as well as several vegetarian options. The downtown location is a plus.

▶ **Eagle's Nest Restaurant**   In the former Buskin River Inn, now the Comfort Inn Kodiak; 800-544-2202 or 907-487-2700.

FUSION | QUALITY ★★★★ | $9–$29 | SUITABLE FOR KIDS? Y

A local favorite for fine dining, despite owner changes. Features an extensive wine-and-spirits list.

▶ **Galley Gourmet**   800-253-6331 or 907-486-5079; kodiak-alaska-dinner-cruises.com.

CRUISE | QUALITY ★★★★ | $95–$120 | SUITABLE FOR KIDS? N

Now *here's* a way to enjoy dinner. Kodiak residents Marty and Marion Owen offer wonderful onboard dinner cruises that explore the island while enjoying exquisite meals provided by Mill Bay Coffee and Pastries' award-winning French chef Joel Chenet (go two listings down for more on Chenet's wonderful cafe). This outing gets our number-one vote.

▶ **Henry's Great Alaskan Restaurant**   512 Marine Way; 907-486-8844.

AMERICAN/SEAFOOD | QUALITY ★★★ | $5–$19 | SUITABLE FOR KIDS? Y

The beer-battered halibut at this downtown institution is a favorite, and the bar is a hopping place on weekends.

▶ **Mill Bay Coffee and Pastries**   3833 Rezanof Dr.; 907-486-4411; millbaycoffee.com.

BAKERY | QUALITY ★★★★ | $2–$9 | SUITABLE FOR KIDS? Y

French-born Martine and Joel Chenet own this superb pastry shop. They roast their own coffee, and Joel creates works of art with pastries and other sweets. Trained in Paris, he is an award-winning spinner of sugar. Not to be missed.

▶ **The Old Powerhouse Restaurant**   516 E. Marine Way, down by the water, near the bridge; 907-481-1088.

JAPANESE | QUALITY ★★★★ | $7–$29 | SUITABLE FOR KIDS? N

The Old Powerhouse might not be the most appropriate name for a restaurant that specializes in Japanese and wonderful sushi, but we love this place just the same. It is indeed housed in a renovated powerhouse, yet it's so much more. The view over the water is wonderful too—sit at the tables and watch sea lions swim by.

▶ **Second Floor Japanese Restaurant**   116 W. Rezanof Dr., right downtown, across from Alaska Commercial Co.; 907-486-8555.

JAPANESE | QUALITY ★★★ | $7–$26 | SUITABLE FOR KIDS? Y

While the atmosphere is not as nice as the Old Powerhouse's, the sushi and sashimi selections are more diverse and less expensive.

▲ On the Town:
What to Do after the Outdoor Adventure

SOUTHCENTRAL COASTAL ALASKA is a funny place. There's so much happening in the great outdoors that in some of the smaller communities, you might not be able to find much to do that doesn't involve hiking, biking, or paddling somewhere. In some of the larger communities, such as Soldotna and Homer, there is enough to keep you busy day and night, whether it's fishing for halibut or fishing for a hot date at the next bar stool.

We've included some of our favorite by-day or by-night things to do in these towns. The pickings get slim in the more remote communities, but don't worry: there's enough outdoors to keep anyone busy.

KENAI PENINSULA

Kenai

▶ **The Backdoor Lounge**   In the Uptown Motel, 47 Spur View Dr.; 800-777-3650 or 907-283-3660. The pub is a popular spot among locals, with a nice ornate wood bar and an old-timey cash register that looks too fancy to actually use. Features lots of TVs for watching sports; pool tables; and complimentary hors d'oeuvres.

▶ **Challenger Learning Center of Alaska**   9711 Kenai Spur Hwy.; 907-283-2000; **akchallenger.org.** It may seem oddly out of place among all the Alaskan-themed visitor attractions, but the Challenger Learning Center of Alaska is the 39th in a worldwide network of Challenger Centers. These are basically living laboratories for youngsters to learn more about space exploration and the value of math and science, but adults will be mesmerized too.

▶ **Kenai Fine Arts Center**   In Old Town, 810 Cook Ave.; 907-283-7040. This aging building provides studio space for members of the Peninsula Art Guild and the Kenai Potters Guild. There are monthly art exhibitions and an artist sales gallery.

▶ **Kenai Visitors and Cultural Center**   11471 Kenai Spur Hwy.; 907-283-1991. The center was built to celebrate Kenai's 200th anniversary and houses museum displays and exhibits, original and traveling art exhibitions, and all sorts of cultural and natural-history programs. Learn more about the Athabascan, Aleut, and Russian cultures, as well as homesteading, mining, commercial fishing, and the oil industry. The natural-history displays are particularly interesting for children. Admission is $3.

▶ **Old Town Kenai Tour**   This is an easy self-guided endeavor; check at the cultural center for details. The city's Russian heritage can be seen here as you walk by the Holy Assumption of the Virgin Mary Russian Orthodox Church, behind the cultural center. The nearby St. Nicholas Chapel is equally as pretty but in a more rustic manner. Fort Kenay is the log structure built during the 1967 Alaska Purchase centennial to commemorate the original Army fort that was there in the late 1800s. Beluga Lookout, at the end of Main Street, is also worth seeing, if only for the commanding view.

▶ **Peninsula Oilers Baseball**   907-283-7133; **oilersbaseball.com.** Take in a baseball game if the team happens to be playing while you're in town. The Peninsula Oilers are three-time national champions in their minor-league division.

▶ **Veronica's Coffee House**   1506 Tyoyn Way, Historic Old Town Kenai, across from the Russian Church; 907-283-2725. This funky cafe features live entertainment Thursdays, Fridays, and Saturdays in a laid-back atmosphere. It's also a teen magnet.

Soldotna

▶ **Decanter Inn**   907-262-5917. A Kasilof favorite with dim lighting and you-never-know-what playing on the jukebox. Lodging is available if you end up needing it; $85 for singles.

▶ **Go Kart Race Track**   Off Funny River Road and Sterling Highway; 907-262-1562. Have a go at outmaneuvering your friends.

▶ **Homestead Museum**   In Centennial Park; 907-262-3832. Wander through the 6-acre park and take a look at some of these historical homesteaders' cabins that have been relocated. No fee, but donations are encouraged.

Homer

Homer is a happening place, and for those who enjoy nightlife, we have a few must-visits for you to check off your list.

▶ **Alaska Islands and Ocean Visitor Center**   95 Sterling Hwy.; 907-235-6961 or 907-226-4624; islandsandocean.org. Learn more about the Alaska Maritime National Wildlife Refuge, Kachemak Bay, and other protected waters in Alaska at this very comprehensive and nicely designed visitor center.

▶ **Alice's Champagne Palace**   195 Pioneer Ave.; 907-235-0630. This is for the rock 'n' roll crowd, with lots of movement going on; open until 5 a.m. for insomniacs.

▶ **Bayside Lounge**   On Pioneer Avenue. This joint offers up country music for those who like a twang in their nightlife.

▶ **Bear Creek Winery**   On Bear Creek Drive, off East End Road; 907-235-8484; bearcreekwineryalaska.com. Take a drive out to this gorgeous winery if only to see how beautiful it is. Wine tastings are held daily in the summer.

▶ **Beluga Lake Lodge**   204 Ocean Dr.; 907-235-5995. Features live entertainment on the weekends.

▶ **Bunnell Street Gallery**   106 W. Bunnell St.; 907-235-2662; **bunnellstreet gallery.org.** A cross-section of Homer and Alaska artwork is on display here, with shows being held regularly. Concerts, readings, and workshops are also featured.

▶ **Carl E. Wynn Nature Center**   East Hill to East Skyline, drive 1.5 miles; 907-235-6667; akcoastalstudies.org. This tucked-away nature center is a great place to explore the meadows above Homer. Wildflower walks are held in the summer.

▶ **Center for Alaskan Coastal Studies**   907-235-6667; **akcoastalstudies.org.** The organization offers natural-history tours across the bay. They are fully guided and a good way to learn more about the flora and fauna of Homer.

▶ **Duggan's Waterfront Irish Pub**   120 W. Bunnell St.; 907-235-9949. This is fast becoming the place to be on the weekends.

▶ **Homer Brewing Company**   1411 Lake Shore Dr.; 907-235-3626. Stop by this out-of-the-way microbrewery for a sampling of some of Alaska's finest microbrew. Buy a growler of your favorite flavor, and take it to the beach for a bonfire—that's the best nightlife of all.

▶ **Homer Family Theatre**   On Pioneer Avenue; 907-235-6728. The small theater shows movies, sometimes double features, in a fun environment. A perk: they sell snacks that are a cut above the bulk junk food that you find at most movie houses.

▶ **Kenai Peninsula Orchestra**   315 W. Pioneer Ave.; 907-235-4899; **kpoalaska.org.** The group often performs publicly. Check ahead of time to see if you can catch a performance.

▶ **Pier One Theatre**   On the Homer Spit; 907-235-7333; **pieronetheatre.org.** Local live theater during the summer on weekends. General admission is $17. Families pay $50.

▶ **Pratt Museum**   3779 Bartlett St.; 907-235-8635; **prattmuseum.org.** This is an excellent museum of natural history with permanent native Alaskan displays and lots of remnants from the early Homer pioneers. Look for the ship-model display, too, which the kids love. Admission is $6 for adults (and worth it).

▶ **Salty Dawg Saloon**   On the Homer Spit; 907-235-6718. A historical monument with wood shavings on the floor. You'll see rugged types ranging from outdoors preps to grizzled fishermen. It would be a crime to visit Homer and not at least set foot into the place.

Seward

▶ **Alaska SeaLife Center**   301 Railway Ave.; 800-224-2525 or 907-224-6300; **alaskasealife.org.** This state-of-the-art research and education facility takes care of injured or orphaned sea animals with the goal of releasing them back into the wild. Meanwhile, we as visitors get to see them up close. Woody the sea lion is an unbelievably playful creature, for instance, and seems to enjoy it when children walk up to his giant see-through water world. Admission is $20 for adults, $15 for youth. It's an excellent destination for children.

▶ **Explore Exit Glacier**   Reached by Exit Glacier Road just outside of Seward; information is available at Kenai Fjords National Park Service visitor center; 907-224-2131; **nps.gov/kefj.** This is one of the few places where you can actually approach the glacier on foot. Beware, though: the glaciers do calve and can injure or even kill you if the ice lands on you. Stay on marked trails and use common sense.

▶ **IdidaRide Sled Dog Tour**   Mile 1.1 Old Exit Glacier Rd.; 800-478-3139 or 907-224-8607; **ididaride.com.** Visit Iditarod Sled Dog race winner Mitch Seavey's kennel and do an IdidaRide dog-lot tour and cart ride.

▶ **Local Watering Holes**   **Yukon Bar** (Fourth Avenue and Washington Street; 907-224-3063) and the seedier **Pioneer Bar** (406 Washington; 907-224-3161).

▶ **New Seward Hotel and Saloon**   209 5th Ave.; 907-224-3095; **hotelseward alaska.com.** This bar is popular not only among the younger folks but also among those who love oysters. The oyster bar is a great place to enjoy fresh shellfish while washing it down with a cold one.

▶ **Seward Museum**   336 3rd Ave.; 907-224-3902. The museum has an interesting mix of Iditarod memorabilia, state and U.S. flag tidbits, and all sorts of military information. Admission is $4.

PRINCE WILLIAM SOUND

Whittier

▶ **The Anchor Inn**   Off the waterfront, near the residential area; 877-870-8787 or 907-472-2354; **anchorinnwhittier.com.** The inn has an attached restaurant-bar that also features nightly entertainment in the summers. It's not New York City (or even Fargo, North Dakota), but people seem to have a great time.

Valdez

In Valdez, there are a couple of options for day cruising for wildlife and glacier viewing. We like **Stan Stephens Wildlife and Glacier Cruises** (866-867-1297; **stanstephenscruises.com**) because Stephens has been in the business long enough to know the sound intimately. Children are welcome, and the food onboard is delicious. The other companies seem a bit stuffy by comparison.

▶ **Local Watering Holes**   There is no shortage of bars in Valdez, but a few of the ones we like include the **Pipeline Club** (112 Egan Dr.; 907-835-4332), which is a bit on the upscale end but has a friendly crowd; the **Egan Street Pub** (210 Egan Dr.; 907-835-3545); and the **Wheelhouse Lounge** at the Valdez Harbor Inn (100 Fidalgo St.; 907-835-5688).

▶ **Maxine and Jesse Whitney Museum**   At the Valdez airport; 907-834-1690. Featuring an impressive—and completely donated—collection of Eskimo artifacts, animal mounts, a native kayak, and more. Prince William Sound

Community College is the official curator, but the location at the airport makes it convenient for everyone. Admission is $5.

▶ **Valdez Museum and Historical Archive**   217 Egan Dr.; 907-835-2764; **valdez museum.org.** Featuring local history exhibits, with information on native culture, the gold rush, Richardson Highway, and the oil spill. Admission is $5 for adults.

Cordova

▶ **Alaskan Hotel and Bar**   On First Street downtown; 907-424-3299. The bar is your typical place until its Wednesday wine tastings take place in the early-evening hours. Belly up to the bar in your Carhartts and make way for some fine vino.

▶ **Cordova Arts Walks**   These community events take place the first Wednesday of the month during the summer. Area businesses featuring Alaska artwork host salmon samples, and street musicians play fun music.

▶ **Cordova Historical Museum**   At the south end of First Street; 907-424-6665. The cultural heritage of the Chugach, Eyak, and Tlingit peoples is highlighted at the museum. It also has coverage of the *Exxon Valdez* oil spill, which decimated much of the sea life in Prince William Sound in 1989 and still is affecting the ecosystem today. The museum is open daily in the summer.

▶ **Powder House**   Mile 2.1 Copper River Hwy.; 907-424-3529. The bar is a nice place to grab a bite and enjoy some drinks with friends. It features bluegrass, country, folk, and even karaoke, to be enjoyed on the deck overlooking Eyak Lake.

KODIAK ISLAND

▶ **Alutiiq Museum & Archaeological Repository**   215 Mission Rd., Suite 101; 907-486-7004; **alutiiqmuseum.com.** Explore 7,500 years of Kodiak native history at this interesting museum. Usually closed on Sundays. Admission is $3 for adults.

▶ **Baranov Museum–Kodiak Historical Society**   101 Marine Way; 907-486-5920; **baranov.us.** This museum, located in the renovated Erskine House, focuses on the Russian influence of Kodiak Island but also has plenty of cultural and natural artifacts from the Alutiiq peoples. Admission is $3 for adults.

▶ **Kodiak Alutiiq Dancers**   713 Rezanof St.; 907-486-4449. This talented group performs daily in the summer, telling stories through music and drumming. Performances are at 2:30 p.m. in a *barabara,* the traditional Alutiiq dwelling.

▶ **Kodiak Launch Complex**   Mile 15.2 Pasagshak Bay Rd.; take the Chiniak Highway to its intersection with the Pasagshak Bay Road; the complex is on the left side. A $38 million low-Earth-orbit launch facility on 27 acres was recently completed at Cape Narrow. It is operated by the Alaska Aerospace Development Corporation and is the only commercial launch range in the United States that is not colocated with a federal facility. You can't go inside the center, and security is pretty tight, but you can drive by just to say you've seen it. Occasionally there will be public events; check at the visitor center for possibilities.

▶ **The Mecca Bar**   302 W. Marine Way; 907-486-3364. The dancing, drinking, and meeting place in Kodiak—the local saying is that you haven't experienced Kodiak until you've been "Mecca-nized." But don't expect anything fancy— this is a fishing town, after all. There are two bars, a dance floor, and live music on the weekends. Clientele runs the gamut.

▶ **Village Bar**   On the mall in downtown Kodiak; 907-486-3412. A cowboy's hangout, although there are wine nights and other special events, as well as big-screen TVs for sports lovers.

PART FOURTEEN

SOUTHEAST ALASKA
home of glaciers and whales

▲ An Overview of the Inside Passage

ON A MAP, Southeast Alaska looks like an afterthought, following the spine of British Columbia like a long, skinny snake. It's easy to wonder why it's even part of Alaska. The narrow, island-studded strip of land seems almost inconsequential. (See Part One, page 8, for a map of the region.)

Of course, that is the furthest thing from the truth. The fact is that Southeast Alaska—or the Panhandle, as it is often called—has some of the most stunning scenery in the state. It has more than 1,000 islands, all of them surrounded by or filled with waterfalls, streams, rivers, and

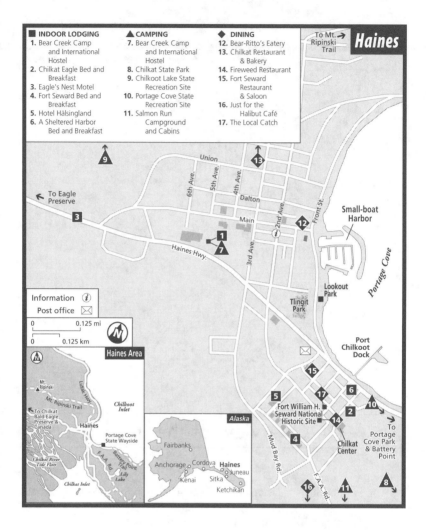

■ INDOOR LODGING
1. Bear Creek Camp and International Hostel
2. Chilkat Eagle Bed and Breakfast
3. Eagle's Nest Motel
4. Fort Seward Bed and Breakfast
5. Hotel Hälsingland
6. A Sheltered Harbor Bed and Breakfast

▲ CAMPING
7. Bear Creek Camp and International Hostel
8. Chilkat State Park
9. Chilkoot Lake State Recreation Site
10. Portage Cove State Recreation Site
11. Salmon Run Campground and Cabins

◆ DINING
12. Bear-Ritto's Eatery
13. Chilkat Restaurant & Bakery
14. Fireweed Restaurant
15. Fort Seward Restaurant & Saloon
16. Just for the Halibut Café
17. The Local Catch

Haines

oceans that create lush old-growth forests. The snow-covered mountains and seemingly infinite number of glaciers are the backdrop to it all.

Southeast is a land of culture and history too. It is home to the Tlingit, Haida, and Tsimshian native peoples who made Southeast Alaska their home before the United States even existed. Their artwork is incredible, with totem poles and carvings that depict a way of life centered on their connections with the land and animals of the area.

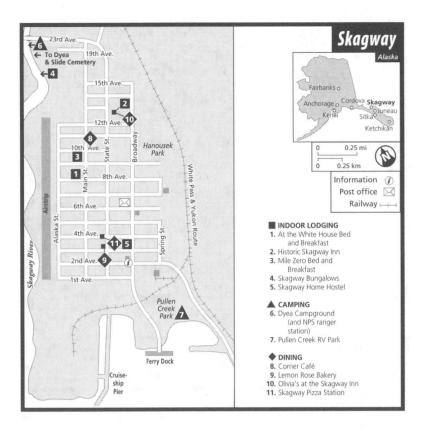

Skagway

Alaska

0   0.25 mi
0   0.25 km

Information ⓘ
Post office ✉
Railway ├──┤

■ INDOOR LODGING
1. At the White House Bed and Breakfast
2. Historic Skagway Inn
3. Mile Zero Bed and Breakfast
4. Skagway Bungalows
5. Skagway Home Hostel

▲ CAMPING
6. Dyea Campground (and NPS ranger station)
7. Pullen Creek RV Park

◆ DINING
8. Corner Café
9. Lemon Rose Bakery
10. Olivia's at the Skagway Inn
11. Skagway Pizza Station

The Panhandle's turn-of-the-century gold-rush history lives on as well. In communities such as **Skagway** and **Juneau,** there are many ways to learn more about the stampede for gold that turned this sleepy sliver of land into a boomtown almost overnight. Museums, businesses, and even entire national parks are devoted to preserving that history, and today's visitor has easy access to it.

About three-fourths of the 500-mile-long Southeast region is part of **Tongass National Forest,** so there is no shortage of land to explore. Southeast is one of the premier spots for water sports such as kayaking and rafting. Backpackers will like some of its historical trails, as well as the trailless adventures that can be had from just about any mountaintop location.

And then there is the **Inside Passage,** the destination of most Alaska adventure cruises available to today's traveler. The Inside Passage is the sheltered

Downtown Juneau

To Mendenhall Valley, Airport, & Auke Bay

Evergreen Cemetery

Cope Park

North Park

Harris Harbor

To Douglas

Alaska

Fairbanks

Anchorage Cordova **Juneau**
Kenai Sitka
Ketchikan

Church
Information
Post office

0   0.125 mi
0   0.125 km

Gastineau Channel

Seaplane Dock

Tourist Info
Marine Park
Cruise-ship Dock

To Thane

INDOOR LODGING
1. Alaska's Capital Inn
2. Juneau International Hostel
3. Westmark Baranof Hotel

DINING
4. Douglas Café
5. El Sombrero
6. Kenny's Wok and Teriyaki

7. Thane Ore House
   and Salmon Bake
8. Wild Spice Restaurant
9. Zen Restaurant

seawater that surrounds the Panhandle, providing excellent protected-water adventures for cruise ships, kayaks, even the occasional rowboat.

The communities that make up the Panhandle are as varied as the scenery, but one thing you will notice immediately is how friendly everyone is. Southeastern Alaskans long ago discovered that one of their greatest assets is their land—the glaciers and whales and mountains that lure so many visitors this far north in the first place. Tourism has become one of the primary industries for the area, and the people know that visitors are their livelihood.

Southeast Alaska's climate is a bit rainier than the rest of the state's, and it is often fogged in or experiences days on end of drizzle and dampness. The temperatures are warmer too, and when the rest of the state is getting snow, Southeast Alaska often just gets more rain. Take one look at a cascading

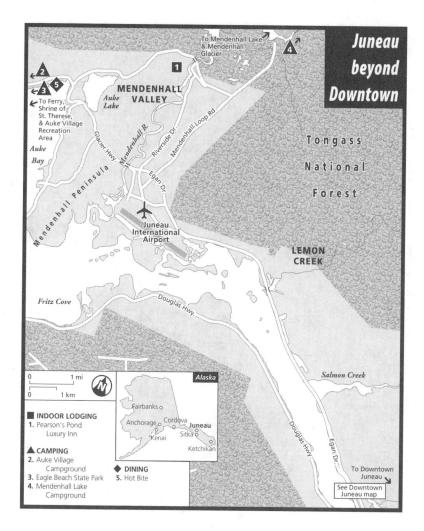

Juneau beyond Downtown

To Mendenhall Lake & Mendenhall Glacier

4

1

2
3 **5**

To Ferry, Shrine of St. Therese, & Auke Village Recreation Area

MENDENHALL VALLEY

Auke Lake

Auke Bay

Mendenhall Peninsula

Glacier Hwy.

Mendenhall R.

Riverside Dr.

Mendenhall Loop Rd.

Egan Dr.

Juneau International Airport

Tongass National Forest

LEMON CREEK

Fritz Cove

Douglas Hwy.

Salmon Creek

Douglas Hwy.

Egan Dr.

0   1 mi
0   1 km

Alaska

Fairbanks

Anchorage   Cordova   Juneau

Kenai   Sitka

Ketchikan

■ **INDOOR LODGING**
1. Pearson's Pond Luxury Inn

▲ **CAMPING**
2. Auke Village Campground
3. Eagle Beach State Park
4. Mendenhall Lake Campground

◆ **DINING**
5. Hot Bite

To Downtown Juneau

See Downtown Juneau map

waterfall or behemoth Sitka spruce, and you'll see that it is this rainy climate that gives the area such beauty.

This chapter focuses on the largest communities through which you may travel while headed for your ultimate outdoor destination. These are the places where you can gear up and move out, but surprisingly, many of them have amenities that rival anything found in cities with millions of

continued on page 410

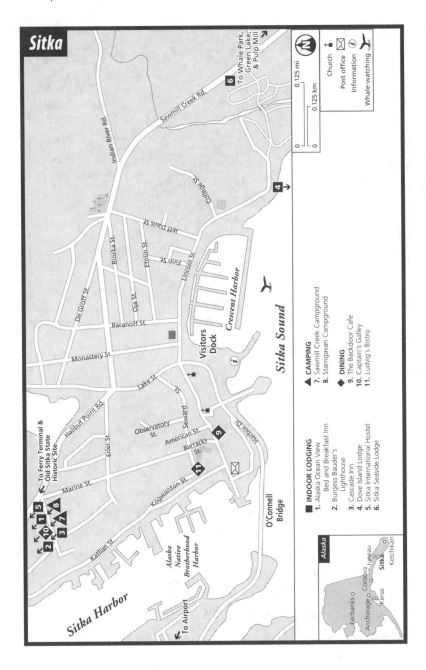

Sitka

To Whale Park, Green Lake, & Pulp Mill

Sawmill Creek Rd.

Indian River Rd.

College St.

Jeff Davis St.

Biorka St.

Etolin St.

Finn St.

Lincoln St.

De Groff St.

Oja St.

Baranoff St.

Crescent Harbor

Monastery St.

Lake St.

Halibut Point Rd.

Visitors Dock

Sitka Sound

Observatory St.

Seward St.

American St.

Barracks St.

Harbor Dr.

Erler St.

Marine St.

Kogwanton St.

Katlian St.

Alaska Native Brotherhood Harbor

O'Connell Bridge

To Ferry Terminal & Old Sitka State Historic Site

Sitka Harbor

To Airport

0.125 mi
0.125 km

† Church
⊠ Post office
ⓘ Information
✈ Whale-watching

■ INDOOR LODGING
1. Alaska Ocean View Bed and Breakfast Inn
2. Burgess Bauder's Lighthouse
3. Cascade Inn
4. Dove Island Lodge
5. Sitka International Hostel
6. Sitka Seaside Lodge

▲ CAMPING
7. Sawmill Creek Campground
8. Starrigavan Campground

◆ DINING
9. The Backdoor Cafe
10. Captain's Galley
11. Ludvig's Bistro

Alaska
Fairbanks
Anchorage Cordova Juneau
Kenai Sitka
Ketchikan

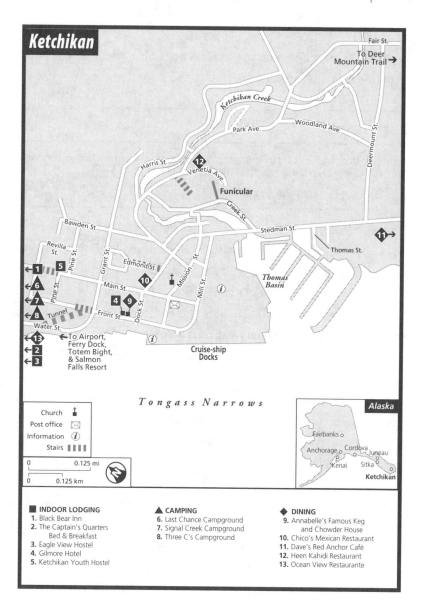

Ketchikan

To Deer Mountain Trail →

Fair St.

Ketchikan Creek

Park Ave.

Woodland Ave.

Deermount St.

Harris St.

12

Venetia Ave.

Funicular

Creek St.

Bawden St.

Stedman St.

Revilla St.

Pine St.

Grant St.

Edmond St.

Main St.

10

Mission St.

Mill St.

(i)

Thomas St.

11→

Thomas Basin

1←

5

6←

7←

8←

Tunnel

Pine St.

4 **9**

Dock St.

Front St.

Water St.

13←

2←

3←

←To Airport, Ferry Dock, Totem Bight, & Salmon Falls Resort

(i)

Cruise-ship Docks

T o n g a s s   N a r r o w s

Church ✝

Post office ✉

Information *(i)*

Stairs ▮▮▮▮

| 0 | | 0.125 mi |
| 0 | | 0.125 km |

Alaska

Fairbanks ○

Anchorage ○

Cordova ○

Juneau ○

Kenai ○

Sitka ○

Ketchikan

■ **INDOOR LODGING**
1. Black Bear Inn
2. The Captain's Quarters Bed & Breakfast
3. Eagle View Hostel
4. Gilmore Hotel
5. Ketchikan Youth Hostel

▲ **CAMPING**
6. Last Chance Campground
7. Signal Creek Campground
8. Three C's Campground

◆ **DINING**
9. Annabelle's Famous Keg and Chowder House
10. Chico's Mexican Restaurant
11. Dave's Red Anchor Café
12. Heen Kahidi Restaurant
13. Ocean View Restaurante

continued from page 407

people. We have created subchapters for Haines, Skagway, Juneau (Alaska's capital), Sitka, and Ketchikan.

▲ Haines

> **HAINES CONVENTION AND VISITORS BUREAU**
>
> 907-766-2234 | haines.ak.us

Haines is one of only two Southeast communities accessible by road. From the Alaska Highway, the northbound traveler can turn onto the Haines Highway and reach a community that has a reputation as one of the driest in the region. At the northern end of America's longest fjord, Haines shares a border with 20 million acres of protected wilderness. It is located on the western shore of **Lynn Canal,** between the **Chilkoot and Chilkat rivers.**

Haines is 80 air miles northwest of Juneau and 600 air miles southeast of Anchorage and Fairbanks. By road, it is 775 miles from Anchorage. It also can be reached by marine ferry. It has cool maritime summers, with temperatures in the 60°F range, and mild winters. Total precipitation averages 52 inches a year, with 133 inches of snowfall.

The community is home to about 1,500 year-round residents and more wildlife than you can count. Whales are common, and bald eagles flock here by the thousands. In fact, Haines is home to one of the largest bald-eagle congregations in the world, and each fall the entire town turns out to celebrate the arrival of the birds there to follow the late salmon runs of November.

Haines was at one time called *Dei Shu* ("end of the trail") by the Tlingit. The first nonnative to settle here was trader George Dickinson, who came to the area in 1880. In 1881, a Presbyterian minister received permission from the Chilkat Tlingits to build a mission and school, which eventually was named in honor of Francina Electra Haines, who was active in the Presbyterian Women's Executive Society of Home Missions. As the area became more and more developed with nonnative people, the name *Haines* stuck.

Haines has a military background too. The first permanent U.S. military installation, Fort William H. Seward, was constructed in 1904, and in 1910 the city was incorporated. Until World War II, it was the only U.S. Army post in Alaska.

Commercial fishing, timber, government, and tourism are the primary employers. Around 45,000 cruise-ship passengers visit every year. The **Chilkat Bald Eagle Preserve** also draws visitors from around the world.

▲ Skagway

> **SKAGWAY CONVENTION & VISITORS BUREAU**
> 907-983-2854 | skagway.com

Skagway is 90 miles northeast of Juneau at the northernmost end of **Lynn Canal,** and the only other Southeast Alaska community that is accessible by road. Take the Klondike Highway from the Alaska Highway, and you will land in this tiny town whose identity is entirely consumed with its rich gold-rush past. You can also reach Skagway by air or marine ferry and cruise ship.

The climate is pleasant in Skagway, with cool summers and mild winters. The average temperature in the summer rarely rises above 65°F, and in the winter there are many days above freezing. With the surrounding mountains as a shroud, the area is also protected from the frequent Southeast rains, so Skagway, like Haines, gets below-average rainfall—averaging 26 inches of precipitation per year, along with 39 inches of snow.

The town is small, with only 850 year-round residents, most of whom make their living through tourism. In fact, much of the town today makes up what is part of **Klondike Gold Rush National Historical Park.** In 1898, when gold was first discovered in the area, the town ballooned with nearly 20,000 would-be prospectors. Many of them were earnest, working hard and finding their gold. Others were up to no good, wreaking havoc wherever they went and turning Skagway into a lawless place.

Those days were short-lived. After the gold disappeared, the town shrank to its original, smaller size, and that's what visitors get to appreciate today. The smaller population is much more conducive to the surrounding area, and a perfect place from which to launch an outdoor adventure.

Primary among the outdoor lures of Skagway is the 33-mile **Chilkoot Pass Trail,** one of two trails used by the gold seekers to reach the headwaters of the **Yukon River,** where the gold was thought to be. The 40-mile **White Pass Trail** began at Skagway and paralleled the present-day route of the **White Pass** and **Yukon Railway.** For more details on hiking the Chilkoot, go to page 91.

▲ Juneau

> **JUNEAU CONVENTION AND VISITORS BUREAU**
> 1 Sealaska Plaza, Suite 305
> Juneau 99801-1245
> 907-586-1737 | traveljuneau.com

Located on the mainland of Southeast Alaska, opposite **Douglas Island,** Juneau was built at the center of the Inside Passage along the **Gastineau Channel** and is the capital of Alaska (many people mistakenly assume that Anchorage is). Juneau is 900 air miles northwest of Seattle and 577 air miles southeast of Anchorage. Most people arrive here by plane, cruise ship, or marine ferry. During the summer, Juneau's population of 31,000 doubles as cruise-ship passengers disembark to explore this city by the water.

And it is a beautiful city. **Mendenhall Glacier, Juneau Ice Field, Tracy Arm Fjord Glacier,** the **Alaska State Museum,** and the **Mount Roberts Tramway** are among the local attractions. There are plenty of hiking and birding opportunities to be found. The fishing is incredible. Outdoor travelers will especially like the kayaking options.

Juneau has mild but often wet weather, which is the norm for most of this region. The average summer temperature ranges 45°F–65°F, although most days it is closer to 60°F. In the winter, the mercury stays around 25°F–

35°F. Annual precipitation is 92 inches in downtown Juneau, and 54 inches 10 miles north at the airport. Snowfall averages 101 inches.

Tlingit Indians were the first known inhabitants of Juneau, and the area was a good source of harvesting salmon. By the late 1800s, as fortune seekers discovered Alaska's wealth of gold, Juneau became yet another gold-rush town. In 1900, the city of Juneau was formed, named for one of those prospectors. At the time, Sitka was the capital of the territory of Alaska, but by 1906, officials moved it to the more bustling Juneau, where active mining was going on.

Today, government is the heart of Juneau, and when the legislature is in session between January and May, the population increases. Tourism also is a major employer, adding about 2,000 seasonal jobs to the area. Nearly 700,000 visitors arrive by cruise ship, and another 100,000 independent travelers visit Juneau each year.

▲ Sitka

SITKA CONVENTION AND VISITORS BUREAU
907-747-5940 | sitka.org

Sitka is on the west coast of Baranof Island along the Pacific Ocean on **Sitka Sound.** Its most noticeable natural feature is **Mount Edgecumbe,** an extinct volcano rising some 3,200 feet above the community. It is 95 air miles southwest of Juneau and 185 miles northwest of Ketchikan. Seattle is 862 air miles to the south. Visitors to Alaska often comment that Sitka is the prettiest town of all, and we tend to agree that it is indeed beautiful. Of all the towns in Southeast Alaska, we think that Sitka is the most picturesque, although outdoor opportunities are more abundant in such places as Skagway and Haines.

Sitka temperatures are a bit cooler than the rest of Southeast Alaska, with winter temperatures dipping into the teens sometimes. In the summer, the temperature range is 48°F–61°F. Average annual precipitation is 96 inches, including 39 inches of snowfall.

About 8,800 people call Sitka home year-round. This historical community was originally inhabited by a major tribe of Tlingits, who called the village *Shee Atika*. It was discovered by Vitus Bering's Russian expedition in
1741, and the site became New Archangel in 1799. A tumultuous few years
followed as the Russians fought for power and the Tlingits fought to keep
their land. By 1808, Sitka was the capital of Russian Alaska, and it remained
the center of trade and commerce for years. After the United States purchased
Alaska in 1867, Sitka remained the capital of the territory until 1906, when
the seat of government was moved to Juneau.

Sitka's economy centers on fishing, fish processing, and tourism. Cruise
ships bring more than 200,000 visitors annually. Access to the area is by
cruise ship, marine ferry, or airlines. The local airport offers daily jet service
from the Lower 48 states and the rest of Alaska.

▲ Ketchikan

KETCHIKAN CONVENTION AND VISITORS BUREAU
131 Front St.
Ketchikan 99901
907-225-6166 | **visit-ketchikan.com**

Ketchikan is on the southwestern coast of **Revillagigedo Island,** opposite Gravina
Island, near the southern boundary of Alaska. It is 679 miles north of Seattle
and 235 miles south of Juneau. Many call Ketchikan the "Gateway to Alaska"
because it often is the first port of call for cruise ships coming from the south.

The 2.2-million-acre **Misty Fjords National Monument** is the highlight of
the Ketchikan area, and it attracts kayakers by the hundreds. But there also
are numerous other outdoor activities to pursue, including hiking, fishing,
birding, and canoeing.

The area lies in the maritime climate zone and enjoys warmer-than-average
winters than its neighbors, with temperatures above freezing for much of the
winter. Summer temperatures are in the 50°F–65°F range. The area gets lots of

rain, though, with an average of 162 inches of precipitation annually, including 32 inches of snowfall.

Ketchikan's population is about 7,600. The town's name comes from the Tlingit word *kitschk-hin,* meaning "thundering wings of an eagle." Fishing and fish processing is one of the mainstays of the local economy, as is timber harvesting, which peaked in the late 1980s and 1990s before declining sharply. Ketchikan's pulp mill closed in 1997, after its 50-year contract with the U.S. Forest Service for timber was canceled.

Tourism is important to Ketchikan, with more than 650,000 cruise-ship passengers visiting the area each summer. Another half-million independent travelers come to the town as well. It is the ideal jumping-off point for such trips as mountain biking on **Prince of Wales Island,** backpacking in Misty Fjords, or kayaking in the Inside Passage.

Regular jet service comes and goes from Ketchikan daily. Access also is via **Alaska Marine Highway** ferry and cruise ship.

> **TRAVELER'S TIP**
>
> ▶ Backpacking in Glacier Bay requires a backcountry permit and orientation. This park, like Denali National Park and Preserve, limits its backcountry visitors to maintain the wild feel of the area. The best way to see the park, however, is by kayak or boat.

▲ Wild Lands

GLACIER BAY NATIONAL PARK AND PRESERVE

GLACIER BAY NATIONAL PARK AND PRESERVE
907-697-2230 | nps.gov/glba

Primary activities:
cruising, kayaking, rafting, mountaineering

Glacier Bay National Park and Preserve has snow-covered mountain ranges rising to more than 15,000 feet, coastal beaches with protected coves, deep fjords, tidewater glaciers, coastal waters, and freshwater lakes. It is the ideal place to visit for paddlers. **Alaska Airlines** provides daily jet service from Seattle via Juneau during the summer and a more limited schedule in the winter. Air taxis in the outlying communities also can take you to the park. There is a passenger ferry to the town of **Gustavus,** but there's no way to bring your own vehicle to the area. A private car-rental operation in Gustavus and a few taxis can get you where you need to go (visit **nps.gov/glba for details**). Otherwise, most lodge and B&B owners provide transportation from the airport to your lodging.

TONGASS NATIONAL FOREST

> **TONGASS NATIONAL FOREST**
> Federal Building
> 648 Mission St.
> Ketchikan 99901
> 907-225-3101 | **fs.fed.us/r10/tongass**

Primary activities: *bear viewing, fishing*

Tongass National Forest, at nearly 17 million acres, is the largest unit in the national-forest system, and recreation opportunities abound here. Mountain biking, backpacking, hiking, fishing, and birding are all popular activities within the forest.

Access to the forest is available from just about every community in Southeast Alaska, but as with most areas here, you'll probably need to fly in to get where you want to go. The Tongass is one of only two national forests in the country to which you can't drive. You can, however, take your vehicle to **Haines** or **Skagway,** get on the **Alaska Marine Highway ferry,** and head to **Ketchikan** or **Juneau. Alaska Airlines** provides daily jet service into the major towns of the Panhandle—Ketchikan, Sitka, and Juneau. From there, charter flights on smaller planes are available to the other towns as well as to remote cabins and lakes.

About 150 cabins are scattered throughout Tongass National Forest. They cost $25–$45 a night and make a great base camp for any outdoor adventure within the area. For specific details on reserving the cabins, go to the special-interest chapters to explore each activity individually.

MISTY FJORDS NATIONAL MONUMENT

MISTY FJORDS NATIONAL MONUMENT
3031 Tongass Ave.
Ketchikan 99901
907-225-2148 | **fs.fed.us/r10/tongass**

Primary activities: *hiking, kayaking, fishing*

The remote Misty Fjords National Monument covers about 3,570 square miles of land and coastal habitat, including several major rivers and hundreds of streams. The monument is part of Tongass National Forest and managed as such. It is located in the southernmost part of the region, from **Dixon Entrance** to beyond the **Unuk River.** The closest community is Ketchikan.

CHILKAT BALD EAGLE PRESERVE–ALASKA STATE PARKS

ALASKA STATE PARKS
Haines Ranger Station
907-766-2292; **dnr.alaska.gov/parks/units/eagleprv.htm**

Primary activities:
birding, fishing, kayaking, rafting

The Chilkat Bald Eagle Preserve was created in 1982 to protect the world's largest concentration of bald eagles and their habitat. It also protects the

TRAVELER'S TIP

▶ Hiking the Chilkoot
Pass Trail, which trav-
els through Klondike
Gold Rush National
Historic Park into Can-
ada, requires permits
and fees. Have your
passport ready too.

natural salmon runs that pass through each year. The
preserve consists of 48,000 acres of river bottomland
of the **Chilkat, Kleheni, and Tsirku rivers** and is an excellent place for water sports. Birders by the thousands
flock to the area in the fall to watch the eagles during
spawning season.

The preserve is accessible by road along the Haines
Highway, or travelers can reach the area by flying
directly into Haines and driving the road from town.
Birding must be done from a distance.

KLONDIKE GOLD RUSH NATIONAL HISTORICAL PARK

KLONDIKE GOLD RUSH NATIONAL HISTORICAL PARK
Second Avenue and Broadway Street
907-983-2921 or 907-983-2921 | nps.gov/klgo/index_old.htm

Primary activities:
backpacking, camping, hiking

Klondike Gold Rush National Historical Park exists to celebrate the Klondike gold rush of 1897–98. It has 15 restored buildings within the Skagway
Historic District and also manages the well-known **Chilkoot Pass Trail,** which
prospectors followed to reach the gold fields. The park also administers a
small portion of the **White Pass Trail.**

About 843,000 visitors came to the 13,000-acre national park last year,
mostly by means of cruise ships that offload thousands of passengers at a
time into the tiny community of Skagway. You can also fly into Skagway from
Juneau or take the South Klondike Highway from Whitehorse, Yukon Territory, into town.

▲ Getting around Southeast Alaska

HAINES

Access is through **Alaska Airlines** (800-252-7522; **alaskaair.com**) by air and **Alaska Marine Highway ferry** (800-642-0066; **ferryalaska.com**) by water. You can also drive to Haines from Canada by taking the Haines Highway off the Alaska Highway.

Affordable Cars   Located in the Captain's Choice Motel, Second Avenue and Dalton Street. Cars are $75 a day, with unlimited mileage. 800-478-2345 or 907-766-3111; **capchoice.com**.

Eagle's Nest Car Rental   Located at Eagle's Nest Motel, Mile 1 Haines Hwy. Cars start at $49 a day, with 100 free miles (40¢ a mile after that). 800-354-6009 or 907-766-2891; **alaskaeagletours.com/carrental.htm**.

SKAGWAY

Access is through **Alaska Airlines** (800-252-7522; **alaskaair.com**) by air or **Alaska Marine Highway ferry** (800-642-0066; **ferryalaska.com**) by water. You can also get to Skagway by taking the Klondike Highway off the Alaska Highway.

Municipal Bus Service   Skagway Municipal and Regional Transit, 1325 State St.; 907-983-2743 or 907-723-3536; $2 to get into town, $5 all-day pass.

Dyea Dave's Shuttle and Tours   907-209-5031. Open seasonally, this outfit can deliver you where you need to go.

Avis Rent A Car   Third Avenue, in the Westmark Hotel; 800-331-1212 or 907-983-2247; **avis.com**. Rates start at $65.

Sourdough Vehicle & Bicycle Rentals   351 6th Ave.; 907-983-2523 or 907-209-5026; **sourdoughrentals.com**. This is our choice because they are family-owned and rent vehicles that can handle the roads; rates are $80–$140 a day.

JUNEAU

Access is through **Alaska Airlines** (800-252-7522; **alaskaair.com**) by air or **Alaska Marine Highway ferry** (800-642-0066; **ferryalaska.com**) by water.

Kipco Auto Rental   Located at the Juneau airport; 907-796-2880. This is a good choice for travelers needing vans or larger-capacity vehicles.

Budget Rent-A-Car   Located at the Juneau Airport; 800-796-1086. An affordable choice for vehicles with unlimited miles.

Hertz Rent a Car   Located at the Juneau Airport; 907-789-9494; **hertz.com.**

Evergreen Taxi   907-586-2121. For around-town destinations.

SITKA

Access is through **Alaska Airlines** (800-252-7522; **alaskaair.com**) by air or **Alaska Marine Highway ferry** (800-642-0066; **ferryalaska.com**) by water.

North Star Rent-A-Car   Located at the Sitka airport; 800-722-6927 or 907-966-2552.

Airport Shuttle   907-747-8443. Provides transportation to the downtown area or to any accommodations during the summer only. Rate is $6 one-way, $8 round-trip.

Ferry Shuttle   907-747-8443. Available at the terminal upon all ferry arrivals. Rate is $8 one-way, $10 round-trip.

Hank's Taxi & Tour Service   907-747-8888; **hankstours.com.** We like Hank because he's smoke-free!

Transit Shuttle   907-747-7290. The shuttle makes regular passes through town, stopping at all the highlights. Get on and drop off as often as you wish; $10 for an all-day pass or $5 for a round-trip.

Yellow Jersey Cycle Shop   Located at 329 Harbor Dr.; 907-747-6317; **yellow jerseycycles.com.** If you want to get around by bike, try this shop, which rents by the day or week.

KETCHIKAN

Access is through **Alaska Airlines** (800-252-7522; **alaskaair.com**) by air or **Alaska Marine Highway ferry** (800-642-0066; **ferryalaska.com**) by water.

Ketchikan Gateway Borough Transit (907-225-8726) operates seven days a week. Fares start at $1; buses run hourly.

▲ Gearing Up

MOST OF THE larger communities of Southeast Alaska have places to resupply or buy gear that you may have forgotten.

Grocery stores in the area are surprisingly well stocked, and fresh food is readily available. Note, however, that you may not have such luck if you travel beyond the major towns covered in this chapter.

Check with the air carriers on which you will be traveling for regulations on carrying items such as knives, guns, campstoves, and camp fuel. Many airlines no longer even allow lighters on board, so these are items you may need to purchase at your destination and leave behind when flying home.

This section of the book is broken down by the main communities in Southeast with shops that will help you find what you're looking for. We list sporting goods/camping supplies and groceries separately, but many stores carry a little of everything—a characteristic of Alaska stores that you will soon notice is commonplace.

> **TRAVELER'S TIP**
>
> ▶ When shopping for food in Southeast Alaska, be prepared to pay higher-than-average prices, especially on perishable items such as milk, vegetables, and fruits.

SPORTING GOODS AND CAMPING SUPPLIES

Haines

▶ **Alaska Backcountry Outfitter Store**   Main Street; 907-766-2876. Offers skiing, snowboard, camping, and climbing gear.

▶ **Outfitter Sporting Goods**   Mile o Haines Hwy.; 907-767-3221. Hiking, camping, and climbing gear; hunting and fishing supplies too.

Skagway

▶ **The Mountain Shop**   355 4th Ave., 907-983-2544; **packerexpeditions.com.**
Gear shop operated by adventure-travel outfitter Packer Adventures;
sells apparel, camping supplies, and sporting goods.

▶ **Sockeye Cycle Co.**   381 5th Ave., 907-983-2851; **cyclealaska.com.**
Offers bike repairs and supplies.

Juneau

▶ **Alaska Paddle Sports**   800 6th St.; 907-463-5678. For paddling gear
and accessories.

▶ **Foggy Mountain Shop**   800 6th St.; 907-586-6780. For backpacking,
mountaineering, and skiing.

▶ **Fred Meyer**   8181 Old Glacier Hwy.; 800-478-9944 or 907-789-6500. Sells camping equipment, sporting goods, fishing licenses, and full-service groceries.

▶ **Juneau Flyfishing Goods**   175 S. Franklin St., Floor 2; 907-586-3754.
Fishing gear and licenses are available here.

▶ **Mountain Gears**   126 Front St.; 907-586-4327. Outdoor gear and
bike supplies.

▶ **Nugget Alaskan Outfitter**   8745 Glacier Hwy.; 907-789-0956; **nuggetoutfitter.com.**
Outdoor clothing, footwear, and raingear.

Sitka

▶ **Baidarka Boats**   201 Lincoln St., Suite 201; 907-747-8996.

▶ **Mac's Sporting Goods**   213 Harbor Dr.; 907-747-6970.

▶ **Murray Pacific Supply**   475 Katlian St.; 907-747-3171.

▶ **Work & Rugged Gear Store**   407 Lincoln St., Suite F; 907-747-6238.
Outerwear and footwear for those frequent rainy days.

▶ **Yellow Jersey Cycle Shop**   329 Harbor Dr.; 907-747-6317;
yellowjerseycycles.com.

Ketchikan

▶ **Alaska Wilderness Outfitting**   3857 Fairview Ave.; 907-225-7335.

▶ **Bob's Guns and Sporting Goods**   685 Pond Reef Rd. N.; 907-247-8139.

▶ **Murray Pacific Supply**   1050 Water St.; 907-225-3135.

▶ **The Outfitter**   201 Dock St.; 907-225-5101.

▶ **Plaza Sports**   2415 Hemlock Ave.; Suite 1110; 907-225-1587.

GROCERY

Haines

▶ **Alaska Meat & Grocery**   420 Main St.; 907-766-2441. Full-service grocery store.

▶ **Howsers IGA**   335 Main St.; 907-766-2040. Full-service grocery store.

▶ **Mountain Market & Mountain Spirits**   289 3rd Ave. and Haines Highway; 907-766-3340. Specializing in natural foods, beer, wine, and spirits.

Skagway

▶ **Fairway Market**   377 State St.; 907-983-2220. Full-service groceries.

▶ **You Say Tomato**   872 State St.; 907-983-2784. Open year-round; more-specialized and organic groceries.

Juneau

▶ **Carrs-Safeway**   3033 Vintage Blvd.; 907-790-5500. Offering full-service groceries; fishing licenses, and some camping and fishing gear.

▶ **Costco Wholesale**   5225 Commercial Blvd.; 888-556-4333 or 907-780-6740. Offering bulk groceries, as well as some camping and sporting goods, depending on supplies. Entrance requires membership.

▶ **Fred Meyer**   8181 Old Glacier Hwy.; 800-478-9944 or 907-789-6500. Offering camping equipment, sporting goods, fishing licenses, and full-service groceries.

Sitka

▶ **Cascade Convenience Center**   2035 Halibut Point Rd.; 907-747-8313. Small selection of groceries.

▶ **Lakeside Grocery**   705 Halibut Point Rd.; 907-747-3317. Full-service groceries.

▶ **Sea Mart**   210 Baranof St.; 907-747-6686. Full-service groceries.

▶ **Sea Mart**   1867 Halibut Point Rd.; 907-747-6266. Full-service groceries.

Ketchikan

▶ **Carrs-Safeway**   2417 Tongass Ave.; 907-228-1900.

▶ **JR's Grocery**   407 Dock St.; 907-225-7489.

▶ **Lighthouse Grocery & Liquor**   10750 N. Tongass Hwy.; 907-247-2626.

▶ **Sea Mart Supermarket**   2417 Tongass Ave.; 907-225-9880.

▶ **Tatsuda IGA**   633 Stedman St.; 907-225-4125.

▶ **Ward Cove Market & Liquor**   7196 N. Tongass Hwy.; 907-247-8200.

▶ **Woodenwheel Cove Trading** Post   29 Port Protection; 907-489-2222.

▲ southeast alaska indoor lodging

NAME	LODGING TYPE	QUALITY RATING	VALUE RATING	COST
HAINES				
Bear Creek Camp and International Hostel	Hostel/ cabins	★★★★	★★★★★	$18–$48
Chilkat Eagle Bed and Breakfast	B&B	★★★★	★★★★	$80
Eagle's Nest Motel	Motel	★★	★★★	$85–$95
Fort Seward Bed and Breakfast	B&B	★★★★	★★★	$95–$259
Hotel Hälsingland	Hotel	★★★★	★★★	$69–$109
A Sheltered Harbor Bed and Breakfast	B&B	★★★	★★★★	$85.
SKAGWAY				
At the White House Bed and Breakfast	B&B	★★★★	★★★	$120–$145
The Historic Skagway Inn	Inn	★★★★	★★★	$119–$189
Mile Zero Bed & Breakfast	B&B	★★★	★★★	$135
Skagway Bungalows	Cabins	★★★	★★★	$125
Skagway Home Hostel	Hostel	★★★	★★★★★	$15–$50
JUNEAU				
Alaska's Capital Inn	B&B	★★★★★	★★★★	$149–$279
Juneau International Hostel	Hostel	★★★★	★★★★	$10
Pearson's Pond Luxury Inn	Inn	★★★★★	★★★	$249
Westmark Baranof Hotel	Hotel	★★★★	★★★	$129–$219

▲ Where to Stay

SOUTHEAST ALASKANS KNOW what the discriminating traveler likes, and you should not have a problem finding adequate lodging in most of the larger communities. Alaska as a whole seems to have many family-run operations

▲ more southeast indoor lodging

NAME	LODGING TYPE	QUALITY RATING	VALUE RATING	COST
SITKA				
Alaska Ocean View Bed & Breakfast Inn	Inn	★★★★	★★★	$89–$249
Burgess Bauder's Lighthouse	Cabins	★★★	★★★★	$125
Cascade Inn	Inn	★★★	★★★★	$115
Dove Island Lodge	Lodge	★★★★	★★★	$85–$200
Sitka International Hostel	Hostel	★	★★★★	$19
Sitka Seaside Lodge	Lodge	★★★	★★★	$1,800/ 4 nights
KETCHIKAN				
Black Bear Inn	Inn	★★★★★	★★★★	$180–$220
The Captain's Quarters Bed & Breakfast	B&B	★★★	★★★★	$100–$110
Eagle View Hostel	Hostel	★★	★★	$28
Gilmore Hotel	Hotel	★★★★	★★★★	$95–$145
Ketchikan Youth Hostel	Hostel	★★	★★★	$15

such as bed-and-breakfasts and lodges, so don't be discouraged if the hotels are sold out. There is likely a place to stay if you look hard enough.

If you're opting for the more outdoorsy options, there are also plenty of choices. Most communities have several campgrounds, some run by the government and others privately owned. We recommend taking advantage of the **Tongass National Forest Service cabins,** which are a steal at $25–$45 a night. However, if you need lodging close to town, you won't have that option.

In this section, we've given you our favorites—places we have tried ourselves and found to be memorable.

HAINES

Indoor Lodging

▶ **Bear Creek Camp and International Hostel**   907-766-2259; **bearcreekcabinsalaska.com.**

QUALITY ★★★★ | VALUE ★★★★★ | $18–$48

This place is about a mile out of town and a good place for backpackers or those traveling on a budget. It's our top pick for the area. Plus, they treat you like an adult, with no lockouts or curfews. Choose from cabins or bunk spaces in the hostel.

▶ **Chilkat Eagle Bed and Breakfast**   907-766-2763; **eagle-bb.com.**

QUALITY ★★★★ | VALUE ★★★★ | $80

Next to the Chilkat Center for the Arts and a favorite among international travelers. The owners speak six languages! Our choice for B&B lovers.

▶ **Eagle's Nest Motel**   800-354-6009 or 907-766-3779; **alaskaeagletours.com.**

QUALITY ★★ | VALUE ★★★ | $85–$95

Near the center of town; not fancy but definitely affordable.

▶ **Fort Seward Bed and Breakfast**   House Number 1 on Officer's Row; 800-615-6676 or 907-766-2856; **fortsewardalaska.com.**

QUALITY ★★★★ | VALUE ★★★ | $95–$259

We really like this spot because of its excellent views and elegant rooms.

▶ **Hotel Hälsingland**   800-542-6363 or 907-766-2000; **hotelhalsingland.com.**

QUALITY ★★★★ | VALUE ★★★ | $69–$109

This is a tourist-oriented place to stay, but we admit it is pretty nice, and the prices are competitive with those of the less-polished places.

▶ **A Sheltered Harbor Bed and Breakfast**   907-766-2741.

QUALITY ★★★ | VALUE ★★★★ | $85

This one is nice because it's on the waterfront. Plus, the owners are super-friendly, and the breakfasts are hearty and filling.

Camping

▶ **Bear Creek Camp and International Hostel**   907-766-2259; **bearcreekcabinsalaska.com.**

QUALITY ★★★★ | VALUE ★★★★ | $12

Good for backpackers or travelers on a budget. Our top pick in the area.

▲ southeast alaska camping

NAME	CAMPING TYPE	QUALITY RATING	VALUE RATING	COST
HAINES				
Bear Creek Camp and International Hostel	Tent	★★★★	★★★★	$12
Chilkat State Park	RV/tent	★★★★	★★★★	$10
Chilkoot Lake State Recreation-site	RV/tent	★★★	★★★★	$10
Portage Cove State Recreation-site	Tent	★★★★	★★★★★	$5
Salmon Run Campground and Cabins	RV/tent	★★★★	★★★	$14–$26
SKAGWAY				
Dyea Campground	Tent	★★★★	★★★★★	$6
Pullen Creek RV Park	RV/tent	★★★	★★★★	$14–$25
JUNEAU				
Auke Village Campground	Tent	★★★	★★★★	$10
Eagle Beach State Park	RV/tent	★★★	★★★★	$10
Mendenhall Lake Campground	RV/tent	★★★★	★★★	$10–$28
SITKA				
Sawmill Creek Campground	Tent	★★★★	★★★★★	Free
Starrigavan Campground	RV/tent	★★★	★★★	$12–$16
KETCHIKAN				
Last Chance Campground	RV/tent	★★★	★★★	$10
Signal Creek Campground	RV/tent	★★★	★★★	$10
Three C's Campground	RV/tent	★★	★★★	$10

▶ **Chilkat State Park**   907-766-2292

QUALITY ★★★★ | VALUE ★★★★ | $10

Located 7 miles south of Haines on Mud Bay Road. Tent and RV camping are available, and the tent sites are right on the beach. A summer host is usually on duty. Run by Alaska State Parks.

▶ **Chilkoot Lake State Recreation-site**   10 miles north of Haines off Lutak Road; 907-766-2292.

QUALITY ★★★ | VALUE ★★★★ | $10

A decent place to pitch a tent, but we like the campgrounds at Chilkat State Park and Portage Cove better (see listings above and following). A summer host is usually on duty. This campground also is run by Alaska State Parks.

▶ **Portage Cove State Recreation-site**   1 mile south of Haines on Beach Road; 907-766-2292.

QUALITY ★★★★ | VALUE ★★★★★ | $5

For backpackers and cyclists only, which means you won't hear the generator buzz of recreational vehicles. Also run by Alaska State Parks.

▶ **Salmon Run Campground and Cabins**   907-766-3240; **karo-ent.com/salmon.htm.**

QUALITY ★★★★ | VALUE ★★★ | $14–$26

This private campground is about a mile and a half from Haines and tucked into the woods, which gives it a very private feeling.

SKAGWAY

Indoor Lodging

▶ **At the White House Bed and Breakfast**   907-983-9000; **atthewhitehouse.com.**

QUALITY ★★★★ | VALUE ★★★ | $120–$145

Yes, the name might seem a little out of place in Alaska, but we like this scenic home in historical Skagway.

▶ **The Historic Skagway Inn**   At Seventh Avenue and Broadway; 888-752-4929 or 907-983-2289; **skagwayinn.com.**

QUALITY ★★★★ | VALUE ★★★★ | $119–$189

You may not be able to resist this inn, which once was a brothel but today offers very respectable rooms. Olivia's Restaurant is inside.

▶ **Mile Zero Bed & Breakfast**   At Ninth and Main streets; 907-983-3045; **mile-zero.com.**

QUALITY ★★★ | VALUE ★★★ | $135

Convenient central location; great views from the deck.

▶ **Skagway Bungalows**   Mile 1 Dyea Rd.; 907-983-2986; **aptalaska.net/~saldi.**

QUALITY ★★★ | VALUE ★★★ | $125

The one-room log cabins are a bit out of town but feel secluded and rustic (although there is indoor plumbing).

▶ **Skagway Home Hostel**   Third Avenue and Main Street; 907-983-2131; **skagwayhostel.com.**

QUALITY ★★★ | VALUE ★★★★★ | $15–$50

The hostel is in a historical building about 10 minutes from the ferry dock. It's a great gathering point for Chilkoot Trail hikers. Offers clean rooms and bunks.

Camping

▶ **Dyea Campground** (and NPS ranger station)   907-983-2921; **nps.gov/klgo/planyourvisit/campgrounds.htm.**

QUALITY ★★★★ | VALUE ★★★★★ | $6

We like this remote spot because the RVers don't come here often. Spaces are first-come, first-served.

▶ **Pullen Creek RV Park**   800-936-3731 or 907-983-2768; **pullencreekrv.com.**

QUALITY ★★★ | VALUE ★★★★ | $14–$25

It's not the most remote site, but the convenient location next to the state ferry dock and right on the water makes this place the choice for the traveler in need of convenient camping.

JUNEAU

Indoor Lodging

▶ **Alaska's Capital Inn**   888-588-6507; **alaskacapitalinn.com.**

QUALITY ★★★★★ | VALUE ★★★★ | $149–$279

This home, located in the historical section of Juneau, is a restored three-level mansion with rooms finely decorated in the Arts and Crafts style.

▶ **Juneau International Hostel**   907-586-9559; **juneauhostel.net.**

QUALITY ★★★★ | VALUE ★★★★ | $10

We like this place in downtown Juneau for its rambling, old-time feel. It has plenty of rooms, but they fill up fast, so don't count on staying here unless you've made reservations in advance.

▶ **Pearson's Pond Luxury Inn**   888-658-6328 or 907-789-3772; **pearsonspond.com.**

QUALITY ★★★★★ | VALUE ★★★ | $249

This outfit is truly luxurious, about 12 miles from downtown Juneau, close to Mendenhall Glacier. Rates are steep but include use of the spas, bikes, and rowboats. Think of these as honeymoon-level accommodations.

▶ **Westmark Baranof Hotel**   800-544-0970 or 907-586-2660; **westmarkhotels.com.**

QUALITY ★★★★ | VALUE ★★★ | $129–$219

This upscale hotel attracts throngs of tourists, but it's conveniently located and usually has openings.

Camping

There are three nice public campgrounds from which to choose in the Juneau area (you won't find much in the way of private camping facilities here).

▶ **Auke Village Campground**   Juneau Ranger District of the Tongass National Forest; 907-586-8800; **fs.fed.us/r10/tongass/recreation/rec_facilities/jnurec.shtml.**

QUALITY ★★★ | VALUE ★★★★ | $10

Located near a scenic beach, with 11 camping sites, picnic tables, and fireplaces. A vault toilet and water faucets are available. First-come, first-served; no reservations taken. Only 1.5 miles from the ferry terminal or 15 miles on the Glacier Highway from downtown Juneau.

▶ **Eagle Beach State Park**   A quarter-mile south of the Eagle Beach Picnic Area, at about Mile 28 of the Glacier Highway; 907-465-4563; **dnr.alaska.gov/parks/aspunits/southeast/eaglebeachsra.htm.**

QUALITY ★★★ | VALUE ★★★★ | $10

The park provides overnight parking for vehicles and tents on a gravel surface in a large open area. A park host is usually on-site. Portable toilets are the only services provided.

▶ **Mendenhall Lake Campground**   Juneau Ranger District of the Tongass National Forest; 907-586-8800; **fs.fed.us/r10/tongass/recreation/rec_facilities/jnurec.shtml.**

QUALITY ★★★★ | VALUE ★★★ | $10–$28

On Mendenhall Lake, in view of the Mendenhall Glacier, about 13 miles from downtown Juneau. There are 68 camping sites and a separate walk-in backpacker section. Water and vault toilets throughout the campground.

SITKA

Indoor Lodging

▶ **Alaska Ocean View Bed & Breakfast Inn**   888-811-6870 or 907-747-8310;
sitka-alaska-lodging.com.

QUALITY ★★★★ | VALUE ★★★ | $89–$249

Three rooms are available in this sunny home overlooking the water. We like
the owners' friendly attitude and the B&B's quick access to the rest of town.

▶ **Burgess Bauder's Lighthouse**   907-747-3056.

QUALITY ★★★ | VALUE ★★★★ | $125

This is a different option for those handy enough to take a skiff to the island
where the lighthouse is built. There are small wooden hot tubs for enjoying
the night sky, a kitchen, and room enough to sleep eight. Great for families or
small groups.

▶ **Cascade Inn**   800-532-0908 or 907-747-6804; **cascadeinnsitka.com.**

QUALITY ★★★ | VALUE ★★★★ | $115

The inn is nothing fancy to look at, but the location is gorgeous and convenient, with private balconies and kitchenettes.

▶ **Dove Island Lodge**   888-318-3474, 907-747-5660, or 907-738-0856;
aksitkasportfishing.com.

QUALITY ★★★★ | VALUE ★★★ | $85–$200

This lodge feels like it's in the middle of nowhere even though you're really
only 5 minutes from the Sitka harbor. Fishing and boating packages are available,
and guests can rent kayaks as well. The hot tub overlooking the water looks
like something out of a movie set.

▶ **Sitka International Hostel**   907-747-8661.

QUALITY ★ | VALUE ★★★★ | $19

The Sitka International Hostel is set in nearly century-old Tillie Paul
Manor, the former infirmary of Sheldon Jackson College and the former
community hospital. Sleeping is in 23 beds in five single-gender dorm rooms
and a family room.

▶ **Sitka Seaside Lodge**   866-747-8113; sitkaseaside.com.

QUALITY ★★★ | VALUE ★★★ | $1,800/4 NIGHTS

This fairly modern lodge won't feel like the rustic log lodges that you may
envision in Alaska, but its location and the stunning views of the water make
you salivate to get out there and enjoy. Fishing packages are incorporated into
each room rate if you wish.

Camping

The Sitka Ranger District of the Tongass National Forest operates two nice public campgrounds in the Sitka area.

▶ **Sawmill Creek Campground**   Sitka Ranger District of the Tongass National Forest; 907-747-4216; **fs.fed.us/r10/tongass.**

QUALITY ★★★★	VALUE ★★★★★	FREE

This is a rustic campground suited to backpackers and located up a steep and windy gravel road. There is no fee to camp at any of the 11 campsites.

▶ **Starrigavan Campground**   Sitka Ranger District of the Tongass National Forest; 907-747-4216; **fs.fed.us/r10/tongass;** National Recreation Reservation System, 877-444-6777 or **recreation.gov.**

QUALITY ★★★	VALUE ★★★	$12–$16

Located 7 miles from Sitka, this campground has three loops with 35 sites. Some are better for backpackers and cyclists, while others are suited to RV drivers. Rates depend on which loop you stay in. Advance registration is accepted for a limited number of campsites, which fill up early.

KETCHIKAN

Indoor Lodging

▶ **Black Bear Inn**   907-225-4343; **stayinalaska.com.**

QUALITY ★★★★★	VALUE ★★★★	$180–$220

This inn offers some great privacy and amenities such as gas fireplaces, Wi-Fi, outdoor lounging area, and soaking tubs.

▶ **The Captain's Quarters Bed & Breakfast**   907-225-4912; captainsquartersbb.com.

QUALITY ★★★	VALUE ★★★★	$100–$110

This custom-built home overlooking the water is one of our favorite places to stay in Ketchikan. Kids aren't allowed here, however.

▶ **Eagle View Hostel**   907-225-5461; **eagleviewhostel.com.**

QUALITY ★★	VALUE ★★	$28

Clean rooms, but the rates are a bit steep as hostels go.

▶ **Gilmore Hotel**   800-275-9423 or 907-225-9423; **gilmorehotel.com.**

QUALITY ★★★★	VALUE ★★★★	$95–$145

Right in town but often overlooked in favor of the larger chain hotels. On the National Register of Historic Places, it shows its age, but also its charm.

▶ **Ketchikan Youth Hostel**   907-225-3319.

| QUALITY ★★ | VALUE ★★★ | $15 |

Your typical no-frills hostel.

Camping

The Ketchikan District of the Tongass National Forest has three nice camp-grounds from which to choose.

▶ **Last Chance Campground**   Ketchikan District of the Tongass National Forest; 907-225-3101; **fs.fed.us/r10/tongass;** National Recreation Reservation System, 877-444-6777 or **recreation.gov.**

| QUALITY ★★★ | VALUE ★★★ | $10 |

This 19-site campground is 10 miles north of Ketchikan on Revilla Road. Advance reservations can be made for a limited number of sites by calling the National Recreation Reservation System; other sites are first-come, first-served.

▶ **Signal Creek Campground**   Ketchikan District of the Tongass National Forest; 907-225-3101; **fs.fed.us/r10/tongass;** National Recreation Reservation System, 877-444-6777 or **recreation.gov.**

| QUALITY ★★★ | VALUE ★★★ | $10 |

There are 24 units in this campground, which is part of the Ward Lake Recreation Area. Advance reservations can be made for a limited number of sites by calling the National Recreation Reservation System. The rest of the sites are available on a first-come, first-served basis.

▶ **Three C's Campground**   Ketchikan District of the Tongass National Forest; 907-225-3101; **fs.fed.us/r10/tongass.**

| QUALITY ★★ | VALUE ★★★ | $10 |

This overflow campground is opened only when Signal Creek fills up. No advance reservations.

▲ Where to Eat

HAINES

▶ **Bear-Ritto's Eatery**   In the Bear Den Mall; 907-766-2117.

| HEALTHY | QUALITY ★★★★ | $5–$13 | SUITABLE FOR KIDS? Y |

A fine choice for those who prefer healthful eating; serves seafood with a Mexican twist.

▲ southeast alaska dining

NAME	CUISINE	FOOD QUALITY	COST
HAINES			
Bear-Ritto's Eatery	Healthy	★★★★	$5–$13
Chilkat Restaurant & Bakery	Cafe/bakery	★★★	$5–$11
Fort Seward Restaurant & Saloon	Steaks/seafood	★★★	$8–$24
Fireweed Restaurant	Pizza/organic	★★★★	$8–$21
Just for the Halibut Café	Seafood	★★★★	$9–$27
The Local Catch	Seafood/Thai	★★★	$7–$19
SKAGWAY			
Corner Café	Burgers/soups	★★★	$6–$12
Lemon Rose Bakery	Bakery/cafe	★★★★	$4–$11
Olivia's at the Skagway Inn	Fusion	★★★★	$9–$30
Skagway Pizza Station	Pizza	★★★	$7–$23
JUNEAU			
Douglas Café	Soups/sandwiches	★★★	$5–$9
Hot Bite	Burgers	★★★	$5–$8
Kenny's Wok and Teriyaki	Sushi/Chinese	★★★	$6–$18
El Sombrero	Mexican	★★★	$6–$19
Thane Ore House and Salmon Bake	Seafood	★★★	$25
Wild Spice Restaurant	Mongolian	★★★	$8–$25
Zen Restaurant	Fusion/Asian	★★★★	$9–$29

▶ **Chilkat Restaurant & Bakery**   Fifth Avenue and Dalton Street; 907-766-3653.

CAFE/BAKERY | QUALITY ★★★ | $5–$11 | SUITABLE FOR KIDS? Y

Open year-round for breakfast and lunch only; dinner on Fridays and Saturdays during the summer.

▲ southeast alaska dining [continued]

NAME	CUISINE	FOOD QUALITY	COST
SITKA			
The Backdoor Cafe	Cafe/soups	★★★	$4–$7
Captain's Galley	American	★★★	$4–$24
Ludvig's Bistro	Mediterranean	★★★★	$9–$29
KETCHIKAN			
Annabelle's Famous Keg and Chowder House	American	★★★	$7–$26
Chico's Mexican Restaurant	Mexican	★★	$4–$17
Dave's Red Anchor Café	American	★★★	$5–$14
Heen Kahidi Restaurant	Fusion	★★★★	$9–$31
Ocean View Restaurante	Italian/Mexican	★★★	$7–$25

▶ **Fireweed Restaurant** In Fort Seward off Portage Street; 907-766-3838.

PIZZA/ORGANIC | QUALITY ★★★★ | $8–$21 | SUITABLE FOR KIDS? Y

They use local and organic food and create some imaginative pizzas.

▶ **Fort Seward Restaurant & Saloon** Mile 0 Haines Hwy., Fort Seward; 877-617-3418 or 907-766-2009.

STEAK/SEAFOOD | QUALITY ★★★ | $8–$24 | SUITABLE FOR KIDS? N

Great steak and seafood. Closed part of the winter.

▶ **Just for the Halibut Café** At the Chilkat Cruises Dock; 907-766-3800 or 907-766-2103.

SEAFOOD | QUALITY ★★★★ | $9–$27 | SUITABLE FOR KIDS? Y

Superb seafood in a waterfront atmosphere.

▶ **The Local Catch** On Portage Street, Fort Seward; 907-766-3557.

SEAFOOD/THAI | QUALITY ★★★ | $7–$19 | SUITABLE FOR KIDS? Y

Their fish tacos and Thai food are marvelous, but they're open only in summer.

SKAGWAY

▶ **Corner Café**   421 State St.; 907-983-2155.

BURGERS/SOUPS	QUALITY ★★★	$6–$12	SUITABLE FOR KIDS? Y

Hamburgers and hearty soups make this a local favorite.

▶ **Lemon Rose Bakery**   330 3rd Ave.; 907-983-3558.

BAKERY/CAFE	QUALITY ★★★★	$4–$11	SUITABLE FOR KIDS? Y

This year-round cafe is another of our favorites. The calzones are big enough to split among three people.

▶ **Olivia's at the Skagway Inn**   Seventh Avenue and Broadway Street; 907-983-2289.

FUSION	QUALITY ★★★★	$9–$30	SUITABLE FOR KIDS? Y

A true fine-dining experience where backpackers in Carhartts are welcome.

▶ **Skagway Pizza Station**   444 4th Ave.; 907-983-2200.

PIZZA	QUALITY ★★★	$7–$23	SUITABLE FOR KIDS? Y

Open year-round, this pizza shop is another local favorite.

JUNEAU

▶ **Douglas Café**   916 3rd St., across the bridge from Juneau; 907-364-3307.

SOUPS/SANDWICHES	QUALITY ★★★	$5–$9	SUITABLE FOR KIDS? Y

Serves some of the best chowder in the city.

▶ **Hot Bite**   Outside of town at the Auke Bay dock, 13 miles from Juneau; 907-790-2483.

BURGERS	QUALITY ★★★	$5–$8	SUITABLE FOR KIDS? Y

Worth stopping at for its burgers. It's open only during the summer, however.

▶ **Kenny's Wok and Teriyaki**   126 Front St.; 907-586-3575.

SUSHI/CHINESE	QUALITY ★★★	$6–$18	SUITABLE FOR KIDS? N

This casual eatery can cook from either country—Japanese sushi or Chinese rice and meat dishes. Quick and friendly service right downtown.

▶ **El Sombrero**   157 S. Franklin St.; 907-586-6770.

MEXICAN	QUALITY ★★★	$6–$19	SUITABLE FOR KIDS? Y

Locals' top choice for Mexican food among the several options in town.

▶ **Thane Ore House and Salmon Bake**   4400 Thane Rd.; 907-586-3442.

SEAFOOD	QUALITY ★★★	$25	SUITABLE FOR KIDS? Y

It's a bit touristy, and a few miles out of town, but on a good day, it's beautiful to sit outside and enjoy salmon fresh-caught in Alaska. Free transportation is provided with reservations.

▶ **Wild Spice Restaurant**   140 Seward St.; 907-523-0344.

MONGOLIAN	QUALITY ★★★	$8–$25	SUITABLE FOR KIDS? N

This restaurant offers fresh, fast foods cooked Mongolian-style on an open grill.

▶ **Zen Restaurant**   51 Egan Dr.; 907-586-5075.

FUSION	QUALITY ★★★★	$9–$29	SUITABLE FOR KIDS? N

This place, in the Goldbelt Hotel, specializes in Asian-inspired creations of coconut shrimp, crispy duck, and lemongrass-infused fishes. The adjacent lounge features jazz music on weekends.

SITKA

▶ **The Backdoor Cafe**   104 Barracks St., behind Old Harbor Bookstore; 907-747-8856

CAFE/SOUPS	QUALITY ★★★	$4–$7	SUITABLE FOR KIDS? Y

A cozy, downtown coffeehouse that serves espresso, handmade bagels, pastries, pies, soups, and fresh-squeezed orange juice. It's a favorite among locals. Closed Sundays.

▶ **Captain's Galley**   1867 Halibut Point Rd.; 907-747-6266.

AMERICAN	QUALITY ★★★	$4–$24	SUITABLE FOR KIDS? Y

Known for its fried chicken, sold by the bucket if you like, with mashed potatoes, country gravy, and biscuits. They also make deli sandwiches, soups, salads, and pizzas, and there's limited seating with great ocean views.

▶ **Ludvig's Bistro**   256 Katlian St.; 907-966-3663.

MEDITERRANEAN	QUALITY ★★★★	$9–$29	SUITABLE FOR KIDS? N

Food with a Mediterranean flair, specializing in Alaska seafood and fresh-baked bread. They also operate the soup cart Ludvig's on Lincoln next to Harry Race Pharmacy. Ludvig's is a bit upscale, so reservations are recommended.

KETCHIKAN

▶ **Annabelle's Famous Keg and Chowder House**   326 Front St., off the lobby of the Gilmore Hotel; 907-225-6009.

| AMERICAN | QUALITY ★★★ | $7–$26 | SUITABLE FOR KIDS? Y |

A somewhat pricey menu but very good food, with lots of healthful choices.

▶ **Chico's Mexican Restaurant**   435 Dock St.; 907-225-2833.

| MEXICAN | QUALITY ★★ | $4–$17 | SUITABLE FOR KIDS? Y |

Basic Mexican fare at affordable prices.

▶ **Dave's Red Anchor Café**   1935 Tongass Ave.; 907-247-5287.

| AMERICAN | QUALITY ★★★ | $5–$14 | SUITABLE FOR KIDS? Y |

A local favorite with a friendly staff and an easygoing atmosphere.

▶ **Heen Kahidi Restaurant**   800 Venetia Way; 907-225-8001.

| FUSION | QUALITY ★★★★ | $9–$31 | SUITABLE FOR KIDS? N |

The name means "tree house on the creek." Has lovely views out to the Tongass Narrows. This is where locals go for a special night out or to celebrate anniversaries. Prices are a bit high, but it's nice for special occasions.

▶ **Ocean View Restaurante**   1831 Tongass Ave.; 907-225-7566.

| ITALIAN/MEXICAN | QUALITY ★★★ | $7–$25 | SUITABLE FOR KIDS? Y |

An Italian menu with lots of variety, and we do mean variety. Can you say pizza, Mexican, seafood, *and* croissants?

▲ On the Town:
What to Do after the Outdoor Adventure

SOUTHEAST ALASKA HAS no shortage of things to do after you've exhausted your outdoor-recreation reserves. Each town has its own character—take Skagway's over-the-top gold-rush theme, for example.

This section will give you a sampling of what you can do when you're relaxing in town before or after your outdoor adventure.

HAINES

▶ **Alaska Indian Arts**   13 Fort Seward Dr.; 907-766-2160; **alaskaindianarts.com.**
See artists at work creating totems, masks, and ceremonial baskets.

▶ **American Bald Eagle Foundation**   907-766-3094; **baldeagles.org.** This nonprofit educational and research foundation features a natural-history museum containing more than 100 full-size specimens.

SKAGWAY

▶ **Corrington Museum of Alaskan History**   525 Broadway; 907-983-2579. With local history and lots of gold-rush history.

▶ **The Days of '98 Show with Soapy Smith**   590 Broadway; 907-983-2545. It's a lot of fun if you like this kind of entertainment. Gives you a glimpse of what the gold rush was all about.

JUNEAU

▶ **Alaskan Brewing Co.**   5429 Shaune Dr.; 907-780-5866; **alaskanbeer.com.** Try the company's award-winning beers on tap during its daily tours, 11 a.m.– 6 p.m. in the summer (last tour is at 4:30 p.m.).

▶ **Alaska State Museum**   395 Whittier St.; 907-465-2901. The Alaska State Museum is home to more than 23,000 artifacts, works of fine art, and natural history. There's a kids' room that simulates Captain James Cook's 18th-century vessel, the *Discovery*.

▶ **Juneau/Douglas City Museum**   Located at Fourth Avenue and Main Street; 907-586-3572. With more than 6,000 historical and fine-art objects, the City Museum offers year-round exhibits and fall and winter community programming.

SITKA

▶ **Alaska Raptor Center**   907-747-8662; **alaskaraptor.org.** The Raptor Center's goal is to release all rehabilitated birds, but some stay behind for visitors to learn from. Admission is $12 for adults, $6 for children.

▶ **Castle Hill**   On Harbor Road, on your way to the airport. Also known as the Baranof Castle site, this area is an early stronghold of the Kiksadi clan. The site is on the National Register of Historic Places.

▶ **Russian Bishop's House**   907-747-6281; **nps.gov/sitk.** The oldest intact Russian building in Sitka was built in 1842. The area is registered as a National Historic Landmark. Admission is $4.

▶ **Sheet'ka Kwaan Naa Kahidi Native Dancers**   888-270-8687 or 907-747-7290; **sitkatribe.org.** The Tlingit Dancers perform in connection with Sitka Tribal Tours at the Sheet'ka Kwaan Naa Kahidi Community House. $7 per person.

▶ **Southeast Alaska Indian Cultural Center**   907-747-8061; **seaicc@gci.net.** The Cultural Center provides a place for local Sitka Tlingits to teach themselves about their own culture. It also helps visitors understand the native people of the area. Admission is $3 per person or $15 for families.

KETCHIKAN

▶ **Creek Street District**   This area off Stedman Street includes a former brothel, called Dolly's House, which has been made into a museum.

▶ **Saxman Native Village**   Mile 2.5 S. Tongass Hwy.. Totem poles can be viewed at this 2½-acre park that has preserved these works of art. Cape Fox Tours 907-225-4846; **capefoxtours.com**) conducts tours as well.

▶ **Tongass Historical Society Museum**   629 Dock St.; 907-225-5600. Houses artifacts from Ketchikan's native past and mining, fishing, and timber history. Admission is $2.

PART FIFTEEN

INTERIOR ALASKA
the heart of the state

▲ An Overview of the Interior

WHEN YOU HEAR the term *Land of the Midnight Sun,* think of Interior Alaska. Here, more than anywhere else, is where a visitor can truly appreciate what that means. In the summer, the sun really *is* still out at midnight. Because of their more southerly locations, the Southcentral and Southeast regions of the state don't experience the same amount of light.

The Interior is warmer as well. Summers in this region can reach 90°F for days at a time, literally giving summer vacationers endless sunshine. This being Alaska, of course, it can get inversely cold in winter—down to –40°F is common. But Alaskans dress appropriately and simply continue to go about their business.

Interior Alaska is a land of vast proportions too. From **Anaktuvuk Pass** to **Denali State Park,** the Interior seems to go on forever. You can drive and drive and see nothing but wilderness. It is the ideal place to gain perspective on just how large Alaska really is. (See Part One, page 9, for a map of the region.)

Interior Alaska is home to some incredible natural wonders. **Mount McKinley,** or **Denali,** as most Alaskans prefer to call it, is in the Interior, looming 20,320 feet above the rest of North America. The mighty **Yukon River,** a river rich in history and overflowing with flora and fauna to be discovered, also flows through the region.

Gold mining brought Interior Alaska into the forefront of the collective imagination, and during the late 1800s and early 1900s, it dominated the thoughts of hopeful prospectors there to find the big vein and become rich overnight.

But once the gold rush ebbed, Alaska's Interior was still the same great mass of land filled with rivers and valleys and mountains. Sure, the gold may have seemed like the region's biggest asset, but in fact, as visitors to this area see on a daily basis, its biggest asset is really the natural beauty. It's a magical place, Interior Alaska, sure to astound you.

Interior Alaska is a culturally diverse region too, with Alaska natives making up a large percentage of its residents. The region's rich Athabascan heritage is on display in museums, stores, villages, and art galleries.

This chapter focuses on the largest communities through which you may travel while headed to your ultimate outdoor destination in Interior Alaska. These are the places where you can gear up and move out. Specifically, we have created subchapters for **Fairbanks,** the communities north of there, and the area around **Denali National Park.**

▲ Fairbanks

FAIRBANKS CONVENTION AND VISITORS BUREAU
(plus information about Circle, Manley Hot Springs, and Coldfoot)
101 Dunkel St., Suite 111
Fairbanks 99701-4806
800-327-5774 | **explorefairbanks.com**

When you think *Interior*, Fairbanks may be the first place that comes to mind. On a map, the city seems smack-dab in the middle of the state—and it is, sort of. About 35,000 people live in Fairbanks, which is a large and sprawling place with its own university, hospital, government, schools, and all the amenities of a large community. There also is a military presence, with **Eielson Air Force** and **Fort Wainwright Army bases** nearby.

Physically, the city is located on the banks of the **Chena River,** in the Tanana Valley. It takes only 45 minutes to fly there from Anchorage, but a road trip will take upwards of 6 hours. The average winter temperatures range from −19°F to −2°F; in the summer the mercury can rise to 72°F on an average day (although days in the 80s and even 90s are not uncommon).

Athabascans have lived in the Fairbanks area for thousands of years, but it was the nonnative Capt. E. T. Barnette who first established a trading post on the Chena River in 1901, marking the beginnings of what would one day be Fairbanks. A year later, gold was discovered 16 miles north of the post, and like every other place affected by the gold, the outpost turned into a city overnight. The town continued to grow and in 1902 was named in honor of Indiana senator Charles Fairbanks, who eventually became vice president. A year later, the third judicial court was moved from Eagle to Fairbanks, followed by more and more government. A jail, post office, and several supply stores opened, and before long, Fairbanks was a thriving city of 3,500, although thousands more were in surrounding areas actively mining.

Today, Fairbanks continues to thrive. Government, transportation, manufacturing, and tourism are its main economic driving factors. Gold mining

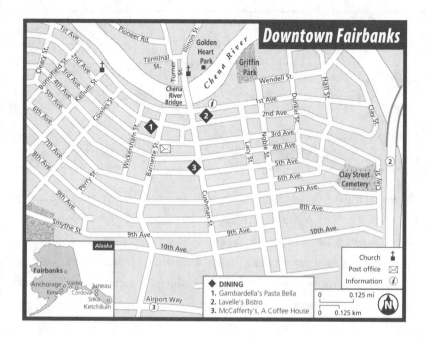

Downtown Fairbanks

DINING
1. Gambardella's Pasta Bella
2. Lavelle's Bistro
3. McCafferty's, A Coffee House

still goes on, but on a much smaller scale than those earlier gold rushes. The **University of Alaska Fairbanks** is also a major employer. Approximately 325,000 tourists visit Fairbanks each summer.

Access to Fairbanks is via the Richardson or Parks highways from the south and the Steese and Elliott highways from the north. There is regularly scheduled jet service from the Lower 48 states, Canada, and Anchorage. The **Alaska Railroad** also provides access, although only from within the state (Anchorage, Seward, and Talkeetna).

▲ North of Fairbanks

CIRCLE

Circle is located on the south bank of the Yukon River at the edge of the **Yukon Flats,** 160 miles northeast of Fairbanks, at the eastern end of the Steese Highway. Because of its subarctic climate, it gets very hot in the summers

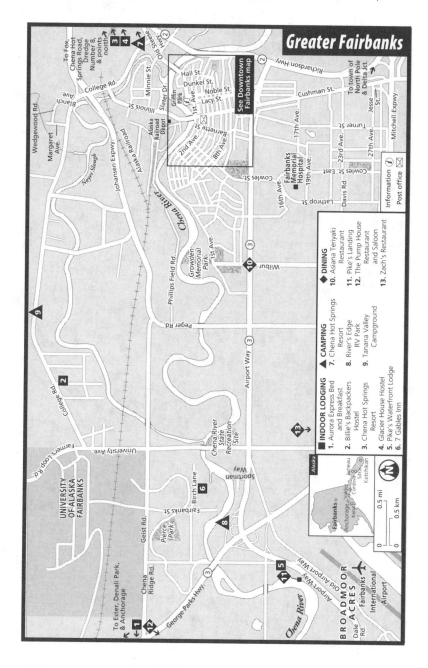

Greater Fairbanks

To Fox, Chena Hot Springs Road, Dredge Number 8, & points north

3
4
7

Old Steese Hwy.
2

Richardson Hwy.

College Rd.

Wedgewood Rd.

Margaret Ave.

Blanch Ave.

Noyes Slough

Illinois St.

Minnie St.

Slater Dr.

Griffin Park

Hall St.
Dunkel St.
Noble St.
Lacy St.
1st Ave.
2nd Ave.
8th Ave.

Alaska Railroad Depot

Barnette St.

See Downtown Fairbanks map

Cushman St.

To town of North Pole & Delta Jct.

Jesse St.

17th Ave.

Turner St.

Mitchell Expwy.

27th Ave.

23rd Ave.

Fairbanks Memorial Hospital

16th Ave.

19th Ave.

Cowles St. East

Davis Rd.

Lathrop St.

Cowles St.

Johansen Expwy.

Chena River

Alaska Railroad

Growden Memorial Park

Phillips Field Rd.

Peger Rd.

1st Ave.

Wilbur

3

10

Airport Way
3

College Rd.

University Ave.

Farmer's Loop Rd.

UNIVERSITY OF ALASKA FAIRBANKS

9

2

Geist Rd.

Pierce Park

Fairbanks St.

Birch Lane

6

Chena River State Recreation Site

Sportman Way

8

13

Chena Ridge Rd.

George Parks Hwy.
3

To Ester, Denali Park, & Anchorage

1
12

Dale Rd.

BROADMOOR ACRES

Old Airport Way

Airport Way

5
11

Fairbanks International Airport

Chena River

◆ DINING
10. Asiana Teriyaki Restaurant
11. Pike's Landing
12. The Pump House Restaurant and Saloon
13. Zach's Restaurant

▲ CAMPING
7. Chena Hot Springs Resort
8. River's Edge RV Park
9. Tanana Valley Campground

■ INDOOR LODGING
1. Aurora Express Bed and Breakfast
2. Billie's Backpackers Hostel
3. Chena Hot Springs Resort
4. Glacier House Hostel
5. Pike's Waterfront Lodge
6. 7 Gables Inn

Alaska

Fairbanks
Anchorage
Valdez
Juneau
Kenai
Cordova
Sitka
Ketchikan

0   0.5 mi
0   0.5 km

N

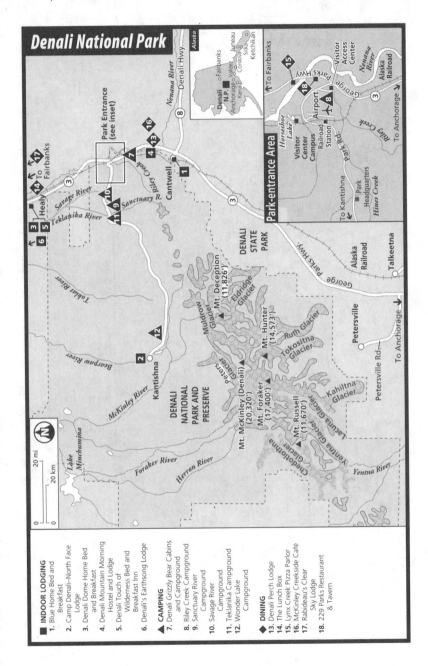

Denali National Park

INDOOR LODGING
1. Blue Home Bed and Breakfast
2. Camp Denali–North Face Lodge
3. Denali Dome Home Bed and Breakfast
4. Denali Mountain Morning Hostel and Lodge
5. Denali Touch of Wilderness Bed and Breakfast Inn
6. Denali's Earthsong Lodge

CAMPING
7. Denali Grizzly Bear Cabins and Campground
8. Riley Creek Campground
9. Sanctuary River Campground
10. Savage River Campground
11. Teklanika Campground
12. Wonder Lake Campground

DINING
13. Denali Perch Lodge
14. The Lunch Box
15. Lynx Creek Pizza Parlor
16. McKinley Creekside Café
17. Rabideau's Clear Sky Lodge
18. 229 Parks Restaurant & Tavern

Park-entrance Area

and very cold in the winters. The temperature range can go from 72°F in the summer to −72°F in the winter. This is a popular spot from which to launch a Yukon River trip, and most people who come this far usually spend some time on the water.

The community was established in 1893 as a supply point for goods shipped up the Yukon River and hauled overland to the gold-mining camps. It got its original name, Circle City, by miners who thought its location was on the Arctic Circle. They were off a bit, but the name remained. During the height of the gold rush, the town bustled with dance halls, mercantiles, lodges, and other businesses. Today, it is home to only about 90 people. Recreation is the largest draw there now, with freshwater fishing and boating as the major attractions.

You can get to Circle from Fairbanks by taking the Steese Highway. Barges deliver goods by the Yukon River during summer. A state-owned gravel airstrip is available too.

MANLEY HOT SPRINGS

At the end of the Elliott Highway, 160 miles west of Fairbanks, you'll come to Manley Hot Springs, a community of about 75 people living along the **Tanana River.** Manley Hot Springs is a community that got its start as a base of operations for gold miners in early 1902. The first resident began farming and raising livestock in the area, quite a feat considering the environmental challenges. The area is cool in the summer, around 55°F, and can dip far below zero in the winter.

The hot springs were a natural draw, though, and as early as 1907, a resort centered on the hot waters was erected and brought passengers via steamers off the Tanana River. At one time, the population in the area climbed to nearly 500. Eventually the resort burned, mining declined, and the community almost disappeared. But in 1959, after the completion of the Elliott Highway, Manley Hot Springs had a road link to the rest of Alaska, and the town began to grow again.

COLDFOOT

A whopping 35 people call this spot in the road home. It is located at Mile 175 of the Dalton Highway at the mouth of **Slate Creek,** on the east bank of the **Middle Fork Koyukuk River.** The temperature swings are not as noticeable as they can be in the more northerly areas, with averages in the 50°F range in the summer and going as low as −20°F in the winter.

Coldfoot originally was named Slate Creek but was renamed after gold seekers at the turn of the century went up the Koyukuk to start searching for their riches and chickened out. When they got cold feet, it is reported, the town became known as such. At the time, Coldfoot really was a town, with two roadhouses, a couple of stores, and seven saloons. Eventually, like so many other gold-rush towns, the gold disappeared and so did the town. There's not much there now except for a motel, a restaurant, a gas station, and an RV park. There are a few other small businesses that serve those traveling the Dalton Highway, but it otherwise is a relatively quiet place.

ANAKTUVUK PASS

CITY OF ANAKTUVUK PASS
907-661-3612 | **cityoakp@astacalaska.net**

This 300-person community is at 2,200 feet on the divide between the Anaktuvuk and John rivers in the central **Brooks Range,** and is the last remaining settlement of the Nunamiut (inland northern Inupiat Eskimo). Because of its high elevation, summers are cool and winters are cold—often −20°F and colder.

Nunamiut bands left the Brooks Range and scattered because of the collapse of caribou populations in 1926–27, and also because of cultural changes brought by the influx of Western civilization. In the late 1930s, however, a group of Nunamiut families returned to the mountains and settled. Others eventually followed, and thus the community formed.

Job opportunities are limited in Anaktuvuk Pass because it is so isolated. Hunting and trapping for the sale of skins, guiding hunters, or making traditional caribou-skin masks or clothing provides income for the residents there. Some residents have seasonal employment outside the community. Caribou is the primary source of meat; other subsistence foods include trout, grayling, moose, sheep, brown bear, ptarmigan, and waterfowl.

Access to the area is by small aircraft, which fly there regularly. In the winter, a snow road can create access to the village by way of the Dalton Highway, but it is only for bringing in supplies.

▲ Denali Area

DENALI VISITORS CENTER
Mile 240 Parks Hwy.
907-683-2294 | nps.gov/dena

DENALI CHAMBER OF COMMERCE
907-683-4636 | denalichamber.com

There is more to the Denali area than just the fact that it is home to the most-visited national park in Alaska. The Denali area includes the communities of **Anderson, Cantwell, Clear, Ferry, Healy,** and **Mount McKinley Village,** which among them all have fewer than 2,000 year-round residents. Most of these people live off the beaten track, and their homes are not easily seen from the road.

> **TRAVELER'S TIP**
>
> ▶ Most people choose to drive to Denali National Park, as it is the least expensive option. However, the **Alaska Railroad** offers a scenic view of parts of the state not seen from the road.

Tourism is the mainstay for those living in the Denali area, and during the summer, residents stay busy showing visitors from the outside world their special corner of the earth. In the winter, however, things slow down. While some winter visitors come to Denali to experience sports such as snow machining, dog mushing, and skiing, for the most part, Denali is quiet in winter.

The town of **Cantwell** is at the crossroads of the Parks and Denali highways, 27 miles south of the entrance to **Denali National Park.** The **Alaska Railroad** passes through town. **Ferry** is the smallest of the communities, at just 29 residents at last count, and is adjacent to the Alaska Railroad. Twelve miles north of Ferry is **Healy,** the largest community in the Denali area, with about 1,000 permanent residents. This is where most supplies for the region can be purchased, although there are no true big-box stores until you get to Fairbanks. **Mount McKinley Village,** just outside the park entrance, and **Anderson** round out the region. For more information on the park, see the listing under "Wild Lands" below.

▲ Wild Lands

DENALI NATIONAL PARK AND PRESERVE

DENALI NATIONAL PARK
Denali Park 99755-0009
907-683-2294 | nps.gov/dena

Primary activities:
birding, backpacking, mountain biking, mountaineering, and dog mushing

This 6-million-acre spread of wild land includes **Mount McKinley,** North America's highest mountain at 20,320 feet tall, as well as countless other mountains and glaciers that seem to go on forever. The park encompasses a complete subarctic ecosystem teeming with wildlife including moose, grizzly bears, Dall sheep, and wolves.

The park was established as Mount McKinley National Park in 1917, but in 1980 the name was changed to honor the Athabascan word for the mountain: **Denali,** or "high one." Today the park gets the most visitors of any in the state—about 400,000 each year.

Access to the park is via the Alaska Railroad from Fairbanks or Anchorage, the Parks Highway via car or bus, or small charter plane.

DENALI STATE PARK

VISITOR CENTER (at Alaska Veterans Memorial)
Mile 147.1 Parks Hwy.
DENALI RANGER STATION
Alaska State Parks/Mat-Su Area Headquarters
907-745-3975 | **dnr.alaska.gov/parks/units/denali1.htm**

Primary activities: *backpacking, fishing, hiking, skiing, mountain biking*

Denali State Park comprises 325,240 acres and often is overlooked as people rush to get to the national park of the same name. It's about 100 air miles north of Anchorage and lies roughly on either side of the Parks Highway. Sandwiched between the **Talkeetna Mountains** to the east and the **Alaska Range** to the west, Denali State Park offers wonderful ridge walks for backpackers, as well as shorter trails for mountain bikers seeking technical singletrack.

Fishing is excellent in the area as well. All five species of Pacific salmon spawn within the waters of the park and share the streams with rainbow trout, arctic grayling, and Dolly Varden. Small numbers of lake trout inhabit **Byers, Spink,** and **Lucy lakes.** Burbot and whitefish can also be found in Byers Lake. The large rivers are clouded with glacial silt, though, and make for poor sportfishing.

Moose, as well as grizzly and black bears, are found throughout the park. Occasionally a wolf or wayward caribou is spotted. Smaller, elusive residents include lynx, coyotes, red foxes, snowshoe hares, land otters, and flying and red squirrels.

There are two campgrounds, accessible by the Parks Highway: **Denali View North Campground,** at Mile 162.7, and **Byers Lake Campground,** at Mile 147.

WHITE MOUNTAINS NATIONAL RECREATION AREA

> **WHITE MOUNTAINS NATIONAL RECREATION AREA**
> blm.gov/ak/st/en/prog/sa/white_mtns.html (for general White Mountains information, mileage between cabins, and a detailed map of the area)

Primary activities: *backpacking, fishing, rafting, skiing, and dog mushing*

That Fairbanks residents have such a huge playground in their backyard, only 30 miles to the north of town, is remarkable. Outdoor recreationists flock to the more than 200 miles of maintained trails in the White Mountains National Recreation Area.

The seeds of the White Mountains National Recreation Area were planted nearly 20 years ago, with the passage of the Alaska National Interest Land Conservation Act, which aimed to set aside valuable acreage for multiple purposes. Unlike most federal land in Alaska, this recreation area is managed by the U.S. Bureau of Land Management. Not only does the BLM maintain a wealth of trails and cabins for winter use, but it has also established two campgrounds and created hiking areas for those visiting the land in the summer. Today, White Mountains is the largest national recreation area in the United States, the only national recreation area in Alaska, and the only one in the nation managed by the BLM.

TRAVELER'S TIP

▶ Because its many wet, boggy areas freeze over and get covered in snow, White Mountains National Recreation Area is a better winter destination than a summer one, but backpackers and boaters still come here in the summer.

Accessing the White Mountain National Recreation Area is easy. From Fairbanks, drive north on the Elliott or Steese highways, depending on where in the recreation area your trip will begin. Four pulloffs, two along each highway, allow for long-term parking. Cross-country skiing and dog mushing are the most popular activities in the winter, although you do share the trail with snowmobiles, so be prepared for some occasional noise. Hiking near **Wickersham Dome** and **Mount Prindle** (the highest point in the White Mountains at 5,286 feet) is popular in the dry summer months. Floating the **Beaver Creek National Wild River** is fast becoming popular. BLM cabins are available up to 30 days in advance for $25 per night. Reservations can be made in person at the BLM Public Room, 1150 University Ave., Fairbanks 99709, or by calling 800-437-7021, 907-474-2251, or 907-474-2252. Trail maps can also be ordered by calling this number.

ARCTIC NATIONAL WILDLIFE REFUGE

ARCTIC NATIONAL WILDLIFE REFUGE
101 12th Ave.
Box 20, Room 236
Fairbanks 99701
800-362-4546 or 907-456-0250 | **arctic.fws.gov**
Go to **arctic.fws.gov/airtaxi.htm** for air-taxi information.

Primary activities:
backpacking, camping, rafting

The 9.6-million-acre Arctic National Wildlife Refuge supports the greatest variety of plant and animal life of any park or refuge above the Arctic Circle in the entire world. That's an impressive superlative, and one that you may not immediately notice when entering this place. The land is so vast that one often feels all alone, but the fact is that the area teems with wildlife, whether it is the pygmy shrew or the giant grizzly bear.

The land is inhabited by 45 species of land and marine mammals and 36 species of fish can be found in the refuge's waters. More than 180 species of birds have been spotted as well.

Most people recognize the Arctic National Wildlife Refuge as the land at the center of an ongoing oil-drilling debate in Congress. Some want to open up the land to oil exploration, while others say the land was set aside for a reason: to stay wild. Outdoor travelers can appreciate this wildness while traveling down one of the many rivers or backpacking across the open tundra. It's a vast and intimidating place, but awe-inspiring at the same time.

The refuge remains roadless, with the exception of the limited access provided by the Dalton Highway, which passes through the western tip of the refuge. Most visitors choose to take a private charter plane into their location of choice and arrange pickup at a later time. Many visitors take a commercial flight to **Fort Yukon, Arctic Village, Deadhorse,** or **Kaktovik,** and charter a smaller plane into the refuge from there.

YUKON FLATS NATIONAL WILDLIFE REFUGE

YUKON FLATS NATIONAL WILDLIFE REFUGE
101 12th Ave.
Room 264, Box 264
Fairbanks 99701
907-456-0440 | **yukonflats.fws.gov**

Primary activities: *birding, rafting, canoeing, kayaking, fishing*

Yukon Flats National Wildlife Refuge is just slightly smaller than Arctic National Wildlife Refuge, with 9 million acres of wild land in eastern Interior Alaska. It includes the **Yukon Flats,** a vast wetland basin bisected by the Yukon River and dotted with a network of lakes, streams, and rivers.

The refuge is home to the largest density of breeding ducks in Alaska making it one of the greatest waterfowl-breeding areas in North America, so it is a bird lover's paradise. Migrating birds pass through the flats by the thousands, but a hardy few species—only about 12—live in the refuge year-round.

Wildlife ranges from grizzly bears to moose to wolves, although none of these creatures are seen as frequently as in other regions of the state. Black bears are more common in the refuge than grizzlies.

The refuge is about 100 miles north of Fairbanks. Access is primarily by boat or aircraft. Get there by taking the Steese Highway from Fairbanks to the Yukon River at Circle. From Circle, you travel down the river via watercraft into the refuge. Charter service to remote lakes and gravel bars along rivers is also available from Fairbanks and Fort Yukon. Visitors may also drive up the Dalton Highway to the Yukon River Bridge and travel upriver about 5 miles to reach the refuge.

> **TRAVELER'S TIP**
>
> ▶ Because of its subarctic climate, Yukon Flats National Wildlife Refuge experiences seasonal extremes in temperature and daylight. It can get as hot as 100°F in the summer and as cold as –70°F in the winter.

▲ Getting around the Interior

FAIRBANKS

Access by air is through **Alaska Airlines** (800-252-7522; **alaskaair.com**). You can also drive to Fairbanks from the Richardson or Parks highways.

▶ **Airport Car Rentals** **Avis Rent-A-Car** (800-331-1212 or 907-474-0900; **avis.com**); **Budget Rent-A-Car** (800-474-0855 or 907-474-0855; **budget.com**); and **Dollar Rent-A-Car** 907-451-4360) all have comparable rates, at $50 and up per day.

▶ **Go North Alaska Travel Center** 866-236-7272 or 907-479-7272; 3500 Davis Rd., Fairbanks 99709, **paratours.net**. They offer camper vans and trucks beginning at about $50.

▶ **National Car Rental** 4960 Dale Rd.; 800-227-7368 or 907-451-7368; **nationalcar.com**. Cars, trucks, and vans available and two locations, one at the airport and one downtown.

NORTH OF FAIRBANKS

▶ **Arctic Outfitters** 907-474-3530; **arctic-outfitters.com.** This outfit rents vehicles for driving the Dalton Highway. The vehicles are gravel-road ready and come with emergency gear in case of breakdowns. Based in Fairbanks, but it is the only outfit that rents vehicles for the areas north of Fairbanks.

▶ **Dalton Highway Express** 907-474-3555; **daltonhighwayexpress.com.** Offers transportation along the Dalton Highway and Fairbanks.

▲ Gearing Up

FAIRBANKS IS YOUR best opportunity to get your gear and supplies in order, although other opportunities are in the region. As is the rule everywhere in Alaska, the more remote the area, the more you will pay. Despite advances in transportation and the higher efficiency of moving goods, it is still difficult to get the freshest or best of anything in outlying communities.

This section of the book is broken down by the main communities in the Interior with shops that will help you find what you are looking for. We list sporting goods and camping supplies and groceries separately, but many stores carry a little of everything—a characteristic of Alaska stores that you will soon notice is commonplace.

SPORTING GOODS AND CAMPING SUPPLIES

Fairbanks

▶ **Alaska Outdoor Rentals and Guides, LLC** 907-457-2453; **2paddle1.com.** Outfitting adventurers with kayaks, canoes, and mountain bikes, plus accessories.

▶ **Alaska Tent & Tarp Inc.** 529 Front St.; 907-456-5501. This outfit sells some of the best cold-weather camping tents on the market today. Locally owned and a local favorite.

▶ **All Weather Sports** 927 Old Steese Hwy.; 907-474-2811; **allweathersports.com.** For all your cycling needs in the area, especially for those brave enough to try snow-biking or riding during winter.

▶ **Beaver Sports** 3480 College Rd.; 907-479-2494; **beaversports.com.** The largest sporting-goods store in the area, carrying names such as The North Face, Marmot, and Dana Designs. Skis, camping gear, kayaks, and more.

▶ **Big Ray's Store** 507 2nd Ave.; 907-452-3458 or 800-478-3458, **bigrays.com.** An excellent source for heavy-duty winter clothing, boots, hats, mittens, Carhartts, and such. A longtime local favorite, Big Ray's serves Bush communities as well.

▶ **Fred Meyer** 3755 Airport Way; 907-474-1415, 930 Old Steese Hwy., #A; 907-459-4200; 19 College Rd.; 907-459-4200. These full-service grocery stores have everything you might need, from camping supplies to fresh vegetables. They sell fishing licenses as well, and have a wide selection of fishing tackle.

Denali Area

▶ **Denali Mountain Morning Hostel and Lodge** Just outside Denali National Park; Mile 244.1 Parks Hwy.; 907-683-7503; **hostelalaska.com.** This is a rustic hostel located in the heart of the Alaska Range, on Carlo Creek with great hiking trails. Proprietor Bill Madsen can direct you to local outlets for backpack or camping gear rental.

▶ **Denali Mountain Works** Across from the McKinley Chalets; 907-683-1542; **akrivers.com.** They sell everything from outdoor clothing to backpacks, stoves, Carhartts, and fuel, as well as guide some awesome raft and river trips under the name of Too-loo-uk River Guides.

GROCERY

Fairbanks

▶ **Asian Food Market** 1616 S. Cushman St., Suite 1a, 907-455-7814. A good place to shop for alternative ingredients that may not be readily available at the typical full-service grocery stores. A great resource for vegetarians.

▶ **Carrs/Safeway** 30 College Rd.; 907-374-4100 and 3627 Airport Way; 907-479-4231. Full-service groceries and limited camping/fishing supplies.

▶ **Fred Meyer** 3755 Airport Way; 907-474-1400. This full-service grocery store has everything you might need, from camping supplies to fresh vegetables.

North of Fairbanks

▶ **Fox General Store** 2226 Old Steese Hwy. N.; 907-457-8903. Known locally for their delicious pies, and it's worth the drive to get them.

Denali Area

▶ **McKinley RV & Campground** Mile 248 Parks Hwy.; 800-478-2562; **mckinleyrv .com.** Under new management, this is the only RV park with a free shuttle to the park entrance. Groceries, fuel, deli, Wi-Fi, laundry, propane, and dump station are available. Campsites start at $20.

▲ Where to Stay

WE THINK OF the lodging situation in Interior Alaska as feast or famine. In the populated areas, your choices are vast. The Denali area has dozens of bed-and-breakfasts, hotels, and hostels from which to choose. Fairbanks has more than we can count.

But head out into the fringe areas, such as the Dalton Highway, north of Fairbanks, or south along the Richardson Highway, and the selections become few and far between. Still, there are a few gems out there.

FAIRBANKS

Indoor Lodging

▶ **Aurora Express Bed and Breakfast**   1540 Chena Ridge Rd.; 800-221-0073; **fairbanksalaskabedandbreakfast.com.**

QUALITY ★★★★ | VALUE ★★★ | $145–$225

Choose from a whole lineup of refurbished rail cars in the side yard of this home. It sounds crazy, but it's not—they're actually pretty neat.

▶ **Billie's Backpackers Hostel**   2895 Mack Rd.; 907-479-2034; **alaskahostel.com.**

QUALITY ★★★ | VALUE ★★★ | $28

This one gets the highest ratings among independent travelers, although we also like the Glacier House Hostel (two listings down). Billie's Backpackers is off College Road, near the university. Everyone loves Billie too. Look for the house with all the international flags hanging out front.

▶ **Chena Hot Springs Resort**   907-451-8104; **chenahotsprings.com.**

QUALITY ★★★★★ | VALUE ★★★★ | $65–$249

This special place is on Chena Hot Springs Road, outside of town but worth the drive. The hot springs are incredible, especially in the winter when paired with northern lights–viewing in subzero temperatures. In summer, rent a yurt for two for just $65 a night.

▶ **Glacier House Hostel**   535 Glacier Ave.; 907-322-4946; **hostelfairbanksalaska.com.**

QUALITY ★★★★ | VALUE ★★★★ | $22

For $10 they'll come pick you up and drop you off at the airport or railroad at this newer hostel in town. Linens are included, and laundry is on-site as well.

▶ **Pike's Waterfront Lodge**   1850 Hoselton Rd.; 877-774-2400; **pikeslodge.com.**

QUALITY ★★★★ | VALUE ★★★★ | $140–$210

By Fairbanks standards, Pike's is one of the nicest places in town, and an enjoybale option for those who might want a little pampering before their outdoor adventure. Great outdoor dining in summer.

▲ interior alaska indoor lodging

NAME	LODGING TYPE	QUALITY RATING	VALUE RATING	COST
FAIRBANKS				
Aurora Express Bed and Breakfast	B&B	★★★★	★★★	$145–$225
Billie's Backpackers Hostel	Hostel	★★★	★★★	$28
Chena Hot Springs Resort	Bunks/ cabins/resort	★★★★★	★★★★	$65–$249
Glacier House Hostel	Hostel	★★★★	★★★★	$22
Pike's Waterfront Lodge	Lodge	★★★★	★★★★	$140–$210
7 Gables Inn	Inn	★★★★	★★★★	$50–$200
NORTH OF FAIRBANKS				
Coldfoot Camp	motel-style	★★	★	$219
DENALI AREA				
Blue Home Bed and Breakfast	B&B	★★★	★★★	$135+
Camp Denali–North Face Lodge	Wilderness lodge	★★★★★	★★★★	$3,535/week
Denali Dome Home Bed and Breakfast	B&B	★★★★	★★	$170–$190
Denali Mountain Morning Hostel and Lodge	Hostel/cabins	★★★★★	★★★★★	$35–$80
Denali Touch of Wilderness Bed and Breakfast Inn	B&B	★★★★	★★★★	$165–$198
Denali's Earthsong Lodge	B&B/ cabins/lodge	★★★★★	★★★★	$155–$195

▶ **7 Gables Inn**   4312 Birch Lane; 907-479-0751; **7gablesinn.com.**

QUALITY ★★★★ | VALUE ★★★★ | $50–$200

Centrally located near major attractions, with affordable rooms or a two-bedroom apartment, private Jacuzzi baths, and a full gourmet breakfast.

▲ interior alaska camping

NAME	CAMPING TYPE	QUALITY RATING	VALUE RATING	COST
FAIRBANKS				
Chena Hot Springs Resort	RV/tent	★★★★★	★★★★	$20
River's Edge RV Park	RV/tent	★★★★	★★★	$21–$42
Tanana Valley Campground	Tent	★★★	★★★★★	$16–$24
NORTH OF FAIRBANKS				
Campgrounds along the Dalton Highway	RV/tent	★★★	★★★★★	Free
Coldfoot Camp	RV/tent	★★	★★★	$15–$30
DENALI AREA				
Denali Grizzly Bear Cabins and Campground	Tent/ RV/ cabins	★★★	★★★	$25–$242
Riley Creek Campground	RV/tent	★★★★	★★★★	$14–$28
Sanctuary River Campground	Tent	★★★★	★★★★	$9
Savage River Campground	RV/tent	★★★★	★★★★	$22–$40
Teklanika Campground	RV/tent	★★★★	★★★★	$16
Wonder Lake Campground	Tent	★★★★★	★★★★★	$16

Camping

▶ **Chena Hot Springs Resort** At the end of Chena Hot Springs Road, Mile 56; 907-451-8104; **chenahotsprings.com.**

QUALITY ★★★★★ | VALUE ★★★★ | $20

Get the most out of the hot springs, but stay in an economical camp spot instead of a pricey room. The hot springs are incredible.

▶ **River's Edge RV Park** 4200 Boat St.; 800-770-3343 or 907-474-0286; **riversedge.net.**

QUALITY ★★★★ | VALUE ★★★ | $21–$42 (FOR TENT OR RV CAMPING)

Offers great views, free showers, and a close-to-the-airport location. Cottages and suites are also available for $155–$205.

▶ **Tanana Valley Campground**   1800 College Rd.; 907-456-7956;
tananavalleyfair.org.

QUALITY ★★★ | VALUE ★★★★★ | $16–$24

This campground is a find for the budget-conscious camper. Tent sites are
cheap, showers free.

NORTH OF FAIRBANKS

Indoor Lodging

▶ **Coldfoot Camp**   Mile 175 Dalton Hwy., in Coldfoot; 866-474-3400 or
907-474-3500; **coldfootcamp.com.**

QUALITY ★★ | VALUE ★ | $219

Rooms are simple and clean, albeit expensive for what you get, as this is the
only place around for miles.

Camping

▶ **Campgrounds along the Dalton Highway**   U.S. Bureau of Land Management
(BLM) camps, various locations; 907-474-2200; **blm.gov/ak/dalton.**

QUALITY ★★★ | VALUE ★★★★★ | FREE

The BLM manages much of the land along the road and has 10 campgrounds,
three of which are primitive camping areas. The locations are **Finger Mountain**
(Mile 98), **Arctic Circle** (Mile 115), **Gobblers Knob** (Mile 131), **Grayling Lake** (Mile
150), **South Koyukuk River** (Mile 156), **Marion Creek** (Mile 179), **Middle Fork Koyukuk River** (Mile 204), **Last Spruce Tree** (Mile 235), **Galbraith Camp** (Mile 274), and
Last Chance (Mile 355). Some sites have pit toilets and other amenities; none
have fees.

▶ **Coldfoot Camp**   Mile 175 Dalton Hwy., in Coldfoot; 866-474-3400 or
907-474-3500; **coldfootcamp.com.**

QUALITY ★★ | VALUE ★★★ | $15–$30

Outside the camp are places for tent and RV camping. Tent camping is free;
RV hook-up sites are $30. Showers are $10.

DENALI AREA

Indoor Lodging

▶ **Blue Home Bed and Breakfast**   In Cantwell, 40 minutes south of Denali;
907-768-2020; **cantwell-bluehome.de.**

QUALITY ★★★ | VALUE ★★★ | $135+

Two guest rooms with lovely mountain views. The owners speak Dutch and
make fine leather artwork. It's the nicest place to stay in Cantwell.

▶ **Camp Denali–North Face Lodge**   907-683-2290; **campdenali.com.**

QUALITY ★★★★★ | **VALUE** ★★★★ | **$3,535/WEEK**

Our choice for end-of-the-road fine wilderness lodging. The owners are longtime Alaskans who've operated the lodge since 1952, and they offer some of the best food, friendship, and stories you will enjoy your entire trip. Daily outings, special naturalist programs, and just about any other outdoor adventure you want is possible. Highly recommended, although admittedly expensive.

▶ **Denali Dome Home Bed and Breakfast**   In Healy; 800-683-1239 or 907-683-1239; **denalidomehome.com.**

QUALITY ★★★★ | **VALUE** ★★ | **$170–$190**

This family-run bed-and-breakfast is hosted by the gracious Miller family, whose friendliness is why we recommend it. Plus, it's open year-round.

▶ **Denali Mountain Morning Hostel and Lodge**   13 miles south of Denali National Park; 907-683-7503; **hostelalaska.com.**

QUALITY ★★★★★ | **VALUE** ★★★★★ | **$35–$80**

This is our lodging choice for those wanting to explore the park but don't want to lodge in the bustling McKinley Village chaos. The hostel has rooms, bunks, and cabins for rent, and welcomes guests of all ages. The creekside bonfire is always nice, too.

▶ **Denali Touch of Wilderness Bed and Breakfast Inn**   In Denali Park; 800-683-2459 or 907-683-2459; **touchofwildernessbb.com.**

QUALITY ★★★★ | **VALUE** ★★★★ | **$165–$198**

This longtime bed-and-breakfast has many rooms from which to choose and a soothing outdoor hot tub. Rates drop in the winter.

▶ **Denali's Earthsong Lodge**   In Healy; 907-683-2863 or 907-460-1451; **earthsonglodge.com.**

QUALITY ★★★★★ | **VALUE** ★★★★ | **$155–$195**

Charming log cabins with private baths and amenities. Longtime Denali residents Jon and Karin Nierenberg offer meals and slide-show programs. They recently added a two-bedroom cabin that is perfect for families. These naturalists can share their knowledge of the area as well as or better than most people in Denali. This is our number-one choice for lodging in the Healy area. The Nierenbergs also offer sled-dog kennel tours. Rates start at $155 for a cabin.

National Park Service Campgrounds

The National Park Service operates the following five campgrounds, three of which are accessible by vehicle. For more information, call 907-683-2294 or visit **nps.gov/dena**. Sites can be reserved by calling 866-761-6629 or 907-272-7275 or visiting **reservedenali.com**.

▶ **Riley Creek Campground**   A quarter mile west of the Parks Highway.

QUALITY ★★★★ | VALUE ★★★★ | $14–$28

Has 150 sites for RVs and tents. Open year-round.

▶ **Sanctuary River Campground**   Mile 23 Park Rd.

QUALITY ★★★★ | VALUE ★★★★ | $9

Has seven sites for tents only. Open seasonally. A one-time reservation fee of $5 is required in addition to the standard nightly fee. Accessible only by camper bus.

▶ **Savage River Campground**   Mile 13 Park Rd.

QUALITY ★★★★ | VALUE ★★★★ | $22–$40

Has 33 sites for RVs and tents. Open seasonally. (The nearby Savage River Group Camp sites are $40.)

▶ **Teklanika Campground**   Mile 29 Park Rd.

QUALITY ★★★★ | VALUE ★★★★ | $16

Three-day passes are now required. Check with Denali officials before registering.

▶ **Wonder Lake Campground**   Mile 85 Park Rd.

QUALITY ★★★★★ | VALUE ★★★★★ | $16

Has 28 sites for tents only. Open seasonally. A one-time reservation fee of $5 is required in addition to the standard nightly fee. Accessible only by camper bus.

Other Denali Campground

▶ **Denali Grizzly Bear Cabins and Campground**   In Denali Park; 866-583-2696 or 907-683-2696; **denaligrizzlybear.com**.

QUALITY ★★★ | VALUE ★★★ | $25–$242

Camping right on the Nenana River (and close to the road, but you probably won't notice it over the river noise). Options range from tents to hotel rooms, small and premium cabins.

▲ Where to Eat

INTERIOR ALASKA DINING

Fairbanks

▶ **Asiana Teriyaki Restaurant**   2001 Airport Way; 907-457-3333.

| ASIAN | QUALITY ★★★ | $8–$18 | SUITABLE FOR KIDS? Y |

Offers an affordable and interesting mix of Korean and Japanese.

▶ **Gambardella's Pasta Bella**   706 2nd Ave.; 907-456-3417; gambardellas.com.

| ITALIAN | QUALITY ★★★★ | $9–$29 | SUITABLE FOR KIDS? N |

Italian cuisine in a hidden-away section of downtown Fairbanks. Fine wines accompany large portions.

▶ **Lavelle's Bistro**   575 1st Ave.; 907-450-0555; **lavellesbistro.com.**

| FUSION | QUALITY ★★★★★ | $11–$32 | SUITABLE FOR KIDS? N |

The wine experts here can help pick the perfect accompaniment to your meal.

▶ **McCafferty's, A Coffee House**   408 Cushman St.; 907-456-6853, mccaffertys.net.

| CAFE | QUALITY ★★★★ | $2–$6 | SUITABLE FOR KIDS? Y |

Their soups are delicious. Live entertainment on weekends.

▶ **Pike's Landing**   4438 Airport Rd.; 907-479-6500; pikeslodge.com/pikes-landing.html.

| BAR/AMERICAN | QUALITY ★★★ | $6–$18 | SUITABLE FOR KIDS? Y |

This restaurant draws the tourists, but the food is very good. We still go here every time we visit Fairbanks.

▶ **The Pump House Restaurant and Saloon**   796 Chena Pump Rd.; 907-479-8452; **pumphouse.com.**

| FUSION | QUALITY ★★★★★ | $9–$34 | SUITABLE FOR KIDS? N |

Established in 1933, the Pump House serves one of the best Sunday brunches in town. The dining area overlooks the Chena River and is an absolutely gorgeous place to eat on a sunny day.

▶ **Zach's Restaurant**   1717 University Ave., second level inside Sophie Station Hotel; 800-528-4916 or 907-479-3650; **fountainheadhotels.com.**

| FUSION | QUALITY ★★★★ | $8–$20 | SUITABLE FOR KIDS? N |

For a hotel restaurant, this one seems to go above and beyond the norm.

▲ interior alaska dining

NAME	CUISINE	FOOD QUALITY	COST
FAIRBANKS			
Asiana Teriyaki Restaurant	Asian	★★★	$8–$18
Gambardella's Pasta Bella	Italian	★★★★	$9–$29
Lavelle's Bistro	Fusion	★★★★★	$11–$32
McCafferty's, A Coffee House	Cafe	★★★★	$2–$6
Pike's Landing	Bar/American	★★★	$6–$18
The Pump House Restaurant and Saloon	Fusion	★★★★★	$9–$34
Zach's Restaurant	Fusion	★★★★	$8–$20
NORTH OF FAIRBANKS			
Manley Roadhouse	American	★★	$9–$25
Truckers Café Coldfoot Camp	American	★★★	$8–$26
DENALI AREA			
Denali Perch Lodge	American	★★★★	$10–$30
The Lunch Box	Asian/Mexican	★★★	$4–$9
Lynx Creek Pizza Parlor	Pizza	★★★★★	$7–$24
McKinley Creekside Café	American	★★★★	$7–$28
229 Parks Restaurant & Tavern	Fusion	★★★★★	$11–$34

We've always had good dining experiences here. Steaks and Alaska seafood dominate the dinner menu.

North of Fairbanks

▶ **Manley Roadhouse**   Mile 152 Elliott Hwy.; 907-672-3161.

AMERICAN | QUALITY ★★ | $9–$25 | SUITABLE FOR KIDS? N

This historical roadhouse offers food, rooms, and cabins for those who drive this far. The roadhouse also features lots of historical artifacts from the area's rich mining past. The food is basic, but the pies and cinnamon rolls are fresh-baked and delicious.

▶ **Truckers Café Coldfoot Camp**   Mile 175 Dalton Hwy., in Coldfoot; 907-474-3500 or 866-474-3400; **coldfootcamp.com.**

AMERICAN	QUALITY ★★★	$8–$26	SUITABLE FOR KIDS? Y

Home-style cooking, and prime rib almost any time. There's also an accompanying bar, the Frozen Foot Saloon, if you want to kick up your heels.

Denali Area

▶ **Denali Perch Lodge**   888-322-2523 or 907-683-2523; **denaliperchresort.com.**

AMERICAN	QUALITY ★★★★	$10–$30	SUITABLE FOR KIDS? N

The locals eat at The Perch Restaurant, and the owners know everyone. The food is great, and the wine selection is surprisingly good for being so far out in the middle of nowhere. There's also the Panoramic Pizza Pub. Private-bath and shared-bath cabins rent for $85–$125 per night.

▶ **The Lunch Box**   Spur Road and Coal Street in Healy; 907-683-6833.

ASIAN/MEXICAN	QUALITY ★★★	$4–$9	SUITABLE FOR KIDS? Y

Offers food that ranges from Asian-American to Mexican—they do it all out here in the middle of nowhere! The prices are right, though, and the service is extra-friendly. The Lunch Box also prepares sack lunches to take into the park with you for your all-day adventures.

▶ **Lynx Creek Pizza Parlor**   Mile 238.4 Parks Hwy., Denali Park; 907-683-2547.

PIZZA	QUALITY ★★★★★	$7–$24	SUITABLE FOR KIDS? Y

It's filled to bursting all the time, but the pizza really earns its reputation. Pizza can be eaten in-house or delivered to your hotel, lodge, or camp.

▶ **McKinley Creekside Café**   Mile 224 Parks Hwy.; 888-533-6254 or 907-683-2277; **mckinleycabins.com.**

AMERICAN	QUALITY ★★★★	$7–$28	SUITABLE FOR KIDS? Y

Near Carlo Creek, 13 miles south of the Denali National Park entrance; offers delicious food and great cabin lodging.

▶ **229 Parks Restaurant & Tavern**   In Denali National Park; 907-683-2567; **campdenali.com.**

FUSION	QUALITY ★★★★★	$11–$34	SUITABLE FOR KIDS? N

This restaurant at the park entrance takes fine food to new levels. Owners Laura and Land Cole know what they're doing. Land was raised in Denali and built the timber-frame restaurant himself. The Coles also run Camp Denali (page 462), one of our choices for lodging in the area.

▲ On the Town:
What to Do after the Outdoor Adventure

WHETHER YOU'RE NURSING blisters from your multiday hike or recovering from a week of paddling on some remote river, you shouldn't have trouble finding ways to unwind once you're back in town: Fairbanks has numerous attractions and entertainment venues to choose from, and even outlying areas such as Denali offer some fun things to do.

FAIRBANKS

▶ **Alaska Salmon Bake & Palace Theatre**   3175 College Rd.; 800-354-7274 or 907-452-7274; **akvisit.com.** *The Golden Heart Revue* is performed by a professional cast and features music by Fairbanks composer Jim Bell. It's a comic look at early and present-day Fairbanks. Rates are $31 for adults, $15 for children.

▶ **Georgeson Botanical Garden**   On the University of Alaska Fairbanks campus, 117 W. Tanana Dr.; 907-474-1944; **georgesonbg.org.** While away an afternoon enjoying the flowers that grow under the power of the 24-hour midnight sun in the northernmost public garden in the United States.

▶ **Large Animal Research Station**   2220 Yankovich Rd.; 907-474-7207; **uaf.edu.** See the large animals of Alaska, thanks to the research efforts of professors at University of Alaska Fairbanks. There are daily guided tours of musk oxen, caribou, and reindeer.

▶ **University of Alaska Museum of the North**   907 Yukon Dr., on the University of Alaska Fairbanks campus; 907-474-7505; **uaf.edu/museum.** This museum is jam-packed with artifacts, natural and historical exhibits, and other interesting tidbits. One of the highlights is Blue Babe, a 36,000-year-old Steppe bison that was recovered from a mining site nearby. Admission is $10 for adults, $5 for youth 7–17.

NORTH OF FAIRBANKS

▶ **Circle District Historical Society**   Mile 128 Steese Hwy., in Central; 907-520-1893; **cdhs.us/Fset.htm.** Learn about the area's mining history, see mammoth tusks and bones, and check out local beadwork, wildflowers, and gold displays.

▶ **Gold Dredge No. 8**   1755 Old Steese Hwy. N.; 907-457-6058; **golddredgeno8.com.**

▶ **Simon Paneak Memorial Museum**   341 Mekiana Rd., in Anaktuvuk Pass;

907-661-3413; **north-slope.org/nsb/53.htm.** Visit America's farthest-north museum to learn about the Nunamiut people.

▶ **Trading Post**   Mile 49.5 Elliott Hwy.; 907-474-3507. At this shop you can get your official certificate stating that you've passed the Arctic Circle. It's slightly touristy, but a milestone nonetheless.

DENALI AREA

▶ **Alaska Cabin Nite**   Performances at the McKinley Chalet Resort; 800-276-7234 or 907-264-4600; **denaliparkresorts.com/alsakan-cabin-nite-dinner-theatre.aspx.** Two shows each night May–September offer a gold-rush tale of adventure in the early 1900s. Heroine Fanny Quigley was a real-life pioneer in the Kantishna area, deep in Denali National Park. Performers tell her story with humor, music, and colorful acting, all while doubling as your servers for the all-you-can-eat buffet. It's a blast, even for those who don't think much of theater. The cost is $62 for adults, $31 for children age 12 and under. Suitable for all ages.

▶ **Husky Homestead Tours**   907-683-2904; **huskyhomestead.com.**Take a tour of an Iditarod Sled Dog Race champion's kennel. Jeff King has a hand-built log cabin in the mountains surrounding the park; daily tours of his kennels introduce the neophyte to the state sport of dog mushing. Cuddle puppies, hear trail stories, and get a feel for what it's like to have the job of dog musher. Tours are $49 for adults, $29 for children age 12 and under, and last an hour and a half. Not recommended for children age 3 or younger.

▲ An Overview of the Roadless Regions

FANNING OUT FROM the Interior is land so remote that it is simply called the Bush. The majority of Alaska's native people choose to reside here, often living off the land by fishing, hunting, and gathering as their ancestors did before them. The largest communities are **Barrow, Nome,** and **Kotzebue,** augmented by dozens of villages scattered across the region. We have also included Southwest Alaska as part of our Bush chapter because of its remote, sparsely populated environment. Its larger communities are **Unalaska–Dutch Harbor, Dillingham,** and **Bethel,** as well as **King Salmon,** a smaller community

Dillingham

Okstokok Cir.
Kokwok Cir.

1
4
7
5
10

Scandinavian Creek

To
← Airport

Lily
Pond

Kenny Wren Rd.

2nd Ave.

Little Airport Rd.

F St.

E St.

E St. W.

Seward St.

D St.

Kanakanak Rd.

2
8
9

Boat
Harbor

C St.

Main St.

Alaska St.

Central Ave.

11

3rd Ave. E.
2nd Ave. E.

Main St.

2nd Ave. W.

1st Ave. W.

3   A St.

B St.

2nd Ave. E.

6

■ INDOOR LODGING
1. Beaver Creek Bed
   and Breakfast
2. Bristol Bay Lodge
3. The Bristol Inn
4. Hillside Haven B&B
5. Thai Inn

7. Round Island
8. Togiak National
   Wildlife Refuge
9. Wood-Tikchik State
   Park

◆ DINING
10. Café Hillside
11. The Muddy Rudder

▲ CAMPING
6. City of Dillingham
   Campground

Nushagak Bay

0   600 ft
0   200 m

N

that serves as a hub for many outdoor adventures. (See Part One, pages 10–13, for maps of the Bush Southwest and Bush Far North regions.)

The Bush's Inupiat, Yup'ik, and Aleut natives depend on boats, snow-mobiles, and dog teams to get around mostly roadless communities. During the winter the rivers freeze, creating ribbon highways for snowmobile and dog-team travel. In summer, boats provide transportation. Today, most com-munities also have air service, connecting the world to these once-inaccessible places. The Bush is where some of the most adventurous of the adventurous roam, rafting rivers that perhaps see fewer than a dozen people in any given year, or fishing lakes that don't know the feel of human footprints.

To be honest, the communities of the Bush are a bit drab at first glance, with the exception of Unalaska, which has some fabulous scenery right off the bat. Barrow, for instance, is flat, treeless, and cold year-round. It seems desolate and lifeless, which is to be expected considering the

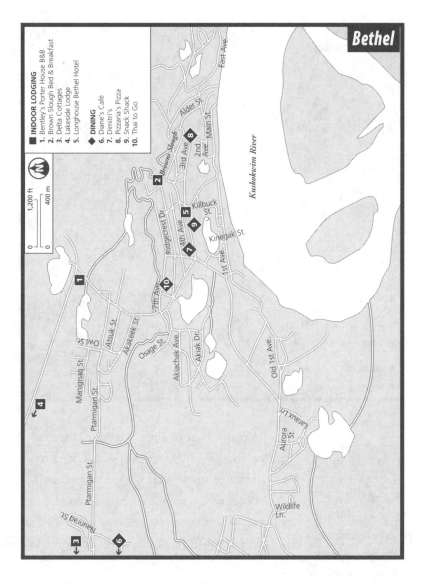

Bethel

INDOOR LODGING
1. Bentley's Porter House B&B
2. Brown Slough Bed & Breakfast
3. Delta Cottages
4. Lakeside Lodge
5. Longhouse Bethel Hotel

DINING
6. Diane's Café
7. Dimitri's
8. Pizzaria's Pizza
9. Snack Shack
10. Thai to Go

extreme climate. Bethel and Dillingham are much the same: flat, expansive, and void.

In the summer, though, the tundra of these places comes alive with colorful wildflowers and varying degrees of green with the other plants that cling to life there. The rivers are great for rafting and fishing. The wilderness beckons to backpackers who want to see new places.

King Salmon

| 0 | | 2,400 ft |
| 0 | 400 m | |

Iris St.

Sylvester St.

Sockeye Rd.

King Salmon St.

Cohoe Rd.

Eskimo Creek

Jensen Dr.

Bluff St.

Bonnie Ln.

2 **6**

5

3 (Access #3 by river.)

Main St.

State St.

B St.

Caribou Rd.

Naknek River

■ INDOOR LODGING
1. Alagnak Lodge
2. King Ko Inn
3. Rainbow Bend Lodges

▲ CAMPING
4. Alagnak Wild River

◆ DINING
5. Eddie's Fireplace Inn
6. King Salmon Café

4

1

TRAVELER'S TIP

▶ The Bush is worth exploring if for no other reason than its remoteness, the fact that your adventure is taking place so far off the beaten path that often no one's even bothered to give the places a name.

The real appeal of Bush Alaska is that, for the outdoors traveler, there are millions of acres of public—and sometimes private—land to explore. Some of Alaska's most remote and rugged national parks, preserves, and other protected lands are located here, and are well worth checking out. It's an adventurous feeling, exploring such uncharted territory. For that reason, most of this chapter focuses on the national parks and preserves, wild rivers, and monuments worth seeing when in this region.

Lodging and eateries are few and far between in the main communities, but we have offered a few suggestions of places that we think are suitable while in towns or resupplying for your backcountry trips.

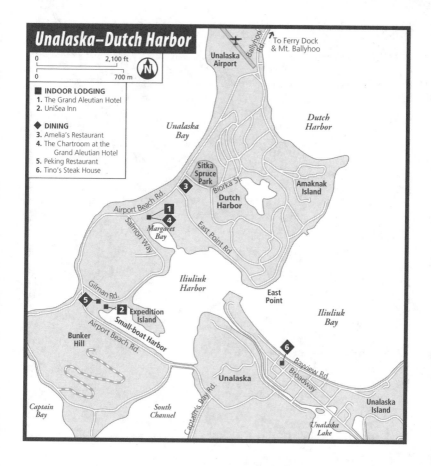

Unalaska–Dutch Harbor

To Ferry Dock & Mt. Ballyhoo

Unalaska Airport

Ballyhoo Rd

Dutch Harbor

Unalaska Bay

Sitka Spruce Park

Biorka St.

Dutch Harbor

Amaknak Island

Airport Beach Rd.

Salmon Way

Margaret Bay

East Point Rd.

Iliuliuk Harbor

East Point

Iliuliuk Bay

Gilman Rd.

Expedition Island

Airport Beach Rd.

Small-boat Harbor

Bunker Hill

Bayview Rd.

Broadway

Unalaska

Captain's Bay Rd.

Captain Bay

South Channel

Unalaska Island

Unalaska Lake

0 2,100 ft
0 700 m

■ **INDOOR LODGING**
1. The Grand Aleutian Hotel
2. UniSea Inn

◆ **DINING**
3. Amelia's Restaurant
4. The Chartroom at the Grand Aleutian Hotel
5. Peking Restaurant
6. Tino's Steak House

▲ Southwest

THIS AREA OF Alaska is often overlooked when travelers come here, in part because what it offers—unparalleled fishing, backpacking, and boating opportunities—can be found in more-accessible areas of the state. Southwest Alaska is composed of the **Aleutian Islands,** which stretch from the end of the Alaska Peninsula almost to Japan; the **Pribilof Islands,** which include **St. George** and St. Paul islands; Bethel, the largest "city" in the region; and the **Iliamna–Lake Clark** region. Some guidebooks include Kodiak Island as part of Southwest Alaska, but we've grouped it with the Southcentral Coastal region because it shares many of the same

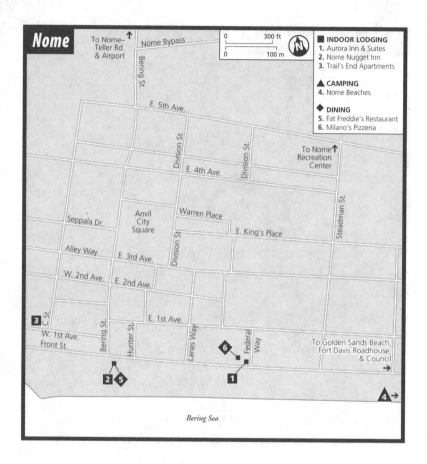

outdoor recreation opportunities found in Southcentral Alaska and is easily accessed from that region.

Southwest Alaska, geographically, is a diverse place, with active volcanoes, wild rivers—the **Yukon** and **Kuskokwim** are two of the better-known ones—and plenty of open wild land in the form of national parks and preserves in which to explore. Among native residents in this region are the Yu'pik Eskimos on the western mainland and the Aleuts on the Aleutian and Pribilof islands.

Our favorite places to visit in this region of the state include the **Lake Clark–Iliamna Lake area** and **Katmai National Park,** both of which have some of the best fishing and bear viewing in the entire state.

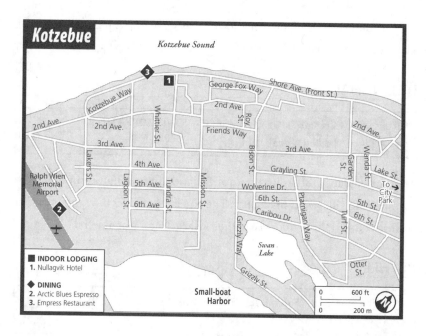

Kotzebue

Kotzebue Sound

Kotzebue Way

Shore Ave. (Front St.)

George Fox Way

2nd Ave.

Roy St.

Friends Way

2nd Ave.

2nd Ave.

2nd Ave.

3rd Ave.

Whittier St.

Bison St.

3rd Ave.

Lakers St.

4th Ave.

Grayling St.

Garden St.

Wanda St.

Lake St.

Ralph Wien Memorial Airport

Lagoon St.

Tundra St.

5th Ave.

6th Ave.

Mission St.

Wolverine Dr.

6th St.

Caribou Dr.

Ptarmigan Way

Turf St.

5th St.

6th St.

To City Park

Grizzly Way

Swan Lake

Otter St.

Grizzly St.

Small-boat Harbor

■ **INDOOR LODGING**
1. Nullagvik Hotel

◆ **DINING**
2. Arctic Blues Espresso
3. Empress Restaurant

0   600 ft
0   200 m

N

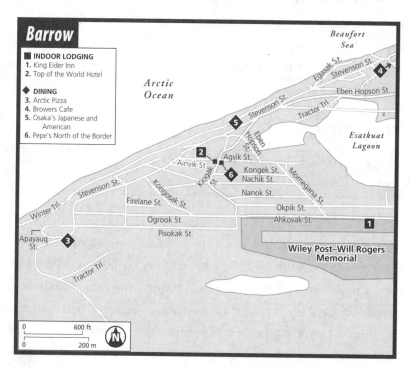

Barrow

Beaufort Sea

■ **INDOOR LODGING**
1. King Eider Inn
2. Top of the World Hotel

◆ **DINING**
3. Arctic Pizza
4. Browers Cafe
5. Osaka's Japanese and American
6. Pepe's North of the Border

Arctic Ocean

Eqasak St.

Stevenson St.

Stevenson St.

Eben Hopson St.

Tractor Trl.

Esatkuat Lagoon

Stevenson St.

Eben Hopson St.

Agvik St.

Ainvik St.

Kiogak St.

Kongek St.

Nachik St.

Momegana St.

Stevenson St.

Kongosak St.

Firelane St.

Nanok St.

Winter Trl.

Ogrook St.

Okpik St.

Ahkovak St.

Pisokak St.

Apayauq St.

Tractor Trl.

Wiley Post–Will Rogers Memorial

0   600 ft
0   200 m

N

Brief descriptions of the major towns that serve as jumping-off points for adventures are provided below and following.

DILLINGHAM

DILLINGHAM CHAMBER OF COMMERCE AND VISITOR CENTER
907-842-5115 | dillinghamak.com

With a population of around 2,400, Dillingham is a hub community for surrounding villages in **Bristol Bay.** The city is located on the north shore of **Nushagak Bay** at the confluence of the **Nushagak** and **Wood rivers.**

BETHEL

BETHEL CHAMBER OF COMMERCE
907-543-2911

Located on the banks of the **Kuskokwim River,** the village of Bethel is home to about 5,800 year-round residents, many of whom fish for a living in the **Bering Sea.** The primary native population consists of Yup'ik Eskimo, and many of them still live a subsistence lifestyle.

KING SALMON

KING SALMON VISITORS CENTER
907-246-4250

With only 400 or so residents, King Salmon is a small village, but it serves as one of the primary starting points for many Southwest Alaska adventures. It is located on the north bank of the **Naknek River** on the Alaska Peninsula, about 15 miles upriver from the village of **Naknek.** The native population is a mixture of Aleuts, Indians, and Eskimos. King Salmon is a transportation hub for Bristol Bay, and fishermen launch from there regularly.

UNALASKA

> **UNALASKA/PORT OF DUTCH HARBOR CONVENTION AND VISITORS BUREAU**
> 877-581-2612 | unalaska.info

Unalaska overlooks **Iliuliuk Bay** and **Dutch Harbor** on Unalaska Island in the Aleutian Chain. It lies 800 air miles from Anchorage and 1,700 miles northwest of Seattle. It is a rapidly growing and diverse community, focused on fishing and fish processing.

LAKE CLARK NATIONAL PARK AND PRESERVE

FIELD HEADQUARTERS	ADMINISTRATIVE HEADQUARTERS
1 Park Pl.	240 W. 5th Ave.
Port Alsworth 99653	Anchorage 99501
907-781-2218	nps.gov/lacl

Primary activities: *backpacking, rafting, fishing*

Lake Clark is one of the least-visited but most spectacular of the national parks in Alaska, and a great starting point for any unique outdoor adventure. Its 4 million acres attract fewer than 5,000 visitors a year, making it the type of place where you can have an adventure in which you cross paths with no one.

Lake Clark National Park and Preserve stretches from the shores of **Cook Inlet,** across the **Chigmit Mountains,** to the open hills of the western Interior. The Chigmits, where the Alaska and Aleutian ranges meet, comprise rugged and jagged-looking mountains and glaciers, which include two active volcanoes, **Mounts Redoubt** and **Iliamna.** The 40-mile-long **Lake Clark** is critical salmon habitat to the Bristol Bay salmon fishery, one of the largest sockeye-salmon fishing grounds in the world. The park is open year-round, although most of its visitors come between June and September.

Access to the Lake Clark region is by small aircraft from Anchorage, Kenai, or Homer. Floatplanes can land on the many lakes throughout the area, or wheeled planes can land on beaches or the few private airstrips in the region. Scheduled commercial flights between Anchorage and Iliamna, 30 miles outside the boundary, provide another means of access. There are no roads in the park. A 2.5-mile trail to **Tanalian Falls** and **Kontrashibuna Lake** is accessible from the town of Port Alsworth. The 50-mile Telaquana Trail, depicted on maps, is an undeveloped historical route from Lake Clark to Telaquana Lake.

KATMAI NATIONAL PARK AND PRESERVE

FIELD HEADQUARTERS	ADMINISTRATIVE HEADQUARTERS
1 King Salmon Mall	240 W. 5th Ave.
King Salmon 99613	Anchorage 99501
907-246-3305	**nps.gov/katm**

Primary activities: *bear viewing, fishing*

Katmai is a 4.7-million-acre national park and preserve located on the Alaska Peninsula, across from Kodiak Island, which also includes the mystical area known as the **Valley of 10,000 Smokes.** The area was named so in the early 1900s, when explorers discovered huge smoldering volcanoes, one of which, Novarupta, had deposited hundreds of feet of volcanic ash across the valley floor. This 40-square-mile area is still stark today, although lush vegetation surrounds it. The National Park Service reports that at least 14 volcanoes in Katmai are considered active, although none of them are currently erupting. Brown bears and salmon are very active in Katmai, which is why it receives so many more visitors than Lake Clark. In 2004, there were about 57,000 visitors, most of them there to see and photograph bears, go fishing, or both. The number of brown bears in the region has grown to more than 2,000, and during the peak of the sockeye-salmon run in July, as many as 60 bears at a time congregate in **Brooks Camp** along the **Brooks River** and the **Naknek Lake** and

Brooks Lake shorelines. However, the bears' range goes beyond this region, and they can be found all along the 480-mile Katmai Coast feeding on clams, crabs, and an occasional whale carcass.

Katmai National Park is open year-round, though most visitors travel there between June and September. Prime bear-viewing months are July and September, although a few bears may be in the area at any time between late May and December.

Access is via small plane. Park headquarters are in King Salmon, about 290 air miles southwest of Anchorage. Several commercial airlines provide daily flights into King Salmon as there is no road access. Brooks Camp, along the Brooks River approximately 30 air miles from King Salmon, is a common destination for visitors to the park. Brooks Camp can be reached only via small floatplane or boat.

> **TRAVELER'S TIP**
>
> ▶ Be prepared for anything when traveling to Katmai National Park. Weather and bears are always a factor here, so plan extra time to work around delays. There are occasions, especially in July, when visitors are unable to get to the falls platform due to time constraints and flight schedules.

ANIAKCHAK NATIONAL MONUMENT AND PRESERVE

ANIAKCHAK NATIONAL MONUMENT AND PRESERVE 907-246-3305	**ADMINISTRATIVE HEADQUARTERS** 240 W. 5th Ave. Anchorage 99501 **nps.gov/ania**

Primary activities: *rafting, fishing, backpacking*

Aniakchak National Monument and Preserve is for those who seek a destination like no other. This area is best suited for rafting, fly-fishing, and hiking, and a trip to the **Aniakchak Caldera** is unparalleled. The caldera is a giant dry crater that is the result of a series of eruptions, the latest dating to 1931 and the earliest as long ago as 3,500 years. It's nearly 6 miles in diameter and covers more than 10 miles, making it a great destination hike. The 2,000-foot caldera was thought to once be a 7,000-foot mountain that collapsed after the eruptions. While exploring the area, you'll see many outstanding examples of volcanic features, such as lava flows, cinder cones, and explosion pits. **Surprise Lake,** located within the caldera, is the source of the **Aniakchak River,** which flows through a giant crack in the caldera wall. The site also contains the **Aniakchak Wild River.**

Access to the park is by plane or floatplane from King Salmon, or by powerboat from any one of the numerous villages along the Pacific Ocean coastline. There are no formal trails within the preserve, although open ash fields make the backpacking and hiking options easier than bushwhacking. Conditions are usually windy within the caldera, and the coastal region is often cloudy and foggy. There are plenty of bears in the area too, so be sure to pack food well away from camp and be on the lookout. While exploring, also look for great birding and wildlife-watching options. The waterfowl and migratory bird habitat of Bristol Bay's coastal plain is west of the caldera. To the east, the Pacific Coast and offshore islands provide habitat for sea mammals and seabirds.

ALAGNAK WILD RIVER

ALAGNAK WILD RIVER
907-246-3305 | nps.gov/alag

Primary activities: *rafting, fishing*

Alagnak Wild River winds through the **Aleutian Range** on the Alaska Peninsula and is a great destination for scenic and whitewater rafting, as well as fishing for rainbow, sockeye, king salmon, northern pike, arctic char, and grayling. The area was designated as a Wild River in 1980, preserving the upper 56 miles of water and protecting the river and its immediate environments for future generations. It's the most popular fly-in fishery in Southwest Alaska and is inaccessible by road.

Access to the Alagnak is by charter flight from Anchorage and King Salmon or by powerboat from one of the villages along the river. The area is great not only for fishing but also for viewing wildlife such as caribou, beavers, lynx, mink, otters, foxes, wolverines, and occasionally wolves.

ALEUTIAN WORLD WAR II NATIONAL HISTORIC AREA

ALEUTIAN WORLD WAR II VISITOR CENTER
907-581-9944 | ounalashka.com
Open year-round

Primary activities: *birding, hiking, interpretive programs, wildlife viewing*

While this area is more dedicated to preserving history, the Aleutian World War II National Historic Area is also a remarkable place in which to explore. Located just outside of the Aleutian Island community of Unalaska, it follows the history of the U.S. Army **Fort Schwatka,** at Ulakta Head on Mount Ballyhoo. The fort is one of four coastal-defense posts built in the early 1940s to protect the **Dutch Harbor Naval Operating Base.** The fort overlooks Dutch Harbor and was key to its protection. Although today many of the bunkers and wooden structures of Fort Schwatka have collapsed, the gun mounts and lookouts are among the most intact in the country. A visitor center is located in the renovated Naval Air **Transport Services Aerology Building** at the Unalaska airport. It's a good place to explore in town.

WOOD-TIKCHIK STATE PARK

WOOD-TIKCHIK STATE PARK
550 W. 7th Ave.
Suite 1390
Anchorage 99501-3561
907-269-8698

WOOD-TIKCHIK RANGER STATION
907-842-2375
dnr.alaska.gov/parks/units/woodtik
Open seasonally, late May through late September

Primary activities: *kayaking, rafting, fishing*

Undeveloped and quite wild, Wood-Tikchik State Park holds the distinction of being the largest state park in the nation, covering 1.6 million acres of wilderness land that managers have worked hard to keep unspoiled. The park embraces a low-impact-camping mentality, so it is the perfect destination for outdoor travelers who appreciate land that remains untouched by vehicles, trails, and other amenities.

TRAVELER'S TIP

> ▶ Although the weather in Wood-Tikchik State Park between late May and early October permits outdoor recreation activities almost daily, flying, boating, and alpine activities are occasionally hampered or unsafe. Prepare for such changes in your schedule should bad weather appear.

The park was created in 1978 to protect fish- and wildlife-breeding habitats and allow an uninterrupted place for native subsistence practices and recreation. Its name is derived from the two lakes that dominate the region, but there are many others, as the park comprises a water-based ecosystem that is perfect for sea kayaking and river running.

Bordered by the **Nushagak Lowlands** on the east and the **Wood River Mountains** to the west, the lake system spans a variety of terrain and vegetative zones that are known for their rugged beauty. Pointed peaks, alpine valleys, and steep V-shaped arms make the western edge of the lakes look almost like a fjord. The lakes, which vary 15–45 miles long, are deep and relatively temperate for this part of the state, with water temperatures ranging 40°F–60°F during the summer.

Access to Wood-Tikchik State Park begins from Dillingham, in Southwest Alaska. Daily commercial-airline service is available from Anchorage, and air charter by floatplane is the most common mode of reaching the park; plus, the entire park is open to private-aircraft landings. You can also get to the Wood River Lakes via Aleknagik, 24 miles north of Dillingham by road, although you won't save a lot of money this way.

The weather is generally cool and moist, with average daily July temperatures in the low 60s. Precipitation is most prevalent in the summer, especially August.

Freshwater sportfish are generally prolific through-out the area and include rainbow trout, grayling, lake trout, arctic char, Dolly Varden, and northern pike. In addition, whitefish are an important subsistence spe-cies in the Tikchik Lakes, and all five species of salmon can be found. Wildlife includes such species as brown bears and occasionally black bears, ungulates such as moose and caribou, and small animals such as rab-bits, otters, beavers, and wolverines. The shrill calls of ground squirrels and marmots are heard frequently.

TRAVELER'S TIP

▶ There are no roads connecting Togiak National Wildlife Refuge to anyplace else, nor are there any trails, campgrounds, or facilities for those look-ing for a comfortable camping experience. Access is by air or water during ice-free months.

TOGIAK NATIONAL WILDLIFE REFUGE

TOGIAK NATIONAL WILDLIFE REFUGE
6 Main St.
Kangiiqutaq Building
907-842-1063 | togiak.fws.gov

Primary activities: *fishing, wildlife viewing, backpacking, rafting, kayaking, birding*

Managed by the U.S. Fish and Wildlife Service in Alaska, this 4.7-million-acre area was designated to conserve fish and wildlife populations. It's located in Southwest Alaska between **Kuskokwim Bay** and **Bristol Bay,** about 350 air miles southwest of Anchorage. It is bordered on the north by **Yukon Delta National Wildlife Refuge** and on the east by **Wood-Tikchik State Park.**

Togiak is a challenging place to reach. Its sea cliffs, fast-flowing rivers, and coastal lagoons are beautiful in the lowlands, and the surrounding **Ahk-lun Mountains** add grandeur in the form of craggy peaks.

One of the primary draws to the refuge is **Cape Peirce,** on the western edge of Bristol Bay and composed of rocky cliffs, ledges, and inaccessible beaches. It is a spectacular place to see such wildlife as Pacific walrus, spotted and harbor seals, puffins, and other rare and common seabirds. Access to the area, however, is limited due to the sensitive nature of the habitat, so visitors must obtain a permit ahead of time.

Access to the refuge is primarily by air taxis based in Dillingham, although there are a couple in King Salmon and Bethel.

U.S. Geological Survey topographic maps of the area may be purchased online at **topomaps.usgs.gov/ordering_maps.html.**

WALRUS ISLANDS STATE GAME SANCTUARY– ROUND ISLAND

WALRUS ISLANDS STATE GAME SANCTUARY
Alaska Department of Fish and Game, Division of Wildlife Conservation
907-842-2334 | **wildlife.alaska.gov** (go to "Walrus Island" link)

Primary activities:
wildlife viewing, backpacking, birding

Visits to this sanctuary, particularly the rugged **Round Island,** are limited because it is a critical habitat to the walrus. Each year in spring and summer, thousands of male walrus gather on this group of seven islands in Bristol Bay. The islands have enjoyed protected status since 1960, and visitors must obtain permits to travel here.

▲ Far North

ANY REGION IN the Far North that is not accessible by road is included in this chapter on the Bush. That includes such far-flung communities as Nome, Barrow, and Kotzebue but also encompasses some vast territories of land owned by the federal government and protected for centuries to come for outdoors travelers to enjoy.

The Far North is quintessential Alaska, the stereotype one often envisions when thinking of Alaska: long, cold winters; lots of dark nights; and plenty of wild animals roaming freely.

It is a land of extremes. At its northernmost reaches, the region enjoys the country's longest period of daylight, with 84 continuous days of constant daylight May 10–August 2. In contrast, during the dark days of winter, it is a cold, lonely place, and the sun remains set for 67 days. This is where polar bears roam—nowhere else in Alaska will you find them, despite what the movies portray. Grizzly bears, caribou, and moose are common, as well as tundra creatures such as arctic foxes and hares.

Among the native people living in the Far North, there are two groups of Eskimos: Inupiat on the mainland and Yu'piks, who reside in **Savoonga** and **Gambell,** on **St. Lawrence Island.**

Like Southwest Alaska, the Far North is home to some of the best national parks and preserves in the state, most of which are a result of the Alaska National Interest Lands Conservation Act, which in the late 1970s set aside millions of acres of land for public protection and use.

These areas are the places we recommend visiting, although stopping at some of the predominantly native communities along the way can remind one of being in a different country altogether, adding a cultural aspect to your trip that really can't be matched elsewhere in the state. Our favorites are **Kobuk Valley National Park,** where you can experience miles of sand dunes, and **Bering Land Bridge National Preserve,** where the Serpentine Hot Springs beckon year-round. We have included a few other options, as well, that are worth exploring.

Brief descriptions of the major towns that serve as jumping-off points for adventures are provided below.

NOME

NOME CONVENTION AND VISITORS BUREAU
907-443-6624 | **nomealaska.org**

This Bering Sea–coast community boomed at the turn of the century, when gold was discovered on its beaches, prompting one of the biggest gold rushes in history. Today, gold and other mineral mining still is the major economic force in Nome, home to about 3,500 residents, more than half of them Alaska natives. Nome is on the Seward Peninsula, some 540 miles from Anchorage, and off the road system. Nome's other claim to fame is the **Iditarod Trail Sled Dog Race,** the annual dog-mushing race from Anchorage to Nome.

KOTZEBUE

KOTZEBUE VISITOR INFORMATION CENTER 154 2nd St. Kotzebue 99752	907-442-3890 (Open during summer months; in the off-season, call and leave a message to arrange a visit.)

The mostly native community of Kotzebue lies 26 miles north of the Arctic Circle and 550 air miles northwest of Anchorage. There's not a lot in the way of visitor amenities here, but Kotzebue is one of the main starting points for forays farther into the wilderness. This is where you will arrange flights into the public lands and get to remote lodges scattered across the land.

BARROW

CITY OF BARROW 907-852-5211	**NORTH SLOPE BARROW PUBLIC INFORMATION DIVISION** 907-852-0215

Barrow is about as far north as you can go in Alaska, and once there you will truly feel that you are on the edge of the earth. The land is vast, open, and flat, and it seems to go on forever. Located 330 air miles north of the Arctic Circle, Barrow is in fact the farthest-north community in the Western Hemisphere. It is easily accessed via daily jet service from Anchorage or Fairbanks.

Barrow is another one of those Alaska communities that doesn't have much for the visitor looking for entertainment. But outdoor travelers are not necessarily seeking that sort of experience. Instead, the remoteness alone is the draw. If that is what you seek, then by all means visit this community— we've eaten at and stayed at a few places there that we recommend. Otherwise, your Far North adventure is likely going to be more outdoors adventurous if embarking from Nome or Kotzebue.

BERING LAND BRIDGE NATIONAL PRESERVE

> **BERING LAND BRIDGE NATIONAL PRESERVE**
> 907-443-2522| nps.gov/bela

Primary activities: *birding, hiking, backpacking, fishing, dog mushing, skiing*

The Bering Land Bridge National Preserve is one of the most remote national-park areas, on the Seward Peninsula in northwest Alaska, with its headquarters based in Nome. It is a remnant of the land bridge that connected Asia with North America more than 13,000 years ago. Archaeologists believe it was across the Bering Land Bridge, also called Beringia, that humans first passed from Asia to populate the Americas.

Camping, hiking, backpacking, and other exploration of the surrounding areas are possible with charter flights that can be arranged from Nome. Access to the preserve, in fact, is via Bush plane or small boat in the summer, and skis, snowmobile, or dog team in the winters. No roads lead directly into it, but that's part of the appeal. The park is open year-round, although most people visit in the summer months.

One of the best-kept secrets of this rarely visited preserve is **Serpentine Hot Springs,** a natural hot spring that offers year-round relaxation and a bunk-house-style cabin for those who don't mind sharing

TRAVELER'S TIP

▶ As is typical in the Bush, Serpentine Hot Springs has always had a casual, relaxed, and sharing atmosphere. Be sure to care for the facilities as you would if you were a guest in someone's home.

with others in exchange for a truly unique experience. The cabin sleeps 15–20 people in two sections and includes a wooden tub for bathing in a small bathhouse, which is fed by the waters of the hot spring. You can't reserve the cabin, and you may have to share it with other visitors who show up at the same time—it's considered Bush etiquette, so please resist the urge to claim first-come, first-served. There is unlimited camping too, for those who want more privacy if others show up. There is no developed water or power, and there are no sanitation facilities.

CAPE KRUSENSTERN NATIONAL MONUMENT

CAPE KRUSENSTERN NATIONAL MONUMENT
907-442-3890 or 907-442-3760

Primary activities:
backpacking, kayaking, dog mushing

Cape Krusenstern National Monument is an interesting study in Alaska beach life, and a place not visited often by outdoor travelers. While you can go backpacking and kayaking in this area, it is often windy and chilly, even in the middle of summer. Winter travel by dogsled is often the best means of travel, although it gets bone-chillingly cold, often –20°F or lower for days on end.

The area is beautiful, though. It is a coastal plain dotted with lagoons and pothole lakes, and surrounded by gently rolling limestone hills. Cape Krusenstern's bluffs and beach ridges are a great place for those curious about archaeology or geology, and the presence of prehistoric inhabitation goes back some 9,000 years.

In summer, wildflowers dot the landscape and huge numbers of migratory birds come from all over the world to nest. They use the lagoons as feeding and staging areas.

Alaska natives still hunt marine mammals along the beaches, and local rural residents are allowed to hunt in the monument. A local zinc mine operates along the northern boundary, so travelers are best suited to choose the southern side for more solitude.

Access to the monument is by private charter plane out of Kotzebue or Nome. Commercial airlines provide service from Anchorage or Fairbanks to Nome or Kotzebue. There are scheduled flights to villages and chartered flights to specific park areas. Summer access may include motorized or non-motorized watercraft, aircraft, or walking. Winter access may include snow-mobiles, aircraft, or walking.

The monument is open year-round, and the headquarters are in Kotzebue. There are no developed facilities such as camping or hiking trails, so be pre-pared for true wilderness travel. Summer hikes are possible, but there also is a lot of private land surrounding the monument, so be sure of where you are traveling. Kayaking is possible on several of the larger lagoons, but constant windy conditions can make it feel quite cold, even in the summer.

KOBUK VALLEY NATIONAL PARK

KOBUK VALLEY NATIONAL PARK
907-442-3890 or 907-442-3760 | nps.gov/kova

Primary activities: *backpacking, wildlife viewing, dog mushing, boating*

The Baird and Waring mountain ranges make up Kobuk Valley National Park, a park that is incredible in many ways but a must-see for those outdoor trav-elers who want a truly unique adventure. Located within the park is the 25-square-mile **Great Kobuk Sand Dunes,** as well as the **Little Kobuk** and **Hunt River dunes.** The unusual sand dunes look oddly out of place in Alaska but are there nonetheless, the result of ancient glaciers grinding together with the wind and rain. The dunes now cover much of the southern portion of the Kobuk Valley, where they are stabilized by vegetation. River bluffs, composed of sand

and standing as high as 150 feet, hold permafrost ice wedges and the fossils of Ice Age mammals.

The closest towns to Kobuk Valley National Park are Kotzebue and Nome, both of which have daily jet service from Anchorage and Fairbanks. Access to the park is by air taxi, which can take you to most places within the park that you'd like to see. You can also travel the Kobuk River by boat to access the area, as well as backpack in, although there are no trails. In the winter, access is via snowmobile, dog team, or skis if you're brave enough. Tundra and river bars are often used for primitive camping. Do not camp in archaeological areas or on private property.

The park is open year-round, although winter conditions are typical of the Arctic, with temperatures routinely plummeting to as low as −50°F. Throughout the year, educational and interpretive programs are offered at the **Kotzebue Public Lands Information Center** (907-442-3760).

NOATAK NATIONAL PRESERVE

NOATAK NATIONAL PRESERVE

907-442-3890 or 907-442-3760 | nps.gov/noat

Primary activities: *backpacking, wildlife viewing, boating, dog mushing, skiing*

As one of North America's largest mountain-ringed river basins with an intact ecosystem, the **Noatak River** environs feature some of the Arctic's finest arrays of plants and animals. The river is classified as a National Wild and Scenic River, and it offers superlative wilderness float-trip opportunities— from deep in the **Brooks Range** to the tidewater of the **Chukchi Sea.**

There are no trails or roads in the park.

Throughout the year programs are offered at the Kotzebue Public Lands Information Center. Activities include occasional guided hikes and slide-show lectures on various features of the preserve.

Noatak National Preserve is open year-round. The headquarters office, located in Kotzebue, is open 8 a.m.–5 p.m. Monday–Friday. The visitor center, also located in Kotzebue, is open for the summer, Tuesday–Friday noon–8 p.m. and Saturday noon–4 p.m.

Commercial airlines provide service from Anchorage or Fairbanks to Nome or Kotzebue. From Kotzebue to the parklands, fly with various air-taxi operators. There are scheduled flights to villages and chartered flights to specific park areas. Summer access may include motorized or nonmotorized watercraft, aircraft, or walking. Winter access may include snowmobiles, aircraft, or walking.

▲ Getting around the Bush

SOUTHWEST

Dillingham

Access by air is through **Alaska Airlines** (800-252-7522; **alaskaair.com**), **Frontier Flying** (800-478-6779 or 907-543-5863; **frontierflying.com**), and **Peninsula Airways** (800-448-4226; **penair.com**).

Cabs are available through **Nushagak Cab Co.** (907-842-4403) or **Issama Cab** (907-842-4881).

Bethel

Access by air is through the following air companies, although there are smaller charter-flight operators in town for forays into the wilderness: **Alaska**

Airlines (800-252-7522; alaskaair.com), **Era Aviation** (907-543-3905; flyera.com), and **Frontier Flying** (800-478-6779 or 907-543-5863; frontierflying.com).

Cab fares within Bethel are set by city ordinance, which makes getting around affordable. A few choices include **Alaska/Checker Cab** (907-543-2040; fares are $4 within the city); **Camai** (907-543-5800); **City Cab** (907-543-4141); and Kusko (907-543-2169).

King Salmon

Access by air is through **Alaska Airlines** (800-252-7522; alaskaair.com) and **Peninsula Airways** (800-448-4226; penair.com).

There are no car rentals or cab companies, but you can pretty much get where you need to on foot.

Unalaska

Access by air is through **Alaska Airlines** (800-252-7522; alaskaair.com) and **Peninsula Airways** (800-448-4226; penair.com), with connecting service also to the Pribilof Islands).

Access by sea is on the **Alaska State Ferry M/V _Tustumena,_** which travels to Unalaska monthly (800-642-0066; ferryalaska.com).

Cars can be rented from **B. C. Vehicle Rental** (907-581-6777), inside the Unalaska Airport; a range of vehicles is available.

FAR NORTH

Nome

Access by air is through **Alaska Airlines** (800-252-7522; alaskaair.com), **Frontier Flying** (800-478-6779 or 907-543-5863; frontierflying.com), and **Bering Air** (907-442-3943; beringair.com).

Cars can be rented from **Stampede Vehicle Rentals** (800-354-4606 or 907-443-3838; aurorainnome.com/Stampede.htm).

For cab service, call **Checker Cab** at 907-443-5136.

Kotzebue

Access by air is through **Alaska Airlines** (800-252-7522; alaskaair.com), **Frontier**

Flying (800-478-6779 or 907-543-5863; **frontierflying.com**), **Baker Aviation** (907-442-3108), and **Bering Air** (907-442-3943; **beringair.com**).

Cars can be rented from **Kikiktagruk Inupiat Corporation** at 907-442-3165.

Cab companies include **B&D Cab Co.** (907-442-2244) and **Kobuk Cab** (907-442-3651).

Barrow

Access by air is through **Alaska Airlines** (800-252-7522; **alaskaair.com**) and **Frontier Flying** (800-478-6779 or 907-543-5863; **frontierflying.com**).

Cars can be rented from **UIC Auto Rentals** (907-852-2700; prices are on the high side, about $75 per day) or **King Eider Inn** (888-303-4337 or 907-852-4700; **kingeider.net**) for those who are lodging there. The other option is to call a taxi: **Alaska Taxi** (907-852-3000), **Arcticab** (907-852-2227), **Barrow Taxi** (907-852-2222), or **City Cab** (907-852-5050).

▲ Gearing Up

YOU'LL SAVE MONEY when traveling to the Bush if you buy most or all of your supplies ahead of time. Some of the larger towns, such as Bethel and Nome, will have supply stores and even grocery stores, but prices are high, especially for perishable items such as milk, vegetables, and fruits. These supplies are also often at less than their peak, and it can be disappointing, say, to buy a bag of overpriced apples and discover that half of them are soft and mushy.

In most chapters of this book, we have broken down the "Gearing Up" sections into sporting goods, camping supplies, and groceries. However, because the communities of the Far North and Southwest Alaska are so small, you won't likely find such diversity. In the Bush, it's not uncommon to see baked beans next

TRAVELER'S TIP

▶ In the Bush, do not count on local grocery, sporting-goods, and camping stores to have what you will need, because many of these shops are sparsely supplied and carry only the basics such as batteries, candles, and other necessities.

to hip waders in the local grocery store, or to buy your fishing license in the same place you'll purchase postage stamps.

Out of necessity, shop owners in the Bush have learned to diversify their stores to meet the needs of their customers. This attitude can make shopping in the Bush convenient; still, your choices will be limited to whatever the local shop owner has on hand. Therefore, we've broken the sections of this chapter into town names and listed the few choices available in each town, and what you can find at each store or shop.

SOUTHWEST

Dillingham

▶ **AC Value Center–Alaska Commercial Company**   First and Main streets; 907-842-5444. The best place in town for groceries. Also a good source for sporting goods, fishing licenses, and some camping supplies.

▶ **Alaska Department of Fish and Game Office**   907-842-2427. Sporting goods, fishing licenses, and permits.

▶ **N&N Market**   10 Main St.; 907-842-5283. Groceries, sporting goods, and fishing licenses.

Bethel

▶ **AC Value Center–Alaska Commercial Company**   907-543-2661 or 907-543-3463. Groceries, some camping supplies, and sporting goods.

▶ **Kwethluk Sport Store**   12 miles from Bethel in the village of Kwethluk; 907-757-6412. Sporting goods and fishing licenses.

▶ **Swanson's**   830 River St.; 907-543-3221. Hardware, sporting goods, fishing licenses, tackle, and camping gear.

King Salmon

▶ **Alaska Commercial Company**   907-246-6109. Groceries, sporting goods, camping supplies, and fishing licenses.

▶ **City Market**   1 Peninsula Ave.; 907-246-6109. Groceries and other limited supplies.

Unalaska

▶ **AC Value Center–Alaska Commercial Company**   100 Salmon Way; 907-581-1245. Sporting goods and fishing licenses.

▶ **Aleutian Commercial Company and Alaska Ship Supply** 907-581-1284; **western pioneer.com.** These two companies, owned by the same outfit, Western Pioneer, provide marine hardware, fishing gear, bait, groceries, clothing, tools, and many other goods and services.

▶ **Eagle Food Center** 2029 Airport Beach Rd.; 907-581-4040. Groceries and fishing licenses.

FAR NORTH

Nome

▶ **AC Value Center–Alaska Commercial Company** 907-443-2243. Groceries, sporting goods, camping supplies, and fishing licenses.

▶ **Hanson's Safeway** 907-443-5454. Groceries and some sporting goods and camping supplies, along with fishing licenses.

▶ **Nome Outfitters** 907-443-2880. Fishing licenses, sporting goods, and camping supplies.

Kotzebue

▶ **Country Store** Off Front Street; 907-443-5666. Groceries, fishing licenses, limited camping supplies, and sporting goods.

▶ **Alaska Commercial Co.** 907-442-3285. The largest grocer, with fishing licenses, limited camping supplies, and sporting goods.

▶ **Rotman Stores** 500 Shore Ave.; 907-442-3123.

Barrow

▶ **AC Value Center–Alaska Commercial Company** 4725 Ahakvoak St.; 907-852-6711. Groceries, fishing licenses, camping supplies, and some sporting goods.

▲ Where to Stay

THE BUSH IS a vast land dominated by wilderness and dotted by only a handful of lodging options. You may have difficulty finding a place to sleep in some of the smaller villages and towns in this region. Many of the options are basic at best, so with a few exceptions, do not expect luxury.

In this section, we've given you a few options, places that we have tried ourselves and found to be acceptable.

▲ bush southwest indoor lodging

NAME	LODGING TYPE	QUALITY RATING	VALUE RATING	COST
DILLINGHAM				
Beaver Creek Bed and Breakfast	B&B/cabins	★★★	★★★★	$95–$155
Bristol Bay Lodge	Wilderness lodge	★★★★★	★★★★	$6,850/week
The Bristol Inn	Hotel	★★★	★★	$160–$190
Hillside Haven B&B	B&B	★★★	★★★	$140–$210
Thai Inn	B&B	★★★	★★★★	$120
BETHEL				
Bentley's Porter House B & B	Hotel/B&B	★★★★	★★★★	$110–$160
Brown Slough Bed & Breakfast	Cabins	★★★★	★★★	$100–$150
Delta Cottages	B&B	★★	★★	$100–$120
Lakeside Lodge	B&B	★★★	★★★★	$105
Longhouse Bethel Hotel	Hotel	★★★	★★★	$149–$189
KING SALMON				
Alagnak Lodge	Wilderness lodge	★★★	★★★	$2,450/3 nights
King Ko Inn	Duplex	★★	★★★★	$210
Rainbow Bend Lodges	Cabins	★★★★	★★★★	$800/2 nights
UNALASKA				
The Grand Aleutian Hotel	Hotel	★★★★★	★★★★	$179–$320
UniSea Inn	inn	★★★	★★★	$110–$130

DILLINGHAM

Indoor Lodging

▶ **Beaver Creek Bed and Breakfast**   866-252-7335 or 907-842-7335; dillinghamalaska.com.

QUALITY ★★★ | VALUE ★★★★ | $95–$155

▲ bush southwest camping

NAME	LODGING TYPE	QUALITY RATING	VALUE RATING	COST
DILLINGHAM				
City of Dillingham Campground	Tent	★★	★★★★	Free
Goodnews, North Fork, or Middle Fork rivers	Tent	★★★★★	★★★★	Free
Kanektok or Arolik rivers	Tent	★★★★	★★★★	Free
Nushagak River	Tent	★★★	★★★★	Free
Picnic Beach and Cape Constantine	Tent	★★★★★	★★	Free
Round Island	Tent	★★★★★	★★★★★	Free
Togiak River	Tent	★★★★	★★★★	Free
Wood-Tikchik State Park and Togiak National Wildlife Refuge	Tent	★★★★★	★★★★★	Free
KING SALMON				
Alagnak Wild River	Tent	★★★★	★★★★★	Free
UNALASKA				
Unalaska Lands	Tent	★★★★	★★★★	Free

We like this place because you have your choice of a room in the main house or your own house or log cabin just a mile down the road. Hosts Susan and Gorden Isaacs couldn't be more gracious.

▶ **Bristol Bay Lodge**   907-842-2500; **bristolbaylodge.com.**

QUALITY ★★★★★ | VALUE ★★★★ | $6,850/WEEK

For the visitor with plenty of cash to spend, a week or two at the Bristol Bay Lodge is luxurious, with great food, lodging, and some of the best fishing in the state, tucked away within Wood-Tikchik State Park. You'll fly out by small plane each day to some of the remotest fishing spots in the world, then come home to meals and fine lodging. Rate does not include gratuities, fishing license, or fishing tackle. You also have the option of staying at small outcamps run by the lodge. Fly out to the small camps for some true solitude, and then return to the main lodge a day or two later.

▲ bush far north indoor lodging

NAME	LODGING TYPE	QUALITY RATING	VALUE RATING	COST
NOME				
Aurora Inn & Suites	hotel	★★★★	★★★	$130–$220
Nome Nugget Inn	hotel	★★★	★★	$120–$160
Trail's End Apartments	apartments	★★★	★★★	$110
KOTZEBUE				
Nullagvik Hotel	hotel	★★★	★★★	$170–$190
BARROW				
King Eider Inn	hotel	★★★★	★★★★	$140–$210
Top of the World Hotel	hotel	★★★	★★★	$145–$200

▲ bush far north camping

NAME	CAMPING TYPE	QUALITY RATING	VALUE RATING	COST
NOME				
Nome Beaches	tent	★★★★★	★★★★★	free

▶ **The Bristol Inn**   104 Main St.; 800-764-9704 or 907-842-2240; alaskaoutdoors.com/bristolinn.

QUALITY ★★★ | VALUE ★★ | $160–$190

This small hotel is downtown and pretty basic, but it's clean and has a free shuttle to the airport; nonsmoking rooms are available.

▶ **Hillside Haven B&B**   907-842-3523.

QUALITY ★★★ | VALUE ★★★ | $140–$210

Donna and Henry Shade make your stay here enjoyable. One of the more popular bed-and-breakfasts in the area, and one of the best places to eat good food. Their Café Hillside features gourmet fare.

▶ **Thai Inn**   907-842-7378; **thai-inn.com.**

| QUALITY ★★★ | VALUE ★★★★ | $120 |

The inn features rooms completely separate from the residence, offering privacy, but the amenities of a B&B. As the name implies, the lodging has an Asian-inspired theme.

Camping

▶ **City of Dillingham Campground**   907-842-5211.

| QUALITY ★★ | VALUE ★★★★ | FREE |

The city has designated seasonal camping sites at the boat harbor.

▶ **Goodnews, North Fork, or Middle Fork rivers**   907-967-8520.

| QUALITY ★★★★★ | VALUE ★★★★ | FREE |

For land-use permits, contact the land manager of Mumtram Pikkai, Inc. at the number above.

▶ **Kanektok or Arolik rivers**   907-556-8289.

| QUALITY ★★★★ | VALUE ★★★★ | FREE |

For land-use permits, contact the land manager at Kanektok, Inc. at the number above.

▶ **Nushagak River**   907-842-5218.

| QUALITY ★★★ | VALUE ★★★★ | FREE |

Camping can be found on state lands along the Nushagak and Mulchatna drainages. There is a three-day limit on stays here. If you're camping above the high-water mark, a use permit from a local native corporation may be necessary. Contact the land manager of Choggiung Ltd. at the number above.

▶ **Picnic Beach and Cape Constantine**

| QUALITY ★★★★★ | VALUE ★★ | FREE |

These spots are most readily accessed by air (thus the relatively low value rating).

▶ **Round Island**   In the Walrus Islands State Game Sanctuary.

| QUALITY ★★★★★ | VALUE ★★★★★ | FREE |

Permit camping is allowed.

▶ **Togiak River**   907-493-5520.

| QUALITY ★★★★ | VALUE ★★★★ | FREE |

For land-use permits, contact the land manager of Togiak Natives Ltd. at the number above.

▶ **Wood-Tikchik State Park and Togiak National Wildlife Refuge**

| QUALITY ★★★★★ | VALUE ★★★★★ | FREE |

Wilderness camping can be found in these nearby public lands.

BETHEL

Indoor Lodging

▶ **Bentley's Porter House B & B**   624 1st Ave.; 907-543-5923 or 907-543-3552.

| QUALITY ★★★★ | VALUE ★★★★ | $110–$160 |

Of the hotels in town, this one is the most highly recommended. There are 26 rooms; rates include breakfast.

▶ **Brown Slough Bed & Breakfast**   923 6th Ave.; 888-543-4334 or 907-543-4334.

| QUALITY ★★★★ | VALUE ★★★ | $100–$150 |

We really like the Alaska log-and-timber-frame houses, and the owners, Grant and Debbie Fairbanks, are friendly and accommodating. Wireless Internet access is available.

▶ **Delta Cottages**   124 Gunderson Ct.; 907-543-3610.

| QUALITY ★★ | VALUE ★★ | $100–$120 |

Rooms are basic but clean.

▶ **Lakeside Lodge**   H-Marker Lake; 907-543-5275; **lakesidelodgebnb.com.**

| QUALITY ★★★ | VALUE ★★★★ | $105 |

There are only three rooms, with two beds per room. The owners are friendly and the atmosphere relaxed. Amenities include free airport pickup and wireless Internet.

▶ **Longhouse Bethel Hotel**   751 3rd Ave.; 866-543-4613 or 907-543-4612; **longhousebethelinn.com.**

| QUALITY ★★★ | VALUE ★★★ | $149–$189 |

Offers the amenities of larger lodgings with a smaller, more intimate feel. High-speed Internet access is available, and all rooms are nonsmoking.

Camping

There are no designated camping areas in Bethel, but most people who prefer to camp seek out riverbank areas along the Kuskokwim River. Practice low-impact camping methods, and be aware that you may be sharing space with subsistence fishermen in the area.

KING SALMON

Indoor Lodging

▶ **Alagnak Lodge**   800-877-9903; **alagnaklodge.com.**

QUALITY ★★★ | VALUE ★★★ | **$2,450/3 NIGHTS**

Yet another great fishing destination, this is on the more affordable end of the remote-lodging options. The lodge is on a bluff over the Alagnak River, affording great views. All meals are provided, and the food is excellent.

▶ **King Ko Inn**   866-234-3474 or 907-246-3377; **kingko.com.**

QUALITY ★★ | VALUE ★★★★ | **$210**

This is the place to stay for those who enjoy socializing and meeting fun people. The King Ko Inn features tidy duplexes nestled in the woods, complete with small kitchenettes that are functional but not fancy. The accompanying King Ko Bar is a great nightspot, although it does not interfere with the peace and quiet of the duplexes. Our choice for "in-town" lodging.

▶ **Rainbow Bend Lodges**   888-575-4249 or 907-246-1500; **bristolbayfishing.com.**

QUALITY ★★★★ | VALUE ★★★★ | **$800/2 NIGHTS**

Rainbow Bend offers small, fully equipped cabins right on the Naknek River, which is a prime spot for fishing. A bit spendy at $800 for two nights and two days, but it's scenic and comes with its own boat rental so you can get out and fish. Plus, the cabins have their own kitchenettes. Our overall favorite.

Camping

▶ **Alagnak Wild River**   907-246-4250.

QUALITY ★★★★ | VALUE ★★★★★ | **FREE**

This area is available for primitive camping only, and permits are recommended for users. They are available at no charge at the King Salmon Visitor Center (see phone number above).

UNALASKA

Indoor Lodging

▶ **The Grand Aleutian Hotel**   498 Salmon Way; 866-581-3844; **grandaleutian.com.**

QUALITY ★★★★★ | VALUE ★★★★ | **$179–$320**

The Grand Aleutian offers luxury in the middle of nowhere. Rooms have expansive views of the surrounding mountains and waterways, and the local artwork on the walls makes you feel as if you're visiting an exclusive museum.

▶ **UniSea Inn**   188 Gilman Way; 866-581-3844; **grandaleutian.com.**

QUALITY ★★★	VALUE ★★★	$110–$130

Offers simple, clean, and comfortable rooms at economical rates.

Camping

▶ **Unalaska Lands**   907-581-1276; **ounalashka.com.**

QUALITY ★★★★	VALUE ★★★★	FREE

The Ounalashka Corporation privately owns much of the land of Unalaska, Amaknak, and Sedanka islands. To camp—or hike, ski, camp, bike, or snowmobile—you must obtain a permit from the corporation's offices at 400 Salmon Way, in Margaret Bay (see contact information above). Camping is free and popular along local creeks and at the beach.

NOME

Indoor Lodging

▶ **Aurora Inn & Suites**   907-443-3838 or 800-354-4606; **aurorainnome.com.**

QUALITY ★★★★	VALUE ★★★	$130–$220

The 68 units, some with kitchenettes, are sort of plain but are the best equipped of any of the hotels in Nome.

▶ **Nome Nugget Inn**   Downtown; 877-443-2323.

QUALITY ★★★	VALUE ★★	$120–$160

Convenient downtown location gives access to the many attractions and areas of interest in this frontier town; the 47 rooms aren't as nice as the Aurora's, but they offer impressive views of the Bering Sea.

▶ **Trail's End Apartments**   308 W. 1st St.; 907-443-3600.

QUALITY ★★★	VALUE ★★★	$110

This modest lodging option is for those staying in town for more than a few days. Not fancy, but the apartment gives you cooking options.

Camping

▶ **Nome Beaches**   907-443-6624; **nomealaska.org.**

QUALITY ★★★★★	VALUE ★★★★★	FREE

The best camping in Nome is on the beaches, where many people still search for gold much like the prospectors who came here in the early 1900s. The camping is free, but there are limitations on locations. Call for details.

KOTZEBUE

Indoor Lodging

▶ **Nullagvik Hotel**   300 Shore Ave.; 907-442-3331; **nullagvik.com.**

QUALITY ★★★ | VALUE ★★★ | $170–$190

The hotel isn't fancy from the outside, but the rooms actually are quite nice.

BARROW

Indoor Lodging

▶ **King Eider Inn**   888-303-4337 or 907-852-4700; **kingeider.net.**

QUALITY ★★★★ | VALUE ★★★★ | $140–$210

Our favorite lodging option by far in Barrow is the King Eider Inn, which has nice log-decor furniture and fully modern rooms. It's also within easy walking distance of the airport.

▶ **Top of the World Hotel**   907-852-3900; **tundratoursinc.com.**

QUALITY ★★★ | VALUE ★★★ | $145–$200

This is one of the more popular lodging options because the hotel is hooked up with tour operators, but the King Eider's rooms are nicer.

▲ Where to Eat

SOUTHWEST EATERIES

Dillingham

▶ **Café Hillside**   907-842-3523.

GOURMET | QUALITY ★★★ | $9–$17 | SUITABLE FOR KIDS? Y

For eat-in or to-go orders; all meals are made from scratch with healthful ingredients. The Portuguese ham-and-bean soup, turkey and veggie wraps, and strawberry-spinach salads are favorites. Menu changes often.

▶ **The Muddy Rudder**   100 Main St.; 907-842-2634.

AMERICAN | QUALITY ★★★ | $7–$20 | SUITABLE FOR KIDS? Y

This centrally located eatery has a diverse menu for breakfast, lunch, and dinner, and a family-friendly atmosphere. Only open seasonally, though.

▲ bush southwest dining

NAME	CUISINE	FOOD QUALITY	COST
DILLINGHAM			
Café Hillside	Gourmet	★★★	$9–$17
The Muddy Rudder	American	★★★	$7–$20
BETHEL			
Diane's Café	American	★★★★	$12–$29
Dimitri's	Greek/American	★★★★	$7–$29
Pizzaria's Pizza	Pizza	★★★	$4–$20
Snack Shack	American	★★★	$6–$12
Thai to Go	Thai	★★★★	$6–$24
KING SALMON			
Eddie's Fireplace Inn	American	★★★★	$6–$28
King Salmon Café	Neighborhood	★★★	$7–$12
UNALASKA			
Amelia's Restaurant	American	★★★★	$12–$27
The Chartroom at the Grand Aleutian Hotel	Fusion	★★★★★	$13–$32
Peking Restaurant	Chinese/sushi	★★★★	$10–$29
Tino's Steak House	Mexican/steaks	★★★	$10–$30

Bethel

▶ **Diane's Café**   1220 Hoffman Hwy.; 907-543-4305.

AMERICAN | QUALITY ★★★★ | $12–$29 | SUITABLE FOR KIDS? N

Diane's has some of the best food in town, especially because the owners keep the menu fresh by changing it seasonally. The prices are a little steep, but if you're staying at the adjoining Pacifica Hotel, they're often lowered.

▶ **Dimitri's**   281 4th Ave.; 907-543-3434.

GREEK/AMERICAN | QUALITY ★★★★ | $7–$29 SUITABLE FOR KIDS? N

The prices are a bit high, but the soups are worth it.

▲ bush far north dining

NAME	CUISINE	FOOD QUALITY	COST
NOME			
Fat Freddie's Restaurant	Diner	★★★	$9–$19
Milano's Pizzeria	Pizza/Chinese	★★★	$9–$24
KOTZEBUE			
Arctic Blues Espresso	Espresso	★★★	$2–$6
Empress Restaurant	Chinese	★★★	$10–$20
BARROW			
Arctic Pizza	Chinese/steaks/pizza	★★★	$9–$29
Browers Cafe	Diner	★★	$7–$16
Osaka's Japanese and American	Japanese/American	★★★	$11–$20
Pepe's North of the Border	Mexican	★★★★	$11–$22

▶ **Pizzaria's Pizza**   942 3rd Ave.; 907-543-1400.

PIZZA | QUALITY ★★★ | $4–$20 | SUITABLE FOR KIDS? Y

Local pizzeria with dine-in or take-out options.

▶ **Snack Shack**   520 3rd Ave.; 907-543-2218.

AMERICAN | QUALITY ★★★ | $6–$12 | SUITABLE FOR KIDS? Y

Basic burger-and-sandwich place.

▶ **Thai to Go**   270 6th Ave.; 907-543-4449.

THAI | QUALITY ★★★★ | $6–$24 | SUITABLE FOR KIDS? Y

A local standby for quick and authentic Thai food.

King Salmon

▶ **Eddie's Fireplace Inn**   907-246-3435.

AMERICAN | QUALITY ★★★★ | $6–$28 | SUITABLE FOR KIDS? N

Full-service restaurant and bar that also offers video rentals.

▶ **King Salmon Café**   907-246-2233.

NEIGHBORHOOD	QUALITY ★★★	$7–$12	SUITABLE FOR KIDS? Y

Standard cafe food; one of the only choices in town.

Unalaska

▶ **Amelia's Restaurant**   907-581-2800.

AMERICAN	QUALITY ★★★★	$12–$27	SUITABLE FOR KIDS? Y

It looks rather like a shack, but the food is fresh and affordable.

▶ **The Chartroom at the Grand Aleutian Hotel**   498 Salmon Way; 866-581-3844; grandaleutian.com.

FUSION	QUALITY ★★★★★	$13–$32	SUITABLE FOR KIDS? N

The Chartroom does great things with seafood plucked right from the sea. Prices are steep, but the food is excellent.

▶ **Peking Restaurant**   Gilmore Road; 907-581-2303.

CHINESE/SUSHI	QUALITY ★★★★	$10–$29	SUITABLE FOR KIDS? Y

Chinese food and dim sum, plus fabulously fresh sushi here.

▶ **Tino's Steak House**   11 N. 2nd St.; 907-581-4288.

MEXICAN/STEAKS	QUALITY ★★★	$10–$30	SUITABLE FOR KIDS? N

We have friends who will walk across town to get to this excellent eatery, which offers delicious Mexican food and steaks.

FAR NORTH EATERIES

Nome

▶ **Fat Freddie's Restaurant**   Front Street; 907-443-5899.

DINER	QUALITY ★★★	$9–$19	SUITABLE FOR KIDS? Y

Honest diner food with a view of the Bering Sea.

▶ **Milano's Pizzeria**   110 W. Front St.; 907-443-2924.

PIZZA/CHINESE	QUALITY ★★★	$9–$24	SUITABLE FOR KIDS? Y

Craving pizza but your traveling companion is in the mood for Chinese? Not to worry—you can get both here.

Kotzebue

▶ **Arctic Blues Espresso**   At the Kotzebue airport; 907-442-2554.

ESPRESSO	QUALITY ★★★	$2–$6	SUITABLE FOR KIDS? Y

Fresh-brewed coffee and snacks, with friendly employees.

▶ **Empress Restaurant**   In downtown Kotzebue; 907-442-4304 or 907-442-4305.

| CHINESE | QUALITY ★★★ | $10–$20 | SUITABLE FOR KIDS? Y |

The restaurant is family-owned, and the Mongolian beef is top-notch.

Barrow

▶ **Arctic Pizza**   125 Upper Apayauq St.; 907-852-4222.

| CHINESE/STEAKS/PIZZA | QUALITY ★★★ | $9–$29 | SUITABLE FOR KIDS? Y |

As you will notice in Alaska, there are restaurants that claim to specialize in everything under the sun—a Chinese, pizza, and steak place isn't all that unusual, and we salute this can-do attitude. Stick with the pizza, though.

▶ **Browers Cafe**   907-852-3663.

| DINER | QUALITY ★★ | $7–$16 | SUITABLE FOR KIDS? Y |

We were a little disappointed when we first saw this cafe—it's weather-beaten and sort of shabby-looking, but it really is the best place in Barrow to get a home-cooked burger and decent french fries.

▶ **Osaka's Japanese and American**   980 Stevenson St.; 907-852-4200.

| JAPANESE/AMERICAN | QUALITY ★★★ | $11–$20 | SUITABLE FOR KIDS? Y |

The American is all right, but go with what the owners know—their great sushi and Japanese dishes.

▶ **Pepe's North of the Border**   1204 Agvik St.; 907-852-8200.

| MEXICAN | QUALITY ★★★★ | $11–$22 | SUITABLE FOR KIDS? Y |

The dining pickings in Barrow are slim, and Pepe's North of the Border is one of the best. Over the years, longtime owner Fran Tate has remodeled the place from a slight two-room affair to a brightly decorated restaurant that can now serve more than 200 guests at a time. Probably the farthest-north Mexican restaurant in which you could ever eat.

▲ On the Town:
What to Do after the Outdoor Adventure

TRUTH IS, THESE small towns don't have much in the way of attractions; still, a few places are interesting to visit if you have time.

SOUTHWEST

Dillingham

▶ **Samuel K. Fox Museum**   D and Seward streets; 907-842-4831. Features carvings, baskets, and other works by local native artists. Artifacts on display include the Shaman's Hands, old Yup'ik masks, and photos from the area. Open noon–4 p.m. Monday–Friday.

Bethel

▶ **Bethel Museum and Cultural Center**   420 Chief Eddie Hoffman Hwy.; 907-543-1819. Showcases traditional and contemporary works by some of the region's most talented artists. Closed Sundays and Mondays.

Unalaska

▶ **Russian Orthodox Church of the Holy Ascension**   907-581-6404. This church is more than 200 years old and is a great subject for photos (no cameras are allowed inside the building, though). Tours take place Saturdays at 6 p.m. and Sundays at 9 a.m.

FAR NORTH

Nome

▶ **Old St. Joseph's Church**   Anvil City Square; 907-443-6624. Newly restored, this is one of the few structures that survived Nome's 1934 fire, which destroyed most of the town.

Barrow

▶ **Inupiat Heritage Center**   National Park Service/INUP, 240 W. 5th Ave., Anchorage 99501; 907-852-0422 or 907-852-4594. The center features exhibits, artifacts, a library, a gift shop, and an impressive display of mounted birds and other small animals. Learn about commercial whaling and the influence of the Far North's native peoples in its growth. Open weekdays year-round. Free admission.

ACCOMMODATIONS/DINING INDEX

SUBJECT INDEX